RAND McNALLY

W9-BRT-963

2018

Best of the Road® Atlas & Guide

CONTENTS

2018 Best of the Road® Travel Guide

Rand McNally presents 25 amazing U.S. road trips through the Northeast, Midwest, South, and West in this 132-page travel guide, all hand-picked from our collection of Best of the Road® trips. From beach vacations to mountain adventures to everything in between—for a weekend or a week—there's something for everyone.

Pages B1-B132

Road Atlas

Locator map: page ii
Road maps: pages 2-128
Map legend: inside front cover
Index: pages 129-136

Mileage Chart

Driving distances between 90 North American cities and national parks.

Page 138

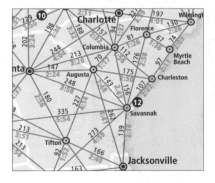

Mileage and Driving Times Map

Distances and driving times between hundreds of North American cities and national parks.

Inside back cover

For licensing information and copyright permissions, contact us at permissions@randmcnally.com.

If you have a comment, suggestion, or even a compliment, please visit us at randmcnally.com/contact or write to:
Rand McNally Consumer Affairs
P.O. Box 7600
Chicago, Illinois 60680-9915

Published in U.S.A.
Printed in China

1 2 3 LE 18 17

FSC
www.fsc.org
MIX
Paper from
responsible sources
FSC® C020056

ATLANTIC PROVINCES Pg. 126

MAINE Pg. 45

NEW HAMPSHIRE Pg. 65

MASSACHUSETTS Pg. 48

RHODE ISLAND Pg. 91

CONNECTICUT Pg. 23

VERMONT Pg. 104

NEW YORK Pg. 69

NEW JERSEY Pg. 65

PENNSYLVANIA Pg. 86

DELAWARE Pg. 24

MARYLAND Pg. 46

VIRGINIA Pg. 106

WEST VIRGINIA Pg. 112

NORTH CAROLINA Pg. 74

SOUTH CAROLINA Pg. 92

GEORGIA Pg. 28

FLORIDA Pg. 26

ALABAMA Pg. 4

MISSISSIPPI Pg. 56

TENNESSEE Pg. 94

KENTUCKY Pg. 42

OHIO Pg. 78

INDIANA Pg. 36

ILLINOIS Pg. 32

MICHIGAN Pg. 50

WISCONSIN Pg. 114

MINNESOTA Pg. 54

IOWA Pg. 38

MISSOURI Pg. 58

ARKANSAS Pg. 10

LOUISIANA Pg. 44

OKLAHOMA Pg. 82

KANSAS Pg. 40

NEBRASKA Pg. 62

SOUTH DAKOTA Pg. 93

NORTH DAKOTA Pg. 77

TEXAS Pg. 98

NEW MEXICO Pg. 68

COLORADO Pg. 20

WYOMING Pg. 116

MONTANA Pg. 60

IDAHO Pg. 31

UTAH Pg. 102

ARIZONA Pg. 8

NEVADA Pg. 64

CALIFORNIA Pg. 12

OREGON Pg. 84

WASHINGTON Pg. 108

MEXICO Pg. 128

HAWAII Pg. 30

ALASKA Pg. 6

QUÉBEC Pg. 124

ONTARIO Pg. 122

MANITOBA Pg. 121

SASKATCHEWAN Pg. 120

ALBERTA Pg. 119

BRITISH COLUMBIA Pg. 118

CANADA Pg. 117

Legend

State / Province Map — Pg. 78

Vicinity Map — Pg. 34

City Map — Pueblo Pg. 20

National Park — Zion NP Pg. 102

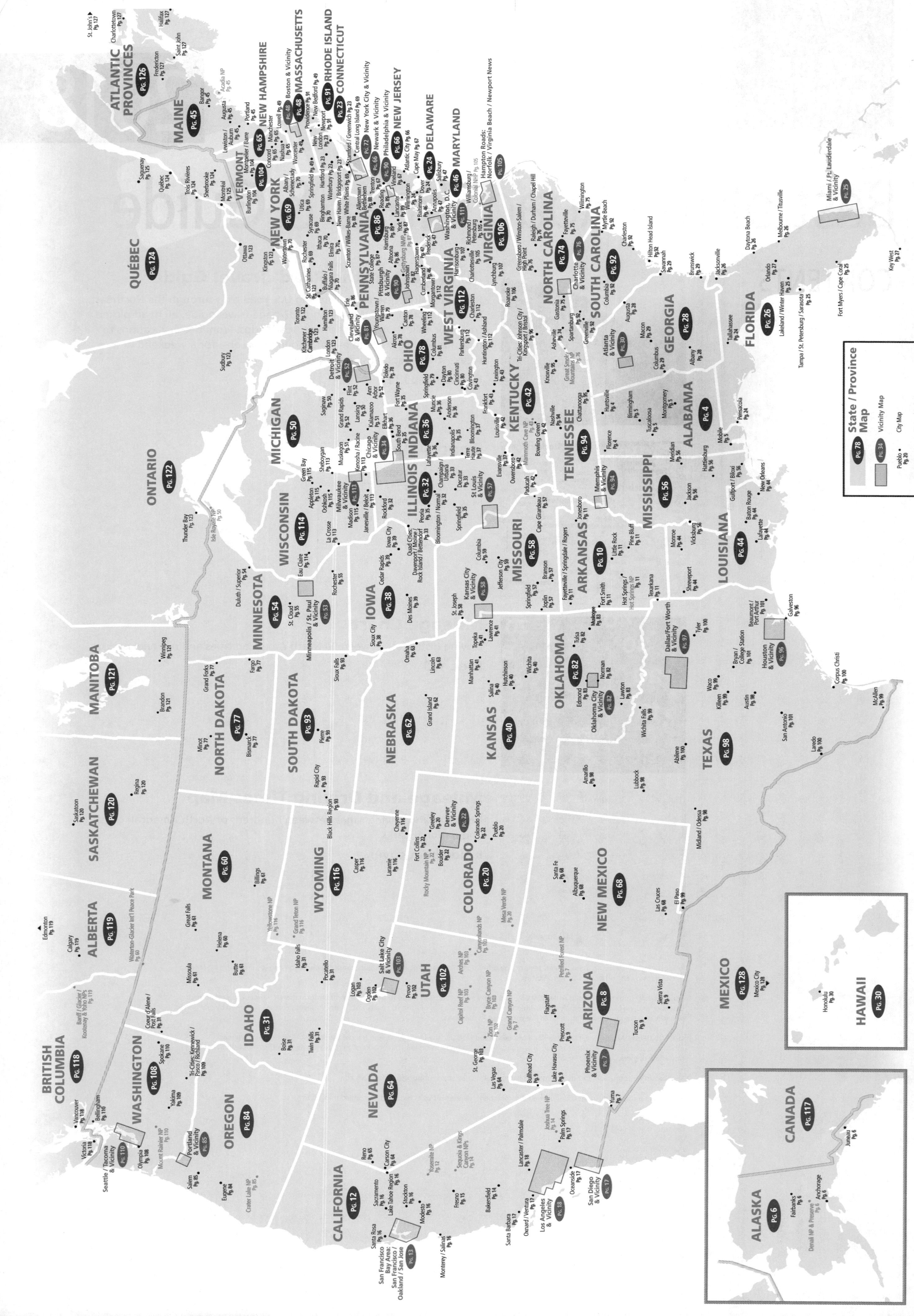

RAND McNALLY

2018

Best of the Road® Travel Guide

West

Midwest

Northeast

South

Portland, ME

Best of the Road® Travel Guide

Northeast

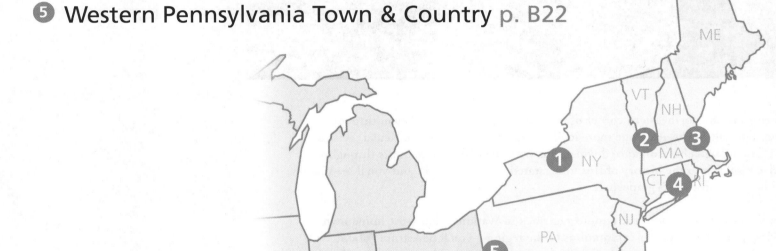

NORTHEAST

MIDWEST

SOUTH

WEST

New York's Finger Lakes: Savor the Flavors

ROUTE TOWNS: Skaneateles | Aurora | Ithaca | Trumansburg | Lodi | Watkins Glen | Horseheads | Elmira | Corning Hammondsport | Dundee | Canandaigua

New York is the nation's third-largest wine-producing state, and its Finger Lakes region tantalizes the palate with flavors from more than 100 wineries and 70 craft breweries. There's no straight shot through the area—not with 11 glacially carved, finger-shaped lakes in the way. Rather, a trip here involves wending your way through idyllic towns and around vineyard-lined shores.

Vineyard on Keuka Lake

This route begins in the northeastern corner of the Finger Lakes, and winds you through several charming small towns, each one more idyllic than the last. Lakes like Keuka, Seneca, Cayuga, and Canandaigua have organized wine trails with themed tasting events throughout the year. Delve deeper into the history of this understated region, though, and you'll see that its roots extend beyond those of its grapevines.

When you're not whipping around the famous racetrack in Watkins Glen—the hometown of motor racing and a good hub for explorations of the region—you'll be learning about revolutionary glass technology and innovation at the world's largest glass museum in Corning.

When you're not hiking near stunning waterfalls—one taller than those up in Niagara—you'll be gliding high in the skies above the Soaring Capital of America, marveling at the same vistas that inspired Mark Twain.

NEW YORK

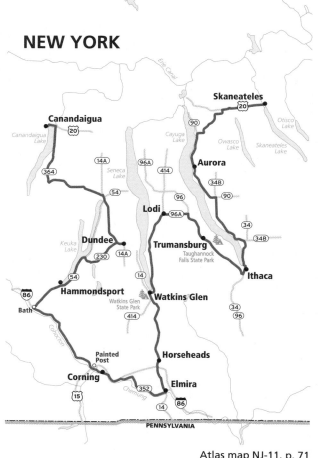

PENNSYLVANIA

Atlas map NJ-11, p. 71

Distance: 222 miles zigzagging point to point.

Type of Trip: Weekend Getaway; Arts & Culture, Great Outdoors, History & Heritage, Picture Perfect, Small Town Gems.

Must Try: Award-winning Rieslings and other cold-climate varietals introduced by wine-making pioneers like Dr. Konstantin Frank and Hermann J. Wiemer.

Must Buy: Whether you shop at one of the region's many art galleries or glass studios or at The Corning Museum of Glass Shops, don't leave the Finger Lakes without taking home a locally made glass treasure. Oh, and a case or two of wine!

Must See: The Corning Museum of Glass, Watkins Glen State Park, Dr. Frank Vinifera Wine Cellars, New York Wine & Culinary Center.

Worth Noting: Among the private operators offering wine and other sightseeing tours is **Experience! The Finger Lakes**, LLC (501 Warren Rd., Ithaca, 607/233-4818, www. experiencefingerlakes.com), whose vineyard and culinary excursions are especially popular.

You can also fly above the scenery in one of **Costa Flying Service's** (324 Victory Hwy., Painted Post, 607/962-0053, www.costaflying.com) four-seater planes and feel the breeze out on Seneca Lake aboard the schooner *True Love* (Schooner Excursions Inc., 1 N. Franklin St., Watkins Glen, 607/535-5253, www.schoonerexcursions.com).

Travel Tips: The Finger Lakes are accessible from many metropolitan areas. The starting point, Skaneateles, is about four hours from Toronto, Philadelphia, and New York City, and roughly five hours from Boston and Cleveland. The Syracuse Hancock International Airport is an easy gateway. Visit in summer to enjoy the lakes, or in fall to view foliage rivaling that of New England.

NORTHEAST

MIDWEST

SOUTH

WEST

Skaneateles

Mid-Lakes Navigation. This is one of a handful of places in the country that still has mail service by water. With Mid-Lakes Navigation, you can watch deliveries being made while learning lake history from your guide. In addition to the popular three-hour U.S. Mailboat cruise around Skaneateles Lake, the company offers sightseeing, lunch, and dinner cruises on the lake and on the Erie Canal. *11 Jordan St., (315) 685-8500, www.midlakesnav.com.*

Aurora

Mackenzie-Childs. MacKenzie-Childs has been handcrafting ceramics and hand-decorating furniture since 1983. Somehow, its floral motifs, checkerboard patterns, and fanciful prints combine successfully to give traditional home décor an Alice-in-Wonderland-like twist. Explore the shop and take a 40-minute tour of the 1800s farmhouse. Its three floors have displays of whimsical furniture, eclectic dishware, and other merchandise that demonstrate how to incorporate the intricate patterns into your own home. *3260 State Rte. 90, (315) 364-6118, www.mackenzie-childs.com.*

Ithaca

Cornell Lab of Ornithology. Serious birders rub elbows with casual enthusiasts at this epicenter of avian research. You can spot some of the more than 200 species found here on guided 45- or 90-minute trail hikes, from windows in the two-story atrium, and through scopes overlooking the birdfeeder garden. Check the latest reports on resident winged creatures using the eBird Trail Tracker kiosk in the visitors center. The Wild Birds Unlimited shop is crammed with field guides and activities kits; birding optics; bird baths; and, naturally, feeders. *159 Sapsucker Woods Rd., (800) 843-2473, www.birds.cornell.edu.*

Trumansburg

Taughannock Falls State Park. Here, hikes along gorge and rim trails afford spectacular views of Taughannock Falls, which, at 215 feet, are taller than those at Niagara. Over time, what is one of the highest waterfalls east of the Rockies penetrated layers of sandstone, shale, and limestone (the bed of an ancient sea), carving out a 400-foot-deep gorge. Cabins (reservations required) and tent and RV sites overlook Cayuga Lake, which has a swimming beach, fishing areas, and a marina and boat-launch sites. *1740 Taughannock Park Blvd., (607) 387-6739, parks.ny.gov.*

Lodi

Wagner Vineyards Estate Winery. Here, each of the 30 or so varietals—from the dry Riesling and Cabernet Franc to the sweet Niagara and Vidal Blanc Ice—has five generations of winemaking expertise behind it. What started with Bill Wagner planting a few vines beside Seneca Lake has grown into a mecca for award-winning Finger Lakes wine, producing more than 50,000 cases annually. The $4 ($6 on Sat.) tasting flights feature four to six pours. For $3, you can try six craft brews at the Wagner Valley Brewing Co. The Ginny Lee Café has superb lunches and lake views. *9322 State Rte. 414, (607) 582-6450, www.wagnervineyards.com.*

Watkins Glen

Watkins Glen State Park. Over the centuries, water carved the gorge that makes this park's scenery so enchanting. The 2-mile Gorge Trail descends some 400 feet and follows a stream past 200-foot cliffs and 19 waterfalls, some so close you feel their spray. Follow the trail out and back on foot from the main entrance or take the $5 shuttle (summer only) to the upper entrance and walk back down to the main one. To see the gorge from above, follow the Indian or South Rim trails along its forested rim. The park also has a seasonal campground with rustic cabins and tent and RV sites. *1009 N. Franklin St., (607) 535-4511, parks.ny.gov.*

Watkins Glen International. Get ready to start your engines! Racing in Watkins Glen began in 1948, and, although these roots are in Formula 1, the town and its track have also seen open-wheel, sports, and stock-car racing. Indeed, today Watkins Glen International hosts the NASCAR Sprint Cup Series, among other events. You can even follow in the tracks of great racers on the Drive the Glen Experience, which features two 3.4-mile laps behind a pace car. *2790 County Rte. 16, (866) 461-7223, www.theglen.com.*

Horseheads

Horseheads Brewing, Inc. You can just about smell the hops down the street from the tiny tasting room of this brewery. After sampling your first selection, you'll understand why Horseheads has twice been named New York State's Best Craft Brewery. Casual beer drinkers and connoisseurs alike are delighted by favorites like Brickyard Red Ale, Horseheads Double IPA, and the unique Hot-Jala-Heim Beer with Bite—which uses hot peppers, including jalapeños and Anaheim peppers, in the brewing process. *250 Old Ithaca Rd., (607) 739-8468, www.horseheadsbrewing.com.*

Marina in the Finger Lakes

Eat & Stay

Blue Water Grill | Skaneateles. A hearty lunch or dinner overlooking Skaneateles Lake is hard to beat. This local favorite offers something for everyone—no kidding—whether you're hankering for a bowl of rich lobster bisque and a crisp salad or sandwich, a tasty burger or fresh tacos, or a full steak or seafood dinner. There's even a separate sushi menu. On a bright summer day, try to score a table out on the deck. *11 W. Genesee St., (315) 685-6600, www.bluewaterskaneateles.com.*

Mirbeau Inn & Spa | Skaneateles. Standing on the bridge that traverses a lily pad–filled pond in the gardens, you might feel as if you've stepped into a Monet masterpiece. Mirbeau, which the hotel loosely translates as "reflected beauty," draws upon elements in the French Impressionist's paintings to create a serene landscape—one with European-style buildings; soft, light colors; and an introspective character. Spend the afternoon getting a Monet's Favorite Fragrance aromatherapy spa treatment. Spend the night in one of 34 rooms, luxuriously appointed with soaking tubs and fireplaces. *851 W. Genesee Street Rd., (877) 647-2328, www.mirbeau.com.*

Moosewood Restaurant | Ithaca. The unassuming, ivy-covered exterior gives no indication that you're about to enter one of *Bon Appétit*'s 13 Most Influential Restaurants of the 20th Century. Since opening in 1973, Moosewood has been a creative force in vegetarian cuisine, through its meals here and its many famous cookbooks. The menu changes based on what's in season and available through the Finger Lakes Organic Growers Cooperative. *215 N. Cayuga St., (607) 273-9610, www.moosewoodcooks.com.*

Watkins Glen Harbor Hotel | Watkins Glen. A V-shaped beacon at the head of Seneca Lake, this luxurious 104-room hotel is a splurge in peak season but offers fantastic off-season deals. It's easy to relax here, thanks, in no small part, to the quintessential pier and lake views. Swim in the indoor pool, dine at the Blue Pointe Grille, or select a Finger Lakes Riesling in the Coldwater Bar. *16 N. Franklin St., (607) 535-6116, www.watkinsglenharborhotel.com.*

NORTHEAST

MIDWEST

SOUTH

WEST

Elmira

Mark Twain Study. Pathways on the Elmira College campus lead to an octagonal, Victorian-style structure where Samuel Clemens (aka Mark Twain) wrote portions of his most-famous works. Though he lived in Hartford, CT, the humorist, lecturer, and writer spent summers visiting his in-laws at nearby Quarry Farm; the study was moved from the farm in 1952. The Mark Twain Exhibit, in neighboring Cowles Hall, has photographs, furniture, and memorabilia. You can also visit Clemens's gravesite in Woodlawn Cemetery. In July and August, narrated Trolley into Twain Country tours depart on the hour (Tues.–Fri. 10–2, Sat. 10–1) from the Chemung Valley History Museum. *1 Park Pl., (607) 735-1941, www.elmira.edu.*

National Soaring Museum. The first national soaring contest was held in Elmira back in 1930, making it the Soaring Capital of America. This museum, atop Harris Hill and overlooking a historic and still-operational airfield, honors that legacy. Artifacts and vintage, classic, and modern gliders provide a comprehensive look at motor-less flight. You can also fly silently over the Chemung River valley on a Harris Hill Soaring Corporation glider ride (weekends Apr.–May and Sept.–Oct., daily June–Aug.). *51 Soaring Hill Dr., (607) 734-3128, www.soaringmuseum.org.*

Corning

The Corning Museum of Glass. The array of cuts, patterns, colors, and consistencies of the glass here will not only dazzle you but also transport you from antiquity to modernity and through Asia, the Middle East, Europe, and America. At the world's largest glass museum, you'll learn about various glass-making processes; watch glass artisans at work; and maybe even fuse, blow, or sandblast your own piece during the popular (book ahead) Make Your Own Glass experience. Plan to spend at least four hours here, more if you explore the museum's enormous shopping area. *1 Museum Way, (607) 937-5371, www.cmog.org.*

Corning

The Rockwell Museum. Local department store owner Bob Rockwell's fascination with the history and art of the American West began as a child on his family's Colorado ranch. His collection of paintings and sculptures is now housed in a striking Romanesque-Gothic building that was once city hall. Themed galleries explore the American experience. The museum's famous pieces of Western art by Frederic Remington and Charles M. Russell are in the Remington and Russell gallery. Other galleries include Visions of America and Wildlife. *111 Cedar St., (607) 937-5386, rockwellmuseum.org.*

Hammondsport

Dr. Frank Vinifera Wine Cellars. In 1962, a decade after emigrating from the Ukraine, Dr. Konstantin Frank ignited the so-called Vinifera Revolution. Having successfully grown grapes in areas where winters were even colder than those Upstate, he knew that Riesling and Chardonnay grapes could survive near Keuka Lake. He went ahead and planted his vines. The result? The state's most award-winning winery with multiple Winery of the Year titles at the New York Wine & Food Classic. There's no charge to taste up to five pours. *9749 Middle Rd., (800) 320-0735, www.drfrankwines.com.*

Glenn H. Curtiss Museum. If it weren't for the giant Curtiss C-46 Commando outside, you'd never know this warehouse-like building contained some of the country's greatest aviation artifacts. Glenn H. Curtiss, Hammondsport's favorite son, was called the Fastest Man on Earth after he clocked 136.4 mph with his Curtiss V8-powered motorcycle in 1907. He went on to build airplanes and was awarded U.S. pilot's license No. 1. Here you'll see Curtiss motorcycles, originals and replicas of his planes, and even his later creation: the camper trailer. *8419 State Rte. 54, (607) 569-2160, www.glennhcurtissmuseum.org.*

Dundee

Hermann J. Wiemer Vineyard. In 1976, German vintner Hermann J. Wiemer introduced the Riesling and Chardonnay varietals that helped put Finger Lakes wine-making on the map. He was convinced that his vinifera vine plantings would, despite harsh winters, thrive on Seneca Lake's western shores. He was right. Today, this vineyard is regarded as one of the region's best: In 2014 and 2015, it made the *Wine & Spirits* list of the world's Top 100 Wineries. The tasting room serves five samples for $5. *3962 State Rte. 14, (607) 243-7971, wiemer.com.*

Canandaigua

New York Wine & Culinary Center. Before there was the Big Apple, there were bushels of little apples . . . and wheat, grapes, black raspberries. Not to mention cheese. This center celebrates the state's agricultural bounty by encouraging you to savor all the flavors. Learn how to cook using New York ingredients in the state-of-the-art kitchen, or sit down to a delicious meal in the Upstairs Bistro, whose balcony overlooks Canandaigua Lake. The center also has a beer- and wine-tasting room and provides information about area wine trails. *800 S. Main St., (585) 394-7070, www.nywcc.com.*

Eat & Stay

Seneca Harbor Station | Watkins Glen. This restaurant's harbor views will have you out snapping pictures, but the steaks, burgers, seafood, and chowders will bring you back to the table soon enough. The building that once housed a train station has been restored to its 1876 heyday—albeit with a nautical rather than a railroad theme. Eat in the dining room, on the covered deck overlooking the lake, on the beach patio, or out on the water with a dinner cruise aboard the *Seneca Legacy. 3 N. Franklin St., (607) 535-6101, www.senecaharborstation.com.*

The Cellar | Corning. This acclaimed restaurant in Corning's historical Gaffer District is a great place to pair fantastic modern fusion food with award-winning wine. Order such seasonally changing entrees as slow-roasted pork belly with ramen noodles or American Kobe beef with duck-fat French fries. *21 W. Market St., (607) 377-5552, www.corningwinebar.com.*

Hickory Hill Family Camping Resort | Bath. Activities here range from wagon rides and pedal carts to disc golf and laser tag. Kids love the Scamper's SprayGround, a pool with a maze of colorful tubes that spray water. Sure you can park your RV or pitch a tent, roast marshmallows, and sleep out under the stars. But you can also stay in a cabin, cottage, or lodge, and get a signature Grape Seed body treatment at the on-site Finger Lakes Wellness Center and Health Spa. *7531 County Rd. 13, (800) 760-0947, www.hickoryhillcampresort.com.*

FLX Wienery | Dundee. When you order a Whole Hog at this gourmet hot dog stand, out comes a massive sausage (your choice of locally sourced bratwurst, Italian, or chorizo), topped with fried onions, bacon, fried egg, cheese curds, and more. Add a side of poutine (French fries with cheese curds and a light brown sauce) and a decadent salted caramel and pretzel milkshake to your order, and you'll never look at fast food the same way again. The menu also has specialty burgers, Korean barbecue, and vegetarian options. *5090 State Rte. 14, (607) 243-7100, www.flxwienery.com.*

The Corning Museum of Glass

Northern New England Summits & Shores

ROUTE TOWNS: Bennington, VT | Manchester | Rutland | Waitsfield | Waterbury | East Barre | Cabot | St. Johnsbury
Bretton Woods, NH | Gorham | Jackson | North Conway | Wolfeboro | Portsmouth | Kittery, ME
Ogunquit | Kennebunkport | Old Orchard Beach | Portland | Freeport

New England is rich in history, color, and flavor. American heritage took root here four centuries ago, and the states of Vermont, New Hampshire, and Maine have proudly preserved much of that legacy.

Henry Covered Bridge
Bennington, VT

On this journey through northern New England, you'll take in many treasured heritage sites, museums, and landmarks—from humble houses and stately mansions to ages-old railways and timeless covered bridges. En route to the coast, you'll also travel along and through a pair of national forests. Each has its own color; both offer mountain vistas, particularly beguiling in the fall, and myriad outdoor activities year round.

Indeed, every season brings its own unique, yet quintessentially New England, experiences. Endless hiking trails double as cross-country ski, snowshoe, snowmobile, and even sleigh-ride routes. Slick downhill ski slopes double as rugged mountain-biking terrain. Grand mountainside, lakeside, and coastal resorts and lodges serve as either romantic or family-friendly refuges amid the varied shades of green in spring and summer, the red-orange-yellow palette of fall, and the pure whites and icy blues of winter.

In terms of flavor, *real* maple syrup is synonymous with this corner of the country. Vermont is renowned for its dairy products, particularly its sharp cheddar cheese; New Hampshire and Maine for their chowders, bisques, and other dishes made with straight-from-the-Atlantic catches. Restaurants old and new throughout the region are also capitalizing on the seasonal bounty of local farms.

Distance: 480 miles point to point.

Type of Trip: Vacation Getaway; History & Heritage, Great Outdoors, Small Town Gems.

Must Try: Cheese at Cabot Creamery, ice cream at Ben & Jerry's, and lobster at a shack (like the one in Ogunquit, ME).

Must Buy: A jug of pure maple syrup from Vermont or New Hampshire (both states have advocates in the debate about which is better). If you drive the auto road, don't deny yourself the badge of honor: a "This Car Climbed Mt. Washington" bumper sticker.

Must See: Covered Bridge Museum, Norman Rockwell Museum, the top of Mount Washington (one way or another), Strawbery Banke, Kittery Trading Post, Old Orchard Beach, Wadsworth-Longfellow House, L.L. Bean.

Worth Noting: Seasons really do matter here. Some businesses still only operate in peak months—which vary depending on whether you're talking about summits or shores. Winter closures aren't unheard of in the highest elevations. Down a ways, things come to life in fall and winter, though more spots once associated only with winter activities are staying open in warmer months. On the coast, many places still operate primarily from May through October, shutting some or all of the time in cooler months.

Travel Tips: Scenic highways and byways are the best way to travel here, and they call for extra driving time. Sometimes you just need a slower, steadier approach (especially when the weather's bad) to manage the curves, switchbacks, and steep hills. Other times you just need more time for stops at overlooks, covered bridges, and farm stands.

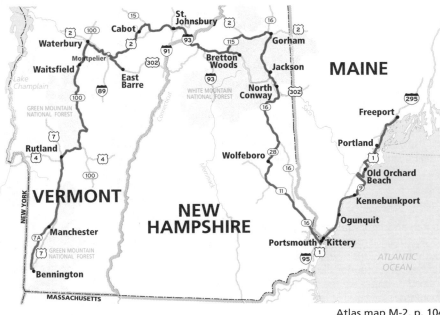

Atlas map M-2, p. 104

Bennington, VT

Bennington Museum. The fine and folk art, furnishings, glass, pottery, and other artifacts at this regional history museum date from as far back as the early 18th century. The highlight, though, is the large collection of works by Anna Mary Robertson "Grandma" Moses, whose colorful, engaging, art-naïf paintings showcase everyday life in rural Vermont. She was a prolific artist, despite not having started to paint in earnest till she was 78 years old. The museum also has Grandma Moses memorabilia, including her childhood schoolhouse. *75 Main St., (802) 447-1571, www.benningtonmuseum.org.*

Bennington Center for the Arts Covered Bridge Museum. This full-spectrum art center has a 300-seat theater and gallery spaces showcasing Native American, nature- and wildlife-themed works, and other visual arts. It also has a gallery dedicated to Vermont's iconic covered bridges, 104 of which are still operational throughout the state. Explore bridge engineering, construction, and creators, and then check out a working model railroad featuring six Vermont rail bridges. An interactive map will help you plan a tour of covered bridges, five of which are nearby. *44 Gypsy Ln., (802) 442-7158, www.thebennington.org.*

Hildene

Manchester

Hildene. This Georgian Revival mansion was built in 1905 by Robert Todd Lincoln, the only son of Abraham and Mary Todd who lived into adulthood. He resided here until 1926, and direct descendants continued the legacy until 1975. The house is filled with original furniture as well as presidential and Lincoln family memorabilia. The 412-acre grounds encompass a farm, gardens, trails, and woods. And, since Robert Todd Lincoln once served as CEO of the Pullman Company, Hildene also explores early rail travel. Be sure to see the well-preserved Sunbeam, a luxury wooden passenger car with its own rich history. Self- or historian-guided tours are available, as are seasonal tractor-drawn wagon rides. *1005 Hildene Rd., (802) 362-1788, www.hildene.org.*

American Museum of Fly Fishing. A specialist's sport requires a specialist's museum. Though modest in size, this one has a remarkable collection of fly-fishing ephemera, photography, and art. Displays showcase tackle used by the sport's most famous enthusiasts, including an early 19th-century wooden rod used by Daniel Webster and gear that helped Babe Ruth, Dwight D. Eisenhower, Ernest Hemingway, Andrew Carnegie, Glenn Miller, and others hook fish. There's also a library, a reading room, and year-round events, including fly-tying lessons. Next door is the flagship outpost of **Orvis** (4180 Main St., 802/362-3750, www.orvis.com), the outdoors outfitter that started out selling fly-fishing gear in 1856. *4104 Main St., (802) 362-3300, www.amff.com.*

Rutland

Norman Rockwell Museum of Vermont. Learn about the artist whose name is practically synonymous with 20th-century Americana. Although this museum spans most of Norman Rockwell's career, the emphasis is on his Vermont years. Displays of more than 2,500 *Saturday Evening Post* and other magazine covers, advertisements, and paintings take you on a journey through his development as an illustrator. Exhibits also explore how his work reflected the country's economics, politics, and culture. A gift shop sells prints and other souvenirs that let you bring home a little piece of Rockwell. *654 Rte. 4 E., (Rte. 100), (877) 773-6095, www.normanrockwellvt.com.*

Waitsfield

The Store. The old 1834 Methodist Meeting House is now home to Vermont's ultimate culinary emporium. In addition to cookbooks, linens, pottery, and every gadget and pot or pan a cook or chef could need, there's an array of Vermont edibles—from maple syrup and maple pumpkin butter to cheese and chocolate. Upstairs you'll find a collection of 19th- and 20th-century English and American country antiques as well as a dream kitchen, where the resident chef offers small-group cooking lessons. *5275 Main St., (802) 496-4465, www.vermontstore.com.*

Waterbury

Ben & Jerry's Factory Tour. Guided half-hour tours of a Ben and Jerry's factory let you lap up the history of a beloved (and politically opinionated) brand. And yes, free ice cream samples are part of the deal. Though schedules vary, tours take place year-round and include a short "moovie," a close-up look at the manufacturing process, and a stop in the ice-cream and gift shop. The grounds also have a cow-viewing area; a picnic spot; and the Flavor Graveyard, where ill-conceived flavors—like the short-lived Economic Crunch—have been laid to rest. On midsummer Saturday evenings, stay late for the free outdoor movie. *1281 Waterbury-Stowe Rd., (866) 258-6877, www.benjerry.com.*

Green in Two Parts

The Vermont portion of the USDA's jointly managed, 416,000-acre **Green Mountain & Finger Lakes National Forests** (802/747-6700, www.fs.usda. gov/gmfl) falls into two zones: the South Zone, roughly from the Massachusetts border to Rutland, and the North Zone, from just north of Rutland to just south of Waitsfield. Route 100 is just one of the scenic roads that edges the forest and travels through charming, amenities-filled hamlets.

Green Mountain hiking highlights include the 272-mile Long Trail, which runs through both zones on up to Canada; the Appalachian Trail, which runs concurrently with the Long until north of Killington and then forks eastward into New Hampshire; and the Robert Frost National Recreation Trail, an easy walk that begins on Route 125 in Ripton. Peaks here rise as high as 4,000 feet, and ski resorts include Sugarbush, Bromley, and Mount Snow. Get more info at the forest supervisor's office in Rutland or ranger stations in Manchester Center, Middlebury, and Rochester. **The Green Mountain Club** (4711 Waterbury-Stowe Rd., Waterbury Center, 802/244-7037, www.greenmountain-club.org) maintains the Long Trail and is another great resource.

East Barre

Vermont Flannel Company. You're in Vermont, so you might as well get cozy and buy local at the same time. This family business has produced high-quality flannel goods—promising better fabric that shrinks less thanks to a tighter weave—at its East Barre location since 1991. A small team "dedicated to world comfort" proudly hand cuts and sews the company's plush, ultra-soft blankets, shirts, shorts, leggings, scarves, hats, and sleepwear. *128 Mill St., (802) 476-5226, vermontflannel.com.*

Cabot

Cabot Creamery & Visitor Center. This country creamery began producing its award-winning cheeses in 1919. Daily guided factory tours show how curd is made from milk, processed into various types of cheese, formed into blocks or wheels, and stored for aging. You'll also get to sample a range of Cabot products and shop for edible and non-edible souvenirs. *1 Home Farm Way, (802) 563-2231, www.cabotcheese.coop.*

St. Johnsbury

Fairbanks Museum & Planetarium. Northern New England's natural history museum was founded in 1889 by Franklin Fairbanks, a wealthy industrialist with a penchant for beautiful and sometimes strange artifacts. Inside a classic Victorian, you can view his "cabinet of curiosities" and thousands of other historical, natural, and ethnological artifacts—from toys, tools, and weapons to fossils, eggs, and preserved creatures. Exhibits and shows at the Lymann Spitzer Jr. Planetarium highlight the solar system, the stars, meteorological events, and mythology. *1302 Main St., (802) 748-2372, www.fairbanksmuseum.org.*

Bretton Woods, NH

Mt. Washington Cog Railway. You'll channel the little engine that could during a ride on the world's second-steepest railway. Built in 1869, this "marvel of 19th-century technology" takes you 3 miles up the northeast's tallest peak pulled by a biodiesel locomotive or, on morning runs, a classic steam engine. This National Historic Engineering Landmark is considered a "must do" on any visit to New England—both for the experience and the views. You can make a full day of it by riding the railway, taking in its museum and gift shop, and dining in the restaurant at its Marshfield Base Station. The train operates on varying schedules between late April and November. *3168 Base Station Rd., 6 mi off Rte. 302, (603) 278-5404, www.thecog.com.*

White and Wild

The **White Mountain National Forest** (603/536-6100, www.fs.usda.gov/whitemountain) stretches across northeastern New Hampshire and into southwestern Maine, encompassing Presidential Range peaks in an area the size of Rhode Island. Presiding over it all is 6,288-foot Mount Washington, cloaked in some of the nation's coldest (-43 degrees F) and windiest (231 mph) weather. A highlight of any visit is climbing to its peak—on foot or by road or rail. In addition, scenic routes like the famous Kancamagus Scenic Byway wind through the forest and into "notches," as gaps or passes are known here.

Over 1,200 miles of trails include 117 often-rugged miles of the Appalachian Trail. Attitash, Loon Mountain, Waterville Valley, and Wildcat ski resorts and several lodges offer year-round R&R opportunities. Get more info at forest headquarters in Campton (weekdays 8–4:30), district ranger stations in Conway and Gorham, or the **White Mountain Visitor Center** (200 Kancamagus Hwy., 603/745-8720, www.visitwhitemountains.com) in North Woodstock. There's also the **Appalachian Mountain Club** (www.outdoors.org), which operates out of its Highland Center Lodge at Crawford Notch (between Bretton Woods and Bartlett).

Gorham

Mount Washington Auto Road. In New England, bumper stickers claiming "This Car Climbed Mount Washington" are ubiquitous. Get yours by driving (May through October during daylight hours) to an elevation of almost 6,300 feet along this famous 7-plus-mile toll road. The route is remarkable for its curves, its views, and the fact that it's been open since 1861. To ensure the best vistas (and see if the road is even open), check conditions before heading out. If you don't feel like driving yourself, guided van tours are available. From December through March, you can also join a 75-minute tour aboard the Mt. Washington Snowcoach, a nine-passenger van tricked out with a four-track system in place of wheels. *Rte. 16, Pinkham Notch, (603) 466-3988, mtwashingtonautoroad.com.*

White Mountains

Eat & Stay

Kismet Kitchen I Montpelier. The best way to top off a trip to Vermont farm country is with a fine farm-to-table dining experience. This popular chef-owned and -operated restaurant serves dinner Wednesday through Saturday and brunch on weekends. The menu mixes well-made American standards with innovative fare like goat cheese gnudi (gnocchi-like dumplings) and pork schnitzel with mustard cress. *52 State St., (802) 223-8646, www.kismetkitchens.com.*

Omni Mount Washington Resort I Bretton Woods, NH. What would a grand, 1902 mountain resort be without a porte-cochère, expansive verandas, sweeping lawns, and breathtaking views? Of course, you also need a Great Hall, a Grand Ballroom, and a Conservatory—all lofty in scale but understated in elegance. Artful leaded-glass windows and period chandeliers keep things bright; area rugs keep things hushed. Reservations and jackets are required for dinner in the Main Dining Room. Stickney's restaurant and The Cave, a former speakeasy, are more laid-back. The hotel also has a spa, an equestrian center, and an acclaimed children's program (ages 4–12). Other activities on site and nearby include golf, biking, and zip lining. Winter sees ice skating, snowshoeing, sleigh rides, and world-class alpine and Nordic skiing at Bretton Woods. *310 Mt. Washington Hotel Rd., (603) 278-1000, www.omnihotels.com.*

Mt. Washington Cog Railway

Snowboarder in White Mountain National Forest

NORTHEAST

MIDWEST

SOUTH

WEST

NORTHEAST

MIDWEST

SOUTH

WEST

Jackson

Mount Washington Observatory & Summit Museum. Set at the highest point in the country east of the Mississippi River, this observatory has played a crucial part in meteorological recording. Atmospheric research conducted here during the 1930s helped us to better understand things like the constitution of clouds, ice physics, and wind speeds. You can learn about this and ongoing research during a tour of the observatory. Don't miss the museum's memorabilia, weather exhibits, and geological artifacts like rock strata more than 400 million years old. Layer up: the summit gets chilly even in summer. *Sherman Adams Visitor Center, Mt. Washington State Park, (603) 356-2137, www.mountwashington.org.*

North Conway

Conway Scenic Railroad. The picturesque journey of this restored 1874 railroad is a great reason to break from your road trip. The Conway Scenic Railroad opened in 1974 after extensive renovations preserved a landmark station and surrounding property in North Conway Village. Today, the company operates vintage railcars on two excursion lines—the Valley and the Notch—over three routes and 35.5 combined miles. Round-trip journeys take as little as an hour or as long as five. Seating is available in coach, first-class, dome, or dining cars; the last includes a prix-fixe, three-course lunch or dinner. Valley trains operate year round, Notch trains only in warmer months; schedules vary. Reservations and/or advance ticket purchases are advised. *38 Norcross Cir., (603) 356-5251, conwayscenic.com.*

Wolfeboro

The Winnipesaukee Belle. For more than a century, Lake Winnipesaukee has been a popular cruising destination. Today, only one vessel offers relaxing waterborne tours of the 72-square-mile lake. The *Winni Belle*, a 2-story, 65-foot paddle-wheeler, makes scenic 90-minute round trips from the town docks in Wolfeboro, also known as "America's oldest summer resort." The season runs from late May to mid-October. *90 N. Main St., (609) 569-3016, www.winnipesaukeebelle.com.*

Historic structures at Strawbery Banke Museum

Portsmouth

Strawbery Banke Museum. History gets real at the museum enclave of Strawbery Banke, where you can experience how people lived and worked four centuries ago. Amid a 10-acre site with 42 restored and furnished historic structures, artisans and other "townsfolk" in period costume go about their chores while you look on. You can even try your hand at weaving or other crafts, play games, or dress up in period clothing. You can buy tickets, good for two consecutive days, at the adjacent visitors center. If you arrive off season (the museum is closed Nov.–Apr.), never fear; the result of strict zoning throughout downtown Portsmouth is a plethora of preserved colonial buildings—many housing boutiques, restaurants, and inns. *14 Hancock St., (603) 433-1100, www.strawberybanke.org.*

Wentworth-Coolidge Mansion. Step back into colonial New England at the Wentworth-Coolidge Mansion, once the home of Benning Wentworth—New Hampshire's Royal Governor from 1741 to 1767— and later of businessman and amateur artist J. Templeman Coolidge III. The gardens are where the first lilacs were planted in the New World, and the mansion is historically prized as the only original surviving residence of a Royal Governor in the United States. Tour this National Historic Landmark and its seaside grounds from May through October. *375 Little Harbor Rd., (603) 436-6607, wentworthcoolidge.org.*

The Press Room. This place has been the region's main live-music club since the 1970s. Longtime patrons and new fans head here seven nights a week to catch jazz, folk, blues, bluegrass, and rockabilly shows. There's also an extensive selection of draft beers and microbrews as well as drink specials and a mix of contemporary and traditional pub fare. *77 Daniel St., (603) 431-5186, www.pressroomnh.com.*

Kittery, ME

Kittery Trading Post. Officially founded in 1647, making it one of Maine's oldest incorporated towns, Kittery is proud of its colonial history. One can only guess at what its early citizens would make of the town's contemporary shopping scene, which includes several sprawling outlet malls. It also, however, features the famous Kittery Trading Post. Outfitting outdoor sports enthusiasts since 1938, this rustic-looking, multilevel emporium sells reliable, affordable gear from major and specialty brands. It also has very knowledgeable staffers, who can help you shop for anything from snowshoes and skis to fishing tackle and kayaks. *301 U.S. 1, (888) 587-6246, www.kitterytradingpost.com.*

Eat & Stay

Wolfeboro Inn I Wolfeboro. Built in 1812 and expanded in 1987, the regal Wolfeboro Inn has long welcomed travelers into its elegant rooms and New England–style pub, Wolfe's Tavern. Today's visitors enjoy its friendly service, traditional-meets-contemporary furnishings, and amenities like free Wi-Fi and fine bath products. Consider booking a suite or deluxe-view room to behold Lake Winnipesaukee. Linger on the inn's private sandy beach, wander its landscaped grounds, or cozy up to its fire pits. The inn is also walking distance from Wolfeboro village and near many access points for hiking, skiing, sledding, and other outdoor activities. *90 N. Main St., (603) 569-3016, www.wolfeboroinn.com.*

The Friendly Toast I Portsmouth. Work up an appetite before heading to this deliciously retro local's favorite. Regardless of the hour, you can get breakfast featuring dishes made with both classic and zesty ingredients like chorizo, goat cheese, and avocado-lime sauce. Sandwiches (on homemade bread), burgers, burritos, and daily specials round out the menu. Definitely try the Babe Benny, an eggs Benedict variation with pulled pork, poached eggs, and both Hollandaise *and* barbecue sauce—all on a warm slab of cornbread. *113 Congress St., (603) 430-2154, www.thefriendlytoast.com.*

Ale House Inn I Portsmouth. You don't have to drink to find yourself intoxicated by this inn. Though housed in the former Portsmouth Brewing Company warehouse (circa 1880), don't expect to find lace doilies, floral draperies, or other traditional trimmings. Here, it's all about industrial-chic (think exposed brick and loft-like design) and contemporary amenities (like complimentary in-room iPads). There's no onsite restaurant, but the inn is within walking distance of downtown Portsmouth's singular cafés, restaurants, bars, and boutiques. *121 Bow St., (603) 431-7760, www.alehouseinn.com.*

Portland, ME

Ogunquit Beach

Maine lobster

Ogunquit

Ogunquit Beach. This broad, gradually sloping, white-sand beach is consistently ranked one of America's 10 best. It covers 1.5 miles of oceanfront and another 3.5 miles along the Ogunquit River, behind frontal dunes. If you can take the chill, dive in around Memorial Day; but prime swimming, volleyball, bocce, and kite-flying season is July and August. Surfers ride waves near the mouth of the Ogunquit River. The scenic Marginal Way runs 1.5 miles along the craggy coast to Perkins Cove. *(207) 646-2939, ogunquit.org.*

Kennebunkport

Seashore Trolley Museum. The collection of rolling stock and memorabilia at this museum, founded in 1939, represents almost every major American city (and a few foreign ones) that has or had a streetcar system. Here you'll learn about the origins of mass transportation as well as the dedicated craftsmanship behind the early workhorse vehicles and their evolution into today's buses, light-rail vehicles, and rapid-transit cars. From May through October, you can take in the 330 acres of grounds aboard a historic trolley as well as tour the museum. *195 Log Cabin Rd., (207) 967-2800, www.trolleymuseum.org.*

Old Orchard Beach

Old Orchard Beach & Pier. This 7-mile stretch of Maine coastline buzzes with seaside activity in warm months, when Old Orchard Beach becomes a hotspot for travelers from New England, Canada, and beyond. At the center of the sandy beach is the Pier, a shop- and restaurant-lined boardwalk. It's all anchored by the 4-acre **Palace Playland** (207/934-2001, www.palaceplayland.com), where kids and playful adults whirl, swirl, and slide on old-school amusements and new-fangled thrill rides. In summer, the beach sparkles with fireworks every Thursday evening. *(207) 934-2500, www.oldorchardbeachmaine.com.*

Portland

Maine Historical Society. Founded in 1822, the country's third-oldest state historical society is the best place to explore Maine's rich history. Its 1-acre campus in the heart of Portland's downtown cultural district consists of the society's museum and store, the Brown Library, and the Wadsworth-Longfellow House. Permanent exhibits bring history to life through housewares, textiles, tools, and toys as well as militaria and archaeological artifacts. Changing exhibits let you dive deeper into local and national history. The society also conducts walking tours and hosts special events both on and off campus. *489 Congress St., (207) 774-1822, www.mainehistory.org.*

Wadsworth-Longfellow House. This treasured National Historic Landmark is the oldest standing structure on the entire Portland peninsula, and the first wholly brick dwelling in the city. The three-story house was built in 1785 by General Peleg Wadsworth, grandfather of poet Henry Wadsworth Longfellow. Today the Maine Historical Society meticulously maintains the house and the family's original household items, art, and artifacts within. Behind it is the beautiful, secluded Longfellow Garden. From June through October, hour-long guided house tours are available daily between 10:30 (noon on Sun. and in May) and 4. *489 Congress St., (207) 774-1822, www.mainehistory.org.*

Portland Discovery Land & Sea Tours. City tours and Casco Bay excursions have long been this outfit's bailiwick. Its narrated, 105-minute City and Lighthouse trolley tour takes you to landmarks like the Portland Head Light (Maine's oldest lighthouse) and a few hidden gems tucked onto city streets and along the rocky coast. Options (all offered May through Oct.; schedules vary) also include shorter land tours, sunset and lighthouse cruises, and land-and-sea combination outings. *170 Commercial St., (207) 774-0808, www.portlanddiscovery.com.*

Freeport

L.L. Bean Flagship Store. The flagship store of this famous, family-run retailer—in business since 1917—never closes. Literally. It's open 24/7. So when you're gearing up for a pre-dawn backpacking or fishing trip and realize that you need a waterproof solar-powered flashlight or that your chest-high waders have sprung a leak, you're covered. You can also shop for Maine souvenirs while browsing the array of outdoor activity clothing and gear.

Test your goods on hiking ramps or learn more about them during demonstrations. Enjoy the indoor trout pond and all the taxidermy. L.L. Bean Outdoor Discovery Schools take things up a notch with private or group lessons (from an hour to as long as a week, both in-store and on-location) on fly fishing, kayaking, bird-watching, archery, and countless other wilderness activities. Note that the L.L.Bean Outlet is nearby. *95 Main St., (877) 755-2326, www.llbean.com.*

Eat & Stay

The Lobster Shack | Ogunquit. This is Maine, so there will be lobster—and and steamers, fresh-caught fish, and crab cakes. A one-time lobstermen's storage shack has been the site of a restaurant since 1947, when lobster and clam steamers were the only menu items, and butter cost extra. A straight-up boiled Maine lobster won't disappoint, but lobster wraps and lobster BLTs are worthy new diversions. *110 Perkins Cove Rd., (207) 646-2941, www.lobster-shack.com.*

Central Provisions | Portland. For a delicious alternative to traditional lobster houses, head to this Old Port restaurant inside a sturdy, 19th-century brick building. Well-prepared raw, cold, hot, or hearty small plates let you sample a range of flavor combinations across a variety of vegetable, meat, and seafood dishes. Try local oysters on the half shell, lobster fritters with bacon and saffron aioli, beet salad with avocado and green peppercorns, or foie gras with blood orange and millet granola. *414 Fore St., (207) 805-1085, www.central-provisions.com.*

The Chadwick Bed & Breakfast | Portland. Inside a restored 1891 house, four guest rooms have private baths, memory-foam mattresses, and electric fireplaces. Rates include a hot gourmet breakfast; Wi-Fi; and 24-hour access to snacks, beverages, DVDs, and books. Relax in an Adirondack chair beside a fire pit; wander the nearby Arts District and Old Port; or get in some hiking, biking, or other outdoor activities along the coast or in forested state parks west of town. *140 Chadwick St., (207) 774-5141, www.thechadwick.com.*

Old Orchard Beach Pier

Massachusetts Maritime Tour

ROUTE TOWNS: Newburyport | Ipswich | Essex | Rockport | Gloucester | Salem | Marblehead | Boston | Quincy Plymouth | New Bedford | Fall River

There's more than 400 years of history in many of the cities and towns that hug the Massachusetts coast. This trip between and through them is truly classic—and just a bit revolutionary.

Fort Pickering Lighthouse, Salem

The close proximity to the Atlantic has long fostered a co-dependence with the sea. To immerse yourself in the (aptly nicknamed) Bay State's rich maritime traditions, start at Newburyport's Custom House Maritime Museum on Boston's North Shore, and then head to Cape Ann to explore the Essex Shipbuilding Museum or board the *Lannon*, a century-old schooner that sails from Gloucester Harbor. Move from water to witches in Salem, home of the infamous witch trials and Nathaniel Hawthorne's House of the Seven Gables. Continuing south you'll soon be ensnarled in Boston's notorious traffic. If you need a break, "paahk the cahhh," and head out on foot to explore this vibrant city, where history meets sports meets culture at every turn.

The South Shore, a quieter but no less historic section of the coast, is just south of Boston. Here you'll find Plymouth, famous landing place of the Pilgrims in 1620; a replica of the *Mayflower*; and Plimoth Plantation, a living-history museum, where you can experience 17th-century life. New Bedford's historic whaling center and Lizzie Borden's hometown of Fall River await you farther along I-195.

Atlas map B-15, p. 49

Distance: 160 miles point to point.

Type of Trip: Weekend Getaway; Arts & Music, History & Heritage, Picture Perfect.

Must Try: Fresh seafood—fried, steamed, grilled, baked, boiled, broiled, battered, breaded, poached—with a side of Boston baked beans and a bottle of Sam Adams beer, followed by a slice of Boston cream pie.

Must Buy: Things that are very, very old. Antique stores abound in town centers, and if you see signs for a yard sale or an off-the-beaten path antiques spot, be sure to stop. Families have been here for several generations, and lots of stuff gets handed down, whether it's wanted or not.

Must See: Faneuil Hall, Boston Tea Party Ships and Museum, New England Aquarium, Custom House Maritime Museum, Salem Witch Museum, Plimoth Plantation.

Worth Noting: The best time to do this trip is the week right before Memorial Day (but not the weekend itself) because the weather is good yet the higher summer rates haven't yet kicked in (and won't do so till mid-June or after July 4th). Early spring sees wildly unpredictable weather. Fall, on the other hand, offers that famous New England foliage. Winter is cold, but the holidays bring craft bazaars and Christmas-themed historic house tours.

Travel Tips: If you're flying, you can start at Boston's Logan International Airport or Providence's T. F. Green Airport (and then do this trip in reverse). To lengthen this itinerary, consider pairing it with the coastal areas of the Northern New England Summits & Shores trip and/or the Connecticut Coast & River Valley trip.

Newburyport

Custom House Maritime Museum. Newburyport was settled in 1653 at the intersection of the Merrimack River and the Atlantic Ocean, almost immediately solidifying its importance as a commercial port. The town was home to a thriving shipyard in the 19th century, and some claim that this is the birthplace of the U.S. Coast Guard. The museum, housed in a handsome Greek-revival building, contains objects that represent this maritime history. There are stunning models and paintings of the clipper ships that once plied their trade in this area, as well as artifacts from actual ships that made it back to port and those salvaged from ships lost at sea. The museum's Coast Guard Room tells its history through art and photos and helps to explain exactly what the Coast Guard does. *25 Water St., (978) 462-8681, www.customhousemaritimemuseum.org.*

Ipswich

Castle Hill on the Crane Estate. This plot of land has been prime real estate since the 1630s, when John Winthrop, Jr., son of the Massachusetts Bay Colony's first governor, got his hands on it. Several generations later, the land was bought by Richard T. Crane, Jr., who hired Frederick Law Olmsted's sons to design 165 acres of terraced gardens. Guided tours of the furnished, 59-room David Adler–designed Stuart-style Great House are offered, as are guided tours of the Olmsted-designed areas. To feel like you're part of the Roaring '20s summer set, book a night at the **Inn at Castle Hill** (280 Argilla Rd., 978/412-2555). In summer, Crane Beach is open to the public. *290 Argilla Rd., (978) 356-4354, www.thetrustees.org.*

Essex

Essex Shipbuilding Museum. This museum tells the story of the town's shipbuilding industry, which produced approximately 4,000 wooden-hulled ships between 1650 and 1950. Exhibits include photos, plans, half-hull and fully rigged models, tools, construction techniques, and hands-on displays at the original shipyard. If you take the tour you'll see a video about traditional shipbuilding and learn first-hand about what is required to craft a seaworthy vessel. A gift shop sells everything for the secret sailor inside of you. *66 Main St., (978) 768-7541, www.essexshipbuildingmuseum.org.*

Rockport

The Paper House. Rockport's a haven for artists of all persuasions and levels of talent, as a casual stroll along the harborfront will attest. The Paper House, which was built out of newspaper in 1922 by Elis Stenman, is a perfect example of this creativity. Stenman, a mechanical engineer—who, incidentally, had a hand in making paper clips—also constructed the furniture for his summer house out of paper, including a piano and a grandfather clock. *52 Pigeon Hill St., (978) 546-2629, www.paperhouserockport.com.*

Gloucester

Gloucester

Schooner sail on the *Thomas E. Lannon.* At this point you've seen the water, you've smelled the water, maybe you've been in the water, but have you been out *on the water?* The *Lannon,* a century-old working schooner, takes people on a two-hour excursion around Gloucester Harbor; you may have to help raise and lower the sails. On the weekends, there's sometimes live music aboard, which makes it all the merrier. Note: Sailing is extremely dependent on the weather. *63 Rogers St., (Rte. 127), (978) 281-6634, schooner.org.*

Salem

The House of the Seven Gables. Yes, the House of the Seven Gables really exists. Built in 1688 by wealthy local merchant John Turner, it eventually became the home of Susanna Ingersoll, Nathaniel Hawthorne's second cousin. Hawthorne visited the house during the five years he worked as a surveyor at the Salem Custom House, which gave him the inspiration for his famous novel of the same name. On your tour of the house take in the wealth of items on display (furniture, carpets, dinnerware, paintings, and other domestic items from the mid-1800s) and the "Secret Staircase," a steep, narrow passage—accessed through the false back of a closet—that leads to the attic. *115 Derby St., (978) 744-0991, www.7gables.org.*

Marblehead

Chandler Hovey Park and Marblehead Light Tower. The iron-frame support structure and rust-orange exterior make Marblehead Light Tower stand out from more traditional Eastern seaboard lighthouses, but that makes it all the more interesting, as it's the only one of its type in New England. Unfortunately, lighthouse access is off limits, but the nearly 4-acre Chandler Hovey Park that surrounds it has spectacular views of the coast and Marblehead Harbor activity. There's a parking area, restrooms, benches, picnic tables, and swimming in season. *Follett St., (781) 631-3350, www.marblehead.org.*

Eat & Stay

Woodman's | Essex. Founded in 1914, Woodman's claims to have invented the fried clam strip, a local culinary classic that you *must* try. The prices are a little high, and the lines are always out the door, but it's all worth it. The lobster rolls and the New England clam chowder, regional food staples, are equally top-notch. *121 Main St., (978) 768-2559, www.woodmans.com.*

Salem: City of Witches

Salem is most known for, of course, the 1692 Witch Trials, one of the strangest episodes in American colonial history. Fourteen women and five men were hanged after being convicted of sorcery, and one man died after being pressed to death over the course of two days. The **Salem Witch Museum** (19½ Washington Sq. N., 978/744-1692, www.salemwitchmuseum.com) has stage sets that use figures and narration to bring this frightening era to life.

The gift shop sells all sorts of one-of-a-kind witchy paraphernalia including Salem witch bottles (small glass vessels filled with sand, salt, a nail, and a charm that colonists used to use to ward off evil). Visit in October for **Salem Haunted Happenings** (www.hauntedhappenings.org), as it's full of Halloween-themed events that culminate on the 31st with tricks and treats, Salem pirates during the day, and the annual Salem Witches' Halloween Ball and fireworks at night.

Salem Witch Museum

city itinerary

Boston: Where It All Began

Today, this very in-the-now city is sports-mad (lifelong devotion to the Sox, Celts, Bruins, and Pats is assumed); rich in intellectual institutions; home to firms and start-ups at the forefront of 21st-century technology; and a place where world-class restaurants, long-time local favorites, and ethnic eateries thrive. But Boston also embraces its rich history at every turn. After all, the city was instrumental in forming the Massachusetts Bay Colony, in the events that led to the American Revolution, and in the early life of the new Republic. It may not be the actual "hub of the solar system" (which is how Oliver Wendell Holmes referred to the Massachusetts State House, on Boston's Beacon Hill, in 1858) but plenty of locals would argue otherwise: Boston's nickname is "The Hub."

Travel Tips: Hundreds of thousands of people drive into, out of, and around Boston daily. Don't be one of them. Consider parking outside the city and taking the ubiquitous subway, known as the "T," to get into and around town. There are also free shuttles from Logan International Airport to the MBTA's Airport station on the Blue Line. Alternately, the Silver Line, a dedicated rapid bus service, stops at all the terminals and continues on to the Red Line's South Station. Amtrak from New York stops first at Back Bay station, with connections to the T's Orange Line, and then at South Station, with connections to the Red Line.

Visitor Info: Greater Boston CVB, 2 Copley Pl., (888) 733-2678, www.bostonusa.com.

1 Boston Common. This lively urban park has paths, fields, shady trees, a duck pond, and benches. It's ringed by handsome commercial and residential buildings and crowned by the Massachusetts State House, with its majestic golden dome. During the mid-1600s, this area was home to some of the colony's first European settlers. For a small fee, residents could graze their livestock on the "common." During the Revolutionary War period, it was a British encampment, and in the 1960s, it was a gathering spot for activists. The Common is also the beginning of the 2.5-mile Freedom Trail, which leads to 15 other Colonial and Revolutionary War sites. *Bordered by Beacon, Park, Tremont, Boylston, and Charles sts. (617) 635-4505, www.cityofboston.gov.*

2 The Freedom Trail. Sixteen sites important to Boston's Colonial and Revolutionary War periods are linked via a 2.5-mile red-lined brick path embedded in the sidewalks. The tour begins at Boston Common and ends at Bunker Hill. It takes you through the heart of Boston and to three historic cemeteries; the Old South Meeting House, where speeches and debates furthered the cause of independence;

the Old State House; Faneuil Hall; and the Paul Revere House. Although some attractions (Old State House and Paul Revere House) charge admission, the self-guided trail is free. Faneuil Hall's first floor has a National Park Service information center with maps and guided tours. *Boston Common Visitors Center, 139 Tremont St., (617) 357-8300, www.thefreedomtrail.org.*

3 The Old State House. Built in 1713, this was the seat of the Massachusetts colony's English government. It was from here that the Declaration of Independence was read to the people of Boston on July 18, 1776. The lion and unicorn atop the building are reproductions, as the originals, which represented the Crown, were burned in post-reading-of-the-Declaration exuberance. Guided and self-guided tours are offered. The Revolutionary Characters exhibit contains artifacts and documents related to people from that era, and the Revolutionary Treasures exhibit has unique items from the period. There's also a multimedia show about the Boston Massacre, which took place just outside. *206 Washington St., (617) 720-1713, www.bostonhistory.org.*

The Old State House

Eat & Stay

4 The Bell in Hand Tavern. This time-honored tavern was founded in 1795 by Jimmy Wilson, the town crier whose job it was to walk the streets, bell in hand, literally crying out the news of the day. Today there's a good selection of beers, cocktails, and American pub fare, with items that the original patrons would have recognized (baked haddock, fish and chips, New England clam chowder) and some they would not (chicken quesadillas, Reuben sandwiches). Try to snag a table near one of the large windows that open in warm weather and provide excellent people watching. *45 Union St., (617) 227-2098, bellinhand.com.*

5 Boston Harbor Hotel. One of the country's finest hotels was built in 1987 and is easily recognizable by its 80-foot central arch, which leads to Rowes Wharf. The 230 rooms and suites are on the 8th through the 16th floors, and all have large picture windows that allow for stunning views of the harbor or the city; some of the grander suites have private balconies. For dining, there's the highly acclaimed Meritage or the informal Rowes Wharf Sea Grille. *70 Rowes Wharf, (617) 439-7000, www.bhh.com.*

George Washington statue in Public Garden

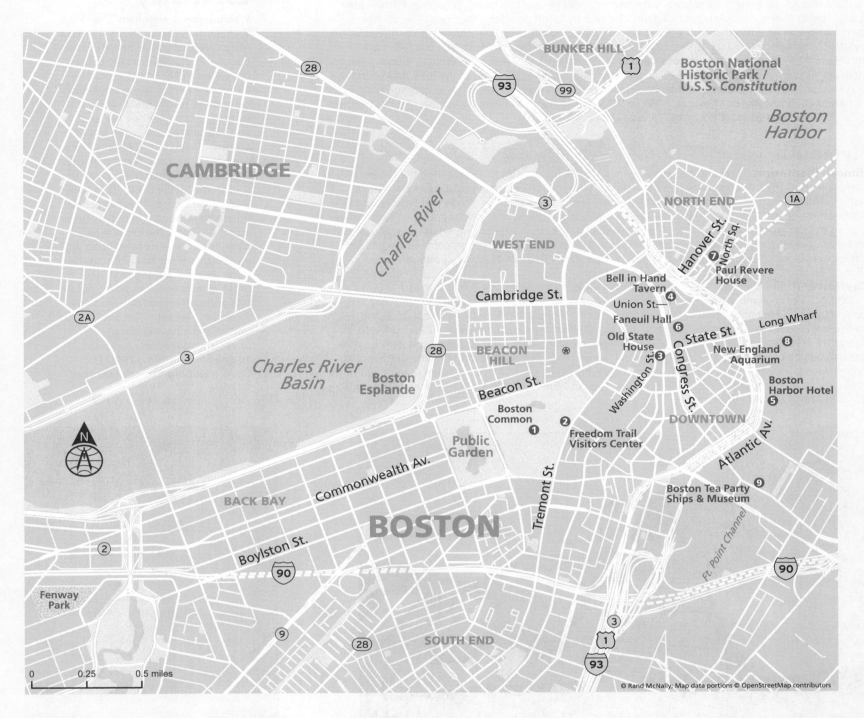

CAMBRIDGE

BUNKER HILL

Boston National
Historic Park /
U.S.S. *Constitution*

Boston Harbor

NORTH END

Paul Revere House ⑦

WEST END

Bell in Hand Tavern ④
Union St.
Faneuil Hall ⑥
Old State House
State St.
Long Wharf
New England Aquarium ⑧

Cambridge St.

BEACON HILL

Boston Harbor Hotel ⑤

Boston Esplande

DOWNTOWN

Beacon St.

Boston Common ①

Public Garden

Freedom Trail Visitors Center ②

Atlantic Av.

BOSTON

Commonwealth Av.

BACK BAY

Boston Tea Party Ships & Museum ⑨

Boylston St.

Fenway Park

SOUTH END

Tremont St.

Hanover St.
North Sq.
Washington St.
Congress St.
Ft. Point Channel

Charles River

Charles River Basin

© Rand McNally; Map data portions © OpenStreetMap contributors

0   0.25   0.5 miles

The Paul Revere House

⑥ **Faneuil Hall.** Wealthy merchant Peter Faneuil built his namesake hall in 1741 to market imported and exported goods (including, sadly, slaves). The building was used by Samuel Adams and other Sons of Liberty in the 1760s and '70s to protest British Colonial rule. Still a venue for political speeches and public meetings, Faneuil Hall now encompasses the original hall, as well as the North, South, and Quincy Market buildings. True to its commercial past, the complex is home to retail outlets, restaurants, and vendors that sell take-away food and souvenirs. *1 Faneuil Hall Sq., (617) 242-5642, www.cityofboston.gov/ freedomtrail.*

⑦ **The Paul Revere House.** Although prosperous silversmith Paul Revere is best known for his "midnight ride" to Lexington and Concord, warning all along the way that the British were coming, as a member of the Sons of Liberty he was also instrumental in establishing an underground revolutionary network. You can tour his restored 18th-century house, where two rooms contain items once owned by his family. The gift shop sells reproductions of Revere's silver and engraving work, along with things like Revere-themed coffee mugs and refrigerator magnets. *19 North Sq., (617) 523-2338, www.paulreverehouse.org.*

⑧ **New England Aquarium.** Penguins, though not native to Boston, take pride of place here, but they are only a fraction of the aquarium's thousands of examples of marine life. Many different environments are re-created such as an Amazon rainforest, a coral reef, coastal Maine, and a harbor seal habitat.

If you want to see whales—right whales, humpbacks, pilot whales—and dolphins, take Boston Harbor Cruises' **New England Aquarium Whale Watch** (1 Long Wharf, 617/227-4321, www.bostonharborcruises.com/ whale-watch), which is a three-hour tour offered in conjunction with the Aquarium. *1 Central Wharf, (617) 973-5200, www.neaq.org.*

⑨ **Boston Tea Party Ships and Museum.** On the evening of December 16, 1773, members of the underground group Sons of Liberty disguised themselves as Mohawk Indians, boarded three British trade ships anchored at Griffin's Wharf, and dumped their payload of tea chests into Boston Harbor. At this museum honoring what came to be known as the Boston Tea Party, you can become a colonial-era participant in a mock meeting where a Sam Adams re-enactor whips the crowd into an anti-tax frenzy. Or, you can board a replica of the *Beaver,* one of the ships at the wharf that night, and throw simulated bales of tea into the harbor. Abigail's Tea Room has tea (ahem), soft drinks, beer and wine, and assorted pastries and sandwiches. *Congress St. Bridge, (866) 955-0667, www.bostonteapartyship.com.*

Quincy

Adams National Historical Park. In 1787, John Adams, the country's second president, purchased the "Old House," which was subsequently the home of four generations of this preeminent American family; Abigail Adams and John Quincy Adams, the country's sixth president, lived here. The 13-acre site encompasses an additional 11 historic structures, including a formal 18th-century style garden, the presidential birthplaces, and the United First Parish Church, where the presidents and first ladies are entombed. All tours start at the **visitors center** (1250 Hancock St.), which has exhibits, a bookstore, and a free 26-minute film about the Adams family. The two-hour trolley tour stops at the John Adams and the John Quincy Adams birthplaces and then continues to the "Old House," which has a collection of Louis XV furniture John Adams purchased in 1780. In the formal garden you'll find a rosebush that has bloomed since 1788. *135 Adams St., (617) 770-1175, www.nps.gov/adam.*

Plymouth

Plimoth Plantation. This living history museum recreates the daily life of Pilgrims and the native Wampanoags in 1627 through recreated homesteads, costumed re-enactors, cooking demonstrations, lectures, and games. There's also a crafts center, where workers use traditional tools and techniques to produce most of the items you'll see in use on the grounds; a working grist mill; and the Nye Barn, where you can meet animals, many of which are direct descendants of the cattle, sheep, goats, pigs, and birds the Pilgrims would have encountered or brought with them from England. The visitors center has a gift shop that features Colonial-era items and a café. *137 Warren Ave., (508) 746-1622, www.plimoth.org.*

Mayflower II. The original, 102-foot-long, 25-foot-wide, four-masted *Mayflower* carried 102 passengers (including three pregnant women) and cargo to the New World in 1620. The replica you see today was constructed in an English shipyard in the mid-1950s using materials faithful to the original, including lumber, hemp ropes, hand-sewn canvas sails, and individually forged nails. *Mayflower II* was sailed to Plymouth in 1957 and is still seaworthy. When you tour the ship, guides and costumed role players share details about life onboard. Spoiler alert: It was pretty grim. Though the ship is part of Plimoth Plantation, it's docked in Plymouth Harbor and can, and probably should, be seen on its own rather than as part of the Plimoth Plantation day-pass option—you don't want to get Pilgrim fatigue. *State Pier, across from 74 Water St., (508) 746-1622, www.plimoth.org.*

Plimoth Plantation

New Bedford

New Bedford Whaling National Historical Park. Whale-oil lamps were ubiquitous in the mid-19th century, and New Bedford was the world's premier whaling port and, thus, its richest city per capita. With a collection of museums, historic homes and buildings, and a working waterfront, the park invites you to explore the town in the context of its golden past and its importance to the nation and the world. The visitors center has self-guided tours and maps, a brief movie, and helpful park personnel. Guided tours of New Bedford leave from the center daily and last approximately one hour. *33 William St., (508) 996-4095, www.nps.gov/nebe/index.htm.*

Fall River

Lizzie Borden Bed & Breakfast Museum. This unusual B&B's motto, "Where everyone is treated like family," might seem a touch ironic, given the children's rhyme that goes: "Lizzie Borden took an axe / And gave her mother 40 whacks / And when she saw what she had done / She gave her father 41." While it might not be true (there's still considerable debate), that's the gist of the story. Even if you don't spend the night, you can tour the house and learn about the events that took place before the August 4, 1892, double murder, Lizzie's indictment, and her subsequent acquittal. Guests staying at the inn are given a "more involved" 90-minute house tour. Note: If you do stay here, you have to make your room accessible for the tours, which are held daily 11–3. *230 2nd St., (508) 675-7333, www.lizzie-borden.com.*

Battleship Cove. The cove's highlight is the USS *Massachusetts*. Nicknamed "Big Mamie," she launched in 1942 and soon saw action during WW II's Allied invasion of North Africa. She participated in numerous other battles, but not a single sailor died while onboard. Despite her illustrious career she was decommissioned and destined for the scrap heap until a group of veterans, aided by Massachusetts schoolchildren, raised the funds to bring her to Fall River in 1965. She's been joined by the destroyer USS *Joseph P. Kennedy, Jr.*, built in 1945 and named after JFK's older brother; the WW II–era submarine USS *Lionfish*; and the *Hiddensee*, a Soviet-built missile corvette that was part of the East German fleet and is the only one of its kind in the United States. *5 Water St., (508) 678-1100, www.battleshipcove.org.*

Newport: Millionaire's Walk

If you're carrying on to Connecticut or New York City, consider stopping in Newport, Rhode Island. You'll see many of the city's famous Gilded Age "cottages" from the 3.5-mile **Cliff Walk** (401/845-5300, www.cliffwalk.com), which is perched high above Newport's shoreline. Here you'll find The Breakers, a 70-room Italianate estate commissioned by Cornelius Vanderbilt; Marble House, built by Cornelius's younger brother, William; and Rosecliff, which was designed by one of the Gilded Age's most famous and talented architects, Stanford White.

Cliff Walk can be accessed from several streets along the way, but most visitors start at Memorial Boulevard on the northern end, where there's a parking lot (the other is at Narragansett Avenue). Much of the walk is fenced, but in some spots you're just a couple of feet from tumbling off the side. Two sets of stairs help you cross some particularly steep sections, and several lookouts provide fine ocean views. Toward the southern end things get a little more treacherous, so proceed with caution, and always look out for poison ivy. Dogs are allowed as long as they are leashed and curbed.

The Breakers mansion

Connecticut Coast & River Valley

ROUTE TOWNS: Mystic I Groton I New London I Old Lyme I Old Saybrook I Essex I East Haddam I Haddam
Middletown I Hartford I New York, NY

For many, Connecticut is a place to drive through between Boston and the Big Apple. But, with centuries of Yankee history and heritage, this state is worth hopping off the highway to explore.

Mystic Seaport

Time-honored rural routes travel through ivy-wrapped, old-growth forests, along waterscapes both fresh and salty, into towns with true village greens, and past Colonial houses with tidy gardens. Indeed, as the scenery and sights suggest, decorum is part and parcel of Connecticut living (no surprise that Martha Stewart started her empire here). So, by all means, head through en route to other urbane or bucolic northeastern destinations . . . just be sure to stop and give this state its due.

This short but sight-rich tour takes you from Long Island Sound estuaries through the Connecticut River Valley and into Hartford. It highlights the contributions of Connecticut's waterside communities—from pre-Colonial days through the Revolutionary War and beyond. Among the coastal treasures are the renowned maritime museum and aquarium in Mystic. Heading north along the Connecticut River, you'll learn about a woman named Arnold who was thankful and a man named Hale who had only one regret. You'll experience the legacy of myriad Connecticut artists, among them the writers Mark Twain and Harriet Beecher Stowe, the actor William Gillette, the playwright Eugene O'Neill, and a group of painters who were inspired enough by the area's landscapes—both wooded and watery—to form America's first Impressionist school.

Distance: 75 miles point to point; 195 miles point-to-point with a New York City excursion.

Type of Trip: Weekend Getaways; Arts & Culture, History & Heritage, Picture Perfect, Small Town Gems.

Must Try: Fresh seafood; a steamed cheeseburger (a culinary innovation that sounds weird but results in a truly juicy, tender burger); brick-oven pizza.

Must Buy: This state was once the home of Danforth Pewter, which supplied most of the nation's tableware between 1755 and the mid-1800s; although it moved to Vermont, Woodbury Pewter has continued the tradition. Its tankards, porringers, candlesticks, and other items are sold in shops throughout the state as well as in Woodbury's own factory outlet.

Must See: Mystic Seaport, Griswold Inn, Gillette Castle, Mark Twain House & Museum.

Worth Noting: Several communities, like Middletown, have town tours that will enrich your visit; inquire at local tourist boards or historical societies. Also, get out on the water aboard a sailing vessel out of Mystic, a riverboat out of Essex, or a motor yacht out of Old Saybrook.

Travel Tips: This trip makes a nice segment on a longer journey to/from the Berkshires (60–90 minutes from Hartford), Vermont's Green Mountains (three hours from Hartford), adjacent Rhode Island, Boston (90 minutes from Mystic), or coastal Massachusetts. It also pairs well with a New York City excursion (three hours from Hartford or Mystic). If you don't want to drive into the Big Apple, Amtrak has service from Hartford or Mystic. Visiting from outside the region? In addition to major urban airports, look into Bradley International near Hartford.

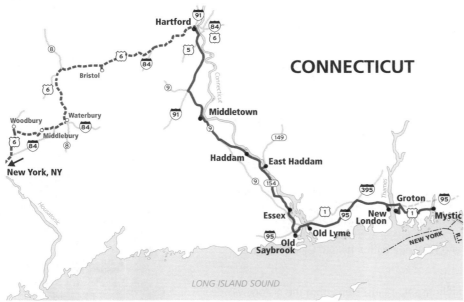

CONNECTICUT

LONG ISLAND SOUND

Atlas map F-13, p. 23

NORTHEAST

MIDWEST

SOUTH

WEST

Mystic

Mystic Seaport. At this spectacular maritime museum, you'll experience 19th-century seafaring life in a re-created village, with period-furnished residences and businesses, and through exhibits of art, ship models, and maritime artifacts. There's also a preservation shipyard, where craftsmen use traditional skills to restore and maintain historic ships, some of which you can climb—or even sail—aboard. Check the calendar. The Seaport hosts many ongoing and seasonal events; some, like the holiday Lantern Light Tours, are especially popular. *75 Greenmanville Ave., (860) 572-0711, www.mysticseaport.org.*

Mystic Aquarium. Sharks, stingrays, jellyfish, reptiles, and birds are among the 6,000 aquatic specimens you'll encounter here. In the Arctic Coast exhibit, underwater windows let you get up close and personal with Beluga whales. The Roger Tory Peterson penguin exhibit has views of its 35 residents above and below the water. In the Pacific Northwest exhibit, you'll see Steller sea lions and Northern fur seals. There are also sea mammal shows and 4-D movies. *55 Coogan Blvd., (860) 572-5955, www.mysticaquarium.org.*

Mystic Seaport

Groton

Submarine Force Museum. Submarines are an integral but often overlooked part of military history. Not at this museum and library operated by the U.S. Navy. More than 80,000 documents, photographs, and artifacts—from models to navigation equipment to weaponry—showcase the contributions of these underwater vessels. The museum, which is on the Thames River, is also the official home of the USS *Nautilus* (SSN 571), the world's first nuclear submarine (launched just downriver in 1955). See firsthand how its crew lived, worked, and made history. *1 Crystal Lake Rd., (860) 694-3174, www.ussnautilus.org.*

New London

Eugene O'Neill Homestead–Monte Cristo Cottage. In the early 1900s, young Eugene O'Neill and his family spent summers in this cottage overlooking the water. Named in honor of O'Neill's father, whose most popular acting role was in *The Count of Monte Cristo,* the 1840s-era cottage was the setting for two of the Nobel Prize–winning playwright's most famous works: *Long Day's Journey Into Night* and *Ah, Wilderness!* The home has an extensive collection of artifacts and memorabilia. *365 Pequot Ave., (860) 443-5378, www.theoneill.org/monte-cristo-cottage.*

Old Lyme

Florence Griswold Museum. Florence Griswold was the patron of such early 20th-century American painters as Childe Hassam, Henry Ward Ranger, and Willard Metcalf. The artists who boarded at her late-Georgian-style mansion between 1900 and the early '30s painted the surrounding landscapes, adopting European techniques and creating one of America's first Impressionist school art colonies. Today, her home, a National Historic Landmark, is an art museum. You can also see changing exhibits in the Krieble Gallery, visit an artist's studio, and stroll 11 acres of grounds. There's also a gift shop and a café (open May–Oct.). *96 Lyme St., (860) 434-5542, florencegriswoldmuseum.org.*

Old Saybrook

General William Hart House. William Hart had made his fortune trading in the West Indies by the time he led Connecticut's Light Horse Militia (and armed his family's merchant ships to harass the British) during the Revolution. He also had built this Georgian-style house (1767), one of Old Saybrook's oldest. Tours highlight intriguing architectural details and authentically planted Colonial gardens, with different areas for vegetables and flowers as well as herbs used for cooking, dyeing, and medicinal purposes. *350 Main St., (860) 395-1635, www.saybrookhistory.org.*

Essex

Essex Steam Train and Riverboat. Take a break from driving with a vintage train trip through the Connecticut River Valley. If you like, combine your ride with a riverboat cruise. You'll depart by rail from Essex station for a 12-mile narrated trip through wetlands and towns to Deep River Landing. Here, you'll board the three-deck *Becky Thatcher* riverboat and glide past coves, inlets, and historical sites like the Goodspeed Opera House. Some trips also combine a train and ferry ride with a hike to Gillette Castle. *1 Railroad Ave., (860) 767-0103, essexsteamtrain.com.*

Connecticut River Museum. In an 1878 steamboat warehouse that's just steps from the historic village of Essex, paintings, artifacts, models, and documents showcase life and industry along the river. Before or after your visit, book a sail aboard the *Mary E,* a 75-foot schooner built in 1906. There are several guided and self-guided museum tours, some of which include a sail, a walk through town, or lunch at the historic (and not to be missed) Griswold Inn. *67 Main St., (860) 767-8269, www.ctrivermuseum.org.*

Eat & Stay

Mystic Pizza I Mystic. This place has been serving pizza since 1973, well before it inspired screenwriter Amy Jones to feature it in the eponymous 1988 movie starring Julia Roberts. Experience the pizza and movie magic by popping in for a slice of the day, a whole pie, or a calzone or grinder. Pick up "A Slice of Heaven" T-shirt or cap on the way out. *56 W. Main St., (860) 536-3700, www.mytogo.co/ Mystic_Pizza.*

S&P Oyster I Mystic. A setting right on the Mystic River and fresh, delicious seafood, often with a Latin American twist, make this place a standout. Dine inside or al fresco on everything from traditional New England clam chowder, lobster rolls, and scallops to seafood white-bean chili, gazpacho, and Chilean sea bass. Of course, a lot of folks come for the oysters, fresh from New England and Canada. Save room for the chocolate pot de crème. *1 Holmes St., (860) 536-2674, sp-oyster.com.*

Steamboat Inn I Mystic. Colonial-contemporary chic, with the occasional nautical touch, best describes the aesthetic of this 11-room inn on the Mystic River—steps from sights, shops, and restaurants. Breakfast, included in the rates, is served in the common room, where you can also help yourself to beverages throughout the day or sip sherry in the evening. The inn also has loaner bicycles for two-wheeled town tours. *73 Steamboat Wharf, (860) 536-8300, steamboatinnmystic.com.*

The Griswold Inn I Essex. The beloved "Gris" has been a hostelry and tavern pretty much since opening in 1776. It rarely gets more authentic than this. The 33 rooms and suites have been modernized for comfort and convenience yet restored and decorated to period. The downstairs dining room specializes in fresh, flavorful, simply prepared American cuisine, sometimes featuring historical menus. The Wine Room has a tapas menu and tastings. The memorabilia-filled Tap Room, one of *Esquire* magazine's 100 Best Bars in America, serves up live music—from sea shanties to Dixieland banjo to rock—with beer, ale, and pub fare. Before leaving, pick up mementos across the street in Goods & Curiosities. *36 Main St., (860) 767-1776, griswoldinn.com.*

Florence Griswold Museum

Nathan Hale Schoolhouse

East Haddam

Gillette Castle State Park. It might have the shape and size of a medieval castle, but the fieldstone exterior gives this hilltop structure a texture unlike any you've seen before. The 24-room home (1914) was the creation of Connecticut native William Gillette, an eccentric actor known for his stage portrayals of Sherlock Holmes. It took local tradesmen five years to finish the main structure, with unusual built-in furnishings like a table that rolls on a track, elaborate hand-hewn woodwork, and 47 uniquely carved doors. The 84 landscaped acres and river views are no less impressive. A tour of both the grounds and the castle is a highlight of a visit to this wooded state park. You can combine a ride on the Essex Steam Train with a hike to the castle. *67 River Rd.,(860) 526-2336, www.ct.gov.*

Nathan Hale Schoolhouse. In 1773, 18-year-old Nathan Hale (already a Yale graduate) spent five months teaching at this one-room schoolhouse (circa 1750). When the Revolution began, Hale joined the Continental Army. In 1776, while spying in New York City, he was captured and executed by the British. His last words were, "I only regret that I have but one life to give for my country." Great words to ponder while touring the restored schoolhouse, complete with authentic desks, tools, and tables. *29 Main St., Rte. 149, (860) 873-3399, www.connecticutsar.org.*

Goodspeed Opera House. William Goodspeed loved theater enough to spend some of his banking and shipping fortune building this opera house. When completed in 1876, the Victorian confection, the tallest wooden structure on the Connecticut River, not only had a theater but also a steamboat terminal. Today, the season runs from mid-April through late-November with three productions of classics like *Bye Bye Birdie* or *Anything Goes.* If you can't get tickets (or musical theater isn't your thing), stop by for one of the hour-long, guided, backstage tours held every Saturday from 11 to 1 June through October. *6 Main St., (860) 873-8668, www.goodspeed.org.*

Haddam

Thankful Arnold House. It was a tradition in early New England for the often-devout colonizers to name their children for virtuous qualities like Chastity, Patience, Prudence, or Temperance. That's no doubt how Thankful Arnold (née Clark) got her unusual name. On the cellar-to-attic tours of this restored and furnished home, you'll learn about life in the late 18th and early 19th centuries as well as about the lives of Thankful, her husband, and their 12 children. Ask about the mysterious finds uncovered during restoration work. *14 Hayden Hill Rd., (860) 345-2400, www.haddamhistory.org.*

Middletown

General Mansfield House. Middletown, home of Wesleyan University, owes its name and its prosperity to a location on the Connecticut River, midway between Hartford and Old Saybrook. It was first settled in 1650 and, by the 1700s, was one of the state's wealthiest communities. It was also known for its Danforth pewter items. This history is documented through art, photographs, decorative arts, and textiles inside the General Mansfield House, one of the town's oldest buildings. Ask about the Middletown Heritage Trail, a walking tour with 20 historical sites. *151 Main St., (860) 346-0746, www.middlesexhistory.org.*

Hartford

Mark Twain House & Museum. In 1874, Samuel Clemens (aka Mark Twain) and his family moved into their beloved, 25-room, Picturesque Gothic Revival home in Hartford's exclusive Nook Farm district. By then, Clemens, a native of Missouri, was a seasoned traveler, journalist, novelist, and lecturer. But he hadn't yet penned his most famous works. He wrote *The Adventures of Tom Sawyer* (1876), *The Adventures of Huckleberry Finn* (1884), and *A Connecticut Yankee in King Arthur's Court* (1889) while living here. You can visit the house—with its many stunning features, including some designed by Louis Comfort Tiffany—on hour-long guided tours. Consider combining a visit here with one to the nearby Harriet Beecher Stowe House. *351 Farmington Ave., (860) 247-0998, www.marktwainhouse.org.*

Harriet Beecher Stowe House. The author of *Uncle Tom's Cabin* (1852) was born in Litchfield, CT, in 1811. The daughter of a minister, she and her 10 siblings were raised to "shape their world." Harriet did so through her writing, which focused on abolition and other social issues of the day. In 1873, Harriet, her husband, and their family settled into this brick cottage in the leafy Nook Farm district, where, the following year, Mark Twain became a neighbor. Tours, which depart from the visitors center inside a former carriage house, take in the first and second floors filled with family possessions. Inquire about combo tours of the Stowe and Twain houses. *77 Forest St., (860) 522-9258, www.harrietbeecherstowecenter.org.*

Wadsworth Atheneum. Highlights of America's oldest continually operating public art museum (since 1844) include a large collection of Hudson River School paintings; American fine and decorative art spanning myriad styles and periods; European Baroque, Renaissance, and Impressionist paintings; and an impressive collection of contemporary American and European art. The 7,500-piece Costume & Textiles collection has everything from gowns to drawings to notions. A gift shop and a café round out the offerings. *600 Main St., (860) 278-2670, www.thewadsworth.org.*

Eat & Stay

O'Rourke's Diner | Middletown. Not only is this shiny, Art-Deco diner a local architectural landmark, but it also serves a local specialty: the steamed cheeseburger. It sounds weird, but this method of preparation results in a truly juicy, truly tender patty with cheese melted into every nook and cranny. The owner's uncle, who opened this diner in 1941, once worked at the gone-but-not-forgotten Jack's Lunch, the Middletown institution where the steamed cheeseburger reportedly originated. *728 Main St., (860) 346-6101, www.orourkesmiddletown.com.*

Inn at Middletown | Middletown. Built as the residence of a wealthy banker in 1810—and large enough to later be used as an armory—this hotel blends stately brick Colonial styling with contemporary amenities. Everything here is well-appointed, from the lobby with its marble floors and two-story flying staircase to the rooms with their mahogany furnishings, flat-screen TVs, and free Wi-Fi. A stay here also puts you within walking distance of shops, the Connecticut River, and Wesleyan University. The on-site Tavern at the Armory restaurant offers an extensive menu for breakfast, lunch, and dinner. *70 Main St., (860) 854-6300, www.innatmiddletown.com.*

Firebox Restaurant | Hartford. Set in a restored redbrick building, the Firebox features a streamlined rustic décor and contemporary cuisine made, as much as possible, with ingredients from Connecticut and elsewhere in New England. Roughly 30% of the staff is also locally sourced—right from the neighborhood. Tuck into mussels in lager beer, rendered duck breast, or perfectly grilled salmon. For a quick bite and lighter fare, check out the adjacent Tavern at Firebox. *539 Broad St., (860) 246-1222, www.fireboxrestaurant.com.*

En Route to NYC

If you drive down to New York City, several places along or just off I-84 are worth a look. First up is a choice of two amusement parks with vintage and high-tech thrill rides: **Lake Compounce** (186 Enterprise Dr., Bristol, 860/583-3300, www.lake-compounce.com) opened in 1846; **Quassy** (2132 Middlebury Rd., Middlebury, 203/758-2913, www.quassy.com) has been around since 1908.

Connecticut has been in the button-making business for more than 200 years. Roughly 3,000 examples of these tiny works of art are displayed at the **Mattatuck Historical Society** (144 W. Main St., Waterbury, 203/753-0381, www.mattatuckmuseum.org), not far from Quassy Amusement Park. If you didn't shop for pewterware earlier, stop at **Woodbury Pewter Factory Outlet** (860 Main St. S., Woodbury, 800/648-2014 www.woodburypewter.com), for deals on this renowned company's creations and those from 40 other manufacturers.

NORTHEAST

MIDWEST

SOUTH

WEST

NORTHEAST

MIDWEST

SOUTH

WEST

city itinerary

New York, NY: Lower Manhattan Highlights

How do you tackle the Big Apple? One slice at a time. This two- or three-day itinerary serves up highlights of its oldest and most layered slice: Lower Manhattan (aka Downtown). Both the Dutch and English settled here. After the Revolution, Washington bade his troops farewell here. In the 19th and early 20th centuries, it gave countless immigrants their first glimpse of America and their first home in it. Of course, Lower Manhattan is also where tragedy struck that fateful September day in 2001. Constants throughout it all? Wall Street fortunes made and lost, goods shipped in and out, and the din and motion of an ever-evolving, never-sleeping city.

Travel Tips: The lack of a grid of numbered streets makes navigation tricky, but Lower Manhattan's history- and culture-rich neighborhoods truly invite exploration on foot. That said, numerous subways and buses serve downtown and can quickly whisk you elsewhere in Manhattan—or Brooklyn, for that matter. Note: A stroll to the latter borough across either the Brooklyn or Williamsburg bridges is a great way to spend an hour or two. So is a free ferry ride out and back to Staten Island from downtown's Whitehall (South) Ferry Terminal.

Visitor Info: NYC & Company, 810 7th Ave., 10019, (212) 484-1200, www.nycgo.com.

Statue of Liberty

Reflecting pool at the National September 11 Memorial & Museum

❶ Castle Clinton National Monument.
If your ancestors arrived in this country via New York between 1855 and 1890, chances are they passed through immigration at Castle Clinton (aka Castle Garden), originally built as part of War of 1812 defenses. All the more fitting that today, this is the jumping off point for Statue Cruises ferries to the Statue of Liberty and Ellis Island national monuments. Before setting sail, take in the splendid harbor views and check out the often-overlooked exhibits showcasing the structure's storied past, which is intrinsically linked to the history of early 19th-century Manhattan. Admission to Castle Clinton, open daily 7:45 to 5, is free as are the 20-minute ranger tours held daily at 10, noon, 2, and 4. *Battery Park, (212) 344-7220, www.nps.gov/cacl.*

Monumental Trips
Statue Cruises (www.statuecruises. com) ferries stop at both of the harbor's national monuments, allowing you to hop off and back on before returning to the starting dock. Book ahead as some cruises do sell out. The Castle Clinton ticket kiosk is open daily 8:30 or 9–4:45 or 6:30, depending on the season; the last ferry departs the mainland at 3:30 or 5, Liberty Island at 5 or 6:45, and Ellis Island at 5:15 or 7.

❷ Statue of Liberty National Monument.
New York's most recognizable landmark was sculpted by Frederic Auguste Bartholdi for the French government, which gave it to the United States on July 4, 1886, to commemorate the French/American alliance during the Revolutionary War. Since then, the 152-foot copper statue has served as a welcome to, in Emma Lazarus's words, the "huddled masses yearning to breathe free." The 45-minute ranger (or self-guided audio) tours cover construction, symbolism, and restoration. Exhibits at the museum inside the pedestal, which also has an elevator up to an observation deck, lend still more insight. The climb to the crown—up the 154 steps of a spiral staircase—rewards you with fantastic harbor views. *Liberty Island, (212) 363-3200, www.nps.gov/stli.*

❸ Ellis Island Museum of Immigration.
The primary East Coast entry point for America's newcomers between 1892 and 1954, the 27.5-acre Ellis Island is now part of the Statue of Liberty National Monument. During the highly recommended ranger-led tours (or self-guided audio tours), you'll learn how 12 million immigrants underwent literacy tests and physicals as part of being processed. You'll also see the Baggage Room, the Great Hall Registry Room, and the Railroad Ticket Office. A searchable database contains over 22 million passenger manifests, theaters show documentaries, and the American Immigrant Wall of Honor is engraved with more than 500,000 names. *Ellis Island, (212) 363-3200, www.nps.gov/elis.*

Eat & Stay
❹ **Delmonico's.** If you like eggs Benedict, you have this place to thank. It's just one of the many firsts at America's first fine-dining restaurant. Before the Delmonico brothers opened their doors in 1837, eating at individual tables and choosing from a selection of dishes printed on menus were unheard of. By the Gilded Age, anyone who had made it in New York dined here. The setting is as stately as ever; dress accordingly. Though not required, reservations are a good idea. *56 Beaver St., (212) 590-1144, www.delmonicosrestaurant.com.*

❺ **Fraunces Tavern.** New York's oldest standing structure (1719) is a tavern—just like in the old days. It's also a museum with permanent exhibits that include the second-floor Long Room, where George Washington bade farewell to his troops in 1783, and the Clinton Room, a recreated Federal-style dining room. Several other galleries host changing exhibits of early Americana. The restaurant, a maze of dining rooms, features standard American fare for brunch, lunch, and dinner. Celebrate the Spirit of 1776 with the specialty chicken pot pie (one of Washington's favorite dishes) and a glass of whiskey or pint of small-batch beer in the Dingle Whiskey Bar. *54 Pearl St., (212) 968-1776, www.frauncestavern.com.*

Lower East Side Tenement Museum

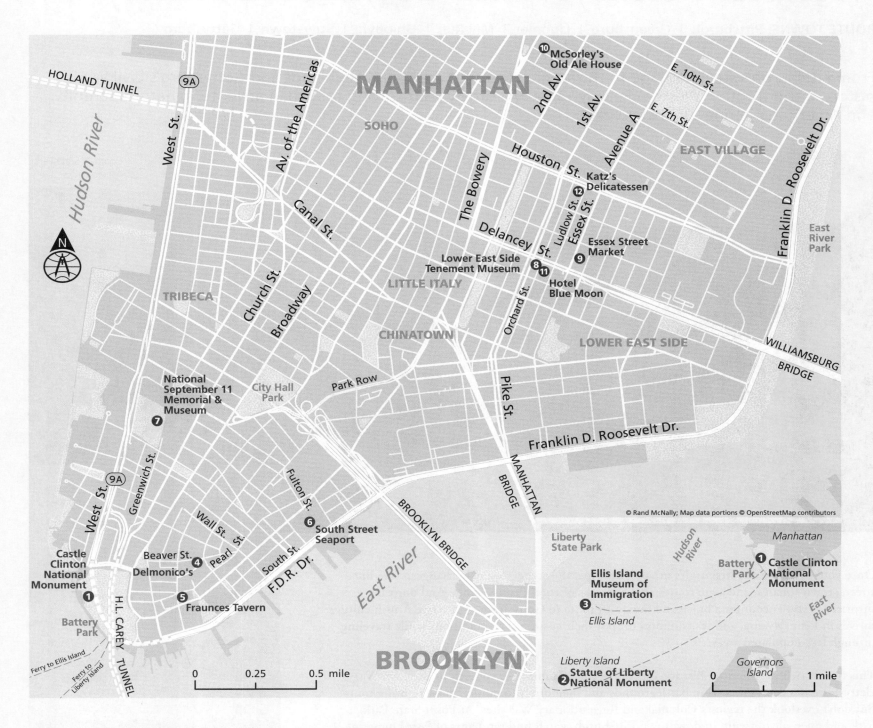

6 South Street Seaport. This restored 18th- and 19th-century port district is fun for the whole family, with landmark architecture; historic ships; and a pirate's booty of exhibits, restaurants, pubs, shops, and vendors. The dock area berths several late 18th and early 19th century ships, some open for tours and/or harbor excursions—a great way to end a day. *12 Fulton St. (212) 748-8600, southstreetseaportmuseum.org.*

7 National September 11 Memorial & Museum. Thoughtful, thought-provoking displays of artifacts and audiovisual clips tell the story of 9/11 before, during, and after the terrorist attacks. The interactive Wall of Faces tells the stories of the nearly 3,000 victims in New York (2001 and 1993), at the Pentagon, and on United Flight 93 in Pennsylvania. At the memorial, water cascades down into two square reflecting pools designed to represent the footprints of the World Trade Center towers and edged by panels etched with the names of those who lost their lives. *180 Greenwich St., (212) 312-8800, www.911memorial.org.*

8 Lower East Side Tenement Museum. For decades, the Lower East Side's rough-and-tumble streets were home to countless immigrants struggling to achieve the American Dream. Some of their stories are shared on tours of several re-created apartments at 97 Orchard Street, a five-story tenement building, National Historic Landmark, and must-see museum. All

told, between 1863 and 1935, some 7,000 people from 20 nations lived at this address. Tours depart from the Museum Shop/Visitors Center and last 60, 90, or 120 minutes; prices vary, and reservations are recommended. *103 Orchard St. (877) 975-3786, www.tenement.org.*

9 Essex Street Market. Combine a visit to the Tenement Museum with one to this bustling Lower East Side institution. It's filled with stalls selling dewy fish, handmade chocolates, specialty ice cream, freshly baked pastries, gourmet cheeses, and farm fresh produce. It's a great place to nosh on the go! *120 Essex St., (212) 312-3603, www.essexstreetmarket.com.*

10 McSorley's Old Ale House. There are older New York saloons—Bridge Cafe (1794), Ear Inn (1817), Chumley's (1830s)—but few retain that old Lower Manhattan working-class patina quite like McSorley's. The date of its establishment is questionable: Most say 1854, some 1862. Little has changed here since then, though, and there's a lingering smell that can only be achieved via a sawdust-covered floor and a bar that's been alternately drenched with beer and rubbed with wood polish for decades. *15 E. 7th St., (212) 474-9148, mcsorleysoldalehouse.nyc*

Eat & Stay

11 Hotel Blue Moon. A stay at this chic, 22-room boutique hotel, steps from the Lower East Side Tenement Museum, not only puts you right in the neighborhood that was once home to many of the "huddled masses" but also in a building where some actually lived. Public areas in this restored 19th-century tenement showcase original woodwork and artifacts, including items found during restoration. Rooms average twice the size of most New York guest quarters and come in several configurations. All are named after early 20th century celebrities. *100 Orchard St., (347) 294-4552, www.bluemoon-nyc.com.*

12 Katz's Delicatessen. This deli has been serving hungry Lower East Siders since 1888. You can't miss the neon sign, which rarely goes dim—a good thing in a city that never sleeps and likes to nosh at all hours. The Rueben, pastrami, corned-beef, brisket, and other sandwiches here are huge and tasty. The bagels, matzo-ball soup, hot dogs, and cheesecake are renowned. *205 E. Houston St., (212) 254-2246, www.katzsdelicatessen.com.*

Western Pennsylvania Town & Country

ROUTE TOWNS: Pittsburgh | Greensburg | Ligonier | Mill Run | Ohiopyle | Stoystown | Gettysburg

From Pittsburgh's steel heritage to the scenic beauty of the Laurel Highlands and Gettysburg's Civil War history, a trip through Western Pennsylvania will satisfy your craving for urban adventure, natural serenity, and Americana in one succinct weekend.

Ohiopyle State Park

Once you're outside of Pittsburgh's urban landscape, the scenery quickly changes. Tree-lined streets, town squares, and state routes are hallmarks of rural Pennsylvania. And don't be surprised if you encounter a horse and buggy en route to Gettysburg—an active Amish culture thrives in Pennsylvania, and it's common to spot their customs and traditions while traveling through less-populated areas.

This tour is rich in American history. Of course you can immerse yourself in the Civil War: Gettysburg has everything from battlegrounds and memorials to quirky ghost-sighting tours. But don't overlook the region's Colonial and Revolutionary War sites. At Point State Park, a park and open-air museum in downtown Pittsburgh, you'll find remnants of Fort Duquesne and other artifacts. At Fort Ligonier, you'll learn about the daily life of a soldier during the French and Indian War and get a chance to experience history through the eyes of George Washington. Fast forward to the 21st century to a field in Stoystown that was forever changed by the tragic events of September 11, 2001.

Atlas map WM-4, p. 87

Distance: 291 miles point to point.

Type of Trip: Weekend Getaway; RV; Arts & Culture, History and Heritage, Sports Fans.

Must Try: Don't pass up a chance to try a Primanti Bros. sandwich. Many a hungry trucker or office worker has devoured this Pittsburgh original. Farnsworth House Inn's main dining room specializes in period fare; try the game pie.

Must Buy: Sports enthusiasts, especially Steelers fans, should pick up an iconic Terrible Towel. Gettysburg finds include Civil War memorabilia ranging from authentic antiques to kitsch replicas. Throughout the region look for folk art inspired by Pennsylvania Dutch and Amish designs.

Must See: The Andy Warhol Museum, Senator John Heinz History Center, Duquesne Incline, Fallingwater, Flight 93 National Memorial, Gettysburg National Military Park.

Worth Noting: Pittsburgh offers three distinct shopping areas: the South Side, with its artsy vibe; the Strip District, with its wholesale and ethnic markets; and Shadyside, with its upscale shops. Restaurants, bars, and concert venues also make these popular destinations for a night out. In Gettysburg, the antiques shops lining Steinwehr Avenue make for a shopping experience that's more like a scavenger hunt.

Travel Tips: Take this trip in the fall to see spectacular displays of autumnal colors.

city itinerary

Pittsburgh

Downtown and the North Shore

❶ The Andy Warhol Museum. Each floor of this seven-story building follows a decade of the life and art of Andy Warhol, who was born in Pittsburgh in 1928. In addition to the well-known Pop Art collection (those Campbell's soup cans) and portraits (Elvis, Marilyn, Jackie O), the museum has extensive archives and about a half-million bits of ephemera such as party invitations, scrapbooks, personal items, and his trademark silver-white wigs. The café is a convenient place for lunch. *117 Sandusky St., (412) 237-8300, www.warhol.org.*

❷ Fort Pitt Museum. A walk to Point State Park, where the Monongahela, Allegheny, and Ohio rivers meet, will lead you to this two-story museum, which details the city's origins as it emerged from the French and Indian War. Displays cover Native American and military history, Colonial settlement, and early industry. There are living history exhibits and events, audiovisual presentations, and a gift shop. After touring the museum, stop by the Fort Pitt Block House, which was built in 1764 and is Pittsburgh's oldest structure. The remnants of Fort Duquesne are just beyond the house. *601 Commonwealth Pl., (412) 281-9284, www.heinzhistorycenter.org.*

Southside and Mount Washington

❸ Duquesne Incline. It was built to haul freight and passengers up Mount Washington, and today its century-old cable cars—whose cherry, oak, and maple interiors have been fully restored—carry commuters as well as visitors. The views are panoramic from the Upper Station observation deck and from several restaurants along Grandview Avenue. There's free parking across the street from the Lower Station. *1197 W. Carson St., (412) 381-1665, www.duquesneincline.org.*

Duquesne Incline

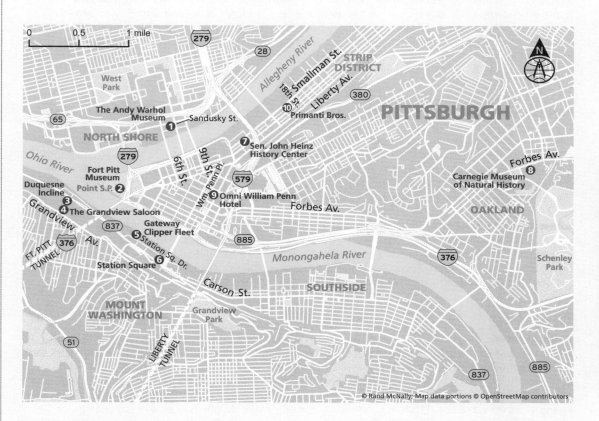

❹ The Grandview Saloon. Atop Mount Washington and a short walk from the Duquesne Incline's Upper Station, the saloon is the ideal place to take in the Pittsburgh skyline. Stop in for lunch, an evening cocktail and appetizers, or dinner. Although known for its steaks, the restaurant also has seafood, sandwiches, and salads. It's the perfect nightcap to a day of sightseeing. *1212 Grandview Ave., (412) 431-1400, www.thegrandviewsaloon.com.*

❺ Gateway Clipper Fleet. Take in the sights of Pittsburgh and experience the significance of the Three Rivers from the deck of a Gateway Clipper boat. Cruise options include a one-hour sightseeing tour, the family-friendly Good Ship Lollipop excursion, and romantic evening and themed dinner sails. Vessels depart year round from the Station Square Dock on the south side of the Monongahela. *350 W. Station Square Dr., (412) 355-7980, www.gatewayclipper.com.*

❻ Station Square. This 52-acre complex on the Monongahela River was once the hub of the Pittsburgh and Lake Erie Railroad. Some of the remaining boxcars have been converted into shops, and the station houses the Grand Concourse restaurant. There are also more than 20 shops and 20 restaurants, a riverboat cruise line, and entertainment venues and nightclubs. Plus, it's a convenient 5-minute walk from the heart of Pittsburgh. *125 W. Station Square Dr., (412) 261-2811, www.stationsquare.com.*

Oakland and the Strip District

❼ Senator John Heinz History Center. Capturing 250 years of Pittsburgh history under one roof, the center successfully tells the story of how the city and its environs shaped the future of medicine, robotics, higher education, and broadcasting. The most memorable exhibit fills two stories and highlights Pittsburgh's tradition of innovation—from the invention of the Ferris wheel to the inception of KDKA (the world's first commercial radio station) and the creation of Heinz Ketchup. Interactive displays let you take a ride on America's first superhighway, the PA Turnpike, and see how the house of the future will impact and improve the next 250 years. *1212 Smallman St., (412) 454-6000, www.heinzhistorycenter.org.*

❽ Carnegie Museum of Natural History. Famous for its Dinosaurs in Their Time exhibit, the museum has 19 skeletons on display, including an Apatosaurus, a Diplodocus, and a Tyrannosaurus rex. But life doesn't stop at the Mesozoic Era. From the Paleozoic to the present, from the North Pole to the South, this museum has life on Earth covered. Note: it's in the same complex as the Carnegie Museum of Art. *4400 Forbes Ave., (412) 622-3131, www.carnegiemnh.org.*

Eat & Stay

❾ Omni William Penn Hotel. Commissioned by wealthy industrialist Henry Clay Frick, the William Penn was completed in 1929 and was, at the time, the largest hotel between Pittsburgh and Chicago. Much of its original splendor remains: Spacious, stately rooms have cherrywood furnishings and crown moldings. Amenities are geared to business travelers as well as families; kids receive a backpack filled with treats on arrival. Breakfast, lunch, and dinner are served in the Terrace Room, the Tap Room and Speakeasy Lounge are great places for a quiet cocktail or casual meal, and the Palm Court is the spot for high tea. *530 William Penn Pl., (412) 281-7100, www.omnihotels.com.*

❿ Primanti Bros. When it opened during the Great Depression, Primanti Bros. was dedicated to serving truckers and shift workers an honest meal at a fair price. This philosophy still holds true, as sandwiches are just as mountainous as they were decades ago, stacked high with your choice of meat and toppings and loaded with fries and coleslaw. Devouring one of these behemoths is a Pittsburgh tradition. This is the original Strip District location, but there are others around town. *46 18th St., (412) 263-2142, www.primantibros.com.*

NORTHEAST

MIDWEST

SOUTH

WEST

NORTHEAST

MIDWEST

SOUTH

WEST

Greensburg

Westmoreland Museum of American Art. Established in 1959, the Westmoreland has become a preeminent museum of American art. Here, works by artists from southwestern Pennsylvania are displayed in perfect harmony with classic pieces by the likes of Mary Cassatt and John Singer Sargent. In addition to the permanent collection of art from the 18th to the 20th centuries, the Westmoreland hosts many noteworthy exhibits. It's also home to the Westmoreland Jazz Society, which adds another layer of innovation to the museum's progressive nature. *221 N. Main St., (724) 837-1500, www.thewestmoreland.org.*

Ligonier

Fort Ligonier. Used from 1758 to 1766 as a garrison during the French and Indian War and Pontiac's War, the fort served as a vital link in British communication and supply lines. Today 8 acres of the original fort have been preserved. Re-created interiors include an officer's mess, barracks, an underground magazine, a commissary, and a guardroom. Outside are a hospital, a log dwelling, bake ovens, a saw mill, and a forge. Combine your tour with a visit to the on-site museum, which showcases artifacts and art, including the George Washington Collection, which features an autobiographical account of Washington's six years on the Pennsylvania frontier. *200 S. Market St., (724) 238-9701, fortligonier.org.*

Idlewild and SoakZone. The oldest amusement park in the state and the third oldest in the nation was developed as a picnic and recreational area by the Ligonier Valley Railroad in 1878. Today its themed areas include Story Book Forest, Old Idlewild, Hootin' Holler, Jumpin' Jungle, and SoakZone. Collectively they offer classic rides, new-fangled thrill rides and water slides, shows, and storybook characters brought to life. It's the perfect place to spend a summer's day. *2574 U.S. Hwy. 30, (724) 238-3666, www.idlewild.com.*

Mill Run

Fallingwater. Designed by Frank Lloyd Wright in 1935 for the Kaufmanns, the prominent Pittsburgh family that owned Kaufmann's department store, the house generated national attention when it appeared on the cover of *Time* magazine in January 1938. It's built on cantilevers over a 30-foot waterfall, so it becomes one with its natural setting. The Kaufmanns used the house as a summer retreat until 1963, when Edgar Kaufmann Jr., following his father's wishes, gave the home to the Western Pennsylvania Conservancy. Fallingwater, now a National Historic Landmark, is the only major Wright–designed house open (since 1964) to the public with its original furnishings, artwork, and setting intact. Tour times and open hours vary by season; to guarantee your place on a house tour, it's imperative that you purchase tickets in advance. Wear comfortable shoes: There's a ¼-mile downhill walk from the visitors center to the house, and, once inside, there are more than 100 stairs to climb. *1491 Mill Run Rd., (724) 329-8501, www.fallingwater.org.*

Ohiopyle

Ohiopyle State Park. The Youghiogheny River passes through this park, providing opportunities for whitewater rafting, kayaking, and canoeing. Overlook platforms ensure great views from the shore, and there are 79 miles of hiking trails, 27 miles of biking trails, and almost 12 miles of bridle paths. Other activities include fishing, rock climbing, hunting, snowmobiling, and cross-country skiing. Reservations are required for all campsites and cabins; note that the campground is open April through mid-December. *124 Main St., (724) 329-8591, www.dcnr.state.pa.us.*

Ohiopyle State Park

Stoystown

Flight 93 National Memorial. On Tuesday morning, September 11, 2001, United Airlines Flight 93 was hijacked. Realizing the goal was to destroy the U.S. Capitol, the passengers and crew devised a plan to crash the plane into a field before it reached Washington. The field is now home to a 2,200-acre National Park Site, where a Wall of Names on the Memorial Plaza honors the 40 passengers and crew aboard the flight and marks a portion of the flight path. A hemlock grove damaged by the crash has been replanted with trees, wildflowers, and native grasses. There's also a Visitor Center Complex that includes site trailheads, an overlook, and a Learning Center. *6424 Lincoln Hwy., (814) 893-6322, www.nps.gov/flni.*

Gettysburg

Gettysburg National Military Park. Today, portions of the Gettysburg battlefield are preserved much as they were that fateful July. You'll also find more than 1,300 monuments along 26 miles of scenic roadways. Self-guided driving tours are popular, or you can hire a licensed battlefield guide to accompany you or join a commercial bus tour with an on-board guide. The National Park Service Museum and Visitor Center has a huge collection of Civil War relics; interactive exhibits; *A New Birth of Freedom*, a 22-minute film; and the massive Gettysburg Cyclorama. There's a bookstore, and the café serves Civil War–era and family-friendly cuisine. There are also several miles of hiking and bridle trails. The adjoining Gettysburg National Cemetery is the final resting place for more than 6,000 soldiers from many American wars, including 3,512 Civil War burials. *1195 Baltimore Pike (Rte. 97), (717) 334-1124, www.nps.gov.*

Fallingwater

Get Your Terrible Towel Ready

Whether you bleed black and gold or are just a sports fan, the **Pittsburgh Steelers Training Camp** (300 Fraser Purchase Rd., Latrobe, 412/432-7800, www.steelers.com/schedule-and-events) is a must see. Art Rooney, Jr., member of the Rooney family who own the Steelers, graduated from St. Vincent College in 1957. When he scouted for the team in the 1960s, Rooney worked so that the team could train at his alma mater, and the Steelers began training at St. Vincent's in 1966.

Today, the camp is open to the public, and offers daily fan activities such as youth football games, field-goal kicks, and quarterback tosses. In the Play 60 Fun Zone, kids (grades 1–12) participate in football-themed activities for an hour on team practice days. Who knows? A chance encounter with Big Ben or another Steelers great could lead to hands-on football tips.

Eat & Stay

Mountain Pines Campground I **Champion.** Lodging options at this country getaway include tent sites, RV sites (with full or partial hookups), cabins, and a lodge. It's long on amenities, too, from laundry facilities and a convenience store to a games room, sports courts, and a playground. In warmer months, swim in Pennsylvania's largest outdoor pool or head out to one of the fishing sites. In cooler months, take a dip in the heated indoor pool, maybe after a day of hiking in the area. The cabins and lodge are open all year. *1662 Indiana Creek Valley Rd., (724) 455-7411, www.mountainpinescamping.com.*

The Civil War's Bloodiest Battle

In the summer of 1863, Confederate General Robert E. Lee began an invasion north of the Mason–Dixon line. As part of this, he was intent on destroying a major railroad bridge at Harrisburg, PA, thus interrupting northern supply routes. At Gettysburg, a chance encounter with George Meade's Union forces led to a three-day battle that saturated the surrounding farmland with blood. It's estimated that 51,000 soldiers were killed, wounded, or reported captured or missing (with the number of losses about equal on both sides), making this the Civil War's bloodiest battle. The South never fully recovered from the losses, both physical and psychological. This Union victory also came one day before another in Vicksburg, MS; the outcomes of these two battles marked a turning point in the war.

Gettysburg National Cemetery. The casualties from the Battle of Gettysburg were so extreme that almost every building in the small town was employed to house the wounded, and most of the dead were hastily buried in shallow graves. Andrew Curtin, then Pennsylvania governor, had David Wills, an influential member of the community, quickly obtain land on which to found a national cemetery. Within four months, the 17-acre site was dedicated with a lavish ceremony featuring Edward Everett, the most popular speaker of his day. When, after more than two hours, Everett finished his speech, President Abraham Lincoln stepped to the podium to deliver his brief remarks. He spoke for only two minutes, but his scant, 272-word Gettysburg Address was so appropriate to the occasion that it has endured, becoming one of the country's most famous speeches. Of the more than 3,500 Civil War soldiers buried here, over 950 were never identified. *Taneytown Rd., (717) 334-1124, www.nps.gov/gett.*

Eisenhower National Historic Site. Dwight Eisenhower, 34th President of the United States, and his wife, Mamie, bought this farm estate in 1950; the present, 690-acre site encompasses four farms, including the 230-acre President's Farm. The estate served as a "temporary White House" while the president recuperated from a heart attack, and the Eisenhowers hosted world leaders including Khrushchev, De Gaulle, and Churchill. Eisenhower lived here until his death in 1969; two years earlier, the couple deeded the property to the National Park Service. Mamie continued to live at the estate until her death in 1979; it was opened to the public in 1980. Rangers offer tours and interpretive walks. To visit the farm, take the shuttle from the Gettysburg National Military Park's visitors center (1195 Baltimore Pike). *243 Eisenhower Farm Rd., (717) 338-9114, www.nps.gov.*

Statue of General Gouverneur Kemble Warren at Little Round Top, Gettysburg National Military Park

Shriver House Museum. Frozen in time, this museum is dedicated to the Shrivers, a prominent Gettysburg family whose lives, like those of so many others, were disrupted by the onslaught of the Civil War and the Battle of Gettysburg. In 1861, George Shriver joined the Union forces, leaving his wife, Hettie, behind to manage their home and raise their two daughters. When the battle erupted, Hettie took her girls to her parents' home outside of town. Their Gettysburg home was quickly occupied by the Confederate Army, and, after the battle, it was used as a hospital. In 1996 the house was fully restored to its original 1860 condition. Mid-19th-century treasures include medical supplies, letters, household items, corset stays, and children's toys. *309 Baltimore St., (717) 337-2800, www.shriverhouse.org.*

Ghosts of Gettysburg Tours. Knowledgeable guides take you on evening excursions to darkened downtown streets whose buildings witnessed conflict and are said to be active with restless spirits. These interactive, history-rich tours may captivate the most skeptical participants and expose you to the bizarre and unexplained sightings that have occurred in and around Gettysburg since the bloody battle of 1863. Tours depart from the Baltimore Street Headquarters, which opens at 2 pm; reservations are recommended. *271 Baltimore St., (717) 337-0445, ghostsofgettysburg.com.*

Farnsworth House Inn. Built in 1810, the inn is steeped in Civil War history and lore. Guides in period dress spin tales of General Farnsworth's ill-fated battle; share stories of how the house came to shelter Confederate sharpshooters; and give an accurate account of Lincoln's procession as it passed the house before he delivered the Gettysburg Address. You can also book a stay in one of the 10 elegant Victorian-era guest rooms, each uniquely decorated and named after historical figures (Abraham Lincoln, General Custer) and some of Gettysburg's memorable characters like Jennie Wade, the only civilian killed during the Battle of Gettysburg. The inn also has a main dining room and Sweney's Tavern. Civil War relics and props from the 1993 movie *Gettysburg* make up much of the décor. A museum and immaculate gardens invite exploration. *401 Baltimore St., (717) 334-8838, www.farnsworthhouseinn.com.*

Eat & Stay

Quill Haven Country Inn | Somerset. Country charm meets modern conveniences at this 1918 farmhouse B&B. The Arts and Crafts–style inn is furnished with antiques and period reproductions. Its four cozy rooms, decorated with stained-glass lamps and other whimsical details, have baths and heated mattress pads. Breakfast is served daily, a complimentary glass of wine is served each evening, and a small kitchenette in the common living room is stocked with free refreshments. There's also a hot tub. Note that discounts are available for area ski resorts and restaurants. *1519 N. Center Ave., (866) 528-8855, www.quillhaven.com.*

Dobbin House Tavern | Gettysburg. Dine by candlelight "in the Colonial manner" in one of the six beautifully—and authentically—restored Alexander Dobbin dining rooms in Gettysburg's oldest historic (1776) home. Or enjoy a light meal in the more casual Springhouse Tavern. Both menus employ Colonial English, so you might order a "hofpitality sallade" before enjoying a "fine fowl with shrimps" or "efcallopes of veal." Homemade breads and desserts are prepared in the restaurant's own bakery. *89 Steinwehr Ave., (717) 334-2100, www.dobbinhouse.com.*

Brafferton Inn | Gettysburg. Handsomely furnished rooms with modern amenities, as well as a location close to Lincoln Square, shops, and restaurants, make this B&B an appealing choice in historic downtown Gettysburg. The 17 rooms, including 9 suites, are decorated in Colonial, Victorian, or shabby-chic style; choose from lodgings in a number of buildings. Ample breakfasts are served in the 1815 dining room, and you can relax in the parlor of this National Register of Historic Places property. Avoid a York Street–facing room if noise bothers you. *44 York St., (717) 337-3423, www.brafferton.com.*

NORTHEAST

MIDWEST

SOUTH

WEST

Pennsylvania Memorial, Gettysburg National Battlefield

Chicago, IL

NORTHEAST

MIDWEST

SOUTH

WEST

Best of the Road® Travel Guide

Midwest

NORTHEAST | MIDWEST | SOUTH | WEST

Columbus and Ohio's Hocking Hills

ROUTE TOWNS: Columbus | Logan | Nelsonville | McArthur | Lancaster

Sure, Columbus has the vitality of a state capital that's home to a Big Ten state university. But it has something more: A mix of contemporary creativity and a traditional, roll-up-your-sleeves mentality gives it a palpable buzz. South of the capital, some of the scenery is expected, some surprising. All of it is lovely.

Columbus

As home to the headquarters of the L Brands—whose family includes Victoria's Secret, Bath & Body Works, and Henri Bendel—Columbus is very fashion forward, attracting designers and other young entrepreneurs from across the globe. The nation's 15th largest city, smack dab in the middle of a state known for its farms, is also known for innovative, field-to-fork dining. Redbrick 19th-century buildings housing art galleries, boutiques, and restaurants fill historic districts like Short North and German Village and make walking tours a joy.

Just south of the capital, flat fertile fields stretch for miles, punctuated only by the occasional stand of trees. About an hour southeast on Route 33, however, the landscape changes dramatically. The trees and brush thicken, and the road winds along in seemingly impossible S-curves, ribboning up and down hills that, time after time, give you the flutters as you crest them. You've reached the Hocking Hills, where sandstone deposited by glaciers has eroded through the eons to create a forest-scape of hollows, gorges, and caverns. It's not just the topography that differs from the surrounding Appalachian foothills—the flora and fauna do, too. The area is home to several state parks and forests as well as some quintessentially American and very charming small towns.

Distance: 191-mile loop (starting and ending in Columbus).

Type of Trip: Weekend Getaway; RV; Great Outdoors, History & Heritage, Picture Perfect, Small Town Gems.

Must Try: Sauerkraut balls (a German tradition); buckeye candies (an Ohio tradition); any of the state's craft beers.

Must Buy: A handmade washboard from the Columbus Washboard Company.

Must See: American Whistle Factory, German Village, Columbus Washboard Company, waterfalls and caves in Hocking Hills State Park, hummingbirds in Lake Hope State Park, the Sherman House Museum.

Worth Noting: You can fully experience the capital's vibrant dining scene with **Columbus Food Adventures** (614/440-3177, columbusfoodadventures.com). Area food blogger Bethia Woolf blends urban history with culinary insight on walking tours that let you eat your way through town, from the trendy Short North arts and shopping district to the classic German Village. She also has offerings for meat lovers, food-truck aficionados, dessert devotees, and coffee connoisseurs.

Travel Tips: This trip takes you along Route 33 from Columbus to Logan, in the heart of the Hocking Hills, and on to Nelsonville. In both towns, you'll find plenty of Americana, craftsmanship, and down-home food. The same is true of Lancaster. To reach it from Nelsonville on the return trip to Columbus, consider looping back through those glorious hills along routes like 56—a stretch so curvaceous that Ford Motor Company has used it as a test road. The state parks have RV sites, but the hills here make it essential to check routing carefully.

Atlas map SB-9, p. 80

city itinerary

Columbus

❶ American Whistle Factory. The only metal whistle manufacturer in the United States supplies everyone from traffic cops to school coaches to professional referees. All ages are welcome on the 45-minute guided tours (by reservation only) of the factory, about 10 miles north of the Short North arts and shopping district. Various "whistle stops" showcase how the metal is stamped, die-struck, and formed before being tumbled in a trough to remove sharp edges. The highlight? Seeing how the cork ball is inserted into the finished version—that and collecting your shiny new whistle at the end of the tour! *6540 Huntley Rd., (614) 846-2918, www.americanwhistle.com.*

❷ Glean. The inventory is ever inventive, ever changing, and ever environmentally friendly. All the wares in this Short North district shop are hand-crafted, most of them locally, using repurposed items. Found objects give ceramics a rich texture. Old spoons engraved with messages become garden markers. Knitted goods are used to make soft toys. Also look for fragrant soaps made with essential oils and pressed flowers or lavender and oats (for an exfoliating effect). *815 N. High St., (614) 515-2490, shopglean.com.*

❸ The Candle Lab. The long-burning, hand-poured candles in this Short North shop come in 120 different scents and are made with natural soy wax, cotton paper wicks, and the purest of fragrant oils. Can't find one that you like? Sit down at the Fragrance Bar and blend your own. There's also a selection of Columbus-made bath and body products. *751 N. High St., (614) 949-1458, www.thecandlelab.com.*

❹ North Market. More than 30 regional farms, orchards, and greenhouses supply this public market, open since 1876. Vendors also sell cookware and a variety of ethnic cuisines. Be sure to try some of Jeni's Splendid Ice Creams. Founded locally in 2002, Jeni's now has scoop shops in several states, and Jeni Britton Bauer's book, *Jeni's Splendid Ice Creams At Home,* won a James Beard Foundation Award. Prefer a savory snack? Check out Pam's Market Popcorn, with flavors both mild (cheese or caramel) and wild (Painful Purgatory Pepper). *59 Spruce St., (614) 463-9664, www.northmarket.com.*

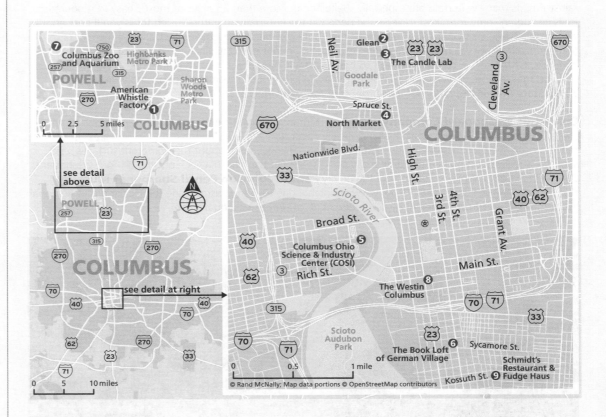

❺ Columbus Ohio Science & Industry Center (COSI). One of the nation's top science centers, COSI is a favorite place for families to explore and learn together. Three floors of hands-on exhibits are featured in themed areas such as Energy Explorers, Space, Lab Spaces, Ocean, Life, Gadgets, Progress, Live Shows, and Little Kid Space. Ride the country's only high wire unicycle—safe for everyone, thanks to a large counterweight and the laws of physics—browse the Science 2 Go shop, and grab a bite in the Atomic Café. Outside, in Big Science Park, don't miss the Giant Lever, which enables anyone to lift a car. *333 W. Broad St., (614) 228-2674, cosi.org.*

❻ The Book Loft of German Village. If you love books, you'll love this warren of new and used tomes. One of the nation's largest independent shops, it has more than 30 volume-filled rooms that meander through buildings dating from the mid-1800s. It's such a labyrinth that the shop hands out printed maps to help you navigate. Three rooms are dedicated to cookbooks. Though the discounts and savings are great here, you can save even more using website coupons. *631 S. 3rd St., (614) 464-1774, www.bookloft.com.*

A Day in the Wilds

If the weather's nice, consider a day trip to the ❼ **Columbus Zoo and Aquarium,** one of the nation's best and set on the banks of the Scioto River, a short drive northwest of the capital. What started with just a few animals in 1927 today has 9,000 creatures representing 800 species. It's also home to "America's Zookeeper," Jack Hanna, the zoo's director emeritus famous for his work with endangered species and his appearances on numerous TV shows.

This zoo saw the first gorilla born in captivity (1956), so these magnificent animals feature greatly in the African forest. Other habitats showcase North American, Asian, and Australian wildlife. The Manatee Coast is a highlight of a 192,000-gallon aquarium. Adjacent to the zoo are Zoombezi Bay water park and other attractions in Jungle Jack's Landing. You can also get in a round on the 18-hole Safari Golf Club course. *4850 W. Powell Rd., Powell, 614/645-3400, www.columbuszoo.org.*

Eat & Stay

❽ The Westin Columbus. Downtown's Great Southern Hotel & Opera House opened its doors in 1897—a true grand dame built of brick in the French Renaissance style. The grandeur continues today under the auspices of the Westin brand. Among the contemporary touches in the 188-room, pet-friendly hotel are Westin's trademark Heavenly Beds and Heavenly Showers. What's more, a stay here puts you within walking distance of not only downtown sights, but also those in the Short North and German Village districts. There are great deals to be had on the smaller rooms; packages make larger ones more budget-friendly. *310 S. High St., (614) 228-3800, www.westincolumbus.com.*

❾ Schmidt's Restaurant and Fudge Haus. Schmidt's was established as a German Village meat-packing business by an immigrant from Frankfurt back in the 1880s. The restaurant, opened in 1967 near the meat-packing plant, is still owned and operated by the Schmidt family. The menu is steeped in tradition, too, with sausage platters, wiener schnitzel, sauerbraten, and spaetzle. This is also a great place to try sauerkraut balls: bratwurst mixed with sauerkraut, rolled into balls, coated in batter, and deep-fried. Don't miss the neighboring Schmidt's Fudge Haus & Gifts, with its hand-crafted chocolates, including Ohio's renowned peanut-butter-and-chocolate buckeyes. *240 E. Kossuth St., (614) 444-6808, www.schmidthaus.com.*

Logan

Hocking Hills State Park. Hemlock shaded hollows and sandstone recesses draw nature lovers to this 2,356-acre park and the adjacent and nearby areas of Hocking State Forest. In spring or after a summer rainstorm, its many waterfalls are especially spellbinding. More than 26 miles of mostly easy to moderate trails (including some for bikes) traverse the park. On the entertaining naturalist-led tours you'll hear about the "magic tree;" visit Old Man's Cave, once the home of a hermit; discover why Canadian hemlocks thrive here; and learn how the recess caves were formed. You might even convince the naturalist to do some bird calls. Of the park's 169 campsites, 156 have electrical hookups. Other amenities here include cabins and cottages, a store, shower and laundry facilities, playgrounds, a swimming pool, and a dining lodge. *19852 State Rte. 664 S., (740) 385-6842, parks.ohiodnr.gov/hockinghills.*

Columbus Washboard Company. Washboards (handy on long camping trips) do a great job removing stains from cuffs and collars. They're also rustically decorative and add rhythmic zing to bluegrass music. Here you can see them assembled by hand (in just 45 seconds), learn about their different surfaces, and shop for a really good board and some really good soap! On the way in, check out the 24-foot washboard, the world's largest. While in Logan, visit the quirky **Paul A. Johnson Pencil Sharpener Museum** (13178 State Rte. 664 S., 740/385-9706, www.explorehockinghills.com), just outside the Hocking Hills Regional Welcome Center. *14 Gallagher Ave., (740) 380-3828, columbuswashboard.com.*

Hocking Hills State Park

Nelsonville

Rocky Outdoor Gear Store. Rocky has been making outdoor boots and work shoes since 1932. Situated in the original Nelsonville factory, the company's outlet store fills three floors with not only footwear, but also outdoor activity clothing and accessories for all four seasons. Prices are reasonable throughout, but, for truly remarkable deals, head straight to the second floor for clearance items. A small on-site café is known for its bison burgers and its great-value-for-money lunch specials. *45 E. Canal St. (740) 753-3130, www.rockyboots.com.*

Hocking Valley Scenic Railway. The collection of rolling stock amassed and restored by this volunteer-run nonprofit railway is inspired: commuter coaches from the 1920s; a B&O passenger coach from the 1940s; bi-level Pullman cars from the 1960s; and locomotives, cabooses, and other utility cars from all periods. On weekends from late May through late October, you can ride in one of the passenger cars pulled by a vintage diesel engine along track that once belonged to the Chesapeake & Ohio Railway. Round-trips between Nelsonville and either Haydenville or Logan are just under and just over 2 hours, respectively. Fall foliage and holiday trains are popular. *33 W. Canal St. (740) 249-1452, www.hvsry.org.*

Starbrick Gallery. The streets on and off Nelsonville's main square are lined with restored Victorian commercial buildings, many of which house galleries containing local works of both art and craft. One of them is the Starbrick, named after the famously durable and elegant paving stones that were, for many years, made in Nelsonville using area clay. Pottery and other ceramic items feature greatly here, but you'll also find hand-crafted jewelry and clothing as well as works in glass, wood, and paper. *21 W. Columbus St., (740) 753-1011, www.starbrick.com.*

From Wild Rides to Gentle Glides

Driving and hiking aren't the only ways to enjoy the scenery of the Hocking Hills. Just as thrilling are the 20- to 60-minute flights over the region throughout the year offered by **Hocking Hills Scenic Air Tours** (Vinton County Airport, 66285 Airport Rd., New Plymouth, 740/649-2207, www.hockinghills.com/airtours). Don't forget your camera. For still more thrills, you can zoom from treetop to treetop with **Hocking Hills Canopy Tours** (10714 Jackson St., Rockbridge, 740/385-9477, www.hockinghillscanopytours.com), just one of several area zip line operations. On the more relaxing end of things are the kayaking trips offered by **Touch the Earth Adventures** (740/591-9094, www.hockinghills.com/earthtouch) on Lake Hope and other area waterways.

Eat & Stay

Inn & Spa at Cedar Falls I Logan. Guest quarters here are named for flora or fauna of the type you'll find on the property's 75 wooded acres. All accommodations offer high-quality bedding and toiletries; a mix of contemporary country-style furnishings and hand-selected antiques; and the chance to experience utter peace. Nine guestrooms with twin or queen beds are in a two-story building with rocking-chair lined porches and a comfy, Wi-Fi-equipped common room. Cottages, which sleep varying numbers of people, have queen or king beds, whirlpool tubs, decks, refrigerators, and microwaves; some are pet-friendly. The spa has a full menu of treatments and a team of highly experienced therapists. In keeping with the overall green philosophy, the restaurant features seasonal, field-to-fork meals. Reservations are a good idea. *21190 State Rte. 374, (740) 385-7489, innatcedarfalls.com.*

FullBrooks Café I Nelsonville. Daily breakfast and light lunch specials are posted on blackboards behind the counter at this tiny café on Nelsonville's Public Square. Sample fresh scones or muffins made with local fruit, or try a classic egg, bacon, and cheese sandwich. The tasty soups, salads, sandwiches, and delicious desserts served later in the day have attracted both locals and visitors for more than a dozen years. *6½ Public Sq., (740) 753-3391, www.fullbrookscafe.com.*

McArthur

Lake Hope State Park. With its rugged terrain and placid lake, it's hard to believe that this heavily wooded, 2,983-acre park—entirely within Zaleski State Forest—was the site of iron-ore smelting operations that supplied the Union Army with armament and ammunition. Today, an old chimney along the Hope Furnace Trail is the main reminder of this industrial past. There are six other moderate hiking trails, as well as eight moderate-to-difficult biking trails, a 21-mile backpacking route, a 23-mile single-track bike route, and 33 miles of bridle trails. The abundance of warblers, woodpeckers, and finches makes this park popular with birdwatchers. And, between July 1 and August 31, you can head over to the nature center for a chance to hand-feed the hummingbirds. Other amenities include a swimming beach; 187 campsites, 46 with electrical hookups; cottages; shower and laundry facilities; and a dining lodge. *27331 State Rte. 278, (740) 596-4938, parks.ohiodnr.gov/lakehope.*

Lancaster

Rockmill Brewery. About the time owner Matthew Barbee was tiring of his fast-paced Los Angeles lifestyle and asking himself "What's next?", he discovered the joys of beer—specifically, Belgian beer from the Wallonia region. After returning to Ohio to work on his family's 1870s former horse farm, he thought about opening a winery, but then he thought, "No. A brewery." Upon testing the water on his family's property, Barbee discovered that it had the same mineral content as that used to make . . . Belgian beer in the Wallonia region. Since 2010, this brewery has been crafting a line of hardy Belgian-style beers. The brewery doesn't serve food (you're welcome to bring your own), but on Sunday it offers cheese boards with the craft brews. *5705 Lithopolis Rd. N.W., (740) 205-8076, www.rockmillbrewery.com.*

Sherman House Museum. This is the house where Civil War General William Tecumseh Sherman and his brother, U.S. Senator John Sherman, were born. The original 1811 section and an 1816 addition contain two parlors, a study, a kitchen/dining area, and bedrooms filled with family memorabilia and period furnishings. In a brick 1870s addition, you'll find Civil War exhibits; one bedroom has a recreation of the general's field tent. On tours of the property, you'll learn about Sherman's early years, his stint at West Point, and his Civil War actions—from that first battle at Bull Run to the March to the Sea campaign to the Confederate surrender in North Carolina. A visit to this house pairs nicely with one to the nearby **Georgian Museum** (105 E. Wheeling St., 740/654-9923, www.thegeorgianmuseum.org), a restored, 13-room Federal house that's also under the auspices of the Fairfield Heritage Association. *137 E. Main St., (740) 687-5891, www.shermanhouse.org.*

Ohio Glass Museum. Between 1890 and the mid-1920s, roughly a dozen glass companies—drawn by the area's natural resources—set up operations in and around Lancaster. This museum honors that history. An overview film and docent-led tours cover the various glass-making processes used through the years. A resident glassblower gives demonstrations and offers classes. Exhibits showcase everything from etched crystal stemware to decorative milk glass pieces to utilitarian but colorful Depression-era glass items. Locally crafted glass items in the gift shop make great souvenirs. *124 W. Main St., (740) 687-0101, ohioglassmuseum.org.*

Starbrick Gallery (above)
Columbus Washboard Company (right)

Eat & Stay

JimBo's Bar and Diner | South Bloomingville. Although many roads in the Hocking Hills region are thrilling and scenic, the ride along Route 56 can be particularly curvaceous. Whether you're in a car or on a motorcycle, you're bound to work up an appetite on this drive. That's where JimBo's comes in. This spic-and-span, no-frills roadside joint is beloved by members of bike and car clubs as much for its location as for its burgers and cheese fries. Portions are large, and service is friendly, fast, and strategic. Alas, JimBo's has limited hours and is only open seasonally. *23356 State Rte. 56, (740) 332-6550.*

The Ridge Inn Restaurant | Laurelville. This is a great place for breakfast, particularly on weekends *and* if you see a sign out front that says, "Jo's Famous Donuts – Ready Now." These melt-in-your-mouth confections are made from scratch in small batches on Thursday through Sunday. And they sell out fast. Don't worry if you miss out. There are plenty of other fresh home-style options on the menu—daily for breakfast, lunch, and dinner—at this locally owned, family-friendly spot. Before or after your meal, head across the street and pick up some fresh peaches, apples, or other seasonal produce at the Laurelville Fruit Company. *16178 Pike St. (740) 332-0300, www.theridgeinnrestaurant.com.*

Glenlaurel Inn | Rockbridge. The theme, design, and decor of this property nod to Scotland and Wales. Amid Hocking Hills forestland are the manor and carriage house—with common areas and seven guest rooms and suites—as well as more than a dozen stand-alone accommodations, including 450-square-foot crofts and 700-square-foot cottages. Some quarters have kitchenettes, living rooms, and private hot tubs; most have stone fireplaces; all have country-contemporary furnishings and are named after a Scottish clan. You'll also find an on-site restaurant (breakfast is included in the rates), a trail through the surrounding 140 acres, and a Scottish links golf course. In-room spa services are available. Many guests come for the romance, making it a less-than-ideal place for families with small children. Some guests come to disconnect: Rooms don't have TV service, though some do have entertainment centers for playing films. *14940 Mount Olive Rd., (740) 385-4070, www.glenlaurel.com.*

Heart of Indiana Tour

ROUTE TOWNS: Indianapolis | Edinburgh | Columbus | Gnaw Bone | Nashville | Beanblossom | Bloomington

There's a lot to explore in central Indiana: from great arts in Indianapolis to great architecture in Columbus; from idyllic wooded scenery in Brown County to lively food and culture scenes in Bloomington.

Eiteljorg Museum of American Indians and Western Art, Indianapolis

This tour samples the cultural vitality, scenic beauty, and increasingly sophisticated food scene in central Indiana. It begins in Indianapolis, the state capital, where families can spend hours at the splendid Children's Museum of Indianapolis—just one of several kid-friendly sites—or at one of the city's world-class art museums.

To the south is Columbus, one of the nation's top destinations for architecture lovers. Its streets contain modernist jewels designed by such acclaimed architects as I.M. Pei, Harry Weese, and Deborah Berke. Just strolling around downtown is a pleasure, but you'll learn even more on one of the guided tours offered by the town's visitors center.

From Columbus, the road winds west into Brown County, a landscape of rolling ridges, mysterious hollows, and mist rising from forested valley floors. A century ago, the American Impressionists of the Hoosier School migrated here to capture the countryside in watercolors and oils. Visit the T.C. Steele State Historic Site to learn more about their stories, and explore the wooded glens yourself in Brown County State Park. A little farther west is Bloomington, a lively college town.

INDIANA

Atlas map J-9, p. 36

Distance: 97 miles point to point (Indianapolis to Bloomington); 152 miles full loop.

Type of Trip: Weekend Getaway; RV; Arts & Music, History & Heritage, Small Town Gems.

Must Try: A Midwestern-fresh meal. Many restaurants here are locally owned *and* use locally sourced ingredients. This is particularly true of Bloomington, where more than 100 one-of-a-kind eateries reflect not only the region's farm-to-fork philosophy but also the community's ethnic diversity.

Must Buy: Creative types have flocked to Brown County for over a century. Crafts like weaving, leatherworking, and quilting are big. You'll also find unique jewelry, hand-painted silk scarves, and original works of art.

Must See: Conner Prairie Interactive History Park, Children's Museum of Indianapolis, Columbus Architecture Bus Tours, T.C. Steele State Historic Site, Tibetan Mongolian Buddhist Cultural Center.

Worth Noting: On this very kid-friendly road trip, sites include the world's largest children's museum, a marionette theater, and several science and history offerings, like the Conner Prairie Interactive History Park, where costumed interpreters will enthrall the entire family with the dramas of daily life in 19th-century Indiana.

Travel Tips: Plan your trip for the fall to take advantage of the brilliant foliage that will line much of the route outside of Indianapolis. Brown County is particularly scenic and sponsors a full slate of fall-themed festivals.

NORTHEAST

MIDWEST

SOUTH

WEST

city itinerary

Indianapolis

❶ Conner Prairie Interactive History Park. One of the nation's premier living-history museums brings 19th-century Indiana to life through costumed interpreters who go about their daily activities in five historic areas. Here you can be part of a Civil War raid, learn to throw a tomahawk or make a basket in the Lenape Indian Camp, dip a candle at the William Conner Homestead, or learn about early aviation history at the 1859 Balloon Village. Note that the park is in the suburb of Fishers, about 20 miles northeast of downtown. *13400 Allisonville Rd., (317) 776-6000, www.connerprairie.org.*

❷ Indianapolis Museum of Art. The 54,000+ works here span 5,000 years of history, with significant collections of African, American, Asian, and European art. Highlights include a large group of Neo-Impressionist paintings by Georges Seurat and his followers, the largest J.M.W. Turner collection outside of Great Britain, and many outstanding Japanese Edo-period paintings and Chinese ceramic pieces. The 152 acres of grounds contain the Virginia B. Fairbanks Art & Nature Park, one of the country's largest contemporary art parks, and the Oldfields–Lilly House & Gardens, a historic estate. *4000 Michigan Rd., (317) 923-1331, www. imamuseum.org.*

❸ Children's Museum of Indianapolis. With 1.2 million visitors a year and nearly 500,000 square feet, this is the world's largest children's museum. Its 11 major galleries cover science, global cultures, history, and the arts. Youngsters love the Playscape and Doc McStuffin areas, while older kids appreciate ScienceWorks, with its hands-on experiments, and Dinosphere with its realistic sound and lighting effects. Other highlights include an 11,000-pound steam engine, a re-created pirate shipwreck, a weather station, a climbing wall, a real Indy racecar, a planetarium, and a theater. What's more, costumed interpreters—like an Egyptian archaeologist—help kids delve more deeply into many exhibits. *3000 N. Meridian St., (317) 334-4000, www.childrensmuseum.org.*

❹ Indianapolis Motor Speedway. Opened in 1909, the racetrack—a National Historic Landmark—hosts a half-dozen major events each year, including late May's famous Indy 500, which celebrated its 100th anniversary in 2016. Year-round you can visit the IMS Hall of Fame Museum with its displays of cars,

Indianapolis Motor Speedway

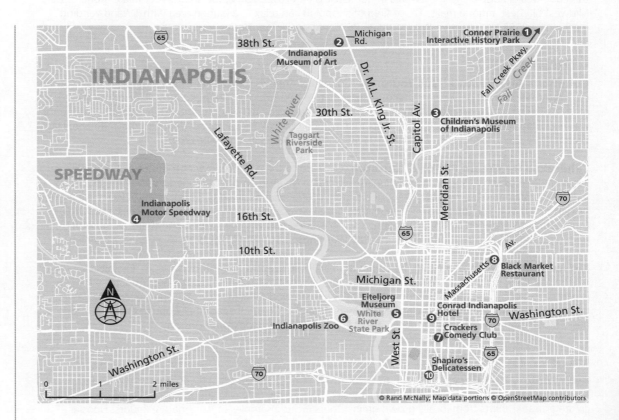

© Rand McNally; Map data portions © OpenStreetMap contributors

awards, and art; video footage of early races; and exhibits on how competitions are timed and scored. Take a Grounds Tour for behind-the-scenes access. Note that several parking lots have RV (with electric hookups) and tent sites. *4790 W. 16th St., (317) 492-8500, www.indianapolismotorspeedway.com.*

❺ Eiteljorg Museum of American Indians and Western Art. Founded by Indianapolis philanthropist Harrison Eiteljorg, this museum celebrates the art, history, and cultures of North America's indigenous peoples and the American West. It has one of the nation's finest collections of contemporary Native American art as well as classic works by the likes of N.C. Wyeth, Frederic Remington, Charles Russell, and Kay WalkingStick. Its café serves Southwestern fare, and its store has many items produced by Native American artists. *500 W. Washington St., (317) 636-9378, www.eiteljorg.org.*

❻ Indianapolis Zoo. The country's largest privately funded zoo is home to about 230 species of animals and more than 2,000 varieties of plants living in different "biomes"—oceans, deserts, plains, forests—as well as three aviaries with birds from around the world. Highlights include the Simon Skjodt International Orangutan Center, the Dolphin Pavilion with daily shows, and zoo babies ranging from lions and giraffes to gibbons and meerkats. Adjacent to the zoo, the 3-acre White River Gardens contains 16,000 plants, including tropical flora inside a glass conservatory. *1200 W. Washington St., (317) 630-2001, www.indianapoliszoo.com.*

❼ Crackers Downtown Comedy Club. Making Indianapolis laugh since 1980 in this and at its Broad Ripple location, Crackers features a full calendar of stand-up comedians—from locals braving weekly open-mike nights to national performers on tour. Children under 17 aren't admitted, so you can laugh at any joke without fear of setting a bad example. *207 N. Delaware St., 2nd Fl., (317) 631-3536, www.crackerscomedy.com.*

Eat & Stay

❽ Black Market Restaurant. Casual but sophisticated Black Market is in the city's lively and eclectic arts district. Chef Micah Frank's sometimes eccentric, but always delicious, comfort food has won praise from both *The New York Times* and local food critics. The seasonal menu might include coffee-rubbed barbecued brisket or cornmeal-crusted catfish and, for dessert, salted chocolate brickle with cream-cheese ice cream. Be sure to try the signature pickle appetizer, which comes with freshly made peanut butter. For the complete experience, sit at the large communal table. FYI: adults 21+ only! *922 Massachusetts Ave., (317) 822-6757, www.blackmarketindy.net.*

❾ Conrad Indianapolis Hotel. For a splurge in downtown Indy, check into this 23-story hotel with 247 luxury rooms, a full-service spa, a fitness center, and an infinity-edge pool. Works by internationally acclaimed artists hang on its first and second floors. The Capital Grille offers upscale dining, while Tastings, a wine bar boasting 200+ wines from around the world, serves wine by the taste, glass, or bottle. *50 W. Washington St., (317) 713-5000, www. conradindianapolis.com.*

❿ Shapiro's Delicatessen. Four generations of the Shapiro family have served pastrami, corned beef, matzo ball soup, and other comfort-food staples to legions of fans at this classic kosher deli. The establishment (still in the same spot where it first opened in 1905) includes a bakery and small grocery as well as a cafeteria-style deli serving breakfast, lunch, and dinner. *808 S. Meridian St., (317) 631-4041, www.shapiros.com.*

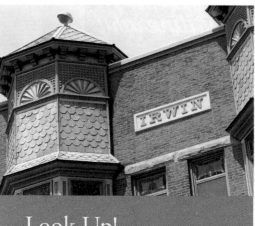

Edinburgh

Exit 76 Antique Mall. There's nothing fancy about this establishment, but treasures abound from more than 330 dealers displaying their wares in 600 booths and cases. Its 72,000 square feet make it one of the Midwest's largest antique malls. Those tired of shopping can relax in a lounge area with TV and vending machines. *12595 N. Executive Dr., (812) 526-7676, www.exit76antiques.com.*

Columbus

Columbus Architectural Bus Tours. The Columbus Area Visitors Center offers a variety of tours of the city's internationally acclaimed architecture. Its signature two-hour, guided bus tour will introduce you to many of the nearly 70 eye-popping churches, commercial buildings, schools, and art installations. Along the way you'll learn about architects and artists that include I.M. Pei, Eliel and Eero Saarinen, Kevin Roche, Harry Weese, Dale Chihuly, and Henry Moore. *506 5th St., (800) 468-6564, columbus.in.us.*

Zaharakos Ice Cream Parlor & Museum. Catering to the collective sweet tooth of Columbus since 1900, Zaharakos serves sodas and homemade ice cream treats in an old-fashioned parlor. With its Tiffany-style lamps, stained-glass windows, imported marble counters, and carved oak furnishings, it looks like it could be part of a movie set. Though sweet treats take pride of place, the menu also has sandwiches and soups. Dining music is provided by an orchestrion, a self-playing organ with 184 pipes, and there's a museum featuring rare 19th-century soda fountains. *329 Washington St., (812) 378-1900, www.zaharakos.com.*

Kidscommons. Youngsters (and the young at heart) will love this three-floor museum. Exhibits include a 17-foot climbing wall, a bubble lab, a laser harp, and a robotic arm. The most famous attraction, though, is part of ExploraHouse, an exhibit on what makes houses work; a giant toilet "flushes" kids down a slide to the floor below. In a nod to the acclaimed architecture of Columbus, another popular exhibit lets kids design their own city. *309 Washington St., (812) 378-3046, www.kidscommons.org.*

Gnaw Bone

Bear Wallow Distillery. Located in the evocatively named hamlet of Gnaw Bone, this woman-owned business is continuing the long tradition of Hoosier moonshine, only with an upscale twist. Its copper stills create artisanal spirits from locally grown grains. Tours include samples of its signature liquors: Hoosier Hooch Corn Whiskey Moonshine, Bear Trap Barrel Strength White Whiskey, and Liar's Bench Rye Whiskey. No need to worry about revenue agents—this moonshine is legal. *4484 E. Old State Rd. 46, (812) 657-4923, www.bearwallowdistillery.com.*

Nashville

Brown County State Park. Founded in 1929, this 16,000-acre oasis is nicknamed the Little Smokies because of its resemblance to the Great Smoky Mountains. Densely forested hills and valleys, rugged ridges, and deep ravines entice hikers and fall-foliage enthusiasts. You can camp or book a motel room or cabin at the **Abe Martin Lodge** (877/563-4371 for reservations), which was built in 1932 and has a restaurant and indoor water park open to nonguests. Other park and lodge amenities include interpretive nature programs, playgrounds, picnic areas, tennis courts, a swimming pool, hiking and biking trails, and 70 miles of equestrian trails. *1801 State Rd. 46 E., (812) 988-6406, www.in.gov/dnr.*

Brown County State Park

Melchior Marionette Theatre. Take a break from shopping in the area's many craft stores and antiques shops with a stop at this outdoor theater run by Peggy Melchior and her daughter, Heidi. You'll enjoy the 20-minute shows featuring handcrafted, half-life-size, colorfully costumed marionettes. Performances charm both kids and adults. Tickets are sold 15 minutes before show time; the popcorn is free. *92 S. Van Buren St., (317) 535-4853, melchiormarionettes.com.*

T.C. Steele State Historic Site. Landscape painter Theodore C. Steele (1847–1926), the most highly respected of Indiana's painters, moved to Brown County in 1907 and helped introduce the area's beauty to an international audience. This state historic site preserves Steele's studio and home—the charmingly named House of the Singing Winds. You can tour both structures as well as gardens planted and tended by Selma Steele, the artist's wife. Five scenic hiking trails, from easy to steep, wind through the property, which also has a gift shop. *4220 T.C. Steele Rd., (812) 988-2785, www.tcsteele.org.*

Beanblossom

Bill Monroe Music Park & Campground. Known as the father of bluegrass music, Bill Monroe spent much of his life in tiny Beanblossom, 5 miles north of Nashville. His former home is now the site of the Bill Monroe Bluegrass Hall of Fame & Country Star Museum, featuring instruments, clothing, and memorabilia from the greats of bluegrass and country music collected during Monroe's 60 years as a performer. A 5,000-seat outdoor theater hosts performances throughout the summer.

This is also where the world's oldest, continuously running bluegrass festival is held: June's eight-day Bill Monroe Memorial Bluegrass Festival, which began in 1967 (make reservations well in advance). The 55-acre site has a campground with more than 600 sites (300 with full RV hookups), as well as shower facilities, dump stations, and other amenities. There are also rustic log cabins for rent. *5163 N. State Rd. 135, (812) 988-6422, www.billmonroemusicpark.com.*

Bloomington

Monroe Lake. The 10,750-acre Monroe Lake has eight state recreation areas along its shores, making it a very popular place to boat, water-ski, fish, and swim; you'll also find hiking trails, camping, and a nature center. **Fourwinds Resort and Marina** (9301 S. Fairfax Rd., 812/824-2628, www.fourwindsresort.com), in Fairfax State Recreation Area, has 118 rooms, two restaurants, a heated pool, boat rentals, a private beach, and mini-golf. *4850 S. State Rd. 446, (812) 837-9546, www.in.gov/dnr.*

Tibetan Mongolian Buddhist Cultural Center. Thubten Jigme Norbu, eldest brother of the Dalai Lama, was a professor of Tibetan studies at Indiana University and founded this center in 1979. Since then, it's become one of the most important centers of its kind in the country, with nearly a dozen buildings on 108 wooded acres in the southeastern corner of Bloomington. The heart of the property is the Kumbum Chamtse Ling Monastery, filled with ornate, brilliantly colored Tibetan iconography. Visitors of all faiths are welcome to walk the grounds and attend services. Don't miss the immense bronze prayer wheels from the center's sister temple, Kumbum Monastery in Tibet. *3655 S. Snoddy Rd., (812) 336-6807, tmbcc.org.*

WonderLab Museum of Science, Health and Technology. Located near Indiana University in the heart of Bloomington's downtown entertainment and arts district, WonderLab is designed to awaken young people's curiosity about the world. More than 50 exhibits on two floors invite kids to touch, explore, question, and learn. Highlights include a Bubble-Airium that teaches concepts such as surface tension and density; an outdoor exhibit on solar power; a magnet wall; tree-house climbing structures; a tropical aquarium; and a gallery with live insects, reptiles, and amphibians. *308 W. 4th St., (812) 337-1337, www.wonderlab.org.*

Upland Brewpub. Although Upland Brewing now has four locations in central Indiana, this cozy spot is where it all started. Since 1998, it's been pouring seasonal craft brews, with 10 on tap at any time. Beer is the focus here, but the dining room also serves an array of pub favorites and pizzas (families are welcomed), often made with locally sourced ingredients. In keeping with Bloomington's indie vibe, art from local artists adorns the walls. In warm weather, the biergarten is an inviting place to sit and sip. *350 West 11th St., (812) 336-2337, uplandbeer.com.*

Indiana University's Eskanazi Museum of Art. With a dramatically angled building designed by famed architect I.M. Pei and 45,000 objects dating from ancient Mesopotamia to the present, this is considered one of the country's top university art museums. There are paintings by Claude Monet, Jackson Pollack, and Pablo Picasso, along with highly regarded collections of ancient gold jewelry and African masks. Angles Café—named for the building's unusual design—refreshes you with beverages and pastries. *1133 E. 7th St., (812) 855-5445, artmuseum.indiana.edu.*

Tibetan Mongolian Buddhist Cultural Center

Monroe Lake

Eat & Stay

Story Inn & Restaurant | Nashville. This hostelry is inside a restored, 1850s general store, complete with well-worn hardwood floors and pressed-tin ceilings. The setting is impressive, too: to reach it, you'll wind along the eastern edge of Brown County State Park. The restaurant is chockablock with antiques and bric-a-brac; is open daily for breakfast, lunch, and dinner; and serves Hoosier-style dishes made with ingredients sourced from the onsite garden or area farms. You can stay in cottages or one of the guest rooms above the restaurant. Accommodations are pet-, horse- (there's a barn), and ghost-friendly (ask about the mysterious Blue Lady). *6404 S. State Rd. 135, (812) 988-2273, www.storyinn.com.*

FARMbloomington Restaurant | Bloomington. Despite his classic European training, Chef Daniel Orr specializes in "real food for real people." This means simple American classics like roasted half chicken, grilled pork loin, grass-fed chopped steak with melted Gruyère cheese, and bison steak with cornbread salad. The FARMhouse fries, served with FARM's own Tailgate Chipotle Catsup, are the best! Burgers, pizzas, and FARMwiches are on the menu, too. And the three-egg breakfast omelets, rashers of peppered bacon, and crispy home fries are a good way to start your day. *108 E. Kirkwood Ave., (812) 323-0002, www.farm-bloomington.com.*

Showers Inn | Bloomington. This elegant inn, built in 1903, was once home to the Showers family, owners of one of the largest furniture companies in the U.S. You can stay in the historic Art Nouveau inn or in the newer Arts and Crafts–style Composer House, where each room is named after a song by an Indiana composer. Enjoy a full breakfast each morning, with many dishes made using local produce. The inn's within easy walking distance of the Indiana University campus and many other attractions. *430 N. Washington St., (812) 334-9000, www.showersinn.com.*

Lake Michigan's Western Shore

ROUTE TOWNS: Chicago, IL | Racine, WI | Milwaukee | Sheboygan | Elkhart Lake | Manitowoc | Two Rivers | Sturgeon Bay | Carlsville | Egg Harbor | Fish Creek | Sister Bay | Baileys Harbor | Green Bay | Rapid River, MI | Garden | Seney | St. Ignace | Mackinac Island

The blue waters of Lake Michigan form the backdrop for this road trip that begins in bustling, big-shouldered Chicago and ends amid the Victorian-era elegance of Mackinac Island.

Wisconsin shoreline

In the Windy City, you'll be introduced to several internationally known attractions, including the Art Institute of Chicago and the Field Museum. In the evening, treat yourself to a Chicago-style pizza at Lou Malnati's and visit the Jazz Showcase or watch the fireworks off of Navy Pier.

Then shift into a slower gear for a winding journey up the western shore of Lake Michigan, passing through the city of Milwaukee (Harley-Davidson fans, in particular, will want to stop here) and several other Wisconsin towns rich in natural beauty and history.

Plan to linger awhile in Door County, WI, for there's much to explore in this narrow peninsula that separates Green Bay from the vastness of Lake Michigan. Its small towns have colorful names like Egg Harbor, Fish Creek, and Sister Bay; take a trolley tour to learn more about their equally colorful histories. You'll find many places here to gaze out over the waters of the lake, tour lighthouses, and sample the agricultural bounty of the region.

After passing through the Packers Capital of Green Bay, the route leads into the Upper Peninsula of Michigan, where the people get fewer, the trees taller, and the sense of vastness grows with each passing mile.

Atlas map C-13, p. 32

Distance: 775 miles point to point.

Type of Trip: Vacation Getaway; Arts & Music, Great Outdoors, History & Heritage, Sports Fan.

Must Try: A Door County fish boil, as much for the cooking spectacle as for the food.

Must Buy: A Chicago Cubs hat from the Windy City, paired with a T-shirt from Milwaukee's Harley-Davidson Museum.

Must See: Art Institute of Chicago, Second City, Kohler Waters Spa, Peninsula State Park, Door County Trolley Tours, Seney National Wildlife Refuge, Grand Hotel.

Worth Noting: Take time to savor the views and soak up the sunshine on Lake Michigan beaches and roadside pull-offs. The massive lake is like a small-scale ocean (without the need to wash off the salt when you get out of the water).

When the weather's pleasant, visit the outdoor attractions first, as Lake Michigan is known for its volatile weather, and you should take full advantage of the favorable conditions.

Travel Tips: This itinerary can easily be done in shorter segments. The farther north you go, the more wild and scenic the route becomes. Travel amenities like gas stations and restaurants become scarcer, so plan accordingly.

city itinerary

Chicago, IL: Breezing Through the Windy City

Chicago has one of the world's most beautiful skylines. Not only is it bordered by the blue waters of Lake Michigan, but it's also dominated by towering architectural masterpieces. This city of bravado, sass, and style has way too many attractions to see in just a day or two. This breeze-in-and-out itinerary includes blockbusters such as the famed Art Institute and the Field Museum; restaurants that introduce you to the city's diverse culinary scene; and some recommendations on how to learn more about the city's architectural legacy.

The best place to get your bearings is Millennium Park, along the lake and amid the downtown district known as The Loop. Since 2004, it's been a magnet for visitors and locals alike, with an ever-changing splash fountain, impressive works of art, a Frank Gehry–designed outdoor music pavilion, and Anish Kapoor's *Cloud Gate,* a sculpture that's become one of the most photographed spots in Chicago (go ahead and call it The Bean—nearly everyone does).

The cosmopolitan stretch of Michigan Avenue known as the Magnificent Mile is the city's premier shopping destination, but many other venues offer bargains and treasures. Try Bucktown for vintage stores, Oak Street for designer wear, and State Street for big-name retailers like Macy's. In the evening, you can choose from dozens of shows, ranging from Broadway blockbusters to experimental productions staged in store fronts. You can also enjoy a night of improv comedy at the world-renowned Second City or an evening of great music at the equally renowned Jazz Showcase.

Travel Tips: The curving shoreline of Lake Michigan is the site of many of Chicago's top attractions. It's also a terrific place to swim, rollerblade, bike, and people watch. From the lake, wander through Grant Park and The Loop, soaking up the city's dynamic vibe. Don't be afraid to look up. Locals love visitors who appreciate the city's architectural landmarks.

Visitor Info: Choose Chicago, 301 E. Cermak Rd., 312/567-8499, www.choosechicago.com.

In and Around The Loop

1 Field Museum. The collection at this world-class natural history museum got its start during the 1893 World's Columbian Exhibition. Upon entering the main hall, you're greeted by the skeleton of Sue, the largest and best-preserved Tyrannosaurus rex skeleton ever assembled: 42 feet long, 13 feet tall at the hips, and with teeth as long as your forearm. Continue on past Sue, and you'll view displays featuring some of the museum's 24 million specimens and artifacts. Highlights include exhibitions on the pre-Columbian Americas and ancient Egypt, the Grainger Hall of Gems, and the Underground Adventure (seen from the perspective of a bug, everything in it is 100 times its normal size). *1400 S. Lake Shore Dr., (312) 922-9410, www.fieldmuseum.org.*

2 Shedd Aquarium. This aquarium has more than 30,000 amphibians, reptiles, mammals, fish, and invertebrates from around the world. Its Abbott Oceanarium highlights the marine life of the Pacific Northwest, with white-sided dolphins, Beluga whales, sea otters, and sea lions. The Amazon Rising exhibit shows what life is like for fish, birds, and people under flooded rain forest conditions, while the Wild Reef is home to sharks, stingrays, and other species that live on a coral reef in the Philippines. The Shedd also has 80 smaller exhibits displaying an amazing variety of aquatic creatures. *1200 S. Lake Shore Dr., (312) 939-2438, www.sheddaquarium.org.*

3 Jazz Showcase. The city's oldest jazz club—founded in 1947 by Joe Segal and now owned by his son Wayne—is within walking distance of several big-deal attractions. Unlike some of its glitzier neighbors, though, this club is the real deal. Virtually all the big names in jazz have played here through the years, and today's performers range from grizzled old-guard cats to relative newcomers. Its 4 pm Sunday matinee is geared toward families, with free admission for kids 12 and under—a great way to introduce them to one of America's greatest inventions. *806 S. Plymouth Ct., (312) 360-0234, www.jazzshowcase.com.*

4 Skydeck Chicago. Formerly known as the Sears Tower, Willis Tower is one of North America's tallest buildings. Visiting the observation deck on its 103rd floor isn't for the faint-hearted. The attraction includes glass balconies that extend 4.3 feet into thin air, giving you a vertigo-inducing look at the busy city streets 1,353 feet below. Or look up and out—on a clear day you can see four states. The Skydeck also includes interactive exhibits on Chicago and a nine-minute film on the city's growth as an architectural powerhouse. *233 S. Wacker Dr., (312) 875-9447, theskydeck.com.*

Art Institute of Chicago

Eat & Stay

5 Lou Malnati's. On March 17, 1971, Lou Malnati opened his first restaurant, and, for the rest of his life, shared his delight in having opened up an Italian pizzeria in a Jewish neighborhood on an Irish holiday. His restaurant helped set the standard for the Chicago-style deep dish: a thick pie with a flaky, buttery crust that's best eaten with a knife and fork. Still owned by the Malnati family, the company now has branches throughout the city. Its South Loop location is within walking distance of many attractions, making it easy to sample Malnati's signature creation in all its cheesy, saucy, aromatic glory. *805 S. State St., (312) 786-1000, www.loumalnatis.com.*

Chicago skyline

6 Chicago Architecture Foundation Tours. The Great Chicago Fire of 1871 and the 1893 World's Columbian Exposition not only led to the transformation of the city, but also put it at the vanguard of urban architectural design the world over. Skyscrapers here are, by turns, intimidating, unusual, and magnificent. The best place to learn about them is on one (or more!) of the outstanding tours offered by the non-profit Chicago Architecture Foundation. Its most popular excursion is a cruise on the Chicago River, but the daily-changing roster also includes walking tours as well as those by bus, trolley, train, bike, or Segway. The Tour Center gift shop has a well-edited selection of architecture-themed items. Not surprisingly, LEGO sets are very popular. *224 S. Michigan Ave., (312) 922-3432, www.architecture.org.*

7 Art Institute of Chicago. The historic wing of the city's premier art museum was originally built for the 1893 World's Columbian Exposition and later transformed to accommodate a permanent collection of ancient through contemporary art. Its Modern Wing, added in 2009, houses 20th- and 21st-century art and makes the institute one of the nation's largest museums. Among the world-famous paintings here are Georges Seurat's *A Sunday on the Island of La Grande Jatte,* Grant Wood's *American Gothic,* and Edward Hopper's *Nighthawks.* You'll find unexpected treasures, too, including a marvelous collection of miniature rooms with intricately detailed interiors. And having your picture taken with the two bronze lions that guard the Michigan Avenue entrance is a Chicago tradition. *111 S. Michigan Ave., (312) 443-3600, www.artic.edu.*

NORTHEAST

MIDWEST

SOUTH

WEST

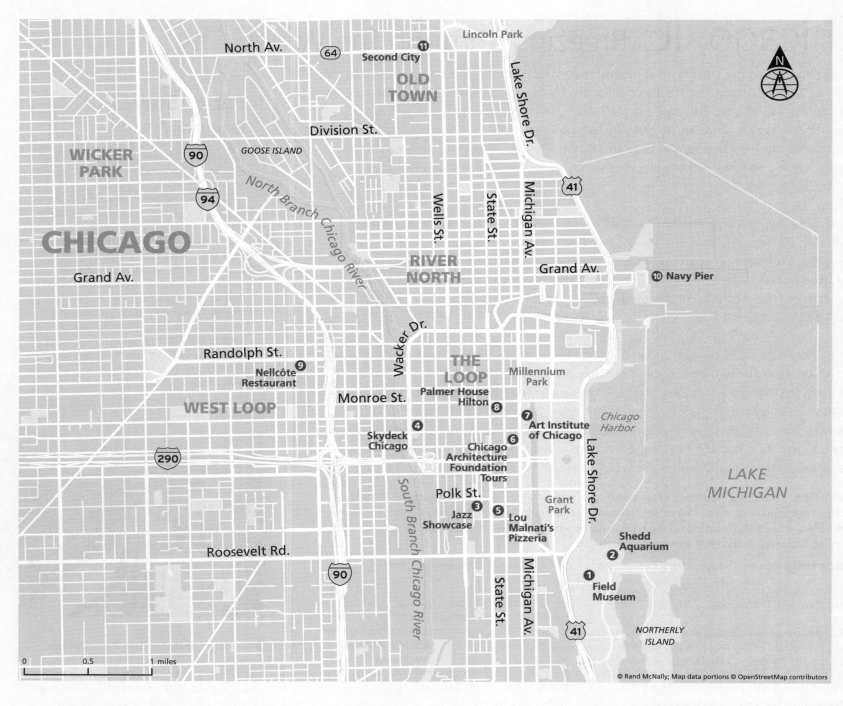

North Av.

Second City ⑪

Lincoln Park

64

OLD TOWN

Division St.

Lake Shore Dr.

WICKER PARK

90

GOOSE ISLAND

94

41

CHICAGO

North Branch Chicago River

Wells St.

State St.

Michigan Av.

RIVER NORTH

Grand Av.

Grand Av.

⑩ Navy Pier

Wacker Dr.

THE LOOP

Millennium Park

Randolph St.

Nellcôte Restaurant ⑨

Monroe St.

Palmer House Hilton ⑧

Chicago Harbor

WEST LOOP

④

⑦ Art Institute of Chicago

Skydeck Chicago

⑥

LAKE MICHIGAN

Chicago Architecture Foundation Tours

Lake Shore Dr.

290

South Branch Chicago River

Polk St.

Grant Park

③

Jazz Showcase

⑤ Lou Malnati's Pizzeria

Shedd Aquarium

Roosevelt Rd.

②

State St.

Michigan Av.

① Field Museum

90

NORTHERLY ISLAND

41

0   0.5   1 miles

© Rand McNally; Map data portions © OpenStreetMap contributors

Eat & Stay

⑧ Palmer House Hilton. The first incarnation of this grand dame was built by businessman Potter Palmer as a wedding gift to his new wife. It burned just 13 days after its opening in the Great Chicago Fire of 1871. Undaunted, Palmer rebuilt an even bigger, grander, and (not surprisingly) more fire-resistant hotel. In addition to 1,641 rooms off its long, warren-like corridors, it offers fine dining in its Lockwood Restaurant and great people watching in Potter's bar. *17 E. Monroe St., (312) 726-7500, www.palmerhousehiltonhotel.com.*

⑨ Nellcôte Restaurant. With its wrought-iron gates, antique crystal chandeliers, and white Italian-marble tables, this West Loop restaurant is the place to go for a special night out. It's elegant but not stuffy—its name, for instance, pays homage to a French villa that was once rented by the Rolling Stones. The restaurant serves a menu influenced by French, Spanish and Italian cuisines, with ingredients sourced from artisan purveyors in the Midwest. *833 W. Randolph St., (312) 432-0500, www.nellcoterestaurant.com.*

North of The Loop

⑩ Navy Pier. What started as a shipping and recreational facility in 1916 became a recruitment training center during World Wars I and II. Today's vibrant multipurpose facility, still evolving, is easily recognized by its giant Ferris wheel. Navy Pier is also home to the Chicago Children's Museum, Chicago Shakespeare Theatre, an IMAX theater, the Driehaus Gallery of Stained Glass Windows, Polk Bros. Park, kiddy rides, a climbing wall, a carousel, restaurants, gift shops, and tour boats—more than enough to please everyone in the family. *600 E. Grand Ave., (800) 595-7437, navypier.com.*

⑪ Second City. Its theater seats a few hundred people, it uses props that look like garage-sale finds, and it features a cast largely made up of former class clowns. Yet, despite its low-budget vibe, Second City is one of the most influential forces in American comedy, delighting Chicago and the larger world with its perceptive, wry brand of improvisational humor. It's launched the careers of luminaries that include John Belushi, Mike Myers, Bill Murray, Tina Fey, and Stephen Colbert. Attend a performance to see if you can spot the next break-out star. *1616 N. Wells, (312) 337-3992, www.secondcity.com.*

Navy Pier

Racine, WI

Larsen's Bakery. No trip to southeastern Wisconsin is complete without sampling the quintessential Danish pastry known as the kringle. This family-owned bakery uses century-old Copenhagen recipes to make 30 varieties of the sweet, a favorite of the region's many Danish-Americans. Here, a three-day process results in a flaky ring filled with nuts or fresh fruits, then topped with icing or glazed sugar. *3311 Washington Ave., (262) 633-4298, www.larsenskringle.com.*

SC Johnson Administration Building. Of Racine's many Frank Lloyd Wright buildings, this is the most famous. It's also the architect's largest commercial structure. Completed in 1939, it attracts Wright devotees from around the world to its forest of dendriform columns (they resemble large golf tees) and its 43 miles of glass tubing used for both natural and artificial light. The furniture was also designed by Wright. The 90-minute Campus Tours (Mar.–Dec., Thurs.–Sun., free; reservations recommended) include the Administration Building; the Wright-designed Research Tower; and Fortaleza Hall, featuring a design by Foster + Partners. *1525 Howe St., (262) 260-2154, www.scjohnson.com/en/company/visiting.aspx.*

North Beach. Wisconsin's first beach to earn certification from the National Clean Beaches Council is the pride of Racine. Enjoy 50 acres of white sand next to the blue waters of Lake Michigan, with lifeguards on duty in summer. There's free parking in nearby lots and streets, a large nautical-themed playground, a bicycle and walking path, a bath house, and a concession stand. No wonder *Parents* magazine named it one of the nation's top beaches. *Hoffert Dr., cityofracine.org/beaches.*

Milwaukee RiverWalk

city itinerary

Milwaukee

❶ Miller Brewery Tour. With the departure of Pabst—the long-gone granddaddy of all Milwaukee's breweries—Miller took over the title of oldest survivor of the city's venerable brewing tradition. The company dates from 1855, and the tour includes the original storage caves. The brewery is one of the largest in the United States. An indoor-outdoor guided walking tour traces the history of the company and shows the high-tech production lines used today. At the end, enjoy an ice-cold brew in the tasting room or outdoor beer garden. *4251 W. State St., (414) 931-2337, www.millercoors.com/breweries.*

❷ Pabst Mansion. This ornate, imposing Flemish Renaissance Revival–style home was built in the 1890s by Captain Frederick Pabst, sea captain, beer baron, and philanthropist. Its 37 rooms are a testimony to Gilded Age excess, with stained-glass windows, plush furnishings, exquisite wood craftsmanship, and fine objets d'art. Although tour guides give the history of the house and describe how Pabst helped shape the city, they also point out amusing details in the home. For example, a painting in the upstairs bedroom depicts an angelic cherub drinking a stein of beer—a true Milwaukee touch. *2000 W. Wisconsin Ave., (414) 931-0808, www.pabstmansion.com.*

❸ Harley-Davidson Museum. This iconic company got its 1903 start as a small machine shop behind the Davidson family's home at 38th and Highland. In 2008 the Harley-Davidson Company (which is still based in Milwaukee) opened this museum. While it's become an international mecca for motorcycle enthusiasts, you don't have to be a Harley rider to appreciate its exhibits. In addition to more than 450 motorcycles and displays that trace the history of the company and its designs, the museum celebrates the eccentricities and creativity of its aficionados. Especially interesting are videos of riders, who reminisce about their cross-country odysseys and more. Before you leave, make sure you get your picture taken on a Harley—the perfect image to impress your friends on Facebook. *400 W. Canal St., (414) 287-2789, www.harley-davidson.com.*

❹ Milwaukee Art Museum. The museum's stunning Quadracci Pavilion is the first Santiago Calatrava–designed building in the U.S. It features a dramatic, 90-foot-high, glass-walled reception hall and is topped by a wing-like sunscreen that folds and unfolds twice each

day. Located on the Milwaukee lakefront, the museum has 25,000 works from antiquity to the present. Highlights include German Expressionist works, American decorative arts, folk and Haitian art, and American art after 1960. *700 N. Art Museum Dr., (414) 224-3200, mam.org.*

❺ RiverWalk District. The scenic RiverWalk follows the Milwaukee River for 2 miles as it winds through the heart of the city. Lined by sidewalk cafes, restaurants, tour boats, pubs, whimsical sculptures, and trendy shops, this is one of the liveliest parts of town. It's also home to the city's most famous fictional resident: Fonzie (aka The Fonz) of *Happy Days* fame. The classic TV show was set in Milwaukee, and the city has erected a life-size bronze statue of Arthur Fonzarelli, who was played by Henry Winkler. *milwaukeeriverwalkdistrict.com.*

❻ Usinger's Sausages. Located on Old World Third Street, a district of restored 19th-century buildings, Usinger's Sausages helps keep Milwaukee's German traditions alive by serving the best of the wurst. Doing business in the same storefront since 1880, it sells 70 varieties of sausages, from fresh bratwursts and Thüringer summer sausages to liverwurst. *1030 N. Old World 3rd St., (414) 276-9105, www.usinger.com.*

Eat & Stay

❼ Iron Horse Hotel. A century-old warehouse was renovated to create this boutique hotel. Although it caters to motorcycle enthusiasts, even those who don't ride in on a Harley will feel welcome here. Its 100 loft-style guest rooms come in a variety of shapes, styles, and configurations, with exposed brick walls and large windows. For dinner, book a table at Smyth, its casual but chic restaurant. *500 W. Florida St., (414) 374-4766, www.theironhorsehotel.com.*

❽ Mader's Restaurant. It's not hard to spot Mader's—just look for the half-timbered building with the stone tower in downtown Milwaukee. Founded in 1902, Mader's serves an array of German favorites in rooms decorated with medieval armor, weaponry, and works of art. The restaurant's Sunday brunch, served by dirndl-clad waitresses, wins accolades as one of the best in the city. *1041 N. Old World 3rd St., (414) 271-3377, www.madersrestaurant.com.*

NORTHEAST

MIDWEST

SOUTH

WEST

Sheboygan

8th Street Ale House. With more than 30 craft beers on tap, the 8th Street Ale House reflects the growing sophistication of the Wisconsin brewing scene. While a few favorites are perennials, the rest of the spigots rotate through beers from around the world, from light lagers to rich, aromatic stouts. You can also choose from 70 bottled brews. Its restaurant serves classic pub grub, including half-pound burgers and (this being Wisconsin) deep-fried cheese curds. *1132 N. 8th St., (920) 208-7540, 8thstreetalehaus.com.*

Elkhart Lake

Sheboygan Broughton Marsh Park & Campground. Sheboygan Marsh encompasses more than 13,000 acres of wetlands and is well-loved by birders, fishermen, and other outdoors enthusiasts. Visit Sheboygan Broughton Marsh Park to learn more about this ecologically rich zone. Its 30 acres include the Marsh Lodge (home to a supper club called Three Guys and a Grill) and a 9-hole foot-golf course. An 80-foot observation tower offers a bird's-eye view of the marsh, and a campground has 64 sites and piers for convenient fishing. *W7039 County Rd. Sr., (920) 876-2535, www.sheboygancounty.com.*

Manitowoc

Wisconsin Maritime Museum. Manitowoc is quite likely the only small Midwestern town with its own submarine. During WWII, 28 of the vessels were built here. Although the USS *Cobia* wasn't one of them, it is nevertheless in the same class of ships and now permanently resides at this museum on the shore of Lake Michigan. In addition to touring the submarine's interior, you can learn about shipwrecks and boat building and how shipping shaped the history of Wisconsin. The Aquatic Species Investigation Lab, meanwhile, tells of an important environmental issue: the growing numbers of invasive aquatic species that threaten the ecosystem of the Great Lakes. *75 Maritime Dr., (920) 684-0218, www.wisconsinmaritime.org.*

Beerntsen's Chocolates. Since 1932, Beerntsen's has crafted its chocolates and other confections by hand in old-fashioned copper kettles. Its downtown shop offers the chance to step back in time, with its striped awning storefront, black-walnut booths and cabinets, and row upon row of hard candies in display jars. A small dining area serves lunch, and a soda fountain dispenses ice cream treats. *108 N. 8th St., (920) 684-9616, beerntsens.com.*

Two Rivers

Rogers Street Fishing Village and Museum. The small town of Two Rivers celebrates its most important industry in this historical site on the banks of the East Twin River. Commercial fishing on the Great Lakes isn't for the faint-hearted, and this museum aptly describes the shipwrecks and other dangers that threaten the lives of those who rely on it for their livelihood. Highlights include an 1886 lighthouse, 1936 wooden fishing tug, and vintage fishing sheds. An exhibit on the Great Lakes Coast Guard tells of valiant search-and-rescue efforts through the years, including those that took place after the famous wreck of the *Rouse Simmons,* lost in a great storm while carrying a load of Christmas trees in November of 1912. *2102 Jackson St., (920) 793-5905, rogersstreet.com.*

Sturgeon Bay

Sturgeon Bay

Door County Maritime Museum. In addition to learning about shipbuilding and commercial fishing at this waterfront museum, you'll meet a colorful cast of characters that include hardy fishermen, ingenious shipbuilders, and stalwart lighthouse keepers. A highlight is the restored tugboat *John Purves,* built in 1919 and used for Great Lakes towing and salvage operations. The Baumgartner Gallery explores the history of lighthouses in Door County—which has one of the nation's greatest concentrations of them—and displays more than 30 model ships. *120 N. Madison Ave., (920) 743-5958, www.dcmm.org.*

Carlsville

Door Peninsula Winery. The oldest and largest winery in Door County has grown into a multilevel complex that also houses a distillery and restaurant. Its tasting room gives samples of more than 45 traditional and fruit wines, which you can purchase along with every conceivable kind of wine-related accessory. The neighboring distillery makes a range of spirits from vodka and gin to single-malt whiskey. From its tasting room you can view the inner workings of the production area. *5806 State Hwy. 42, (920) 743-7431, store.dcwine.com/winery.*

Kohler Style

The Kohler Company is known for its elegant plumbing and bath fixtures; its Ann Sacks collection of stylish ceramic tiles; and its Baker and McGuire lines of contemporary furniture. But when it was founded in Sheboygan back in 1873, it focused on making plows and other farm tools—including an enameled horse trough, which, ". . . . when furnished with legs, will serve as a bathtub." You could say the rest is history, but there's more.

In 1899, Kohler decided to move its operations outside Sheboygan. The company later hired landscape designers Olmsted Brothers of Boston to create a plan for the company town—a greenery-filled village that remains protected by strict zoning and preservation regulations. Today, the town of Kohler makes a lovely side trip from Sheboygan as well as a great place to stay, thanks to the Kohler Waters Spa, and to play thanks to its Pete Dye–designed championship Whistling Straits and Blackwolf Run golf courses.

Whistling Straits golf course, Kohler

Eat & Stay

Kohler Waters Spa I Kohler. Given the company's history, it seems natural that Kohler would open a resort with a spa known for its water treatments and exquisitely landscaped grounds. You can stay at the American Club, a historic property next to the spa, or the nearby Inn on Woodlake. All rooms are luxuriously appointed with the company's lines of fixtures, tiles, and furniture. In the spa, body treatments, massages, and facials are often incorporated into hydrotherapies: acoustic baths with calming sounds and vibrations, jetted tubs with soothing colored lights, Vichy showers, and Turkish hammam rituals. There are also treatments just for men or teens as well as fitness facilities and salon services. *501 Highland Dr., (855) 444-2838, www.americanclubresort.com.*

Two Rivers

Door County

Egg Harbor

Wood Orchard Market. Door County is famous for the market stands that sell the delectable produce of its farms, orchards, and vineyards. The Wood Orchard Market is among the best. Watch for its giant apple as you drive north on State Highway 42. Inside you'll find fresh fruits, jams, baked goods, and cherries in a multitude of forms. You'll be amazed at all the ways they use the fruit here. While you shop, your kids can enjoy the property's go-cart track. *8112 State Hwy. 42, (920) 868-2334, www.woodorchard.com.*

Door County Trolley. These bright red trolleys are a familiar sight along this region's byways, and a narrated trip on one of them lets you concentrate on the scenery instead of the road. Several themed tours are offered, from those focusing on wineries to those highlighting lighthouses. There's even one that introduces you to the ghost stories of the peninsula originally known as Death's Door—later changed to the friendlier Door County. In cold weather, take a Winter Wonderland Tour that includes a sleigh ride. *8030 State Hwy. 42, (920) 868-1100, www.doorcountytrolley.com.*

Fish Creek

Peninsula State Park. This 3,776-acre expanse of woods, wetlands, meadows, and dolostone cliffs is bordered by 8 miles of Green Bay shoreline. In addition to camping, swimming, boating, hiking, golfing, and biking, you can also visit one of Door County's loveliest lighthouses, Eagle Bluff. A docent-led tour gives insights into the isolated lives of those who guided ships to safety along the dangerous shoreline from 1868 until the light was automated in 1926. In summer, the park hosts performances by the **Northern Sky Theater** (920/854-6117, www.northernskytheater.com). An open-air amphitheater surrounded by tall trees provides a sylvan setting for the troupe's professional productions of original plays. *9462 Shore Rd., (920) 868-3258, dnr.wi.gov/topic/parks.*

Sister Bay

Shoreline Cruises. With 300 miles of coastline, some of Door County's best views are from the water. Shoreline Cruises, one of several tour boat companies on the peninsula, offers a number of excursions from the harbor in Sister Bay. A Lighthouse Islands Cruise heads south past multimillion-dollar, clifftop mansions, then cruises beside Peninsula State Park and past small islands rich in history. A Coastline, Cliffs and Caves Cruise takes a northern route to Ellison Bay and Ellison Bluff, with views of the Sister Islands bird sanctuary along the way. For a leisurely end to the day, book a Sunset Cruise (you're encouraged to bring along snacks and beverages to accompany the view). *Sister Bay Marina, 10733 N. Bay Shore Dr., (920) 854-4707, www.shorelinecharters.net.*

Baileys Harbor

Cana Island Lighthouse. Located on a spit of land reached by a causeway, Cana Island is arguably the most picturesque of the nearly dozen Door County lighthouses. You can climb the 89-foot tower for a panoramic view of Lake Michigan and Door County. Displays in the attached house give information on the lonely but vitally important occupation of lighthouse keeper in the days before electric power. Here at Cana Island, the lighthouse was lit by heated lard oil, which had to be changed every three hours through the night. Even in inclement weather this is an evocative spot, with fog often swirling around the island and lighthouse. *8800 E. Cana Island Rd., (920) 743-5958, www.dcmm.org.*

Green Bay

Green Bay Packers Hall of Fame. The Packers have long been at the center of Green Bay—as well as Wisconsin—culture. The Hall of Fame, the first built to commemorate a single professional American football team, celebrates Packers history with exhibits of artifacts and memorabilia. Located at Lambeau Field, it includes a re-creation of legendary coach Vince Lombardi's office. You can also tour the stadium, arguably the most famous in the NFL, and buy a vast array of green-and-gold items in the Packers Pro Shop. *1265 Lombardi Ave., (920) 569-7512, www.packers.com/lambeau-field.*

National Railroad Museum. With more than 70 locomotives and railroad cars, this is one of the largest rail museums in the U.S. Exhibits include a 600-ton Union Pacific Big Boy, a British-made A4 Class locomotive named in honor of Dwight D. Eisenhower, an Aero-Train built by General Motors, and the world's largest collection of passenger train drumheads (the illuminated signs on the back of trains). An exhibit on Pullman Porters explores labor and civil rights history as well as railroad heritage. The 33-acre grounds have an 85-foot observation tower overlooking the Fox River and Green Bay. Rides on vintage trains are offered daily from May through September and on weekends in October. October sees a Pumpkin Train; in December, there's the Polar Express. *2285 S. Broadway, (920) 437-7623, www.nationalrrmuseum.org.*

Eat & Stay

Pelletier's Restaurant & Fish Boil | Fish Creek. When dinner time rolls around, look for Door County's unique culinary treat: the fish boil. The dramatic preparations with outdoor kettles and sudden flashes of fire are shows in themselves. Those at Pelletier's Restaurant are renowned. After watching the pyrotechnics, you'll tuck into a meal of whitefish steaks, small red potatoes, and sweet onions. For dessert, have a piece of cherry pie. *4199 Main St., (920) 868-3313, www.doorcountyfishboil.com.*

Whistling Swan Inn & Restaurant | Fish Creek. Door County's oldest-operating inn has a peripatetic past. It was built in 1887 in Marinette, WI, and, during the winter of 1907, was transported across frigid Green Bay by horses to its present Fish Creek location. In addition to seven guest rooms, the inn has an outstanding restaurant that takes its locavore mission seriously: an ever-changing menu lists the farms that provided the produce, meats, herbs, and cheeses used in each day's dishes. Dine on an enclosed veranda for a lovely view of Fish Creek's charming downtown. *4192 Main St., (920) 868-3442, www.whistlingswan.com.*

Wood Orchard Market, Egg Harbor

Rapid River, MI

Peninsula Point Lighthouse. Built at the end of the Civil War, this lighthouse was illuminated by an oil lamp until 1922. Located at the tip of the Stonington Peninsula, it's now operated by the U.S. Forest Service as a historic site. Climb its 40-foot circular staircase for an expansive view of Lake Michigan, and then head back down to hunt for fossils along the limestone shore. The bird-watching here is good, too, especially during the spring and fall migrations (more than 200 species have been spotted). This remote, scenic spot is also on the fall migration route for monarch butterflies. *County 513 T Rd., (906) 428-5800, www.fs.usda.gov.*

Garden

Fayette Historic State Park. This 711-acre park preserves the remains of an iron-smelting town that was abandoned in 1891. The furnaces and restored buildings offer glimpses into the rigors of industrial work on the Upper Peninsula. The park has a 61-site campground, and the adjoining Snail Shell Harbor offers boating and scuba diving. *4785 II Rd., (906) 644-2603, www.michigan.gov/dnr.*

Seney

Seney National Wildlife Refuge. Established in 1935 to protect migratory birds and wildlife, Seney is a testimony to the resilience of nature. In the 19th century, the land here had been heavily logged, drained, cultivated, and burned before efforts to make it commercially productive were abandoned. Today, about a quarter of its nearly 100,000 acres are designated as wilderness. A highlight is the Strangmoor Bog National Natural Landmark, a rare peat bog ecosystem with carnivorous plants such as the purple pitcher plant and sundew. The visitors center has information on how best to explore this wild environment. *1674 Refuge Entrance Rd., (906) 586-9851, www.fws.gov/refuges.*

St. Ignace

Museum of Ojibwa Culture and Father Marquette Mission Park. At this museum you'll learn how the Ojibwa, Huron, and French cultures shaped this region in the 17th century. Exhibits trace the migration of the Ojibwa tribe from the Atlantic Ocean to the Great Lakes, the multitude of skills that allowed them to survive the region's harsh winters, and the family dynamics of life in an extended clan. Outside the museum, a replica of a Huron long house gives insight into the tribe most associated with the Upper Peninsula. The site also includes the grave of Father Jacques Marquette, the French Jesuit missionary who helped map the northern portion of the Mississippi River. During July and August, the museum sponsors walking tours on the history and culture of the region. *500 N. State St., (906) 643-9161, www.museumofojibwaculture.net.*

Fort Mackinac

Mackinac Island

Fort Mackinac. The British established the original fort in the 1780s; the Americans took it over in the 1790s; and, although the British recaptured it briefly during the War of 1812, it again served the U.S. up until the late 19th century. Many of its 14 original buildings were restored as part of a 1930s WPA project. Today you can explore the guardhouse, command headquarters, schoolhouse, canteen, commissary, storehouse, bath house, barracks, officers' quarters, and hospital—taking in displays of military artifacts along the way. There are walking tours and re-enactments throughout the day, including cannon- and rifle-firings, drills, and even a court martial. *7127 Huron Rd., (906) 847-3328, www.mackinacparks.com.*

Island Time

Between Michigan's Upper and Lower peninsulas, Mackinac Island stands as a reminder of a different time. The French adapted the Native American name, calling it Michilimackinac (Land of the Great Turtle); the British shortened it to Mackinac and built the fort that bears that name. In the late 19th-century, it became a Great Lakes vacation destination for those escaping the summer heat of cities like Cleveland, Chicago, and Detroit.

Today, many of the island's 500 or so permanent residents live in a small village, where charming Victorian-era structures house restaurants, inns, nightspots, and boutiques (don't miss the confectioner shops selling the island's famous fudge!). About 80 percent of Mackinac, however, is state park, where roads and trails take you to curious rock formations and limestone cliffs, a War of 1812 battlefield, and the restored Fort Mackinac itself. An island-wide ban on automobiles means that you'll travel everywhere by foot, bike, and (believe it or not) horse-drawn carriage.

Eat & Stay

Nahma Inn I **Nahma.** The town of Nahma was built in the 1880s by the Bay de Noquet Lumber Company, which used it as a base of operations for Michigan's Upper Peninsula. The company's hotel is now the Nahma Inn, located on the shore of Lake Michigan. Its 14 guest rooms are quaint and comfortable rather than luxurious (half of them have shared baths). The inn also has a restaurant that serves lunch and dinner and a bar where you can hang out with the locals. Afterward, relax around a fire pit on the patio. *13747 Main St., (906) 644-2486, www.nahmainn.com.*

Grand Hotel I **Mackinac Island.** An endless porch is lined with white rockers, bloom-filled flower boxes, and American flags hung as if to salute the Great Lakes—all this, and you've only just arrived. Built in 1887, the Grand is a study in Victorian refinement, albeit one filtered through a contemporary lens. Many rooms have canopy beds as well as bold floral wallpaper and broad-stripe draperies tied together in a coordinated mix of jewel-tones and pastels. Rates are high but include breakfast, a luncheon buffet, and a five-course dinner. Lawn and vintage-league baseball games, carriage tours, garden strolls, and spa treatments are among the leisurely pursuits. You can also golf on the 18-hole Jewel course; play tennis on a clay court; swim in the huge pool; and bike, hike, or run along trails. There are children's programs and plenty of package deals. *286 Grand Ave., (906) 847-3331, www.grandhotel.com.*

Grand Hotel, Mackinac Island

Great River Road: North

ROUTE TOWNS: Minneapolis/St. Paul, MN | Bloomington | Red Wing | Wabasha | Winona | La Crosse, WI
Prairie du Chien | McGregor, IA | Dubuque | Galena, IL | Savanna | Moline | Rock Island | Nauvoo
Hannibal, MO | St. Louis

Of all the ways to get from Minneapolis/St. Paul to St. Louis, the most fun option is behind the wheel along
the Great River Road, a combination of routes that follows the flow of the Mississippi River.

Pikes Peak State Park, Iowa

It's been years since anyone called sophisticated St. Paul "a river town," yet the state capital
sets a high bar for riverfront development. Its downtown district is adjacent to the river as is
its science museum, which houses a Mississippi River Visitors Center staffed by rangers. In
St. Louis, the river is the backdrop for a baseball stadium complete with a huge entertainment
complex, a national park, and the iconic Arch (aka the Gateway to the West).

In between are mid-size metropolitan areas, like the famous Quad Cities of Illinois and Iowa,
and small towns like Red Wing and Winona, MN, where legacy brands long known for their
pottery, boots, and drugstore sundries are part of both local and national history. Other storied
places include Galena, IL, where Ulysses S. Grant
once lived; Nauvoo, IL, first settled by
Mormons; and Hannibal, MO, hometown
of Samuel Clemens. Pack your bags,
load the cooler, and fill the gas tank.
Adventures await in these and other
places along Mississippi River.

Atlas map O-9, p. 55

Distance: 688 miles point to point.

Type of Trip: Vacation Getaway; RV;
Arts & Culture, History & Heritage, Small
Town Gems.

Must Try: *MN:* Fresh thick, white,
walleye in fillets or even on a stick.
WI: Racine kringles, flaky fruit-and-nut-
filled pastries. *IA:* Dubuque's soft, creamy
Trappistine caramels. *IL:* the official snack
is popcorn—plain or buttered, cheese
or caramel coated. *MO:* St. Louis–style
pizza, with its cracker-thin crust.

Must Buy: *MN:* Jewelry made with
Thomsonite, a rare silicate mineral.
WI: Cheese—soft or hard, sharp or mild.
IA: The khaki Pikes Peak State Park
bandanna map has over 11 miles of
screen-printed trails. *IL:* Anything with
that iconic John Deere logo. *MO:* A copy
of *The Adventures of Tom Sawyer* to
read or re-read.

Must See: Science Museum of
Minnesota, Mall of America, Red Wing
Pottery, Red Wing Shoe Company,
Watkins Heritage Museum, National
Mississippi River Museum, Grant's Home,
John Deere Pavilion and Headquarters,
Historic Nauvoo, Mark Twain Boyhood
Home, Gateway Arch, Anheuser Busch
Brewery.

Worth Noting: Try to catch a festival
along the way, maybe the Minnesota
State Fair (Aug.), St. Paul Winter Carnival
(Jan./Feb.), La Crosse's Oktoberfest USA
(Sept./Oct.), Dubuque's American River
Festival (Jun.), Great Galena Balloon
Race (Jun.), or Hannibal's National Tom
Sawyer Days (Jul.).

Travel Tip: This route is identified
by green-and-white signs showing a
riverboat pilot's wheel with the words,
"Great River Road" encircling the top
and the name of the state you're in at
the bottom. Contact the **Mississippi
River Parkway Commission** (www.
experiencemississippiriver.com) for info.

city itinerary

Minneapolis/ St. Paul, MN

Downtown Minneapolis

❶ Walker Art Center. The Walker is one of America's most celebrated contemporary art museums. Franz Marc's *The Large Blue Horses* (1911) was its first acquisition of modern art, purchased in 1942. Other favorites include Edward Hopper's *Office at Night*, Georgia O'Keeffe's *Lake George Barn*, and Andy Warhol's *16 Jackets*.

The center offers tours of its contemporary building, its collection, and the Minneapolis Sculpture Garden, which displays 50 pieces, including the iconic, whimsical *Spoonbridge and Cherry*. (The massive aluminum-and-stainless-steel sculpture and fountain by Claes Oldenburg and Coosje van Bruggen depicts a giant spoon balancing a plump, red cherry. The spoon weighs 5,800 pounds; the cherry tips in at 1,200.) Together the building and garden total 19 acres on the edge of downtown. *1750 S. Hennepin Ave., (612) 375-7600, www.walkerart.org.*

❷ American Swedish Institute. By 1920, over a million Swedes had immigrated to the United States and settled in the upper Midwest, with Minnesota being a favorite destination. The abundance of low-cost land (coupled with religious freedom) was the catalyst. In 1929, the Turnblad family founded the American Institute for Swedish Arts, Literature, and Science and donated their home to house it. Today, the mansion is on the National Register of Historic Places, and the organization, now called the American Swedish Institute, is set in both it and the Nelson Cultural Center. Its programs and collections celebrate the contributions and roles Swedes play in U.S. culture and history. Displays include glass, textiles, and artwork. *2600 Park Ave. S., (612) 871-4907, www.asimn.org.*

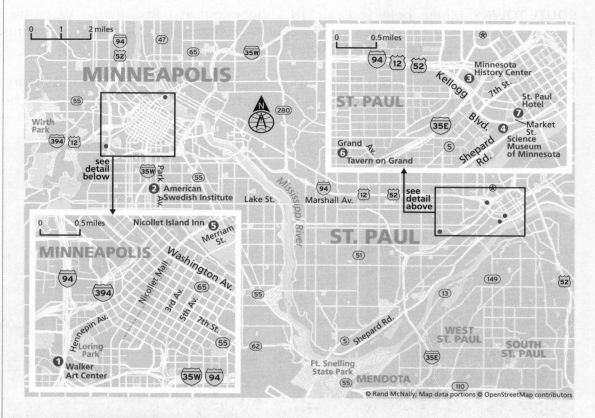

Walker Art Center

Downtown St. Paul

❸ Minnesota History Center. Exhibits here are often as engaging as they are informative. Weather Permitting, for instance, lets you experience how Minnesotans handle the challenging elements in their neck of the north woods. And it's hard not to react during the multimedia tornado presentation, when a simulated call urges you to, "Get to the basement!" Traveling exhibits highlight experiences of everyday life elsewhere in the world. *345 W. Kellogg Blvd., (651) 259-3000, www.minnesotahistorycenter.org.*

❹ Science Museum of Minnesota. The first floor of this science complex has a Mississippi River Visitor Center manned by rangers, who share plenty of info about Big Muddy, which is right outside the door. If the five permanent galleries of interactive exhibits don't entice you to stick around and explore, the hum from the world's largest seismograph strung through the atrium will. You can also learn by playing in the Big Back Yard, where a nine-hole miniature golf course is themed to showcase the river's biodiversity. *120 W. Kellogg Blvd., (651) 221-9444, www.smm.org.*

Science Museum of Minnesota

Eat & Stay

❺ Nicollet Island Inn. Awnings and flower boxes on the windows of an 1873 factory are clues that this building has moved from the realm of commerce to that of romance. Often recognized as the most romantic lodging in the Twin Cities, the 23-room inn offers views of the storied Mississippi River from its rooms and its lauded restaurant. The seasonally changing menu of dishes made from locally sourced meat and produce make it a local dining favorite. So do Sunday's five-course champagne brunches. *95 Merriam St., (612) 331-1800, www.nicolletislandinn.com.*

❻ Tavern on Grand. Walleye is always on the menu at Tavern on Grand, where Minnesota's official state fish is served in ceviche or in cakes topped with béarnaise. Find it on a sampler plate and in spring rolls. The most popular menu item is the Walleye Basket. For lighter fare, consider walleye on a stick, state-fair style. Theme nights include half-price wine on Monday, a Mexican menu on Wednesday, and trivia games on Thursday. *656 Grand Ave., (651) 228-9030, www.tavernongrand.com.*

❼ St. Paul Hotel. Built in 1910, the 254-room grand dame of St. Paul hospitality is in the heart of the capital. Amenities include a rooftop fitness facility and the first-floor St. Paul Grill, with its prime steaks. Rooms are elegant, with mahogany armoires and poster beds; tufted velvet chairs; and granite bathroom vanities. Many have views of Rice Park and its charming bronze sculptures of Charlie Brown and the gang—a nod to the fact that the city is the birthplace of *Peanuts* cartoonist Charles M. Schulz. *350 Market St., (800) 292-9292, www.saintpaulhotel.com.*

Paddle-wheeler on the Mississippi River, La Crosse

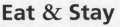
Bald eagle over the Mississippi River

Bloomington, MN

Mall of America. Enjoy a sales-tax-free day of wardrobe and accessories shopping in the 500+ stores at one of the world's largest shopping malls, situated in Bloomington, just 15 minutes southwest of the center of the Twin Cities. How big is it? Big enough to house a roller coaster and other amusement rides. You can literally shop for miles here; some people even walk the mall for exercise, following marked Mayo Clinic mile, 5K, and 10K routes. *60 E. Broadway, Hwy. 494 and Cedar Ave., (952) 883-8800, www.mallofamerica.com.*

Red Wing

Red Wing Pottery Museum. Red Wing's salt-glazed stoneware pottery—used for food storage before the time of refrigeration—was featured at the Minnesota State Fair back in the 1920s and is considered highly collectible today. Its free museum displays some 6,000 pieces of dinnerware, crocks, jugs (including one that holds 70 gallons), folk art, and early-1900s advertising pieces. Watch for the unique shapes, patterns, and glazes of items designed by Eva Zeisel and other great American ceramicists. *Pottery Place Annex, 240 Harrison St., (651) 327-2220, www.potterymuseumredwing.org.*

Red Wing Shoe Company Museum and Store. Free, self-guided tours of this museum showcase the history of the American-made work boot company. You can't miss the world's largest boot: size 638-D, which reportedly weighs more than a ton; was made to the same (but larger) specs as Red Wing's classic work boot; and, at 16-feet high and 20-feet long, would be too big for even the Statue of Liberty. Find shoes your own size at the outlet store. *315 Main St., (651) 388-6233, www.redwing.redwingshoestore.com.*

Wabasha

National Eagle Center. Because the Mississippi River doesn't freeze near Wabasha, you can see bald eagles in the wild here almost any time of year. You'll definitely see them, as well as golden eagles and other raptors, at the National Eagle Center. Check out the five resident rescue birds (Angel, Columbia, Donald, Harriet, and Was'aka) and one of the live, 45-minute, naturalist-led presentations held daily at 11, 1, and 3. *50 Pembroke Ave., (651) 565-4989, www.nationaleaglecenter.org.*

Winona

Winona County Historical Society Museum. Three levels of exhibits and vignettes showcase such unique artifacts as a 1930s marble bank counter with bulletproof glass in the teller windows and holes in the framework to balance shotgun barrels. In Walking Through Time, children can explore a cave, a tepee, and a riverboat. Downtown Winona has more than 100 Victorian buildings on the National Register. Printed architectural walking tours are available at the information desk here. *160 Johnson St., (507) 454-2723, www.winonahistory.org.*

Minnesota Marine Art Museum. Set on a secluded channel of the Mississippi River, MMAM has a permanent collection of marine, maritime, and otherwise water-themed art. Here you can see everything from classic works by Turner, Homer, and the Hudson River School to realist works by Wyeth; modernist works by O'Keeffe; and Impressionist and abstract works by Monet, Renoir, Matisse, Van Gogh, Kandinsky, and Picasso. *800 Riverview Dr., (507) 474-6626, www.mmam.org.*

Watkins Heritage Museum and Store. From horse-and-buggy distribution to manufacturing to e-commerce, the history of J.R. Watkins natural remedies and products, founded in 1868, unfolds here. One of the company's first products—a muscle liniment made from Asian camphor and red pepper extract—is still sold today. Pick some up in the on-site store, or try new formulas at the samples table during one of the free museum tours. *150 Liberty St., (507) 457-6095, www.jrwatkins.com.*

La Crosse, WI

City Brewing Company. This contract brewer has 70 fermentation tanks inside its production complex. Yet it's the six silos/tanks used to create the world's largest six-pack that get most folks to pull over for a social-media moment. The tanks can hold enough beer to fill 7 million actual cans. That's 140 cans, or nearly 24 six-packs, for each of the town's 50,000+ residents. *1111 3rd St. S., (608) 785-4200, www.citybrewery.com.*

Grandad Bluff. Along the Mississippi there's no bluff quite as impressive as the 590-footer affectionately called Grandad. It was opened to the public as a park in 1912, and a shelter atop it provides expansive views of La Crosse, the river, and the bluffs along the Minnesota side. There's a parking lot only 300 feet from the viewpoint. *3020 Grandad Bluff Rd., (608) 789-7533, www.cityoflacrosse.org.*

Eat & Stay

St. James Hotel I Red Wing. Built to lodge wheat traders arriving by rail or steamboat, the St. James opened on Thanksgiving Day, 1875. At four stories, it was the highest building for miles and was ahead of its day, with amenities like steam heat and hot-and-cold running water. Today, rooms nod to the past with stately Victorian styling and classic river and downtown views, while the hotel maintains a cutting-edge reputation. Here, you can request just about anything, including your choice of body pillows and water, isotonic, or buckwheat head pillows—there's even an option with high-quality, built-in speakers. Restaurants range from the gourmet to the casual, including a whiskey bar with pub food. *406 Main St., (651) 388-2846, www.st-james-hotel.com.*

Rudy's Drive-In I La Crosse. The largest root beer stand in the Midwest, Rudy's Drive-In bills its triple-patty Monster Burger as a "sensational sandwich." But it also offers lighter fare such as a 1/3-pound turkey burger and the Walnut Burger (seasoned walnut and cheese patty fully dressed on a bun), which was made famous by the historic Trempealeau Hotel, Restaurant, and Saloon, situated upriver some 20 miles from La Crosse. Rudy's menu appeals to those who pull over simply to be served by an honest-to-goodness carhop. Summertime's themed Cruise or Bike nights add to the fun. *1004 La Crosse St., (608) 782-2200, www.rudysdrivein.com.*

NORTHEAST

MIDWEST

SOUTH

WEST

Prairie du Chien

Villa Louis. Throughout the 1800s, the Dousman family made a fortune in lumber, real estate, and other businesses. Their Victorian summer estate, built along the Mississippi, has a celebrated British Arts-and-Crafts style interior and is filled with period furnishings. Costumed docents lead tours through 25 rooms highlighting family history; the everyday life of the 19th century's elite; and the art, architecture, and restoration of the mansion. *521 North Villa Louis Rd., (608) 326-2721, villalouis.wisconsinhistory.org.*

McGregor, IA

Pikes Peak State Park. Here, just south of the town of McGregor, a 500-foot bluff overlooks the point where the Mississippi and Wisconsin rivers meet, a confluence that feeds millions of gallons of fresh water into Old Muddy. Because settlers weren't allowed to stake claims in this driftless area, it's now one of Iowa's most pristine natural preserves. Hike up for a breathtaking view of the twin suspension bridges connecting Iowa and Wisconsin. The park is also home to Bridal Veil Falls; Sand Cave; some Indian mounds; and a campground with 77 sites (60 electrical), shower and restroom facilities, a dump station, and a park concession. *15316 Great River Rd., (563) 873-2341, www.stateparks.com.*

Shopping Alert

McGregor (563/873-3795, www.cityofmcgregoriowa.com) has a colorful past that includes deep Scottish roots thanks to the namesake clan who settled the area. Its downtown district is lined with 19th-century buildings repurposed as restaurants and shops. Seven of those retailers specialize in antiques.

Dubuque river view

Dubuque

National Mississippi River Museum & Aquarium. This massive museum complex lets you fully explore the Mississippi River as it wends from Minnesota to Louisiana. Follow along as naturalists guide you through various types of river flora and fauna in the Woodward Nature Wetland Trail exhibit. Learn about paddle-wheelers and other craft in the Fred W. Woodward Riverboat Museum and the Pfohl Family Boatyard, where hands-on activities include virtually navigating a barge using a pilot's wheel, much like the one emblazoned on Great River Road signposts. See exotic marine life in Rivers to the Sea aquariums; tour a dredge boat; or sit a spell on a bench sculpture that includes Samuel Clemens, who appears to be contemplating the Mississippi. *350 E. 3rd St., (563) 557-9545, www.mississippirivermuseum.com.*

Fenelon Place Elevator Company. Fenelon Place Elevator Company's funicular railway is steep, short, and fun to ride. The 296-foot line takes you up 189 feet, from Fourth Street to Fenelon Place, with views of Dubuque, the river, and beyond to Wisconsin and Illinois. Built for private use in 1882 and opened to the public two years later, Fenelon Place Elevator is credited with inaugurating cable-car technology that's still used today. *512 Fenelon Pl., (563) 582-6496, www.fenelonplaceelevator.com.*

Galena, IL

Ulysses S. Grant Home State Historic Site. In 1854, after several years in the U.S. Army, Ohio-born Ulysses S. Grant retired from military service and tried his hand (unsuccessfully) at other things. In 1860, he moved his family to Galena, where they rented a small Federal-style house, and Grant worked as a clerk in his father's store. With the outbreak of the Civil War a year later, he returned to the army as a colonel in the 21st Illinois Volunteer Infantry Regiment. And the rest, as they say, is history. In 1865, the people of Galena gave General Grant this Italianate-style house as a gift for his service. Filled with period furnishings, including many Grant family possessions, it's one of Galena's must-see historic sites. *500 Bouthillier St., (815) 777-3310, www.granthome.com.*

Galena Cellars Vineyard & Winery. Tucked inside a restored granary near the floodgates in Galena, this tasting room and gift shop features the varieties produced by the Galena Cellars Vineyard located north of town. Sip dry or semi-dry reds and whites as well as fruit and dessert wines inside or out on the shaded patio. *515 S. Main St., (800) 397-9463, www.galenacellars.com.*

Eat & Stay

Fried Green Tomatoes | Galena. Downtown Galena's popular, upscale eatery serves up a lot of history with its steak, chop, and seafood dishes. Its building has housed an iron-stove shop, a theater, a tombstone carver's studio, and the Jo Daviess County Courthouse. Don't leave without trying the eponymous appetizer: green tomatoes that are lightly breaded, delicately sautéed, and sprinkled with cheese. *213 N. Main St., (815) 777-3938, www.friedgreen.com.*

DeSoto House Hotel | Galena. Abraham Lincoln once spoke from a balcony at this 55-room property, the state's oldest operating hotel. Ulysses S. Grant used it as headquarters for his presidential campaign. Samuel Clemens, Susan B. Anthony, and Theodore Roosevelt were other notable guests. Today, modern rooms with Victorian styling solidify the hotel's historic place on Galena's main street. *230 S. Main St., (815) 777-0090, www.desotohouse.com.*

Hotel Blackhawk | Davenport, IA. This hotel opened in downtown Davenport back in 1915 with such amenities as a bowling alley. A restoration jazzed things up, giving the 130-room property an oh-so-contemporary décor with a hip, colorful palette. And that bowling alley? Still here and now complete with a chic martini bar. Room amenities include iPhone docks and bathroom mirrors with TV screens in them. There's also an indoor pool and a spa/salon. Dining options include Beignet Done That and Bix Bistro and Lounge. *203 E. 3rd St., (888) 525-4455, www.hotelblackhawk.com.*

Fenelon Place Elevator Company, Dubuque

Savanna

Mississippi Palisades State Park. This 2,500-acre park, 3 miles north of Savanna at the confluence of the Mississippi and Apple rivers, features erosion-carved cliffs, or palisades, and two noteworthy rock formations: Indian Head and Twin Sisters. Its 13 miles of trails weave along some paths once used by Native Americans. Stands of white birch and other deciduous trees provide autumnal color; in warmer months, look for fiddlehead ferns among brilliant lobelia, bluebell, and yellow ladies' slipper blooms. Winter sees eagles feeding at the confluence. The park has 241 first-come-first-served tent or RV sites (110 with electrical hookups) in both shaded and open areas. Hot-water showers, flush toilets, and a concession building are open May–October. *16327A IL Rte. 84, (815) 273-2731, dnr.state.il.us.*

Moline

Lagomarcino's. Family-owned Lagomarcino's started making fine chocolates in 1908, a tradition that continues several generations later. Today, though, it also has a soda fountain and is an overall favorite for light dining. Tiffany lamps, mahogany booths, terrazzo flooring, and tin ceilings hint at the confectioner's past. Try a Lago—similar to a Dr. Pepper—with a simple sandwich for lunch. Follow it with a sundae whose ice cream and bittersweet fudge are homemade. *1422 5th Ave., (309) 764-1814, www.lagomarcinos.com.*

John Deere Pavilion. Admission is free at downtown Moline's John Deere Pavilion, where you can climb aboard giant tractors and combines or slip into a simulator and try driving through a planted field. The adjacent John Deere Store is the best place in the Quad Cities to find toy tractors, clothing, and other items featuring that iconic leaping-deer logo. *1400 River Dr., (309) 765-1000, www.deere.com.*

John Deere World Headquarters. Designed by architect Eero Saarinen, Deere's 1,400-acre world headquarters complex has won numerous awards for its innovative use of materials. The lobby, with displays of antique and new equipment, is open to the public for free visits. A three-dimensional mural by Alexander Girard uses more than 2,000 farming artifacts to depict 177 years of agricultural history. *One John Deere Pl., (309) 765-9588, www.deere.com.*

John Deere Pavilion

Rock Island

Mississippi River Visitor Center. A series of locks and dams makes it possible to navigate the Mississippi River. You can learn more about them at this information center and museum in Rock Island. Depending on the time of year, it's also a great place to observe raptors and other birds, given its location on the Mississippi Flyway. Note that you'll need to show identification on the approach to Arsenal Island and Locks & Dam 15. *1575 Rodman Ave., Bldg. 328, (309) 794-5338, www.mvr.usace.army.mill/Missions/Recreation.*

Nauvoo

Historic Nauvoo. At the Historic Nauvoo Visitors Center, displays and films highlight the town's 1839 founding by Mormons. It's also a great place to pick up maps and find out about the many tour options. Horse-drawn wagon rides present an overview of the area and its dramatic past, including the late night, winter exodus of the Mormons as they fled west to avoid religious persecution. Another trek lets you pull or push a handcart along a trail, just as the Mormons did 150 years ago on their journey from Illinois to Utah. You can also visit historical buildings, enjoy musical theater, and stroll through shops manned by costumed interpreters. All sites, tours, shows, and rides in Historic Nauvoo are free. *Main and Hubbard Sts., (217) 577-2603, www.historicnauvoo.net.*

Hannibal, MO

Planters Barn Theater. At this theater inside an 1849 barn, you can experience the humor and drama that made Samuel Clemens (aka Mark Twain) famous the world over. May through July features Richard Garey's one-man show, *Mark Twain Himself.* Group Twain-themed walking tours are also available, and, in December, the resident theater troupe performs *A Shepherd's Tail. 319 N. Main St., (573) 231-0021, www.heritagestage.com.*

Mark Twain Boyhood Home and Museum. Samuel Clemens's hometown experiences certainly influenced his writing. Likewise his writing greatly impacted his hometown. If you're looking for Mark Twain—or Tom Sawyer, Huck Finn, and Becky Thatcher—you'll definitely find them here. Start at the Interpretive Center, where you can pick up a ticket admitting you to Twain's restored 1840 boyhood home; the one-time home of Laura Hawkins, his childhood sweetheart and model for the fetching Becky; and the Museum Gallery, with Norman Rockwell illustrations of Tom and Huck and a first-floor bookshop with an impressive selection of Twain's works. The statue of Tom and Huck at the foot of Cardiff Hill is a favorite spot for group photos. *120 N. Main St., (573) 221-9010, www.marktwainmuseum.org.*

Mark Twain Riverboat. Step aboard this 400-passenger sternwheeler, built in 1964 by the Dubuque Boiler and Boatworks, to sail along the river and learn its legends and lore. On sightseeing cruises you can grab a bite at the snack bar. Dinner cruises include a buffet, soft drinks, live music, and dancing. *100 Center St., Center Street Landing, (573) 221-3222, www.marktwainriverboat.com.*

Eat & Stay

Mark Twain Family Restaurant | Hannibal. The Mark Twain Dinette (aka Family Restaurant) has long been a downtown riverfront fixture, serving three squares a day since 1942. The menu is full of such Southern staples as catfish or fried-chicken dinners, pork-tenderloin sandwiches, and frosty mugs of homemade root beer. *400 N. 3rd St., (573) 221-5511, www.marktwaindinette.com.*

Java Jive Coffee House | Hannibal. The riverfront Java Jive claims to be the first coffee house west of the Mississippi. Step inside; sink into a sofa; and indulge in a coffee, freshly brewed from locally roasted beans, and some baked goods. The café, which occasionally hosts live music and readings, serves its fare on dishes made by a local potter. *211 N. Main St., (573) 221-1017, www.javajiveonline.com.*

Reagan's Queen Anne B&B | Hannibal. At this bed-and-breakfast, an 1899 Queen Anne–style residence is surrounded by grounds with flowering gardens, a gazebo, a koi pond, and a waterfall. Inside, the six guest rooms feature details like lace curtains, stately cast-iron or wood bedsteads, and the occasional bit of chintz; four rooms have private baths. The downtown property can also arrange a visit from Mark Twain, as portrayed by actor Richard Garey, noted for his one-man Clemens shows at the nearby Planters Barn Theater. *313 N. 5th St., (573) 221-0774, www.reagansqueenanne.com.*

Hannibal

NORTHEAST

MIDWEST

SOUTH

WEST

city itinerary

St. Louis, MO: A Gateway Getaway

What started as a five-street village named for Louis IX became a major crossroads after President Thomas Jefferson's fortuitous Louisiana Purchase. Indeed, the 630-foot stainless-steel Gateway Arch, on the banks of the Mississippi River, honors the city's role in westward expansion. Today, though millions stop here, few have any intention of heading very far west, thanks in no small part to the city's many attractions.

You can revel in St. Louis heritage at the museums and venues in Forest Park, or jam with some of the 300,000-plus residents in trendy neighborhoods like the Delmar Loop. You can sample the city's renowned beer, or cheer at a Cardinals game. The upshot? You really don't need to be in a rush to head west—or any other direction.

Travel Tips: From Hannibal to St. Louis, MO 79 is one of the most scenic stretches along the Mississippi River, passing thickly wooded islands and towering limestone bluffs. In town, Attraction Corridor signs point the way to popular sites. Use the Kingshighway, Grand, or Broadway exits to reach many of them. Also note that downtown St. Louis has plenty of parking—almost 50,000 spaces, in fact.

Visitor Info: St. Louis Convention & Visitors Commission, *701 Convention Plaza, (800) 916-0092, explorestlouis.com.*

St. Louis skyline and Gateway Arch

Delmar Loop/University City and Forest Park

❶ St. Louis Zoo. This renowned zoological park—which is free and open 365 days a year—is the most popular site in town, attracting nearly 3 million animal-loving visitors annually. Don't miss the bears at Grizzly Ridge (new in 2017); Red Rocks (aka Big Cat Country); Historic Hill (birds, primates, amphibians); and Cypress Swamp, featuring spoonbills, herons, and other species that thrive along the Mississippi. Hop on the Zooline Railroad for a ride through it all. *1 Wells Dr., (314) 781-0900, www.stlzoo.org.*

St. Louis Zoo

Downtown

❷ Gateway Arch. Soaring 630 feet above the Mississippi River, the distinctive stainless-steel Gateway Arch commemorates both the city's founding and President Thomas Jefferson's successful efforts for westward expansion via the Louisiana Purchase. The Arch is the centerpiece of the Jefferson National Expansion Memorial. Security measures require you to pass through a checkpoint; allow 30 minutes for this (more time in summer) before your scheduled tram ride to the top of the arch. Tip: Avoid summer crowds and long security-line waits by visiting the Arch at night. *11 N. 4th St., (877) 982-1410, www.nps.gov/jeff.*

❸ Busch Stadium and Ballpark Village. Busch Stadium is home to Major League Baseball's St. Louis Cardinals. A downtown landmark since 1966, the latest incarnation of it opened in April 2006 with seats for 46,861 fans. Tours are offered. A statue of Hall of Famer Stan "The Man" Musial stands outside Gate 3 of the stadium, and the **Ballpark Village** (stlballparkvillage.com) entertainment complex is adjacent to it. Here, in Cardinals Nation, you can dine and drink; catch games from the ATT Rooftop (tickets required); or tour the amazing

Eat & Stay

❹ Blueberry Hill. This restaurant and music club is filled with pop-culture memorabilia. Think: *The Simpsons,* the Beatles, *Star Wars,* and rock-and-roll legends like Chuck Berry featured on lunch boxes and toys. Grab a made-to-order burger in the Dart Room, or step downstairs into the Duck or the Elvis rooms for live music. Step across the street for a selfie by Chuck Berry's statue. You can also see his star (and those of other famous citizens) on the St. Louis Walk of Fame, which runs along Delmar Boulevard. *6504 Delmar Blvd., (314) 727-4444, www.blueberryhill.com.*

❺ Moonrise Hotel. The Moonrise—a moderately priced boutique hotel in the trendy Delmar Loop neighborhood—is both eco- and pet-friendly. It's also taken the moon to new heights, with space-age décor and lighting and lots of lunar-themed artwork and memorabilia. Rooms are wired for lift-off with 32-inch plasma TVs, iPod docking stations, and free Wi-Fi. The Eclipse restaurant serves contemporary American fare in a Jetsons-like setting, and the rooftop bar serves craft cocktails beneath the world's largest moon sculpture. *6177 Delmar Blvd., (314) 721-1111, moonrisehotel.com*

❻ Pi Pizzeria. This place made St. Louis pizza famous—and did so by word of mouth. No ads, no commercials, just delicious pies with cracker-thin crusts and all-natural toppings. The dining area at the Delmar Loop location, one of three in the city, spills onto a super-wide sidewalk with great people watching, thanks to the legendary Pageant Theater across the street. Favorite pies include the thin-crust East Loop, with chicken, mushrooms, onions, pesto sauce, and mozzarella. If deep dish is more your thing, try the Delmar, with chicken, barbecue sauce, and fresh cilantro. *6144 Delmar Blvd., (314) 727-6633, pi-pizza.com.*

collection of memorabilia in the Cardinals Hall of Fame. The Village is also home to a FOX Sports Midwest studio and several other restaurants and bars (after 9 pm, no one under 21 is allowed in the Village). *250 Stadium Plaza, (314) 345-9600, stlouis.cardinals.mlb.com.*

❼ Anheuser-Busch Brewery Tour. At the oldest and largest Anheuser-Busch complex, brewery tours are first-come, first served, so arrive early. See, feel, and smell the ingredients while watching the brewing process unfold. The 1885 stables house the company's majestic Clydesdale horses, dray animals that stand up to 18-hands (6 feet) and weigh up to 2,000 pounds. Stops also include the Beechwood Aging Cellars and the Biergarten, where AB products and soft drinks are available. *1 Busch Pl. (12th & Lynch Sts.), (314) 577-2626, www.budweisertours.com.*

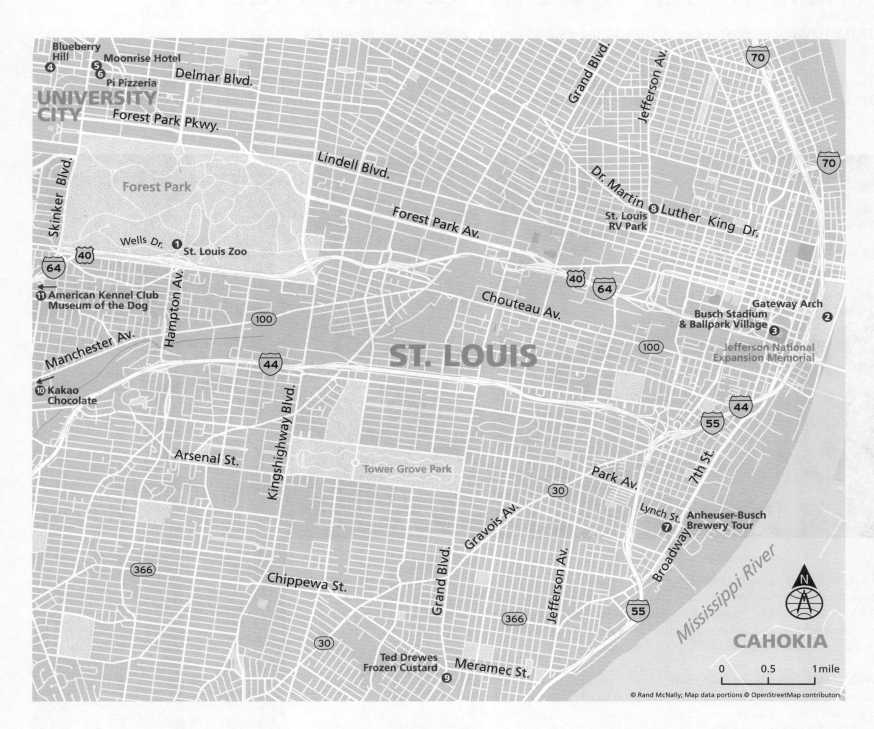

ST. LOUIS

© Rand McNally; Map data portions © OpenStreetMap contributors

0   0.5   1 mile

CAHOKIA

NORTHEAST

MIDWEST

SOUTH

WEST

Eat & Stay

8 St. Louis RV Park. Location, location, location works for RV parks, too. This one in downtown St. Louis isn't large, but it does offer a lot of amenities like large pull-through sites with full hook-ups, clean restrooms, and a swimming pool. The park is also close to public transit, a rental-car office, and a bike trail that follows the Mississippi toward a bridge to Illinois. The Riverfront Walk, Anheuser-Busch Brewery, Gateway Arch, and several free museums at Forest Park are also nearby. *900 N. Jefferson Ave., (800) 878-3330, www.stlouisrvpark.com.*

9 Ted Drewes Frozen Custard. Ted Drewes has drawn crowds to its serving windows since 1929. They don't come for a particular flavor but rather a specific style—one so frozen that it's called "concrete." Customers delight in taking selfies holding the serving cups upside down. Try a Terramizzou (pistachios and Ted's secret blend of chocolate) or a Lemon Crumb (lemon-vanilla with graham crackers). *4224 S. Grand Blvd., (314) 352-7376, teddrewes.com.*

Western Reaches of St. Louis

10 Kakao Chocolate. In this neighborhood shop on the western edge of St. Louis, the chocolate-filled display cases are as mesmerizing as the confectioners at work in the open kitchen. Here, chocolates are made on large sheets, just like in Switzerland, using all-natural ingredients—including a few unique seasonings like chili pepper and curry powder. Pick up delicious truffles, brittles, hot-chocolate mixes, or even a cocoa grilling rub for truly tasty souvenirs. *7272 Manchester Rd., (314) 645-4446, www.kakaochocolate.com.*

11 American Kennel Club Museum of the Dog. Man's best friend is both heralded and welcomed at this museum. More than 700 works of art, decorative arts, and photography depict dogs of all breeds, both famous and simply friendly. Permanent exhibits include the All-Star Dogs Hall of Fame, with murals and storyboards, and a collection honoring canines that have served in the military. The gift shop has as many items for four-legged friends as it does for their humans. *1721 S. Mason Rd., (314) 821-3647, www.museumofthedog.org.*

Side Trip to St. Charles

Main Street in St. Charles, 25 miles west of the Gateway Arch, bustles with artisans, tradespeople, and shoppers—much like it did when it was founded in 1769. Thousands of pioneers stopped in what was Missouri's first state capital to replenish supplies before heading into the "new territory." And the people of St. Charles have labored lovingly to preserve their rich river town heritage.

Today almost a million people visit each year, but instead of stocking up on sundries, they're stocking up on wares from boutiques; art galleries; or jewelry stores, like **Cassandra Erin Studio** (112 S. Main St., 636/573-0133, www.cassandraerin.com). Rather than eating at campsites or taverns, they're dining in one of the 150-odd restaurants.

If you decide to join them, consider booking a horse-drawn carriage ride; visiting the **Lewis & Clark Boat House and Nature Center** (1050 S. Riverside Dr., 636/947-3199, www.lewisandclarkcenter.org); or exploring some of the Boone Lick Trail, which starts here.

Missouri Family Fun & Fine Fiddling

ROUTE TOWNS: Jefferson City | Lake of the Ozarks Area | Springfield | Republic | Branson

The middle of Missouri, from the capital south, offers plenty of family fun, down-home food, and lake and Ozark Mountain scenery. Of course Branson is the hub for fine music—on the fiddle and other instruments.

Ozark Mountain fall scenery

Nearly 200 years ago, Lohman's Landing (aka Jefferson Landing), a sleepy but central and scenic steamboat stop, was chosen as the site for a new state capital. The Missouri River and its bluffs are still an impressive sight, and so is Jefferson City. Downtown, hanging baskets overflow with flowers, and patterned, tree-lined sidewalks invite strolling and window shopping. Benches and cafes encourage lingering.

South of the capital is the Lake of the Ozarks, where you can swim, paddle, fish, or just relax waterside. In Springfield, catch a minor league baseball game at Hammons Field or visit Fantastic Caverns, one of several caves in the region. In nearby Republic, tour the site of the first Civil War battle west of the Mississippi. Highway 65 south takes you to the Tri-Lakes Area (Table Rock Lake, Lake Taneycomo, and Bull Shoals Lake) and Branson, playgrounds for the child in everyone.

The entertainment in Branson all started in the 1960s, when the Presley Family (no relation to the King) began performing in an area cavern. Their shows featured local mountain music with lots of two- and three-part harmony accompanied by a fiddle, banjo, flat-top guitar, washboard, and a percussion instrument fashioned from the jawbone of a mule. The tradition continues with the *Presleys' Country Jubilee,* in the family's own 1,500 seat theater, Branson's first. It's since been joined by about 50 others in town and the surrounding hills.

Atlas map G-14, p. 59

Distance: 210 miles point to point.

Type of Trip: Weekend Getaway; RV; Arts & Music, Great Outdoors, History & Heritage, Small Town Gems, Sports Fan.

Must Try: Central Dairy ice cream, a "throwed" roll experience at Lambert's Café, a cooking class through *Midwest Living* Culinary & Crafts School at Silver Dollar City.

Must Buy: Tickets to at least one Branson show, a spa treatment at The Lodge of Four Seasons or Chateau on the Lake.

Must See: Missouri State Museum, Missouri State Penitentiary & Museum, Fantastic Caverns or the Ozark Cavern, Wilson's Creek National Battlefield, Silver Dollar City.

Worth Noting: South and west of Jefferson City are more than 10 vineyards and wineries in what's part of the officially designated Ozark Mountain American Viticultural Area. As the area's 19th-century German settlers discovered, soil and climate conditions here are similar to those of another famous wine region: the Rhine River valley. The **Missouri Wine and Grape Board** (missouriwine.org) has information on the Ozark Mountain and other state viticulture areas; its website also has a winery-tour planning tool. To this we say, *"Prost!"*

Travel Tips: Although this trip is short enough for a weekend getaway, there are so many things to see and do and great places to stay—including some stellar campgrounds—it's probably better to make it a more leisurely journey. To lengthen it, though, consider adding on a visit to St. Louis. From the Gateway to the West, it's just a 2-hour, 130-mile drive, most of it along I-70, to Jefferson City. You could also readily combine this trip with one to Arkansas. Branson is a mere 50 miles northeast of Eureka Springs.

NORTHEAST MIDWEST SOUTH WEST

Jefferson Landing State Historic Site (above)
Missouri State Capitol (right)

Jefferson City

Missouri State Capitol & Museum. The third Missouri State Capitol on this downtown site was modeled after the U.S. Capitol, built of Missouri-quarried marble, and completed in 1917. A tour of its grounds, interior, and on-site state history museum provides a great overview of both Missouri and Jefferson City as well as the architecture of the building itself. Interior highlights include murals—some by such significant artists as Thomas Hart Benton and Sir Frank Brangwyn—depicting state history. The grounds also feature memorials to Lewis & Clark, Missouri Law Enforcement, and Missouri Veterans.

In the first-floor Missouri State Museum, changing and permanent exhibits showcase the state's diverse history and resources. One of the highlights is a rare collection of over 130 Civil War battle flags—at least one of which is always on display—that belonged to or were captured by Missouri units on both sides of the conflict. As you might recall, Missouri was one of the most divided states during the Civil War. It's one of many fascinating stories that you can learn more about here. Admission to the capitol and the museum is free, and so are the 45-minute guided tours, which take place on each hour (except for noon) Monday through Saturday 9–4 and Sunday at 11 and 2. *201 W. Capitol Ave., (573) 751-2854 or (573) 751-4127 (tour info), mostateparks.com.*

Jefferson Landing State Historic Site. The Lohman Building is set up just as it would have been in the days when river boats and, later, the railroads, first stopped in what became the state capital. Be sure to check out the informative video, *Welcome to Missouri's State Capital.* You can also visit the Rozier Gallery, inside the landing's Union Hotel, where there are rotating exhibits of memorabilia, photographs, and art. Admission to the site is free. *100 Jefferson St., (573) 751-2854, mostateparks.com.*

Missouri State Penitentiary & Museum. Before being decommissioned in 2004, this was the oldest continuously operating prison west of the Mississippi. In 1836, when it opened, the Battle of the Alamo was going on, and Andrew Jackson was in his second term. By the time Alcatraz began accepting prisoners, MSP was 100 years old. In 1967, *Time* magazine called it the "bloodiest 47 acres in America" because of its incredibly high number of serious assaults. Many of its inmates were equally notorious, among them James Earl Ray and heavyweight champion Sonny Liston, who learned to box during his stint here.

Tours take you to their cells as well as to the gas chamber—where 40 men and women were executed—housing units, and the upper yard. History, ghost, and other tours are available. Tickets must be purchased in advance. For still more prison history, be sure to visit the nearby **Missouri State Penitentiary Museum** (100 High St.). Memorabilia-filled displays, including a recreated cell, showcase various aspects of life inside the walls. Admission is free. *115 Lafayette St., (866) 998-6998, www.missouripentours.com.*

Lake of the Ozarks Area

Lake of the Ozarks State Park & Ozark Cavern. Missouri's largest state park comprises 17,626 acres. It has 89 miles of shoreline, two swimming beaches, horseback riding, and more than 10 developed trails—one of which, the Ozarks Aquatic Trail, is designed for boaters, with 14 designated buoy stops along the shore. Take time for a guided tour of Ozark Caverns, a parks-operated cave, where you might spot the elusive blind grotto salamander. A highlight is the unusual Angel Showers formation. The never-ending shower of water comes out of a seemingly solid rock ceiling. Though not part of the park, Bridal Cave and Jacob's Cave are two other popular caverns in the Lake Ozark area. *403 Hwy. 134, Kaiser, (573) 348-2694, mostateparks.com.*

Eat & Stay

Central Dairy | Jefferson City. In business since 1932, Central Dairy is a longtime favorite not only of locals but also of visitors from throughout the Midwest and beyond. The "fresh as a Missouri morning" ice cream comes in such traditional flavors as French or cherry vanilla, fudge ripple, double-chocolate chip, and strawberry. The preparations are equally classic, with everything from cones and sundaes to sodas, malts, and shakes. *610 Madison St., (573) 635-6148, centraldairy.biz.*

The Grand Cafe | Jefferson City. This restaurant in the historic downtown focuses on fresh American fare in a setting that combines tin ceilings, pale walls, and wooden floors for a contemporary look. Lunch choices include sandwiches and salads such as pulled pork on a roll and a vegetable antipasto salad. The dinner menu lists small-plate options such as crab cakes and meatballs but also has rib eye and other meat options as well as fish and pasta. Try a custom cocktail for a treat. *107 E. High St., (573) 635-7842, www.grandcafe-jc.com.*

Capitol Plaza Hotel | Jefferson City. It's probably no surprise that one of the city's highest-rated hotels is part of downtown's largest conference center. The pet-friendly property also has free Wi-Fi, a restaurant and lounge, an indoor pool, a fitness center, a business center, and a 24-hour gift shop. A stay here puts you close to all the downtown sights, government buildings, and shops in the Capital Mall and The Crossings. *415 W. McCarty St., (573) 635-1234, www.capitolplazajeffersoncity.com.*

The Lodge of Four Seasons | Lake Ozark. This swanky, amenities-rich (and dog-friendly) resort, nestled along the Lake of the Ozarks shore, has surprisingly reasonable prices. Rooms and suites, many with lake views, are in several buildings throughout the property. Find serenity in the Japanese Garden or the Asian-inspired spa, where Himalayan Salt Stone massages and Seaweed Rejuvenation facials await. Several pro-designed courses offer 54 holes of golf. Restaurants and lounges include the more formal HK's off the main lobby; the casual Shutters at the Lake, open seasonally; and the Fire & Ice Patio and Bar, beside one of four swimming pools. A marina offers cruises and water-sports activities. *315 Four Seasons Dr., (573) 365-3000, www.4seasonsresort.com.*

NORTHEAST

MIDWEST

SOUTH

WEST

Bridal Cave, Lake of the Ozarks area

Springfield

Hammons Field. This $32-million minor-league ballpark is home to the Springfield Cardinals, a Texas League team affiliated with the St. Louis Cardinals. Even though the 7,000-plus-seat park looks good enough for the majors, tickets are affordable. The rookie players sign autographs, and family-friendly, sideline entertainment abounds. Munch on a meaty hot dog or a pretzel. The season runs early April through Labor Day. *955 E. Trafficway St., (417) 863-2143, www.milb.com.*

Fantastic Caverns. The temperature in Fantastic Caverns is a constant 60 degrees, and the trip through them is easy because all the work is done by a Jeep-drawn tram. Along the way, you'll see limestone stalactites, stalagmites, and other formations. You'll learn about cavern inhabitants, like the blind Ozarks cave fish, and past cavern uses—as a place to grow mushrooms, a speakeasy, and a music hall. *4872 N. Farm Rd. 125, (417) 833-2010, www.fantasticcaverns.com.*

Republic

Wilson's Creek National Battlefield. The first major Civil War battle fought west of the Mississippi River claimed the life of Nathaniel Lyon, the first Union general to die in the conflict. Although it was considered a Confederate victory, they suffered heavy losses and were prevented from making inroads into Missouri. The land around the so-called Bloody Hill remains much as it was when the battle raged here on August 10, 1861. Even the home of farmer John Ray, who watched the event from his porch as his family took refuge inside, is well preserved from the time when it was used it as a Southern field hospital. The Ray House (open Memorial Day to Labor Day; check ahead for days and hours) displays the bed upon which General Lyon's body was placed for examination.

The visitors center has military exhibits, a 30-minute video, a fiber-optics battle-strategy map, and a well-stocked bookstore. You can take a self- or cell-phone-guided 4.9-mile driving tour, featuring 8 interpretive sites, or explore on foot along one of 5 short trails off the tour road. In addition, 7 miles of hiking and horseback-riding trails wind through the park. On select summer weekends, volunteers in period costume gather here for living-history demonstrations that re-enact both civilian and military life. Each year, the anniversary of the battle sees a special program that includes keynote speeches. *6424 W. Farm Rd. 182, (417) 732-2662, ext. 227, www.nps.gov/wicr.*

Branson

Silver Dollar City. Folksy, 1880s-themed Silver Dollar City, situated 5 miles west of Branson off Highway 76, emphasizes Ozark crafts and culture. The entertainment complex has more than 40 thrill and kiddy rides; historic structures like a 19ᵗʰ-century homestead, school, and church; and a colony of 100 resident artisans. Showcased crafts include woodcarving, glass-blowing, pottery making, blade smithing, and basket weaving. You can also try your hand at preparing traditional Midwestern dishes in daily 60-minute classes at the *Midwest Living* Culinary & Crafts School.

Affiliated with Silver Dollar City are the **White Water Park**, with its watery rides and slides; the nearby **Wilderness RV Park,** which has a free shuttle to and from the theme parks; and the 278-foot *Branson Belle* paddle-wheeler. Two-hour, three-course lunch and dinner cruises come with spectacular views of Table Rock Lake from the showboat's three decks and entertainment from the best of Branson's singers and dancers. The ship sails from the boardwalk at White River Landing, just south of Branson, where several shops sell clothing, accessories, gourmet items, and souvenirs. *399 Silver Dollar City Pkwy., (800) 475-9370, www.silverdollarcity.com.*

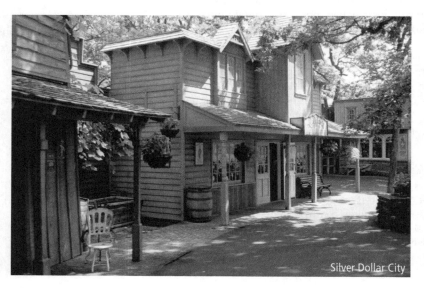
Silver Dollar City

Eat & Stay

Majestic Oaks Family RV Park & Campground | Eldon. A mix of back-in and pull-through sites—all of them with full hookups and many of them secluded—accommodate rigs small and large at this woodsy campground in the Lake of the Ozarks area. Tent sites, cabins, and JayFlight rental trailers round out the lodging options. And there are amenities for everyone in the family, including a playground; a pool; games and TV rooms; shuffleboard, basketball, and volleyball courts; hiking trails; and a dog park. There are also two shower facilities and a laundry room. The calendar fills up with pot-luck dinners, barbecues, and other seasonal events. *8 Majestic Oaks Rd., (573) 365-1890, majesticoakscampground.com.*

Lambert's Café | Ozark. At Lambert's Café, folks stand in line to get food thrown at them. This quirky spot serves famously large portions of ham, fried catfish, barbecue ribs, and chicken and dumplings. But, it's best known for its "throwed rolls"—freshly baked, toque-shaped dinner rolls that the "pitcher" on duty hurls across the dining room to seated customers. So, heads up! On this and on the fact that they don't take credit cards here. *1800 W. State Hwy. J, (417) 581-7655, www.throwedrolls.com.*

That's Entertainment

Branson's 50-plus theaters are often filled to capacity by music-lovers who come for gospel, Motown, Cajun, bluegrass, and, of course, country—performed by many of the genre's biggest names. Also on the various billboards are tributes to the likes of the Blues Brothers, the Beatles, the Rat Pack, Johnny Cash, and others. The mix continues with headliner comedians, performing animals, variety shows, magic acts, murder-mystery productions, Chinese acrobats, Irish tenors, and . . . well, you get the idea.

On a visit here, it's hard to wrap your head around all the entertainment offerings, let alone organize your schedule. Your best bet is to check out what's going on through the **Branson Tourism Center** (220 Branson Hills Pkwy., 800/785-1550, www.bransontour-ismcenter.com), which sells tickets and has all kinds of show, lodging, and dining packages and information.

The Shepherd of the Hills. This outdoor drama features a cast of more than 90 actors, as well as horses, donkeys, mules, and sheep. It's held on the grounds of the Ross family homestead (site of a cabin that's on the National Register of Historic Places) and is adapted from Harold Bell Wright's novel, which ignited America's fascination with the Ozark mountain country. Other attractions include horseback riding, zip-lining, and a Jeep-drawn tram tour with stops at numerous points of interest. *5586 W. State Hwy. 76, (417) 334-4191, theshepherdofthehills.com.*

Dick's 5&10. With an inventory of 50,000 items—give or take—you could explore this store for hours. Shelves are packed with games and toys, gifts and crafts, and housewares and hardware. If you're not a collector, you might just become one after seeing the aviation, train, sports, and other memorabilia. And it's hard to resist picking up a few sweets in the old-time candy aisle. *103 W. Main St., (417) 334-2410, www.dicks5and10.com.*

The Butterfly Palace & Rainforest Adventure. More than a thousand colorful butterflies and other creatures inhabit the indoor tropical gardens here. Before entering this world, visit the Rainforest Theater for a 15-minute 3D movie documenting the life cycle of butterflies. Then make your way through the tangle of vines and other obstacles in the Banyan Tree Adventure, or reflect on your path while navigating the Emerald Forest Mirror Maze. In the Science Center, you can learn about many rainforest creatures, including the skink. (They have one here with a blue tongue. His name is Harry, and you can meet him!) *4106 W. State Hwy. 76, (417) 332-2231, www.thebutterflypalace.com.*

Ride the Ducks. Get a unique view of Branson's mountain and lake scenery in the all-terrain vehicle known as the "Duck," an amphibious open-air truck originally developed for use in WWII. You'll experience its extraordinary land and water capabilities on one of two 70-minute excursions to Table Rock Lake or Lake Taneycomo. Both take in the highlights in and around Branson, and both feature a splashdown, followed by a 30-minute or so "sail." *2320 W. State Hwy. 76, (417) 266-7600, branson.ridetheducks.com.*

Table Rock State Park. Table Rock Lake has an 800-mile shoreline, and this park takes great advantage of it. The fishing is excellent, especially in the spring, and there are designated swimming areas and lots of other water-sports opportunities. At the public marina, you can rent scuba equipment and take lessons or arrange catamaran excursions, parasailing trips, and WaveRunner outings. Camping—at primitive or RV sites—is also an option. *5272 State Hwy. 165, (417) 334-4704, mostateparks.com.*

Showboat *Branson Belle* paddle-wheeler (above)
The Butterfly Palace & Rainforest Adventure (right)

Eat & Stay

Danna's Bar-B-Que & Burger Shop | Branson. The owner, a Texas transplant, grew up watching her aunt prepare brisket and dreamed of running her own barbecue joint one day. Today, she runs three: this one in Branson proper, another in Branson West, and the third in nearby Kirbyville to the east. The pork, beef, and chicken are marinated, rubbed, hickory smoked and slow cooked. The ribs are "big, bold, and very meaty." Burgers, sandwiches, nachos, and stuffed baked potatoes round out the list of entrees. Sides include French fries, onion rings, coleslaw, beans, and Memphis rolls. There's also a children's menu. *963 State Hwy. 165, (417) 337-5527, dannasbbq.com.*

Branson KOA Campground & Convention Center | Branson. This Ozark Mountains RV park and resort has more than 140 RV sites—from luxury pull-throughs to basic back-ins. There are also tent-camping sites as well as efficiency, 1-, and 2-room cottages and lodges that sleep from 2 to 10 people. You can also arrange discounted Branson show tickets and packages here. The morning pancakes are complimentary, as are use of the hot tub, swimming pool, playground, and fitness center. Be sure to bring the pooch—dogs can run free at Kamp K9. *397 Animal Safari Rd., (417) 334-4414, bransonkoa.com.*

Chateau on the Lake Resort Spa and Convention Center | Branson. Hard to believe that Branson's entertainment strip is just a short drive from this bluff-top retreat overlooking Table Rock Lake. Water is a feature inside as well as out: The 10-story atrium lobby has a waterfall. Many of the 300-plus rooms and suites have either lake or Ozark Mountain views. You can indulge in a European-style treatment at the Spa Chateau; have breakfast, lunch, or dinner in the Chateau Grille, known for its prix-fixe Chef's Table menu with wine pairings; or grab a more casual meal or snack at the Atrium Café & Wine Bar, the Sweet Shoppe, or the Downstairs Deli. Other amenities include tennis courts, a fitness center, a kids club, indoor and outdoor pools, and water sports (arranged at the on-site marina). *415 N. State Hwy. 265, (417) 334-1161, www.chateauonthelake.com.*

Key Largo, FL

Best of the Road® Travel Guide

South

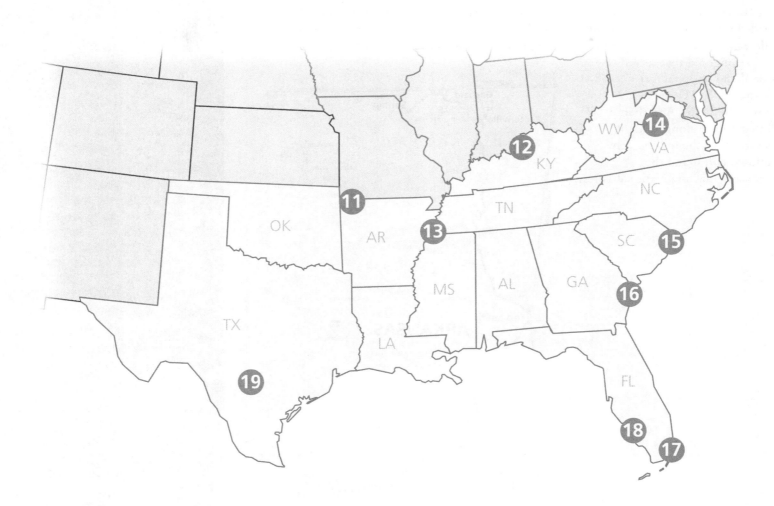

NORTHEAST

MIDWEST

SOUTH

WEST

Arkansas Springs Eternal

ROUTE TOWNS: Eureka Springs I Garfield I Bentonville I Fort Smith I Hot Springs

Arkansas is called the Natural State for good reason: Start with almost 3 million acres of wildlife-filled national forest. Add in 600,000 acres of lakes, 9,700 miles of streams and rivers, and countless mineral springs with waters known for their curative properties—and "Eureka!" You have it.

Hot Springs National Park

This trip starts and ends with those curative waters. In the hillside resort of Eureka Springs, the Victorian architecture is so well preserved that the entire downtown district is on the National Register of Historic Places. There are more than 60 springs in the town itself, including the restored Blue, Basin, Grotto, and Crescent. To the south and east is Hot Springs, whose thermal waters put it on the map first as a healing center, then as a national park, and then as a gangster getaway.

There's a lot of colorful history in and between these communities. Pea Ridge is the site of a pivotal battle in the Civil War. Bentonville showcases the beauty of the region and the nation with a collection of American art housed in a museum surrounded by woods and water. Fort Smith has a stronghold that served as a territorial and national fort (1817–24 and 1838–71) and as a federal court (1872–96). And then there's all that nature along and through swatches of the million-acre Ozark National Forest and the 1.8-million-acre Ouachita National Forest.

Atlas map B-3, p. 10

Distance: 280 miles point to point.

Type of Trip: Weekend Getaway; RV; Arts & Culture, Great Outdoors, Quirky & Oddball, Small Town Gems.

Must Try: A spa treatment in a Eureka Springs resort and/or the Buckstaff Bathhouse in Hot Springs. A sweet treat from an old-time soda fountain at the Fort Smith history museum or one of the **Dixie Café** (dixiecafe.com) locations statewide.

Must Buy: Eureka Springs is home to more than 200 artists and artisans, so a handcrafted work from here is a must. Hot Springs also has its share of craftspeople, particularly potters.

Must See: Crescent Hotel, Thorncrown Chapel, Crystal Bridges Museum, Pea Ridge National Military Park, Fort Smith National Historic Site, Fordyce Bathhouse in Hot Springs National Park, Gangster Museum.

Worth Noting: The main office of Ozark National Forest is in Russellville, 85 miles east of Fort Smith and 72 miles north of Hot Springs. That for Ouachita National Forest is in Hot Springs. Throughout both forests there are numerous ranger stations, recreation areas, and tent and RV campgrounds, both rustic and developed.

Travel Tips: This trip picks up just about where the Missouri Family Fun and Fine Fiddling trip leaves off. You can also follow the 19-mile Pig Trail Scenic Byway as well as segments of the Ozark Highlands Scenic Byway, Arkansas Scenic 7 Byway, and Talimena Scenic Byway.

NORTHEAST MIDWEST SOUTH WEST

Eureka Springs

Eureka Springs Historical Museum. Permanent first-floor exhibits include Our Native American History, The City that Water Built, and Fires: The Big Ones, making this museum a good first stop on a visit to the town. There's also a roster of changing exhibits and a second-floor gallery with works by the many artists and artisans who've made Eureka Springs their home. *95 S. Main St., (479) 253-9417, www.eurekaspringshistoricalmuseum.org.*

Eureka Springs Tram Tours. This company's highly popular, 90-minute, narrated tram tours take you up and down the town's hilly streets lined with always-stately and often-colorful Victorian architecture. Stops include the Crescent Hotel and Grotto Spring. Tours often sell out; reserve ahead. *137 W. Van Buren St., (479) 253-9572, www.eurekaspringstramtours.com.*

Thorncrown Chapel, Eureka Springs

Magic Water

In 1856, Dr. Alvah Jackson found the Great Healing Spring of Native American legend. He called it Basin Spring and claimed its water could cure eye ailments. Reportedly, he sold it as Dr. Jackson's Magic Eye Water, and, during the Civil War, also used it to treat wounded soldiers in his "cave hospital." After the war, word of the springs here spread wider, especially when Ozarka Water Company and others began bottling the water for sale.

The town was formally incorporated in 1879, but its early years were difficult. Portions of it were destroyed by a series of fires. In 1882, the Eureka Springs Improvement Company was founded to develop more and better civic services and improve safety. Houses and hotels—like the Crescent, the Grand Central, and the Palace—were increasingly built of brick and stone rather than wood. The legacy of all this history is an entire spa-resort community on the National Register of Historic Places.

Quicksilver Gallery. This two-floor shop in the heart of downtown Eureka Springs sells works by about 120 artists, artisans, and craftspeople, some based in town and others regionally or nationally known. The inventory includes watercolors, photography, tapestries, mobiles, jewelry, ceramics, and blown glass. There's also a selection of musical instruments that you can try out. *73 Spring St., (479) 253-7679, quicksilvergallery.com.*

Thorncrown Chapel. What is, according to the American Institute of Architects, one of the best buildings (circa 1980) of the 20th century has only one 24x60-foot rectangular room. But what a room it is. A gabled, 48-foot-high, sky-lighted roof seems to balance atop a frame of pine columns and latticework beams. The walls are made of glass—6,000 square feet of it. The result is a soaring, light-filled Ozark Gothic building that's perfectly at home amid the surrounding hardwood forest. *12968 Hwy. 62 W., (479) 253-7401, www.thorncrown.com.*

Belle of the Ozarks. A great way to take in the Ozark scenery is aboard this vessel out on Starkey Park's Beaver Lake, just 10 miles southwest of Eureka Springs. The seasonal, 75-minute, narrated *Belle of the Ozarks* cruises take you past 60 miles of shoreline. Along the way, you'll hear about a pristine island wildlife sanctuary, a Native American burial site, a submerged homestead, the Beaver Dam, White House Bluffs, and more. There are restrooms and concessions aboard. *4024 Mundell Rd., (479) 253-6200, www.estc.net/belle.*

Garfield

Pea Ridge National Military Park. In early March of 1862, Union soldiers were deployed to block Confederate movement toward St. Louis. Some 26,000 men fought here for control not only of Missouri, but also northern Arkansas. Difficulty traveling and a break in the supply line led to a Confederate loss. The two-day battle, much of which took place near Elkhorn Tavern, resulted in more than 3,000 casualties.

This 4,300-acre site commemorates the pivotal event. Its visitors center shows the 30-minute film, *Thunder in the Ozarks,* and has Civil War exhibits as well as a bookstore and gift shop. It's also the departure point for a 7-mile self-guided driving tour of the battlefield with a re-creation of the Elkhorn Tavern and 10 interpretive stops. There are also 7 miles of hiking trails and 9 miles of horse trails. *15930 Hwy. 62 E., (479) 451-8122, www.nps.gov/peri.*

Bentonville

Crystal Bridges Museum of American Art. Alice Walton, longtime art collector and daughter of the Walmart founder, was instrumental in establishing this truly special place. Integration with the wooded and watery landscape was key to renowned architect Moshe Safdie's design. In the sleek, interconnected pavilions, the American art–filled galleries are as compelling as the views through the window-lined corridors. Admission to the permanent collection is free.

Highlights of the collection include a Charles Willson Peale painting of George Washington and Norman Rockwell's *Rosie the Riveter* as well as works by the likes of Winslow Homer, John Singer Sargent, Georgia O'Keeffe, George Wesley Bellows, and Edward Hopper. In addition to taking in the art, you can hike or bike the 120-acre site along seven short trails. The on-site Eleven restaurant serves contemporary American comfort food. *600 Museum Way, (479) 418-5700, crystalbridges.org.*

Eat & Stay

Mud Street Café | **Eureka Springs.** The muffins at this popular breakfast and lunch spot get high praise, though you can also start the day with the Chef's Scramble and other omelets. Lunch sees a selection of burgers, croissant and other sandwiches, and salads. This is also a great place to grab some tea, an espresso (the coffee drinks have won awards), and a dessert, and just relax in the sitting area amid all the oak furnishings and Victorian-style fixtures. *22G S. Main St., (479) 253-6732, www.mudstreetcafe.com.*

The Grand Taverne | **Eureka Springs.** The sage used on your pork chop or the chives used on your walleye might have come straight from the chef's balcony herb garden. That's just one of the things that make this dinner spot special. Another is its setting inside the Grand Central, one of several historic spa hotels in downtown Eureka Springs. Note that the prix-fixe, six-course Chef's Table Menu is a great value for the money. Reservations are a good idea here. *37 N. Main St., (479) 253-6756, grandcentralresort.com.*

The Crescent Hotel | **Eureka Springs.** This rusticated-stone aerie sprawls amid 15 wooded acres high above downtown. Imagine the views! Some rooms have balconies that take full advantage of them; all rooms have a true-to-period feel and current creature comforts. Completed in 1886 and originally operated by the Eureka Springs Improvement Company, the "castle in the clouds" has so much lore that it offers self-guided walking tours. And, yes, all that lore includes tales of resident spirits: An on-site operator offers guided tours of America's Most Haunted Hotel. You can also hike the grounds, relax in the New Moon Spa, and dine in the Crystal Dining Room. *75 Prospect Ave., (855) 725-5720, www.crescent-hotel.com.*

Fort Smith

Fort Smith National Historic Site. At the confluence of the Arkansas and Poteau rivers on the Oklahoma border, Fort Smith was once a far western outpost of the United States. Established in 1817 to mediate Native American disputes and protect the area's few settlers, it was briefly abandoned and later rebuilt to serve as a military supply depot. The fort's early years were rough and tumble ones: Out here, on the far edge of civilization, shady characters accompanied westward-bound pioneers, causing considerable trouble for newcomers and Native Americans alike. Things were no less turbulent during the antebellum, Civil War, and Reconstruction periods. In 1872, Fort Smith was transformed from fort to court in an attempt to instill order.

Exhibits in several restored buildings on this 37-acre site cover the military; area outlaws; the U.S. Marshal Service; and the Trail of Tears, the route along which thousands of Native Americans died during an 1838–39 forced march west. Be sure to see the courthouse's dank basement jail. Before citizens demanded that a new one be built, this small space could hold as many as 150 criminals at once and was known as Hell on the Border. There's also a grisly but compelling reproduction gallows and displays of authentic handcuffs, leg irons, and guns—all testaments to life on the edge of lawlessness. *301 Parker Ave., (479) 783-3961, www.nps.gov/fosm.*

The Hangin' Judge

Three years after Fort Smith became a federal court, Judge Isaac C. Parker arrived to clean up rampant corruption. During his 21-year tenure, more than two-thirds of some 13,500 cases resulted in guilty verdicts. He sentenced more than 150 hardened murders and rapists to death by hanging. Though only 79 of them were actually hanged, Parker nevertheless became known as the Hanging Judge.

To his credit, he did clean things up. He was also known as an advocate for Native American rights and for judicial reform involving criminal cases. It's even said that he was personally against capital punishment, using it only as prescribed by law at the time. After his death in 1896, he was buried at the National Cemetery in Fort Smith.

Fort Smith (top), The Clayton House (above)

Fort Smith Museum of History. The Atkinson-Williams Warehouse (circa 1907) is now the storehouse of about 40,000 artifacts from Fort Smith's fascinating past. Exhibits take you through its days as a frontier town in Indian Territory to its post–Civil War federal court period and beyond. Highlights include a re-creation of the courtroom presided over by Judge Isaac C. Parker (aka the Hanging Judge), a replica 19th-century woodworking shop, a 1920s drugstore with a working soda fountain, and a display of vintage telephones. There are also photographs and memorabilia related to the four-story brick building, which is on the National Register of Historic Places. It's also on many a list of haunted places: museum staff and visitors have reported seeing a small child or hearing a gavel slamming. *320 Rogers Ave., (479) 783-7841, www.fortsmithmuseum.org.*

The Clayton House. Although built in the 1850s, it was only in the 1880s that the house was transformed into this eight-room Italianate Gothic mansion. William Henry Harrison Clayton lived here with his large family between 1882 and 1897 while serving as a federal prosecutor. On 30- to 60-minute tours, you'll see the formal areas as well as the sitting room, study, and upstairs bedrooms—all beautifully restored and furnished.

The grounds are equally well maintained, with an old-fashioned herb garden and a gazebo. It's easy to imagine the lives of the Victorian-era owners. Indeed, you might not have to merely imagine them. Some people claim to have been touched when no one was near them. Others have heard heavy footsteps or slamming doors. Still others have seen the ghostly figure of a well-coiffed gray-haired woman. *514 N. 6th St., (479) 783-3000, claytonhouse.org.*

Ozark National Forest. This forest spans roughly 1.2 million acres from the northwestern corner of Arkansas south to the Arkansas River valley. The mountains here, part of the Boston Range, are actually plateaus made rugged over the millennia by swelling rivers and erosion. Among the beautiful vistas are those of deeply V-shaped valleys and bluffs of sandstone or limestone. You can take advantage of those views in spots along several scenic byways as well those along more than 400 miles of trails.

This is also an ideal place to fish for bass and trout; canoe or kayak; and whitewater raft along one of six designated Wild and Scenic Rivers. Spring sees the dogwoods and redbuds in bloom; fall sees the maple, oak, and hickory trees ablaze with color. There are plenty of developed recreation areas as well as campgrounds with lakeside or overlook settings. *Main Office: 605 W. Main St., Russellville, (479) 964-7200, www.fs.fed.us.*

Hot Springs

Hot Springs National Park. The historic resort community of Hot Springs, nestled in the Zig Zag Range of the Ouachita Mountains, and this eponymous national park are entwined. Several of the opulent bathhouses along Central Avenue (aka Bathhouse Row) have been restored. The Fordyce contains a park visitors center and museum, where you can see original dressing rooms, a short film about spa bathing rituals, a music room, state rooms, and a gymnasium. The Lamar Bathhouse houses the park's gift shop. To take the waters yourself, head to the Buckstaff—the only functioning bathhouse open within the park—or the Quapaw Bath & Spa.

At the end of the Grand Promenade, by De Soto Rock, you can get a sense of what the springs were like in the earliest days, before all the landscaping. The promenade is also the jumping off point for a hike up to the 216-foot Hot Springs Mountain Tower, with its 360-degree views. From here you can link up with other trails in the park, which has 26 miles of them. In addition there are two scenic park drives; many picnic areas; and the Gulpha Gorge Campground, which has 44 first-come, first-served campsites (28 with hookups). *369 Central Ave., (501) 620-6715, www.nps.gov/hosp.*

Eat & Stay

Ralph's Pink Flamingo BBQ | Fort Smith. To the owner-chef of this unpretentious restaurant, barbecue is both a passion and a sport. He's perfected his cooking techniques competing in (and winning) competitions across the country, including those sponsored by the prestigious Kansas City BBQ Society. But the proof is in the eating, and the barbecue here gets raves. The pulled pork, baby-back ribs, chicken, and brisket are all highly recommended. Sides include baked beans, slaw, and potato salad. And a bottle of the restaurant's own barbecue sauce makes a great souvenir. *2801 Old Greenwood Rd., (479) 649-7427, www.pinkflamingobbq.com.*

Beland Manor Inn | Fort Smith. Each of the seven rooms here has a unique layout; a Federal- or Victorian-style décor; and a private bath. Given that all offer lots of charm, you're better off making your choice based on varying amenities: the Ruth and Louis Suite, for instance, has a king-size four-poster bed, an old-fashioned tub, and an extra large separate shower while the Eugenia Beatrice Suite has a queen-size feather bed, a fireplace, and a two-person spa tub. Among the thoughtful touches are comfy robes, free snacks and beverages, Wi-Fi, and cable TV. Some rooms include candlelight breakfast service. *1320 S. Albert Pike, (479) 782-3300, fort-smith.net.*

Bathhouse Row

Healing Waters

Soon after the Louisiana Purchase, the mineral-laden, 143-degree-Fahrenheit waters here began attracting a steady stream of people suffering from arthritis and other ailments. Bathhouses were built at the foot of Hot Springs Mountain, where many major springs still flow to the surface at a rate of 700,000 gallons a day. As the city grew and prospered, so did the splendor of its bathing palaces. Canvas tents were supplanted by wooden structures that were in turn replaced by more elaborate Italianate or Mediterranean style structures.

Along the stretch of Central Avenue known as Bathhouse Row were the Buckstaff, Fordyce, Hale, Lamar, Maurice, Ozark, Quapaw, and Superior. Each was filled with marble, stained-glass, tile mosaics, and other elaborate ornamentation. In the 1960s, more advanced medical treatments began replacing therapeutic bathing, and, one by one, the bathhouses closed. Restoration efforts didn't begin till the 1980s.

The Gangster Museum of America. Ah, the good old bad old days, when gambling and booze were illegal—but that didn't stop anyone from enjoying them—and Hot Springs was a hot attraction for ne'er-do-wells. Al Capone vacationed here, enjoying the horse races, the spa, and his own special room at the Arlington Hotel. He has his own special exhibit at this museum, too. Memorabilia, photographs, and recorded accounts also highlight Owen "Owney" Madden, who's credited with really putting Hot Springs on the gangster map in the mid-1930s and '40s; Maxine Jones, once the city's richest madam; and Mayor Leo Patrick McLaughlin and Judge Verne Ledgerwood, who famously corrupted local politics. *510 Central Ave., (501) 318-1717, www.tgmoa.com.*

Maxine's Live. This late 19th-century brick building was once a bordello owned by Maxine Jones, the area's richest madam back in the 1960s. Today, it's an acclaimed club with live music Wednesday through Saturday nights and plenty of cold beer and personality every night. Acts here include regional performers as well as touring bands making their way between Nashville and Austin. And there's something for everyone in the line-up: Southern to indie rock, rockabilly to country, folk to swing. The menu includes burgers, pizza, and other pub fare. *700 Central Ave., (501) 321-0909, www.maxineslive.com.*

Arkansas Alligator Farm and Petting Zoo. This place has been handling alligators since 1902. There are more than 100 of the critters here—you can even pet one—and summer months see feeding shows. A small museum has natural history exhibits, including a skeleton of a purported merman; a petting zoo has deer, sheep, pygmy goats, and other docile animals; and other zoo areas feature wolves, primates, a mountain lion, and more. *847 Whittington Ave., (501) 623-6172, www.alligatorfarmzoo.com.*

Fox Pass Pottery. This studio and shop, founded in 1973, features pieces by Jim and Barbara Larkin. He works at the potter's wheel, while she hand-builds her pieces. Although they're known for their unique glazes, the wood-fired salt kiln they use can create a pleasing finish without a traditionally applied glaze. Most pieces are dishwasher and microwave safe. *379 Fox Pass Cutoff, (501) 623-9906, foxpasspottery.com.*

Ouachita National Forest. First established in 1907 as the Arkansas National Forest and later renamed, Ouachita (pronounced wash-i-tah) is the South's oldest national forest. It's also the region's largest, with more than 1.8 million acres of mountainous terrain, myriad rivers and lakes, and a mix of pine and hardwood trees. Most of the forest is in Arkansas, extending for about 100 miles from Hot Springs west to the state border, where almost 355,000 acres spill over into southeastern Oklahoma.

You can swim or fish for bass, crappie, catfish, and bluegill in secluded, crystal-clear waters; canoe or whitewater raft along one of several rivers; or spend a day boating on the man-made, 40,000-acre Lake Ouachita. Recreation areas have picnic sites, campgrounds, and trailheads. A system of more than 700 miles of hiking, biking, and horseback riding routes includes the 192-mile Ouachita National Recreation Trail, which cuts along the peaks of the Ouachita Mountains and spans the entire forest from west to east. *100 Reserve St., (501) 321-5202, www.fs.fed.us.*

Eat & Stay

Arlington Resort Hotel and Spa | Hot Springs. This twin-towered Art Deco grand dame opened with a gala dinner-dance on New Year's Eve 1924. Many of its magnificent public spaces are in use today, including its spa, where you can still indulge in thermal mineral-water baths and other treatments. There's lots of history here; maybe a bit too much for some. Word is that guest rooms are truly tired. Still, it's hard not to be captivated by the hotel where Al Capone stayed (Room 442) when he vacationed in Hot Springs. And, yes, this property is reportedly haunted by several ghosts, including a little girl in a pink dress and a bellman often seen going about his business on the 11th floor. *239 Central Ave., (501) 623-7771, www.arlingtonhotel.com.*

McClard's Bar-B-Q | Hot Springs. In the 1920s, Alex and Alice McClard ran a motor court. The story goes that they accepted payment from one traveler in the form of a secret barbecue recipe, which they then made their own. Folks soon came from miles around for the couple's delicious beef and pork barbecue. And they still do. The fourth generation of the family runs this restaurant, where portions are still generous, prices are still reasonable, and bottles of McClard's sauces and seasonings are for sale. *505 Albert Pike Rd., (501) 623-9665, www.mcclards.com.*

Mr. Whiskers | Hot Springs. What's a trip to the South without enjoying some catfish? Or hush puppies? Fresh, Southern comfort food—prepared with love and care by a Hot Springs native—is just what you'll find at Mr. Whiskers. There are also chicken tenders, burgers, and New Orleans-style po-boy sandwiches. And the menu has grilled as well as fried options. *4195 Malvern Ave., (501) 262-3474, www.greatcatfish.com.*

Ozark National Forest

NORTHEAST

MIDWEST

SOUTH

WEST

Kentucky Bluegrass & Bourbon

ROUTE TOWNS: Louisville | Clermont | Elizabethtown | Hodgenville | Bardstown | Lawrenceburg | Versailles | Lexington | Frankfort

Ah, Kentucky. Home of so many American classics—Bluegrass Country and bourbon among them. Here you'll also find the birthplaces of both Abraham Lincoln and his wife, of a legendary baseball bat, and of a boxing legend. A journey through this state is truly as iconic as it is idyllic.

Kentucky landscape

This trip starts in Louisville, home of Churchill Downs and birthplace of two famous American sluggers of very different types. From here it travels south through Elizabethtown to Bardstown, the so-called Bourbon Capital of the World, and the place where songwriter Stephen Foster—famous for such classics as "Oh! Susanna," "Camptown Races," and "Swanee River"—was inspired to write the state song, "My Old Kentucky Home."

From here it's over to Lexington, home of more than one stately racecourse, and then to Frankfort, the state capital. Along the way are stops at the birthplaces of both Abraham Lincoln and Mary Todd as well as at several of the historic distilleries that are part of the Bourbon Trail. And all this history and refined tradition unfold amid rolling blue-green pastures—corralled by wooden fences and dotted with grazing Thoroughbreds. Nothing captures this aspect of Bluegrass Country quite like a visit to the Kentucky Horse Park.

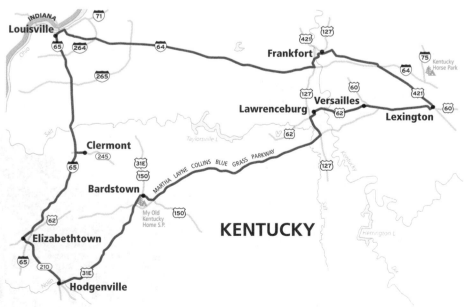

Atlas map G-8, p. 42

Distance: 240-mile full loop.

Type of Trip: Weekend Getaway; RV; History & Heritage, Picture Perfect, Small Town Gems, Sports Fan.

Must Try: A hot brown (although there are variations, essentially it's an open-faced turkey sandwich drizzled with Mornay sauce and broiled); any of the state's world-renowned spirits; breakfast in the Track Kitchen at the Keeneland Racetrack (as much for the atmosphere and the chance to watch early-morning horse-training sessions as the food).

Must Buy: Silver-plated mint julep cups and commemorative Derby glasses. Both make great, collectible souvenirs and both are perfect for serving up that traditional minty concoction back at home.

Must See: At least one distillery (of course), Churchill Downs/Kentucky Derby Museum, Abraham Lincoln Birthplace, Oscar Getz Museum of Whiskey History, Kentucky Horse Park, Liberty Hall.

Worth Noting: Several events lead up to the early May running of the Derby: an air show; a marathon with a route through Churchill Downs; a balloon race; the Fillies Derby Ball; the Pegasus Parade; and the Fest-a-Ville and Chow Wagon food, drink, and music extravaganzas.

Travel Tips: This trip covers many of the distilleries on the official **Kentucky Bourbon Trail** (kybourbontrail. com). For more information and maps (including a bike route), check out its website or that of the **Louisville Visitors Center** (301 S. 4ᵗʰ St., 888/568-4784, www.gotolouisville.com).

city itinerary

Louisville

① **Churchill Downs.** There's been horse racing in Louisville since the 1780s, when events took place on Main Street. Although the first Kentucky Derby wasn't held till 1875, "the most exciting two minutes in sports"—on the first Saturday in May—is the nation's oldest continuously held sporting event. Its home, Churchill Downs, is as steeped in tradition as the Derby itself. The 1.25-mile course near downtown also hosts the Kentucky Oaks on the Friday before the Derby and more than 30 other Thoroughbred stakes races throughout its spring and fall seasons. A walking tour of the track is included with admission to the on-site Kentucky Derby Museum, which offers several other, more in-depth tours. *700 Central Ave., (502) 636-4400, www.churchilldowns.com.*

② **Kentucky Derby Museum.** Gate 1 of the stately Churchill Downs is the perfect place for this museum. First-floor exhibits focus on the race itself, with displays that both entertain and engage. You can hear first-hand accounts of race fans, see how best to enjoy the Derby as a spectator, learn about the art of "calling" (announcing) the race, and watch historical race footage. Second-floor displays highlight owners, jockeys, and horse breeding. Admission includes a walking tour of Churchill Downs. Spring through fall also see the Barn and Backside Van Tour and/or the Inside the Gates Tour. Combo tickets are available, so, if you have a full day, you can do all three tours, visit the museum, have lunch in the Derby Café, and shop in the gift store. *704 Central Ave., (502) 637-1111, www.derbymuseum.org.*

③ **Louisville Slugger Museum & Factory.** A steel, 68,000-pound, 120-foot-tall baseball bat, the world's largest, welcomes you to this museum and adjacent factory where the world-famous Louisville Sluggers are made. Begin your visit with a short film in the 100-seat theater, and then climb on a 17-ton baseball glove carved from ancient Kentucky limestone. In Bud's Batting Cage, practice using replicas of bats swung by all the greats. In the Grand Slam Gallery and Gallery 125, check out baseball collectibles and memorabilia, including the Louisville Slugger Babe Ruth used to hit 60 home runs in 1927. On a factory tour, watch artisans use lathes to turn out baseball bats for major and little leaguers alike. *800 W. Main St., (877) 775-8443, www.sluggermuseum.com.*

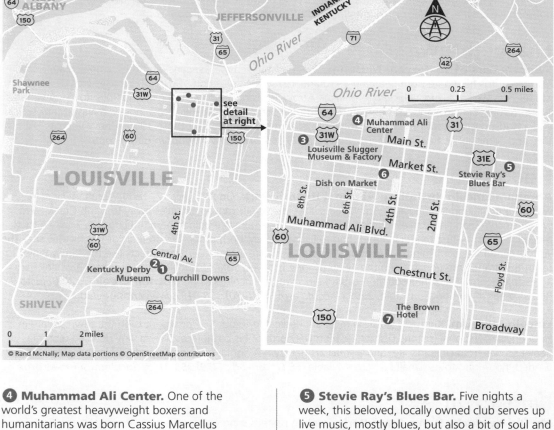

Louisville Slugger Museum

Kentucky Derby at Churchill Downs

④ **Muhammad Ali Center.** One of the world's greatest heavyweight boxers and humanitarians was born Cassius Marcellus Clay in Louisville on January 17, 1942. The interactive exhibits, films, and memorabilia at this downtown museum document his life, his career, and his philosophy. Six immersive pavilions are named for and contain displays that illustrate Ali's core values: Confidence, Conviction, Dedication, Respect, Giving, and Spirituality. In the Train with Ali exhibit, you can punch a speed bag or shadow box in a room that re-creates the late champ's Deer Lake Training Camp. *144 N. 6ᵗʰ St., (502) 584-9254, www.alicenter.org.*

⑤ **Stevie Ray's Blues Bar.** Five nights a week, this beloved, locally owned club serves up live music, mostly blues, but also a bit of soul and classic rock. The setting, inside a restored 1906 building with exposed brick walls, is intimate and laid-back, making this the perfect place to unwind, hang with the locals, and sip a Maker's Mark Old Fashioned. *230 E. Main St., (502) 582-9945, www.stevieraysbluesbar.com.*

Eat & Stay

⑥ **Dish on Market.** State pride is evident at this relaxed restaurant, where the tag line is "Kentucky Food and Drink. . . at Prices That Are Hard to Beat." And you can get that value for money and those Southern-style dishes at breakfast, lunch, and dinner. Tuck into Kentucky fritters to start, perhaps followed by a Bluegrass rib-eye steak (served with a bourbon glaze), shrimp and grits, or a Market Street burger. Sweet-potato fries, mac and cheese, and sweet cornbread are among the comforting side dishes. There are also salads and other veggie offerings as well as a kids menu. *434 W. Market St., (502) 315-0669, dishonmarket.com.*

⑦ **The Brown Hotel.** Opened in 1923, this 16-story, 293-room property is a downtown classic, one that's also on the National Register of Historic Places. Restoration work in the 1980s brought the property back to its original English Renaissance style. Rooms have a sophisticated mix of patterns and color schemes. Beds have Egyptian cotton sheets and European white-down comforters. Free Wi-Fi and shuttle service are givens here—unusual perks for a luxury hotel. Locals and visitors consider the on-site English Grill to be one of the city's best restaurants. It's also the place to try a hot brown, a Kentucky specialty sandwich that originated in this hotel back in 1926. *335 W. Broadway, (502) 583-1234, www.brownhotel.com.*

NORTHEAST

MIDWEST

SOUTH

WEST

Clermont

Jim Beam American Stillhouse. Tours of this all-American distillery, operating since 1795, feature a hospitable, down-home vibe. It's named after James B. Beam, who helped re-establish the brand as one of the world's best-selling bourbons in 1933 after Prohibition. What is now the seventh generation of the Beam/Noe family is still involved in the business. Guided tours include a tasting and last about 90 minutes (reservations are a good idea). Afterward, pop over to Fred's Smokehouse for some barbecue, beans, and bourbon ice cream. *526 Happy Hollow Rd., (502) 543-9877, www.jimbeam.com.*

Elizabethtown

Swope's Cars of Yesteryear Museum. The roadsters, coupes, sedans, and other immaculately restored autos here date from between 1910 and 1972. The collection of over 60 vehicles includes several Model Ts as well as luxury vehicles from Pierce Arrow, Packard, Cadillac, Lincoln, and Rolls Royce. A vintage T-bird, Cobra, Camaro, and Mustang are among the sportier models. Rarer cars include a Nash Metropolitan and a Hudson Commodore. And isn't there something irresistible about those 1960s Chevy Impalas? All this, and admission is free. *1100 N. Dixie Ave., (270) 765-2181, www.swopemuseum.com.*

Hodgenville

Abraham Lincoln Birthplace National Historic Park. On February 12, 1809, Abraham Lincoln was born at Sinking Spring Farm. A few years later, the family moved 10 miles away to Knob Creek Farm, where Lincoln made his earliest childhood memories. The family remained here until he was 7, when they moved yet again—first to Indiana and then to Illinois. Today, both properties are part of this historic site. The visitors center has a 15-minute film about Lincoln's early life and displays of artifacts like the family Bible. To reach the granite memorial, climb the 56 steps, one for every year of Lincoln's life, or follow a wheelchair-accessible boardwalk. A reproduction cabin marks where Lincoln was born. **Knob Creek** (7120 Bardstown Rd.) also has a reproduction cabin. *2995 Lincoln Farm Rd., (270) 358-3137, www.nps.gov/abli.*

Lincoln Museum. Kentucky's official museum dedicated to our 16th president is on the town square in Hodgenville's National Historic District, just 3 miles north of his birthplace. Twelve very detailed dioramas depict scenes from Lincoln's life, and a small art gallery has displays of Lincoln and Civil War memorabilia. Guided, hour-long tours (small fee) are available. *66 Lincoln Sq., (270) 358-3163, lincolnmuseum-ky.org.*

Bardstown

My Old Kentucky Home State Park. Stephen Foster's song was inspired by Federal Hill, the Georgian-style home that belonged to his cousin, Judge John Rowan, and that Foster visited in 1852. The restored site includes Judge Rowan's law office, a carriage house, a barn, and gardens. Guided tours by docents in period costume take place throughout the year. The park is also home to a 39-site campground facility, a picnic area, a visitors center, and a gift shop. *501 E. Stephen Foster Ave., (502) 348-3502, parks.ky.gov/parks.*

Jim Beam American Stillhouse

Bourbon with a Capital "B"

Bardstown bills itself as "Bourbon Capital of the World" for good reason. Distillers have been operating in and around the town since 1776. Today, in addition to the Oscar Getz Museum of Whiskey History, the town is home to Heaven Hill Distillery and is a Kentucky Bourbon Trail "trailhead" for visits to other big-name producers like Maker's Mark, Jim Beam, Wild Turkey, and Woodford Reserve.

The community also hosts September's **Kentucky Bourbon Festival** (www.kybourbonfestival.com). For seven days, distillers engage in competitions for the best specialty cocktail, best window display, and fastest 500-pound-barrel roller. For everyone else there are cooking (with bourbon) demonstrations, a Bourbon Hold'em Tournament, barrel-making demonstrations, walking tours, food and crafts vendors, a scavenger hunt, a hot-air balloon glow, and amusement rides and games. There are also samplings galore.

Heaven Hill Brands. Although founded in 1935, this distillery is a "newcomer" compared with some other Kentucky operations. It is, nevertheless, the country's seventh-largest supplier of distilled spirits and the largest that's still family owned. Their line includes not only bourbon, but also vodka, rum, tequila, and liqueur. The focus is on whiskey, though, at its **Bourbon Heritage Center** (www.bourbonheritagecenter.com), which offers several tours with tastings that showcase both the modern distillery and the history of bourbon. *1311 Gilkey Run Rd., (502) 337-1000, www.heavenhill.com.*

Oscar Getz Museum of Whiskey History. Housed in stately, redbrick Spalding Hall, a one-time college and seminary, this museum has an extensive collection of whiskey artifacts, some from as far back as colonial days. You'll see moonshine stills, old-time jugs and bottles, advertisements, and more. Spalding Hall also houses the Bardstown Historical Museum, where displays give you 200 years of additional context for all that whiskey history. Look for Native American artifacts, pioneer items, Lincoln documents, and Stephen Foster and Jesse James memorabilia. *114 N. 5th St., (502) 348-2999, www.whiskeymuseum.com.*

Lawrenceburg

Wild Turkey Distillery. The Ripy brothers established their distillery on Wild Turkey Hill back in 1869. In the subsequent decades, the operation flourished enough for them to take their bourbon to the 1893 Chicago World's Fair. The rest, as they say, really is history—one filled with the innovations of three generations of master distillers in the Russell family. Tours are offered daily on the hour. There's also a gift shop so you can stock up on the merchandise. *1417 Versailles Rd., (502) 839-2182, wildturkeybourbon.com.*

Eat & Stay

Back Home Restaurant | Elizabethtown. Fried green tomatoes, country ham, pinto beans, cornbread, hot browns, fresh cobbler. . . if you're not hungry yet, you will be upon smelling all that great Southern cooking. The aromatic experience continues in the on-site shop, filled with Candleberry candles, fudge, antiques, and crafts. Upstairs there's also O'Neals, a boutique selling unique accessories and clothing to suit all tastes. *251 W. Dixie Ave. (270) 769-2800, www.backhomerestaurant.com.*

Jailer's Inn Bed & Breakfast | Bardstown. History is palpable at this unique bed-and-breakfast in the former Nelson County Jail (circa 1819). Despite the iron bars on the windows, 20-inch-thick walls, and heavy steel doors, the 6 guest rooms are homey, and each has a period theme, with antiques, wallpaper, and upholstery to match. A full breakfast is included in the rates. For a contrasting look at life behind bars (and, perhaps, an encounter with one of the more ethereal former prisoners who reportedly linger here) visit the preserved 1874 jail at the back of the inn. *111 W. Stephen Foster Ave., (502) 348-5551, www.jailersinn.com.*

My Old Kentucky Dinner Train | Bardstown. Hop aboard this vintage train for a two-hour lunch or dinner excursion through forested countryside. The three-course meals, included in your ticket price and served in restored 1940s cars, might feature chicken couscous salad or Kentucky "hot brown" for lunch and prime rib or seared salmon for dinner. A full bar service (for an extra cost) is available. Note that the train adheres to a business-casual dress code: pants or reasonable-length skirts/dresses for women, collared shirts and slacks or khakis for men. *602 N. 3rd St., (502) 348-7300, www.kydinnertrain.com.*

Versailles

Three Chimneys Farm. Many a remarkable racehorse—including 2008 Derby winner Big Brown—has found a home on this 2,300-acre Thoroughbred stud farm. Get a look at its operations and equine celebrities on 60- to 90-minute tours of the palatial barns. You'll also visit the life-size memorial to Seattle Slew (a Triple Crown winner and one of the farm's most famous residents) and meander through the stallion cemetery. Tours of the Stallion Division are by appointment only (book well ahead), and the $15 (cash only) fee is donated to equine-related charities. *1981 Old Frankfort Pike, (859) 873-7053, www.threechimneys.com.*

Woodford Reserve. It's hard not to appreciate elegant small-batch bourbon packaged in glass bottles that recall oversize (and also elegant) flasks. On the daily Distillery Tours (which include a tasting) of the 42-acre Woodford Reserve, founded in 1812, you'll learn how master distillers create their rich amber spirits using five sources of flavor. The visitors center has a tasting room, Glenn's Creek Café, and a shop. *7855 McCracken Pike, (859) 879-1812, www.woodfordreserve.com.*

Lexington

Kentucky Horse Park and Training Grounds. Only mildly curious about horses? You'll still need a day just for the highlights of this enormous complex. True horse lover? Plan on the two days allowed for with a general admission ticket. There's always something happening in the show and training rings, arenas, stadium, amphitheater, steeplechase course, and 24 barns. Stop at the visitors center to see what's on, then take an orientation trolley or horse-drawn carriage tour (yup, this place is that big!).

The International Museum of the Horse showcases saddles and tack; horse-drawn conveyances; and equine-themed paintings, folk art, photography, and sculpture. The American Saddlebred Museum highlights a beautiful and uniquely American breed of show horse. Options for the younger set include the Kids Barn, with interactive exhibits, storytelling sessions, and the chance to groom some ponies. Rounding things out are an amenities-loaded campground; gift, tack, and farrier shops; organized tours of area horse farms; and, of course, horseback riding! *4089 Iron Works Pkwy., (859) 233-4303, www.kyhorsepark.com.*

Saddlebreds Steal the Show

Although Kentucky is known for its Thoroughbred racers, it's also recognized for a breed of stately, high-stepping show horses. First developed in Kentucky and Virginia as riding and carriage horses back in the 1800s, Saddlebreds (aka Kentucky Saddlers) are descended from breeds that were, by the time of the Revolution, recognized as truly American. Even-tempered, elegant, and strong, these horses were often ridden by Confederate cavalry officers during the Civil War.

The Red Mile Racetrack. Here, it's all about the trotters! Founded in 1875, the world's second-oldest harness-racing track takes its name from its distinctive 1-mile red-clay oval. Although it has a regular schedule of Standardbred races from midsummer to early fall, a highlight is October's Kentucky Futurity, the third leg of the Triple Crown of Harness Racing for Trotters. *1200 Red Mile Rd., (859) 255-0752, www.redmileky.com.*

Keeneland Racetrack. A visit to this track, opened in 1936, is truly an authentic Bluegrass Country experience. Although Thoroughbred races are only held for three weeks in both April and October, you can visit year-round to watch the morning training sessions (free, 6 am–10 am); grab breakfast and rub elbows with jockeys, trainers, and owners in the Track Kitchen; and take a free, self-guided tour of the paddock. *4201 Versailles Rd., (859) 254-3412, www.keeneland.com.*

Mary Todd Lincoln House. When Mary Todd was born here in 1818, Abraham Lincoln and his family had left the second of their Kentucky farms and were living in Indiana. Many years later, the two ended up in Springfield, IL. When they met, Mary was being courted by Lincoln's Democratic Party rival, Stephen A. Douglas. Although their shared political party must have helped unite Abraham and Mary, it's nice to think that their shared Kentucky roots also played a role. Insightful docents lead hour-long tours through the brick, 14-room, late-Georgian house that was Mary's home until she was 21. What's considered the "first shrine to a first lady" is filled with period furniture, portraits, and personal items from both the Todd and Lincoln families. *578 W. Main St., (859) 233-9999, www.mtlhouse.org.*

Frankfort

Thomas D. Clark Center for Kentucky History. Don't let the modern exterior fool you. Inside is a repository of all things Kentucky from across the ages. The permanent A Kentucky Journey exhibit has some 3,000 artifacts—among them, Abraham Lincoln's pocket watch (still ticking!)—that illustrate state history from prehistoric to contemporary times. There's also a roster of changing exhibits, talks, and other events. Admission here also gets you entry to and tours of the Kentucky Military History Museum and the Old State Capitol, both nearby and part of the Kentucky Historical Society's History Campus. *100 W. Broadway, (502) 564-1792, history.ky.gov.*

Liberty Hall. When statesman John Brown began building his estate in 1796, Thomas Jefferson wrote to him with design tips. Today, it's considered one of the country's finest examples of Federal architecture. On the 75-minute guided tours, you'll learn about the Brown family and the many dignitaries they hosted, early 19th century life, and state history. You'll also hear about the Gray Lady, the spirit that reportedly haunts the estate. The gift shop has a well-curated inventory—from garden accessories and holiday ornaments to doll dresses and Kentucky cookbooks. *202 Wilkinson St., (502) 227-2560, www.libertyhall.org.*

Buffalo Trace Distillery. Named for an ancient buffalo river crossing, Buffalo Trace has been a successful distillery for more than two centuries and has the awards and National Historic Landmark status to prove it. Free hour-long Trace Tours (no reservations needed) talk you through the bourbon-making process. They also take you into a centuries-old brick warehouse, fragrant from white-oak, charred-interior barrels full of aging bourbon, some of which you'll taste. More in-depth hour-long tours (free, reservations required) focus on the distillery's history—or its ghosts. *113 Great Buffalo Trace, (502) 696-5926, www.buffalotracedistillery.com.*

NORTHEAST
MIDWEST
SOUTH
WEST

Eat & Stay

Eighth Pole Inn | Lexington. Set amid 20 acres on what is now known as Hillside Farm, this inn (formerly Swann's Nest Inn) is in the heart of Bluegrass Thoroughbred Country and just 8 miles west of downtown Lexington. New owners renovated the entire property in 2015. Their emphasis on quality and style blends perfectly with an informal ambience and true Kentucky hospitality. The six rooms and suites in the main house and annex are spacious and elegantly appointed. A Continental breakfast is included in the rates. *3463 Rosalie Rd., (859) 226-0095, eighthpoleinn.com.*

Cheapside Bar & Grill | Lexington. This busy pub in the heart of downtown has been serving up good cheer and good food for about 30 years. You can dine indoors or outside on the patio and deck. The menu features Southwestern and modern Mexican dishes for brunch (on Saturday), lunch, and dinner. There's live music, generally R&B, on weekends and plenty of craft brews and cocktails all week. What you won't ever find, though, is a cover charge. *131 Cheapside St., (859) 254-0046, www.cheapsidebarandgrill.com.*

Mary Todd Lincoln House, Lexington

Great River Road: South

ROUTE TOWNS: Memphis, TN | Clarksdale, MS | Indianola | Vicksburg | Natchez | St. Francisville, LA | Baton Rouge
New Orleans

The scenery on the southern stretch of the Great River Road changes from industrial to agricultural; the music, from bluesy guitar riffs to the fiddles and washboards of Cajun and zydeco to Dixieland jazz. And, between Beale Street and Bourbon Street, there's rarely a skyline in sight.

Mississippi River with New Orleans skyline

This trip is bookended by two of America's music capitals—Memphis, a bastion of the blues and rock-and-roll, and New Orleans, the birthplace of jazz. In between, you'll learn about the music that greatly influenced Elvis and many before and after him at the Delta Blues Museum in Clarksdale, Mississippi. You'll also take in Vicksburg, site of a key Civil War battle, and Natchez, where dozens of antebellum mansions were spared from destruction by Union forces.

The rhythm of the river changes yet again as it runs into Louisiana, past the plantations in and near St. Francisville. In Baton Rouge, the state's politics are often as spicy as its food. This lack of pussyfooting around is even evident on the state university campus, where a live tiger serves as the mascot. You'll find the bayou zest for the good life, which includes enjoying great music and food, in New Orleans. Here, though, the clubs vibrate with jazz, Cajun, zydeco, blues, and rock nightly, and the menus kick things up a culinary notch or two in several legendary kitchens.

Distance: 590 miles point to point.

Type of Trip: Vacation Getaway; RV; Arts & Music, History & Heritage, Quirky & Oddball, Small Town Gems.

Must Try: *TN:* dry-rubbed barbecue ribs, pulled pork, or beef brisket. *MS:* catfish, here delicious and fresh however it's prepared. *LA:* any Cajun or Creole dish; you also can't go wrong with a po-boy or a beignet.

Must Buy: *TN:* Elvis memorabilia (maybe a Jailhouse Rock swinging-legs clock?). *MS:* a book, pin, magnet, or other treasure depicting a Natchez estate. *LA:* Café du Monde chicory coffee and beignet mix; Mardi Gras baubles.

Must See: Graceland, National Civil Rights Museum, Delta Blues Museum, Vicksburg National Military Park, Natchez Trace National Historic Park, Myrtles Plantation, Jackson Square, Voodoo Museum, WW II Museum, Maple Leaf Bar.

Worth Noting: Immerse yourself in culture at a festival: Memphis in May/ Beale Street Music Festival, Elvis Week (mid-Aug), B.B. King Homecoming (Jun.), Natchez Pilgrimages (Mar.–Apr and Sept.–Oct.), Mardi Gras (varies based on Lenten calendar), New Orleans Jazz & Heritage Festival (Apr.– May).

Travel Tips: This route is identified by green-and-white signs showing a riverboat pilot's wheel with the words, "Great River Road" encircling the top and the name of the state you're in at the bottom. Contact the **Mississippi River Parkway Commission** (www. experiencemississippiriver.com) for info.

Atlas map G-2, p. 94

Memphis, TN

1 Mud Island River Park. Hop on the monorail at Front Street to access Mud Island River Park, a 52-acre entertainment complex at the tip of a Mississippi River peninsula. Check out the River Walk and the Mississippi River Museum. Island concessionaries sell food; rent pedal boats, kayaks, and bikes; and purvey tickets for riverboat sightseeing, dinner, and sunset cruises. Summertime sees concerts in the 5,000-seat amphitheater. *125 N. Front St., (800) 507-6507, www.mudisland.com.*

2 The Peabody Memphis. Word is that someone once put baby alligators and, later, turtles in the lobby fountain of the stately Peabody hotel. But a 1930s general manager thought ducks were more fitting. His first wooden decoys were soon replaced by live North American mallards, which were trained by a staffer who was once a circus performer. Thus began a tradition that continues to this day: the duck parade.

At 11 each morning, one drake and four hens leave the rooftop Royal Duck Palace and take the elevator to the lobby. John Phillip Sousa's "King Cotton March," plays as they waddle off the elevator, along a red carpet, and into the travertine marble fountain, where they spend the day. The ceremony is reversed at 5 each evening. Watching the duck parade is free; meals in this landmark hotel's restaurants (where duck is *never* served), or stays in its luxurious rooms, are pricier—but worth it if you're up for a splurge. *149 Union Ave., (901) 529-4000, www.peabodymemphis.com.*

3 Sun Records. In 1954, a truck driver named Elvis Presley dropped into Sam Phillips's studio to record a song as a birthday present for his mother. The rest, as they say, is history. Phillips and his label not only gave Elvis his start but also laid down tracks for Jerry Lee Lewis, B.B. King, Howlin' Wolf, Roy Orbison, Johnny Cash, and Carl Perkins. Original instruments and recording equipment give you a real feel for those early days of rock and roll. It's also still a working studio, with sessions scheduled at night to accommodate the steady stream of daytime visitors. Tours are offered daily 10:30–5:30 at the bottom of the hour. *706 Union Ave., (800) 441-6249, www.sunrecords.com.*

4 Beale Street Brass Notes Walk of Fame. W.C. Handy perfected his version of the

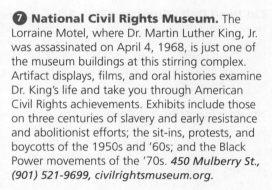

Mississippi Delta blues in Beale Street clubs. Elvis Presley frequented the neighborhood, absorbing the musical inflections that would distinguish him from others. Today this restored historic district flourishes as a commercial and nightlife center. Follow the 150 large, brass, musical notes embedded in the sidewalk between 2nd and 3rd streets. Each honors someone who made a difference in the blues genre. *203 Beale St., (901) 526-0115, www.bealestreet.com.*

5 A. Schwab Dry Goods Store. Founded in 1876, this dry goods emporium stocks corncob pipes, suspenders (44 different kinds of them!), American flags, Raggedy Anne dolls, and penny candy. Quirky souvenirs like voodoo supplies, bongo drums, and ukuleles mix with more traditional T-shirts and baseball caps. There's also a kiosk of Elvis-themed wares. *163 Beale St., (901) 523-9782, a-schwab.com.*

6 B.B. King's Blues Club. This renowned venue is festooned with authentic memorabilia from B.B.'s illustrious career and those of other legendary Memphis musicians. Listen to live music nightly performed by an array of Memphis-based players, and dine on fried dill pickles, barbecue ribs, shrimp and grits, and other Southern favorites. *143 Beale St., (901) 524–5464, www.bbkingclubs.com/memphis.*

7 National Civil Rights Museum. The Lorraine Motel, where Dr. Martin Luther King, Jr. was assassinated on April 4, 1968, is just one of the museum buildings at this stirring complex. Artifact displays, films, and oral histories examine Dr. King's life and take you through American Civil Rights achievements. Exhibits include those on three centuries of slavery and early resistance and abolitionist efforts; the sit-ins, protests, and boycotts of the 1950s and '60s; and the Black Power movements of the '70s. *450 Mulberry St., (901) 521-9699, civilrightsmuseum.org.*

8 Graceland. Elvis Presley's Colonial Revival estate is one of America's most-visited homes. Mansion Tours take in the entryway, living room, kitchen, and jungle-themed family room. On-site museums showcase the King's collection of 20 vehicles, including his famed 1955 pink Cadillac; his gold records and other awards; his Vegas period (think of all those jumpsuits); and his custom jets. The shopping's good here, too, with books and CDs, Elvis-themed togs, art and collectibles, and stuff for kids. *3734 Elvis Presley Blvd., (901) 332-3322, www.graceland.com.*

Eat & Stay

9 Charles Vergos' Rendezvous Restaurant. Ham-and-cheese sandwiches are still on the menu here, but most folks pass them up for the award-winning, dry-rub barbecue—especially the ribs. At this favorite stop for locals as well as celebrities, the credo is simple: "As long as you love ribs, and your mama taught you how to behave, you're welcome at our table." *52 S. 2nd St., (901) 523-2746, www.hogsfly.com.*

10 Heartbreak Hotel. The 128-room Heartbreak Hotel, named for Elvis's famous song, features suitably kitschy décor: think red funky furniture in the lobby and totally retro rooms. Hard-core fans reserve the Graceland Suite, where the aesthetic is inspired by that at Elvis's famous mansion—just next door. *3677 Elvis Presley Blvd., (901) 332-1000, www.graceland.com.*

Beale Street

Hopson Plantation (above)
Delta Blues Museum (above left)

Clarksdale, MS

Delta Blues Museum. Established in 1979 by the Carnegie Public Library, this museum has an extensive collection of books, recordings, videos, and memorabilia—some of it extremely rare. Exhibits trace the blues from its origins in the cotton fields through to today, and the gift shop has hard-to-find recordings and publications. Check to see what seminars, museum programs, or live music performances are on offer. Or, better yet, visit during the museum-sponsored Sunflower River Blues and Gospel Festival held every August. Before leaving, ask a staffer about who's playing where in Clarksdale. *1 N. Edwards Ave. (1 Blues Alley), (662) 627-6820, www.deltabluesmuseum.org.*

Ground Zero Blues Club. If it doesn't have a pool table, mismatched chairs, and strings of holiday lights, it's not a true blues club. You'll find all three, and more, at this dilapidated-on-purpose juke joint co-owned by Academy Award–winning actor (and Mississippi Delta native) Morgan Freeman. Veterans such as Guitar Shorty and T-Bone Pruitt play here Wednesday through Saturday evenings. The kitchen serves up WeekDay Plate Lunches and specialty sandwiches like grilled catfish BLTs. If you're looking for a 24/7 blues experience, rent one of the retro upstairs apartments for a night. *387 Delta Ave., (662) 621-9009, www.groundzerobluesclub.com.*

Cat Head Delta Blues and Folk Art. Delta Avenue is a blues fan's kind of street. Just steps from Cat Head Delta Blues & Folk Art, a Mississippi Blues Trails Marker identifies the original site of the WROX radio station, which once featured live broadcasts by the likes of Ike Turner, Sam Cook, and Elvis. Step inside Cat Head itself to get some blues CDs for the road. This eclectic shop has occasional live performances or book signings; it's also the place to get info on the local music scene. *252 Delta Ave., (662) 624-5992, www.cathead.biz.*

Hopson Plantation & Commissary. A few miles from the crossroads of U.S. highways 61 and 49, said to be the place where Robert Johnson sold his soul to the devil for the ability to play music like no other, lies Hopson Plantation & Commissary. Once one of the South's largest cotton farms and unchanged from its days as a working plantation, Hopson takes you back in time with a walk around sharecropper shacks and seed houses. Some of the farming equipment displayed here is particularly significant, given that Hopson was the first to take a cotton crop from planting to baling entirely by machine back in the 1930s. The commissary, which is generally open only by appointment, hosts live music shows just about every Saturday. *8141 Old Hwy. 49 S. (at Pixley Rd.), (662) 624-5756, www.hopsonplantation.com.*

Indianola

The B.B. King Museum and Delta Interpretive Center. The Mississippi Delta is filled with blues museums, but this one ranks at the top. Well-designed, multimedia exhibits tell the story of B.B. King's remarkable life and times. Highlights include his beloved guitar, Lucille; his home recording studio; and, adjoining the museum, an old brick cotton gin where he worked in the 1940s. The Interpretive Center includes insights into the cotton fields, street corners, and juke joints that spawned the Mississippi Delta's contribution to world music: the blues. *400 2ⁿᵈ St., (662) 887-9539, www.bbkingmuseum.org.*

Vicksburg

Biedenharn Coca-Cola Museum. Although Coca-Cola was developed by Dr. John S. Pemberton of Atlanta, GA, in 1866, he originally sold it to soda fountains in syrup form. It wasn't until 1894 that someone thought of selling it in individual bottles. This is the site where Joseph Biedenharn first did so. Here you can see the earliest Coke bottles (well before it had those Mae West curves) as well as other memorabilia related to the classic soft drink. You can also get souvenirs; candy; ice cream; and, of course, an ice cold Coke. *1107 Washington St., (601) 638-6514, www.biedenharncoca-colamuseum.com.*

Vicksburg National Military Park. The Vicksburg National Military Park commemorates the campaign, siege, and defense of Vicksburg, which was a critical chapter in the American Civil War. Highlights include the U.S.S. *Cairo* Gunboat and Museum and the Vicksburg National Cemetery. On a visit here you'll learn how, throughout the war, the Union Army made it a priority to gain control of the Mississippi River, despite the Confederate imperative to hold it. This struggle truly came to a head in strategically situated Vicksburg. *3201 Clay St., (601) 636-0583, www.nps.gov/vick.*

Eat & Stay

Shack Up Inn | Clarksdale, MS. For a culturally immersive overnight experience, stay at the Shack Up Inn on the Hopson Plantation & Commissary grounds. It rents out a row of authentic, nostalgically furnished shotgun shacks, updated with indoor plumbing, air-conditioning, and other basics. You can all but see musicians sipping a cold one on the rickety porches and belting out some impromptu blues. *001 Commissary Cir., (662) 624-8329, www.shackupinn.com.*

The Tomato Place | Vicksburg. Part old-fashioned produce stand, part café, and part crafts gallery, this colorful, quirky place sits along U.S. 61 just south of Vicksburg. It offers locally grown fruit and vegetables, homemade jams and preserves, all-fruit smoothies, and fresh-squeezed lemonade. You can also enjoy tasty po-boys, BLTs, sweet-potato fries, and peach cobbler. *3229 Hwy. 61 S., (601) 661-0040, www.thetomatoplace.com.*

Vicksburg National Military Park

The Siege of Vicksburg

In early 1863, General Grant launched the complex Vicksburg Campaign, which involved marching the Union Army of the Tennessee south along the river to take the city. Although the Union had more troops, the Confederates had the advantage of already being entrenched in fortifications amid hilly area terrain. A series of Union assaults and naval bombardments failed to break through, and, in May, both sides settled into a siege, punctuated by skirmishes, that lasted roughly two months. The Confederates ultimately surrendered, though, on July 4, 1863—a day after the Union victory at Gettysburg. Historians posit that the outcomes of these two battles marked the turning point of the war.

Natchez

Natchez Trace National Historic Park. In the early 18th century, the French established a trading post on a southern stretch of the Mississippi. Natchez was passed to Spanish hands, and then, finally, to the U.S. in 1798. During the next 60 years, it developed into one of the South's most important ports because it linked "King Cotton" to British textile mills via the river, then the ocean. Southern wealth displayed itself in the grand homes of planters and merchants. Two of this park's sites trace over a century of that history.

Melrose was the 80-acre estate of cotton planter John T. McMurran. On a guided tour of the Greek Revival mansion, note the original furnishings—especially the floor coverings. On the grounds, trails lead to several outbuildings, including slave quarters, where exhibits enrich your understanding of how much work (and how many people) it took to maintain these substantial Southern estates. Afterward, continue your tour through history at the William Johnson House, the home of a free black man. His personal story and that of his barber shop unfold through the lens of his diary.

Note that Melrose tours last about 45 minutes and are offered at the top of the hour daily between 9 and 4. There's a nominal entrance fee, and you're encouraged to arrive at the visitors center a few minutes early. Admission is free to the William Johnson House, where the tours are self guided, though a ranger is on hand to answer questions. *1 Melrose Montebello Pkwy., (601) 446-5790, www.nps.gov/natc.*

Longwood mansion, Natchez

Natchez Pilgrimage Tours. A relatively quick 1862 surrender to Union Admiral David Farragut (of "Damn the torpedoes, full speed ahead" fame) meant that Natchez's many antebellum homes survived the Civil War intact. And, thanks to the arduous long-time efforts of preservationists, many of these confections still stand. Several are open to the public year-round. During special spring and fall house pilgrimages, privately owned properties also open, bringing the count you can visit up to around 24.

Natchez Pilgrimage Tours offers several packages including the popular three-house tour, carriage ride, and lunch at the Carriage House restaurant. Mansions featured include: Melrose (1848), Longwood (1861), Stanton Hall (1857), Monmouth Plantation (1818), Magnolia Hall (1858), House on Ellicott's Hill (1798), Rosalie (1832), Auburn (1812), and Linden (1800). Each has a story, often told by hoop-skirted docents who also point out the hand-painted wallpaper, mahogany furnishings, bone china, and old-time household contraptions like crystal flytraps.

Note that you can also tour Melrose as part of a visit to the Natchez Trace Historic National Historic Park. Of the others, Longwood best encapsulates a tumultuous history in its octagonal walls—it's finished on the exterior but unfinished within because laborers left at the outbreak of the war. Palatial Stanton Hall features gilded mirrors, original Stanton family furnishings, and an enormous entry hall (16x72 feet). At the impressive Monmouth, you can also stay in the former 1818 Greek Revival Governor's Mansion, an award-winning hotel, or enjoy a five-course meal at Restaurant 1818. *640 S. Canal St., (601) 446-6631, www.natchezpilgrimage.com.*

Old South Winery. Natchez's hot and humid climate favors the growth of muscadine grapes, a varietal that produces wine ranging from sweet whites to dry reds. Inspired by his grandmother's winemaking, a local veterinarian founded the Old South Winery, which offers tours and tastings and has a gift shop. *65 S. Concord Ave., (601) 445-9924, www.oldsouthwinery.com.*

Darby's Famous Fudge. Chocolate, vanilla, and peanut butter are among the flavors of fudge that have been made at this downtown shop for more than 20 years. The perennial favorite, though, is chocolate praline. Whatever you select will be made using the freshest ingredients, often including homegrown Natchez pecans. *410 Main St., (601) 446-9737, www.darbysfudge.com.*

Natchez Museum of African-American History & Culture. This museum, in the former post office, chronicles the story of African-American life in Natchez. Exhibits cover the periods from enslavement through WW II, highlighting the community's struggles and accomplishments through art, photographs, and artifacts. Works by the author Richard Nathaniel Wright, who was born in Natchez, are also displayed. *301 Main St., (601) 445-0728, visitnatchez.org.*

Eat & Stay

Roux 61 Seafood and Grill | Natchez. The "Roux Crew" wears shirts that read "Let the food coma happen." The family-owned restaurant's reputation is secure with a menu well beyond étouffée and fried green tomatoes. Expect bold Southern flavor and super-sized portions of everything from seafood po-boys to crawfish pasta to shrimp-and-alligator cheesecake. And there's live music to boot. *453 Hwy. 61 S., (601) 445-0004, roux61.com.*

Fat Mama's Tamales | Natchez. As its name suggests, the focus at this small log cabin–style restaurant is tamales: served by the dozen (or half dozen) and handmade according to a recipe well-honed over time. You can also get taco soup, chili, boudin sausage, and po-boy sandwiches. Be sure to try the famous fire-and-ice pickles (spicy but served cold) or the Knock You Naked margaritas. If you like the latter, pick up some margarita mix on the way out. *303 S. Canal St., (601) 442-4548, www.fatmamastamales.com.*

A New Way to Trace the Old

Generations of Native Americans, Natchez, Choctaw, and Chickasaw among them, used a series of long-blazed trails along the Mississippi River. The same trails were followed by early European explorers and settlers. Later came the boatmen—the so-called Kaintucks—who floated down both the Ohio and Mississippi rivers to Natchez. There, many of them sold their goods and vessels (for use as lumber) and used the trails, which collectively became known as the Natchez Trace, to return north. By the early 19th century, the Trace was important not only to commerce but also the military. Andrew Jackson marched his troops along it during the War of 1812.

Traversing the Old Trace took about 35 days on foot and 20 days on horseback. Today, you can do it in just a few days (with stops) along the scenic, 444-mile **Natchez Trace Parkway** (www.nps.gov/natr). It runs between Nashville, TN, and Natchez, MS, with additional access points in Jackson and Tupelo, MS, and Cherokee, AL. It passes Native American burial mounds, rocky outcroppings, cypress swamps, clear streams and lakes, and unspoiled woodlands of dogwoods and redbuds. It also passes plenty of places to stop the car; get out; and hike, bike, camp, or explore history.

Under-the-Hill Saloon. Though the whiskey's no longer the firewater served back in the day, the setting and ambiance at this friendly watering hole do evoke earlier times. A 200-year-old building filled with eclectic memorabilia and music provided by the occasional piano player or jazz band help you recall the days when Under-the-Hill was Natchez's red-light district. *25 Silver St., (601) 446-8023, www.underthehillsaloon.com.*

Grand Village of the Natchez Indians. Natchez is a gumbo of many cultures. Native Americans were the first to inhabit the region, and the Natchez Indian chiefdom gave the city its name. This National Historic Landmark, just southeast of downtown, has three burial mounds, a ceremonial plaza, and a re-created Natchez Indian dwelling. *400 Jefferson Davis Blvd., (601) 446-6502, www.nps.gov/nr.*

The Myrtles Plantation, St. Francisville

Spanish moss covered trees at Melrose plantation, Natchez Trace National Historic Park

St. Francisville, LA

The Myrtles Plantation. Although not as grand as many River Road properties, in many ways the Myrtles epitomizes plantation styling. The 1½-story clapboard residence has a wraparound gallery porch—complete with elaborate wrought-ironwork and rocking chairs—and a truly opulent interior. It also has a lot of history. It was established in 1796 by General David Bradford (aka Whiskey Dave), who fled to Louisiana, then a Spanish colony, after taking part in the Whiskey Rebellion. In the 1800s, it was sold and remodeled twice, first by the Woodruff family, then by the Stirling family, whose members lived here through the 1890s.

Where there's history, there's lore, and here some of it is tragic and haunting—literally. A visit to what's billed as One of America's Most Haunted Houses is not for the faint of heart. Learn about the property and its many well-documented ghosts on a tour (held daily on the half hour). Skeptical? Spend the night inside the mansion, which is also a B&B, and see for yourself. *7747 U.S. Hwy. 61, (225) 635-6277, www.myrtlesplantation.com.*

Rosedown Plantation State Historic Site. This state historic site and national landmark, a two-story Greek Revival manor fronted by upper and lower gallery porches, was built in the mid-1800s by wealthy cotton planter, Daniel Turnbull, and his wife, Martha. She was responsible for the property's renowned gardens—some 28 acres of them. Tours (held daily on the hour) take in these gardens, the elegant main house with its many original family-owned pieces, and some of the 13 historic outbuildings on the surrounding 371 acres. *12501 LA Hwy. 10, (225) 635-3332, www.crt.state.la.us/louisiana-state-parks.*

Grandmother's Buttons. Housed in a restored 1905 bank, this shop has a vast array of jewelry made using antique buttons sourced from all over the world. Pieces here include delicate bracelets and hairpins, elegant drop earrings, chunky rings, and statement-piece necklaces. There's also a selection of gifts, clothing, and other accessories. *9814 Royal St., (225) 635-4107, www.grandmothersbuttons.com.*

Baton Rouge

Louisiana State Capitol. The interior of this 34-story, limestone, Art Deco skyscraper—a truly unique capitol—features exquisite marble and bronze details and a polished-lava floor (in Memorial Hall). Sculptures showcase state history; a 27th-floor observation deck showcases the Mississippi River and surrounding area. The grounds include the Capitol Gardens and a memorial to the famous (some say infamous) Governor Huey P. Long, who conceived the capitol. *N. 3rd St. at State Capitol Dr., (225) 342-7317, louisiana.gov.*

USS Kidd. The *Kidd,* a WW II–era Fletcher-class destroyer, has been restored to its 1945 appearance. You can explore more than 50 of the ship's interior areas. Displays at the Veterans Museum include ship models, a full-scale replica of Old Ironsides's gun deck, a P-40 Flying Tiger, and a Corsair A-7E jet. *305 S. River (Government St. at the levee), (225) 342-1942, www.usskidd.com.*

Old Governor's Mansion. Built in 1929 by Governor Huey P. Long, the mansion bears a striking resemblance to the White House in Washington, D.C. Indeed, its design is based on an original design by Thomas Jefferson, with the same exterior Corinthian columns and wing structure as the president's abode. This is actually the second mansion to sit here: Despite political opposition, the often-controversial Governor Long razed the original antebellum mansion. Its replacement cost the state $150,000, a huge sum in lean Depression times. *502 North Blvd., (225) 387-2464, www.oldgovernorsmansion.org.*

Mike's Habitat (LSU Campus). Since 1935, the tiger mascot on campus at Louisiana State University in Baton Rouge has been named Mike, to honor the athletic director who spearheaded the idea of a live mascot in 1936, Chellis Mike Chambers. Today's habitat is considered one of the largest of its kind in the world: more than 15,000 square feet. *N. Stadium Rd. (near Pete Maravich Assembly Center), (225) 578-5030, www.mikethetiger.com.*

Eat & Stay

Eola Hotel | Natchez. A classic since 1840 and today on the National Register of Historic Places, the Eola is a stately inn with four massive columns marking its entrance. The interior is equally impressive, with 19th-century reproduction furnishings and fixtures in the 16 guest rooms and public areas. Rooms are named after historic people who helped settle Natchez. The hotel offers contemporary amenities, and each stay includes a full southern breakfast. Downtown's Antiques Row shopping district and the Under-the-Hill dining and nightlife district are both nearby. *201 N. Pearl St., (601) 442-8848, eolahotel.com.*

Butler Greenwood Plantation & Bed and Breakfast | St. Francisville, LA. The antebellum Butler Greenwood Plantation has remained in the same family since the 1790s. It's filled with priceless antiques, portraits, and heirlooms and has an exceptional formal Victorian parlor. Enchanting cottages on the oak-lined grounds offer privacy for overnight guests. *8345 U.S. Hwy. 61, (225) 635-6312, www.butlergreenwood.com.*

Magnolia Café | St. Francisville. Here you can try Louisiana favorites like the muffaletta, a large round sandwich layered with meats, cheeses, and an olive relish. Also on the menu: fried alligator, sweet-potato fries, crawfish salad, and spicy shrimp or other po-boys. Friday nights see live music. *5689 Commerce St., (225) 635-6528, www.themagnoliacafe.net.*

USS *Kidd,* Baton Rouge

New Orleans, LA: Big Easy Basics

Despite many challenges—epidemics, fires, war, natural disasters—over the course of almost 300 years, New Orleans has not only survived but taken things in stride. In the aptly named Big Easy, a palpable sense of perseverance complements an equally palpable joie de vivre, whether that means bar-hopping on Bourbon Street, antiques shopping on Royal Street, sipping coffee at Café du Monde, or rattling Uptown on the St. Charles Avenue streetcar (they *aren't* called trolleys here). Throughout town, things are often spiced with a bit of "lagniappe" (pronounced lan-yap) in which merchants, barkeeps, and restaurateurs often give customers a little something extra for nothing. What better way to let the good times roll?

Travel Tips: Neighborhoods here also embrace the good with the bad; one block might be perfectly safe, the next a bit dicey. Get your bearings on a tour (or two), and don't hesitate to call for a cab, especially at night, and even if you're only going a short distance.

Visitor Info: New Orleans Convention & Visitors Bureau, *2020 St. Charles Ave., (800) 672-6124, or 529 St. Ann St., (504) 568-5661; www.neworleanscvb.com.*

St. Louis Cathedral, Jackson Square

The Quarter

① Jackson Square. Dating from 1718, the French Quarter, or Vieux Carré (Old Square), is the oldest section of New Orleans, with architecture reflecting primarily Spanish and French influences. At its heart is Jackson Square. Here, facing the Mississippi, street performers and sidewalk artists entertain visitors and locals, some of whom live in the historic apartment buildings on either side.

In the center of it all is the St. Louis Cathedral, one of the country's oldest churches. It's fronted by a statue of Andrew Jackson, victor in the Battle of New Orleans, and flanked by the Cabildo, once the seat of the Spanish government, and the Presbytere, designed as a residence for Capuchin monks but used instead for commercial purposes. The two buildings are part of the Louisiana State Museum.

Nearby streets include Royal, pedestrian-only by day and famous for its antiques shops, and Bourbon, pedestrian-only by night and legendary for its bars and clubs. That said, the entire grid of streets surrounding Jackson Square buzzes. So does the French Market, just along Decatur, with its crafts and produce stands, shops, and restaurants. *Bounded by Chartres, St. Ann, Decatur, and St. Peter Sts., (504) 658-3200, www.nola.gov/parks-and-parkways.*

② Café du Monde. The original French Market coffee house opened in 1862, and the menu at this 24/7 café remains simple: dark-roasted coffee, here brewed with chicory, and beignets—deep-fried pastries heavily dusted with powdered sugar (you'll leave with a dusting of it yourself!). A plate of three beignets with a steaming cup of café au lait is the best deal in town for under $10. *800 Decatur St., (504) 525-4544, cafedumonde.com.*

③ New Orleans Historic Voodoo Museum. Most visitors expect to be scared with creepy tales of curses and black magic. The museum delivers, but it also offers an explanation of voodoo as a religion and how it plays into the history of New Orleans. See piles of artifacts, dolls, potions, and gris-gris bags (filled with herbs and essential oils blessed by a voodoo practitioner). Items in the gift shop let you get some good mojo to go. The museum also offers cemetery walking tours. *724 Dumaine St., (504) 680-0128, www.neworleansonline.com.*

④ Pat O'Brien's Bar. The original Pat O'Brien's was a speakeasy that turned legitimate after Prohibition. Popularity forced it to relocate to its current, larger location on St. Peter's Street. Locals make room for visitors—including lots of college kids celebrating football games or just celebrating—in the courtyard area or in the piano bar, where dueling players are a common sight. The signature drink is the Hurricane, a super-sweet, rum-based concoction that goes down easily (be careful). Upon ordering, you'll pay a deposit for the souvenir glass, which you can take home or return for a slight refund. *718 St. Peter St., (504) 525-4823, www.patobriens.com.*

Eat & Stay

⑤ Muriel's Jackson Square. Here, the location, with its view of Jackson Square, rivals the contemporary Creole menu. A resident ghost keeps things interesting, too. Strange shadows have been seen posturing in the courtyard; disembodied voices have been heard in the Seance Bar. Muriel's management even keeps a table set for the spirit of Mr. Jourdan, on whose 18th-century property the restaurant is set. Join him for a meal, perhaps one with goat cheese–filled crepes topped by Gulf shrimp in a buttery sauce of Chardonnay, onion, tomato, and bell pepper. *801 Chartres St., (504) 568-1885, www.muriels.com.*

⑥ Lafitte Guest House and Gallery. This boutique hotel provides privacy and comfort only steps from the lively nightlife. It was built in 1849 as a mansion for the Gelieses family, and today it has 14 crisply elegant guestrooms overlooking either a courtyard or a street. All rooms have en suite baths; some have private balconies, though the hotel invites all guests to its shared balcony for an insider's view of the Quarter and beyond. *1003 Bourbon St., (800) 331-7971, www.lafitteguesthouse.com.*

⑦ Johnny's Po-Boys. The sandwiches are scrumptious at the city's oldest family-owned po-boy restaurant. Each creation starts with fresh, grilled French bread that's then "dressed" (i.e., slathered with mayo and adorned with lettuce and tomato) and piled with oysters, crawfish, shrimp, or roast beef. Tables in the front fill quickly; try venturing into the back room for an open spot. Note that it's cash-only here. *511 St. Louis St., (504) 524-8129.*

⑧ Mother's. Since opening in 1938 on what was called "restaurant row," the menu at this lived-in diner-like eatery features some of the city's best down-home staples like baked ham, po-boys, gumbo, jambalaya, and red beans and rice. And nothing beats breakfast at Mother's: ham, eggs, buttery grits, and flakey biscuits or maybe an étouffée omelet. *401 Poydras St., (504) 523-9656, www.mothersrestaurant.net.*

NORTHEAST

MIDWEST

SOUTH

WEST

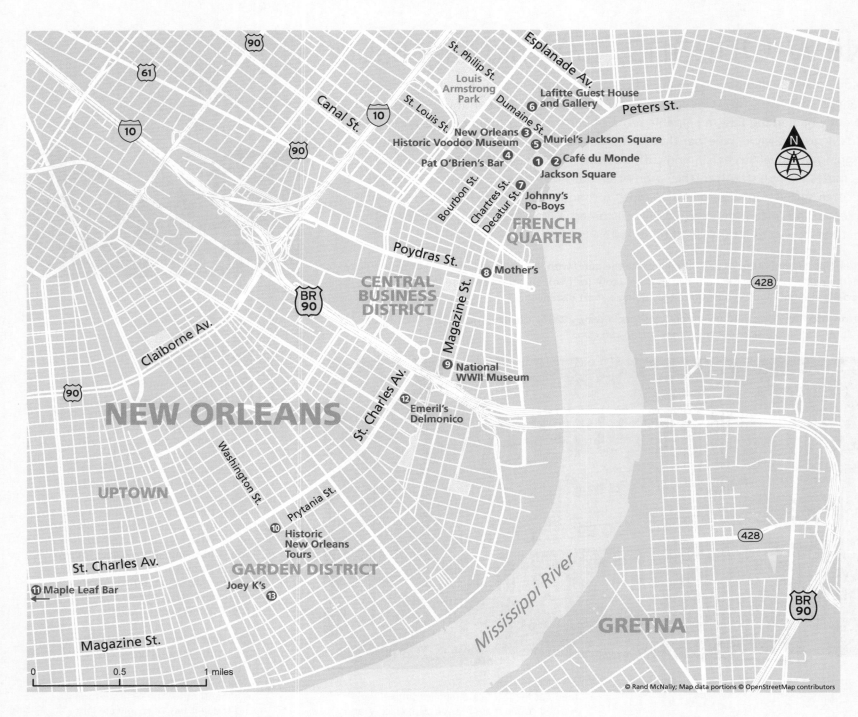

CBD and the Warehouse District

9 The National WW II Museum. Why does the Big Easy have a multiplex museum honoring the service men and women of WW II? Well, Higgins Industries, headquartered in New Orleans, designed and built the Higgins Boat, which was the linchpin in D-Day operations as it was used to transport troops from ship to shore. Tom Hanks narrates a 4D film, *Beyond All Boundaries,* that tells the dramatic story of America's entry into and participation in the war. Galleries and exhibits showcase all aspects of WW II in the European and Pacific theaters. *945 Magazine St., (504) 528-1944, www.nationalww2museum.org.*

Garden District and Uptown

10 Historic New Orleans Tours. This outfit offers two-hour walking tours of the Treme district, the French Quarter, and other neighborhoods. But its cemetery and Garden District combo tour, offered daily at 11 and 1:45, is particularly popular. Other offerings include music, literary, and other themed city tours as well as excursions outside town to swamps and plantations. Reservations are recommended. *2727 Prytania St. (Washington and Prytania), (504) 947-2120, www.tourneworleans.com.*

11 Maple Leaf Bar. Though light on frills, this bar is heavy on frolic (and ambience), thanks to lots of live music shows featuring local headliners and hot bands on the Southern circuit. Located on Oak Street in the Carrollton area of Uptown, this renowned venue is well worth the trip from anywhere in the city. Arrive in the afternoon or early evening by St. Charles Avenue streetcar, but take a cab back. *8316 Oak St., (504) 866-9359, www.mapleleafbar.com.*

St. Louis Cemetery #1, New Orleans

Eat & Stay

12 Emeril's Delmonico. Take the St. Charles Avenue streetcar to one of the city's culinary institutions, Delmonico's, which opened in 1895 and was re-invented by famed TV personality and oft-honored chef Emeril Lagasse in 1998. His modern interpretations of Creole cuisine include entrées like glazed pork chop with red-bean-and-rice congri, Gulf shrimp étouffée, or crisp duck-leg confit. Lagasse, who owns 13 restaurants, keeps his company headquarters and test kitchen in New Orleans. *1300 St. Charles Ave., (504) 525-4937, www.emerilsrestaurants.com/emerils-delmonico.*

13 Joey K's. Located inside a century-old building, and once featured on Guy Fieri's *Diners, Drive-Ins and Dives* show, Joey K's specializes in down-home Louisiana soul food. The signature dish is shrimp Magazine—large butterflied shrimp sautéed in olive oil, white wine, garlic, artichoke hearts, ham, and green onion and served over angel hair pasta. *3001 Magazine St., (504) 891-0997, www.joeyksrestaurant.com.*

The Inspirational Blue Ridge Parkway

ROUTE TOWNS: Charlottesville, VA I Grottoes I Lyndhurst I Natural Bridge I Ferrum I Floyd I Pinnacle, NC
Blowing Rock I Valle Crucis I Linville I Newland I Marion I Asheville I Chimney Rock
Hendersonville Area

Running from Virginia's Shenandoah Valley to North Carolina's Great Smoky Mountains is one of this country's greatest treasures: the Blue Ridge Parkway. Be prepared to slow down, enjoy the views, and be inspired by it all.

Blue Ridge Parkway near Asheville, NC

To create jobs during the Great Depression, President Franklin D. Roosevelt started the Works Progress Administration (WPA). One of its projects was building the Blue Ridge Parkway (BRP), a 469-mile-long mountain road from Afton Mountain, Virginia, through the Appalachians to Cherokee, North Carolina. This two-lane stretch remains one of America's greatest drives.

This journey starts near Virginia's Shenandoah National Park, travels through several state and national forests as well as some 29 counties, and finishes near North Carolina's Great Smoky Mountains National Park. The trip is interspersed with wonderful rock-framed tunnels and more than 200 scenic overlooks, ranging in elevation from 600 to 6,000 feet. Just off the picturesque parkway, you'll find charming communities with general stores, folk-art marketplaces, down-home restaurants, and cultural museums. Enjoy the drive.

Atlas map H-10, p. 106

Distance: Counting out-and-back side trips off the BRP, this point-to-point trip is 799 miles.

Type of Trip: Vacation Getaway; RV; Arts & Music, Great Outdoors, History & Heritage, Picture Perfect, Small Town Gems.

Must Try: *VA*: Hearty, fresh, mountain fare. *NC*: barbecue, perhaps washed down with a Pepsi, which was invented in this state.

Must Buy: Traditional, locally made arts and crafts, including quilts and other housewares, preserves, clothing, walking sticks, and musical instruments.

Must See: Monticello, Natural Bridge State Park, Mabry Mill Restaurant, The Blowing Rock, Original Mast General Store, Grandfather Mountain, Biltmore Estate, Thompson's Store.

Worth Noting: Many sights along the BRP are located using milepost markers (MPs). Note that, although the route is off limits to commercial vehicles, RVs are welcome; just check tunnel clearances in advance.

Travel Trips: To fully experience the nature that surrounds the BRP, why not stay in one of its campgrounds? Otter Creek (MP 61), Peaks of Otter (MP 86), Rocky Knob (MP 167), Doughton Park (MP 241), Julian Price Park (MP 297), and Linville Falls (MP 316) have both tent and primitive RV sites.

Find details on camping and other lodgings through the **National Park Service** (www.nps.gov/blri), **Recreation.gov** (877/444-6777, www.recreation.gov), and **ReserveAmerica** (www.reserveamerica. com). Reservations are highly recommended.

NORTHEAST

MIDWEST

SOUTH

WEST

Thomas Jefferson statue (above) and house (right) at Monticello

Charlottesville, VA

Monticello. Thomas Jefferson was a true Renaissance man. The author of the Declaration of Independence, third president of the U.S., and founder of the University of Virginia put his vast knowledge of the arts and sciences to good use throughout his 5,000-acre estate. On guided tours, you'll learn that he was an agriculturalist, horticulturist, etymologist, archaeologist, paleontologist, mathematician, cryptographer, surveyor, author, lawyer, inventor, and violinist. He was also a bibliophile, whose personal collection of 6,487 books was the cornerstone of the Library of Congress.

On his 1,000-foot-long terrace and in his orchards and vineyards, Jefferson grew more than 300 varieties of vegetables and 170 varieties of fruits. The interior of the manse has many of his innovations, too. A dumbwaiter hoisted wines from the cellar to the dining room from within the fireplace mantel. A rotating bookstand held open five books at once. A "polygraph" machine allowed Jefferson to create duplicate letters as he wrote. *931 Thomas Jefferson Pkwy. (Rte. 53), (434) 984-9800, www.monticello.org.*

Grottoes

Grand Caverns. America's oldest show caves were discovered in 1804, when Bernard (Barnette) Weyer was hunting. Two years later, he opened them to curious paying guests. Civil War soldiers often explored them, and more than 200 Union and Confederate signatures remain. Tours take in popcorn, flowstone, drapery, shield, and soda-straw formations in chambers with evocative names like the Persian Palace, Grand Ball Room, Dante's Inferno, Jefferson's Hall, Bridal Chamber, and Cathedral Hall (the largest at 280 feet long and 50 feet high). Bring a jacket: temperatures are a constant 54 degrees. *5 Grand Caverns Dr., (540) 249-5705, www.grandcaverns.com.*

Humpback Rocks, Lyndhurst

Lyndhurst

Humpback Rocks. About 6 miles into your BRP drive, you'll see a huge greenstone outcropping (or hump), jutting 3,000 feet into the air. In the 1840s, this natural landmark helped guide wagon trains over the Howardsville Turnpike through the Appalachian Mountains. Today, it's a BRP landmark, with a visitors center and a farm museum surrounded by nearly 3,000 forested acres. Stop by to see the one-room log cabin; several outbuildings that reflect regional, late-1800s architecture; and costumed interpreters demonstrating weaving, basket making, and gardening. *Blue Ridge Pkwy., MP 5.8, (540) 943-4716.*

Natural Bridge

Natural Bridge State Park. Before the advent of billon-dollar theme parks, an entrepreneur only had to discover a natural attraction, set up a gate, and charge admission. That's what happened at the Natural Bridge. In the 19th and 20th centuries, the 215-foot-high, 90-foot-span arch became particularly popular with European travelers, and visitors could opt to be lowered over the edge in a steel cage while a violinist played. The bridge regularly appeared on Wonders of the World lists. Today the majestic formation is part of a 1,500-acre state park that includes 6 miles of trails and a visitors center. *6477 S. Lee Hwy., (540) 291-1324, www.dcr.virginia.gov/state-parks.*

Navigating the BRP

The BRP's marketing website (www. blueridgeparkway.org) has a plethora of helpful trip-planning information, as does the National Park Service's site (www.nps.gov/blri). If you're looking specifically for dining and lodging info, the park service has a website (www.nps.gov/blri/planyourvisit/eatingsleeping.htm) for that, too.

Out on the road, at Milepost 384 and beside offices for the BRP and the Blue Ridge National Heritage Area, you'll find the **Blue Ridge Parkway Visitor Center** (195 Hemphill Knob Rd., Asheville, 828/298-5330). There's a 24-minute video about the route and western North Carolina's unique culture as well as information desks, exhibits, a gift shop, and a 22-foot-long interactive BRP map.

Linn Cove Viaduct, Linville, NC

Eat & Stay

Michie Tavern | Charlottesville, VA. What satisfied travelers in 1784, when this tavern opened, satisfies them today. In the lunch-only Ordinary dining room, 18th-century recipes are used to create classics like fried chicken, hickory-smoked pulled pork, mashed potatoes and gravy, black-eyed peas, stewed tomatoes, cornbread, and biscuits. Walk off your meal with a visit to the tavern's general store (housed in a grist mill), metal smith store, and gift shop. *683 Thomas Jefferson Pkwy., (434) 977-1234, www.michietavern.com.*

Peaks of Otter Lodge | Bedford, VA. Here, you immediately get a sense of what life was like in the mid-1800s. There's the old Polly Woods's Ordinary (aka tavern), which provided travel necessities as early as 1840 (no longer operational), and about a mile walk from the visitors center is the Johnson Farm, which offers living-history demonstrations. And then there's the 63-room Peaks of Otter Lodge, which was built in 1964 and also has tent and RV sites (book through ReserveAmerica), a restaurant, and a gift shop. Trails in the extensive system here are popular thanks to cooler summer temperatures, abundant wildlife, and hardwood forests. Hiking to the top of Sharp Top (one of the three Peaks of Otter) is a tradition. *85554 Blue Ridge Pkwy., MP 85.5, (540) 586-1081 (lodge), (540) 586-4496 (visitors center), www.peaksofotter.com.*

NORTHEAST

MIDWEST

SOUTH

WEST

Ferrum

Blue Ridge Institute & Museum. Ferrum College founded this institute in the early 1970s to document, interpret, and present the folk heritage of the Blue Ridge region. Its free galleries have changing folk art and cultural exhibits, and its Blue Ridge Farm Museum (admission charged), a re-created Virginia-German farmstead, has costumed interpreters preparing meals over open hearths, driving oxen, blacksmithing, and doing a host of other chores. The BRI also hosts the October **Blue Ridge Folklife Festival** (www.blueridgefolklifefestival.org), which has music and storytelling stages, old-time crafts, local produce and homemade treats, horse-pulling contests, a moonshiner's still, and more. *20 Museum Dr., (540) 365-4416, www.blueridgeinstitute.org.*

Floyd

Rocky Knob/Rock Castle Gorge. In 1978, one of the BRP's older gas stations (circa 1948) was converted into the seasonal, weekend-only Rocky Knob Visitor Center, operated by the National Park Service. It's a great place to get information on Rock Castle Gorge, one of the parkway's most floral-rich sections with an extensive trail system. If you'd like to stay the night, there are tent and RV sites (book through ReserveAmerica) available from early May to late October. *Blue Ridge Pkwy., MP 174.1, also accessible from MPs 167–169, (540) 745-9662, www.nps.gov/blri.*

Mabry Mill Restaurant. This complex offers so much more than just a place to eat. It also offers a glimpse at life in the early 20th century, with a gristmill, sawmill, blacksmith shop (complete with a working smithy), and the Matthews Cabin. Costumed interpreters conduct craft demonstrations; visit on weekends in late September and October, and you'll see them churning out apple butter. Sunday afternoon concerts of traditional Appalachian music are another highlight.

A gift shop features Virginia crafts and foods as well as mill- and BRP-inspired clothing, books, music, and souvenirs. You can also get grits, cornmeal, and buckwheat flour made at the on-site mill, which was built circa 1908 by Ed Mabry. The restaurant's country-style menu features barbecue pulled pork, chicken pot pie, creamed corn, and blackberry cobbler. Another plus? Breakfast is served all day. Be sure to try one of the pancake choices ranging from cornmeal and buckwheat to blueberry and apple. *Blue Ridge Pkwy., MP 176.1, (276) 952-2947, www.mabrymillrestaurant.com.*

Mabry Mill Restaurant, Floyd

Pinnacle, NC

Pilot Mountain State Park. If you watched *The Andy Griffith Show,* you'll remember him referring to Mount Pilot. Well, the park that sparked the name covers more than 3,700 wooded acres. Drive to the top of the monolithic mountain, rising 1,400 feet above the Upper Piedmont Plateau, for views of Winston-Salem to the south. Rock climbing and rappelling are adventurous options, but hiking and picnicking are the primary attractions. If you're in the mood and suitably equipped, there's fishing and canoeing on the Yadkin River, about 20 miles away but part of the same park. Primitive campsites are open mid-March and late November; there's also seasonal RV camping (no hook-ups). *1792 Pilot Knob Park Rd., (336) 325-2355, www.ncparks.gov.*

Blowing Rock

Moses Cone Manor House. Along with his brother, Caesar, Moses Cone established one of North Carolina's largest textile empires in the late 19th and early 20th centuries. He and his wife, Bertha, used some of their wealth to create this country estate. In 1949, the Colonial Revival–style Flat Top Manor and its surrounding 3,500 acres were given to the federal government to be operated as a "public park and pleasuring ground."

In summer and fall, staffers offer tours of the 23-room mansion, short talks on the porch, and guided walks to the Cone Cemetery. While you're here, visit the Parkway Craft Center, which sells art, photography, pottery, glass items, woodworks, jewelry, quilts, and more created by members of the Southern Highland Craft Guild. *Blue Ridge Pkwy., MP 294, (828) 295-7938, www.blueridgeparkway.org.*

Eat & Stay

Mayberry Motor Inn | Mt. Airy, NC. It's just the basics at this traditional single-level motor lodge, which offers 27 rooms, a Continental breakfast, and 10 surrounding acres. Although you can't sleep in Aunt Bee's Room, you can see items the owners purchased from the Raleigh estate of Frances Bavier, who played the family matriarch on *The Andy Griffith Show.* *501 N. Andy Griffith Pkwy., (336) 786-4109, www.mayberrymotorinn.com.*

The Real Life Mayberry

If **Mt. Airy** (Visitors Center, 200 N. Main St., 336/786-6116, www.visit-mayberry.com) seems familiar, it's because Andy Griffith's hometown inspired the fictional utopia of Mayberry in *The Andy Griffith Show.* And Mt. Airy has since adopted more of the Mayberry veneer by promoting show-related sites like Wally's Service Station and Floyd's City Barber Shop.

In addition to seeing a re-creation of the courthouse, you can take a guided town tour in a replica Mayberry squad car, or stay at **Andy Griffith's Home Place** (711 E. Haymore St., 336/789-5999). You can also buy a car at Mayberry Auto Sales, shop in the Mayberry Flea Market, take in a show at the Andy Griffith Playhouse, or visit the **Andy Griffith Museum** (218 Rockford St., 336/786-1604, www.andygriffithmuseum.com). Festivals include September's Mayberry Days (www.surryarts.org/mayberry-days), when fans come out in droves for myriad events.

Wally's Service Station, Mt. Airy, NC

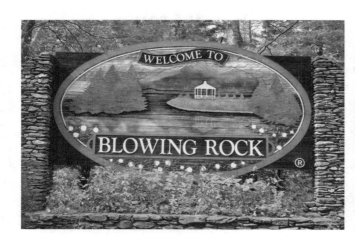

Tweetsie Railroad, Blowing Rock

The Blowing Rock. Talk about truth in advertising. Stop at this natural attraction, and you'll understand how it and its nearby town got their names. When you stand at the precipice 3,000 feet above the Johns River Gorge, powerful gusts of wind sweep up and over the rim like invisible ocean waves. Hours are always weather permitting; call ahead before you visit. *432 The Rock Rd., (828) 295-7111, www.theblowingrock.com.*

Tweetsie Railroad. Owing to its shrill whistle, locals gave the original East Tennessee and Western North Carolina Railroad this nickname. It stuck, becoming identified with the original steam-locomotive attraction that evolved into one of the nation's first theme parks. Today, rides include a carousel, a Ferris wheel, a drop tower, a Tilt-a-Whirl, and the Wild West Train Adventure. Add to this gold panning, Diamond Lil's Can-Can Revue at the Tweetsie Palace, the Deer Park zoo, gift shops, restaurants, and events like Fourth of July fireworks and October's Ghost Train Halloween Festival, and you've got yourself a heap o' fun. *300 Tweetsie Railroad Ln., (828) 264-9061, www.tweetsie.com.*

Valle Crucis

Original Mast General Store. Just a few miles north of Boone and the BRP is a country store that opened around 1883, when it doubled as a doctor's office and meeting place. Things haven't changed much since then. A pot-bellied stove sits in the center of the store, and racks and shelves are stocked with suspenders, birdhouses, knives, marbles and other old-time toys, cornmeal, hoes, plus a lot of things you didn't know people made any more. They also sell items made by more modern brands like Carhartt, Dansko, Columbia, and Merrell. There are several Mast General Stores in North Carolina, but this is the original. *3565 Hwy. 194 S., (828) 963-6511, www.mastgeneralstore.com.*

Linville

Grandfather Mountain. At 5,946 feet, this is the highest peak in the Blue Ridge Mountains. A long and winding road leads to the top, and the popular Mile-High Swinging Bridge—a 228-foot-long steel-cable suspension bridge above a chasm—leads to breathtaking vistas. The park also has 11 trails that vary in degrees of difficulty from a gentle walk to a rigorous trek. The Nature Museum has a collection of North Carolina gems and minerals as well as displays on regional wildlife like bears, cougars, and otters. Mildred's Grill, in the museum building, serves a basic menu of soups, sandwiches, and salads. The Fudge Shop serves freshly made batches, often in seasonal flavors like pumpkin pie or peppermint candy. *2050 Blowing Rock Hwy., (828) 733-1354, www.grandfather.com.*

Linn Cove Viaduct. Due to an environmentally sensitive 7-mile section that defied cut-and-fill road construction, for years the BRP was left unfinished. Eventually environmentalists, landowners, engineers, and architects put their skills together to skirt the rugged slopes of Grandfather Mountain. The solution was a 1,243-foot-long bridge consisting of 153 50-ton segments. Since its completion in 1987, the viaduct has received 11 design awards. Scientists also continue to study the unique ecology of this mountain habitat, currently home to dozens of globally endangered plant and animal species. *Blue Ridge Pkwy., MP 304, (828) 733-1354, www.visitnc.com.*

Newland

Christa's Country Corner. If you exit at Pineola Gap, near MP 312, you'll find Christa's Country Corner, which carries many things you didn't know you needed but will want once you arrive. There's udder balm (for the cow in your life), cans of snuff, homemade preserves, mountain honey, molasses, and Moon Pies. There are also shelves of body care and beauty supplies as well as vests, jackets, boots, and socks. If you have a hankering for comfort foods, Christa whips up daily specials like meat loaf, chicken and dumplings, barbecue pork, and beans and cornbread. *1600 Jonas Ridge Hwy. (Hwy. 181), (828) 733-3353, www.christas.com.*

Marion

Linville Caverns. After Henry Colton saw fish swimming out of a solid rock wall, he did a little sleuthing and found a cave system with an underground stream populated by native trout. That was back in the early 1800s. In the late 1930s, North Carolina's only show cave opened to the public. Well-lit paths make your cave exploration easier than Colton's was. Guides point out highlights such as the Frozen Waterfall and a natural bridge. Temperatures are a steady 52 degrees; bring a jacket. Five minutes away, at Linville Falls, there are tent and RV sites that you can book through ReserveAmerica. *19929 Hwy. 221 N., (828) 756-4171, www.linvillecaverns.com.*

Eat & Stay

The Westglow Resort & Spa | **Blowing Rock.** Relaxation here starts with deep breaths of clean mountain air and continues with the setting—in an impeccably restored Georgian-style estate that was once the home of an early-20th-century landscape painter. It follows that the views are spectacular. Six Mansion Rooms feature crisp white linens and dark-wood Colonial-style furnishings; three Lodge Suites are more contemporary and have fireplaces and decks. Immerse yourself in the surroundings on short hikes and bike rides, or try one of the comprehensive fitness-class offerings. You can also arrange to go fly-fishing, canoeing, kayaking, horseback riding, or whitewater rafting with a local outfitter. Of course, you could simply sink blissfully into a facial, a body wrap, or a massage. *224 Westglow Cir., (828) 295-4463, www.westglowresortandspa.com.*

The Omni Grove Park Inn | **Asheville.** E.W. Grove made his fortune in patent medicines, but his lasting legacy is this elegant inn. Opened in 1913, the 513-room lodge seems perfectly suited to Asheville, framed by a forested backdrop and fronted by an expansive lawn. Inside you'll find exquisite and original Arts & Crafts décor, including 700 custom-made pieces of furniture and 600 hand-hammered copper light fixtures. If you're an F. Scott Fitzgerald fan, request Room 441, which is where he stayed and worked. Guest rooms throughout have solid-oak Stickley and Roycroft furnishings and cottage-style windows that open to mountain, golf course, or courtyard views. The Main Inn has the most traditional atmosphere; the Vanderbilt and Sammons wings are more modern. The spa here is critically acclaimed. The spectacular golf course was designed by Donald Ross in 1926. *290 Macon Ave., (828) 252-2711, www.groveparkinn.com.*

NORTHEAST MIDWEST SOUTH WEST

Asheville

Folk Art Center. With a mission to preserve and interpret the folk arts of the southern Appalachians, this center has exhibition galleries with changing displays, a library, a bookstore, and the Allanstand Craft Shop. After a visit here, you'll better understand the artisans who create, sew, throw, weave, and whittle crafts unique to the Blue Ridge region. A BRP information desk will acquaint you with other area attractions, and a nearby trail will entice you to stretch your legs a bit more. *Blue Ridge Pkwy., MP 382, (828) 298-7928, www.southernhighlandguild.org.*

Biltmore Estate. Modeled after a 16th-century chateau in France's Loire Valley, George W. Vanderbilt's 250-room mansion was completed in 1895. America's largest privately owned home has more than 4 acres of floor space, 65 fireplaces, 43 bathrooms, 34 bedrooms, and 3 kitchens. You need a full day to explore the mansion, the gardens, and beyond; an estate tour is only part of the experience.

You can also visit the winery for tastings or tours, or stop by the Antler Hill Village, once the center of life for Vanderbilt employees who raised crops, tended livestock, worked in the Biltmore Dairy, and cared for the mansion. Today, the village is alive with blacksmiths, woodworkers, and other artisans. The Smokehouse serves barbecue, sandwiches, and traditional southern dishes. Note that reserving tour tickets in advance can save you a few bucks. *1 Lodge Rd., (800) 411-3812, www.biltmore.com.*

Chimney Rock

Chimney Rock Park. In Asheville, take U.S. 64 past Bat Cave (yes, Bat Cave) to Chimney Rock Park, where a 500-million-year-old rock tower, rising 1,200 feet above the Hickory Nut Gorge, dominates the landscape. Enjoy the view as well as the hiking trails and catwalks that stretch from rock to rock. (An elevator to the top has had issues; call ahead for its status.) After you explore, head a few miles farther east on U.S. 64 to picturesque Lake Lure. Its wide sandy beach will coax you to pause and enjoy the scenery. *Hwy. 64/74A (431 Main St.), (800) 277-9611, www.chimneyrockpark.com.*

Chimney Rock Park

Hendersonville Area

Curb Market. Since 1924, the only items sold at this indoor Hendersonville market are those grown, homemade, or handcrafted by Henderson County residents. Retail spaces are so prized that they're passed down through the generations. Drop by for blueberry jam, pickled okra, fried pies, moonshine jelly, walking sticks, and a heapin' helpin' of Southern hospitality. *221 N. Church St., (828) 692-8012, www.curbmarket.com.*

Pisgah National Forest. Closely associated with the Blue Ridge Parkway and abutting the Great Smoky Mountains National Park, Pisgah covers more than a ½-million mountainous western North Carolina acres. Within its boundaries are 138 miles of the Appalachian Trail, clear mountain streams known for excellent trout fishing, waterfalls surging into deep gorges, slippery Sliding Rock, and the Cradle of Forestry in America (once part of the Biltmore Estate, this was the nation's first forestry school). Fishing, whitewater rafting, and horseback riding are among the activities here. There are primitive backcountry campsites and established campgrounds with RV sites, which you can book through Recreation.gov. *1600 Pisgah Hwy., (828) 877-3265, www.fs.fed.us.*

Carl Sandburg Home. Carl Sandburg won Pulitzer Prizes for his poetry and his biography of Abraham Lincoln. The 245-acre Connemara estate in Flat Rock was his home for the last 22 years of his life. Inside the 22-room, circa-1838 residence, a three-year preservation project is under way through fall 2018. The Sandburgs' furniture and books have been removed from the rooms, but you can still explore the house's history through temporary exhibits that also discuss conservation efforts. Guided tours take about 30 minutes.

Outside, you can stroll along 5 miles of trails; visit outbuildings, including the goat barn, milk house, and springhouse; and savor the estate's hills, orchards, pastures, and lakes. If you're a real Sandburg fan, Connemara hosts presentations by authors and historians and cultural events like Memorial Day's Sandburg Folk Music Festival. The on-site bookstore offers volumes about Sandburg, Lincoln, Americana, and the national parks. *81 Carl Sandburg Ln., (828) 693-4178, www.nps.gov/carl.*

Thompson's Store. How country is the town of Saluda? Well, each Independence Day it's the site of the Coon Dog Day celebration, when mountain families come down to show off their hunting dogs. In the heart of this small community is the state's oldest shop: Thompson's Store was established in 1890 and still has its heart-pine flooring and tongue-and-groove walls. There's lots of Coon Dog Day merchandise, but the signature product is Thompson's Sage Sausage, made with a secret family recipe handed down since the 1940s. Next door, Ward's Grill serves down-home breakfasts, chili-cheeseburgers, and super-thick milkshakes. *24 Main St., (828) 749-2321, thompsons-store.com.*

Folk Art Center, Asheville

River Arts District, Asheville

That High Lonesome Sound

Like the landscape that gave it heart and soul, the root music of the Appalachians is spare, haunting, and spirited. Shaped by the inward focus of isolated communities, it's alternately called Appalachian, hill-billy, mountain, or old-time music. Instruments like the fiddle, banjo, mandolin, and dulcimer blend with pitched, harmonized vocals to make its characteristic "high lonesome sound."

Grand Ole Opry radio broadcasts, started in 1925, helped bring mountain music to the masses. And, in 1927, a western Virginia family, the Carters, made some of the first country music recordings at the now-famous Bristol Sessions. Their traditional Appalachian material, framed by guitar and autoharp, typifies the music still picked, plucked, and played in country stores, on porch stoops, and at regional festivals.

South Carolina: Highlights of Lowcountry

ROUTE TOWNS: North Myrtle Beach | Myrtle Beach | Murrells Inlet | Pawleys Island | Georgetown | Charleston | Beaufort | St. Helena Island

From the 60-mile stretch of golden Grand Strand beaches to the mansions of historic Charleston and Beaufort to the plantations and seaside towns in between, Lowcountry charms you with its historical and natural beauty, great food, and Southern hospitality.

Marsh near Charleston

A road trip along coastal South Carolina means a relatively straight shot through seaside towns, many of which seem frozen in the elegance of a different era. This trip begins near popular Myrtle Beach in the north and journeys south into cities steeped in some of that history—and draped in Spanish moss.

Plan to spend a few days exploring the vibrant city of Charleston, ranked the No. 1 city in the U.S. by *Travel + Leisure*. In the Holy City, so named for its many houses of worship, it's as if the past is living and breathing in the present. Antebellum mansions seemingly frozen in time are shaded by old-growth trees. Church bells, ships' horns, and the clip-clap of horses pulling touring carriages blend to create a time-honored symphony. Sweet tea and that fabled Southern hospitality charm all who visit.

Elsewhere along the road, when you're not learning to dance the shag in North Myrtle Beach, you'll be touring centuries-old plantations and snapping pictures of flowers at some of the oldest public gardens in the country. When you're not perfecting your backswing at famed golf courses on Kiawah Island, you'll be following in the footsteps of movie stars in Beaufort, which served as the backdrop for classics like *Forrest Gump*.

Atlas map E-13, p. 92

Distance: 220 miles point to point.

Type of Trip: Weekend Getaway; RV; Arts & Music, Great Outdoors, History & Heritage, Picture Perfect.

Must Try: Calabash-style seafood (fish or shrimp coated in a cornmeal batter and lightly pan-fried), a preparation that originated in North Carolina but is prevalent in Lowcountry South Carolina as well. Also, chicken bog: a thick, creamy chicken-and-rice dish that's slow cooked in a single pot.

Must Buy: A cotton rope hammock from the Original Hammock Shop; a handwoven sweetgrass basket.

Must See: Fat Harold's Beach Club, Myrtle Beach Boardwalk, Brookgreen Gardens, Fort Sumter National Monument, Middleton Place.

Worth Noting: Charleston is home to many interesting festivals including Charleston Fashion Week (Mar.), Spring Festival of Houses and Gardens (mid-Mar.–mid-Apr.), and Spoleto Festival USA, celebrating performing arts (late May–early June).

Travel Tips: In terms of the beach, things are at their best (weather-wise) and busiest June through August. Spring and fall bring cheaper prices and cooler temperatures, though you can still enjoy a beach vacation. Charleston is best enjoyed between March and May or September and November—without all that midsummer heat.

Note that in October 2016, Hurricane Matthew hit the coast, causing flooding, beach erosion, and tree loss. Some piers in Myrtle Beach sustained damage, and state parks, notably Hunting Island State Park and Huntington Beach State Park, closed temporarily. Although time inevitably brings a return to normalcy, it's worth checking the status of hard-hit sites.

North Myrtle Beach

Fat Harold's Beach Club. You can't blend in with the locals until you can dance like them, and in Lowcountry that means learning the shag. This is one of the best places to get in step. The king of shag and founder of this club, Harold Bessent, wouldn't have had it any other way. The Society of Stranders (SOS), a group devoted to the shag, holds events here, and the calendar is chockablock with dancing lessons—some of them free—and a revolving roster of DJs. *212 Main St., (843) 249-5779, www.fatharolds.com.*

Myrtle Beach

Myrtle Beach Boardwalk and Promenade. The heart of Myrtle Beach is its boardwalk, which runs from a pier at 14th Avenue North to another at 2nd Avenue North. For a gull's-eye view of all that sea and sand, take a spin on the SkyWheel. **Broadway at the Beach** (www.broadwayatthebeach.com) has that classic seaside carnival atmosphere, with more than 15 restaurants; several theaters; myriad specialty shops; and attractions like WonderWorks, Ripley's Aquarium, and the Hollywood Wax Museum. The nearby Pavilion Nostalgia and Carousel Park has tamer, more vintage offerings like funnel cake stands, kiddy rides, and the 1912 Herschell-Spillman Carousel. Mellower still are leisurely hand-in-hand strolls on the sand or along paved paths. *14th Ave. N. to 2nd Ave. N., myrtlebeachdowntown.com.*

Myrtle Beach

Murrells Inlet

Huntington Beach State Park. Find exceptional wildlife viewing in one of South Carolina's best-preserved state parks. Hiking and interpretive trails wind through habitats ranging from freshwater lagoons to salt marshes. More than 300 recorded species make it a premier birding site. The park also incorporates the historic Atalaya Castle, including the studio of sculptress Anna Hyatt Huntington, who, with her husband, Archer Huntington, also founded nearby Brookgreen Gardens. Visit in September to shop for jewelry, glassworks, ceramics, basketry and other works at the renowned Atalaya Arts and Crafts Festival. Outside the "royal" walls during the festival, fantastic music, Lowcountry cuisine, and beach parties reign. *16148 Ocean Hwy., (843) 237-4440, www.southcarolinaparks.com.*

Brookgreen Gardens. In 1931, four rice fields were transformed into public gardens that, today, often make top-10 lists of the nation's best. Themed landscape areas include Live Oak Allee, with trees planted as far back as the 18th century, and the Palmetto Garden, which features the Sabal palmetto, South Carolina's state tree. The gardens also showcase 1,400 works by 350+ American figurative sculptors—the country's largest collection. Kids love the zoo filled with Lowcountry creatures; the Enchanted Storybook Forest, with storybook playhouses; and the Children's Discovery Room and Sensory and Nature Trail. Seasonal offerings include a Butterfly House and Gullah cultural programs. Daily offerings include guided sculpture tours. *1931 Brookgreen Dr. (843) 235-6000, www.brookgreen.org.*

Pawleys Island

The Original Hammock Shop. It's hard to believe these soft, handmade, cotton-rope hammocks were first designed in 1889 out of sheer need to improve less-than-ideal sleeping conditions on a riverboat. Captain Joshua John Ward, who transported rice from plantations to the nearby coastal towns of Georgetown and Waverly Mills, wanted something to replace his grass-filled mattress, which was particularly uncomfortable on hot summer nights. Sailors told him about woven hammocks from Central America that allowed for cool, comfortable, shipboard sleep. Realizing he wouldn't be able to travel abroad to get one, he fashioned his own airy yet strong cotton version. It was so sturdy that it has withstood the test of time. Today you can visit the shop's weaving shed, where craftspeople weave a ¼-mile of white cotton rope into each classic hammock. The weave is then attached to a frame and finished off with traditional, self-tightening nautical knots. *10880 Ocean Hwy., (843) 237-9122, hammockshop.com.*

Georgetown

Cap'n Rod's Lowcountry Plantation Tours. Discover the histories and mysteries of the South during three- to four-hour boat tours, taking you past plantations, slave cabins, and abandoned rice fields. You'll even visit a beautiful lighthouse on Shell Island. Watch for wildlife along the way! Tours, offered Monday through Saturday, depart from the Harbor Walk behind the Rice Museum. All boats have shaded decks and on-board refreshments. Note that this is a cash-only operation. *701 Front St., (843) 477-0287, www.lowcountrytours.com.*

Rice Museum. The rice grown in South Carolina between the mid-18th and mid-19th centuries helped to feed the nation and to build many a planter's fortune. At this museum housed in two buildings—a one-time hardware store and a former market hall with an iconic clock tower—you'll learn just how important this crop was through exhibits of tools, maps, and dioramas. Watch video presentations, take a one-hour guided tour, and view displays of works by area artists. *633 Front St., (843) 546-7423, www.georgetown-sc.com.*

Eat & Stay

Original Benjamin's Calabash Seafood | Myrtle Beach. Nautical memorabilia sets the scene at the restaurant that introduced North Carolina's Calabash-style seafood (cornmeal battered and lightly pan-fried) to Myrtle Beach more than 30 years ago. This unique culinary style and a 170-item prix-fixe buffet have led locals to consistently name Benjamin's as a Best on the Beach restaurant. *9593 N. Kings Hwy., (843) 449-0821, www.originalbenjamins.com.*

Island Vista Oceanfront Resort | Myrtle Beach. This Grand Strand resort offers the perfect combination of luxury and family fun. Not only will you find elegant dining and relaxing spa treatments but also free programs for kids ages 5 to 12, including sandcastle building contests, scavenger hunts, pool games, and craft activities. *6000 N. Ocean Blvd., (843) 449-6406, www.islandvista.com.*

Ocean Lakes Family Campground | Myrtle Beach. This acclaimed mega-park's 859 campsites, complete with full hookups and Wi-Fi access, are nestled among 310 acres with eight lakes and prime Atlantic Ocean shore—all just 4 miles south of Myrtle Beach city limits. Pitch a tent or rent a trailer or beach house. On-site amenities include pools, miniature golf course, arcade, restaurant, store, and coin-op laundry. There's also a nature center with programs and exhibits geared to all ages. *6001 S. Kings Hwy. (843) 238-5636, www.oceanlakes.com.*

Lee's Inlet Kitchen | Murrells Inlet. Sample some award-winning Lowcountry cuisine at this family-owned restaurant that first opened its doors in 1948. Named one of South Carolina's Top 10 Seafood Restaurants by *Southern Living* magazine, this local favorite serves up such popular dishes as she-crab soup, oyster stew, shrimp Creole, and the catch of the day—caught off the Carolina shores and prepared in distinctive Murrells Inlet style. *4460 U.S. 17 Business, (843) 651-2881, www.leesinletkitchen.com.*

Mansfield Plantation | Georgetown. A mile-long canopy road, created by live oaks draped with Spanish moss, leads to a circa 1816 Federal-style main house on over 900 acres of plantation grounds. It's a Southern setting so beautiful it was used in Mel Gibson's *The Patriot*. Accommodations, with breakfast included, are in the redbrick Kitchen House (1800), School House (1840), and North Guest House (1930). Some of the nine rooms have four-poster beds; others have wrought-iron beds; all have private baths. *1776 Mansfield Rd., (866) 717-1776, www.mansfieldplantation.com.*

NORTHEAST

MIDWEST

SOUTH

WEST

city itinerary

Charleston

❶ Fort Sumter National Monument.
There's an eerie calmness at Fort Sumter, the same place that was shaken by explosions, setting in motion the American Civil War. In the early hours of April 12, 1861, the fort came under Confederate attack and surrendered 34 hours later. It was left a smoldering heap of ruins in Charleston Harbor. Over time, the fort was rebuilt and is now listed on the National Register of Historic Places, standing testament to the struggles of the past. View Fort Sumter from the Battery, then take a narrated ferry ride to the site, where rangers talk about the fort's history. Vessels operated by **Fort Sumter Tours** (843/722-2628, fortsumtertours.com) depart several times daily from Liberty Square, near the Fort Sumter Visitor Education Center. Trips last just over two hours. *Liberty Square, 340 Concord St., (843) 883-3123, www.nps.gov/fosu.*

❷ Charleston Museum. Though it closed for a short time during the Civil War, this museum, founded in 1773, is considered America's oldest. It's been steadily collecting artifacts, crafts, and antiques since the late 18th century and now paints a complete picture of South Carolina's natural and social history. Highlights include a large collection of silver items, displays of WW I and II weaponry, and mounts of extinct indigenous species like the Carolina parakeet. The Kidstory area has hands-on exhibits for youngsters and their families. *360 Meeting St., (843) 722-2996, www.charlestonmuseum.org.*

❸ Palmetto Carriage Works. Seeing the sites via horse-drawn carriage is a must-do in Charleston, and, as the oldest company of its kind in the city, Palmetto Carriage Works has perfected the one-hour, narrated experience. Each tour starts and ends at the Big Red Barn, where you can interact with the horses before or after being taken past mansions, gardens, and churches in the historic district. *8 Guignard St., (843) 723-8145, palmettocarriage.com.*

❹ Bulldog Tours. Wandering along tree-lined streets past colorful historic homes is a great way to soak up Charleston's Southern charm; taking one of the tours offered by this company is another. Guided history walks and immersive culinary experiences are among the options. For a spirited look at the city by the sea, though, look into one of the ghost-hunting expeditions, during which you'll visit cemeteries, churches, hidden alleyways, and the Old City Jail. *18 Anson St., (843) 722-8687, bulldogtours.com.*

❺ The Shops of Historic Charleston Foundation. Here you can select gift items and furnishings to bring home some local style and also support the foundation's ongoing preservation work. Whether you seek elegant reproduction china, pretty placemats, or a handy Charleston tote or dish towel, there are choices at all prices. You can even pick up Carolina rice, honey, or grits. Another store location is in City Market. *108 Meeting St., (843) 724-8484, www.historiccharleston.org.*

❻ Sound of Charleston. Every strum of the guitar and every tickle of the piano keys lulls you into the rhythm of the South. The Circular Congregational Church, in the heart of the historic district, is the site of these performances, featuring a revolving line-up of some of the city's top musicians and singers. Each 75-minute show takes you through four musical sets—from gospel to Gershwin. The songs of the Civil War era are

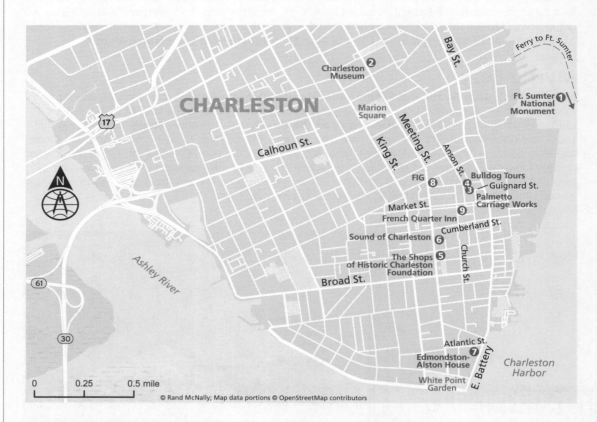

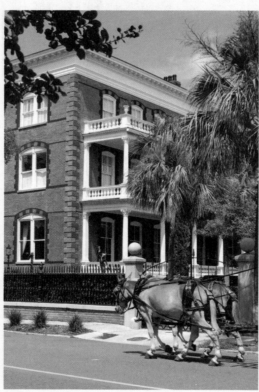

Charleston

plucked on banjo strings; spirituals once sung by slaves are belted by acclaimed gospel singers. *150 Meeting St., (800) 838-3006, soundofcharleston.com.*

❼ Edmondston-Alston House. This 1825 Greek Revival mansion offers unparalleled views of the Charleston Harbor from its seaside perch in the High Battery District. It was here that General P. T. Beauregard witnessed the attack on Fort Sumter in 1861, and where General Robert E. Lee retreated during a city fire. Today, the home showcases Southern affluence, filled with period furniture, artifacts, documents, silver, and china. Guided 30-minute tours are offered daily. If you feel too enchanted with the property to leave, you can spend the night at 21 East Battery B&B, a luxurious, privately owned home on the grounds. *21 E. Battery, (843) 722-7171, www.edmondstonalston.com.*

Eat & Stay

❽ FIG. A short but varied menu features such tantalizing dishes as cornflower-dusted grouper and the suckling-pig rice bowl, confirming something we all know to be true: Food Is Good (FIG). And here it's made with locally sourced ingredients to truly showcase the flavors of the Lowcountry. It's also served in an eclectic atmosphere FIG dubs "one part retro diner, one part neighborhood café, and one part elegant bistro." No surprise for this local favorite that in 2015 Chef Jason Stanhope won the James Beard Foundation's Best Chef Southeast award. *232 Meeting St., (843) 805-5900, www.eatatfig.com.*

❾ French Quarter Inn. If the numerous award plaques and accolades hung on the wall in reception don't convince you that this is one of the city's best hotels, then the grandeur of the lobby and its spiral, sky-lighted staircase probably will. Of course, pricy rates accompany all the critical acclaim, but there's really no better place to stay in the heart of Charleston's French Quarter. The spacious rooms are sumptuously appointed with European bedding; red medallion-patterned valences; ornate furniture; and rich gold, black, and white upholstery. Evenings see wine-and-cheese receptions and free milk and cookies; mornings see Continental breakfast. Bike rentals are complimentary, and you can arrange a massage in your room. *166 Church St., (843) 722-1900, fqicharleston.com.*

Middleton Place estate (above)
Cannon at Fort Sumter (right)

A Drive Into the Past

Before heading south from Charleston along the coast, consider a day trip northwest of downtown to sights that highlight the city's earliest days. About 6 miles out you'll come to the **Charles Towne Landing State Historic Site** (1500 Old Towne Rd., 843/852-4200, www.southcarolinaparks.com), an unusual park/museum that marks the site of the first English settlement in South Carolina. Highlights include interpretive facilities and tours; the Animal Forest, a natural habitat zoo showcasing creatures encountered by the first settlers; and the *Adventure*, a replica 17th-century trading ketch.

Another 12 miles northwest is **Middleton Place** (4300 Ashley River Rd., 843/556-6020, www.middletonplace.org), the estate of Henry Middleton, President of the First Continental Congress. Decorative and fine arts from the mid-18th to the mid-19th centuries document the history of this affluent South Carolina family in the 1755 South Flanker house. It's the only surviving residential structure of the three that were originally here. In addition to taking a 45-minute guided house tour, you can explore America's oldest formally designed garden, a vast landscape planted so that there's something blooming just about year round: camellias in the winter; azaleas in the spring; magnolias, crepe myrtles, and roses in the summer. You can also observe a working plantation, kayak down the Ashley River, or go horseback riding. This National Historic Landmark site also has a restaurant serving Lowcountry cuisine for lunch and dinner and an inn offering modern accommodations.

Beaufort

Kazoo Factory. This unconventional museum is always buzzing with activity—it *is* dedicated to kazoos, after all! Learn the history of this unique musical instrument through a fun video and guided tour. After you've seen the manufacturing process in the factory, you'll be able to make your own kazoo. *12 John Galt Rd., (843) 982-6387, www.kazoofactory.com.*

Beaufort Tours. Beaufort has been voted America's Happiest Seaside Town, and Beaufort Tours aims to show you why. Follow in the footsteps of Tom Hanks and Julia Roberts on the Beaufort Movie Tour, and see locations used in films like *Forrest Gump* and *Something to Talk About*. Visit a cotton plantation on the Plantation and Gullah Tour, or join a two-hour walking tour of Beaufort's historic district. *1006 Bay St., (843) 838-2746, www.beauforttoursllc.com.*

Beaufort Kayak Tours. All that water surrounding this beautiful city offers a unique way to take in the sights. Enjoy a history lesson while paddling around with a professional guide on one of six tours, each two to three hours in length. Visit Hunting Island State Park for some fishing and shell collecting; kayak past antebellum mansions and abandoned rice fields, or glide through salt marshes, keeping an eye out for blue crabs and bottlenose dolphins. *(843) 525-0810, www.beaufortkayaktours.com.*

St. Helena Island

Hunting Island State Park. Along with miles of sandy beaches and a lighthouse that's open to the public, this island has more than 5,000 acres waiting to be explored. White egrets, great blue herons, osprey, bald eagles, pelicans, loggerhead turtles, and alligators are some of the creatures that make their homes here. The park also has nature trails and a nature center, a fishing pier, a boat ramp, and a park store. In addition, there are tent and RV campsites (all of the latter have electric and water hookups) as well as cabins. Note that a two-night minimum stay is required, and reservations are a good idea. *2555 Sea Island Pkwy., (843) 838-2011, southcarolinaparks.com.*

Eat & Stay

Kiawah Island Golf Resort | Kiawah Island. The public Beachwalker Park on this barrier island 21 miles south of Charleston consistently makes Dr. Beach's list of America's best beaches. It's just one reason to visit. Golf is another. The island, much of which is a gated resort community, has five championship courses. Experience the resort side of things with a stay at the Sanctuary Hotel, a 255-room luxury property evoking a grand Southern manor. In addition to getting in a round or two of golf, you can play tennis on one of 24 courts, rent a bike and explore 30 miles of paved trails, and book a spa treatment. The property also has restaurants and shops. *1 Sanctuary Beach Dr., (843) 768-2121, www.kiawahresort.com.*

Lowcountry Produce Market & Café | Beaufort. This market and café strives to take you back to a time when family recipes were the only ones, and all the ingredients used for them *had* to be locally sourced. You can't go wrong with shrimp and grits, chicken salad, or a burger. Browse the retail area, and take home hand-packed and canned goods made on premises. *302 Carteret St., (843) 322-1900, lowcountryproduce.com.*

The Rhett House Inn | Beaufort. Although this award-winning 17-room inn looks like something out of *Gone with the Wind*, Tom Hanks stayed here while filming *Forrest Gump*. It's hosted other Hollywood stars, too: Barbra Streisand, Robert Redford, Sandra Bullock, Ben Affleck, Gwyneth Paltrow, Kevin Bacon, Kyra Sedgwick. Perfect for a romantic escape, girls' getaway, or even a golf retreat, this inn serves up Southern hospitality at its finest, from the glass of champagne on arrival to the homemade desserts in the evening. *1009 Craven St., (843) 524-9030, www.rhetthouseinn.com.*

We're Ready for Our Close-Up . . .

With such evocative scenery and architecture, it's no surprise that Charleston has served as the backdrop for many a Hollywood movie. But charming Beaufort has quite a few cinematic credits as well. Here's just a short list of productions shot in one or both of these cities:

Charleston: *The Prince of Tides* (1991); *Die Hard: With a Vengeance* (1995); *Legend of Bagger Vance* (2000); *The Patriot* (2000); *Cold Mountain* (2003); *The Notebook* (2004); *Dear John* (2010).

Beaufort: *The Big Chill* (1983); *The Prince of Tides* (1991); *Forrest Gump* (1994); *Something to Talk About* (1995); *G.I. Jane* (1997); *Legend of Bagger Vance* (2000).

NORTHEAST

MIDWEST

SOUTH

WEST

Historic Georgia: In and Around Savannah

ROUTE TOWNS: Savannah I Pin Point I Skidaway Island I Isle of Hope I Fort Pulaski I Tybee Island

In the so-called Hostess City of the South, you know folks are sincere when they say, "Ya'll come back now, ya hear?" And you'll find that same welcoming spirit everywhere you go—in town and out along the coast.

Forsyth Park, Savannah

This is the perfect weekend escape for, well, anyone: couples, families, best friends, beach lovers, history buffs. Although it takes you on side trips—east to Tybee Island and its beaches and southeast to several sites—it centers on Savannah's 2.2-square-mile Historic District. Here, trees are draped in Spanish moss, and streets are lined with buildings designed in Georgian, Greek Revival, Gothic, and other 18th- and 19th-century architectural styles. You can't help but feel like you've stepped back in time. Indeed, given that it was founded in 1733 by General James Oglethorpe, Savannah has seen every important moment in this country's history.

Hence the city that was the only major one to survive General Sherman's March to the Sea not only has Civil War and Underground Railroad sites, but also those dating from the Colonial and Federal periods. Savannah is also a bustling port. If you get the chance, be sure to see it from the water. Riverboat cruises provide a great perspective, as do boat tours of the riverfront and surrounding waterways. *The Waving Girl,* in the waterfront Morrell Park, is a statue of a young girl who "greeted" ships that came and went between 1887 and 1931. She's just one of many testaments to the bond between Savannah's people and its port.

Atlas map K-13, p. 28

Distance: 45 miles point to point (Savannah to Tybee Island via sights to the south); 18 miles point to point (Savannah to Tybee Island).

Type of Trip: Weekend Getaway; RV; Arts & Culture, History & Heritage, Picture Perfect.

Must Try: The fried chicken, buttered beans, sweet potatoes, okra, and other dishes served at Mrs. Wilkes Dining Room. Also: pimento sandwiches (yes, pimento); seafood (fried, grilled, or blackened); and crab stew.

Must Buy: Anything from the River Street complex's boutiques, galleries, and studios. Also, pottery, jewelry, handbags, clothes, and other items crafted by Savannah College of Art and Design (SCAD) students and sold in the **shopSCAD** (340 Bull St., 912/525-5180).

Must See: Telfair Museums, Forsyth Park, Bonaventure Cemetery, Pin Point Heritage Museum, Tybee Island.

Worth Noting: This town is up for a good time, with plenty of nightspots that you can hop between, drink in hand (just put it in a plastic cup). Savannah also has one of the country's largest St. Patrick's Day celebrations. "Midnight" the Book and Movie Tour, led by **Savannah Heritage Tours** (912/224-8365, www. savannahheritagetour.com), hits all the hot spots and then some from John Berendt's best-selling book, *Midnight in the Garden of Good and Evil.*

Travel Tips: Park the car and walk, particularly in the Historic District, bordered by the Savannah River to the north, Gwinnett Street to the south, Martin Luther King, Jr. Boulevard to the west, and Broad Street to the east. If you get tired, hail one of the ubiquitous pedicabs.

NORTHEAST MIDWEST SOUTH WEST

city itinerary

Savannah

1 Savannah History Museum. Housed in a converted railway station in Tricentennial Park, this museum offers a great introduction to the city's rich legacy. Exhibits highlight English settlement in 1733, the 1779 Siege of Savannah, the Civil War, the Industrial Revolution, and Savannah's music and arts scene. Across the street, Battlefield Memorial Park honors those who fought in the American Revolution's second-bloodiest battle. The site is also home to the Georgia State Railroad Museum and the **Savannah Children's Museum** (912/651-4292). Discounted combo tickets are available. The neighboring City of Savannah visitors center has maps and other information. *303 Martin Luther King, Jr. Blvd., (912) 651-6825, www.chsgeorgia.org.*

2 Green-Meldrim House. Savannah's 2.2-square-mile Historic District contains some of the nation's most important examples of 18th- and 19th-century architecture. Among the noteworthy buildings is the Green-Meldrim House, where General William Tecumseh Sherman stayed during Union occupation on the March to the Sea. Sherman considered Savannah too pretty to burn. Instead, he sent a letter to Abraham Lincoln giving him the city as a Christmas gift in 1864. Built in the early 1850s for a cotton magnate, the house (on the west side of Madison Square) is a beautiful example of antebellum Gothic Revival architecture; tours are offered. *14 W. Macon St., Madison Sq., (912) 233-3845, www.stjohnssav.org.*

3 Telfair Museums. Founded in 1886, the South's oldest art museum has three buildings, each containing works that correspond to the era in which it was built. Telfair Academy is home to 19th- and 20th-century American and European art; the Owens-Thomas House has a collection of late 18th- to early 19th-century decorative arts and an exhibit featuring an intact urban slave quarters; and the contemporary Jepson Center has the Glass House and the Sculpture Terrace. The terrace is a great place to take in the views of Telfair Square and the gold-domed City Hall. Another highlight is Sylvia Shaw Judson's *Bird Girl,* a statue made famous for being on the dust jacket of John Berendt's novel *Midnight in the Garden of Good and Evil.* *121 Barnard St., (912) 790-8800, www.telfair.org.*

4 Juliette Gordon Low Birthplace. The birthplace of Girl Scouts of the USA founder Juliette Gordon Low is a restored, 1821, Federal-style home. Located in the Historic District, "the birthplace," as it's called by Girl Scouts across the country, was the city's first National Historic Landmark. About 60,000 people tour the home each year, including 15,000 scouts on organized trips. *10 E. Oglethorpe Ave., (912) 233-4501, www.juliettegordonlowbirthplace.org.*

5 Forsyth Park. The southern edge of the Historic District is home to a 30-acre park with one of Savannah's most photographed attractions—the white, two-tiered, cast-iron fountain made famous in *Midnight in the Garden of Good and Evil.* Adults love the peacefulness of the park; kids love the open space. Saturday sees a great farmers' market here. *Bordered by Gaston St., Whitaker St., Drayton St., and Park Ave., (912) 651-6610, visithistoricsavannah.com/ forsyth-park.*

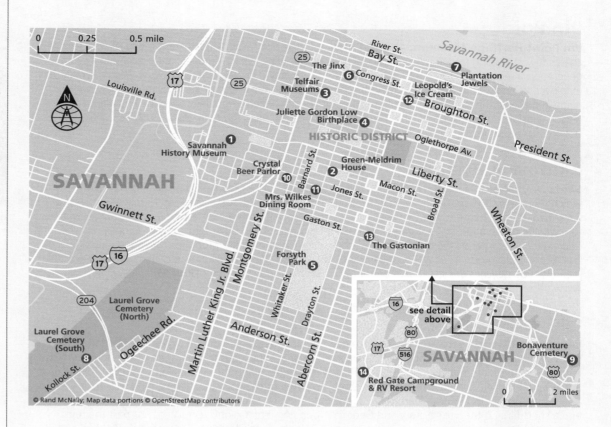

6 The Jinx. Deejays and touring bands perform alternative, hip-hop, and hardcore rock in a club where the aesthetic is punk meets Goth. Don't let the décor deter you. As one fan said, "You know how popular/awesome a place is by the number of bikes parked outside." *127 W. Congress St., (912) 236-2281.*

7 Plantation Jewels. Growing up in Savannah, the Chance brothers were constantly digging up bits of glass, ceramic shards, and antique buttons from construction sites. Many years later, those treasures have been turned into the unique jewelry you'll find at Plantation Jewels in the River Street plaza. It's a great way to take home a piece of Savannah history. There are plenty of pubs and restaurants in the complex as well. *502 East River St., Stall 71–72, (912) 667-4608, www.plantationjewels.com.*

8 Laurel Grove South Cemetery. Built in 1850, this historic cemetery has two sections. The 90-acre Laurel Grove South has more free African-Americans from the era of slavery buried in it than in any other Southeastern cemetery. Across the road, Laurel Grove North is the final resting place of more than 1,500 Confederate soldiers as well as Girl Scouts founder Juliette Gordon Low. *2101 Kollock St., (912) 651-6772, www.savannahga.gov.*

9 Bonaventure Cemetery. This gorgeously haunting cemetery is the final resting place for soldiers; statesmen; and such favored sons and daughters as the writer Conrad Aiken, singer-songwriter Johnny Mercer, and a young girl known as Little Gracie. Born in 1883, she died just 6 years later of pneumonia and was memorialized here with a life-size likeness by sculptor John Walz. Don't expect to find the figure of a girl that graced the cover of John Berendt's novel *Midnight in the Garden of Good and Evil.* After people trampled adjacent graves in their quest for the "bird girl," the statue was moved to Telfair Museums. Free, guided Bonaventure Historical Society tours are offered on the second Sunday (and preceding Saturday) of each month. *330 Bonaventure Rd., (912) 651-6843, www.bonaventurehistorical.org.*

Eat & Stay

10 Crystal Beer Parlor. Photos here regale the storied past of the city's second-oldest restaurant. What's rumored to have been a speakeasy during Prohibition was one of America's first restaurants to serve alcohol when the 18th Amendment was repealed. Stop in for the crab stew or a burger, but stay for the peach cobbler. Oh, and did we mention the beer? There's a varied list of American-made brews including "Beers of Our Fathers," with brands like Lone Star, Dixie, Iron City, and Genesee. *301 W. Jones St., (912) 349-1000, www.crystalbeerparlor.com.*

11 Mrs. Wilkes Dining Room. One of Savannah's most famous eateries always has a line out the door. Diners sit at tables of 10, which are set with every delectable Southern dish imaginable: fried chicken, meatloaf, black-eyed peas, collard greens, butter beans, red rice, candied yams. Menu options change daily, but you'll never be disappointed. It's family style, and, just like at home, you help yourself and clear your own plates. And this place doesn't take credit cards. *107 W. Jones St., (912) 232-5997, mrswilkes.com.*

12 Leopold's Ice Cream. In 1919, the Leopold brothers arrived from Greece in search of la dolce vita. The result of their quest was this ice cream parlor, where they served malts, milk shakes, black-and-white sodas, and club and pimento sandwiches—along with their famous ice cream. Today, there are more than 24 classic and seasonal flavors, from rum raisin and tutti frutti to Thin Mints & Cream. *212 E. Broughton St., (912) 234-4442, www.leopoldsicecream.com.*

(Savannah Eat & Stay cont. on p. B82)

NORTHEAST

MIDWEST

SOUTH

WEST

Pin Point

Pin Point Heritage Museum. About 11 miles southeast of Savannah, Pin Point is one of the Georgia coast's few remaining traditional Gullah-Geechee communities, where residents are descendants of first generation freed slaves. From 1926 until 1985, A.S. Varn & Son Oyster Seafood Factory was the area's main employer. Its closure threatened not only the community but also a way of life. This museum, however, helps to preserve the area's unique culture. Though you can take self-guided tours, the knowledge and personal insights of the docents who lead tours are priceless. *9924 Pin Point Ave., (912) 355-0064, www.chsgeorgia.org.*

Skidaway Island

Skidaway Island State Park. You can follow stretches of the Colonial Coast Birding Trail, along which more than 300 species have been spotted, through this 588-acre site about 13 miles southeast of Savannah. It's also home to the 1-mile Sandpiper and 3-mile Big Ferry trails as well as a boardwalk that leads to a wildlife observation tower. Keep an eye out for waterfowl and other birds as well as deer, raccoon, and fiddler crabs. An interpretive center has reference materials and ranger programs for young and old. Picnic facilities and playgrounds, as well as cabins and tent and RV sites (reservations required), are also available. Tybee Island's beaches are less than an hour away. *52 Diamond Causeway, (912) 598-2300, www.gastateparks.org/SkidawayIsland.*

Isle of Hope

Wormsloe Historic Site. In the 1730s, colonist Noble Jones carved out an impressive plantation just 8 miles southeast of Savannah. Today, a 1.5-mile, oak-lined avenue leads to what's left of the house, which remained in the Jones family until 1973. Like many residences along the Georgia and South Carolina coast, it was a "tabby house," built using cement that's a mixture of coastal materials like sand, water, lime, wood ash, and oyster shells. You can learn more about this at the on-site museum, which has excavated artifacts and a short film on the site's history and Georgia's founding. The Colonial Life Area, just past the ruins, often has docents in period costume demonstrating Colonial-era skills. *7601 Skidaway Rd., (912) 353-3023, www.gastateparks.org/Wormsloe.*

Fort Pulaski

Fort Pulaski National Monument. Although it predates the Civil War, this fort is most famous for a 30-hour 1862 bombardment that resulted in Union forces seizing it from the Confederates. This seizure proved that no fortress is invincible, changing military defense strategies the world over. Fort Pulaski is also notable for having been the first assignment of Robert E. Lee upon his graduation from West Point. The visitors center has historical exhibits and the 17-minute film, *The Battle for Fort Pulaski,* as well as a bookstore and gift shop. Ranger-led walks through the fort's interior are available. Self-guided tours of the fort's marshland territory range from ¼-mile to 2-miles long. Other recreational opportunities include fishing and biking. *U.S. Hwy. 80 E., (912) 786-5787, www.nps.gov/fopu.*

Tybee Island

Tybee Light Station and Museum. Given its 3-mile strand of gorgeous white sand and a location just 18 miles east of Hostess City, this barrier island serves as Savannah's public beach. Though it's walkable year round, peak season runs from Memorial Day through Labor Day. When temperatures rise to the 80s or high 90s, city dwellers come here to swim, sunbathe, gather shells, and play volleyball. There are special events, too, including the Beach Bum Parade in May and the Pirate Fest in October. Amenities include restrooms, snack bars, and restaurants. The island is also home to Georgia's oldest and tallest lighthouse, **Tybee Light Station and Museum** (30 Meddin Dr., 912/786-5801, www.tybeelighthouse.org). Georgia founder Gen. James Oglethorpe ordered its construction, which was completed in 1736; climb the tower's 178 steps for a view of the entire island. *802 1st St., (912) 786-5444, tybeeisland.com.*

Tybee Island

Green-Meldrim House, Savannah

Eat & Stay

13 **The Gastonian** I **Savannah** *(see map, p. B81).* Just a few blocks from beautiful Forsyth Park in the heart of the Historic District, The Gastonian offers Southern hospitality at its finest, thanks, in part, to the made-to-order breakfast, afternoon hors d'oeuvres, and evening dessert with coffee. Built in 1868, the B&B consists of two Regency Italianate-style mansions that are connected by an elevated walkway above a formal garden. The inn and its 17 rooms (many with fireplaces) are furnished with English antiques that provide 19th-century ambience amid modern comfort and service. *220 E. Gaston St., (912) 232-2869, www.gastonian.com.*

14 **Red Gate Campground and RV Resort** I **Savannah** *(see map, p. B81).* The 200-acre, former dairy farm that's home to this campground is about 8 miles west of Savannah's Historic District and about 22 miles from Tybee Island. It's easy to get off and on the highways, making it a good bet for larger RVs. Though few sites have much shade, there's plenty of room between them, and they're easy back-ins. The family-owned and family-friendly property has hiking and bridle trails and a clubhouse with a big screen TV and a pool table. The saltwater pool has an adjacent playground and covered deck, the ponds are stocked, and small boats are allowed. Laundry facilities and showers round out the amenities. *136 Red Gate Farms Trail, (912) 272-8028, www.redgatecampground.com.*

A-J's Dockside Restaurant I **Tybee Island.** When you're near the ocean, nothing's better than a classic beach-shack meal. Throw in great service and a deck (they call it a dock) that overlooks the Black River, and you've got A-J's. You'll be set with a selection of 46 beers; fresh fish choices like mahi mahi and flounder; and fried favorites like oysters, shrimp, and scallops. There are non-seafood choices, but why bother, when the crab stew is said to make your mouth water? You can also rent kayaks and paddle boards to explore the river. *1315 Chatham Ave., (912) 786-9533, ajsdocksidetybee.com.*

Miami and the Keys: Destination Paradise

ROUTE TOWNS: Miami | Coral Gables | Homestead | Key Largo | Islamorada | Marathon | Big Pine Key | Key West

There are few destinations in the Lower 48 that travelers might consider exotic, but, in south Florida, balmy, laidback Miami and Key West definitely qualify as tropical paradises.

Bahia Honda

With Miami's large and growing Cuban and Hispanic population—one that finds bilingual billboards joining bilingual radio, television, and newspapers—this vivacious city could be considered South America's northernmost capital. From here, you need only connect the dots via a 113-mile-long chain of islands to arrive in Key West.

This one-time hangout for pirates and—thanks to Jimmy Buffett ballads—drifters has become a bit busy in recent years, thanks to cruise ship docks, four-star resorts, and south Florida's gravitational pull siphoning travelers off from Orlando's theme parks. Additionally, improved relations with Cuba have increased the desire (and ability) to travel there, which likely means that Miami's popularity will surge as it becomes the departure point for a flood of Havana-bound travelers.

But when you make the decision to search for Buffett's fictional utopia, Margaritaville, and you leap from key to shining key, you'll find there are plenty of places that remain relatively untouched, undiscovered, and ready to reveal Florida in its natural state.

Distance: 170 miles point to point.

Type of Trip: Vacation Getaway; RV; Arts & Culture, Great Outdoors, History & Heritage.

Must Try: Lazing on the beach at Lummus Park along Ocean Drive; a Cuban sandwich in South Beach (better yet, Little Havana); conch fritters en route to the Keys.

Must Buy: If you're traveling to the capitals of Florida kitsch, why not invest in a couple of gems? A few favorites: a tropical Florida shirt, a conch shell, and a coconut carved like a face.

Must See: Sunrise from the News Café in Miami's Art Deco District. America's only living coral reef at the John Pennekamp Coral Reef State Park in Key Largo. Once-sunken treasures now displayed at the Mel Fisher Maritime Museum in Key West.

Worth Noting: Summer in south Florida is *hot, hot, hot,* though crowds are thin and rates are low. But if your schedule and budget allow a trip between late fall and early spring, you'll come to understand why fashion photographers schedule wintertime shoots here.

Travel Tips: There's only one road (U.S. 1) between Miami and the Florida Keys. If you miss something heading south, you'll have a chance to see it on the return trip. Some places on the Keys use a U.S. 1 address, but most use mile markers (MM). And "oceanside" or "bayside" in addresses refer to the south side (Atlantic Ocean) or north side (Florida Bay) of U.S. 1.

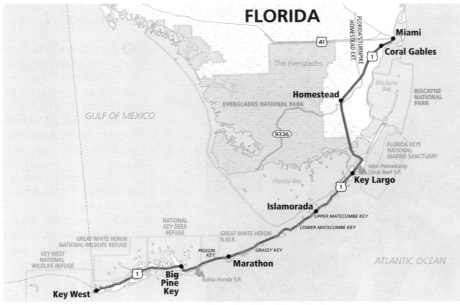

Atlas map P-13, p. 27

city itinerary

Miami, FL: An Art Deco Dream

In 1894, Julia Tuttle—a Miami resident who owned 640 acres—read that a winter frost had killed central Florida's citrus trees. Hers still had fresh orange blossoms, so she promptly wrote a letter to Henry Flagler, the multi-millionaire who was then developing a railroad along Florida's Atlantic coast. Enclosing some of the blossoms, she informed Flagler that Miami never freezes, and if he'd build a hotel there, she'd give him the land.

Flagler's arrival marked Miami's first boom; a second followed in the 1920s and a third in the 1950s. Miami's most recent renaissance began in 1984, when it was showcased on a hot new show (*Miami Vice*), introducing European fashion photographers to a new backdrop for wintertime shoots. When a famed Art Deco hotel was almost razed, a woman named Barbara Baer Capitman stepped in front of bulldozers—ultimately establishing the Art Deco District, on the National Register of Historic Places since 1979.

Travel Tips: Keep in mind that Miami is the city on the mainland. The focus of this itinerary is on Miami Beach, which anchors the south end of the barrier island off the coast of Miami and includes the Art Deco District and South Beach. And although it's only about 170 miles from Miami Beach to Key West, don't drive it in a single day—the culture, the scenery, and the sights call for a more leisurely pace.

Visitor Info: Greater Miami Convention & Visitors Bureau, *701 Brickell Ave., (305) 539-3000, www.miamiandbeaches.com.*

Miami

South Beach

❶ Art Deco Museum. The museum at the Miami Design Preservation League's welcome center showcases examples of Mediterranean Revival, Art Deco, and Miami Modern (MiMo) design. After viewing the exhibits, head out on either a 90-minute guided tour or a self-paced audio tour. You'll wander several blocks of South Beach while learning more about these architectural styles and why they suit the landscape. *1001 Ocean Dr., 2nd fl., (305) 531-3484, www.mdpl.org.*

❷ News Café. Every destination has a place where locals like to hang out. In Miami Beach, it's this little cafe that's the perfect place to grab a bite, read the paper, and people-watch anytime—it's open 24 hours. It's also fronted by Lummus Park, a palm-lined stretch along the Atlantic that runs from 5th to 15th streets. Bordering the News Café to the north and south are classic Art Deco Historic District buildings painted in bold colors and housing classic hotels, classy boutiques, a mix of simple and sophisticated restaurants, and a cool tropical vibe. *800 Ocean Dr., (305) 538-6397, www.newscafe.com.*

❸ The Wolfsonian–Florida International University. Sometimes you don't realize how much beauty there is in the world until you visit a place like the Wolfsonian. A former storage facility, built during Miami Beach's 1920s boom, somehow seems the perfect setting for the collection's 180,000-plus items. You'll be astounded by the variety of styles and pieces gathered from Europe and the U.S. Everything from Arts & Crafts and Art Nouveau to Art Deco and Industrial is reflected in the propaganda posters; rare books; furniture; and works in glass, ceramic, and metal. Tours, lectures, and films reveal how art and design simultaneously shape and reflect mankind's experiences. In a word: gorgeous. *1001 Washington Ave., (305) 531-1001, www.wolfsonian.org.*

❹ The Holocaust Memorial. In complete contrast to the surrounding joie de vivre of Miami Beach is this poignant tribute to the millions who suffered at the hands of the Nazis in WW II death camps. The somber memorial features a black-granite wall bearing the names of victims; a meditation garden; the Arbor of History; the Dome of Contemplation; and the 42-foot bronze *Sculpture of Love and Anguish,* a towering arm upon which figures climb in search of safety. *1933-1945 Meridian Ave., (305) 538-1663, holocaustmemorialmiamibeach.org.*

Eat & Stay

❺ Hotel Impala. The peaceful, tropical setting of this Mediterranean Revival–style hotel is just part of its appeal. Warm earth tones and accents of iron, stone, and mahogany lend a sense of tranquility. Rooms are clean, comfortable, and stylish, with upholstered Florentine-style headboards and brass and Murano-glass fixtures. Elegant without pretension, accommodations also feature a large bathtub or oversized walk-in shower. A cozy courtyard is an ideal place to relax; shops, restaurants, and nightlife are conveniently close on Ocean Drive and Lincoln Road; and the Atlantic is just two blocks away. The hotel offers a concierge, free Wi-Fi, and valet parking, and is pet-friendly. *1228 Collins Ave., (305) 673-2021, www.impala-miami.com.*

❻ Joe's Stone Crab Restaurant. Since 1913, this Miami Beach institution has served tons of stone-crab claws—backed up by butter, lemon wedges, and mustard sauce. Such a long-lived spot has the right to make its own rules: It doesn't take reservations, it has a dress code (casual but neat, no beach attire, no athletic wear, no cut offs), and its staff doesn't like to be in Miami in the summertime (it's closed May through mid-October, the off-season for stone crabs). *11 Washington Ave., (305) 673-0365, www.joesstonecrab.com.*

Art Deco architecture

Map labels:

MIAMI BEACH

Biscayne Bay

MIAMI

907

Meridian Av.

4 Holocaust Memorial

VENETIAN CAUSEWAY

Books & Books

7 Lincoln Rd. Mall

A1A

8 16th St.

The Abbey Brewing Company

SOUTH BEACH

Jungle Island 9

The Wolfsonian-Florida Int'l University

10th St.

5 Hotel Impala

3 Art Deco Museum

887

A1A

MACARTHUR CAUSEWAY

8th St.

1

Alton Rd.

Washington Av.

2 News Café

DOWNTOWN

5th St.

Ocean Dr.

Lummus Park

DODGE ISLAND

6

LITTLE HAVANA

Joe's Stone Crab Restaurant

South Pointe Park

S.W. 15th Rd.

FISHER ISLAND

ATLANTIC OCEAN

Miami River

RICKENBACKER CAUSEWAY

VIRGINIA KEY

S. Miami Av.

10 Vizcaya Museum & Gardens

Biscayne Bay

N

0   0.5   1 mile

© Rand McNally; Map data portions © OpenStreetMap contributors

NORTHEAST

MIDWEST

SOUTH

WEST

7 Books & Books. Miami is the perfect place to grab a good book and settle beneath a palm tree, at a sidewalk café, or on the beach. This independent, locally owned store (its other Florida locations include Bal Harbour and Coral Gables) specializes in books on art, design, fashion, architecture, and local culture; it regularly hosts evenings with recognized authors. The shop is amid the always-buzzing Lincoln Road pedestrian mall. *927 Lincoln Rd., (305) 532-3222, www.booksandbooks.com.*

8 The Abbey Brewing Company. What goes best with a warm, sunny beach? A cold, frosty brew. Join locals a few blocks south of popular Lincoln Road Mall and taste-drive four house beers—Immaculate IPA, Father Theodore's Stout, Brother Dan's Double, and Brother Aaron's Quadruple—all brewed by the Indian River Brewing Company, just up the coast. There are also 10 guest drafts, fine spirits, port wines, pub grub, and quality cigars. This place doesn't open till 1 pm, so you work on your tan before grabbing a cold one. *1115 16th St., (305) 538-8110, www.abbeybrewinginc.com.*

Biscayne Bay

9 Jungle Island. Opened in 1936 as Parrot Jungle, this park was later moved to Watson Island and renamed. It blooms with bananas, coconut palms, bromeliads, and banyan and sausage trees, which you can explore via 1.35 miles of trails. It's home to hundreds of birds from

myriad species as well as multitudes of animals ranging from alligators and snakes to llamas and leopards—even a set of twin orangutans. There's also a playground, a petting zoo, and a show featuring trained birds. *1111 Parrot Jungle Trail, (305) 400-7000, www.jungleisland.com.*

10 Vizcaya Museum and Gardens. One of the Northerners who took an interest in Miami during the 1920s boom was Chicago industrialist James Deering, who built his 34-room, neoclassical winter mansion on Biscayne Bay. It's as close to a palace as you'll find in America and has welcomed the world's notables, including Queen Elizabeth II, Pope John Paul II, Ronald Reagan, Bill Clinton, and Boris Yeltsin. The mansion is only part of the draw: The 10-acre estate includes gardens that are equally attractive. *3251 S. Miami Ave., (305) 250-9133, vizcaya.org.*

Vizcaya Museum and Gardens (above)
Jungle Island (left)

Venetian Pool, Coral Gables

Coral Gables

Venetian Pool. One of the most picturesque and refreshing places in the Miami area is smack dab in the middle of a residential district. In the 1920s, when George Merrick was designing the planned community of Coral Gables, he enlisted his uncle, Denman Fink, to do something creative with an empty rock quarry. Fink came up with a community swimming pool with a twist: it would incorporate a Venetian scene scape with gondolas and waterfalls amid a lush tropical landscape. Nearly 100 years after its premiere, the freshwater 820,000-gallon Venetian Pool is still making a splash. Amazingly, the pool is emptied and refilled each night from the aquifer below. Lockers, concessions, showers, and vintage photos round out this shaded, quiet retreat. *2701 De Soto Blvd., (305) 460-5306, www.coralgables.com.*

Homestead

Coral Castle. The story behind Coral Castle is almost as interesting as the attraction itself. After his 16-year-old sweetheart gave him the brush-off, 26-year-old Edward Leedskalnin left his homeland of Latvia to explore America. In 1936, he ended up in Homestead, bought 10 acres, and kept himself busy constructing a small village created from coral rock. Using only hand tools, it took Leedskalnin 28 years to construct what you see, preserved forever as a National Historic Site. How the 5'1", 100-pound amateur architect single-handedly maneuvered 1,100 tons of stone into place is a mystery no one has solved. *28655 S. Dixie Hwy., (305) 248-6345, coralcastle.com.*

Robert Is Here. South of Miami you'll find some of the state's most fertile farmland. To appreciate the variety of local crops, stop at this fruit stand, here since 1959. Sample small-batch honey with distinct flavors, find tropical produce, and order up a thick fresh-fruit milkshake. *19200 S.W. 344th St., (305) 246-1592, robertishere.com.*

Key Largo

John Pennekamp Coral Reef State Park. Here's a state park with a twist: Most of it is underwater. It starts a foot off shore, flows outward 3 miles into the Florida Straits, and encompasses the only living coral barrier reef in the continental United States and roughly 200 islands and islets. Nearby dive shops can get you ready to discover this underwater world. It's said there are 55 varieties of coral and 500 species of fish, ranging from blue-striped grunts to green moray eels. Shipwrecks here date from as far back as the 1600s.

Non-divers will also find plenty to do. There's a 30,000-gallon aquarium to explore and four types of boat tours, including one aboard glass-bottom vessels that let you stay high and dry while viewing the reefs. You can also rent a canoe or kayak or simply park yourself by the lagoon and enjoy the calm waters and sunshine. Campsites are available, and RVs are welcome. Nearly 50 sites have full hookups; each site has a picnic table and grill. If you stay here (or anywhere in the Keys), bring a telescope or binoculars to watch the night sky. It's clearer here than nearly anywhere else in Florida. *102601 Overseas Hwy. (MM 102.5, Oceanside), (305) 451-1202, www.floridastateparks.org.*

African Queen. Through a series of complicated events, the original *African Queen,* used in the film of the same name starring Humphrey Bogart and Katharine Hepburn, ended up in Key Largo (then again, Bogart did star in the 1948 film *Key Largo* . . .). Anyway, after receiving a $70,000 makeover, the *African Queen* was once again shipshape and now departs on two-hour canal cruises or semi-private dinner cruises off Key Largo (times vary; reservations recommended); she's even been named a National Historic Site. Even if you don't set sail, you can see her moored beside the Holiday Inn—well worth a quick stop for a selfie. *99701 Overseas Hwy. (MM 100), (305) 451-8080, www.africanqueenflkeys.com.*

Islamorada

Anne's Beach. On Lower Matecumbe Key, you can stretch out on the sand and slip your toes into turquoise water. Enjoy a swim in the calm, clear Atlantic Ocean while kiteboarders take advantage of tropical sea breezes. See fishermen, stone crabbers, and lobster divers capture their bounties. Linger along a secluded boardwalk, walk your dog, and picnic at shaded tables among the native mangroves. Park in either of two small lots ¼ mile apart. The best news? It's all free. *Overseas Hwy. (MM 73.5, Oceanside), annesbeach.com.*

Eat & Stay

Biltmore Hotel I **Coral Gables.** Had you attended its premiere in January 1926, you would have entered one of Miami's most elegant hotels. The $10 million palace served as "the center of sports and fashion" as well as a retreat for the Duke and Duchess of Windsor, Ginger Rogers, Judy Garland, Bing Crosby, and assorted Roosevelts and Vanderbilts. Following decades of disrepair, a multimillion dollar renovation in the 1980s restored its Spanish Mediterranean grandeur. Today its 145 guest rooms and 130 suites feature European feather beds, tropical-patterned duvets, and sofas and easy chairs. On-site amenities include French and Mediterranean restaurants, an 18-hole golf course, a fitness center and spa, 10 lighted tennis courts, and one of the country's largest hotel swimming pools. *1200 Anastasia Ave., (305) 445-1926, www.biltmorehotel.com.*

Lorelei Restaurant and Bar I **Islamorada.** How will you know when you've reached this low-key hangout? Just look for the massive mermaid billboard—a clear sign of the region's tropical vibe. A popular spot for motorists and motorcyclists who want to take a jaunt without going the full distance to Key West, Lorelei's bayside setting and island-style veneer capture the look and feel of an authentic Florida hangout. Along with coconut shrimp, conch chowder, draft beers, and tropical drinks, each evening at sunset there's a celebration to a soundtrack of live music. *81924 Overseas Hwy. (MM 82, Bayside), (305) 664-2692, loreleicabanabar.com.*

Key Largo reef

Marathon

Dolphin Research Center. This marine research and educational facility also helps the area's injured marine animals and is the only federally licensed facility in Florida that's allowed to help injured manatees. Atlantic bottlenose dolphins and California sea lions are the center's main residents; learn about their personalities and behaviors. In addition to educational tours and shows, for an extra fee you can enter the water and interact with the dolphins (reservations are required). *58901 Overseas Hwy. (MM 59), Grassy Key, (305) 289-1121, www.dolphins.org.*

Pigeon Key. In the early 1900s, the Overseas Railroad (the brainchild of Henry Flagler) was being constructed to connect Miami to Key West. This 5-acre island was the base camp for hundreds of men working on the project, until the Labor Day Hurricane of 1935 wiped out as much as 40 miles of track. The rail was never rebuilt, and today the original tin-roofed, wood-clapboard buildings form a museum on the National Register of Historic Sites. There are snorkeling, picnicking, and photo ops aplenty. Tours are offered by the Pigeon Key Foundation via a ferry that departs for the island three times daily for a 2.5-hour visit. *1 Knights Key Blvd. (MM 47), (305) 743-5999, www.pigeonkey.net.*

Big Pine Key

Bahia Honda State Park. It was just another island until Henry Flagler's railroad connected the mainland to Key West. Even though the railroad is gone, Bahia Honda became one of the southernmost state parks in America. If you stop before reaching Key West—a little more than a half hour away—you'll find camping (full-facility campsites and vacation cabins), fishing, diving, snorkeling, hiking, kayaking, and one of the country's top beaches. Snap photos of Flagler's historic railroad trestle, and enjoy the Atlantic and Gulf of Mexico views. Relax on the beach; take a swim in the calm, clear water; explore the nature trail; or picnic in one of the pavilions. For a few hours or a few days, the park has year-round appeal. *36850 Overseas Hwy. (MM 37), (305) 872-2353, www.floridastateparks.org.*

National Key Deer Refuge. Standing just about 2 feet high, key deer are miniature versions of their much larger cousins, the white-tailed deer. When their numbers were rapidly dwindling in the 1950s, they were given the protection of this 9,200-acre refuge comprised of pine rockland forests, freshwater wetlands, saltmarsh wetlands, and mangrove forests. Within its boundaries, deer numbers have increased to nearly a thousand, an indication that they, like other refuge wildlife, are thriving. There are walking trails, wildlife viewing areas, and a visitors center less than a mile from the intersection of U.S. 1 and CR 940. *28950 Watson Blvd. (MM 33), (305) 872-0774, www.fws.gov/nationalkeydeer.*

Key West

Sloppy Joe's. Sometimes it seems that this is the most popular bar on earth. While it's not the original bar that Ernest Hemingway frequented (that was around the corner), its inspiration (the Blind Pig) opened after Prohibition ended. The current incarnation has been on the corner of Duval and Greene since 1937. Its clientele includes a mix of locals, cruise ship passengers, college students, and hardcore barflies. When you're here working on a cold beer, a margarita, or something less potent, there's a palpable satisfaction knowing that you're experiencing tropical history—not to mention some live music, which is often played here until the wee hours. *201 Duval St., (305) 294-5717, sloppyjoes.com.*

Ernest Hemingway Home, Key West

Ernest Hemingway Home and Museum. In the 1930s, Ernest Hemingway made Key West his home. Some say it was the idyllic setting of Key West that inspired him to write classics like *For Whom the Bell Tolls, To Have and Have Not,* and *A Farewell to Arms* from the privacy of his second-story writing room. Others say it was sheer coincidence. Regardless, the works earned him the 1954 Nobel Prize for Literature. Today, his former home is a museum whose popularity often results in crowded tours—but it's considered a Key West must. Stroll the grounds for a more peaceful experience and to see descendants of Hemingway's legendary six-toed cats. Note that the museum is a cash-only enterprise. *907 Whitehead St., (305) 294-1136, www.hemingwayhome.com.*

Mel Fisher Maritime Museum. Mel Fisher spent decades searching for treasure-laden Spanish galleons sunk by hurricanes in the Florida Straits. In 1985, he hit the mother lode when he found the circa 1622 wrecks of the *Santa Margarita* and *Nuestra Senora de Atocha*—the *Atocha* carried $450 million in gold, silver, and emeralds. Much of what Fisher didn't cash in on (to cover expenses and investors and to finance a comfortable lifestyle) is on display here, including a 6-pound gold bar and a 77-carat uncut emerald. *200 Greene St., (305) 294-2633, www.melfisher.org.*

National Key Deer Refuge, Big Pine Key

Touring the Keys

Upon arriving in Key West, consider climbing aboard the kitschy **Conch Tour Train** (303 Front St., 305/294-5161, www.conchtourtrain.com). Its 90-minute tours sweep through Key West's popular spots, providing information about the area's history and heritage and the progress it's made over the years. After the tour, you'll have a better sense of what you'd like to see more of—and how to get there.

If sightseeing from the water's your thing, there are numerous options for reef snorkeling, parasailing, jet skiing, or kayaking. A host of charter services and pleasure excursions depart from the marina near Mallory Square. One of these is **Fury Water Adventures** (313 Margaret St., 305/294-8899, www.furycat.com). Its catamaran trips are especially popular. We suggest a sunset cruise, which includes live music and champagne, beer, wine, or soda to toast the setting sun.

For a completely unique Key West experience, sign up for an evening tour with a macabre, costumed host from **Ghost Tours of Key West** (432 Greene St., 305/294-9255, www.hauntedtours.com). It might convince you that this is the country's most haunted place. Tours take you through the heart of the town, filling you in on ghost sightings, unexplained happenings, and a very weird and animated doll named Robert.

Harry S. Truman Little White House. Believe it or not, Key West became popular because Harry Truman was poor. Even as president, Truman never had much money, so when he needed a vacation he had to narrow down his choices to government facilities. Ultimately, he chose the naval station at Key West, and, over the course of his 11 visits, the press traveled in tow, propelling the legend of Key West around the world through newspapers and magazines. Today, 45-minute guided tours take you through the well-preserved (and very down-to-earth) home that served as the wintertime "Little White House." You'll see where Truman worked, the table where he played poker with his pals, and the beautiful gardens surrounding his paradise retreat. *111 Front St., (305) 294-9911, www.trumanlittlewhitehouse.com.*

Key West Lighthouse and Keepers' Quarters Museum. There are only 14 lighthouses in America older than this one, which was activated in 1848, and, uniquely, with a woman as keeper. Climb the 88 steps to the top, where you can take in a wonderful view of the island; it's a perfect vantage point for photographs. Afterward, tour the Keepers' Quarters filled with instruments, maps, and photos that depict a rich maritime history. *938 Whitehead St., (305) 294-0012, www.kwahs.org.*

Fort Zachary Taylor Historic State Park. Although it was active during both the Spanish-American and Civil wars, this fort wasn't completed until 1866. It was one in a series of forts designed to defend the nation's southeastern coastline. There are guided and self-guided tours of the National Historic Landmark. Bring a camera for the incredible fort-top view of the confluence of the Atlantic Ocean and Gulf of Mexico. Barbecue in the shade of trees, lie on the sandy beach, or do some geocaching. Snorkel and see reef fish, coral, lobster, sponges, and stingrays in the calm, clear water. The park's beachfront Cayo Hueso Café offers snacks, cold beverages, beach sundries, and souvenirs. *601 Howard England Way (end of Southard St. on Truman Annex), (305) 292-6713, www.floridastateparks.org.*

Mallory Square Sunset Celebration. In a tradition dating from the 1960s, about an hour before sunset, crowds gather at the waterfront to watch street performers put on nightly shows (some of which are quite extraordinary) for free, though there's a not-so-subtle hint to leave a tip in their hats. An assortment of entertainers—tightrope walkers, jugglers of torches or chainsaws, musicians, strongmen, trained acrobatic cats—make this sunset celebration one of the most popular shows in Florida. After the sun has set, stay to shop. This is a great place to find hand-painted T-shirts, jewelry, and other crafts displayed by artists and crafters. *1 Whitehead St., www.sunsetcelebration.org.*

Southernmost Point. One of the country's most photographed landmarks, the giant yellow, red, and black, buoy-shaped monument marks the Southernmost Point in the continental United States and notes that Cuba is only 90 miles away (if you're up for a swim). It can get very crowded during the day; arrive early and catch a sunrise photo. *Whitehead and South St., southernmostpointwebcam.com.*

Audubon House. This ambitious restoration project is housed in and around the 19th-century home of Captain John H. Geiger. It honors the work of John James Audubon, the famed ornithologist and painter who visited the Florida Keys in 1832. A self-guided tour of the gardens offers a close look at tropical flora such as orchids, bromeliads, and herbs. A bonus: The mansion houses 28 first editions of Audubon's books. *205 Whitehead St., (305) 294-2116, audubonhouse.com.*

Key West aerial view

Eat & Stay

Half Shell Raw Bar | **Key West.** Once a destination becomes popular, it seems small restaurants are shoved aside to make room for chains. Thankfully, the fiercely independent Half Shell Raw Bar retains the vintage feel that it established back in 1972, when it was created within an old shrimp warehouse. If you'd like to see what Key West looked like before it was tamed by cookie-cutter hotels and stores, this cavernous dockside barn is a good place to start. Plus, the menu's loaded with oysters, chicken, burgers, ribs, crab, lobster, conch, grouper, mako, wahoo, and other fish—broiled, grilled, blackened, or fried. *231 Margaret St., (305) 294-7496, www.halfshellrawbar.com.*

Paradise Inn | **Key West.** The light tan, white, and beige palette will soothe you; the sun streaming through wooden-louvered blinds will cheer you; and the gentle whir of ceiling fans will keep you calm and cool. Gardens filled with fragrant flowers and trees surround the old-time cigar-makers' cottages and traditional Bahamian-style houses containing spacious rooms and suites. You'd never know that Key West's lively Old Town—with all its nightspots, restaurants, and shops—is just steps away. And, although the architecture and setting nod to Old Florida, the décor and amenities are all Florida contemporary. Relax still further by the pool or lotus pond or by taking a dip in the Jacuzzi. Continental breakfast and afternoon wine and cheese are included in the rates. *819 Simonton St., (305) 293-8007, www.theparadiseinn.com.*

Fort Jefferson

From Ponce de Leon to National Park

Though these islands were first seen by Ponce de Leon in 1513, it wasn't until 1846 that construction began on Fort Jefferson, then the nation's largest coastal fortification. In 1908, decades after serving as a Civil War military prison, the area was designated a wildlife refuge. In the century since, **Dry Tortugas National Park** (Ranger station in Homestead, 305/242-7700, www.nps.gov/drto) has become a valuable, relatively undisturbed sanctuary. Shallow, blue-green waters cover coral reefs teeming with underwater life, including the loggerheads, hawksbills, and green sea turtles that frequent this 100-square-mile area.

Be advised that, before you see any of this, you'll first have to get here—either by ferry (from the foot of Grinnell St. in Key West) or by float plane—which is no small feat (and no small fee), since it's 70 miles offshore. Once here, however, you can take a ranger-led tour, stay the night at one of 10 primitive campsites, snorkel around Garden Key, fish from the dock, or go farther afield and boat to Loggerhead Key and its circa 1856 lighthouse. Between February and September, binoculars will help you focus on an estimated 100,000 sooty terns nesting on nearby Bush Key.

Southernmost Point Marker, Key West

NORTHEAST

MIDWEST

SOUTH

WEST

Florida's Cultural West Coast

ROUTE TOWNS: Fort Myers | Sarasota | Bradenton | St. Petersburg

Western Florida's sandy shores, Gulf waters, and warm days attract vacationers year-round. But it's more than just sun, sand, and surf that sparkle here. There are also many shining cultural, art, and historical attractions.

Fort Myers

Among the notables you'll encounter on this journey are Hernando de Soto, Thomas Edison, Henry Ford, and John Ringling. In Fort Myers and Sarasota, you can tour elegant gardens and grand estates, get inside the heads of two of the country's greatest 20th-century innovators, step right up to see what life was like behind the scenes and in the rings of "The Greatest Show on Earth," and follow in the footsteps of early Spanish conquistadors.

St. Petersburg has a trio of world-class museums. One showcases everything from American master photographers, like Ansel Adams and Alfred Stieglitz, to Europe's grand masters. Another contains the largest American collection of works—across all media—by surrealist Salvador Dali. A third highlights the colorful, awe-inspiring works of American glass artist and sculptor Dale Chihuly. Along the way, you can sample Southern fare and seafood, stay in a hotel that's been the property of choice since the Roaring Twenties, dance the salsa, sip sangria, and, of course, bask in all that sparkling sun, sand, and surf.

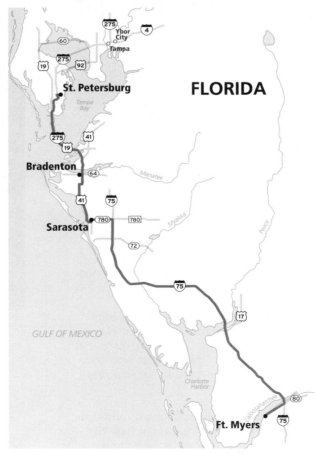

FLORIDA

Atlas map N-9, p. 27

Distance: 117 miles point to point.

Type of Trip: Weekend Getaway; Arts & Culture, History & Heritage, Picture-Perfect.

Must Try: Stone crabs in season (mid October to mid May) at Pinchers in Fort Myers; Cuban sandwiches at Columbia restaurant in Ybor City, Tampa's Latin district.

Must Buy: A surreal souvenir at the Dali Museum.

Must See: Edison & Ford Winter Estates, Circus Museum at The Ringling, Dali Museum, Chihuly Museum, manatees at the South Florida Museum, Aquarium & Planetarium.

Worth Noting: Northeast of downtown Tampa, roughly 30 miles across the bay from St. Pete, is the historic Ybor City district, established in the 1880s as a cigar-manufacturing community and populated by Cuban, Spanish, Italian, and other immigrants. It's now considered Tampa's Latin Quarter and makes a great side trip from St. Pete, thanks to its coffee shops, where you can smell the beans roasting; restaurants, including some classic Cuban and tapas spots; and clubs where the salsa music begs you to dance.

Travel Tips: To reach St. Petersburg from Bradenton (via Terra Ceia), you'll no doubt follow I-275/US 19 across the magnificent 4-mile Sunshine Skyway Bridge. Additionally, three bridges connect St. Petersburg with Tampa, though if you're heading directly to Ybor City, the Howard Frankland is your best bet. This trip is a great complement (or alternative) to visits to Orlando's theme parks. Sarasota is only about 130 miles southwest of Orlando—a really quick trip along I-4 to I-75. Tampa is a straight 85-mile shot from Orlando along I-4.

Fort Myers

Edison & Ford Winter Estates. There's a lot to explore at this truly unique sight, which includes two estates along the Caloosahatchee River (Thomas Edison's Seminole Lodge and Henry Ford's The Mangoes), remarkable gardens, and a memorabilia-filled museum. Edison spent part of each year in Fort Myers from 1886 until his death in 1931. His good friend, Henry Ford, bought the neighboring property in 1916, and the two innovators not only socialized but also collaborated.

Though the gardens are beautiful, Edison actually designed them to be utilitarian rather than decorative—a sort of proving ground for plants. Edison, Ford, and their friend Harvey Firestone were on a quest for a domestic rubber source, so Edison established a botanical research company and laboratory on the grounds of his estate. Today, you'll find more than 1,700 types of plants. Don't miss the banyan tree, one of the nation's oldest, or the Heritage Gardens, which once provided food for the tables of both families.

Highlights in the museum include Edison inventions (and a timeline of them), the custom Model T that was a gift from Ford himself, botanic research lab artifacts, and many pictures and documents. One exhibit even showcases the camping trips the two friends took across the United States, complete with Ford's 1918 custom-built Model T camper. Self-guided audio tours are available, but the historian-led tours (1¼ hours, departing daily on the hour 10–4) are highly recommended. *2350 McGregor Blvd., (239) 334-7419, www.edisonfordwinterestates.org.*

Circus painting from The John and Mable Ringling Museum of Art (top)
Ca' d'Zan Estate at The Ringling (above)

Sarasota

Ca' d'Zan Estate at The Ringling. The Ringlings built their bayside, Venetian Gothic–style palazzo and gardens in 1924–25 and named it Ca' d'Zan (House of John). The best way to see the 41-room, 15-bathroom property is on the 45-minute Private Places tour, which gets you access to the upstairs rooms and, on nice days, the 81-foot Belvedere Tower. It's easy to see where the original $1.5 million construction budget went, with such luxuries as the living room's painted cypress ceiling, the Sienna marble tub in Mr. Ringling's bathroom, and the circus-themed games room. Donated to the state in 1936 upon John Ringling's death, Ca' d'Zan had fallen into utter disrepair by the 1990s. It took 6 years and $15 million to bring it back. After your visit, you might agree it was money well spent.

Circus Museum at The Ringling. Step right up to see all the wonders of the circus—from costumes and props to banners and posters to wagons of all types. You can even check out the elegant railcar that John and Mable used when traveling with the family business. Don't miss the miniature model circus that took master model builder Howard C. Tibbals *50 years* to create. It features 8 tents and more than 42,000 hand-carved pieces.

Museum of Art at The Ringling. First opened in 1931, the footprint of this museum recalls that of the Uffizi Gallery in Florence. The collection is no less grand, with paintings by European Old Masters as well as American and Asian art and artifacts. There's also a sculpture-filled courtyard and a wing for special exhibitions. Guided tours of the permanent collection include one that offers just the European highlights and another that provides a more in-depth look. You can also arrange docent-led tours of the temporary exhibitions.

Historic Asolo Theater at The Ringling. This majestic, 18th-century theater was originally constructed in Asolo, Italy, for the Queen of Cyprus. Dismantled and hidden away during WW II, it was purchased by John Ringling in 1949 and reconstructed at The Ringling Complex. Today, it hosts plays, lectures, movie screenings, and dance and music performances. *Box Office: (941) 360-7399.*

The Ringling Complex

Given that Sarasota was the one-time winter home of the Ringling Brothers and Barnum & Bailey Circus, it's no surprise that John Ringling and his wife, Mable, built an estate here. Its restored buildings and grounds now make up a veritable arts campus—with something for everyone in the family and complete with a café, a restaurant, and a museum store. You could easily fill a day or two, and possibly an evening, here.

Admission to the 66-acre complex includes access to all but the theater performances (at the Asolo and the Florida State University Center for the Performing Arts, also on the grounds). Three-day passes are also available, and the guided tours, particularly of Ca' d'Zan, are well worth the extra fees. If you're here in October, don't miss the Ringling International Arts Festival. *5401 Bay Shore Rd., (941) 359-5700, www.ringling.org.*

Dale Chihuly sculpture (above)
The Dali Museum (right)

Bradenton

South Florida Museum, Aquarium & Planetarium. Florida's natural and cultural history are the focus here. In the museum, two floors of galleries display prehistoric animal skeletons and Native American pottery and jewelry, as well as colonial artifacts and Americana ranging from cut-glass "trading beads" used by the Spanish to medical equipment from the 19th and early 20th centuries. At the 60,000-gallon Parker Manatee Aquarium, you'll learn about Florida's state marine mammal and meet the beloved Snooty, the world's oldest known manatee. The Bishop Planetarium features astronomy shows and virtual journeys into space. *201 10th St. W., (941) 746-4131, www.southfloridamuseum.org.*

De Soto National Memorial. In 1539 Spanish explorer Hernando de Soto landed on the Florida coast. Searching for gold, he and his conquistadors spent four years marching through the southeastern section of the present-day United States. De Soto died in 1542, but his men followed the Mississippi south, ultimately reaching Mexico. This memorial gives you a taste of their journey. The visitors center has a short film and changing displays of artifacts that include weaponry and a suit of armor.

December through April, in the re-created Camp Uzita, docents in period costume demonstrate how the conquistadors survived in their new and sometimes hostile environment. You can also follow a ½-mile Nature Trail through mangrove forest, perhaps spotting pelicans, herons, and other birds or animals that de Soto and his men would have encountered as well. Plaques discuss the expedition and the vegetation and wildlife. Plan to spend about an hour at the De Soto National Memorial—or at least some time walking the dog. Leashed pets are permitted. *8300 De Soto Memorial Hwy., (941) 792-0458, www.nps.gov/deso.*

St. Petersburg

The Dali Museum. Who knew that South Florida had the world's most comprehensive collection of Salvador Dali's oils, watercolors, drawings, graphics, photographs, sculptures, and objets d'art? Exhibits are themed and arranged to help you understand relationships between the pieces and key transition periods in the Spanish surrealist's career. In addition to guided tours, there are daily kids programs and a roster of film series, curator talks, and Sunday Yoga + Dali sessions. The gift store is a great place to pick up a "melting clock" ornament or other surreal souvenirs. *1 Dali Blvd., (727) 823-3767, thedali.org.*

Chihuly Collection. What do Native American baskets, marine life, chandeliers, and Japanese flower arrangements have in common? They all influence the colorful, textural, blown-glass sculptures of Dale Chihuly. The Washington State artist draws from his background in architecture, interior design, and art. To learn his craft, he studied under American masters as well as those at Italy's prestigious Venini glass studio. His singular pieces and full—often enormous—installations have been exhibited in museums throughout the world, including the Smithsonian, the Louvre, and the New York Botanical Garden.

A purpose-built facility houses the magnificent pieces in this permanent collection; visits here are truly stunning visual experiences. A 30-minute video introduces you to the artist and his works, docent-led tours lend still more insight, and a gift shop sells Chihuly merchandise. The collection is affiliated with the Morean Arts Center, directly across the street, which is known for its on-site Glass Studio and Hot Spot where you can watch master glass-blowers at work and enjoy your own personal glass-blowing experience. *720 Central Ave., (727) 822-7872, www.moreanartscenter.org/chihuly.*

Museum of Fine Arts. This museum has one of the finest photography collections in the South, with works by Alfred Stieglitz, Ansel Adams, and Walker Evans, among others. The collection also includes European and American masterpieces, a Steuben glass gallery, Asian and African art, and pre-Columbian, Greek, and Roman antiquities. Docent-led tours, a café, and a gift shop round out the offerings. *255 Beach Dr. N.E., (727) 896-2667, www.fine-arts.org.*

Eat & Stay

Renaissance Vinoy Resort & Golf Club | St. Petersburg. From the Roaring '20s to the 1960s, this was the Gulf Coast accommodation of choice for celebrities, politicians, and socialites. Following a descent into near oblivion, a $93-million renovation in the 1990s included a restoration of the hand-painted frescoes on the dining room's cypress ceilings. Indeed, the Vinoy is so meticulously preserved that you can even take a historical tour of it. You can't beat the location, either, which overlooks a marina and a cultural district that includes Straub Park, the shops and restaurants of Beach Drive, and two museums: Museum of Fine Arts and Museum of History. Amenities include two pools, a fitness center, a spa, tennis courts, and a golf course. *501 5th Ave. N.E., (727) 894-1000, www. vinoyrenaissanceresort.com.*

The Moon Under Water | St. Petersburg. This place has a great location, a great menu, and a great vibe! Don't let the Mediterranean-style exterior fool you: The interior is all British pub. Grab a pint at the bar and order up some sausage rolls (here, made with English bangers) or a curry. And the name? Well that has British-colonial origins, too—just ask your bartender about it. *332 Beach Dr. N.E., (727) 896-6160, www.themoonunderwater.com.*

Columbia Restaurant | Tampa. Although it's a good 25 miles from St. Pete—in Tampa's historic Ybor City Latin district—this restaurant is worth the trip. It opened in 1905, making it one of Florida's oldest eateries, and, with more than a dozen dining rooms, including a café and courtyard space, it's also one of largest. The staff—many of them fourth- and fifth-generation members of the Cuban founder's family—serves up history along with the delicious Spanish bean soups and paella and Cuban sandwiches and roast pork dishes. Sangria, cerveza, or any of several "family wines" will complement your meal. Try to time dinner with a flamenco show, held twice nightly Monday through Saturday (reservations required). The gift shop is a great place to find gourmet souvenirs. *2117 E. 7th Ave., (813) 248-4961, www.columbiarestaurant.com.*

A beach in St. Petersburg

Texas Hill Country

ROUTE TOWNS: San Antonio I Bandera I Fredericksburg I Johnson City I Austin

In this huge state, the miles just keep passing and passing until you finally understand why Texans boast that everything is bigger here. A trip through Hill Country, though, is very manageable, packing a lot of history and culture into a compact area that includes both San Antonio and Austin.

The Alamo

San Antonio seems to embody the full history of Texas, from its days under Spanish and Mexican rule to its struggle for independence ("Remember the Alamo," as the saying goes) and eventual statehood. Strolls or cruises along the picturesque River Walk, built in the 1930s, seem to transport you back in time, too. Cutting-edge Austin, on the other hand, is the repository of all that history. You can spend your days in the capital's world-class history museums and your nights in its world-class music venues. Between the major cities, you'll discover Wild West towns that seem in no hurry to leave the 19th century.

Fredericksburg's pioneer feel has a Bavarian twist, thanks to the region's many German settlers. You can sample that European flavor in brew pubs and restaurants along its main street. In Johnson City, you can drop by the LBJ Ranch to see where the larger-than-life politician made his bids for public office and where his wife, Lady Bird, realized that by simply adding wildflowers, America's highways could become things of beauty.

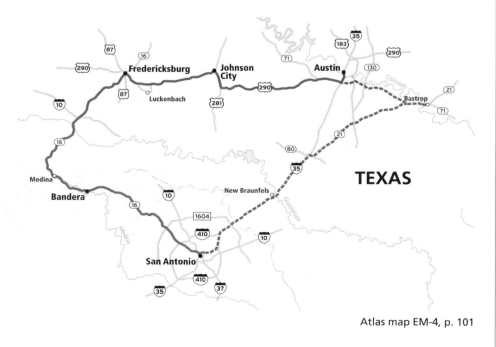

TEXAS

Atlas map EM-4, p. 101

Distance: 203 miles point to point; 328 miles full loop (with stop in Bastrop).

Type of Trip: Weekend Getaway; RV; Arts & Music, History & Heritage.

Must Try: Texas barbecue. Also: a Western swing dance at Arkey's, a basement honky-tonk in Bandera, especially if you dress for the part: blue jeans, cowboy hat, and boots.

Must Buy: Speaking of cowboy hats and boots—could there be any better Texas souvenirs? Well, maybe. While in the capital, look for T-shirts emblazoned with the city's unofficial motto: "Keep Austin Weird."

Must See: The Alamo, River Walk, Bandera, Luckenbach, a live show in Austin.

Worth Noting: This region is in the heart of Texas wine country, where some **51 wineries** (texaswinetrail.com) between Austin and Fredericksburg and from Lampasas to New Braunfels participate in seasonal (self-guided) tour/tasting events. Also, consider timing your trip to experience a festival: South by Southwest (Mar.), Austin's premier music festival; Fiesta San Antonio (Apr.), whose roots go back to the 1890s; Celebrate Bandera (Labor Day); and Fredericksburg's Oktoberfest. When can you see the Texas state flower? Well, those bluebonnets are blooming best during the first two weeks of April.

Travel Tips: It can get supernaturally hot here in summer, with temperatures easily exceeding 90 degrees on most days—so plan accordingly. If you're heading into remote areas, pack some ice and water as well as snacks. Also, flash floods are common during heavy downpours; check weather reports before heading out and pay attention to signs indicating flood zones.

city itinerary

San Antonio

❶ The Alamo. Ask anyone visiting San Antonio for the first time, and they'll likely tell you that they didn't expect to see The Alamo as it is: in the middle of a very active downtown district. Most, it seems, expected it to be in an open and endless desert—as depicted in the 1960 film starring John Wayne. Regardless, the preserved mission originally called San Antonio de Valero still has the power to tell a story of heroism against all odds.

In 1836, nearly 200 farmers, lawyers, surveyors, frontiersmen (including Jim Bowie and Davy Crockett), and others barricaded themselves inside the Alamo, determined to protect what they hoped to establish as the provisional capital of the Republic of Texas. Despite desperate requests for reinforcements, fewer than 100 men answered the call. Outside the walls, Mexico's Santa Anna marshaled his 1,800 men and waited. On March 6, the 13th day of the siege, Mexican soldiers breached the walls and killed all but a few women, children, and slaves, who were told to share what they had seen.

Hearing what happened on fact-filled ranger-led or self-guided-audio tours of the Alamo provides insight into one of the most unforgettable stories in American history. So does touring the museum within the Long Barrack, where the defenders made their final stand, and exploring the grounds, built as part of a WPA project. Admission is free (donations accepted). *300 Alamo Plaza, (210) 225-1391, www.thealamo.org.*

❷ The History Shop. It's definitely worth stopping in this shop just across the street from the Alamo. The inventory of museum-grade antique maps, books, militaria, and weapons will jumpstart your education on the Spanish Colonial era, the Texas Revolution, the Republic era, and the Civil War. What's more, the Alamo Diorama, an audio and light show, fully explains the 1836 battle. *713 E. Houston St., (210) 229-9855, www.thehistoryshop.com.*

❸ Buckhorn Saloon & Museum. At the Buckhorn's gift shop, known as The Curio Store, the inventory celebrates the days when shelves were stocked with silver belt buckles and Native American–made beaded gloves. Today you'll still find Bowie knives and cowboy hats amid T-shirts, mugs, and contemporary Texas-centric souvenirs. You can also tour the museum, with its pioneer and wildlife artifacts. Next door, the Buckhorn Saloon has a similar vintage feel, with a ceiling decorated with the horns and antlers that the owner accepted as payment for drinks and artwork made from rattlesnake rattles. *318 E. Houston St., (210) 247-4000, www.buckhornmuseum.com.*

❹ River Walk. Quiet, secluded, and picturesque—it's hard to believe that one of San Antonio's top attractions was once in danger of being replaced with storm sewers. That was the initial response after a deadly flood, but, when cooler heads prevailed, it was designer Robert Hugman's vision of a lovely "scenescape" called Paseo del Rio, or River Walk, that caught the imagination of citizens. It was completed as a WPA project, and, to this day, the sinuous canals capture the imagination, whether you walk along the promenade with its restaurants, cafés, bars, hotels, and boutiques, or embark with **San Antonio Cruises** (210/244-5700, www.riosanantonio.com) on a sail past scenes of old San Antonio. *110 Broadway, (210) 227-4262, www.thesanantonioriverwalk.com.*

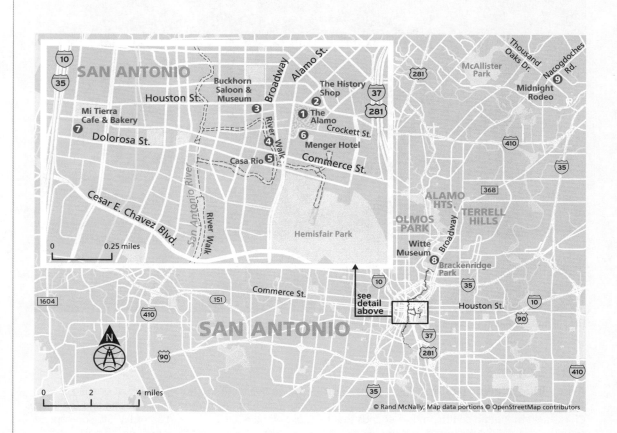

Eat & Stay

❺ Casa Rio. This little River Walk restaurant opened in 1946 and was popular from the start. The owners, however, wanted to keep patrons waiting for tables entertained. The answer? Excursions aboard canoes, gondolas, and paddle boats that went on to become the legendary canal cruises of today. The restaurant still serves diners at waterfront tables beneath colorful umbrellas at its original location—one of the prettiest and most photographed spots on the Paseo del Rio. *430 E. Commerce St., (210) 225-6718, www.casa-rio.com.*

❻ Menger Hotel. In 1859, German businessman William A. Menger looked at the wreckage of the Alamo and, for some reason, decided what was needed across the street was a luxury hotel. Enter the three-story lobby, and you'll see grand gold-capped columns, Victorian accents, antique furnishings, brass light fixtures, rare paintings, and upscale shops. Choose from among 316 rooms, some overlooking The Alamo, and grab a bite in the Colonial Room restaurant or a martini in the Menger Bar. Throughout the hotel, you can almost see the wheeler-dealers striking bargains for cattle, oil, and political office. *204 Alamo Plaza, (210) 223-4361, www.mengerhotel.com.*

❼ Mi Tierra Cafe & Bakery. It's rare when you can buy a hot jelly roll and a cool margarita in the same place, but that's the case at Mi Tierra. What began in 1941 as a small eatery with three tables is now a round-the-clock dining destination for Tex-Mex dishes, imported beers and tequilas, and fresh-from-the-oven baked goods. Enjoy all the flavors while listening to the sounds of los trovadores (strolling musicians). *218 Produce Row, (210) 225-1262, www.mitierracafe.com.*

❽ Witte Museum. Here, history, science, and nature are bonded into an alloy of fun. Once you've learned how settlers managed to make a home for themselves in South Texas (take a look at the pioneer cabins from the 1800s), visit the two-story H-E-B Body Adventure, which is filled with exhibits related to health and wellness. Then peruse some of the 300,000 artifacts in the research and collections center, and enjoy exhibits on dinosaurs and Native American artifacts—all part of Texas history. A visit here pairs nicely with other sites in Brackenridge Park, including the Japanese Tea Garden, San Antonio Zoo, and Eagle Miniature Train. *3801 Broadway, (210) 357-1900, www.wittemuseum.org.*

❾ Midnight Rodeo. When Midnight Rodeo opened, punk and New Wave were just edging out disco. Although it's natural to assume a nightclub of that era would now be a relic, this one's still going strong. Why? Patrons credit its atmosphere, concerts, contests, drink specials, and range of musical genres. Add to all that a wide-open dance floor in a 25,000 square-foot club, and you've got yourself a great honky-tonk. Hint: If you plan to party, bring a designated driver. *12260 Nacogdoches Rd., (210) 655-0040, midnightrodeosanantonio.com.*

River Walk

Field of Indian Paintbrush and Bluebonnets

Bandera

Arkey Blue's Silver Dollar. When you head down the stairwell into this honky-tonk that opened in 1901, you'll understand why Bandera is called the Cowboy Capital of the World. Willie Nelson and the Dixie Chicks are among the country music legends that have played here. On Friday and Saturday, Stetson-capped cowboys and their ladies boot-scoot boogie across the sawdust-covered floor to the red-hot rhythms of a Western swing band. Neon lights, pinball machines, and a jukebox add to the ambience. Call ahead for info on the afternoon jam sessions. *308 Main St., (830) 796-8826.*

Frontier Times Museum. Back in the day, museum displays consisted of whatever curiosities anyone cared to donate. That's the philosophy J. Marvin Hunter Sr., publisher of the *Frontier Times* newspaper and magazine, had in mind when he opened Bandera County's only public museum back in 1933. What will you see? How about some shrunken heads, a two-headed goat, a 2,000-year-old corn cob, and a Medieval birthing chair. More traditional exhibits include Western art, a Hall of Texas Heroes, tributes to great rodeo cowboys, and occasional "pickers circles." Yippee-yi-yay! *510 13th St., (830) 796-3864, www.frontiertimesmuseum.org.*

Fredericksburg

National Museum of the Pacific War. When Chester Nimitz was growing up in landlocked Fredericksburg, no one could have predicted that he would become one of the most respected admirals of WW II, namely the Commander-in-Chief of the U.S. Pacific Fleet. He has a special place in the hearts of residents, as evidenced by this complex, which includes not only the Admiral Nimitz Museum but also the Center for Pacific War Studies, Plaza of Presidents, Memorial Courtyard, and Japanese Garden of Peace. Displays here are full of unique and varied items like a PT boat, a Quonset hut, a mock field hospital, a midget Japanese sub that tried to reach Pearl Harbor, and the casing for a spare Fat Man atomic bomb. *340 E. Main St., (830) 997-8600, www.pacificwarmuseum.org.*

Dooley's 5-10-25. This place is a blast from the past, selling everything from broomstick toy ponies to Mexican jumping beans. What else can you stock up on? How about Radio Flyer wagons, cast-iron cookware, kitchen gadgets, wind-up alarm clocks, plastic flowers, coonskin caps, Beemans gum, Blue Waltz perfume. . . the list goes on. *131 E. Main St., (830) 997-3458.*

Fredericksburg Brewing Company. In 1994, Texas decided to permit the operation of brewpubs. The Fredericksburg Brewing Company opened just months later, making it the state's oldest. Along with first-place finishes in statewide competitions, it earned a gold medal at the 2008 Great American Beer Festival Competition for its Hauptstrasse Helles (Mainstreet Light). It's set in a historic 1890s home and has a dining area, a biergarten, and even a 12-room "bed-and-brew" upstairs. *245 E. Main St., (844) 596-2303, www.yourbrewery.com.*

Ausländer. Combine a Bavarian biergarten with country music, and you get the Ausländer. Drop in for authentic German cuisine and select from roughly 70 beers, including those from Texas, Colorado, California, and Pennsylvania, as well as those from Mexico, Holland, Belgium, Germany, and England. *323 E. Main St., (830) 997-7714, theauslander.com.*

Johnson City

Lyndon B. Johnson National Historic Park. President Lyndon B. Johnson's boyhood home—filled with period pieces reflecting small-town, 1920s Texas—the Johnson Settlement, and the LBJ Ranch are all just 15 miles east of Fredericksburg on U.S. 290. A block away from the home, a visitors center has films and exhibits detailing Johnson's life; it's also the place to pick up self-guided audio tours or sign up for 90-minute ranger-led excursions. A walking trail leads you to the settlement, where Johnson's grandfather built a log cabin for his family and headquartered his cattle-droving business in the late 1860s and early 1870s.

From here, you can visit the so-called Texas White House, a ranch purchased and enlarged by the Johnsons in the 1950s. Other attractions include the one-room schoolhouse that Johnson attended; a nature trail; a Hill Country botanical exhibit; wildlife enclosures stocked with bison, white-tailed deer, wild turkey, and longhorn cattle; and the family cemetery, where President and Mrs. Johnson are buried. *U.S. 290, (830) 868-7128, www.nps.gov/lyjo.*

Eat & Stay

Old Spanish Trail Restaurant I Bandera. Bandera County's oldest continuously operating restaurant (circa 1921) still serves up down-home cooking, from chicken-fried steak to fresh Tex-Mex. While you're here, check out the John Wayne Room (you'll recognize it by hundreds of pictures of The Duke) or grab a seat at the bar, where the stool seats are cowboy saddles. *305 Main St., (830) 796-3836.*

Medina Highpoint Resort I Medina. Texas covers 268,000 square miles of ground—and much of it is quite remote. Such is the case en route to Fredericksburg, where it really seems like you won't see anything. Then, on Highway 16, there's something. The Medina Highpoint Resort is an unexpected find that's perfect for all types of travelers. It has RV sites, bunkhouses, tent camping, cabins, and even a bed-and-breakfast. Inside a well-stocked market, pick up maps that will direct you to local attractions and stock up on food, ice, beverages, and supplies. Sitting atop Edwards Plateau (elevation 2,000 feet), the resort provides a great view along with a great overnight. *23195 State Hwy. 16 N., (830) 589-4695, rvcoutdoors.com/medina-highpoint-resort.*

Living Large in Little Luckenbach

Per capita, Luckenbach (population: 3) might just be one of the world's most famous towns. Located about 10 miles southeast of Fredericksburg, the town—really more like a big ranch—was purchased in 1970 by Hondo Crouch and two partners. Why? Well, Crouch figured that, if he owned it, he could set the rules on when he could drink and how long he could dance.

The dance hall here saw the recording of its first live album (by Jerry Jeff Walker) in 1973, but it became legendary thanks to the 1977 smash, "Luckenbach, Texas (Back to the Basics of Love)" by Waylon Jennings and Willie Nelson. Today folks from around the world come out of curiosity, to take pictures, and buy some souvenirs in the post office and gift shop. Some come in the evening, when the open-air dance hall fills Luckenbach's 9 acres with music and the kind of revelry that Crouch envisioned when he bought the town—for just $30,000. *www.luckenbachtexas.com.*

city itinerary

Austin

1 **Bullock Texas State History Museum.** You can't miss this museum: Just look for the giant, bronze Lone Star sculpture. The highlight of the first floor is the preserved hull of the doomed 17th-century French sailing ship *La Belle*. Second-floor exhibits focus on Texas history from 1821 to 1936, with artifacts and documents from the days of early Mexican settlers, the Republic of Texas, the Civil War, and the Great Depression. The third level features modern Texas, with exhibits ranging from ranching artifacts and oil field tools to local music and NASA. *1800 Congress Ave., (512) 936-8746, www.thestoryoftexas.com.*

2 **Texas State Capitol.** On the free, 30-minute, guided tours (daily every 20–30 minutes) of the majestic capitol, docents share stories about characters such as Stephen F. Austin (the Father of Texas), Sam Houston (renowned general and statesman), and Angelina Eberly (the so-called Savior of Austin). The Capitol Visitors Center, on the southeast corner of the grounds, has information about the capitol, Austin, and beyond. *1100 Congress Ave., (512) 463-0063, www.tspb.state.tx.us.*

3 **Waterloo Records.** Music is the motor that moves Austin, and that motor is fueled by places like Waterloo Records. One of the city's finest record shops is packed with new and used CDs and LPs, including alternative/indie, rock/pop, folk/country, or blues/jazz. Texas artists are well represented, and the music-loving staffers will help you find new sounds. *600A N. Lamar Blvd., (512) 474-2500, www.waterloorecords.com.*

4 **Congress Avenue Bridge Bat Colony.** More than a million Mexican free-tail bats, comprising North America's largest urban colony, hang out beneath the Ann W. Richards Congress Avenue Bridge. Just after sunset, you can stand on its span and watch the entire colony emerge for its nightly food foray. The viewing "season" runs March through November, after which the bats head to Mexico. If you visit in late July or early August, you'll see lots of young pups starting to fly. Want viewing-time information? Call the Austin office of Bat Conservation International. *(800) 538-2287 (BATS), www.batcon.org.*

5 **The Continental Club.** In the late 1950s and '60s, it was a supper club and then a burlesque hall. In the 1970s, show girls and jazz gave way to rockabilly, blues, and roots. You can still find the latter mix today, along with the occasional swing band. A retro, 1950s décor makes it an Austin classic in every sense of the word. *1315 S. Congress Ave., (512) 441-2444, www.continentalclub.com.*

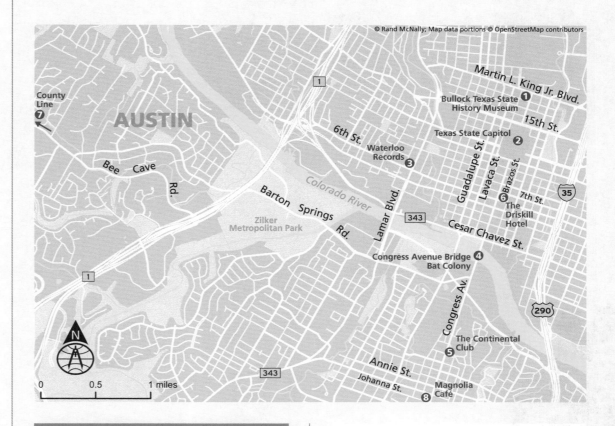

What do Real Cowboys Wear?

Blue Jeans: A lot of cowboys wear Wranglers, rather than Levi's or Lees. Why? Wrangler sponsors many Professional Bull Rider and Professional Rodeo Cowboys Association events. Indeed, its Cowboy Cut model is the official ProRodeo Competition jean.

Hats: The famous Stetson brand has been around since 1865; the Resistol brand started up in 1927. Today the two are sister companies based in Garland, where they both still hand-make high-quality, fur-felt hats worn by real cowboys and in-the-know wannabes.

Boots: Boots made by the Anderson Bean Boot Company are the official footwear of the Texas and Southwestern Cattle Raisers Association. In addition, several companies, like J.B. Hill, still custom-make cowboy boots. In Hill Country, though, a great place to shop for boots is the **Texas Boot Company** (733 Old Austin Hwy., Bastrop, 512/332-0865, texasbootcompany.com)—33 miles southeast of Austin—which also has a museum of historical Western footwear and other gear.

Eat & Stay

6 **The Driskill Hotel.** From its elaborate redbrick and white-limestone exterior to its multihued marble- and stained-glass-adorned public areas, this 1886 confection is all Victoriana. The 189 guest rooms are equally stately; all have plush robes, fine toiletries, and free Wi-Fi. Both the décor and the history are rich and layered. Built by cattle baron Colonel Jesse Driskill, the hotel's been sold in lean times and traded (for a California ranch and vineyard) in high times. It's even rumored to have been lost in a poker game. *604 Brazos St., (512) 439-1234, www.driskillhotel.com.*

7 **County Line.** The County Line reportedly has the best barbecue in a state that itself claims to have the best barbecue in the nation. Regardless, this place is beloved by students, politicians, celebs, families, and anyone else who likes big food and good service. Traveling in a group? Order the Cadillac, a massive platter of (pick five) brisket, beef or pork ribs, chicken, pulled pork, turkey breast, or sausage, plus potato salad, coleslaw, beans, bread, and ice cream. There are two locations on Austin's west side and a half-dozen statewide. *6500 W. Bee Cave Rd., (512) 327-1742, www.countyline.com.*

8 **Magnolia Café.** This place is always buzzing, and waits of up to 45 minutes aren't uncommon on weekends. The air smells spicy, the walls are bright yellow, and the funky decor includes a small painted wooden dinosaur skeleton hanging from the ceiling. Breakfast is a favorite meal. The menu mixes Tex-Mex dishes like tacos and morning *migas* (tortillas with scrambled eggs, beans, salsa, and cheese) with standards like omelets and pancakes. Both this and **Magnolia Café West** (2304 Lake Austin Blvd., 512/478-8645) are open, as they like to say, "24/8." *1920 S. Congress Ave., (512) 445-0000, themagnoliacafe.com.*

Congress Avenue Bridge Bat Colony

Bryce Canyon National Park

Best of the Road® Travel Guide

West

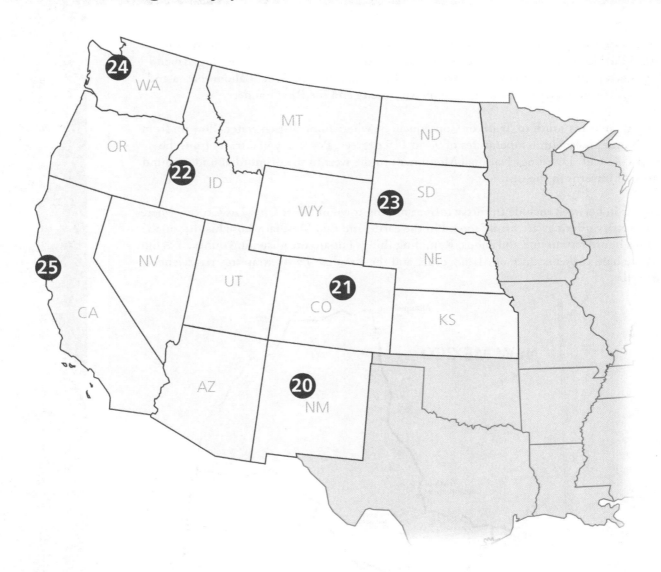

Earth & Sky in Southern New Mexico

ROUTE TOWNS: Albuquerque I Truth or Consequences I Silver City I Gila I Deming I Las Cruces I Alamogordo
Roswell

In southern New Mexico, things seem to center on either earth or sky. This trip covers both in equal measure, from snow-white sand dunes and ancient caverns to pueblo aeries and bastions of stellar exploration.

Albuquerque International Balloon Fiesta

It all starts in Albuquerque, established in 1706 and layered with culture and history, from the Ancestral Pueblo tribes and Spanish conquistadors to the American pioneers of long ago and the high-tech pioneers of today. It's also home to the annual International Balloon Fiesta and plenty of year-round opportunities to soar above the city and the Rio Grande.

The trip then heads south to Truth or Consequences, where mineral-rich waters flow up from the earth into pools with temperatures of 98 to 115 degrees. Beyond, you'll travel from the aeries of Gila Cliff Dwellings National Monument in the west to the primordial underground of Carlsbad Caverns in the east.

Highlights in between include the artsy former mining town of Silver City; Las Cruces, where state university offerings are firmly rooted in the earth; and Old Mesilla, whose historic adobe structures house restaurants and shops. Rounding things out are the glistening dunes of White Sands, the hard rocket science of Alamogordo, and the less-than-hard extraterrestrial science of Roswell.

Atlas map E-4, p. 68

Distance: 805-mile loop (starting and ending in Albuquerque), with another 226 miles out and back for a side trip to Carlsbad Caverns.

Type of Trip: Vacation Getaway; RV; Great Outdoors, History & Heritage, Science & Technology, Small Town Gems.

Must Try: At least one New Mexican dish *with* chile peppers—red or green—perhaps at Mary & Tito's Café in Albuquerque or a restaurant in Old Mesilla, just south of Las Cruces.

Must Buy: Native American crafts, especially silver-and-turquoise jewelry.

Must See: Rattlesnake Museum, Turquoise Museum, Indian Pueblo Cultural Center, Gila Cliff Dwellings, Deming Luna Mimbres Museum, White Sands National Monument, UFO Museum, Carlsbad Caverns.

Worth Noting: Ten private establishments in Truth or Consequences offer day-pass access to their mineral pools. Many also have guest rooms and stay-and-soak packages. For more information, contact **Sierra County Recreation and Tourism** (301 S. Foch St., 575/894-1968, www. sierracountynewmexico.info).

Travel Tips: Allow a couple hours for the winding, 44-mile trip on NM 15—along ridgelines and through canyons—from Silver City to the Gila Cliff Dwellings visitors center. Note: NM 15 between Silver City and the junction with NM 35 is steep, narrow, and winding. Look into alternate routes (e.g., NM 35 through Mimbres) if you have a motor coach or trailer longer than 20 feet—or if you're driving after dark!

city itinerary

Albuquerque

❶ Old Town Tours. A walking tour of Old Town is a great way to start your Albuquerque visit, and this company has been in business for more than 50 years. History-themed walks are held daily at noon; lantern-lit ghost tours are held nightly at 8. Private tours are offered most days year-round at 10, 2, and 4. *Plaza Don Luis, 303 Romero St. N.W., (505) 246-8687, www. toursofoldtown.com.*

❷ Turquoise Museum. Although this small museum sits in a nondescript strip mall, its collection is worldly, representing some 60 mines and all of the major turquoise-producing areas, from the United States to Mexico to China. Other displays highlight mining, lapidary arts, and silversmithing. There are two, guided, 90-minute tours each day; space is limited, so book ahead. Docents happily advise you on what to look for when buying turquoise jewelry, useful knowledge on any southwest trip. *2107 Central Ave. N.W., (505) 247-8650, www.turquoisemuseum.com.*

❸ American International Rattlesnake Museum. Some find the live exhibits here creepy; others find them cool. Regardless, you have to admit this animal conservation museum is truly unique. Small, re-created natural environments house rattlesnakes of every stripe (or other pattern), including Eastern Massasaugas, Western diamondbacks, twin-spotteds, Panamint speckleds, Chihuahuan ridge noses, and Arizona blacks. Prefer the theoretical to the actual? Check out the snake-themed memorabilia—from movie posters to apparel to vintage snakebite kits. *202 San Felipe N.W., (505) 242-6569, www.rattlesnakes.com.*

❹ New Mexico Museum of Natural History and Science. Two life-size, bronze dinosaurs greet you at the entrance. Inside, you can walk through a glowing volcano; learn about Triassic-era dinosaurs; wander through realistic caves both dry and damp; and experience a time when New Mexico was covered by an inland sea. In FossilWorks, watch trained volunteers extract finds from rock. In The Hall of Stars, test your knowledge of the constellations. In STARTUP, see the history of personal computers unfold. *1801 Mountain Rd. N.W., (505) 841-2800, www.nmnaturalhistory.org.*

❺ Indian Pueblo Cultural Center. Changing exhibits and events here highlight the rich dance, crafts, and other traditions of New Mexico's 19 sovereign Pueblo communities. This is also a good place to pick up etiquette tips for visits to area Pueblos such as Santa Ana, Sandia, Isleta, Laguna, and Acoma. Also on-site are a gift shop and a restaurant. *2401 12th St. N.W., (505) 843-7270, www.indianpueblo.org.*

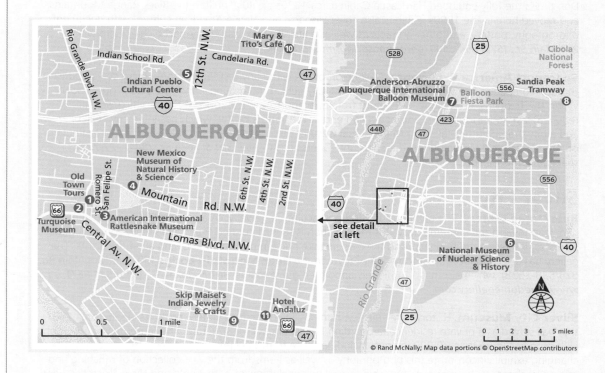

Sandia Peak Tramway

❻ National Museum of Nuclear Science & History. The only museum of its type chartered by Congress has exhibits geared to all ages. They touch on pioneers like Marie Curie and the scientists who worked on the Manhattan Project, and they document historical and current applications in the fields of nuclear energy and medicine. Displays on Hiroshima and Nagasaki and the Cold War highlight darker periods; those on how the Atomic Age affected pop culture lighten the mood. *601 Eubank Blvd. S.E., (505) 245-2137, www.nuclearmuseum.org.*

Up, Up, and Away

When it comes to aerial sightseeing, few cities are more obliging. The world-renowned **Albuquerque International Balloon Fiesta** (www.balloonfiesta.com), held for nine days early each October, sees more than 650 pilots offering rides and demonstrations day and night. Plenty of local operators can take you on lighter-than-air adventures year-round. Inquire about them at the **7 Anderson-Abruzzo Albuquerque International Balloon Museum** (9201 Balloon Dr. N.E., 505/768-6020, www.balloonmuseum.com), where you can also learn how balloons are flown.

A 15-minute, 2.7-mile ride on the **8 Sandia Peak Tramway** (30 Tramway Rd. N.E., 505/856-7325, www.sandiapeak.com), takes you from desert foothills to the windy top of 10,378-foot Sandia Peak. The view from the observation platform extends 11,000 square miles; a ranger station provides trail and wildlife information. Look into combining a late-afternoon tram ride with dinner at the High Finance Restaurant, where picture windows frame spectacular sunsets. In winter, families flock to the summit's ski area. In summer, many folks ride up (on the tram or the chairlift) and hike or bike down.

❾ Skip Maisel's Indian Jewelry & Crafts. A lot of folks shop for turquoise jewelry and Native American crafts in Old Town, but there are often better deals elsewhere. One such place is Skip Maisel's on Central Avenue (aka Route 66), which sells jewelry from several tribes, pottery from all the New Mexican pueblos, Hopi kachina dolls, hand-woven Navajo rugs, and more. *510 Central Ave. S.W., (505) 242-6526, skipmaisels.com.*

Eat & Stay

❿ Mary & Tito's Café. If you want a New Mexican culinary experience that's as memorable as it is authentic, head to this unassuming restaurant. It's been on the local foodie radar since 1963, and it received national attention in 2010, when it won the James Beard Foundation's American Classic Award. The specialty *carne adovada* (pork braised for a really long time and served with a red chile sauce) comes in everything from burritos and enchiladas to pizzas and omelets. *2711 4th St. N.W., (505) 344-6266.*

⓫ Hotel Andaluz. The earth-tone palette and architecture say "traditional Southwest," but the design details, creature comforts, and amenities are all contemporary at this 107-room boutique hotel. Opened in 1939, it was built by New Mexico native Conrad Hilton—the fourth hotel in what would become an empire. Although no longer part of the Hilton chain, it maintains a luxury status. The Wi-Fi and gym access are free, and pets are welcome. Grab a small bite and some great wine at the MÁS tapas bar or a classy cocktail at the Ibiza rooftop patio bar. *125 2nd St. N.W., (505) 242-9090, www.hotelandaluz.com.*

NORTHEAST

MIDWEST

SOUTH

WEST

Truth or Consequences

Geronimo Springs Museum. For background on Truth or Consequences (T or C, as it's called around here), stop by this repository of local pioneer and ranching tools, household items, and farm equipment. Don't miss the fully equipped Hardcastle Cabin (circa 1930s or '40s), built in the Black Range Mountains and moved here in the 1990s. Exhibits also cover Hispanic and Native American culture, with documents, photography, pottery, and other artifacts as well as a life-size wax statue of Apache chief Geronimo. *211 Main St., (575) 894-6600, geronimospringsmuseum.com.*

Spaceport America Experience. Despite problems with early test flights, commercial space tourism through companies like Virgin Galactic will eventually get off the ground—and safely back down again. When this happens, their flights will depart from Spaceport America. Tours of this facility (reservations required) last about four hours and begin and end at the visitors center, which has interactive exhibits and a gift shop. Shuttles take you to the actual (secure) site, where you can "ride" the G-Shock simulator or interact with crew members in the Spaceport Operations Center. *301 S. Foch St., (844) 727-7223, spaceportamerica.com.*

Silver City

Blue Dome Gallery. The paintings, illustrations, sculpture, jewelry, ceramics, textile art, and other works here lean toward the contemporary. But the selection is so well-curated that there's really something for all tastes, interests, and budgets. And the owners take pride in personally knowing all of the artists. The gallery has a second location at the edge of town in the **Bear Mountain Lodge** (60 Bear Mountain Rd., 575/538-2538), which also has 11 uniquely appointed guest rooms. *307 N. Texas St., (575) 534-8671, www.bluedomegallery.com.*

Silver City Museum. History here starts with the building itself—a stately, brick, Italianate (circa 1881) that has served as a private residence, a boarding house, and a civic structure. The museum's photography collection has more than 20,000 images, including those from the late 18th and early 19th centuries. Themed changing exhibits incorporate this photography as well as items from the vast collection of ranching and mining implements; housewares, furnishings, and personal items of both Anglo and Hispanic settlers; and Native American art and artifacts. *312 W. Broadway, (575) 538-5921, www.silvercitymuseum.org.*

Gila Cliff Dwellings

Gila

Gila Cliff Dwellings National Monument. As early as 4000 BC, possible ancestors of modern-day Pueblo Indians settled near the Gila River. The communities thrived for centuries, expanding from pit houses into pueblos. By the 1270s, one such pueblo village was built in lofty caves. By 1300, though, it was abandoned. What happened? Archaeologists still don't know. But the clues and speculation are part of the fun on a visit here.

The visitors center has a small museum of pottery, baskets, tools, and other area artifacts; a bookstore; and a 15-minute interpretive video. From here, it's a 2-mile drive to the trailhead for the 1-mile loop hike up and through the dwellings and their amazing variety of pictographs. Also, try to spend time in the surrounding, 3.3-million-acre **Gila National Forest** (3005 E. Camino del Bosque, 575/388-8201, www.fs.usda.gov/gila), which has plenty of picnicking, camping, hiking, and fishing opportunities. *National Monument: State Hwy. 15, MM 43, (575) 536-9641, www.nps.gov/gicl.*

Deming

Deming Luna Mimbres Museum. There's a lot to see here, from classic cars and military vehicles to old-time schoolroom memorabilia, medical instruments, farm implements, quilts, and lace. There's also a chuck wagon exhibit and a Transportation Annex, highlighting the town's ties to the transcontinental railroad and the famous "silver spike" hammered here back in 1881. The collection of Mimbres Indian pottery is renowned. Also popular are the Military, Doll, and Early 1900s rooms; the displays of minerals and geodes; and the selection of beer steins, bells, and unusual liquor bottles. *301 S. Silver Ave., (505) 546-2382, www.lunacountyhistoricalsociety.com.*

Eat & Stay

Little Toad Creek Brewery & Distillery | Silver City. At the tasting room of an area craft brewery and distillery, the burgers, sandwiches, and other pub grub are often made with locally sourced ingredients. On tap are small-batch blond, amber, and pale ales as well as stouts, porters, and lagers. Word is that the green chili vodka, just one of the spirits made using a hand-built copper still, gives bloody Marys an extra kick. You can also sample rum and whiskey. *200 N. Bullard St., (575) 956-6144, littletoadcreekbrewerydistillery.com.*

Gila Hot Springs Ranch | Gila. Lodgings at this family run outfit include primitive riverside tent sites, RV sites with water hookups, and three self-catering apartments. As the "ranch" in the name implies, horseback riding is one of the favorite activities here, with half- and full-day trail rides in the Gila wilderness. On site, Doc Campbell's sells groceries, sundries, and souvenirs, and Gila Country Corner has locally made crafts. *State Hwy. 15, MM 39, (575) 536-9551, www.gilahotspringsranch.com.*

Hotel Encanto | Las Cruces. Both common areas and the 204 guest rooms are rich in Spanish Colonial style, with wrought-iron work, ornate dark-wood furnishings, and earth-tone textiles. Garduño's of Mexico Restaurant and Cantina serves (poolside upon request) New Mexican and Mexican dishes, and the Azul Ultralounge is a great place to sip a cocktail. The pet-friendly hotel has an on-site day spa and is close to many in-town attractions. *705 S. Telshor Blvd., (575) 522-4300, www.hotelencanto.com.*

Hacienda RV Resort | Las Cruces. Most of the sites are pull-through; all are expansive, level, and have full hookups. An adobe-style clubhouse and several patio areas are among the places to relax and socialize. There's also an enclosed pet area (and a package of goodies for your pet on arrival), a coin-op laundry room, well-equipped restroom and shower facilities, and a fitness room. A tidy, colorful gift shop sells items made in New Mexico. *740 Stern Dr., (575) 528-5800, www.haciendarv.com.*

White Sands National Monument

Las Cruces

New Mexico State University Chile Pepper Institute. To learn about the hottest crop around, stop by the university's unique Chile Pepper Institute. They sell seeds, condiments, cookbooks, and many other things chile pepper. You can also check out the institute's gardens, with more than 150 varieties. Both self-guided (free) and guided (fee, reservations required) tours are available, and the best time to visit is between July and September. By the time you leave, you'll know your greens and jalapeños from your reds and cayennes—very useful when ordering at New Mexico restaurants. While on campus, stop by the Fabian Garcia Botanical Gardens or the University Museum, where exhibits pull from a vast collection of Native American, Hispanic, and colonial artifacts. *945 College Ave., Gerald Thomas Hall, Room 265, (575) 646-3028, www.chilepepperinstitute.org.*

Alamogordo

White Sands Missile Range Museum. This region was the site of the world's first atomic bomb test and where scientists tested the German V-2 and other rockets that eventually took America into space. The main draw at this museum is the Missile Park, with more than 50 projectiles and plaques about each. Indoor exhibits highlight rocket and missile science and the people behind it. A gift shop sells souvenirs and Native American crafts. The museum, though privately operated, is on the U.S. Army's missile range. To enter, stop at the visitors center near the gate and be prepared to show your vehicle registration, driver's license, and proof of auto insurance. *State Hwy. 213, 3 mi. off Hwy. 70 (btw. MM 169 and 170), (575) 678-3358, www.wsmr-history.org.*

New Mexico Museum of Space History. Moon rocks, missiles, rockets, and cinematic "tours" of the night sky are all part of this ultramodern hillside complex, which includes the indoor International Space Hall of Fame and New Horizons Dome Theater & Planetarium and the outdoor John P. Strapp Air & Space Park, Daisy Decelerator Track, and Astronaut Memorial Garden. Numerous interactive multimedia exhibits celebrate human achievement in space technology and space travel. *3198 State Rte. 2001, (575) 437-2840, www.nmspacemuseum.org.*

White Sands National Monument. Here, great wave-like dunes of glistening snow-white sand have engulfed 275 square miles of desert and created the world's largest gypsum dune field. Several trails and a boardwalk let you explore on foot, and there's also a paved 16-mile (round-trip) Dune Drive. But the best way to experience the dunes is by sledding down them! Pick up a plastic saucer sled (you are near Roswell, after all) and some tips at the visitors center, choose a dune, and go! Note that park roads are closed during missile tests at nearby White Sands Missile Range; check ahead. *19955 Hwy. 70 W., (575) 479-6124, www.nps.gov/whsa.*

Roswell

International UFO Museum & Research Center. Did a UFO really crash near Roswell in July 1947? Find out at this museum, founded in 1991 by two participants in the "Roswell incident." Through photographs, witness statements, and other items, you'll learn about reported extraterrestrial sightings—and purported government cover-ups of them. A gift shop has books, DVDs, toys, and many truly unique souvenirs. *114 N. Main St., (575) 625-9495, www.roswellufomuseum.com.*

International UFO Museum, Roswell

Eat & Stay

La Posta de Mesilla | Mesilla. This compound once housed all the goods and services a traveler would need at a stop along the Butterfield Stagecoach line between St. Louis, MO, and San Francisco, CA. That was back in the 1850s. Since 1939, the Territorial-style adobe structures in Old Mesilla have housed the dining rooms of La Posta restaurant. The guacamole, steak, and *tostadas compuestas* (toasted corn tortilla cup filled with frijoles, red chile con carne, lettuce, tomatoes, and cheese) are house specialties. For dessert, try the *sopaipillas,* light pastry puffs served with warm honey for drizzling. The cantina has 100 or so tequilas, and the lobby features a small, exotic aviary. *2410 Calle de San Albino, (575) 524-3524, www. laposta-de-mesilla.com.*

Big D's Downtown Dive | Roswell. The owner promises that "nothing we make comes from a tin can or sits months on end on a shelf somewhere," the first indication that this casual, down-home burger joint is a good bet. And folks do rave about the green chile burger, the garlic fries, and the Monte Cristo sandwich. Prices are reasonable, even more so on specials nights (e.g., 2 for $12 cheese steaks). Word is that seating (and parking) is limited; best not to arrive starving in case there's a wait. *505 N. Main St., (575) 627-0776.*

Side Trip Way Down Under

Some 280 million years ago, the area of the Chihuahuan Desert that's now home to the 119 (known) limestone caves of **Carlsbad Caverns National Park** (727 Carlsbad Caverns Hwy., 575/785-2232, www.nps.gov/cave) was a reef in an inland sea. You can make the steep, 1¼-mile descent (some 79 stories down!) along the Natural Entrance trail into the Big Room, with its interesting formations and marine-life fossils. Alternatively, head down by elevator at the visitors center, 27 miles southwest of Carlsbad proper and 7 miles from the park entrance at White City along US 62/180.

Another highlight of the caverns (for some, anyway) involves one particular type of wildlife. From mid-May through late October, 400,000 Brazilian (aka Mexican) free-tail bats make their home in the caves. Weather permitting, you can watch them depart for their nightly feeding. This experience is accompanied by ranger talks in the amphitheater. The visitors center also has the 16-minute *Hidden Worlds* movie featuring high-def footage of the caves and bats in flight.

The logical jumping off point for a visit (best done as an overnight) to Carlsbad Caverns is Roswell, 113 miles to the north. There are plenty of chain hotels in Carlsbad as well as the **Carlsbad RV Park and Campground** (4301 National Parks Hwy., 888/878-7275, www.carlsbadrvpark.com), which is close to the park's entrance road. North of Roswell along Routes 285 and 60, there's not a lot of, well, anything . . . for the trip back to Albuquerque, it's not a bad idea to tank up and stock up on snacks!

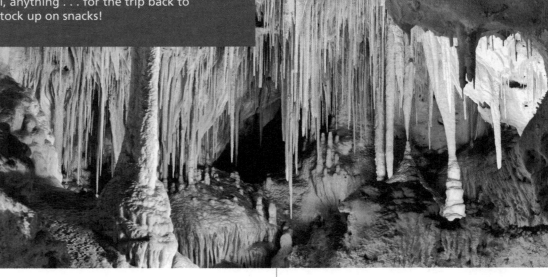
Carlsbad Caverns

Canyon Country

ROUTE TOWNS: Denver, CO | Golden | Georgetown | Grand Junction | Moab, UT | Boulder Town | Bryce Canyon City
Leeds | Springdale | Page, AZ | Flagstaff | Sedona | Williams | Grand Canyon | Las Vegas, NV

You might think that a road trip with this title would simply cover the greatest canyon of them all. But, on this journey, the Grand Canyon is just one of many magnificent canyons and other natural wonders.

Colorado River in Grand Canyon

Denver is a great place to start a visit to Canyon Country, since the Mile High City will help you acclimate to higher elevations and set the stage for the frontier history that unfolds as you travel westward. Of course, Colorado is famous for a few things, like the Gold Rush and early railroads. Get a taste of them in Georgetown and Golden, where you can also taste some refreshing lager at the MillerCoors Brewery.

Near the Utah border, western Colorado's majestic Rocky Mountains are replaced by glowing-red sandstone peaks and valleys. This gorgeous landscape accompanies you to Moab and into Arches National Park, with its ages-old, awe-inspiring stone formations. Farther along, the deep canyons and towering spires of both Bryce Canyon and Zion national parks further elevate and inspire your thinking about how our planet evolved over so many billions of years.

In Arizona, you'll travel along a stretch of historic Route 66, perhaps visiting the Lowell Observatory in Flagstaff, the Glen Canyon National Recreation Area and Lake Powell in Page, and the enchanting town of Sedona. Then, it's on to the Grand Canyon, a place that's older than time, with views that never get old. The final stretch of the trip winds northwest toward the legendary Hoover Dam before cruising into the equally legendary Las Vegas, where everything is illuminated, including your senses.

Atlas map E-13, p. 21

Distance: 1,500 miles point to point.

Type of Trip: Vacation Getaway; RV; Great Outdoors, History & Heritage, Picture Perfect, Science & Tech.

Must Try: Thirsty or not, a milkshake from the vintage Galaxy Diner in Flagstaff is a must. And, in Las Vegas, the nickel slots are always worth a try—just don't get carried away!

Must Buy: A commemorative coin celebrating an event in U.S. history from the U.S. Mint–Denver is a distinctive souvenir and a potentially wise numismatic investment.

Casinos regularly "retire" and then sell their cards; decks with the logo of your favorite Vegas establishment make great small gifts or souvenirs.

Must See: U.S. Mint–Denver; Arches, Bryce Canyon, and Zion national parks; the Grand Canyon; Hoover Dam; Neon Museum.

Worth Noting: Although you'll drive down into canyons, this itinerary traverses some of the highest elevations in the U.S. West—up to 9,000 feet. Take the necessary precautions to prevent altitude sickness, like ascending gradually, staying hydrated (water is best), avoiding alcohol, and allowing time to acclimatize before participating in rigorous activity.

Travel Tips: The national parks and monuments on this trip call for advance planning, especially in terms of booking in-park campsites or lodge rooms and double-checking seasonal access. Highways might close on short notice due to inclement weather; call for the latest information, as online alerts aren't always the most current.

NORTHEAST   MIDWEST   SOUTH   WEST

city itinerary

Denver, CO

1 Denver Museum of Nature & Science. You'll need about a day to fully explore one of the world's largest natural history museums. Highlights include gem and mineral specimens in the Coors Mineral Hall, prehistoric skeletons from La Brea Tar Pits, and Egyptian mummies. An IMAX theater with a 4.5-story-tall screen airs a changing roster of nature, travel, and history films. The Gates Planetarium offers several galactic presentations for all ages, with special shows for children. *2001 Colorado Blvd., (303) 370-6000, www.dmns.org.*

2 Denver Zoo. Established in 1896, Denver Zoo's 80 acres are home to more than 3,500 animals, including rare Amur leopards, Arctic wolves, grizzly and black bears, African lions, vampire bats, and many more fascinating creatures. Primate Panorama is home to a vast variety of apes and monkeys. Tropical Discovery's indoor rainforest has streams, waterfalls, temple ruins, and coral reefs with remarkable fish, amphibians, reptiles, and mammals. Don't miss the Komodo dragon habitat or the 2-mile Toyota Elephant Passage with Asian elephants, one-horned rhinos, and Malayan tapirs. *2300 Steele St., (720) 337-1400, www.denverzoo.org.*

3 Denver Botanic Gardens. Among the many treasures at this 24-acre oasis of greenery is an outstanding collection of rare orchids and a selection of plants native to the West, including yucca, prickly pear, and prairie grasses. Art exhibits are often held throughout the galleries and grounds, which you can take in on one of several themed 60-minute tours. There's also a 3-acre Children's Garden with six ecosystems to explore. *1007 York St., (720) 865-3500, www.botanicgardens.org.*

4 Colorado State Capitol. Built in the 1890s of Colorado white granite and capped by a dome leafed with Colorado gold, the capitol makes a fitting seat for this state's government. Along with portraits of important figures and stained-glass windows depicting historical events, the interior is finished with the entire known supply of rose onyx mined in Beulah, CO. Weekdays see free guided Historical, Legislative (Jan.–May only), and Attic/Dome tours; reservations for all are strongly advised. *200 E. Colfax Ave., (303) 866-2604, leg.colorado.gov.*

5 Denver Art Museum. This museum, established in 1893, has an internationally recognized Native American collection as well as fine collections of modern and contemporary, Asian, pre-Columbian, European, and decorative arts. The museum dramatically increased in

Denver Art Museum

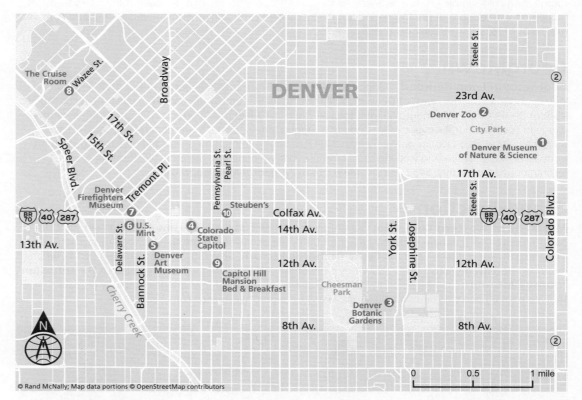

© Rand McNally; Map data portions © OpenStreetMap contributors

size with the 2006 addition of the spectacular Hamilton Building. Designed by renowned architect Daniel Libeskind, its wildly cantilevered design mimics the crags and cliffs of the Rocky Mountains. Daily docent-led tours are free. You can also see resident artists at work, shop in the gift store, and grab a bite in the on-site café or restaurant. *100 W. 14th Ave. Pkwy., (720) 865-5000, www.denverartmuseum.org.*

6 U.S. Mint–Denver. In 1859, a year after gold was discovered in Colorado, the U.S. Government established this bastion of both gold and silver bullion. It's been manufacturing all denominations of D-series circulating and commemorative coins and coin dies ever since. The current facility, built in 1906 to resemble a Florentine palace, stands as one of the state's most treasured institutions. Free, guided, 45-minute tours (reservations required) cover the mint's impressive architecture and artifacts, the coin-making process, and special exhibitions. *320 W. Colfax Ave., (303) 405-4761, www.usmint.gov.*

7 Denver Firefighters Museum. Downtown's original 1909 Firehouse No. 1 showcases an extensive collection of firefighting memorabilia new and old—from gear and vehicles to fire alarms and suppression devices. There are also hands-on exhibits, fire-safety lessons, and photographic archives. The museum gift shop is filled with great souvenirs, including DFD-insignia clothing, housewares, key chains, and money clips. *1326 Tremont Pl., (303) 892-1436, www.denverfirefightersmuseum.org.*

8 The Cruise Room. Opened the day after Prohibition was repealed in 1933, this bar inside downtown's Oxford Hotel is gloriously old school and authentically Denver. The *Queen Mary* ocean liner inspired its Art Deco chrome- and neon-filled decor. On one side of the bar is a classic jukebox; on the other side, some of the state's best bartenders mixing locally distilled spirits into unique concoctions, including the bar's renowned martinis. *1600 17th St., (303) 628-5400, theoxfordhotel.com.*

Colorado State Capitol

Eat & Stay

9 Capitol Hill Mansion Bed & Breakfast. The eclectic architecture of this inn—built in 1891 of rusticated pink stone, with both Romanesque and Queen Anne elements—is typical of Denver's Millionaire's Row and the Capitol Hill district. And staying here puts you in the heart of it all. The eight rooms and suites are distinctively decorated in Victorian style filtered through a contemporary lens. Some have balconies or grand windows (imagine the Rocky Mountain views); others have whirlpool tubs or gas fireplaces; all have fresh-cut flowers. In addition to a full breakfast, an evening wine and beverage service is included in the rates. *1207 Pennsylvania St., (800) 839-9329, www.capitolhillmansion.com.*

10 Steuben's. Between its daily lunch and dinner specials, retro-style décor, and reasonable prices, this centrally located Denver eatery has been a mile-high staple since 2006. Steuben's sources much of its food and beverages from local purveyors, resulting in a delicious mash-up of classic fare with local, seasonal flair. Along with weekend brunch, there's also a tempting weekday happy hour from 2 pm to 6 pm and a 10 pm-to-close "late nite" cheeseburger, fries, and beer special. *523 E. 17th St. (305) 830-1001, www.steubens.com.*

Golden

MillerCoors Brewery. Free tours of this enormous facility offer a taste of MillerCoors history since 1873. Visit for a half-hour self-paced walk through the brewing process, which includes a stop in the "fresh beer room" for a cold sample inside a refrigerated space. Other product tastings are also on the tour's to-do list, topped off with exhibits of photos, neon signs, historical beer cans, and other memorabilia. *13th and Ford Sts., (800) 642-6116, www.millercoors.com/breweries.*

Georgetown

Georgetown Loop Railroad. During the 75-minute, 3-mile train ride between Georgetown and Silver Plume, about 45 minutes west of Denver, you'll traverse a 19th-centruy railroading marvel: the reconstructed 95-foot Devil's Gate High Bridge. All told, the line climbs 640 feet in a "corkscrew" route along a narrow-gauge (3-foot-wide) track over trestles and amid rugged terrain. Diesel trains depart Georgetown several times daily (May–mid-Oct.) or on weekends (mid-Oct.–Jan.); summertime sees additional daily departures from Silver Plume. Hour-long walking tours of an 1870 silver mine also are available. Reservations are recommended for all trips. *646 Loop Dr., (888) 456-6777, georgetownlooprr.com.*

Grand Junction

Museums of Western Colorado. Grand Junction is home to the **Museum of the West** (462 Ute Ave., 970/242-0971), where exhibits highlight 1,000 years of history—from the ancient Anasazi and other tribes to old-west outlaws—and the **Cross Orchards Historic Site** (3073 F Rd., 970/434-9814), where costumed docents demonstrate Grand Valley pioneer life. Also affiliated with this complex is the **Dinosaur Journey Museum** (550 Jurassic Ct., 970/858-7282) in nearby Fruita, where paleontology displays showcase fossils and cast dinosaur skeletons. *www.museumofwesternco.com.*

Delicate Arch, Arches National Park

Moab, UT

Arches National Park. Here, an azure sky contrasts with a crimson and gold panorama of graceful arches, spires, and fins. Made a national monument in 1929 and a national park in 1971, Arches protects more than 76,000 acres of desert landscape and more than 2,000 arches, the world's largest concentration. The rock formations—some fanciful, some bizarre, all breathtaking—were carved over millennia by erosion and exfoliation of the Entrada sandstone that formed over thick salt beds more than 150 million years ago. As the salt dissolved, it warped and cracked the sandstone into vertical ridges that, in turn, eroded into fins. Repeated freezing and thawing chipped away at these, resulting in windows and arches. The process continues today, as rock falls destroy older formations and new ones emerge from eroding fins.

The scenic park drive winds more than 20 miles each way, extending as far as the Devils Garden Trailhead. You can see plenty of awe-inspiring scenery from your car window, but be sure to get out and follow a couple of short trails up to the formations. Some, such as the famous Delicate Arch and Landscape Arch, with its seemingly impossible 306-foot span, require moderate hikes to view at close range. (A fully accessible 100-yard trail leads to a good, albeit distant, viewpoint of Delicate Arch.)

Before setting out, stop by the visitors center near the park entrance to see the short video (shown every half-hour) on park history, pick up a self-guided tour booklet, and browse in the bookstore. You can also make reservations and buy tickets for the ranger-led tour through the Fiery Furnace. There aren't any food concessions in the park (pack accordingly), but drinking water is available at the visitors center and Devils Garden. The Devils Garden Campground fills to capacity every night between March and October, so plan ahead and check in early. *N. Hwy. 191, (435) 719-2299, www.nps.gov/arch.*

Boulder Town

Anasazi State Park & Museum. Here you can explore the ruins of an Anasazi village, where archaeologists have uncovered more than 100 structures thought to have been occupied by an Ancestral Pueblo community from AD 1050 to 1200. You can also tour unexcavated ruins and a replica of a six-room dwelling. A museum has galleries, and interactive exhibits contain thousands of artifacts, including artful ceramics showcasing the Anasazi's sophisticated pottery skills. *460 N. Hwy. 12, (435) 335-7308, stateparks.utah.gov.*

Georgetown Loop Railroad

Eat & Stay

Butterhorn Bakery | Frisco, CO. Do biscuits taste better at 9,097 feet? See for yourself at this bakery and restaurant, serving hungry locals since the 1970s. Butterhorn has mastered virtually every type of egg dish, from scrambles to frittatas to huevos rancheros. Lunchtime brings homemade soups and sandwiches—including buffalo meatloaf burgers and New Orleans muffalettas—all served on house-baked breads. Just be sure to leave room for a pastry. *408 Main St., (970) 668-3997, www.butterhornbakery.com.*

Junction West RV Park | Grand Junction. This friendly RV park has tent sites, pull-through RV sites with electric hookups, and boat storage. Amenities also include free Wi-Fi, spotless shower facilities, air-conditioned laundry facilities, and play areas. *793 22 Rd., (970) 245-8531, www.junctionwestrvpark.com.*

Jailhouse Café | Moab, UT. This humble breakfast spot (a great place to fill up before exploring Arches National Park) has a curious history. It was built in 1885, and has since served as a post office, general store, private home, and county courthouse. Today, the kitchen occupies the same space inmates did a century ago. Had those poor mugs tasted the eggs Benedict, ginger pancakes with apple butter, or other lauded dishes now served here, their time might have been a lot more pleasant. *101 N. Main St., (435) 259-3900.*

Sorrel River Ranch Resort & Spa | Moab. What started as a homestead in 1903 became a cattle ranch in 1947, and is now a Western-style resort. Cabins dot the 160 acres of grounds alongside the Colorado River, 20 miles east of Arches National Park. Don't let the architecture's rusticity fool you: things here are luxurious. In rooms and suites, knotty, light-wood furniture and flooring and crisp white linens create a sense of place and serenity matched only by the river or mountain views—through picture windows or from private decks. A concierge can arrange horseback riding, hiking, and other outings, and reserve your table at the River Grill dining room. Relax in the spa with a Rancher's Deep Tissue massage, and then chill out in the Epic Bar and Lounge. *Mile 17 Hwy. 128, (435) 259-4642, www.sorrelriver.com.*

Bryce Canyon City

Bryce Canyon National Park. Paiute lore has it that Coyote became displeased with the Legend People who lived in Bryce Canyon, turned them to stone, and left them frozen in time. Geologists have it that the fantastic spires, bridges, and hoodoos are the work of water erosion that's far from frozen in time. The limestone, shale, and sandstone of the Paunsaugunt Plateau continues to wear away at the rate of a foot every 50 years or so.

Declared a national monument in 1923, the 56-square-mile national park takes its name from 1870s pioneers Ebenezer and Mary Bryce. A drive along the 37-mile round-trip park road is a great way to see the ever-changing panorama from the many overlooks lining the east shoulder. Rangers suggest driving to Rainbow Point—where, on clear days, your view is obstructed only by the curvature of the earth—and taking in the overlooks on the return trip.

Although you can see the park's majesty without leaving the car, you'll miss the full experience if you don't get out and walk. A high elevation ensures daytime summer temperatures that are perfect for hiking, but be prepared for the mercury to drop after sunset. Several trails, most between 1.5- and 5.5-miles long, originate near the visitors center, itself near the historic Bryce Canyon Lodge and the Sunset and North campgrounds.

The visitors center is also a great place to learn more about the park's history and amazing geology and to find out about scheduled activities. Ranger-led talks and walking tours take place all year (with snowshoes in winter) and span a variety of subjects including wildlife, prehistoric history, and stargazing. Astronomy lovers take note: In the average rural area, 2,500 stars are visible; at Bryce Canyon, close to 7,500 can be seen. *Entrance a few miles south of intersection of Hwy. 12 & Hwy. 63, (435) 834-5322, www.nps.gov/brca.*

Leeds

Silver Reef. In the late 1800s, Main Street was a mile long and Silver Reef boasted 2,000 people, two dance halls, two newspapers, and a thriving Chinatown. Today, it's essentially a ghost town, where you can see remnants of its former glory days in the historic town center. The landmarked Wells Fargo Express office has been converted to a museum and art gallery, where you can step into the original vault, learn about local geology and the silver trade, and view artifacts and photography from the frontier days. *Leeds Exit off I-15, (435) 879-2254 (museum), www.silverreefutah.org.*

Springdale

Zion National Park. For the past 15 million years, the North Fork of the Virgin River has been carving Zion Canyon out of the Navajo sandstone that colors its walls. At the Grand Canyon, some of the best views are from above; here they're from below. Indeed, the rugged terrain, sprawling 229 square miles of high plateau country, is a hiker's paradise, with everything from forests of piñon and juniper pine to red rock canyons that shelter springs, waterfalls, and hanging wildflower gardens. Peregrine falcons, golden eagles, mountain lions, and mule deer are among the creatures that find refuge here.

Exhibits at the Zion National Park Visitor Center, in Springdale on the park's southern end, introduce you to the geology, flora, and fauna. Rangers here give talks, lead guided walks, and help plan independent hikes and drives. Just north is the Zion Human History Museum, where you can learn more about early area inhabitants. Nearby you'll also find the only in-park hotel, the Zion Lodge, which has rooms, suites, and cabins, as well as the South Campground (tent and primitive RV sites) and the Watchman's Campground (tent and electric-hookup RV sites).

Although you can drive along the park's main highway year round, during the busy April through October season, park shuttles—mandatory for all except hikers and bikers—take you from the Springdale visitors center along the Zion Canyon Scenic Drive to the upper canyon. You can also drive between the Springdale and the East entrances along the Zion–Mt. Carmel Highway, which runs through two man-made tunnels, one over a mile long. On the long tunnel's west side are sheer canyon walls almost 3,000 feet high; on its east side are white-, rose-, and salmon-colored slick rocks. Note that bikers, hikers, and vehicles taller than 13 feet aren't allowed along this road.

Zion's northern reaches consist mostly of scenic backcountry, characterized by the Finger Canyons of the Kolob, accessible from Exit 40 off I-15 and along Kolob Canyons Road, which takes you to a scenic viewpoint. The Kolob Canyons Visitor Center offers information on backcountry hiking and camping as well as the primitive sites available at the seasonal Lava Point Campground. *State Rte. 9, (435) 772-3256, www.nps.gov/zion.*

Zion National Park

Eat & Stay

The Lodge at Bryce Canyon | Bryce Canyon. Since 1925, this 114-room, log-and-stone lodge has been the sole hotel inside Bryce Canyon National Park. Choose from Western Cabins with gas fireplaces, renovated Sunset and Sunrise Point rooms with porches and balconies, or more compact studios or suites. In keeping with the tranquil atmosphere, none of the accommodations has a TV. And who cares that you can only access Wi-Fi in the main building when you can readily access all the surrounding nature? The lodge is steps from world-class hiking trails into the canyon and along the rim. A general store, fine-dining restaurant, pizzeria, and coffee shop round out the civilized offerings. *1 Lodge Way, Hwy. 63, (435) 834-8700 or 877/386-4383, www.brycecanyonforever.com.*

Red Mountain Resort | Ivins. With the red rocks of Snow Canyon State Park in its backyard and the formations of Zion just an hour away, slick-rock hiking is a part of each day's experience at this spa resort. All-inclusive Wellness or Adventure retreat packages—some of which include a spa treatment—are good value for money. What's more, the weight-loss programs here are critically acclaimed, so you know the food is healthful and seasonal. The spa itself has many facial and body treatments; some massages reinvigorate tired muscles, others simply leave you in a trance. Rooms, done in soothing earth tones, are standard in terms of size and amenities; try to book one with a mountain view. For more space and a fireplace, opt for a Villa Suite. *1275 E. Red Mountain Cir., (877) 246-4453, www.redmountainresort.com.*

Zion National Park

NORTHEAST

MIDWEST

SOUTH

WEST

Page, AZ

Glen Canyon National Recreation Area. For eons the Colorado River and its tributaries carved breathtaking walls, cathedral-like recesses, and natural bridges out of soft layers of sandstone, creating wonders such as the Grand Canyon and this, its smaller sibling, Glen Canyon. Here, reddish sandstone formations contrast strikingly with the sleek blue waters of Lake Powell. Named after Major John Wesley Powell, who first explored the river in 1869, this 186-mile-long lake was formed when the Glen Canyon Dam was completed in 1966. The 710-foot structure (just 16 feet shorter than the Hoover Dam) not only aided irrigation and harnessed the Colorado's power, it also created the 1.2-million-acre Glen Canyon National Recreation Area—a prime spot for boaters, swimmers, anglers, and hikers since 1972.

At the Carl Hayden Visitors Center, on the lake's southwestern shore, ponder exhibits on area history and geology, find out about trails, and arrange a Glen Canyon Natural History Association tour of the dam. Boating is the best way to get around and take in the scenery, though. Arrange to haul in your own vessel, rent one, or set up guided boat excursions or river-rafting trips through **Lake Powell Resorts & Marinas** (www.lakepowell.com). This outfit also offers a variety of lodging options both out on the lake— in fully equipped houseboats—or beside it in hotels or at campgrounds with both tent and full-hookup RV sites. *691 Scenic View Dr., (928) 608-6200, www.nps.gov/glca.*

Lake Powell

Flagstaff

Lowell Observatory. Founded in 1894 and today a National Historic Landmark, Lowell Observatory is where astronomer Clyde Tombaugh discovered Pluto in 1930. Its hands-on exhibit hall lets you peer through mighty telescopes, including a specially equipped solar one. The Steele Visitors Center has evening multimedia presentations on constellations and deep-sky objects, and the SlipherVision "immersive space theater" offers planetarium shows. Guided tours take place several times daily. *1400 W. Mars Hill Rd., (928) 774-3358, lowell.edu.*

Walnut Canyon National Monument. During the 12th century, Sinagua Indians settled in the shallow caves of Walnut Canyon and built 300 rooms in the shelter of its walls. The community thrived for about 150 years before moving on and living among the Hopi in northeastern Arizona. Walnut Canyon National Monument was established in 1915 to preserve the cliff dwellings they left behind and protect both archaeological and natural resources across 3,600 acres. The visitors center has displays on Sinaguan culture and area geology and natural history. Two primary trails—the challenging Island Trail and the shorter Rim Trail Loop—offer fascinating self-guided or summertime ranger-led hikes. *6400 N. Hwy. 89, (928) 526-3367, www.nps.gov/waca.*

Sedona

Chapel of the Holy Cross. As unexpected as it is inspirational, this sleek, slim chapel soars 250 feet from between two enormous red-rock formations, themselves atop a 1,000-foot bluff. The chapel was the dream of Marguerite Brunswig Staude, a local rancher with big-city ideas (the Empire State building was her model). In the early 1930s, Frank Lloyd Wright, famous for his "organic architecture," was consulted for the design. But plans were left on the table until the 1950s, when a San Francisco firm known for its California modernist works was hired. The chapel finally opened in 1956, winning the 1957 American Institute of Architects Award of Honor. It's part of Sedona's Catholic St. John Vianney Parish and hosts a prayer service every Monday at 5 pm. *780 Chapel Rd., (888) 242-7359, www.chapeloftheholycross.com.*

Willams

Grand Canyon Railway. A wonderful way to begin your trip to Grand Canyon National Park is on the 65-mile rail line established by the Santa Fe Railroad in 1901. Trains depart daily from Williams at 9:30 am, traveling more than 7,000 feet above sea level and through the Colorado Plateau's prairielands and ponderosa- and piñon-pine forests. They arrive at 11:45 in Grand Canyon Village, with all its South Rim touring options, historical sites, and amenities. You can return on the same day, departing at 3:30 and arriving in Williams at 5:45—though many people book overnight stays at one of the Grand Canyon lodges.

Seats are in everything from Pullman cars and Budd coaches to Observation Dome or Luxury Parlor cars, most of them historically significant and superbly restored. They're pulled by diesel locomotives dating from the 1950s and retrofitted to burn recycled restaurant cooking oil—a surprisingly green fuel that respects the region's ecosystem. The railway has many package deals that include meals and/or lodging. Reservations for all trips are essential. *233 N. Grand Canyon Blvd., (800) 843-8724, www.thetrain.com.*

Eat & Stay

Galaxy Diner | Flagstaff. This place has all the fixtures and fittings you'd expect of a Route 66 classic circa 1955—from glitzy neon outside to lots of stainless steel and checkered tile within. Select a tune from the jukebox before settling into a banquette for a chopped-steak burger and Galaxy fries. Or belly up to the counter for a creamy, perfectly blended milkshake. *931 W. Rte. 66, (928) 774-2466, jbsfamily.com/galaxy-diner.*

Starlight Pines Bed & Breakfast | Flagstaff. Starlight Pines is a tranquil base for exploring the Grand Canyon, Sedona, and other memorable sites in and near Flagstaff. The B&B offers four rooms with private baths: Lily has a private balcony that overlooks 9,300-foot Mt. Elden, Dragonfly has a wood-burning fireplace, Art Deco has Tiffany-style lamps, and Peacock has a salvaged 6-foot claw-foot bathtub. Wi-Fi and a gourmet breakfast are included in the rates. *3380 E. Lockett Rd., (928) 527-1912, starlightpinesbb.com.*

Amara Resort & Spa | Sedona. Playful throw pillows and works of art lend pops of color to the taupe and gray color schemes of this boutique hotel's rooms. It's a contemporary-chic enclave that's near Sedona's uptown promenade as well as places to go hiking and biking. There's also plenty of opportunity to chill: by the infinity pool, in the spa, or during each evening's hosted wine hour. The SaltRock Southwest Kitchen serves tantalizing, regionally inspired dishes. *100 Amara Ln., (928) 282-4828, www.amararesort.com.*

Agave89 | Sedona. Sedona locals get great guacamole fresco, street-style tacos, asadas, and other Mexican dishes at Agave89. Among the refreshing libations are margaritas with flavors like pomegranate, blackberry, jalapeño, or prickly pear; the Red Rock sangria; and the Canyons Edge caipirinha. *254 N. Hwy 89A, (928) 282-7200, www.89agave.com.*

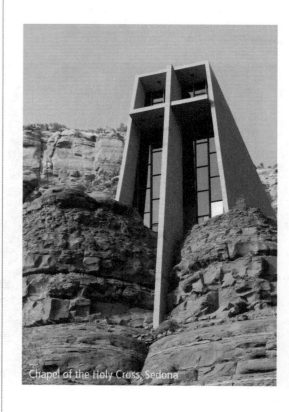

Chapel of the Holy Cross, Sedona

Lookout Studio, Grand Canyon Village

Hopi House, Grand Canyon Village

Grand Canyon

Grand Canyon National Park. Erosion over 5 or 6 million years carved out a natural wonder that merits its name. The Grand Canyon, a mile deep and up to 18 miles across, cuts across 277 miles of northern Arizona. The golds, oranges, and blues of the exposed rock—some an estimated 2 billion years old—change with the sunlight, making for varied panoramas throughout each day. Inner canyon trails lead from the rims to the floor, where the mighty Colorado River twists and turns, alternating stretches of tranquil water with exciting rapids.

Evidence suggests that people have been living in and around the canyon for almost 10,000 years, though the first Europeans didn't come upon it till 1540, and the first settlers, many of them prospectors, didn't stake their claims until the late 1800s. They soon realized that it was easier to make a living accommodating the increasing number of sightseers. Among the more eccentric entrepreneurs was Louis Boucher, the hermit of Hermits Rest, who mined his claim and raised goldfish in a trough at Dripping Springs. There was also Ralph Cameron, who fought in the Arizona courts to retain his right to operate Bright Angel Trail as a toll road. And there were the Kolb Brothers, who photographed (for a fee) visitors embarking on mule rides at their canyon-rim studio.

Although long protected as a forest preserve (1883) and national monument (1908), the canyon wasn't made a national park until 1919. What once attracted some 50,000 visitors annually today attracts 5 million. And there are now so many ways to take it all in: bus tours, mule rides, air excursions, short hikes, multiday adventures across the canyon floor or along the Colorado.

The most popular point of entry is the South Rim, with the main visitors center at Mather Point and Grand Canyon Village, with its many services and amenities, including the depot for the railway from Williams and free shuttle buses that run through the village and to overlooks. Fewer people visit the North Rim, where amenities (namely the Grand Canyon Lodge and its adjacent visitors center) are fewer, and access is seasonal (May 15 to Oct. 15, weather permitting). With elevations of 7,600 to 8,800 feet, though, the North Rim offers some of the most spectacular views. To visit the West Rim, nearer to Las Vegas, consider a walk on the famous (if time-consuming) Skywalk.

Regardless of when or where you visit, make reservations (for everything!) as far ahead as possible. For the mule treks, this means up to 11 months out! Also look into the many park offerings—among them guided and self-guided tours, free ranger-led programs, and special exhibits—via its website or that of the Grand Canyon Association. *(928) 638-7888, www.nps.gov/grca.*

Grand Canyon Village. The village was founded in 1883 as a modest prospecting South Rim settlement. By 1901, the Santa Fe Railroad had completed a line from Williams, AZ, followed by a log and wood-frame rail depot in 1910, to accommodate the tourist boom—which never ended.

Be sure to visit some of the historic district buildings. Hopi House (1905), built by the Santa Fe Railroad as a studio and dwelling for artisans, still sells Hopi and Navajo crafts. Nearby, Verkamp's Visitor Center has pioneer history exhibits in the 1906 structure where Verkamp's Curios once sold souvenirs. Canyon-edge Kolb Studios houses a gift shop in what was a photography concession (1904) run by two brothers, who further supplemented their income by screening movies, holding dances, and running a soda fountain. The Kolbs' competition was Lookout Studio, established by the Fred Harvey Company in 1914, and built of rough-cut limestone to blend with the surrounding cliffs. Today, it has a bookstore with memorable views.

Another Fred Harvey creation is the 1915 El Tovar Hotel, home to the Harvey Girls, waitresses who were later made famous in a movie starring Judy Garland. It has parlors, a fine-dining room, a wide porch with rocking chairs, gift shops, and 78 relatively pricey guest rooms just yards from the canyon rim. Additional lodges stretch beside it, including the modern Thunderbird and Kachina Lodges and the historic Bright Angel Lodge. Other options include the more rustic Maswik Lodge and the Mather Campground and Trailer Village, which accommodates tent and RV campers.

Book park lodges well in advance. It's also good to make reservations for fine-dining restaurants, though you can also just drop into any of several casual eateries and snack bars or the Maswik Lodge food court. *(888) 297-2757 (central reservations), www.nps.gov/grca/planyourvisit.*

En Route to Vegas

If you visit the Grand Canyon via the railway from Williams, it makes sense to stay south of the canyon en route to Vegas, traveling along a stretch of old Route 66 and passing the Hoover Dam.

In Kingman, AZ, the **Historic Route 66 Museum** (120 W. Andy Devine Rd., 928/753-9889, www.route66museum.net) is packed with murals, artifacts, maps, photos, and dioramas highlighting the Mother Road. Across the street is the retro **Mr. D'z Route 66 Diner** (105 E. Andy Devine Ave., 928/718-0066, www.mrdzrt66diner.com).

Just 75 miles northwest of Kingman and some 33 miles southeast of Vegas is the **Hoover Dam** (Hwy. 93, 702/494-2517, www.usbr.gov/lc/hooverdam). This massive 726-foot engineering marvel was constructed during the Great Depression and created Lake Mead, the nation's largest reservoir. A walk across the dam's crest takes you from Arizona to Nevada in just 15 minutes. Guided 60-minute dam and 30-minute power-plant tours are also options. A private operator, **Black Canyon River Adventures** (blackcanyonadventures.com, 800/455-3490), offers raft trips to the dam's base.

city itinerary

Las Vegas, NV: Neon Navigations

It's hard to believe, but, back in 1829, this was a sleepy desert hamlet that a Spanish trader dubbed "The Meadows," or Las Vegas, due to its prairie grasses and spring waters. Today, of course, it's a city with many faces, most framed by glitter and spotlights. In terms of visiting, the modern city is divided into two main areas: historic Downtown, with its early days casinos and its Fremont Street Experience, and the 3-mile Strip, in all its large-scale, glimmering glory.

Exploration of the Strip takes you past pirates battling sexy sirens at Treasure Island, more than 1,000 fountains dancing to the voices of Pavarotti and Sinatra at The Bellagio, and a volcano spewing smoke and fire outside The Mirage. Here it's wise to practice keeping your eyes (and mind) open and your wallet closed. This trip focuses less on the Strip casinos, and more on the other types of sights around them and downtown.

Travel Tips: It's best to lodge centrally and strategically cab or Uber it (fares are reasonable) to places from which you can wander, ponder, and game. This isn't a self-driving kind of town, given the need to park and re-park, often using expensive valet services. Buses merely lumber along, and the monorail stops at only a half-dozen Strip casinos.

Visitor Info: Las Vegas Convention and Visitors Authority, *3150 Paradise Rd., (702) 892-0711, www.lvcva.com.*

The Strip

North of the Strip and Downtown

❶ Las Vegas Natural History Museum. There really is more to Vegas than glitz and big-time glamour, as this museum on the north end of town demonstrates. Exhibits include International Wildlife, Treasures of Egypt, African Savanna and Rainforests, Geology, and Wild Nevada (which, despite its name, doesn't cover rowdy gamblers). The Marine Life Gallery's 3,000-gallon tank is home to sharks and stingrays. Other galleries feature exhibits on prehistoric mammals or dinosaurs. *900 N. Las Vegas Blvd., (702) 384-3466, www.lvnhm.org.*

❷ Neon Museum. In ever-changing Vegas, the stunning and often elaborate neon signs of yesterday and today are regularly replaced by the gleaming marquees of tomorrow. Many a beloved old sign has ended up at this one-of-a-kind museum, just north of downtown. Its La Concha Visitors Center, inside a hotel saved from demolition in 2005, is a remarkable Mid-Century Modern sight in its own right. And the "boneyard" has more than 200 timeless

large- and small-scale illuminated relics. For an enlightening look at them, book advance tickets for the guided Boneyard Tours offered daily on the hour or half-hour. *770 N. Las Vegas Blvd., (702) 387-6366, www.neonmuseum.org.*

❸ Mob Museum. The museum that showcases how Al Capone, Charles "Lucky" Luciano, Bugsy Siegel, Meyer Lansky, and other notorious figures had a hand in shaping Sin City is inside a former federal courthouse. Ironic? Not necessarily. What's formally called the National Museum of Organized Crime and Law Enforcement gives you both sides of the mob story. Displays detail the key characters and the legacy of organized crime—past and present, in Las Vegas and around the world. They also debunk a few myths, highlight a few scams, and outline a few conspiracies. *300 Stewart Ave., (702) 229-2734, themobmuseum.org.*

Eat & Stay

❹ Downtown Grand Hotel. Downtown's old Lady Luck Hotel & Casino was transformed into this fashionable-yet-affordable property (not to be confused with MGM Grand or The D Las Vegas). Despite having 634 spacious rooms in an 18-story tower, it nevertheless has a boutique hotel aesthetic, with bright color schemes, plush furnishings, and amenities like flat-screen HD TVs and pillow-top mattresses. There's also Picnic—an expansive rooftop pool and lounge area—and seven retro-vibe restaurants and bars that can accommodate all palates and budgets. And, of course, there's gambling: at tables and blingy slot or video-poker machines or in sports-betting areas. *206 N. 3rd St., (702) 953-4343, www.downtowngrand.com.*

❺ Hecho en Vegas. If you like authentic Mexican food, try this friendly restaurant in the MGM Grand Hotel on the Strip. The guacamole isn't just made to order, it's made to taste. The menu also has handmade tamales, street tacos, and sweetly salty margaritas. Not only is this dinner spot reliable, but the prices are reasonable—for central Vegas, anyway. Great happy hours make things even more affordable. *3799 Las Vegas Blvd. S., (702) 891-3200, www.mgmgrand.com/restaurants.*

Neon boneyard

❻ One Million Dollar Display. A prominent downtown casino since 1951, Binion's serves patrons according to its founding guidelines: "Good food. Good whiskey. Good gamble." But, in recent years, more folks have been attracted to the casino for its display of precisely $1 million—perhaps in hopes that some big-buck luck will rub off. To join them, head to the Club Binion's Player's Club area, where you can snap a selfie (if you're 21 or older) next to cash in denominations ranging from $1 to $100 bills and encased in clear boxes, arranged in a pyramid atop a poker table. *128 E. Fremont St., (702) 382-1600, www.binions.com.*

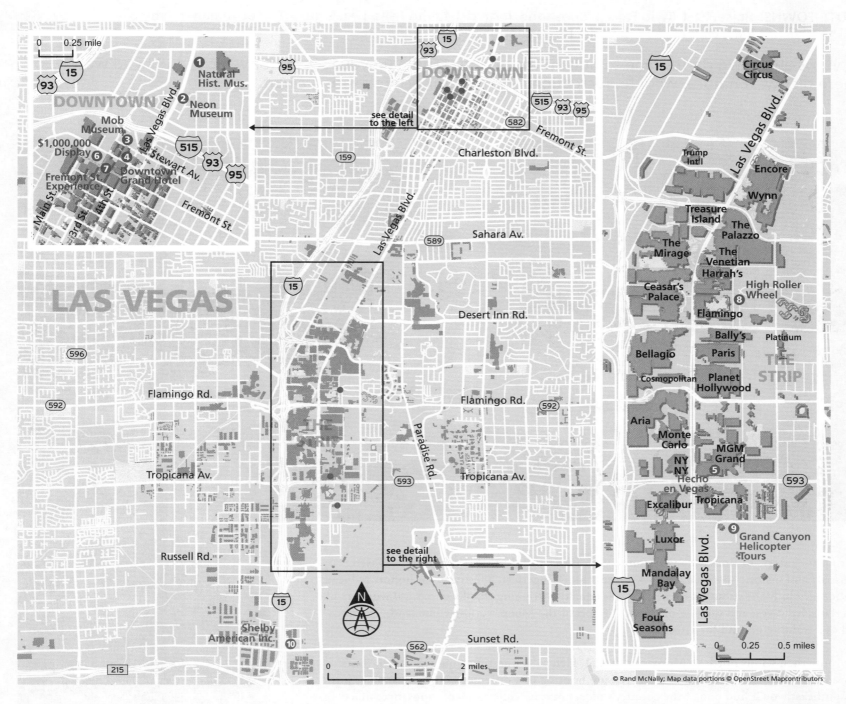

0   0.25 mile

93 15

DOWNTOWN

1 Natural Hist. Mus.

2 Neon Museum

Mob Museum

$1,000,000 Display

Las Vegas Blvd.

3 515

6 Stewart Av.

93 95

7 Downtown Grand Hotel

Fremont St. Experience

Main St. 3rd St. 4th St.

Fremont St.

LAS VEGAS

596

Flamingo Rd.

592

Tropicana Av.

Russell Rd.

215

15

Shelby American Inc.

10

N

0   1   2 miles

562

Sunset Rd.

95

DOWNTOWN

93

15

515 93 95

582

Fremont St.

Charleston Blvd.

159

Las Vegas Blvd

589 Sahara Av.

see detail to the left

Desert Inn Rd.

Paradise Rd.

Flamingo Rd.

592

593 Tropicana Av.

15

593

see detail to the right

15

Circus Circus

15

Las Vegas Blvd.

Trump Int'l

Encore

Wynn

Treasure Island

The Mirage

The Palazzo

The Venetian

Harrah's

High Roller Wheel

Ceasar's Palace

8

Flamingo

Bally's Platinum

Paris

THE STRIP

Bellagio

Cosmopolitan

Planet Hollywood

Aria

Monte Carlo

NY NY

Hecho en Vegas

MGM Grand

5

Excalibur

Tropicana

Luxor

9 Grand Canyon Helicopter Tours

Mandalay Bay

Las Vegas Blvd.

15

Four Seasons

0   0.25   0.5 miles

© Rand McNally; Map data portions © OpenStreet Mapcontributors

NORTHEAST

MIDWEST

SOUTH

WEST

7 Fremont Street Experience. Before the Strip, there was Glitter Gulch, today known as the Fremont Street Experience. It's a five-block entertainment district and open-air pedestrian mall—flanked by shops and such famous casinos as the Golden Nugget, the Four Queens, and Binion's—in historic downtown.

Above it all is Viva Vision, the 1,500-foot-long, 90-foot-high video screen that's the world's largest. Its 12.5 million LEDs and 550,000-watt sound system flash and blast out 6-minute light-and-music shows hourly every night. If you're intrepid, check out SlotZilla, a slot machine–themed zip line with two runs: The lower one launches you from 77 feet up and travels half the length of the mall; the upper Zoom Line launches you, "Superman style," from 114 feet up and runs the mall's entire length. *Fremont St., between Main and 4th Sts., (877) 834-2748, vegasexperience.com.*

Along and Around the Strip

8 High Roller Wheel. The LINQ entertainment district is home to shops, restaurants, nightspots, the LINQ hotel, and yet another impressive Vegas attraction: the High Roller. The world's largest observation wheel rises 550 feet, its 2,000 colorful LEDs rivaling the sparkle of the surrounding Strip. Completing a rotation takes 30 minutes, during which time you (and up to 39 other passengers) are comfortably

ensconced inside an air-conditioned, pod-like "cabin" with benches. Glorious windows afford priceless views day or night. *3545 Las Vegas Blvd. S., (702) 322-0593, www.caesars.com/linq.*

9 Grand Canyon Helicopter Tours. Although none of the tours comes cheap, getting above the fray for breathtaking Vegas views might be worth it. The least expensive option loops around the Strip for an exhilarating 10 to 15 minutes. If money is less of an object, you can fly not only over Vegas, but also the Grand Canyon, Hoover Dam, and other regional points of interest. Reservations are a top-flight idea. *275 E. Tropicana Ave., (702) 835-8477, www.grandcanyonhelicopter.com.*

10 Shelby American Inc. You don't have to be a racing fanatic to enjoy the vehicles produced by Carroll Shelby International, one of the country's premier auto manufacturers since 1962. While taking in the changing displays of shiny, cherry-red racers and other sleek (and fast) vintage cars at the Shelby Heritage Center, located near McCarran Airport, you'll also learn about the first Cobras, as well as the new Mustangs, and how the GT 350 got its name. Visit the center and its shop on your own, or join one of the free guided tours offered once or twice a day Monday through Saturday. *6405 Ensworth St., (702) 942-7325, www.shelbyamerican.com.*

LINQ High Roller Wheel

Wide Skies of the West

ROUTE TOWNS: Boise, ID | Twin Falls | Shoshone | Arco | Idaho Falls | Helena, MT | Bozeman | Pray
Yellowstone, WY | Cody | Thermopolis | Cheyenne

Cowboys and cowgirls, it's time to pull up your boots, saddle up your . . . motor vehicle, and head west,
where plenty of nature, wildlife, recreation, and mineral-rich relaxation await.

Yellowstone National Park

Your journey starts in Boise, Idaho's capital, with its beautiful riverside parks; repurposed
industrial and historic spaces; and quirky events like Gingerfest, a festival that honors redheads.
The scenery in Idaho's southeastern reaches is equally intriguing thanks to natural wonders like
waterfalls, ice caves, and the one-of-a-kind Craters of the Moon—a lunar-like landscape once
used as a training ground for astronauts.

The route then winds north to Montana's capital, Helena, a one-time gold rush town that's
now an adventure destination noted for treasure hunting of a different kind: geocaching. Just to
the southeast, you'll find one of the country's most amazing collections of dinosaur artifacts in
Bozeman and some truly relaxing thermal waters in Pray, where Chico Hot Springs Resort &
Spa has been attracting travelers since the 1890s. It's the perfect rest stop before heading into
Wyoming and embarking on a tour of the nation's first national park: Yellowstone—established
in 1872 by President Ulysses S. Grant.

Farther south, Western history is alive and well in many a frontier town. Cody was named
for Buffalo Bill himself. Thermopolis has still more hot springs, made historic (and free to
the public) thanks to an 1896 treaty between Native Americans and the U.S. government.
Then there's Cheyenne, yet another state capital rife with annals and legends, well-preserved
architecture, and hearty cowboy fare.

Distance: 1,448 miles point to
point.

Type of Trip: Vacation Getaway;
RV; Great Outdoors, History &
Heritage, Picture Perfect, Quirky &
Oddball, Small Town Gems.

Must Try: A dip in a mineral pool
at Hot Springs State Park—a regular
stop for Butch Cassidy and the
Sundance Kid. For cowboy cravings,
take a side trip to Missoula, MT, for
the chicken-fried steak at the Oxford
Saloon; or visit Wyoming's Rib & Chop
House for premium strips and rib eyes.

Must Buy: Cowboy boots from one
of the many Western-wear outfitters
throughout the region.

Must See: Old Idaho State
Penitentiary, Shoshone Falls and Ice
Caves, Craters of the Moon National
Monument, Museum of the Rockies,
Yellowstone National Park, Buffalo
Bill Cody Center, Wyoming Dinosaur
Center, Cheyenne Trolley Tours.

Worth Noting: This territory
is famous for its snowy peaks and
wide-open plains—where sudden
downpours or snowstorms can occur.
Be ready to slow down, detour, or
find a bunk for the night in the event
of bad weather.

Travel Tips: Yellowstone National
Park and other forests and preserves
might close or limit hours seasonally
or for stormy weather. Yellowstone's
many highways also regularly
undergo repair work. Travel with
patience, and build in extra time for
sluggish park traffic.

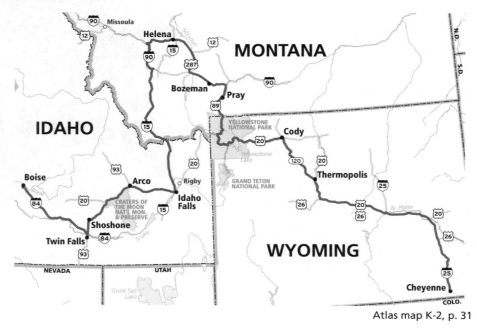

Atlas map K-2, p. 31

Boise, ID

Julia Davis Park. This 89-acre municipal park is considered the first and most central of Boise's so-called String of Pearls (the multiple lush green parks lining the Boise River). It's home to some of the city's most prominent attractions including Zoo Boise, Boise Art Museum, Discovery Center of Idaho, Idaho Black History Museum, and Idaho State Historical Museum (relocated temporarily to 214 Broadway Avenue, until renovations are complete in spring 2018).

It also has the customary amenities, as well as bocce courts, horseshoe pits, a boathouse, paddle boats, barbecue pits, and plenty of flower-lined walkways. A footbridge connects to Boise State University across the river. A section of the 25-mile-long pathway known as the Boise River Greenbelt also traverses the park. *700 S. Capitol Blvd., (208) 608-7650, www.juliadavispark.org.*

Old Idaho Penitentiary. Built in 1870, the penitentiary served the state until 1973. Guided tours now take you to the cell blocks and solitary confinement, and guides spice things up with tales of desperate folks. There's an exhibit of prison tattooing, the J. Curtis Earl Memorial Exhibit of firearms, and seasonal events such as Gingerfest for redheads and Romancing the Pen Valentine's Day tours. *2445 Old Penitentiary Rd., (208) 334-2844, history.idaho.gov/old-idaho-penitentiary.*

Idaho Botanical Garden. The Idaho penitentiary's original farm and nursery is now this lush, 33-acre landscaped space. It features English-style, rose, and meditation gardens; a children's adventure space; a tea house; and the Lewis and Clark Native Plant Garden, which showcases plants collected on the expedition between Great Falls, Montana, and The Dalles, Oregon. You'll also find a varied collection of sculpture throughout the property. *2355 Old Penitentiary Rd., (208) 343-8649, idahobotanicalgarden.org.*

Twin Falls

Shoshone Falls. Located 3 miles east of the city of Twin Falls, these 212-foot cascades have been welcoming people since the early 20th century. Not only are they 45 feet higher than Niagara Falls, but they carry an equivalent volume of water during the spring runoff season. For the most spectacular view, visit October through April, before irrigation diversions diminish the Snake River's flow. The surrounding parkland also has trails, playgrounds, swimming areas, picnic tables, a boat launch, and scenic overlooks. *Shoshone Falls Park Entrance: Falls Ave., (208) 736-2265, www.tfid.org.*

Boise

Shoshone

Shoshone Ice Caves. Even when summer brings temperatures of over 100 degrees, the thermometer in these south-central Idaho caves—17 miles north of Shoshone—consistently registers between 18 and 28 degrees. Freezing air currents inside a lava tube created these remarkable formations some 90 feet down. Layer up and sport sturdy shoes for the daily, 45-minute, guided tours (you can't explore on your own). The on-site museum has gems, minerals, and Native American artifacts. *1561 N. Hwy. 75, (208) 886-2058, www.shoshoneicecaves.com.*

Arco

Craters of the Moon National Monument and Preserve. This preserve's seemingly desolate and bizarre appearance—windswept landscape, lava flows, craters—inspired its lunar name and gave NASA a place to train the Apollo astronauts. Although volcanic activity is thought to extend back 6 million years, it's estimated that the surface was formed only during the last 15,000 years, the result of some 60 lava flows from 25 volcanoes. The last eruption took place 2,000 years ago, but more are anticipated.

Although the preserve appears lifeless, at least 2,000 species of insects thrive here, as do more than 160 species of birds and numerous mammals, reptiles, and amphibians. Spring and summer see a vivid carpet of wildflowers; in winter, the park is groomed for cross-country skiing and snowshoeing. Short trails off the 7-mile Loop Road lead to spatter cones, lava tube caves, and volcanic craters. A visitors center has exhibits and a video that explain the forces that shaped the landscape. *Hwy. 20/26/93, (208) 527-1335, www.nps.gov/crmo.*

Idaho Falls

Idaho Falls. Incorporated in 1891, humble Idaho Falls is the state's second-largest city (Boise's the largest). Its name honors the waterfalls created when a series of Snake River rapids were enhanced in 1911 with the construction of the Lower Idaho Falls Dam. Water spilling over that dam now forms a picturesque cascade, with the Idaho Falls Temple and other urban landmarks in the background. If you have time, combine a visit to the falls with a self-guided walking tour of historic downtown (free map available at downtownidahofalls. com). *Idaho Falls Visitors Bureau, 425 Capital Ave. (208) 523-1010, www.visitidahofalls.com.*

Idaho Botanical Garden

Eat & Stay

10 Barrel Brewing Company Boise Pub | Boise. In a city that conjures images of hearty cowboys and lumberjacks, this pub fits in perfectly. Many of its craft ales, lagers, and stouts are brewed in Boise; all are served up inside a large industrial-style space. A burger, pizza, nachos, or other pub fare will help absorb all those delicious hops. The menu also has lighter fare like salmon wraps, whole-grain salads, and fish tacos. It's a casual place, and minors are welcome at all hours—they'll miss out on the beer, but will undoubtedly enjoy the Nutella fudge brownie. *830 W. Bannock St., (208) 344-5870, www.10barrel.com/agegate.*

The Modern Hotel | Boise. Sleek and stylish, hip and high-tech, eco-friendly and affordable—not bad for a former Travelodge. The Modern features 39 "intelligently designed" rooms with mid-century modern styling. It also offers reliable Wi-Fi; Continental breakfast (included in the rates); and a location near the Boise River waterfront, Julia Davis and Ann Morrison parks, and other attractions. Modern Bar, the on-site restaurant, serves tasty fare with a twist, especially for weekend brunch. With live music some nights, tasty bar food, and inventive cocktails, the bar and its courtyard are great hangouts. *1314 W. Grove St. (208) 424-8244, themodernhotel.com.*

Blue Heron Inn | Rigby, ID. With so many chain hotels dotting the region, this inn on the banks of the Snake River, about 20 miles north of Idaho Falls, is a welcome respite. Its log-cabin styling perfectly suits the lush, pastoral surroundings, both on the property's 3.5 acres and in the greater vicinity, which includes Sun Valley Ski Resort and Yellowstone and Grand Teton national parks. Birding and fishing from the river's edge are both popular activities. Many of the peaceful guestrooms have water views, and a hearty breakfast is included in the rates. *706 N. Yellowstone Hwy., (866) 745-9922, www.idahoblueheron.com.*

NORTHEAST

MIDWEST

SOUTH

WEST

Last Chance Gulch architecture, Helena

Helena, MT

Montana Historical Society Museum. Founded in 1865, the institution that's often referred to as Montana's Museum has more than 50,000 artifacts that bring the state's unique past—from its prehistory through WW II—to life. You'll also see works by such renowned locals as Charles M. Russell, the so-called cowboy artist. Interpretive exhibits, a research center, archives, and a museum store round out the offerings. Note that the historical society also administers and offers guided tours of the original Governor's Mansion. *225 N. Roberts St., (406) 444-2694, mhs.mt.gov/museum.*

Last Chance Train Tours. Climb aboard this open-air train for an hour-long immersion in Montana's capital. Tours depart from the historical society, just east of the Capitol, several times a day during the summer. They cruise by some of Helena's most picturesque sights—from the opulent mansion district and governor's homes (old and new) to the grand St. Helena Cathedral and eye-catching architecture of Last Chance Gulch. *225 N. Roberts St., (406) 442-1023, lctours.com.*

Helena: Capital of Adventure

One of Helena's top outdoor-recreation outfitters, the **Base Camp** (5 W. Broadway, 406/443-5360, www.thebasecamp.com) has everything you need for backpacking, climbing, skiing, kayaking, and geocaching—a game where players hide waterproof containers the world over and challenge others to find them using a GPS device or app. The Base Camp rents GPS units with caches pre-loaded, and locals will gladly add tips and guidance to your search.

If mountain biking's more your thing, you'll be happy to know that the International Mountain Bicycling Association named Helena an official Bronze Level Ride Center, which seems appropriate given the myriad in-town bike lanes and the more than 70 miles of single-track area trails. The family-owned **Big Sky Cycling and Fitness** (801 N. Last Chance Gulch, 406/442-4644, bigskybikes.com) has rentals and tune-up services with on-staff seasoned riders ready to answer any questions.

Bozeman

Museum of the Rockies. Take a walk through more than 4 billion years of Montana's history. A highlight here is one of the world's largest collections of dinosaur fossils, featuring specimens like the Tyrannosaurus rex and the Triceratops. There are also regional and Native American history exhibits; the Taylor Planetarium; and the Living History Farm, featuring the Tinsley House and Heirloom Gardens. The Martin Children's Discovery Center has interactive displays and educational activities explaining the wonders of Yellowstone. *600 W. Kagy Blvd., (406) 994-2251, www.museumoftherockies.org.*

Pray

Chico Hot Springs Resort & Spa. Imagine a morning spent white-water rafting, horseback riding, or dog-sledding followed by an afternoon soak in a 96-degree pool with snow-covered peaks in the distance. Welcome to Chico Hot Springs, where springs were recorded as early as 1865; the first "pools" didn't arrive till the 1890s. In 1900, more formal pools were created and the main lodge was built, drawing people from everywhere who needed to "treat" anything and everything. The resort caters to day and overnight guests alike, so pop in for a dip, schedule various spa treatments, or spend a couple of days combining your soaks with organized resort excursions or your own outings to nearby Yellowstone National Park. Along with a gift shop and café that sells made-in-Montana souvenirs and espresso, there's also a saloon, poolside grill, and formal dining room. *163 Chico Rd., (406) 333-4933, www.chicohotsprings.com.*

Yellowstone, WY

Yellowstone National Park. Established in 1872 and situated in Wyoming (primarily), Montana, and Idaho, this is America's first national park. Preserved within it are Mammoth Hot Springs; Yellowstone Canyon; Lake Yellowstone; and, of course, Old Faithful Geyser. The abundant wildlife here includes grizzly bears, wolves, bison, elk, and bald eagles. Stay on one of 1,000-plus miles of trails, some of which have boardwalks, and follow all rules and guidelines to stay safe and minimize your impact. The park has many interpretive programs and ranger-led walks and talks offered in summer.

If you plan to overnight, there are 12 RV and tent campgrounds, plus nine guest lodges (two are open year round). Dining options—from snack bars to full-service restaurants—abound as do recreational outfitters and general stores. In summer, options for touring (guided and self-guided) include not only scenic drives and hikes but also llama or horseback treks, boating (non-motorized) expeditions, and biking excursions. Fishing is also an option. In winter, you can snowmobile, cross-country ski, or snowshoe. *495 Old Faithful, (307) 344-7381, www.nps.gov/yell.*

Eat & Stay

Oxford Saloon & Café | Missoula, MT. The Ox, as it's affectionately known, occupies a refurbished corner space in downtown Missoula, attracting everyone from local businessmen and cowboys to bikers and college kids. The menu has the sort of filling saloon fare you'd expect from a western-Montana classic: chicken-fried steak with JJ's special gravy; ½-pound burgers; 1-pound rib-eyes; and, of course, breakfast all day. Poker games are held nightly at 8, with stakes starting at 25 cents. *337 N. Higgins Ave., (406) 549-0117, www.the-oxford.com.*

Goldsmith's Bed & Breakfast | Missoula, MT. In 1988, this historic 1911 brick house skirted demolition when the audacious Goldsmiths sawed it in half and moved it to the Clark Fork River's northern bank. It's now a top local inn that has seven homey rooms with private baths and modern amenities. Downtown's eateries and shops are a short walk away. *803 W. Front St., (866) 666-9945, missoulabedandbreakfast.com.*

Cateye Café | Bozeman. Located near the galleries, shops, and vintage architecture of downtown Bozeman's main drag, this compact café serves up family-style hospitality with its cowboy-caliber breakfasts and lunches. Folks line up for reasonably priced dishes like an open-faced meatloaf sandwich or "catastrophe" veggie and cheese scramble. The café also offers playful suggestions like, "Clean your plate—expect chastisement if you don't." *23 N. Tracy Ave., (406) 587-8844, www.cateyecafe.com.*

Buffalo Bill's Irma Hotel | Cody. The hotel built by Buffalo Bill Cody in 1902 and named for his daughter has hosted many famous Old West personalities, including Annie Oakley, Frederic Remington, and Calamity Jane. Although various owners have expanded and renovated the place, it's still in its original, prime, corner location. The Irma Restaurant, open daily for all meals, is famous for its prime-rib dinners and "Wild West salmon." Guestrooms are simple and updated, with air-conditioning, free Wi-Fi, coffeemakers, and hair dryers. *1192 Sheridan Ave., (307) 587-4221, www.irmahotel.com.*

Museum of the Rockies, Bozeman

Cody

Buffalo Bill Center of the West. The Buffalo Bill Museum first opened in 1927 in a log cabin in downtown Cody. Today, it's part of a complex of five Western-themed museums. Here you can learn about the history of the American cowboy, dude ranching, Western conservation, frontier entrepreneurship, and Colonel William F. "Buffalo Bill" Cody—town founder, buffalo hunter, U.S. Army scout, Pony Express rider, and Wild West Show founder.

Exhibits in the Draper Natural History Museum, Plains Indian Museum, and Whitney Western Art Museum lend still more insight into local culture and wildlife. The Cody Firearms Museum has one of the world's most comprehensive collections of American guns. The center also hosts lectures, readings, workshops, and film screenings, and the large gift shop is filled with souvenirs, fine art, and housewares. *720 Sheridan Ave., (307) 587-4771, centerofthewest.org.*

Yellowstone National Park

Thermopolis Hot Springs

Thermopolis

Hot Springs State Park. This unique natural wonderland is one of Wyoming's most relaxing attractions. Each day, more than 8,000 gallons of mineral-rich water flow in at a constant temperature of 135 degrees. The site was preserved thanks to an 1896 treaty between Shoshone Chief Washakie, Arapaho Chief Sharp Nose, and the U.S. government, stipulating that the springs would always have free access.

The treaty has endured: the park is still free to the public, as is its bathhouse, where you can take a therapeutic soak in 104-degree indoor or outdoor pools (bring your own swimsuits and towels, or rent them on site). There are also 6.2 miles of trails; comfort stations; boat docks; picnic shelters; the large Big Spring pool; and a swinging suspension footbridge that offers the best views of the fascinating terrain. *538 N. Park St., (307) 864-2176, wyoparks.state.wy.us.*

Wyoming Dinosaur Center. The 1993 discovery of fossils on Warm Springs Ranch turned Thermopolis into a major center for paleontological research and led to the creation of the Wyoming Dinosaur Center. In addition to the 12,000 square feet of exhibitions that cover the prehistoric record from around the world, the center is headquarters for the scientists who are working on approximately 10 of the 60 surface sites at a time.

You can visit both the museum and the dig sites, which are a few miles away. The Dig for a Day program, which operates from spring through fall, allows you to work side-by-side with the paleontologists who are collecting Jurassic-period dinosaur fossils from the ancient sandstone riverbed (reservations are recommended). *110 Carter Ranch Rd., (307) 864-2997, www.wyodino.org.*

Cheyenne

Cheyenne Trolley Tour. The storied history of Wyoming's capital is encapsulated during the trolley tours offered by this operator. Expert guides regale you with lore and humor as you cruise past the Governor's Mansion, the Capitol, and Cheyenne Frontier Days Old West Museum. The journey also spotlights century-old mansions built by cattle barons, legendary cowboy and railroad sites, and even a handful of reportedly haunted buildings. Purchase tickets at the Visit Cheyenne desk inside the landmark Cheyenne Depot Museum. *121 W. 15th St., (307) 778-3133, www.cheyennetrolley.com.*

Wyoming State Museum. Housed on two floors of the Barrett Building, southeast of the Capitol, this museum's eight permanent galleries interpret Wyoming wildlife; Native American life and culture; and the stories behind everything from the state's military and archeological sites to its trails, trains, and geology. Highlights include a wildlife diorama, the Hands-on History Room, and a life-sized cast of the dinosaur Camptosaurus—one of the state's first dinosaur discoveries. *Barrett Bldg., 2301 Central Ave., (307) 777-7022, wyomuseum.state.wy.us.*

Eat & Stay

Eagle RV Park | **Thermopolis.** Campsites, log cabins, and RV sites are available at this grassy, well-shaded campground 3 miles south of Hot Springs State Park. Pull-through RV parking allows for large vehicles. Electric and cable hookups are available, and Wi-Fi is free throughout the park. You'll also find laundry facilities, a playground, and a general store. Other on-site activities include badminton and horseshoes. *204 Hwy. 20 S., (307) 864-5262, www. eaglervpark.com.*

Wyoming's Rib & Chop House | **Cheyenne.** This hot spot a block from the Cheyenne Depot Museum has a hearty and filling selection of steaks, ribs, and roasts. But there are also plenty of seafood dishes, salads, and sandwiches—plus tasty Cajun classics like po-boys, gumbo, and fried catfish. Locals advise trying the unexpected-but-delicious fried green tomatoes and taking advantage of sociable weekday happy hours. *400 W. Lincolnway, (307) 514-0271, ribandchophouse.com.*

Nagel-Warren Mansion Bed & Breakfast | **Cheyenne.** Building this sandstone confection took two years and cost local entrepreneur Erasmus Nagel $50,000 in 1888—the equivalent of $1.2 million today. The current owner has also spared no expense on restoration. Though each guest room is unique, all have the hallmarks of Victorian elegance: sumptuous patterned fabrics and wallpapers; period-appropriate art; and ornate woodwork and furnishings. The parlor, library, and other common areas are equally rich. Modern amenities include flat-screen TVs, free Wi-Fi, an exercise room, and a hot tub. A full breakfast and afternoon tea are included in the modest rates. *222 E. 17th St., (800) 811-2610, naglewarrenmansion.com.*

Cheyenne

NORTHEAST

MIDWEST

SOUTH

WEST

South Dakota's Black Hills

ROUTE TOWNS: Rapid City | Sturgis | Deadwood | Hill City | Keystone | Custer | Hot Springs

The Lakota Sioux called them Pahá Sápa (Black Hills) for good reason: the pine forests are so dense that the landscape really does appear black from a distance. And this drive through South Dakota's western edge affords plenty of chances to admire and experience all the storied, eerie beauty.

Mount Rushmore National Memorial

Though Wyoming has a sliver of the 125-mile-long, 65-mile-wide Black Hills National Forest, most of it is in South Dakota. The region also encompasses prairies, gulches, caves, lakes, streams, and reservoirs. Deer, mountain goats, elk, and other species find refuge in the forests, and small herds of bison roam the plains while feisty black-tail prairie dogs dig dens beneath them.

Routes like curvaceous US-385 cut swaths right through the Black Hills, north from Rapid City and Deadwood down through Hill City, Custer, and Hot Springs. In Keystone, four of our nation's great presidents, memorialized in Mount Rushmore granite, overlook the forest's eastern reaches. Custer State Park, with its bison herd, and Wind Cave National Park, with its 104 miles of known passages, abut the forest's southeastern edge.

Archaeologists have dated human habitation here back 10,000 years, and, for centuries, the Black Hills have been considered sacred not only by the Sioux but also the Arapaho, Cheyenne, and Kiowa. And this sacred earth has safeguarded precious minerals and ores as well as gigantic prehistoric creatures. This trip offers plenty of opportunities to see renowned geological and paleontological finds. It also takes you through former pioneer and mining towns, where locals are on a first-name basis with long-dead gunslingers.

Distance: 210 miles full loop (starting/ending in Rapid City).

Type of Trip: Weekend or Vacation Getaway; RV; Great Outdoors, History & Heritage, Picture Perfect, Quirky & Oddball, Science & Tech, Small Town Gems.

Must Try: A buffalo burger (many places serve buffalo as well as beef patties).

Must Buy: A dinosaur or mineral dig kit; Lakota Sioux bead- or quill-work items or other crafts.

Must See: Journey Museum, Sturgis Motorcycle Museum, Original Deadwood Tours, Mount Rushmore, Crazy Horse Memorial, Custer State Park, Wind Cave National Park, Black Hills Wild Horse Sanctuary.

Worth Noting: Learn all about **Black Hills National Forest** (www.fs.usda.gov/blackhills, 605-343-8755) and its amenities and activities at the Pactola Visitor Center along US-385, near the Pactola Reservoir Dam, or at ranger stations in Spearfish, Rapid City, and Custer (supervisor's office).

Travel Tips: Southeast of Rapid City, Badlands National Park's jagged formations loom like monuments to a lost civilization. You can readily add an overnight visit, beginning in the Ben Reifel Visitor Center and its Cedar Pass Lodge and Campground. Head out along I-90, stopping at the Minuteman Missile National Historic Site, and loop back along SD-44 through the park (about 300 miles round trip). Short on time? Take a day trip to Wyoming's Devils Tower National Monument, just 78 miles west of Sturgis, mostly along I-90.

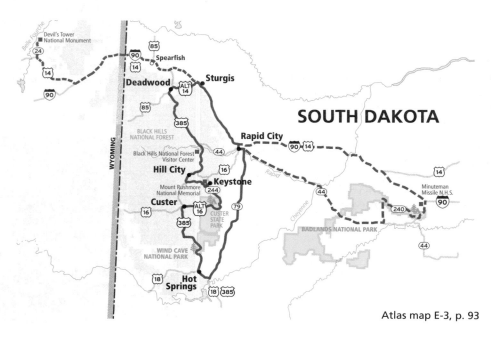

Atlas map E-3, p. 93

Rapid City

The Journey Museum & Learning Center. This museum tells the story of the Northern Plains, from the geological upheaval that created the Black Hills to Native American and frontier settlement. The Sioux Indian Museum has ceremonial garments, containers, dolls, moccasins, and other everyday items highlighting the culture and craftsmanship of the Lakota. The Minnilusa Pioneer Museum features mining, military, and settler artifacts and the stories of such historical figures as Wild Bill Hickok, George Armstrong Custer, Sitting Bull, and Crazy Horse.

Many artifacts on display are provided by the South Dakota Archaeological Research Center, affiliated with the state historical society. Some geological and paleontological finds come from the South Dakota School of Mines and Technology. If fossils and dinosaurs or minerals and gemstones are your thing, consider visiting its free, on-campus **Museum of Geology** (O'Harra Hall, 3ʳᵈ Fl., 501 E. St. Joseph St., 605/394-2467, www.sdsmt.edu), where a gift shop sells prehistoric creature excavation and assembly kits, mineral dig kits, and other cool stuff. *222 New York St., (605) 394-6923, journeymuseum.org.*

Prairie Edge Trading Co. & Galleries. No "Made in China" tags here! Most of the Native American fine art, traditional apparel, jewelry, and other items in Prairie Edge, which focuses exclusively on Plains Indians culture, are created by local artists and artisans. Prices are on the high side, as befits the high quality and authenticity of the work. If you're planning to splurge on a cherished memento, this would be one place to do it. If not, you'll find more affordable items in the bookshop. *606 Main St., (605) 342-3086, www.prairieedge.com.*

Prairie Edge Trading Company

Chapel in the Hills. In the late 1800s, many Norwegians settled in the Dakotas and Minnesota to grow wheat and raise cattle in the fertile plains, and, today, nearly 14% of South Dakota's residents claim Norwegian ancestry. This 1960s Evangelical Lutheran chapel—a replica of the famous 1150 AD, triple-nave Borgund Stavkirke in Laerdal, Norway—honors their forebears. It's hard to believe such a marvel of wood architecture, artisanship, and artistry could be constructed in contemporary times, let alone in the 12ᵗʰ century. *3788 Chapel Ln., (605) 342-8281, www.chapel-in-the-hills.org.*

Reptile Gardens. What started small back in 1937 today has very large collections of reptiles, amphibians, and, yes, bugs, in its three-story Sky Dome and other themed enclosure areas. It's also a strong promoter of conservation. Rounding out the offerings are botanical gardens, gator and snake shows, a playground, a café, and a gift shop. *8955 S. Hwy. 16, (605) 342-5873, www.reptilegardens.com.*

Bear Country USA. As its name suggests, this 250-acre drive-through wildlife park has lots of bears, particularly black ones. But on a drive through its natural Black Hills habitat, you'll also spot freely roaming elk, bighorn sheep, buffalo, mountain goats, timber and Arctic wolves, bobcats, cougars, grizzly bears, and other North American animals. You can also walk through the Babyland area, home to smaller and younger animals, including lots of cubs. *13820 S. Hwy. 16, (605) 343-2290, www.bearcountryusa.com.*

Dinosaur Park. Built in 1936 as part of the WPA program, this quirky park sits atop a sandstone ridge with 100-mile views. Paved walkways take you up past the five original life-size, concrete-and-steel dinosaurs—an Apatosaurus, a Tyrannosaurus rex, a Triceratops, a Stegosaurus, and a Trachodon—which were placed on the National Register of Historic Places in 1990. The other two dinosaurs were built in the 1950s. Admission is free, and the site has a visitors center, café, and gift shop. *940 Skyline Dr., (605) 343-8687, www.blackhillsbadlands.com/dinosaurpark.*

Sturgis

Sturgis Motorcycle Museum & Hall of Fame. For a week each August, the Black Hills rumble with the full-throttled roar of motorcycles thanks to the Sturgis Motorcycle Rally, held since 1938. It draws a half-million people—more than half South Dakota's entire population—to events that include races, concerts, parties, and scenic tours. The epicenter, though, is downtown Sturgis, where bikes line Main Street outside music halls and roadhouses, and the partying goes on all night. Year-round, you can get a taste of the rally spirit at the Sturgis Motorcycle Museum & Hall of Fame. Although vintage bikes and memorabilia feature greatly, there's also an emphasis on honoring the culture and community of motorcyclists. *999 Main St., (605) 347-2001, www.sturgismuseum.com.*

Eat & Stay

Wine Cellar Restaurant | Rapid City. Set in a 100-year-old downtown building with hardwood floors and tin ceilings, this dinner-only restaurant serves small plates as well as full entrées. You might choose root vegetable au gratin, pulled-pork sliders, beef-tenderloin skewers, *poulet en croûte* (chicken wrapped in pastry and then baked), or pan-seared salmon. Thin-crust pizzas come with toppings like pesto and artichoke or smoked chicken and caramelized onions. There's also a robust wine and beer list, seasonal specials, and house-made desserts. *513 6ᵗʰ St., (605) 718-2675, winecellarrestaurant.com.*

Hotel Alex Johnson | Rapid City. The enormous scale of this 1928 structure is typical of many hotels of the day, particularly those founded by captains of industry like Alex Johnson, a vice president of the Chicago and Northwestern Railroad. What's atypical is the German Tudor–style architecture and the interior filled with Native American symbols. Public spaces are as grand as you'd expect; the 143 guest rooms and suites are as comfortable as you could want, with rich woods, leather club chairs, and pillow-top beds. The Wi-Fi is free, the TV is high def, and there's a fitness center, a salon and day spa, a gift shop, and a mix of casual and more formal eateries and lounges. Views from the sleek Vertex Sky Bar are as captivating as the stories about the Lady in White and other restless souls who reportedly haunt these hallowed halls. *523 6ᵗʰ St., (605) 342-1210, www.alexjohnson.com.*

Black Hills

NORTHEAST

MIDWEST

SOUTH

WEST

Deadwood

Original Deadwood Tours. This company's one-hour narrated bus tours take you through the storied streets of this Wild West mining town. Among the many stops is Mt. Moriah (aka Boot Hill) Cemetery, where you can stroll amid the graves of Wild Bill Hickok, Calamity Jane Canary, Preacher Smith, Potato Creek Johnny, and local madam Dora DuFran—whose pet parrot was buried with her. Departures are from the Midnight Star Casino, which, like the tour company itself, is owned by the actor Kevin Costner, who fell in love with South Dakota while filming *Dances with Wolves*. The company also offers guided visits to Tatanka: The Story of the Bison, a museum that's another of Costner's enterprises. *677 Main St., (605) 920-1177, www.deadwoodtour.com.*

Old Style Saloon No. 10. Sawdust still covers the floor in the saloon where Wild Bill Hickok met his death, an event that's re-enacted here several times a day. The walls and rafters are hung with original Old West gunslinger and miner memorabilia, making it something of a living museum. Belly up to the bar for a cold beer or root beer. Kids are welcome here till 8:30 pm, when the live music begins. A second-floor bar is adjacent to the Deadwood Social Club restaurant, which serves a mix of steak and Italian dishes. Gaming options include blackjack, low-limit poker, and slots. *657 Main St., (605) 578-3346, www.saloon10.com.*

Wild Bill Hickok (top)
Old Style Saloon No. 10

Where the West Went Wild

Deadwood's history would be a Wild West cliché if it weren't for one thing: What happened here inspired some of those clichés to begin with. An 1874 expedition under General Custer himself found gold in the Black Hills. Though the government had, with the 1868 Treaty of Fort Laramie, given the hills to the Lakota Sioux, by 1876, thousands of prospectors had entrenched themselves in a mucky tent- and shack-filled camp. They were joined by gunslingers, gamblers, and other opportunists, who frequented the inevitable brothels and saloons.

For a spell, daily life included skirmishes with the Lakota and general lawlessness. Although the brothels are long gone, and the only gun slinging you'll see is during re-enactments of Wild Bill Hickok's tragic end, the casinos are still around (their revenue helps pay for preservation works). So are many of the places where key events unfolded; indeed, much of the town is a National Historic Landmark District.

Hill City

Black Hills Institute of Geological Research. Noted for its paleontological field work and many remarkable discoveries, this institute loans or sells fossil specimens to museums throughout the world. Exhibits in its on-site museum change frequently, as major new finds are featured and loaners—such as Stan, the museum's famed Tyrannosaurus rex—come home for return engagements. In addition to dinosaur skeletons and animal fossils, there's also a collection of agates, minerals, and meteorites. The Everything Prehistoric gift shop has a huge selection of toys, books, games, and crystal items. *117 Main St. (U.S. 385), (605) 574-4289, www.bhigr.com.*

1880 Train. From May through October, the 1880 Train makes the two-hour, round-trip journey several times daily between Hill City and Keystone. Pulled by a classic Baldwin steam engine, it follows the original route of the Chicago, Burlington and Quincy Railroad (CB&Q) over steep gradients through Black Hills National Forest. You can board in either town for one-way or round-trip rides. Snacks are sold on the train and at depot cafés. *222 Railroad Ave., (605) 574-2222, www.1880train.com.*

Keystone

Big Thunder Gold Mine. During hour-long, easy (and accessible) walking tours into this fully preserved mine, you'll learn how, in the late 1800s, two German immigrants teamed up to stake their claim and extract gold using tools and techniques that kept the mine's infrastructure intact. In the adjacent museum, you can see some of this mining equipment—and try your luck panning for gold. *604 Blair St., (605) 666-4847, www.bigthundermine.com.*

Rushmore Tramway Adventures. You can smell the Ponderosa pines as you ride one of 36 chairlifts over the Black Hills and to a unique view of Mt. Rushmore from a nearby hilltop. At the summit, placid pursuits include wandering garden paths, dining in the café, and browsing in the gift shop. Adventurous activities include tackling the Aerial Adventure Park, with its zip lines, suspended bridges and ladders, nets, and other challenges. Feel the need for speed? Consider sledding back down on the Alpine Slide. *203 Cemetery Rd., (605) 593-4923, www.rushmoretramwayadventures.com.*

Mount Rushmore National Memorial. "There is not a monument in this country as big as a snuff box," said sculptor Gutzon Borglum before setting out to give America a grand memorial. In 1927, he began carving the heads of Washington, Jefferson, Lincoln, and Theodore Roosevelt into a granite outcropping atop Mount Rushmore. The project took almost a million dollars, 400 workers, 14 years, and loads of dynamite. By the time Borglum's son Lincoln completed the work in 1941, roughly 450,000 tons of rock had been blasted away to create the 60-foot-high faces. Today one of the world's largest and most recognizable sculptures attracts 3 million visitors annually.

The parking area Information Center has details on each day's events; you can pick up self-guided audio tours here or in a building across the way. The paved, half-mile Presidential Trail has an exhibit on area Native Americans and takes you beneath the sculpted heads. The Lincoln Borglum Visitor Center, directly below the Grand View Terrace, has exhibits and shows the film *Mount Rushmore: The Shrine* every 20 minutes. In warmer months, check out the ranger talks in the Sculptor's Studio or the 45-minute evening program with a ranger presentation, the film *Freedom: America's Lasting Legacy,* and the dramatic illumination of the faces to the sound of the National Anthem. There aren't any picnic or camping facilities, but there is a restaurant, a gift shop, and Mount Rushmore Bookstores. *13000 SD Hwy. 244, (605) 574-2523, www.nps.gov/moru.*

Eat & Stay

Prairie Berry Winery & Miner Brewing Co | **Hill City.** Sandi Vojta's family has been making wines from chokecherries, raspberries, crab apples, rhubarb, and other South Dakota fruit since 1876. The free daily tastings at her winery, founded in 1999, feature up to five varieties. If beer is more your thing, head next door to the tap room of the Miner Brewing Company, where Sandi has been brewmaster since opening in 2013. Brews to sample here might include Black Currant Maibock, India Pale or Irish Red ale, and Oatmeal Stout. The winery restaurant is a great stop for lunch or an afternoon snack, with cheese or charcuterie boards, fresh salads, open-face or flat-grill sandwiches, and a kids menu. *23837 U.S. 385, (877) 226-9453, www.prairieberry.com.*

Trailside Park Resort | **Hill City.** It's in Hill City, with its many attractions and ready access to area sights, yet it's also in a woodsy area, near a great fishing creek and just off the Mickelson Trail through Black Hills National Forest. There are tent sites as well as 35 large RV sites with full hookups. The eight cabins, which can sleep up to four or five people, all have full baths and kitchenettes; some also have decks with grills. Regardless of your lodging choice, the Wi-Fi and the cable are free. *24024 Main St. (U.S. Hwy. 16/385), (605) 574-9079, trailsideparkresort.com.*

Custer

Crazy Horse Memorial. From 1947 until his death in 1982, visionary sculptor Korczak Ziolkowski worked on the large-scale granite sculpture of Lakota Chief (and hero) Crazy Horse. And the work continues through the nonprofit Crazy Horse Memorial Foundation. In addition to a viewing verandah, the campus is home to the Indian Museum of North America, the Native American Educational & Cultural Center, and the sculptor's original studio and home. A roster of events includes laser light shows (May–mid-Oct.), storyteller van tours, and biannual (June and Sept.), 6.2-mile Volksmarches up to the work site and back. The campus also has a gift shop, a restaurant, and a snack bar. *12151 Avenue of the Chiefs, (605) 673-4681, crazyhorsememorial.org.*

Custer State Park. This park's 71,000 acres extend south from the granite peaks of the Black Hills to the northern reaches of Wind Cave National Park. You can also follow the scenic, 17-mile Iron Mountain Road north from the state park to Mount Rushmore. Though Custer's wildlife includes elk, deer, antelope, mountain goats and sheep, burros, and prairie dogs, its main attraction is its 1,300-head bison herd, best seen from along the 18-mile Wildlife Loop Road. What's more, the park is a great area hub thanks to its many outstanding lodging and dining options. *Park Headquarters: 13329 U.S. 16A, (605) 255-4515, www.gfp.sd.gov/state-parks.*

Custer State Park

Hot Springs

Wind Cave National Park. Sioux legend holds that a constant wind from the inner reaches of a Black Hills cave blew the buffalo herds from beneath the Earth to feed the Lakota people. It might well have been this cave. The fourth-longest in the United States and sixth-longest in the world, the 104 miles of known passages are believed to represent only 5% of the cave. And size isn't its only unique quality. Owing to a relatively dry atmosphere, there aren't any of the stalactites or stalagmites found in most caves. Rather, Wind Cave has unusual popcorn, flowstone, frostwork, and boxwork formations.

Outstanding ranger-led tours (mid-Apr.–early Oct.) depart from the visitors center. The Garden of Eden Tour, the least strenuous with just 150 steps, takes in boxwork, popcorn, and flowstone formations. The Natural Entrance Tour features lots of boxwork and involves 300 stairs (mostly down). The Fairgrounds Tour (summer only), the most strenuous with the most stairs, offers the widest array of features. Above ground are 28,295 acres that are home to elk and bison herds and prairie dog communities. More than 30 miles of trails lace the park, among them Elk Mountain, a somewhat strenuous mile-long loop around the campground of the same name. *26611 U.S. 385, (605) 745-4600, www.nps.gov/wica.*

Evans Plunge. Fed by 5,000 gallons of 87-degree, crystal-clear water from springs once fought over by the Sioux and Cheyenne, Evans Plunge is reputed to be the world's largest natural, warm-water, indoor swimming pool. Established as a mineral spa in the 1890s, the modern version is more of a water park with slides, tubes, kiddy pools, and a health club. *1145 N. River St., (605) 745-5165, www.evansplunge.com.*

The Mammoth Site. Ice Age mammoths and other creatures, in search of water fed by ancient hot springs, fell to their deaths in a sinkhole on this site. The sediment that later filled it preserved their remains, which were discovered in the 1970s. In addition to Columbian and woolly mammoths (ancestors of the elephant), the site contains precursors of the bear, camel, llama, wolf, and other species. The museum offers exhibits and a 30-minute guided tour during which you'll see fossilized skeletons still embedded in the ground. *1800 U.S. 18 Bypass, (605) 745-6017, mammothsite.com.*

Black Hills Wild Horse Sanctuary. Ponderosa pines dot the vast grasslands of this sanctuary, where over 600 Choctaw ponies and American, Spanish, and Curly mustangs run wild. Tour fees are high, but proceeds go toward funding this entirely nonprofit operation, whose residents include many rescue horses. Among the offerings are two-hour bus excursions, three-hour 4WD cross-country expeditions, and four-hour photo safaris. Overnight visits with tours and stays in a rustic cabin are also an (expensive) option. At the on-site gift shop, 89% of sales go toward mustang care. *12165 Highland Rd., (605) 745-5955, www.wildmustangs.com.*

Eat & Stay

Sage Creek Grill | Custer. The food is as fresh and as locally sourced as possible, which explains why the menu changes regularly. What does stay the same is the promise to use local meats, wild seafood, and fresh herbs in straightforward, American bistro–style dishes. Starters might include hot artichoke dip with Parmesan or field greens with goat cheese. For dinner, you might tuck into a 10-ounce buffalo steak served with potato or grilled wild sockeye salmon with lemon-parsley butter served over risotto. The lunch menu has burgers and sandwiches (the BLT gets rave reviews). There are also vegetarian options. *611 Mt. Rushmore Rd., (605) 673-2424, sagecreekgrille.com.*

Custer State Park Resort | Custer. Pick from this state park resort's four amenities-filled lodges based on your favorite outdoor activity. Trail rides and nightly hayride chuck-wagon cookouts depart from the Bluebell Lodge, with its four-person log cabins. Legion Lake Lodge rents paddleboats and other water craft. The lodge and motel-style rooms at the State Game Lodge, a grand 1920s wood-and-fieldstone structure on the National Register of Historic Places, are amid forest near a trout-filled creek. The romantic Sylvan Lake Lodge, inspired by Frank Lloyd Wright and built in 1937, is near the trail to 7,242-foot Harney Peak and along the scenic, 14-mile Needles Highway. Myriad tent and RV campgrounds—from modern to primitive—round out the offerings. *Resort offices (State Game Lodge): 13389 U.S. 16A, (605) 255-4772, (888) 875-0001 (reservations), custerresorts.com.*

Wind Cave National Park

NORTHEAST

MIDWEST

SOUTH

WEST

A Pacific Northwest Passage

ROUTE TOWNS: Seattle | Bainbridge Island (Winslow) | Port Angeles | Aberdeen | Astoria, OR | Cannon Beach
Forest Grove | Portland

Water, woods, and historic wonders await on this trip between two great metropolises of the Pacific Northwest: the Emerald City (Seattle) and the City of Roses (Portland).

Cannon Beach

Few cities balance culture and commerce, nature and architecture, the past and the future as well as Seattle. Because of this, the Emerald City—the perfect nickname for an urban hub surrounded by rich evergreen forests—is a highlight of any visit to the Pacific Northwest. It makes a great jumping off point for a visit to the Olympic National Park and Forest and to the ocean mists and maritime legends along the Pacific Coast Highway/Scenic Byway. Waves crash at the base of jagged cliffs, and dense forests loom over nearly every bend.

From Seattle, you'll head west and north to Olympic National Park and Forest via the Bainbridge Island Ferry and the Hood Canal Floating Bridge, which connects the Kitsap and Olympic peninsulas as part of State Route 104. The coastal route south from forested Washington to Oregon is as fun to drive as it is breathtaking. It also promises unique maritime experiences in towns like Aberdeen, WA, and Astoria, OR— the region's oldest settlement, set where the notoriously treacherous Columbia River meets the Graveyard of the Pacific.

Farther south, follow in the steps of Lewis and Clark, look for migrating whales, or wander along beaches with intriguing rock formations. The route inland takes you to two of Oregon's renowned wineries before heading to Portland, straddling the Willamette River. The City of Roses is as renowned for its green spaces and gardens as it is for its storied past. Here, as in Seattle, expect great food, great views, and great stories—old and new.

Atlas map F-7, p. 108

Distance: 442 miles point to point, though you can readily shorten or lengthen this.

Type of Trip: Weekend or Vacation Getaway; RV; Arts & Culture, Great Outdoors, History & Heritage, Picture Perfect, Quirky & Oddball.

Must Try: Oysters at Emmet Watson's in Seattle; herb artichoke pie at Pizza a'Fetta in Cannon Beach; wine from any winery in either state.

Must Buy: *Hammering Man* T-shirt or hand-crafted Native American jewelry from the Seattle Art Museum; a wool Pendleton camp blanket or throw (think classic stripes or tartans in rich earthy or primary colors), woven in Oregon since 1863.

Must See: Pike Place Market, Space Needle, Seattle Art Museum, Elliott Bay Book Company, Hoh Rain Forest in Olympic National Park, Columbia River Maritime Museum, Pittock Mansion, Powell's City of Books.

Worth Noting: You can explore both Seattle and Portland below ground on tours of the Seattle Underground network of tunnels or excursions into Portland's Shanghai Tunnels. And, oh, if these passageways could talk. . . .

Travel Tips: To shorten the point-to-point trip to 300 miles—without missing a thing—head south of Seattle through Olympia (the state capital and home to the national forest headquarters) to Aberdeen, down the coast, and inland to Portland. To lengthen it into a full 625-mile loop, continue north from Portland through **Washington State wine country** (www.washingtonwine.org) in Vancouver, Longview, and Centralia before returning to Seattle via Olympia.

city itinerary

Seattle, WA: Emerald City Essentials

Settled in 1851 and named for a Duwamish Indian leader, Seattle first flourished thanks to the timber industry. The very thing that helped to build the town, however, contributed to its downfall during the Great Fire of 1889. By then, Seattle was a key port, so rebuilding began immediately. Seven years later came the Klondike Gold Rush. As a major waypoint and supply depot for prospectors heading north, Seattle again grew. In subsequent decades the global success of such local innovators as Boeing, Microsoft, Starbucks, and Amazon also brought prosperity. Today the city balances old-time character with forward-thinking civic pride.

Travel Tips: Many of Seattle's must-see sights are also favored by locals, who keep things real. The Bainbridge Island Ferry draws sightseers and day-to-day commuters. Pike Place Market attracts visitors and local fresh-food shoppers. Pike Place is also a great place to anchor an in-town stay. Though you can set out from here on foot or by bike, the city has some steep hills—which is why buses are outfitted with bike racks. Outside of rush hours, traffic isn't bad, but parking in and around downtown can be. The solution? Use the reliable Sound Transit (light rail) and King County Metro (bus) systems.

Visitor Info: Seattle Visitor Center at the Market, *1st Ave. and Pike St., (866) 732-2695, visitseattle.org.*

In and Around the Market

❶ Pike Place Market. Founded in 1907, "the Market," (as locals refer to it) is one of the oldest continually operating farmers' markets in the United States. It's in a multilevel complex overlooking Elliott Bay and part of a 9-acre historic district. At street level on its western side are produce, fish, meat, flower, and craft stands, with various other retailers filling out downstairs shops. Across the narrow cobblestone street that is Pike Place are storefronts and walkways leading into yet more shops and restaurants.

Watch fishmongers toss salmon, visit the first Starbucks outpost, enjoy the antics of talented street performers, and soak in the flavor of Seattle's most popular attraction. You can also grab a treat (or several) and stroll down to Victor Steinbrueck Park at the Market's northern end for an impromptu picnic looking out across the Sound to the Olympic Mountains. A 15-minute walk north of here will take you to the Seattle Art Museum's Olympic Sculpture Park. *85 Pike St., (206) 682-7453, www.pikeplacemarket.org.*

❷ Dimitriou's Jazz Alley. Since opening in 1979, Dimitriou's, on downtown's northern edge, has been one of the country's premier jazz clubs. Taj Mahal, Dr. John, Dizzy Gillespie, and McCoy Tyner are among the internationally known stars who've performed here. While it's less compact than many long-running supper clubs, it still serves up an intimate bistro feeling—though most patrons come for the impressive acoustics and nightly lineups rather than the food. *2033 6th Ave., (206) 441-9729, www.jazzalley.com.*

North to Seattle Center

❸ Space Needle. The 605-foot-tall Space Needle, built for the 1962 World's Fair, offers the best view of the Emerald City and its majestic surroundings. Glass elevators travel up to 10 mph to the observation deck, where you'll find informative displays, shops, and a lounge along with a 360-degree view 500 feet in the air. The revolving SkyCity restaurant offers the same sweeping vistas, with direct access to the observation deck for patrons willing to pay a premium for reliable local fare. *400 Broad St., (206) 905-2100, www.spaceneedle.com.*

Eat & Stay

❹ Inn at the Market. If it's all about location, then this boutique property, the only hotel within Pike Place Market, has them all beat. It has 70 well-appointed guestrooms and one spectacular roof deck overlooking Puget Sound. It also offers easy access to downtown landmarks, the waterfront, Pioneer Square, Belltown, and Capitol Hill. Despite its busy surroundings, this is an intimate "hideaway," known for its attentive staff and unique collection of Northwestern art. *86 Pine St., (206) 443-3600, www.innatthemarket.com.*

❺ Emmett Watson's Oyster Bar. Reaching one of Seattle's best-kept secrets means winding through Pike Place Market's oft-confusing corridors. Don't hesitate to ask for directions. A meal of oysters, chowder, clams, salmon, or other Pacific-centric seafood—as fresh as what the rubber-boot-clad fishmongers are hawking—makes it worth the effort. Named for co-founder and local newspaperman Emmett Watson, this oyster bar has kept its old-school style and flavor ever since shucking its first bivalve back in 1979. Its trademark blue-and-white-checked tablecloths lend to the throwback-diner feel, as do the handwritten menus printed on paper bags. *1916 Pike Pl., Ste. 16, (206) 448-7721.*

❻ Experience Music Project. Conceived as a space for billionaire Paul Allen to display his enormous collection of Jimi Hendrix memorabilia, EMP, in Seattle Center and next to the Space Needle, has grown into a truly unique museum. From the eye-catching Frank Gehry building to the rare memorabilia and state-of-the-art exhibits within, it reflects the rebellious essence of rock 'n' roll. Galleries honor hip-hop; music history in the Pacific Northwest; the relationship between punk and skateboarding; and, of course, legendary guitarist Jimi Hendrix. In the Sound Lab, you can jump onstage for a piercing guitar solo, beat out rhythms on the Big Drum, or cut grooves in the DJ Hallway. *325 5th Ave. N., (206) 770-2700, www.empmuseum.org.*

Space Needle, Monorail, Experience Music Project exterior

A Trip to Century 21

In 1962 Seattle hosted the World's Fair. With the theme "Century 21," it looked to the science and technology of the future for inspiration and left a legacy of icons, the Space Needle among them. Today this 74-acre campus a mile from downtown has myriad attractions. Be sure to arrive via the **Monorail**, also built for the World's Fair. It zips (in about 2 minutes!) between the Seattle Center Station and downtown's Westlake Center Station (5th Ave. and Pine St.), a 5-minute walk northeast of Pike Place Market. The Monorail runs every 10 minutes from 7:30 am to 11 pm weekdays, and 8:30 am to 11 pm weekends.

In addition to the Experience Music Project, Seattle Center museums include the **❼ Pacific Science Center** (200 2nd Ave. N., 206/443-2001, www.pacificsciencecenter.org), with interactive exhibits as well as a butterfly house, planetarium, and IMAX theater, and the **❽ Seattle Children's Museum** (305 Harrison St., 206/441-1768, thechildrensmuseum.org), where kids 10 and under learn by playing. The Key Arena sporting and concert venue, shops, and restaurants round out the offerings that make Seattle Center a social hub for locals and visitors.

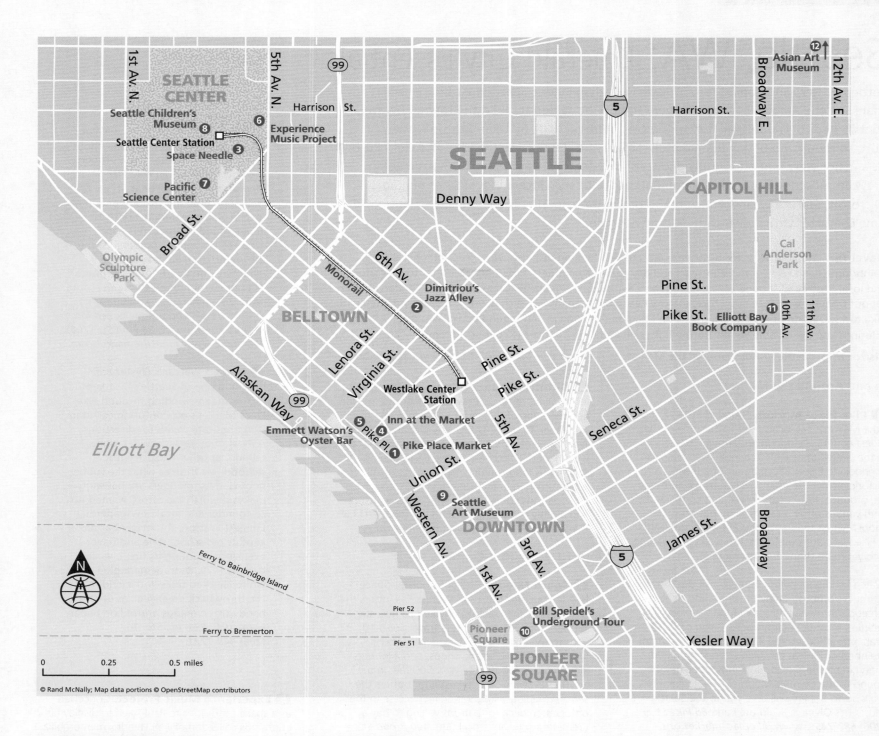

© Rand McNally; Map data portions © OpenStreetMap contributors

South Toward Pioneer Square

⑨ Seattle Art Museum. The city's premiere art museum opened in 1933 and today has more than 25,000 works. Its main building is in the heart of downtown, marked by Jonathan Borofsky's famous 48-foot-tall kinetic sculpture *Hammering Man.* Three stories of galleries contain pieces from many periods and regions, but the Pacific Northwest Native American art and artifacts are highlights. *1300 1st Ave., (206) 654-3100, www.seattleartmuseum.org.*

⑩ Bill Speidel's Underground Tour. This fun, 90-minute guided tour travels along today's sidewalks and down beneath Pioneer Square to 1890s walkways, where many storefronts and some interiors remain intact. Along the way, you'll learn about Seattle's early timber days and famous Skid Row. You'll also get the backstory of this three-block area, where the street level was raised from 8 to 35 feet as part of rebuilding efforts after the Seattle fire of 1889. The tour's founder and namesake was an ardent preservationist, who led a citizen's campaign to designate Pioneer Square a historic district—saving portions of its underground and its topside Victorian-Romanesque buildings. *608 1st Ave., (206) 682-4646, www.undergroundtour.com.*

Capitol Hill

⑪ Elliott Bay Book Company. For many, no visit to Seattle is complete without roaming this independent bookstore's well-stocked aisles. Opened in 1973, it relocated from Pioneer Square to Capitol Hill in 2010—taking its original charm, homey décor, incredible selection, wildly knowledgeable staff, and mellow café with it. Even in the digital age, patrons flock here to fill their reading lists, hear authors from every genre, and delight in the written word. *1521 10th Ave., (206) 624-6600, www.elliottbaybook.com.*

⑫ Asian Art Museum. In 1994, to house its noteworthy collections from Japan, China, and Korea, SAM opened the Asian Art Museum in Capitol Hill's Volunteer Park. SAM also oversees the Olympic Sculpture Garden, just north of Pike Place Market. Wander on your own amid large-scale works by Alexander Calder, Richard Serra, and others, or be enlightened by the museum's guided, 60-minute Site, Sculpture, and Shoreline tour. *1400 E. Prospect St., (206) 654-3100, www.seattleartmuseum.org.*

Pike Place Market

Hoh Rain Forest, Olympic National Park

Bainbridge Island Ferry

Bainbridge Island (Winslow)

Bainbridge Island Ferry. The Washington State Ferry system is the nation's largest, carrying more than 10 million vehicles and 22 million passengers annually. The biggest ferries of its fleet serve the Seattle-to-Bainbridge Island route, transporting well over 6 million riders a year on jumbo-sized boats that can carry as many as 202 vehicles. For many, that 35-minute ride across Puget Sound is a simple daily commute; for others, it's by far the most scenic and relaxing segment of a Pacific Northwest road trip.

Traveling from Seattle is as simple as queueing up at Colman Dock (Pier 52, 801 Alaskan Way S.) for the 9-mile sail to Winslow on Bainbridge Island, where the Kitsap and Olympic peninsulas await. Note that the Washington State Ferry website (www.wsdot.wa.gov/ferries) has real-time images of vehicle waiting areas and estimates of the remaining of spaces for each vessel. *Winslow dock: 270 Olympic Dr. S.E., (888) 808-7977, www.bainbridgeisland.com.*

Port Angeles

Olympic National Park. Three distinct ecosystems make up this 1,427-square-mile peninsular park: Pacific shoreline, subalpine forest and meadowland, and coastal-Northwest rain forest. In addition, many rivers meander through its glacier-carved mountain range. Indeed, glaciers isolated the peninsula from the continent during the Ice Age, resulting in more than 20 unique kinds of wildflowers and animals. The Ice Age also kept out flora and fauna found elsewhere in the region. You won't see grizzly bears or porcupines here. Instead, watch for gray whales, harbor seals, river and sea otters, salamanders, Olympic marmot, Roosevelt elk, black-tailed deer, bobcats, cougars, and black bears.

You can readily combine a trip to here with explorations of Olympic National Forest—which essentially rings the park—and the coast. Beaches in the south tend to be sandy; those to the north are rocky. The drive along U.S. 101 (aka the Pacific Coast Highway/Scenic Byway) has many overlooks and short trails down to the beach. Not far from shore, in the park's southwestern reaches, is the Hoh Rain Forest. Learn about the mild climate and lush vegetation at its visitors center, just off 101. Then consider taking the mile-long Hall of Mosses or one of eight other forest trails to see conifer and maple trees covered in licorice ferns and club moss, as well as towering spruce, hemlock, and western red cedar.

The main visitors center is in Port Angeles, on the park's northeastern edge; there are also park and forest information centers farther west, in the town of Forks, and a forest ranger station farther south in the town of Quinault. Park lodges (www.olympicnationalparks.com/accommodations) include Lake Crescent Lodge, Sol Duc Hot Springs Resort, and the Log Cabin Resort; the latter two also have RV parks, as does Lake Quinault Lodge. All told the park has 16 campgrounds with 900 sites. *3002 Mount Angeles Rd., (360) 565-3130, www.nps.gov/olym.*

Aberdeen

Grays Harbor Historical Seaport. You can do more than just visit this port town's waterfront. You can actually live its maritime history. On dock tours, docents in period costume stand ready to answer questions about the port and its vessels, which include authentic, functional replicas of two 18th-century merchant ships: the *Lady Washington* and the *Hawaiian Chieftain*. Hop aboard these tall ships and explore, or test your sea legs on one of the two- or three-hour adventure, battle, evening, or educational sailings, during which the sailors might tell tall tales or sing sea shanties. Dock tour times and offerings vary, depending on when the ships themselves are in port. *500 N. Custer St., (360) 532-8611, historicalseaport.org.*

Astoria, OR

Clatsop County Historical Society. This outfit operates a trio of museums. Start at the Carriage House Visitors Center (7th and Exchange streets). It's right behind the Captain George Flavel House, an 1885 Queen Anne–style mansion whose hexagonal tower and many wings leave no doubt as to why it was chosen as a location for the 1985 movie, *The Goonies*. Some have also reported mysterious tunes emanating from the Music Room, the apparition of a woman in the hallway, and the sense of being watched in the Library. Most likely, though, you'll just sense the history amid all the elegant period furnishings and fixtures. You can also visit the Heritage Museum, where cultural and historical displays include a partially recreated saloon, or the Uppertown Firefighters Museum with its vintage trucks and gear. *714 Exchange St., (503) 325-2203, cumtux.org.*

Eat & Stay

Lake Quinault Lodge | Quinault. This grand, 1920s, Shingle-style lodge is perfectly at home in its woodsy, lakeside setting. Main Lodge rooms are down-home comfy; some have lake views. For even more coziness, opt for a Fireplace Room. Some Lakeside Rooms are more contemporary, and there's also the Boathouse, which can accommodate groups. The lodge offers lake and rain forest tours; rents kayaks, canoes, and rowboats; and helps you plan hiking, biking, skiing, hot springs, and other excursions in Olympic National Park and Forest. The Roosevelt Dining Room serves breakfast, lunch, and dinner. *345 South Shore Rd., (800) 562-6672, www.olympicnationalparks. com/accommodations.*

Fort George Brewery | Astoria. Recycle, reuse, re-imagine are recurring themes in Oregon. They're definitely key to this brewpub housed in what was once an automotive repair shop built in 1924 on the site of a fur trading post that was part of Astoria's 1811 founding. Belly up to the bar for a Belgian-style Quick Wit or an 1811 Lager, both of which pair well with the house-made sausage sampler and other menu items. Sunday night sees live-music shows; Thursday night features lectures. Neither night has a cover. *1483 Duane St., (503) 325-7468, www.fortgeorgebrewery.com.*

Cannery Pier Hotel | Astoria. The Columbia River views from the public areas and all—yes, all—the chic guest rooms at this hotel are unbelievable. Not surprising given that it was built over the pilings of the Union Fisherman's Cooperative Packing Company, established in the 1890s by fisherman, many of them Finnish, who united against big-time canneries. You'll appreciate the Finnish influence even more in the spa's authentic sauna and during the free Continental breakfast featuring Finnish delicacies. Other amenities include an exercise room, hot tub, free Wi-Fi, and library. Astoria's historic trolley line is nearby, as are many restaurants, brewpubs, and shops. The hotel also has free chauffeur-driven rides in vintage cars and free use of retro-style bikes. *10 Basin St., (888) 325-4996, www.cannerypierhotel.com.*

NORTHEAST

MIDWEST

SOUTH

WEST

Columbia River Maritime Museum. At this museum, a massive window overlooks the Columbia River and the vessels that travel along it slowly and with care. Here you'll learn the stories of such vessels, their river pilots, and the dangers that await them on "the bar" at the mouth of the Columbia. Indeed, the impressive collection of 30,000 maritime artifacts includes items salvaged from wrecks in the so-called Graveyard of the Pacific. Look for the 1820 copper-and-brass token, an example of the de facto currency of the regional fur trade, and the chunk of beeswax from a 17th-century galleon. Step into a simulator to see what it's like to pilot a tugboat before visiting the lightship *Columbia. 1792 Marine Dr., (503) 325-2323, www.crmm.org.*

Astoria Column. The concrete, 125-foot-tall Astoria Column Lighthouse has stood on 600-foot Coxcomb Hill for over 80 years. It was modeled after Trajan's Column in Italy. When it was first constructed, Italian artisans were even brought in to create the bas-relief murals that wind their way up the column. The view from the hill is grand, but the view from atop the lighthouse is spectacular—truly worthy of the 164-step climb. *Coxcomb Hill, (503) 325-2963, astoriacolumn.org.*

Fort Clatsop National Memorial. After a grueling journey through the uncharted Louisiana Purchase and Oregon Territory, Lewis and Clark and the Corps of Discovery reached the Pacific Ocean in mid-November 1805. At Fort Clatsop, named after the local Clatsop tribe, the weary men and one woman (Native American guide, Sacagawea, of course!) spent three months preparing for the return trip. In this 125-acre park at the mouth of the Columbia River, you can learn how the courageous, hardy group of explorers opened up the West.

A short walk from the visitors center, where exhibits and films reacquaint you with the history of the expedition, is a replica of the original fort. Mid-June through Labor Day, rangers in period costume demonstrate survival skills vital to Lewis and Clark's journey, such as bullet- and candle-making and hide tanning. If you're especially adventuresome, you can lend a hand, pulling tallow candles or striking sparks from flint and steel. Nearby trailheads take you to the 6.5-mile Fort to Sea Trail or the 1.5-mile Netul River Trail. *92343 Fort Clatsop Rd., (503) 861-2471, www.nps.gov/lewi.*

Cannon Beach

Ecola State Park. This state park has two beautiful beaches. Crescent Beach is a half-mile long and sandy; it offers picnic shelters and restrooms. Indian Beach is about the same length and has both sandy and rocky sections (though amenities include only pit toilets). Kayakers, surfers, and swimmers like the waters, though there aren't any lifeguards. Among the hiking options is a trail to a spot overlooking the 19th-century Tillamook Rock Lighthouse (in spring and fall, watch for migrating gray whales). The viewpoint is just off the 2.5-mile Clatsop Loop Trail, which takes you through forests of giant Sitka spruce in the footsteps of Lewis and Clark. There's a campsite near both the viewpoint and the trailhead of a 4-mile route that loops you back. *Off Hwy. 101, (503) 436-2844, www.oregonstateparks.org.*

Cannon Beach & Haystack Rock. Named after a cannon that washed up here in 1846, this popular beach is noted for its 235-foot Haystack Rock. The rock's tide pools are filled with colorful starfish, anemone, crabs, chitons, and nudibranchs. In summer, lanky, greenish-black pelagic cormorants take up residence on the south-facing cliffs, while squatty orange-billed tufted puffins claim the grassy north slope. Note that the areas above and below the high-tide line are protected, so you can't climb on Haystack Rock or remove anything living within 300 meters of it. *Cannon Beach Chamber of Commerce, 207 N. Spruce St., (503) 436-2623, www.cannonbeach.org.*

Forest Grove

Apolloni Winery. Pinot grapes grow well in Oregon's terroir, and the Noir, Grigio, and Blanc wines made from them feature greatly here. But so do Italian varieties like Soleggio and Sangiovese, a nod to the origins of the family who established and run this winery. Its tasting room is just off Route 26 (Milepost 6 at Highway 6). Weekends are a good time to visit. *14135 N.W. Timmerman Rd., (503) 359-3606, www.apolloni.com.*

David Hill Vineyards and Winery. First established by a German pioneer family in the late 1800s, David Hill has some of Willamette Valley's oldest Pinot Noir vines. Given its heritage, it's no surprise that the winery also produces Gewürztraminer and Riesling. Stop by the tasting room inside the original farmhouse, just off Route 26, any day of the week to sample these and other varieties. *46350 N.W. David Hill Rd., (503) 992-8545, www.davidhillwinery.com.*

David Hill Vineyards and Winery

Pittock Mansion, Portland

Eat & Stay

Pizza a'Fetta | Cannon Beach. So many people—locals, visitors, food critics—rave about this family owned pizzeria, that it's just about become a Cannon Beach icon. The atmosphere is informal and convivial, the tablecloths are checked, and the pizzas are formed and seasoned to perfection. Build your own, or select from such specialty pies as the Princess Marguerite, the Crab, or the Herb Artichoke, all three of which feature an acclaimed house-made Montrachet sauce. The salad menu is robust, and there's beer on tap. *231 N. Hemlock, (503) 436-0333, pizza-a-fetta.com.*

The Waves at Cannon Beach | Cannon Beach. It's easy to find a comfortable, contemporary place to stay thanks to these locally owned properties along or near Cannon Beach. The Waves collection consists of six oceanfront or ocean-view properties, each with studios or suites. The Argonauta Inn collection has a beach house that can accommodate as many as nine people; a two-bedroom remodeled 1906 house, one of the oldest in town; and two other houses with various suites. The White Heron Lodge collection features a modern Victorian-style house with four suites near Ecola Creek and another more contemporary house with two suites. Many accommodations have fireplaces and kitchenettes; all have laundry facilities, DVD players, and free Wi-Fi and parking. *188 W. 2nd St., (503) 436-2205, www.thewavescannonbeach.com.*

Cannon Beach RV Resort | Cannon Beach. Paved, tree-lined drives lead to this park's 100 paved sites, 11 of them pull-through and all of them with full hookups. On site, you'll find a heated indoor pool and spa tub, a games room, laundry and shower facilities, and a convenience store and gift shop. The cable and Wi-Fi are free, there's overflow parking, and Cannon Beach is just a few blocks away. What's more, this family- and pet-friendly RV resort is open year-round. *340 Elk Creek Rd., (503) 436-2231, cbrvresort.com.*

city itinerary

Portland

❶ Pittock Mansion. Mansion is an understatement. This place is more like a castle, or, more precisely, a French Renaissance–style chateau. In the 1850s, Henry and Georgiana Pittock each traveled west along the Oregon Trail before meeting and marrying in Portland. Henry took over the *Daily Oregonian* newspaper, and made a fortune in several endeavors. Construction of their 22-room sandstone estate—just northwest of what is today Washington Park—was completed in 1914. Though Henry and Georgiana lived here for just a few years, the mansion stayed in the family until the 1960s, when it was taken over by the city, restored, and opened to the public.

Tours of the 46-acre National Historic Landmark estate highlight family possessions, unusual architectural features, and the Pittocks themselves, some of whom might still be here. There have been reports of apparitions, heavy footsteps, and the inexplicable smell of roses. Georgiana, it seems, was quite partial to the blooms and even helped found the annual festival honoring their role in Portland (aka the City of Roses). *3229 N.W. Pittock Dr., (508) 823-3623, pittockmansion.org.*

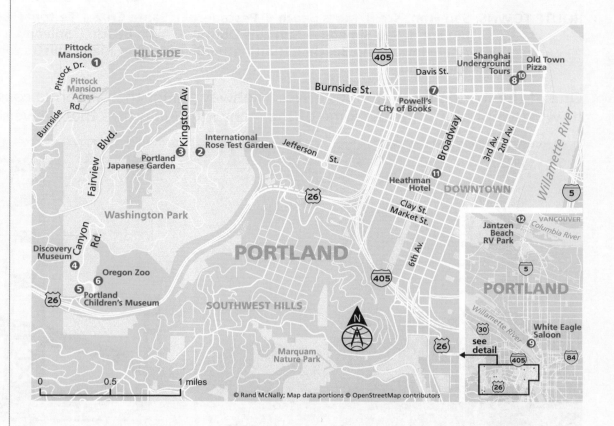

© Rand McNally; Map data portions © OpenStreetMap contributors

A Day in the Park

You can easily fill a day (or two) in Washington Park, west of downtown. The **❷ International Rose Test Garden** (400 S.W. Kingston Ave., 503/823-3636, www.portlandoregon.gov/parks) has over 550 varieties on its 6,800 bushes, which peak from June through August. Consider pairing a visit here with one to the **❸ Portland Japanese Garden** (611 S.W. Kingston Ave., 503/223-1321, japanesegarden.com), which have five Asian-style landscapes. Both gardens have stores with items to create your own tranquil home or garden setting.

At the **❹ Discovery Museum** (4033 S.W. Canyon Rd., 503/228-1367, www.worldforestry.org), affiliated with the World Forestry Center, take a simulated raft ride or learn about different types of forests on "trips" to Russia, China, South Africa, and Brazil. The **❺ Portland Children's Museum** (4015 S.W. Canyon Rd., 503/223-6500, www.portlandcm. org), geared to ages 10 and under, is all about play. Kids can go shopping in the Grasshopper Grocery, go dramatic in the Theater, go artistic in the Maker Studio, or go wild in the Zany Maze.

At the **❻ Oregon Zoo** (4001 S.W. Canyon Rd., 503/226-1561, www.oregonzoo.org) marvel at the creatures of Africa's rainforest and savannah, visit with Asian elephants, watch chimpanzees play, listen to tigers chuff, and watch penguins swim. Several habitats also showcase the wildlife of the Pacific Northwest.

❼ Powell's City of Books. Like the Strand in New York or the Elliott Bay Book Company in Seattle, this is one of those independents where the inventory could be measured in miles. It's also been around for a while, stocks new and used tomes, and has staffers and customers who truly love to read. Stop by to pick up books on local history or lore, scan the national best sellers, grab a cheap paperback, and have a cuppa at the locally owned World Cup Coffee & Tea. Though hours vary, all six locations are open 365 days a year. *1005 W. Burnside St., (503) 228-4651, www.powells.com.*

❽ Shanghai Underground Tours. Hobo's Restaurant is the departure point for the **Cascade Geographic Society's** (www. shanghaitunnels.info) Friday and Saturday evening Shanghai Underground Tours. The fascinating network of passageways was used by dock workers to transport goods to and from the Willamette River—as well as by more nefarious types to shanghai men into service at sea and women into service as ladies of the night. Before or after your tour, hit the lounge for a drink and some mac-and-cheese. The dining room also has a full menu of seafood and steak dishes. *Hobo's Restaurant: 120 N.W. 3rd Ave., (503) 224-3285, www.hobospdx.com.*

❾ White Eagle Saloon. From its opening in 1905 until Prohibition, the White Eagle was a true saloon, with heavy drinking, barroom brawls, prostitution, and other rough-and-tumble goings-on. Indeed, locals once referred to it as the "Bucket of Blood." Today, most patrons only go wild for the live nightly blues or rock shows, the McMenamins Hammerhead pale ale or Terminator stout, the pub grub, and the historical ambience. Spend the evening or the night—upstairs in one of the cozy, reasonably priced hotel rooms. If you dare, that is. Word is, this place is haunted. *836 N. Russell St., (503) 282-6810, www.mcmenamins.com.*

Eat & Stay

❿ Old Town Pizza. The setting: In the former lobby of the 1880 Merchant Hotel. The scenery: Brick walls, aubergine-velvet settees, rustic wooden tables, candlelight. The menu: Fresh salads, toasty Italian sandwiches, pizzas made with hand-tossed dough. It seems a comforting, cozy place to get rid of the drizzly Pacific Northwest chill—or is it? Some patrons report a different kind of chill here. Many claim Old Town Pizza is haunted by the ghost of Nina, a Native American woman who was reportedly murdered in the hotel. *226 N.W. Davis St., (503) 222-9999, www.oldtownpizza.com.*

⓫ Heathman Hotel. Although this downtown hotel has been in business since 1927, today it's all about modern luxury. Its 150 rooms (some of them pet-friendly) feature soothing earth tones; rich, dark woods; and such thoughtful touches as robes and slippers, free Wi-Fi, L'Occitane toiletries, and Portland Roasting French-press coffee. Service is also a hallmark here. And so are ghostly hi-jinks, particularly in Room 703. *1001 S.W. Broadway, (503) 241-4100, portland.heathmanhotel.com.*

⓬ Jantzen Beach RV Park. It's all about location at this RV resort on Hayden Island, in the Columbia River and just 7 miles from downtown. Amid mature trees are over 160 full-hookup sites, including 60-foot pull-throughs. Amenities include free Wi-Fi and cable, a heated pool, and a fitness center. Shops (shopping here is tax free) and a restaurant are nearby. *1503 N. Hayden Island Dr., (503) 289-7626, www.jantzenbeachrv.com.*

NORTHEAST

MIDWEST

SOUTH

WEST

California's Coastal Highway

ROUTE TOWNS: San Francisco | Moss Beach | Pescadero | Santa Cruz | Felton | Boulder Creek | Monterey | Carmel
Big Sur | San Simeon | San Luis Obispo | Avila Beach | Solvang | Santa Barbara | Los Angeles
Anaheim | Long Beach | Huntington Beach | San Juan Capistrano | San Clemente | Carlsbad
San Diego

One of the world's most glorious drives, Highway 1 hugs the California coast, showing off at every turn.
Its windswept bluffs are just some of the many intriguing sites that deliver a memorable vacation.

Golden Gate Bridge, San Francisco

On this trip, you'll eat your way through San Francisco, get up close with nature along the
Northern California coast, and then ride the historic roller coaster on Santa Cruz's Beach
Boardwalk. This is also a great jumping-off point for a side trip to Felton and Boulder Creek
in Redwood Country. South of Santa Cruz, you'll weave along the Central Coast to Monterey,
Carmel, and Big Sur—the route's so stunning that you might want to pull over and admire the
views to avoid plunging into the ocean.

The highway then travels inland to the college community of San Luis Obispo, where you
might want to set up camp to explore the Central Coast wine country. Just 100 miles south
is Santa Barbara, a seaside university town favored by the rich and famous. And then, like an

explosion, you reach Los Angeles. The
best way to explore California's largest
city is one area at a time, picking and
choosing from beach regions, museum-
dotted urban streets, or studio-studded
environs.

Continuing south, the highway crawls
past the upper-class beach towns of
Huntington Beach, Laguna Beach,
and San Clemente before hitting San
Diego, a surprisingly cultural (and
large) beach city and the last stopping
point before the Mexico border.

Atlas map NM-5, p. 12

Distance: 671 miles point to point.

Type of Trip: Vacation Getaway; RV;
Arts & Culture, Great Outdoors, History
& Heritage, Picture Perfect.

Must Try: California cuisine. It's all
about fresh, locally sourced ingredients.
You can purchase your own at
myriad farmer's markets, or sample
market-fresh cuisine at places like San
Francisco's Ferry Building and L.A.'s
Rustic Canyon.

Must Buy: Art. Highway 1 is an artist
mecca. Consider picking up renderings
of the coast along your drive. In Big Sur,
Nepenthe Restaurant's Phoenix Shop
makes a great stop for locally made
creations.

Must See: Ferry Building, Santa Cruz
Boardwalk, Monterey Bay Aquarium,
Point Lobos State Reserve, Hearst
Castle, Venice Beach, Disneyland,
Legoland, San Diego Zoo.

Worth Noting: California beaches
are known for their sun, but fog and
wind can make things chilly. Always
bring a sweatshirt, even in summer.
In the cities, pick up a CityPass for
admission and other discounts at many
sites. While in Santa Cruz, consider
driving north on Route 9 to explore
Redwood Country.

Travel Tips: You can tackle this
trip in a week but two would better
enable you to fully enjoy it. Allow time
for traffic delays. Congestion in Los
Angeles, for instance, can mean you
need well over an hour to cover just
20 miles. In summer, beach regions
get packed; reserve well in advance
for hotels and campsites. Visit in fall
for fantastic weather and a relatively
empty coast.

San Francisco

❶ Fisherman's Wharf. Millions of tourists flock to this neighborhood on cable cars to sample clam chowder in sourdough bowls, hop on ferries to Alcatraz, indulge in chocolate treats at Ghirardelli Square, ride the historic carousel on Pier 39, or take photos of the sea lions that reside at the pier's edge. Cluttered with enough souvenir shops to make anyone sick of seeing the same tacky San Francisco sweatshirt or Alcatraz snow globe, the draw here is that unmistakable feeling of being on vacation. Grab a **Wharf Pass** (www.wharfpass.com) if you plan to visit the five main attractions—Ripley's Believe It or Not, Madame Tussauds Wax Museum, the San Francisco Dungeon, Blue & Gold Bay Cruise, or Aquarium of the Bay (an educational glimpse at the sea life in San Francisco Bay). *Jefferson St., (415) 391-2000, visitfishermanswharf.com.*

❷ Alcatraz. One of America's most famed prisons, Alcatraz lies in the center of San Francisco Bay. Once home to infamous inmates including Al Capone and George "Machine Gun" Kelly, it now houses elaborate gardens, fantastic bay views, and a museum detailing "The Rock's" storied past. Over a million people ferry over from Fisherman's Wharf year-round for guided multi-lingual audio tours, so book early. Mid-afternoon offers the best chance of avoiding the fog, though be sure to dress for warmth whatever time you depart. Night Tours are fun as well. *Fort Mason, B201, (415) 561-4900, www.nps.gov/alca/index.htm.*

Alcatraz

❸ Musée Mécanique. One of San Francisco's quirkiest attractions, this free museum has more than 300 coin-operated musical instruments and antique arcade machines—all in their original working condition. It's an impressive collection of antique carnival games, Skeeball, Whack-a-Mole, mechanical figures like Laffing Sal (the iconic statue guard of the Santa Cruz Boardwalk), and wacky attractions like a carnival constructed of toothpicks and racy viewfinders. *45 Pier, (415) 346-2000, www.museemecanique.com.*

❹ Ferry Building. San Francisco has an epic food scene, and the Ferry Building Marketplace is the epicenter. Where else can you find organic hot dogs, zillions of mushroom varieties, locally grown lavender and heirloom tomatoes, grass-fed beef and fresh-off-the-boat Dungeness crab, pumpkin milkshakes, rose-flavored gelato, Blue Bottle Coffee lattes, and views of the bay? It seems as if the entire city comes out for the Farmers Market—you might run into one of the city's famous chefs. Don't miss bayside oysters at Hog Island Oyster, a steamed bun at Out the Door, a triple cream brie tasting at Cowgirl Creamery, chocolate at Recchiuti, gingerbread cupcakes at Miette, or souvenir shopping at The Gardener. *1 The Embarcadero, (415) 983-8030, www.ferrybuildingmarketplace.com.*

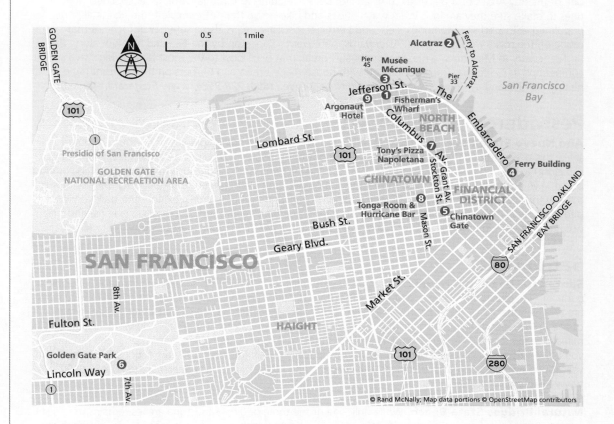

❺ Chinatown Gate. An obligatory photo stop, the red-and-gold, pagoda-topped Chinatown Gate—a gift from the Republic of China to represent peace, love, respect, and prosperity—guards the largest Chinese quarter outside of Asia. Chinatown's 24-block community was settled when the first immigrants arrived in 1848. Meandering down Grant and Stockton streets is an attraction in itself: Hordes of people push down the sidewalk, shopping for everything from live chickens to jade statues. Notable destinations include the Kong Chow Temple, Pacific Heritage Museum, and the Golden Gate Fortune Cookie Factory. If you're hungry, Great Eastern Restaurant serves dim sum and a mean Peking duck. *Grant Ave. at Bush St., (415) 391-2000, www.sanfranciscochinatown.com.*

❻ Golden Gate Park. In the heart of San Francisco, the 1,017-acre Golden Gate Park boasts hundreds of miles of running trails, the Strybing Arboretum Botanical Garden, a Japanese tea garden, the Conservatory of Flowers, two world-class museums, windmills, and lakes. While many visitors flock to museums—California Academy of Sciences and the M.H. de Young Memorial Museum—others explore the AIDS Memorial Grove paths or the Koret Children's Corner with its historic carousel and massive slides. You can also paddle-boat on Stow Lake, join the Hippie Hill drum circle near Haight-Ashbury, enjoy house-brewed beer and thick mac and cheese at Park Chalet, or wave hello to the bison herd by Ocean Beach, here since 1891. *7th Ave., between Lincoln Way and Fulton St., (415) 831-5510, www.golden-gate-park.com.*

Japanese tea garden, Golden Gate Park

Eat & Stay

❼ Tony's Pizza Napoletana. Award-winning pizza maker Tony Gemignani slings nine types of pies in his seven ovens. Located in North Beach, the center of San Francisco's Italian population, it's just a short stroll from Fisherman's Wharf. Scoring a table can be challenging on summer weekend nights. Be patient. It's worth it, especially for Tony's Margherita pizza. *1570 Stockton St., (415) 835-9888, tonyspizzanapoletana.com.*

❽ Tonga Room and Hurricane Bar. Since 1945, stepping into this hole in the wall at the bottom of the historic Fairmont San Francisco has been like taking a trip to the tropics featured in *South Pacific*. The massive subterranean restaurant and Hurricane Bar circle a lagoon that gets rained on once an hour—you don't need an umbrella, save the one in your fruity cocktail. The live band plays music often found at weddings, and, just after Happy Hour, when the drinks take effect, everyone takes to the dance floor. The Pacific Rim cuisine features sweet meats and a mean Kung Pao for a hefty price, but the Pupu platter is the way to go. Reserve well in advance for dinner. *950 Mason St., (415) 772-5278, www.tongaroom.com.*

❾ Argonaut Hotel. Located in a 1908 warehouse overlooking Fisherman's Wharf, this nautical themed 252-room hotel partners with the Maritime Museum, offering a dash of history with your bay views. Original brickwork and Douglas fir beams grace tech-friendly rooms. Amenities include a gym, Blue Mermaid Restaurant, a business center, a helpful concierge, a wine hour, an on-site museum, and parking (hefty fee). *495 Jefferson St., (415) 563-0800, www.argonauthotel.com.*

Moss Beach

Fitzgerald Marine Reserve. South of San Francisco, hidden in a hamlet along Highway 1, you'll find one of the Bay Area's best places to spot sea life. Before heading to this unassuming beach, check the tides to make sure they are low. Wear water-shoes and hike down the cliff to explore the rich tidal pools populated with starfish, anemones, eels, and hermit crabs. This area is also a safe haven for seals that reside on the rocks with their pups. Afterwards, pop over to Princeton-by-the-Sea and hike out along the bird sanctuary to Mavericks, a massive winter surf break that plays host to the most famous big wave surf competition in California. Cap your day off with house-made brews and burgers on the bayfront patio at nearby Half Moon Bay Brewing Company. *200 Nevada Ave., (650) 728-3584, www.fitzgeraldreserve.org.*

Pescadero

Año Nuevo State Park. Home to one of the world's largest breeding colonies of northern elephant seals, this oceanfront state park provides year-round adventurers with the chance to get up close (but not too close) to these massive sea mammals. Winter's the best time to visit, because the elephant seals come to breed, give birth, and molt, but you must reserve a guided tour. Be prepared to hike about a mile on dunes to view the spectacle of their often bloody mating ritual. During other seasons, explore the trails to view bird sanctuaries, the smaller population of seals who reside here year round, sea otters, sea lions, and the occasional great white shark. *1 New Years Creek Rd., (650) 879-2025, www.parks.ca.gov.*

Santa Cruz

Santa Cruz Beach Boardwalk. Set on a beautiful mile-long beach, this seaside amusement park offers a mix of "nostalgia" and "new." Not only is it a State Historic Landmark, but among its more than 30 rides are two National Historic Landmarks: the 1911 Looff Carousel and the 1924 Giant Dipper coaster. State-of-the-art attractions include Undertow, a unique spinning roller coaster. There's also bowling, laser tag, miniature golf, boardwalk games and an arcade, shops, and food vendors. Park admission is free, though you'll need tickets or day passes/wristbands (a good deal!) for all rides and some attractions. There are year-round events, along with summer's free concerts and movie nights. *400 Beach St., (831) 423-5590, www.beachboardwalk.com.*

Natural Bridges State Beach. While only one of the three original sandstone arches remains, this is still very photo-worthy. So are the whales, seals, sea otters, and birds that you might spot off, on, or above the shore. In addition, tidal pools are home to starfish, crabs, and other marine life. The most unique feature, though, is Monarch Grove, a preserve that's home to hundreds of thousands of monarch butterflies from mid-October to early February. Stop by the visitors center to learn more about butterflies—and other area flora and fauna—and to arrange docent-led nature tours and trail hikes. Other amenities include picnic tables, barbecues, and restrooms. *2531 W. Cliff Dr., (831) 423-4609, www.parks.ca.gov.*

Felton

Roaring Camp Railroads. You could chug through dwarfing redwoods on an open-air, narrow-gauge steam train, gliding along trestles on a 75-minute round trip. Or you could (Apr. thru Sept.) make a three-hour round-trip excursion through Henry Cowell Redwoods State Park and then to the Santa Cruz Boardwalk. Round trips commence at the Roaring Camp in Felton or the beach in Santa Cruz. The railroad also has themed dinner trains and special seasonal rides. *5401 Graham Hill Rd., (831) 335-4484 www.roaringcamp.com.*

Boulder Creek

Big Basin Redwoods State Park. The oldest of the California State Parks, Big Basin Redwoods is a hiker's dream destination. Straddling the Santa Cruz Mountains towards Los Gatos, Big Basin's collection of redwood tree hikes is extensive and ideal for all levels of outdoor adventurer. Favorite trails include the Skyline to Sea, Boulder Creek, Berry Creek Canyon (it's tough, but it rewards you with waterfalls), Sempervirens Falls, and Redwood. There are 146 tent campsites in the park, plus RV sites with hookups and tent cabins. Grab a trail map at the visitors center and reserve campsites in advance. *21600 Big Basin Way, (831) 338-8860, www.parks.ca.gov.*

Monterey

Monterey Bay Aquarium. Located in the heart of Monterey Bay in Cannery Row, the Aquarium showcases sea otters, kelp forests, sharks, jellyfish, a dancing school of sardines, and an informative children's area with touch tanks and interactive exhibits. It also offers the chance to step into the sea air and spot mammals and birds from the shore. Come early: There's more to see than you might imagine—not to mention an assortment of special tours. And, if time allows, rent a kayak for some time on the bay. *886 Cannery Row, (831) 648-4800, www.montereybayaquarium.org.*

Elephant seal, Pescadero

Eat & Stay

The Picnic Basket | Santa Cruz. This place celebrates the best of the Santa Cruz food scene, with dishes that feature local, seasonal ingredients. Grab hearty sandwiches accompanied by house-made pickles, fresh-as-can-be salads, and Santa's Cruz's best ice cream from sister-venture Penny Lane. Good coffee, outdoor tables, and ocean views add to your Boardwalk experience. *125 Beach St., (831) 427-9946, thepicnicbasketsc.com.*

Santa Cruz Harbor RV Park | Santa Cruz. Land vessels meet sea vessels at this RV park operated by the Santa Cruz Port District. Situated on the city's harbor, there are few facilities, but sites do offer full hookups, and you can't beat the location. Follow the walking trails around the harbor or head to the beach, just a mile away, to enjoy its volleyball courts and concessions. Within walking distance are some fun restaurants and bars like Crows Nest, which features live music and a rocking beachfront party on Thursday nights in summer. Nightly rates are reasonable; given this and the location, you'd be wise to reserve a site ahead of your visit. *135 5th Ave., (831) 475-3279, www.santacruzharbor.org.*

Monterey Fish House | Monterey. On the outskirts of Monterey, this old school seafood joint charms diners with quality ingredients and spot-on service. The décor is nothing to write home about, but, once you try the cioppino (San Francisco fish stew) or seafood pastas, you'll know why locals want to keep this place a secret. Splurge on oysters when they're in season; the nightly specials are also noteworthy. Expect a wait, especially for dinner on weekends. *2114 Del Monte Ave., (831) 373-4647, www.montereyfishhouse.com.*

Steinbeck: A California Boy

John Steinbeck was truly a great writer, one who captured the unique American experiences of his day in fictional works like the *Grapes of Wrath* and in newspaper articles during his time as a WW II correspondent. But did you know that Steinbeck was born in Salinas, educated at Stanford, and lived for a time in Pacific Grove?

He also had ties to neighboring Monterey, particularly its aquarium. First, the aquarium is on the site of a former sardine cannery, one of several that collectively became known as Cannery Row. Second, the man behind the aquarium's overall "environment" concept was marine biologist Edward F. Ricketts, a friend of Steinbeck's and the inspiration for the character of "Doc" in the 1945 novel, *Cannery Row.*

Cannery Row, Monterey

Monterey State Historic Park. This park preserves Monterey's historic Mexican- and Victorian-inspired adobe houses and gardens. Call to book a guided tour, or grab a "Path of History" map at the Stanton Center and follow sidewalk markers. Don't miss the Custom House, California's oldest government building, or Colton Hall, home to the state's first constitution. Other notable stops include the pink Larkin House; the Presidio of Monterey Museum; and the Stevenson House, a tribute to Robert Louis Stevenson who, unknown and near death, stayed here in 1879. Fame—and improved health—followed, and his life and work are remembered here. *20 Custom House Plaza, (831) 649-7118, www.parks.ca.gov.*

Architectural detail, Carmel Mission

Carmel

Carmel Walks. When it comes to visiting Carmel (aka Carmel-by-the-Sea), the town itself is the sight, thanks to all the storybook buildings; inns and B&Bs; unique shops, day spas, and restaurants; and beautiful beaches (with beautiful sunsets). One of the best ways to take it all in and get the back story is on a two-hour guided walking tour—on and off the beaten path—with Carmel Walks, a well-established and well-regarded tour company. This outfit also provides private tours of the area, including wine country excursions. Guides are well-versed in the hamlet's history, the worth-a-peek galleries, and the best restaurants. *Ocean Ave. and Lincoln St., (831) 373-2813 (info), (888) 284-8405 (tickets), carmelwalks.com.*

Point Lobos State Natural Reserve. First inhabited by Rumsien Indians 2,500 years ago, the central coast's Point Lobos is a wonderful hiking destination, with sweeping views, hidden cypress groves, and bounties of birds. Tag along on free docent-led tours (reservations are a must), or embark along the windswept paths on your own. Favorite hikes include the Cypress Grove Trail and Bird Island Trail (bring binoculars to check out the cormorants' mating ritual; that shock of blue is like nothing you've seen in nature). At the Whaler's Cabin Museum, you can observe relics from Portuguese whaling times, including harpoons, photographs, and whale vertebrae. *62 Hwy. 1, (831) 624-4909, www.pointlobos.org.*

Big Sur coastline

Big Sur

Julia Pfieffer Burns State Park. Big Sur's most dramatic state park showcases 3,762 acres of spectacular coastal cliffs and an 80-foot waterfall plunging into the ocean. Trails meander along bluffs, offering peeks of migrating gray whales in winter, plus sea lions and seals year round. Birdwatchers appreciate the array of black cormorants, seagulls, brown pelicans, condors, and black oystercatchers. Scuba divers flock to the 1,680-acre underwater preserve at Partington Cove—a kelp forest here is abundant with sea life. Two very rustic campsites, Saddle Rock and South Garden, are in a lovely cypress grove ¼-mile west of the parking lots. *Big Sur Station #1, (831) 667-2315, www.parks.ca.gov.*

Nepenthe Restaurant. Road trippers sojourn to Nepenthe mainly for the views and the legend of Big Sur's most talked about restaurant (although some diners suggest the buzz far surpasses both the food and the service). Either way, the sights are right. Below, the ocean crashes into the cliffs, which shelter endangered California condors; whales, sea otters, dolphins, and sea lions dot the water. If the weather's nice, sit outside. Should the fog be too intense, dine indoors. Downstairs, the less expensive Café Kevah serves take-away sandwiches and snacks. Save time to explore the Phoenix Store, Big Sur's emblematic shop, hawking locally made art and body products, books, toys, and much more. *48510 Hwy. 1, (831) 667-2345, www.nepenthebigsur.com.*

San Simeon

Hearst Castle. William Randolph Hearst's spectacular, 165-room mansion—built between 1919 and 1947 through a collaboration with architect Julia Morgan—contains thousands of priceless antiques and works of art. Its 127 acres of grounds are equally spectacular, with gardens, terraces, guesthouses, and a Greco-Roman pool overlooking the Pacific. Many dignitaries and celebrities have visited the castle, and you can, too, on a half-dozen different guided tours. At the base of the mountains is San Simeon (pop. 462), which is dwarfed by the castle and part of the 3,409-acre Hearst San Simeon State Historical Monument. Campgrounds and RV sites with hookups are available; reservations are highly recommended. *750 Hearst Castle Rd., (805) 927-2010, hearstcastle.org.*

Eat & Stay

Portola Hotel and Spa | Monterey. Guests rave about the friendly service, the convenient bayside location, and the value for money. And this place has something for everyone—a spa for relaxing "me" time; a Pirate Program with goodies, on-site activities, and area adventures for kids ages 3–12; and pet-friendly amenities. Rooms have a nautical feel, with louvered wooden window blinds, rattan club chairs, fluffy white linens, and bold touches of red and blue. *2 Portola Plaza, (800) 342-4295, www.portolahotel.com.*

Lamp Lighter Inn | Carmel. In the heart of Carmel, just a few blocks from the ocean, you'll happen upon the Lamp Lighter's cottages, rooms, and suites, which were constructed in 1912. Rooms have luxurious antique furniture, marble baths, cascade showers, flat screen TVs, and Wi-Fi; some have ocean views and fireplaces, creating the ideal space for a post-hike glass of sherry. The friendly staff serves continental breakfast in the den, though you can also enjoy the pastries, fruit, and coffee in the colorful gardens. Pets are welcome for an additional fee. *Ocean Ave. and Camino Real, (831) 624-7372, www.carmellamplighter.com.*

The Intriguing 17-Mile Drive

Located in the Del Monte Forest, **17-Mile Drive** (CA Hwy. 1, 831/624-3811, www.pebblebeach.com) curves between Carmel and Pacific Grove, with the ocean on the right and multimillion-dollar estates and world-famous golf courses on the left. Of the five entrances, the one at Pacific Grove (accessible via Sunset Drive) is the most popular. The route is free to bikers and pedestrians, but drivers must pay a per-car fee. Note that motorcycles are prohibited.

Along the way, numbered pull-offs have intriguing names like Spy Glass Hill (#12). Be sure to look out on the rocks for the Lone Cypress (#16). This very wind-swept tree, a symbol of Pebble Beach, is estimated to be more than 250 years old. Ghost Tree (#17) is near Pescadero Point, where signposts warn of "large unexpected waves that will sweep people off their feet."

Mission San Luis Obispo de Tolosa

San Luis Obispo

Mission San Luis Obispo de Tolosa. One of the original nine California missions founded by Father Junipero Serra, this one, named after Bishop Louis of Toulouse, France, was the fifth in line and established in 1772. The mission offers free self-guided tours daily and afternoon docent-led tours.

Areas available to the public include the church, the gardens, and a museum, which features everything from photos of architectural influences on the buildings over the years to a large collection of arrowheads donated by a local Chumash family. The gift shop sells traditional nativity scenes and crosses, ceramic habit-clad nun sculptures, and books. As this is an active Catholic parish, early morning masses are held on weekends; donations are accepted. *751 Palm St., (805) 781-8220, www.missionsanluisobispo.org.*

Avila Beach

Avila Hot Springs. Oil drillers struck a different kind of gold over a century ago in this sweet beach community. Two miles from the sand, and a short drive from downtown San Luis Obispo, this famed thermal hot springs lures soakers and families to its waterslides, lap pool, and traditional soaking pool; massages are available. The hotel features a modest restaurant as well as summer movie nights, a laundromat, and bike rentals; there are also rental cabins and tent sites. *250 Avila Beach Dr., (805) 595-2359, www.avilahotsprings.com.*

Solvang

Hans Christian Andersen Museum. The life and writings of Danish writer Hans Christian Andersen are honored at this small museum. You'll find first editions of his work, artist renderings, and correspondence and photos. Downstairs, purchase copies of *The Ugly Duckling*, *The Little Mermaid*, and some of his other 160 fairy tales at the on-site Book Loft. After learning about Mr. Andersen, take a stroll through the Danish-style village of Solvang. The cobblestone streets and cottages house wine tasting rooms and Scandinavian shops and restaurants. *1680 Mission Dr., (805) 688-2052, www.bookloftsolvang.com.*

Santa Barbara

Municipal Winemakers. Favorites at this hip downtown winery include an old vine Blanche Chenin Blanc and several hearty reds. The décor is funky with walls of filing cabinets and shabby chic wooden tables; there is a tasting fee. The winery is on Santa Barbara's Urban Wine Trail, which is a collective of local wineries with tasting rooms within downtown. *22 Anacapa St., (805) 931-6864, www.municipalwinemakers.com.*

Eat & Stay

Firestone Grill | San Luis Obispo. Meat eaters unite over hefty burgers and shredded-pork sandwiches at this beloved barbecue joint. Lighter options include fish tacos, creative salads, and avocado sandwiches. In the bar, locals slurp sudsy brews and watch sports on the flat screens; families tend to congregate at picnic tables outside. *1001 Higuera St., (805) 783-1001, www.firestonegrill.com.*

Madonna Inn | San Luis Obispo. Opened in 1958, this internationally recognized inn goes beyond "over the top" with 110 themed rooms honoring all things kitsch. Some have Imperial antiques, others rock an Austin Powers vibe, but all offer you access to the tennis courts, pool, hot tubs, spa, shops, restaurants, bakery, bars, and fitness center. Even if you're just passing through, stop and marvel at the humor and imagination that created a landmark. *100 Madonna Rd., (805) 543-3000, www.madonnainn.com.*

Los Arroyos | Santa Barbara. Wildly popular Los Arroyos delivers traditional Mexican cuisine for all palates. The South of the Border décor invites diners in from the streets of downtown Santa Barbara to order favorites like fish enchiladas, veggie tostadas, chicken burritos, and heaping bowls of guacamole. *14 W. Figueroa, (805) 962-5541, www.losarroyos.net.*

El Capitan Canyon | Santa Barbara. Above the beach and hugged by 300 acres of woodlands, this canyon provides an outdoorsy lodging experience with the comforts of home. Choose from wood-floor yurts, whose cozy beds are topped with thick duvets; creek-side cedar cabins with kitchenettes and fire pits; or safari tents decked out with willow beds and Western-style blankets. Behind a barn door, a rustic market sells locally made gifts and serves breakfast, lunch, and dinner year round. *11560 Calle Real, (805) 685-3887, www.elcapitancanyon.com.*

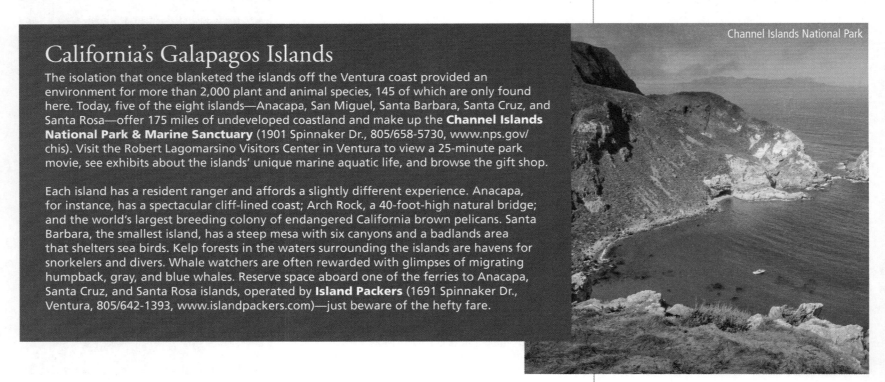
Channel Islands National Park

California's Galapagos Islands

The isolation that once blanketed the islands off the Ventura coast provided an environment for more than 2,000 plant and animal species, 145 of which are only found here. Today, five of the eight islands—Anacapa, San Miguel, Santa Barbara, Santa Cruz, and Santa Rosa—offer 175 miles of undeveloped coastline and make up the **Channel Islands National Park & Marine Sanctuary** (1901 Spinnaker Dr., 805/658-5730, www.nps.gov/chis). Visit the Robert Lagomarsino Visitors Center in Ventura to view a 25-minute park movie, see exhibits about the islands' unique marine aquatic life, and browse the gift shop.

Each island has a resident ranger and affords a slightly different experience. Anacapa, for instance, has a spectacular cliff-lined coast; Arch Rock, a 40-foot-high natural bridge; and the world's largest breeding colony of endangered California brown pelicans. Santa Barbara, the smallest island, has a steep mesa with six canyons and a badlands area that shelters sea birds. Kelp forests in the waters surrounding the islands are havens for snorkelers and divers. Whale watchers are often rewarded with glimpses of migrating humpback, gray, and blue whales. Reserve space aboard one of the ferries to Anacapa, Santa Cruz, and Santa Rosa islands, operated by **Island Packers** (1691 Spinnaker Dr., Ventura, 805/642-1393, www.islandpackers.com)—just beware of the hefty fare.

Los Angeles: In and Around Tinseltown

At first glance, the City of Angels overwhelms with its sprawl and excess. Yet, as you enter each community, the city unravels, revealing a diverse wonderland of amazing eats, world-class museums, stellar beaches, and dazzling night spots.

With just a couple of days to explore, consider starting in the Santa Monica area, where attractions within a few blocks of the beach offer a respite from the heat and traffic. Next, take in the cultural riches of the Mid-City museums and food trucks before weaving into Hollywood's glamorous tribute to the movies. Last, don't miss a chance to explore downtown—the new face of So-Cal cool.

Travel Tips: Los Angeles is known for good weather and bad traffic year round. Summers tend to be more crowded, but the city really gets packed during winter awards season, when celebrities fill the luxury hotels. Spring and fall are ideal times to visit. Freeways tend to look like parking lots all day long, so add additional drive time.

Visitor Info: Discover Los Angeles, *6801 Hollywood Blvd., (323) 467-6412, www.discoverlosangeles.com.*

Graffiti wall at Venice Beach (top)
Coastline near Venice Beach (bottom)

Santa Monica and Venice Beach

1 Santa Monica Pier. Over a century old, the pier stays of-the-moment by inviting kids of all ages to ride the thrilling wooden roller coaster or the 1922 Carousel, challenge their balance at the trapeze school, play state-of-the-art video games, or win massive stuffed animals at the array of carnival games. The Heal the Bay Aquarium, the old-fashioned soda fountain, kitschy shops, seafood restaurants and bars, and the beach keep visitors around all day. Don't miss the free walking tours and events like summertime's Twilight Dance Series, which features big-name musicians for free, and autumn's outdoor movies. Just up the street is Third Street Promenade, a car-free commercial stretch. *200 Santa Monica Pier, (310) 458-8901, santamonicapier.org.*

2 Venice Beach. There's never a dull moment at this legendary Los Angeles beach, where people watching is a major spectator sport. Here you'll see magicians, jugglers, mimes, musicians, singers, impersonators, and fortune tellers. And, if you're inclined to take a more active role in the fun, you can try skateboarding, rollerskating, in-line skating, surfing, or bicycling. Shops renting equipment for these activities as well as souvenir stores and restaurants can be found along the boardwalk.

The Venice Beach and Boardwalk is the busiest site run by the L.A. Department of Recreation and Parks, drawing around 30,000 people daily to its paddle tennis, handball, and basketball courts—and of course its famous Muscle Beach Outdoor Gym. There are also two children's play areas and a renowned skate park. Worthy places to grab a bite to eat include Poke Poke, The Sidewalk Café, and Figtree's Café. Beer lovers will appreciate the Venice Ale House, which serves craft brews alfresco. *1800 Ocean Front Walk, (310) 396-6794, www.laparks.org/venice.*

Mid-City Museums

3 J. Paul Getty Museum at the Getty Center. Housed in the gleaming, travertine-clad Getty Center, overlooking Los Angeles and the Pacific Ocean from atop the Santa Monica Mountains, the museum offers a wealth of European paintings, drawings, illuminated manuscripts, sculpture, decorative arts, and American and European photographs. Changing exhibitions and a wide range of programs draw visitors of all ages; gallery talks, lectures, film screenings, concerts, and family activities are

offered in both English and Spanish. Admission is free, but there's a fee for parking. *1200 Getty Center Dr., (310) 440-7300, www.getty.edu.*

4 Petersen Automotive Museum. Wrapped within ribbons of stainless steel, this world-class museum is a vibrant visual celebration of southern California's car culture. Renovations completed in late 2015 added enhanced displays, 22 new galleries, hundreds of classic automobiles, and a changing roster of exhibits. Whether you're a die-hard motor head or you just love great design, this is a must-see museum. *6060 Wilshire Blvd., (323) 930-2277, www.petersen.org.*

5 Los Angeles County Museum of Art. This world-class complex houses one of the country's largest collections of fine art. Among the samplings from pre-history through modern civilization are the museum's two sculpture gardens, one offering contemporary work and the other masterpieces by Rodin. Ongoing exhibits are inspiring, while rotating special exhibits showcase fashion, sculpture, film, and more. The on-site restaurant serves simple lunch options at outdoor tables, and L.A.'s outstanding food trucks line up along Wilshire Boulevard near the museum. *5905 Wilshire Blvd., (323) 857-6000, www.lacma.org.*

Santa Monica Pier

Eat & Stay

6 Hotel Erwin. You can't beat the location: in the heart of Venice Beach and just a block from the sea. Colorful, beach-hued rooms have modern furnishings and fixtures, balconies, and big windows that invite in that luxurious California sunshine. The Barlo Kitchen and Wine Bar is open for breakfast and dinner, and the attractive High Rooftop Lounge is great for small bites and creative cocktails. *1697 Pacific Ave., (800) 786-7789, www.hotelerwin.com.*

7 Rustic Canyon. This much-hyped dining spot features executive chef Jeremy Fox—so reservations are a good idea. Seasonal menu items might include the ricotta dumplings, grilled lamb sausage, or *pozole verde* (Mexican hominy stew) with Hope Ranch mussels. The artisanal beers, hand-crafted cocktails, and wines by the glass are as pleasing as the cuisine. *1119 Wilshire Blvd., (310) 393-7050, rusticcanyonwinebar.com.*

city itinerary

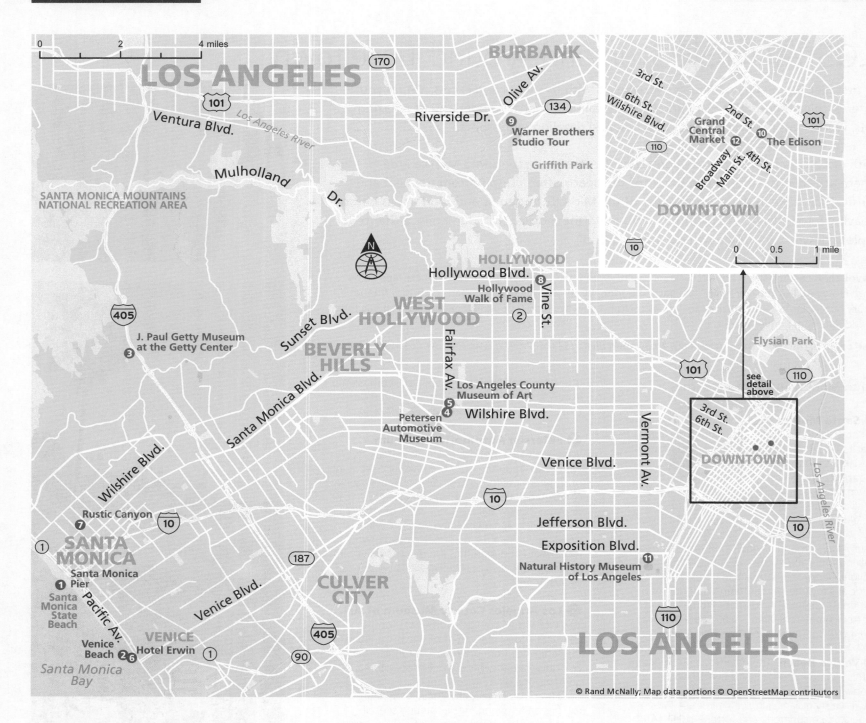

© Rand McNally; Map data portions © OpenStreetMap contributors

NORTHEAST

MIDWEST

SOUTH

WEST

Hollywood and the Studios

8 Hollywood Walk of Fame. Embedded in the sidewalk for more than a mile along Hollywood Boulevard are stars with the names of 2,500-plus directors, actors, musicians, producers—and a few fictional characters—honored for their contributions to Hollywood. You'll also find Mann's Chinese Theater, the historic movie house whose forecourt is paved with roughly 200 cement blocks featuring celebrity signatures and hand- and footprints. Nearby are the Microsoft Theater (home to awards shows and concerts) and the historic El Capitan Theater, where you can join Disney film sing-alongs with live performers dressed as animated characters. *Hollywood Blvd. and Vine St., (323) 469-8311, www.walkoffame.com.*

9 Warner Brothers Studio Tour. This two-hour tour showcases the famed Warner Brothers Studio and includes interactive experiences from films like *Gravity*, *Harry Potter*, and *Lord of the Rings*. You'll end at Stage 48: Script to Screen—a self-guided exhibition area where you can sip espresso at a re-created Central Perk (from the show *Friends*). Plan ahead to join the audience ~~wa~~tching Ellen DeGeneres or Conan O'Brien. ~~Chec~~k www.tvtickets.com for advance tickets to ~~taping~~s of shows like *Mom. 3400 Riverside Dr.,* ~~(8~~2-8687, vipstudiotour.warnerbros.com.

In and Around Downtown

10 The Edison. A downtown power-plant-turned-nightclub invites night owls to experience shows—from burlesque to jazz to indie rock—while sipping artisanal cocktails and craft beers. The vibe is both hip and kitsch, retro and futuristic. Darkened nooks decked out with rich textured seating, candlelight, and memorabilia link the Edison to yesteryear clubs like Ciro's and the Cocoanut Grove. There's a dress code ("old-world style and a sense of romance"), and reservations are recommended. *108 W. 2nd St. #101, (213) 613-0000, www.edisondowntown.com.*

11 Natural History Museum of Los Angeles. The museum's massive collection inspires children of all ages to get up close to animals displayed in artful dioramas. The superstar attraction is the Dinosaur Hall, which houses a staggering collection of bones, including a T-Rex growth series (the only one on earth), flying species, and even giant plant-eating reptiles. Other exhibits include the Butterfly Pavilion, Gem and Mineral Hall, and Becoming Los Angeles. Although you'll need a separate ticket, the La Brea Tar Pits & Museum is just 15 minutes away. *900 Exposition Blvd., (213) 763-3466, www.nhm.org.*

Eat & Stay

12 Grand Central Market. Since 1917, this downtown food hall has celebrated the city's ethnic diversity by housing dozens of take-out restaurants. With the resurgence of downtown's dining scene, serious chefs have also staked claim to food stalls, making this warehouse a destination du jour. From Thai street food to haute barbecue, perfectly crafted lattes to delightful egg sandwiches, you can find just about everything imaginable (and more) housed in this block-long space. You'd want a week to sample the offerings at places like La Tostadería, Horse Thief BBQ, China Café, and Wexler's Deli. *317 S. Broadway, (213) 624-2378, www.grandcentralmarket.com.*

Anaheim

Disneyland. A true original, Disneyland's Magic Kingdom was the first theme park of its kind. It's wise to stay a couple of days to visit Disney's California Adventure Park, the Downtown Disney entertainment complex, and three Disney hotels (which together make this larger than many California cities). Rides are geared towards kids of all ages, with staples like It's a Small World and Jungle Cruise for the whole family, and more thrilling rides like Space Mountain and Matterhorn for older visitors. Grab a Park Hopper pass to Disney's California Adventure to ride Tow Mater and Lightning McQueen in Cars Land. The live performances, character breakfasts, light shows like *Fantasmic* and *Power of Imagination,* parades, fireworks, princess makeovers, and much more are not to be missed. *(714) 781-4000, 1313 Disneyland Dr., disneyland.disney.go.com.*

Long Beach

Queen Mary. In service as an ocean liner from the 1930s to the '60s, the *Queen Mary* now sits in Long Beach harbor, attracting thousands of guests each year. Tour the historic cruise ship that served as a WW II troopship, and visit its onboard galleries while learning about the restoration project that helped land the *Queen Mary* on the National Register of Historic Places. Dine in one of the three restaurants, grab a cocktail in the Observation Bar, or stay at one of the 346 Art Deco staterooms-turned-hotel rooms. For a real treat, take a ghost tour of the ship, though, if you've booked a room, you might not sleep too well that night. *1126 Queens Hwy., (877) 342-0738, www.queenmary.com.*

Catalina Island Ferry. Hop on an express ferry—you might see dolphins and whales in winter—to arrive at majestic Catalina Island in about an hour. Just 22 miles from the mainland, it seems worlds away with its bird sanctuaries, active bison population, and pristine beaches. Ferries also depart from Dana Point, San Pedro, and near the *Queen Mary.* Reservations are recommended especially in summer. Bring some Dramamine as rides can be very bumpy. *320 Golden Shore, (800) 613-1212, catalinaexpress.com.*

Queen Mary

Huntington Beach

Huntington Beach

Huntington City Beach. This might just be southern California's most iconic beach. Known for its dependable surf, thin blonde sand, and miles of uninterrupted coastline, Huntington Beach hosts its share of surf and volleyball contests year round. Take a surf lesson from one of the instructors hanging out by the pier, shop for souvenirs at Kite Connection, or grab a cocktail on the patio of Shorebreak Hotel. Off-season, park your RV along the beach and camp for the night. *Hwy. 1 and 2nd St., (714) 969-3492, www.surfcityusa.com.*

San Juan Capistrano

Mission San Juan Capistrano. Founded in 1775, this mission brought religious settlers to San Juan Capistrano. After almost a century of decay, Catholic conservationists refurbished the original Great Stone Church and the acres of lush grounds. Today the mission lures visitors with guided audio tours of the property. For a treat, explore the Serra Chapel, California's oldest operating church. You can picnic in the gardens, join weekly art walks, and participate in activities like basket weaving or gold panning. *26801 Ortega Hwy., (949) 234-1300, www.missionsjc.com.*

San Clemente

San Clemente State Beach. Near the south end of San Clemente, this camping beach is popular with surfboarders and body surfers. There are a few notable surf breaks in the park, including a nice easy beach break right in front of the campground. More advanced surfers should walk about 15 minutes south of the parking area to Cottons, a local favorite. The campground (www.reserveamerica.com) sits atop a bluff offering lovely sunset views of the Pacific Ocean. There are RV sites with hookups as well as tent camping, picnic areas, and restrooms with showers. *225 W. Califia Ave., (949) 492-3156, www.parks.ca.gov.*

Carlsbad

Legoland California Resort. Even if your clan is not addicted to Legos, a visit to this imaginative amusement park should rank high on your list. Featuring over 60 million Lego bricks throughout the park and resort, Legoland is comprised of over 60 rides, including roller coasters for all ages, thrilling water adventures in the CHIMA waterpark, a movie experience, a Sea Life Aquarium packed with water creatures from the nearby California coastal waters, and Lego Minilands of everything from *Star Wars* to Las Vegas.

There's also a hotel complex designed by the world's most creative Lego builders (check out the mural at hotel reception), restaurants scattered through the parks, and plentiful toy shops. Fun tip: ask any employee for the Lego mini on their nametag, and they're required to trade it for yours! *One Legoland Dr., (760) 918-5346, california.legoland.com.*

Eat & Stay

Casa Mariquita | Santa Catalina Island. If splurging on a room takes a backseat to exploring the island, this moderately priced family-owned hotel might fit the bill. It's in the heart of Avalon and just a block from the beach, so put on your walking shoes (or rent a golf cart or bicycle) and discover shops and restaurants, food markets, and diving charters. Some rooms have ocean views; in others, the views come with a balcony. The cozy courtyards are great spots to unwind. *229 Metropole Ave., (800) 545-1192, casamariquitacatalina.com.*

Big Fish Tavern | Laguna Beach. Not much beats toasting a Pacific sunset over a casual seafood dinner. Although peak hours draw crowds, you can still saunter in without a reservation and find yourself enjoying a mojito and a decadent pot of lobster fondue or lobster mac and cheese. Midday happy hour makes a great post-beach pit stop—especially if you're sampling the large beer selection. Reservations are recommended on busy weekend nights. *540 S. Coast Hwy. #200, (949) 715-4500, bigfishtavernlaguna.com.*

Montage Laguna Beach | Laguna Beach. The 250 rooms and suites of this 30-acre oceanfront property pay homage to California living. The waves lapping in the distance, three pools fronting the shore, the simple beach-colored interiors that breathe of comfort and decadence without being showy, the marble bathrooms, and the Craftsman architecture allow the whole family to relax and behold luxury at its finest. Other on-site amenities include three restaurants, a spa, a children's program, beach activities, and several boutiques. *www.montagehotels.com/lagunabeach.*

NORTHEAST

MIDWEST

SOUTH

WEST

city itinerary

San Diego

❶ San Diego Air and Space Museum.
The museum houses full-scale mock-ups of
Gemini and Mercury spacecraft as well as the
command module from the Apollo IX mission.
There are nearly 70 flying machines, including
replicas of Wright gliders from 1901 and 1902,
a Messerschmidt mock-up, and a Lockheed A-12
Blackbird. For an extra fee, you can test Max Flight
Simulators that surround you with a widescreen
view outside your "jet" or let you feel the effects
of 36-degree pitch, roll, spin, and spiral.

The museum is in Balboa Park, San Diego's largest
public area, where attractions also include the
Museum of Man and the San Diego Museum
of Art, the internationally acclaimed Old Globe
Theater, a carousel, gardens, restaurants, play
areas, and trails. Plan a day to enjoy the park with
a Balboa Park Explorer Pass, which grants entry
into many of the city's cultural arenas.
*2001 Pan American Plaza, (619) 234-8291,
www.sandiegoairandspace.org.*

❷ San Diego Zoo. Considered by many
to be the country's finest zoo, this spectacular
100-acre establishment houses more than 3,700
animals from more than 650 species—including
the largest colony of koalas outside of Australia
and the Giant Panda from China. Spaces mimic
the animals' natural habitats as much as possible.
Kids can view animals their own size at the

Eat & Stay

❸ Hotel del Coronado | San Diego.
Since its construction in 1888, just
across the bay from downtown San
Diego, this Coronado Island luxury
resort has lured celebrities and
statesmen to its oceanfront rooms,
suites, and cottages. The wooden,
Victorian-style beach resort is a
National Historic Landmark—and
famous for its supporting role in
Some Like it Hot. Rooms feature
modern amenities, including plush
bedding and flat-screen TVs; many
have balconies. The free summer
shuttle around the island, the lively
pool, the spa, a beach, kids' club, and
seven restaurants and bars make the
property feel like a summer camp.
*1500 Orange Ave., (800) 468-3533,
hoteldel.com.*

**❹ Stone Brewing World Bistro
and Gardens | Escondido.** Beer and
food lovers rejoice at this stone,
bamboo and water tribute to hops
and California cuisine. Relying on
the bounty of produce that giddily
pops up from the soil in sunny San
Diego, Stone Brewing has taken the
area's dining scene to a new level. Sit
outside around the fire pit in the beer
garden and sip a Stone Cali-Belgique
IPA paired with the "Really Stinky
Cheese Plate." Or head inside to the
windowed loft brewery for Cubano
pork or duck tacos. For an additional
fee, tours of the brewery are available,
but come early as tours fill up and
reservations aren't accepted.
*1999 Citracado Pkwy., (760) 294-7866,
www.stonebrewing.com.*

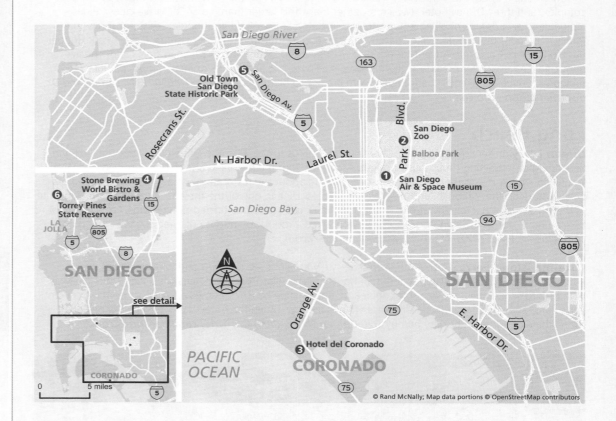

Children's Zoo, and everyone can view the park
from the Skyfari aerial tram or a double-decker
tour bus.

The 10 on-site dining options range from full-
service joints like Albert's Restaurant to snacks at
Poppy's Patio. Note: The affiliated, 1,800-acre San
Diego Zoo Safari Park is about 30 miles north.
This wildlife sanctuary showcases 3,500 animals
from Africa and Asia in large field exhibits much
like their native habitats. *2920 Zoo Dr.,
(619) 231-1515, zoo.sandiegozoo.org.*

**❺ Old Town San Diego State Historic
Park.** Stroll through the first Spanish settlement
in California, where five of the original structures
still stand, and several others have been restored.
Costumed volunteers depict the history and
culture and give cooking demonstrations. Most
people stroll through the park and end up
exploring the shops, restaurants, art galleries,
and museums of Old Town. *San Diego Ave. at
Twiggs St., (619) 220-5422, www.parks.ca.gov.*

**❻ Torrey Pines State Natural Reserve
& Beach.** Oceanfront bluffs at this 2,000-acre
reserve are dotted with wildflowers as well as fine
examples of one of the rarest types of pine on
the planet. Trails weave down to quiet beaches
along sandstone shelves and offer peeks of gray
whales migrating between Mexico and Alaska.
Although parking areas can get crowded with
hikers, photographers, and artists, you can almost
always find solace and inspiration along these
strands, especially early in the morning or near
sunset. *12600 N. Torrey Pines Rd., (858) 755-
2063, torreypine.org.*

San Diego Zoo (top right)
Old Town San Diego State Historic Park (above)

see detail

Road Atlas 2018

MAPS

Quick Map References

2 United States

Capital: Washington, G-17
Land area: 3,531,905 sq. mi.

Selected National Park Service locations

- Acadia National Park C-20
- Arches National Park G-6
- Badlands National Park E-9
- Big Bend National Park L-8
- Biscayne National Park M-18
- Bryce Canyon National Park. G-5

- Canyonlands National Park G-6
- Capitol Reef National Park. G-5
- Carlsbad Caverns National Park. J-7
- Channel Islands National Park H-1
- Congaree National Park. I-17
- Crater Lake National Park D-2

- Cuyahoga Valley National Park F-16
- Death Valley National Park G-3
- Denali National Park L-4
- Dry Tortugas National Park M-17
- Everglades National Park M-17
- Glacier Bay National Park. M-6

- Glen Canyon Nat'l Recreation Area . . G
- Grand Canyon National Park. . . . . H
- Grand Teton National Park . . . . E
- Great Sand Dunes Nat'l Park & Pres. . H
- Great Smoky Mountains Nat'l Park. . H-1
- Guadalupe Mountains Nat'l Park . . . . J

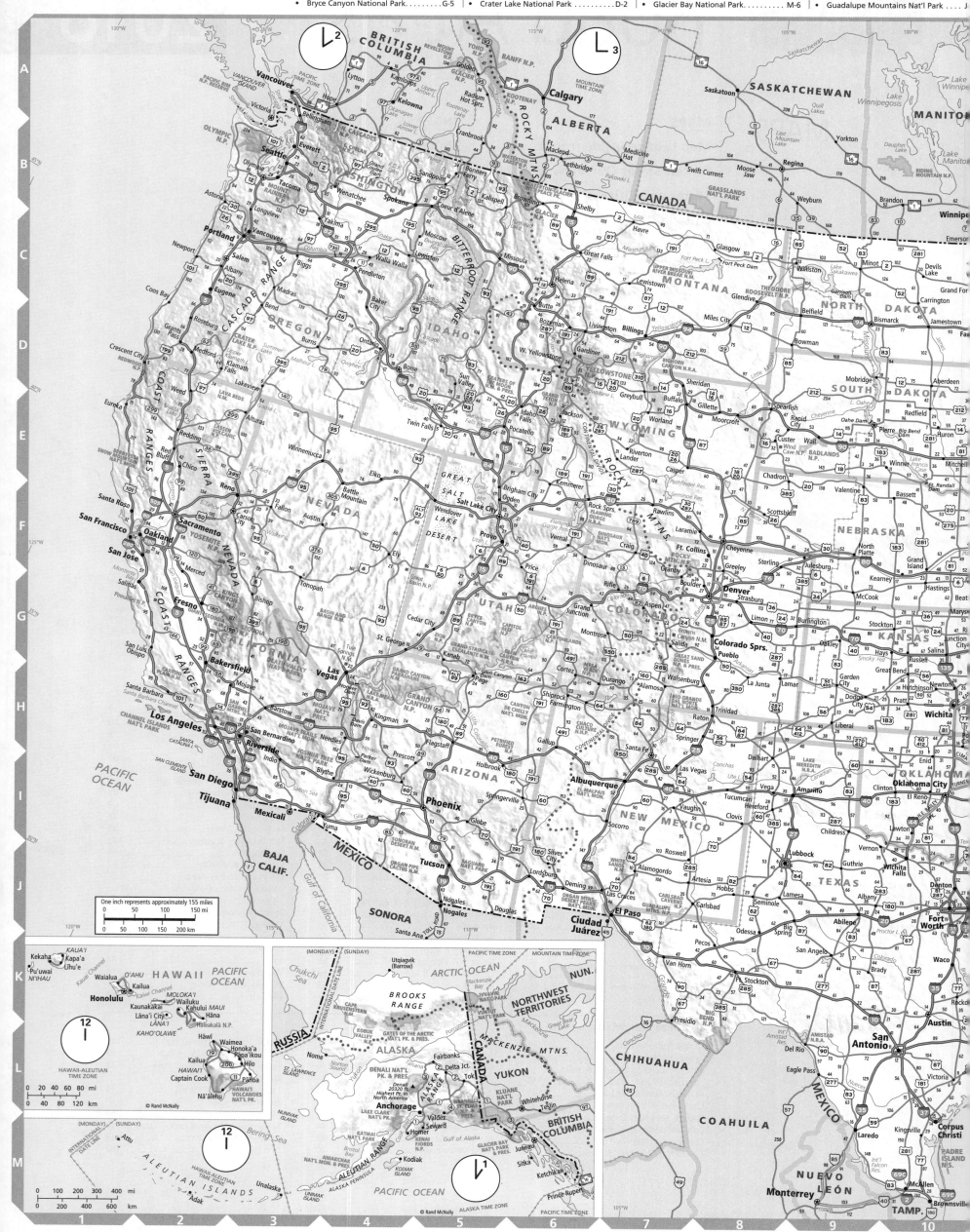

Population: 308,745,538
Largest city: New York, 8,175,133, E-18

Selected National Park Service locations

Haleakalā National Park L-2
Hawai'i Volcanoes National Park L-2
Hot Springs National Park I-12
Isle Royale National Park C-13
Kings Canyon National Park G-2
Lake Mead Nat'l Recreation Area H-4

Lassen Volcanic National Park E-2
Mammoth Cave National Park H-14
Mesa Verde National Park H-6
Mount Rainier National Park B-3
North Cascades National Park B-4
Olympic National Park B-3

Petrified Forest National Park I-5
Redwood National Park D-1
Rocky Mountain National Park F-7
Sequoia National Park G-2
Shenandoah National Park G-17
Theodore Roosevelt National Park . . .D-8

Voyageurs National Park C-12
Waterton-Glacier Int'l Peace Park B-5
Wind Cave National Park. E-8
Yellowstone National Park. D-6
Yosemite National Park F-2
Zion National Park G-5

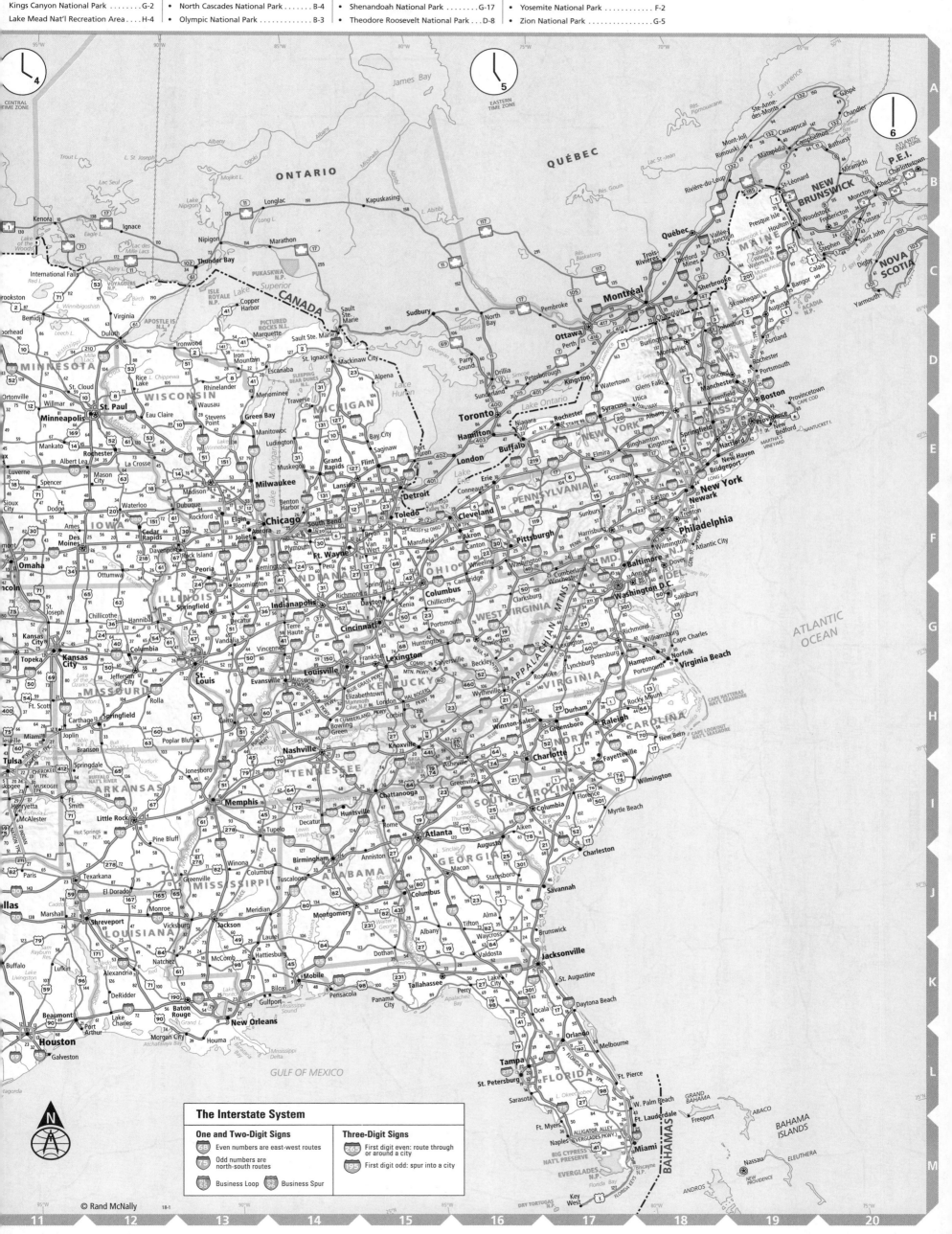

The Interstate System

One and Two-Digit Signs

Even numbers are east-west routes

Odd numbers are north-south routes

Business Loop   Business Spur

Three-Digit Signs

First digit even: route through or around a city

First digit odd: spur into a city

© Rand McNally   18-1

Nickname: The Heart of Dixie
Capital: Montgomery, J-8
Land area: 50,645 sq. mi. (rank: 28th)
Population: 4,779,736 (rank: 23rd)
Largest city: Birmingham, 212,237, F-7

Index of places   Pg. 129

Travel planning & on-the-road resources

Tourism Information
Alabama Tourism: (800) 252-2262, (334) 242-4169;
www.alabama.travel

Toll Road Information
Beach Express (Baldwin Co.): (251) 968-3415; www.beachexpress.com
Montgomery Expressway (Montgomery): (334) 290-2002; www.montgomeryexpressway.com
Tuscaloosa By-Pass (Tuscaloosa): (205) 752-2003; www.tuscaloosabypass

Road Conditions & Construction
(888) 588-2848; www.dot.state.al.us,
alitsweb2.dot.state.al.us/RoadConditions

(Freedom Pass)

Determining distances along roads
Highway distances (segments of one mile or less not shown):
Cumulative miles (red): the distance between red arrows
Intermediate miles (black): the distance between intersections & places

Interchanges and exit numbers
For most states, the mileage between interchanges may be determined
by subtracting one number from the other.

Inset maps: Huntsville; Florence; Georgia Pg. 28

Regional references: Tennessee Pg. 94; Mississippi Pg. 56

Major cities: Huntsville, Decatur, Florence, Muscle Shoals, Sheffield, Tuscumbia, Gadsden, Anniston, Oxford, Birmingham, Bessemer, Hoover, Tuscaloosa, Auburn, Opelika, Phenix City, Columbus, Montgomery, Prattville, Selma, Demopolis, Jasper, Cullman

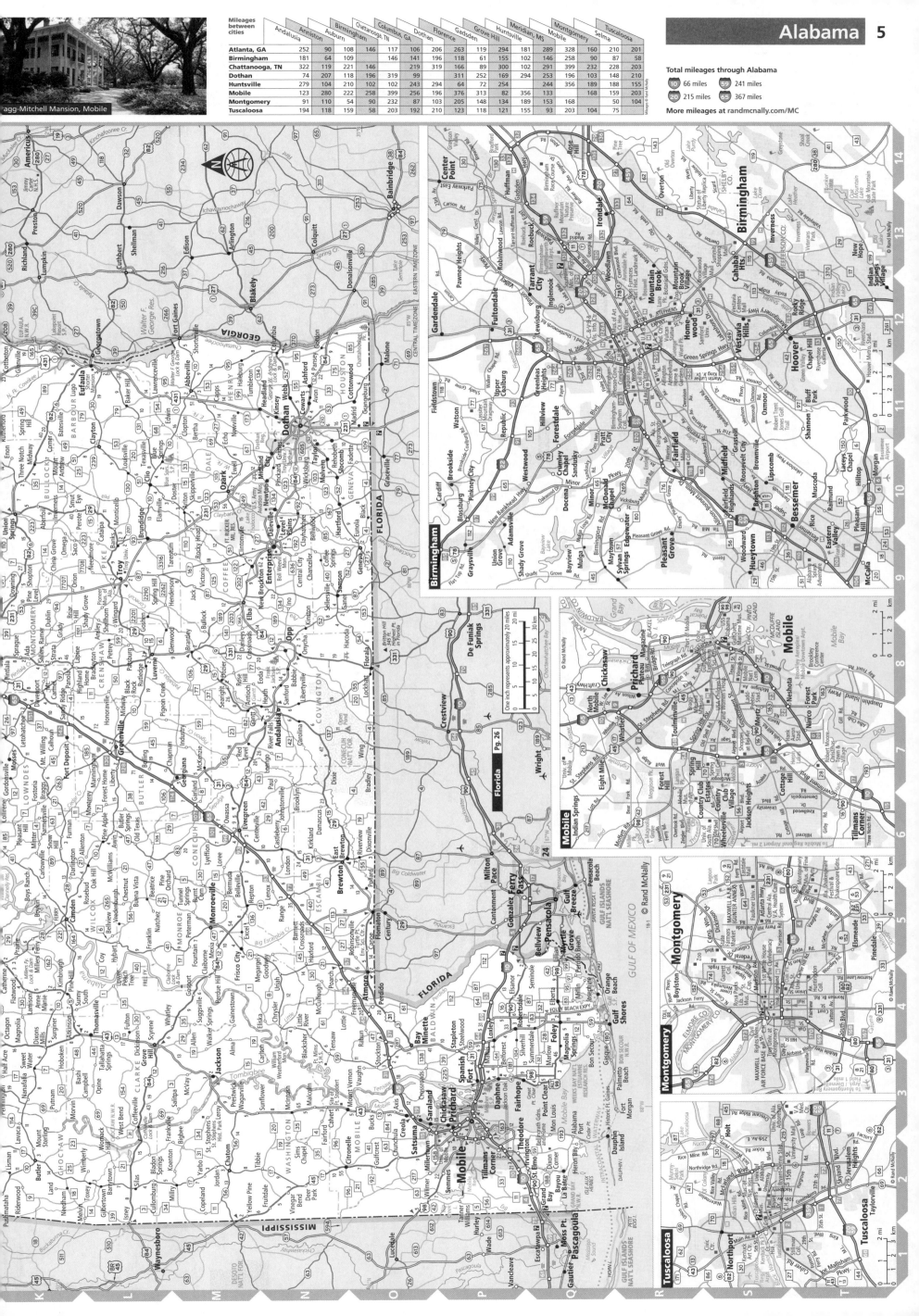

...agg-Mitchell Mansion, Mobile

Mileages between cities	Andalusia	Anniston	Auburn	Birmingham	Chattanooga, TN	Columbus, GA	Dothan	Florence	Gadsden	Grove Hill	Huntsville	Meridian, MS	Mobile	Montgomery	Selma	Tuscaloosa
Atlanta, GA	252	90	108	146	117	106	206	263	119	294	181	289	328	160	210	201
Birmingham	181	64	109		146	141	196	118	61	155	102	146	258	90	87	58
Chattanooga, TN	322	119	221	146		219	319	166	89	300	102	291	399	232	228	203
Dothan	74	207	118	196	319	99		311	252	169	294	253	196	103	148	210
Huntsville	279	104	210	102	102	243	294	64	72	254		244	356	189	188	155
Mobile	123	280	222	258	399	256	256	376	313	82	356	133		168	159	203
Montgomery	91	110	54	90	232	87	103	205	148	134	189	153	168		50	104
Tuscaloosa	194	118	159	58	203	192	210	123	118	121	155	93	203	104	75	

Total mileages through Alabama

10 = 66 miles 20 = 215 miles 59 = 241 miles 65 = 367 miles

More mileages at randmcnally.com/MC

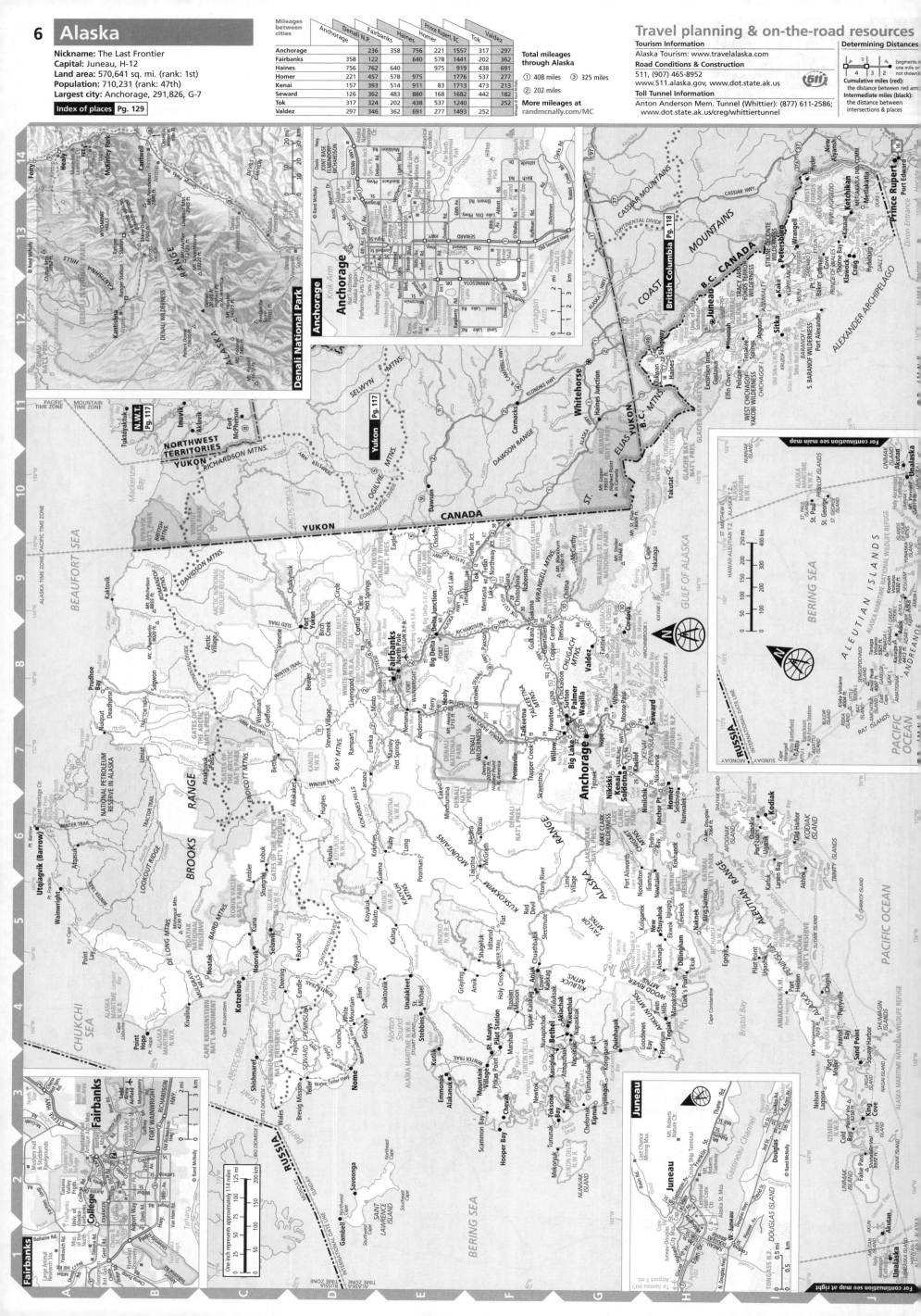

6 Alaska

Nickname: The Last Frontier
Capital: Juneau, H-12
Land area: 570,641 sq. mi. (rank: 1st)
Population: 710,231 (rank: 47th)
Largest city: Anchorage, 291,826, G-7

Index of places Pg. 129

Mileages between cities	Anchorage	Denali N.P.	Fairbanks	Haines	Homer	Prince Rupert, BC	Tok	Valdez
Anchorage		236	358	756	221	1557	317	297
Fairbanks	358	122		640	578	1441	202	362
Haines	756	762	640		975	919	438	691
Homer	221	457	578	975		1776	537	277
Kenai	157	393	514	911	83	1713	473	213
Seward	126	362	483	880	168	1682	442	182
Tok	317	324	202	438	537	1240		252
Valdez	297	346	362	691	277	1493	252	

Total mileages through Alaska
① 408 miles ③ 325 miles
② 202 miles

More mileages at randmcnally.com/MC

Travel planning & on-the-road resources

Tourism Information
Alaska Tourism: www.travelalaska.com

Road Conditions & Construction
511, (907) 465-8952
www.511.alaska.gov, www.dot.state.ak.us

Toll Tunnel Information
Anton Anderson Mem. Tunnel (Whittier): (877) 611-2586;
www.dot.state.ak.us/creg/whittiertunnel

Determining Distances
Cumulative miles (red): the distance between red arrows
Intermediate miles (black): the distance between intersections & places

Folklorica dancers

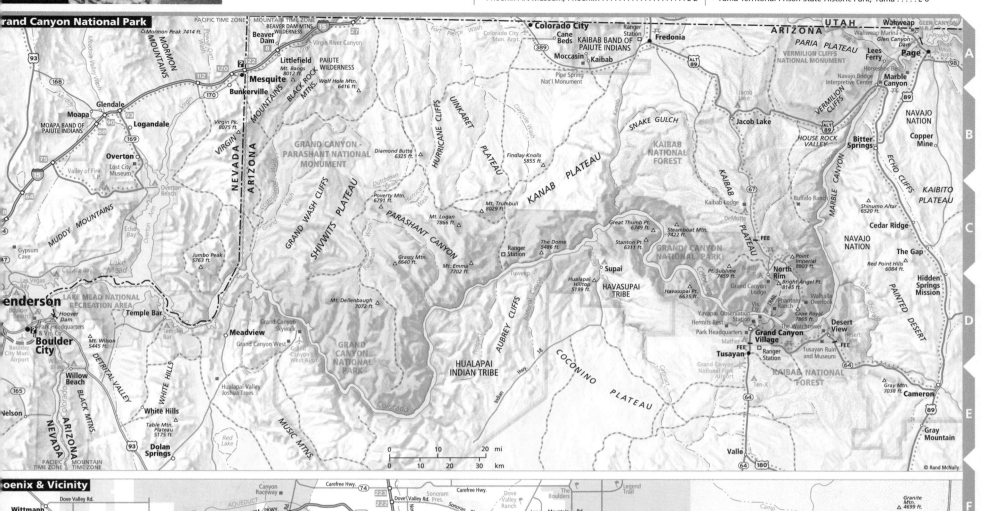

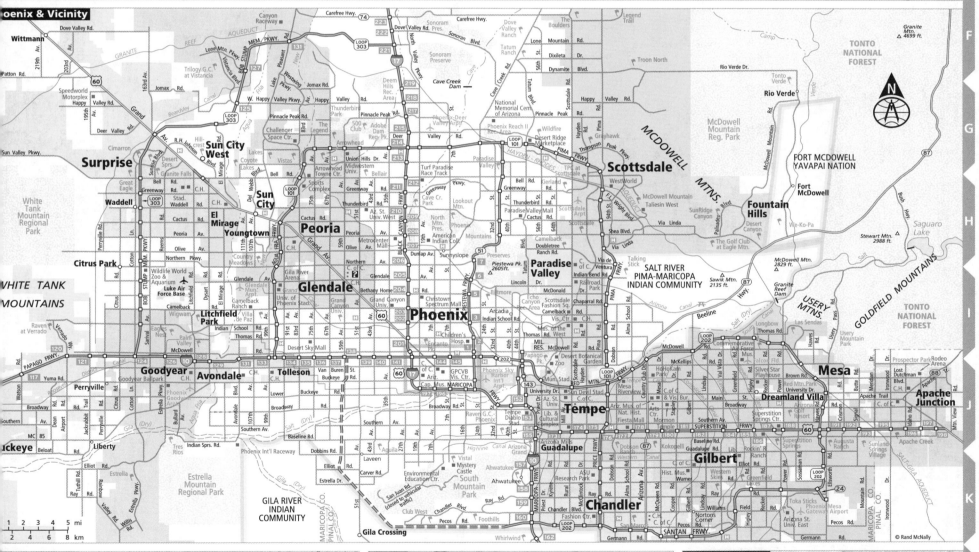

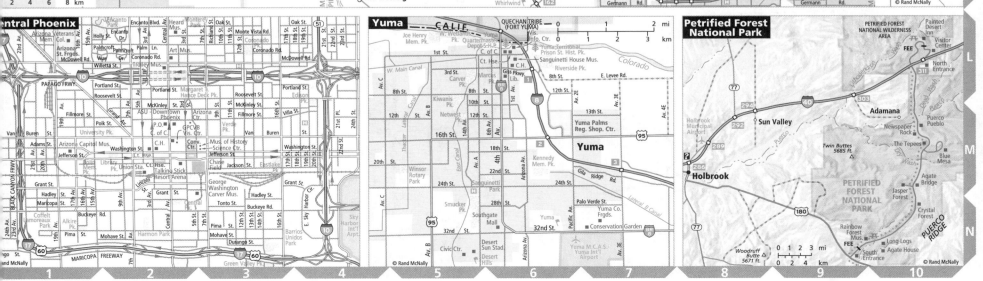

8 Arizona

Nickname: The Grand Canyon State
Capital: Phoenix, J-7
Land area: 113,594 sq. mi. (rank: 6th)
Population: 6,392,017 (rank: 16th)
Largest city: Phoenix, 1,445,632, J-7

Index of places Pg. 129

Travel planning & on-the-road resources

Tourism Information
Arizona Office of Tourism: (866) 275-5816, (602) 364-3700; www.arizonaguide.com

Road Conditions & Construction
511, (888) 411-7623, (888) 411-7624; www.az511.com, www.azdot.gov

Toll Road Information
No toll roads

Determining distances along roads

Highway distances (segments of one mile or less not shown):
Cumulative miles (red): the distance between red arrows
Intermediate miles (black): the distance between intersections & pla

Interchanges and exit numbers
For most states, the mileage between interchanges may be determi
by subtracting one number from the other.

Mileages between cities	Casa Grande	Chinle	Eagar	Flagstaff	Gallup, NM	Grand Canyon	Holbrook	Kingman	Lake Havasu City	Las Vegas, NV	Lordsburg	Nogales	Page	Phoenix	Tucson	Yuma
Flagstaff	191	213	176		185	79	90	146	204	250	374	321	133	139	255	318
Holbrook	220	123	86	90	94	167		237	295	340	264	304	214	230	238	409
Las Vegas, NV	336	463	427	250	435	275	340	104	152		538	467	271	285	401	292
Page	324	204	301	133	255	137	214	281	340	271	499	455		275	390	453
Phoenix	48	353	226	139	324	230	182	198	285	262	179	275	275		116	181
Prescott	148	306	270	93	278	126	184	148	206	251	368	278	227	97	213	214
Tucson	66	361	238	255	333	334	238	297	314	401	156	66	390	116		236
Yuma	172	532	399	318	502	397	409	213	155	292	392	301	453	181	236	

More mileages at randmcnally.com/MC

Total mileages through Arizona
8 178 miles   17 146 miles
10 392 miles   40 359 miles

k Creek Canyon, Sedona

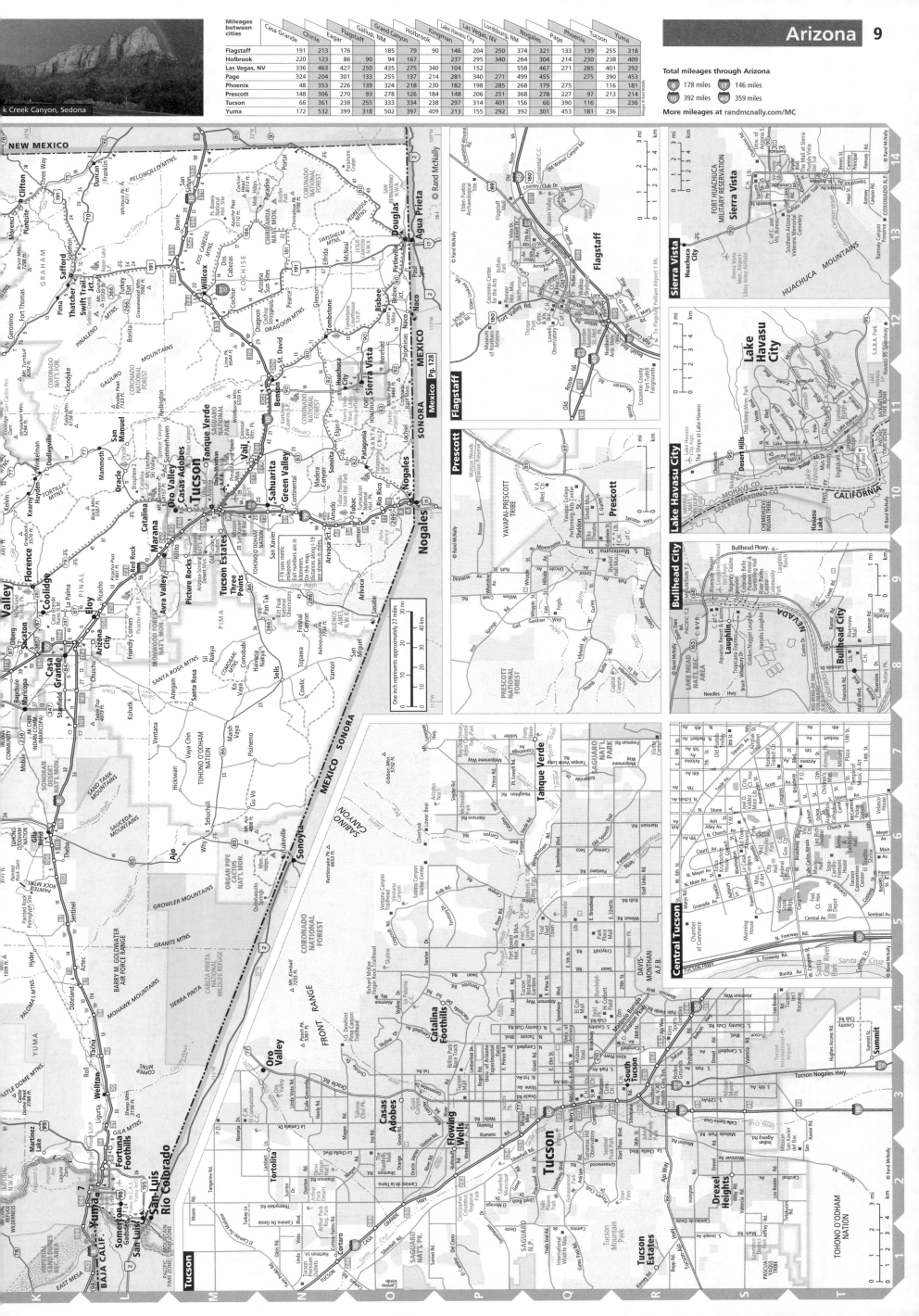

Nickname: The Natural State
Capital: Little Rock, G-7
Land area: 52,035 sq. mi. (rank: 27th)
Population: 2,915,918 (rank: 32nd)
Largest city: Little Rock, 193,524, G-7

Index of places Pg. 129

Travel planning & on-the-road resources

Tourism Information
Arkansas Parks & Tourism; (800) 628-8725, (501) 682-7777; www.arkansas.com

Road Conditions & Construction
(800) 245-1672, (501) 569-2374, (501) 569-2000; www.arkansashighways.com, www.idrivearkansas.com

Toll Road Information
No toll roads

Determining distances along roads

Highway distances (segments of one mile or less not shown):
Cumulative miles (red): the distance between red arrows
Intermediate miles (black): the distance between intersections & pla

Interchanges and exit numbers
For most states, the mileage between interchanges may be determin
by subtracting one number from the other.

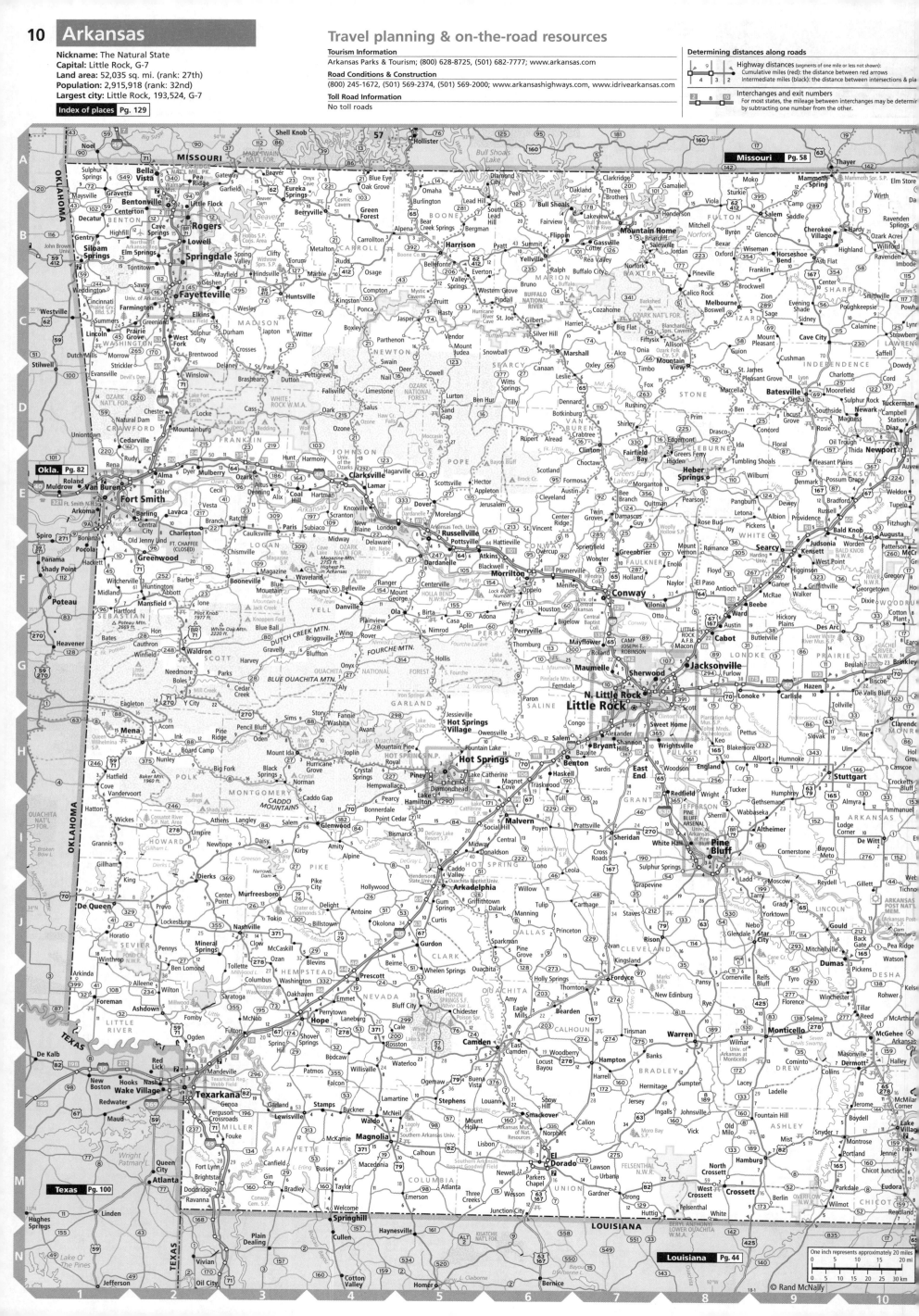

© Rand McNally

Whitaker Point, Ozark National Forest

Mileages between cities	Batesville	Branson, MO	DeQueen	El Dorado	Fayetteville	Fort Smith	Greenville, MS	Hot Springs	Jonesboro	Little Rock	Memphis, TN	Mountain Home	Pine Bluff	Russellville	Texarkana
El Dorado	209	287	141		304	227	109	121	245	118	250	268	91	325	190	88
Fayetteville	251	98	184	304		58	335	184	250	188	318	123	231	24	115	236
Fort Smith	219	158	130	227	58		304	130	261	158	286	187	199	81	84	182
Jonesboro	68	203	272	245	250	261		219	182	130	70	126	171	253	173	270
Little Rock	94	172	143	118	188	158	147	54	130		137	151	43	208	74	142
Memphis, TN	119	274	278	250	318	286	152	188	70	137		195	152	339	204	276
Mountain Home	78	83	287	268	123	187	298	198	126	151	195		194	126	125	287
Texarkana	234	306	54	88	236	182	198	110	270	142	276	152	258	209	

Total mileages through Arkansas

30 — 143 miles   55 — 72 miles
40 — 284 miles   530 — 309 miles

More mileages at randmcnally.com/MC

Jonesboro

Hot Springs / Hot Springs National Park

Fayetteville / Springdale / Rogers

Pine Bluff

Little Rock

Fort Smith

Texarkana

Nickname: The Golden State
Capital: Sacramento, NK-7
Land area: 155,799 sq. mi. (rank: 3rd)
Population: 37,253,956 (rank: 1st)
Largest city: Los Angeles, 3,792,621, SJ-11

Index of places Pg. 129

Travel planning & on-the-road resources

Tourism Information
California Tourism: (877) 225-4367, (916) 444-4429; www.visitcalifornia.com

Road Conditions & Construction
(800) 427-7623; www.dot.ca.gov;
Sacramento region: 511; www.sacregion511.org
San Francisco Bay area: 511; www.511.org

Toll Bridge Information *(both use FasTrak)*
Golden Gate Bridge (San Francisco Bay area):
(415) 921-5858; www.goldengate.org
Bay Area Toll Authority (all other San Francisco Bay
area bridges): (415) 778-6703; bata.mtc.ca.gov

Determining distances along roads
Highway distances (segments of one mile or less not shown):
Cumulative miles (red): the distance between red arrows
Intermediate miles (black): the distance between intersections & places

Interchanges and exit numbers
For most states, the mileage between interchanges may be determined by subtracting one number from the other.

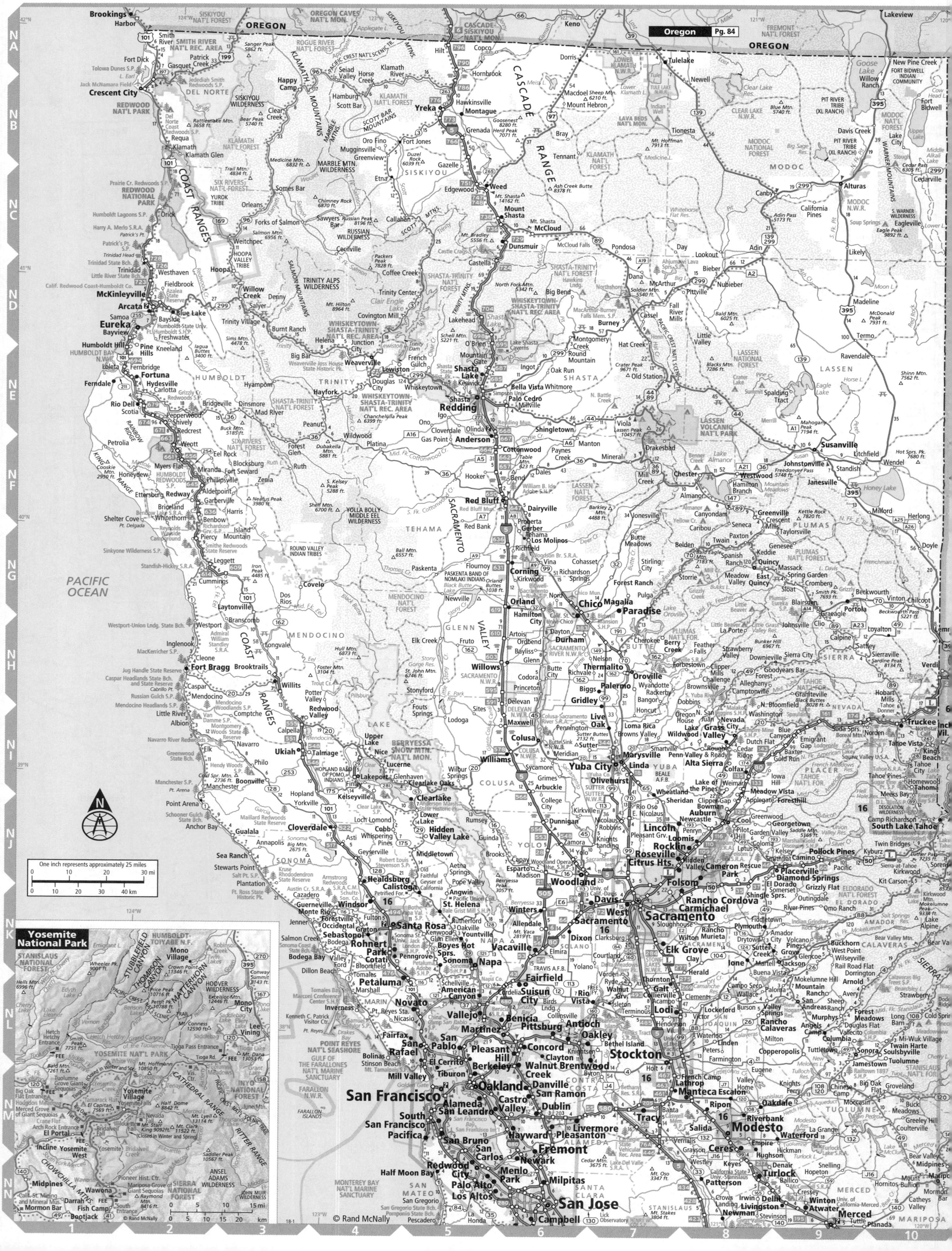

One inch represents approximately 25 miles

© Rand McNally

Yosemite National Park

Mileages between cities	Crescent City	Bishop	Los Angeles	Oroville	Redding	Sacramento	San Francisco	San Jose	Santa Rosa	S. Lake Tahoe	Stockton	Susanville	Ukiah	Vallejo	Yosemite N.P.	Yreka
Alturas	371	280	648	225	144	302	357	385	228	349	103	330	329	392		176
Bishop	614		265	326	400	269	295	290	364	176	224	286	418	328	138	454
Eureka	546	81	544	222	146	289	272	315	217	392	325	259	158	262		98
Redding	400	208	544	94		161	216	244	198	264	209	112	188	187	332	98
Sacramento	269	372	383	68	161		87	115	95	100	47	217	145	58	160	257
San Francisco	295	355	380	150	216	87		45	55	187	82	303	115	30	189	312
San Jose	290	396	340	178	244	115	45		96	215	74	330	156	64	182	340
S. Lake Tahoe	176	472	445	157	264	100	187	215	195		147	143	248	159	189	311

San Francisco Bay Area: San Francisco / Oakland / San Jose

Total mileages through California
5 797 miles   101 791 miles
199 199 miles
More mileages at randmcnally.com/MC

© Rand McNally

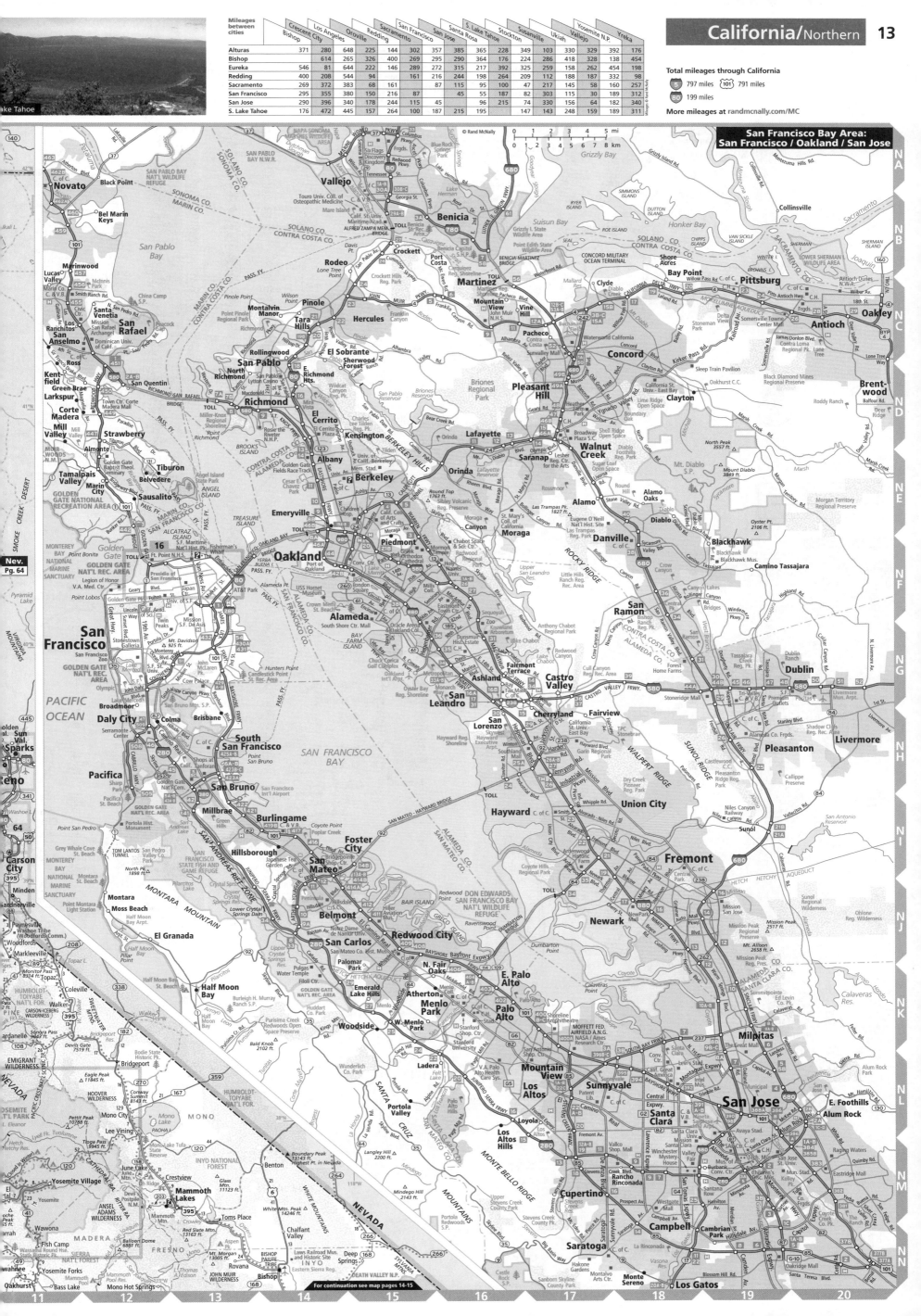

Nickname: The Golden State
Capital: Sacramento, NK-7
Land area: 155,799 sq. mi. (rank: 3rd)
Population: 37,253,956 (rank: 1st)
Largest city: Los Angeles, 3,792,621, SJ-11

Index of places Pg. 129

Travel planning & on-the-road resources

Tourism Information
California Tourism: (877) 225-4367, (916) 444-4429; www.visitcalifornia.com

Road Conditions & Construction
(800) 427-7623; www.dot.ca.gov
Los Angeles area: 511; www.go511.com
San Diego area: 511, (619) 661-7070; www.511sd.com

Toll Road Information
The Toll Roads of Orange Co. (FasTrak): (949) 727-4800; www.thetollroads.com
Pebble Beach Resorts (17-Mile Dr.): (800) 654-9300; www.pebblebeach.com
South Bay Expwy. (San Diego Co.) (FasTrak): (619) 661-7070; www.southbayexpressway.com

Determining distances along roads
Highway distances (segments of one mile or less not shown):
Cumulative miles (red): the distance between red arrows
Intermediate miles (black): the distance between intersections & places
Interchanges and exit numbers
For most states, the mileage between interchanges may be determined by subtracting one number from the other.

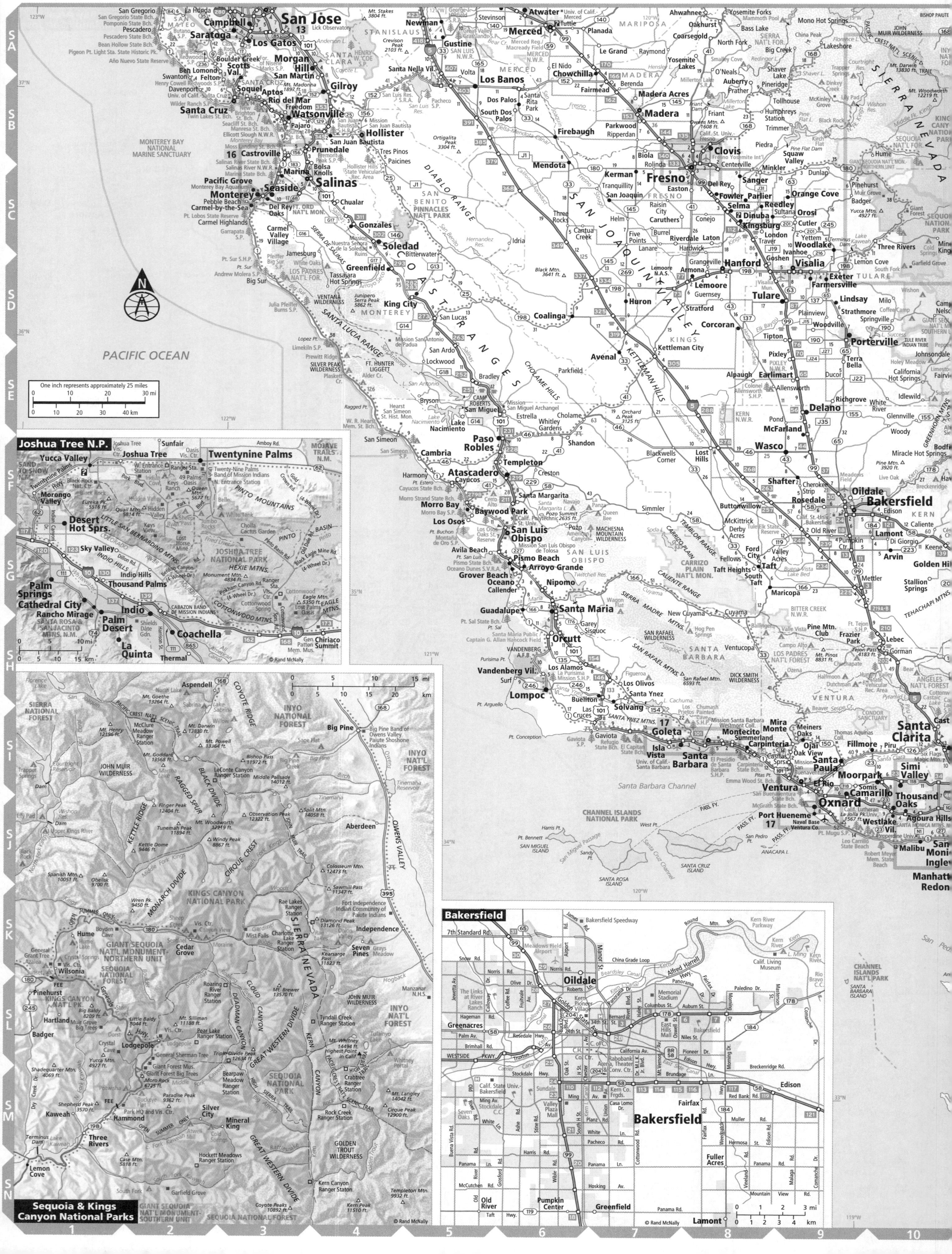

One inch represents approximately 25 miles
0 10 20 30 mi
0 10 20 30 40 km

PACIFIC OCEAN

Joshua Tree N.P.

Sequoia & Kings Canyon National Parks

Bakersfield

© Rand McNally

Alabama Hills, Lone Pine

Mileages between cities

	Bakersfield	Barstow	El Centro	Fresno	Las Vegas, NV	Los Angeles	Monterey	Needles	Palm Springs	Riverside	San Bernardino	San Diego	San Francisco	San Luis Obispo	Santa Barbara	Sequoia N.P.
Bakersfield		129	322	109	286	112	222	272	216	166	166	232	284	130	147	122
Fresno	109	239	429		395	218	150	381	323	271	273	339	183	130	254	77
Las Vegas, NV	286	156	312	395		270	507	110	278	234	225	331	569	415	358	410
Los Angeles	112	114	212	218	270		319	256	107	54	60	120	380	189	94	232
Monterey	222	350	530	150	507	319		494	424	372	373	439	112	142	237	226
Palm Springs	216	123	108	323	278	107	424	188		52	54	139	486	296	201	338
San Diego	232	176	113	339	331	120	439	317	139	97	106		501	313	214	352
Santa Barbara	147	203	306	254	358	94	237	345	201	148	150	214	325	94		268

Total mileages through California
- 5 — 797 miles
- 15 — 287 miles
- 10 — 243 miles
- 40 — 155 miles

More mileages at randmcnally.com/MC

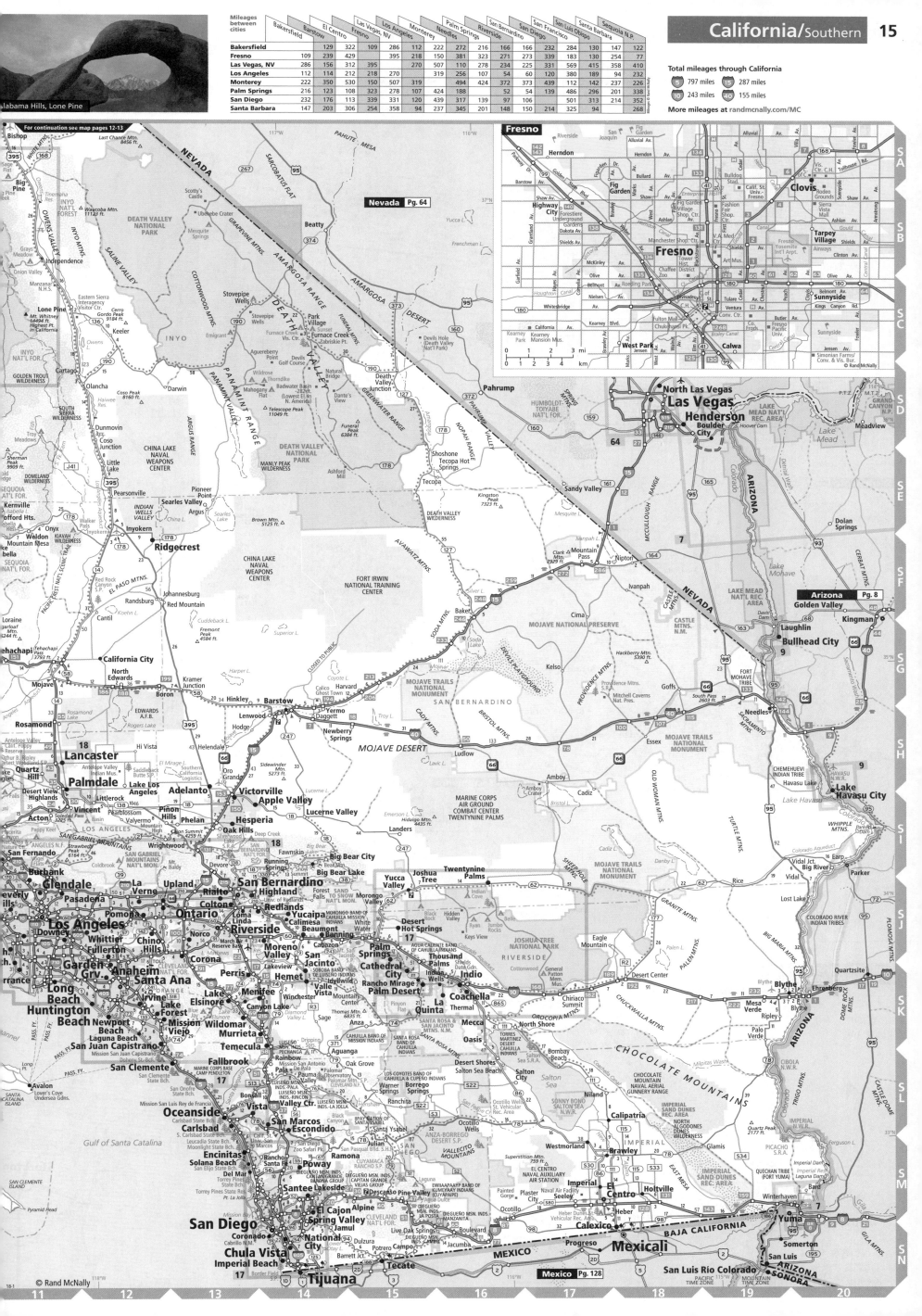

Sights to see

San Francisco Fort Mason Center

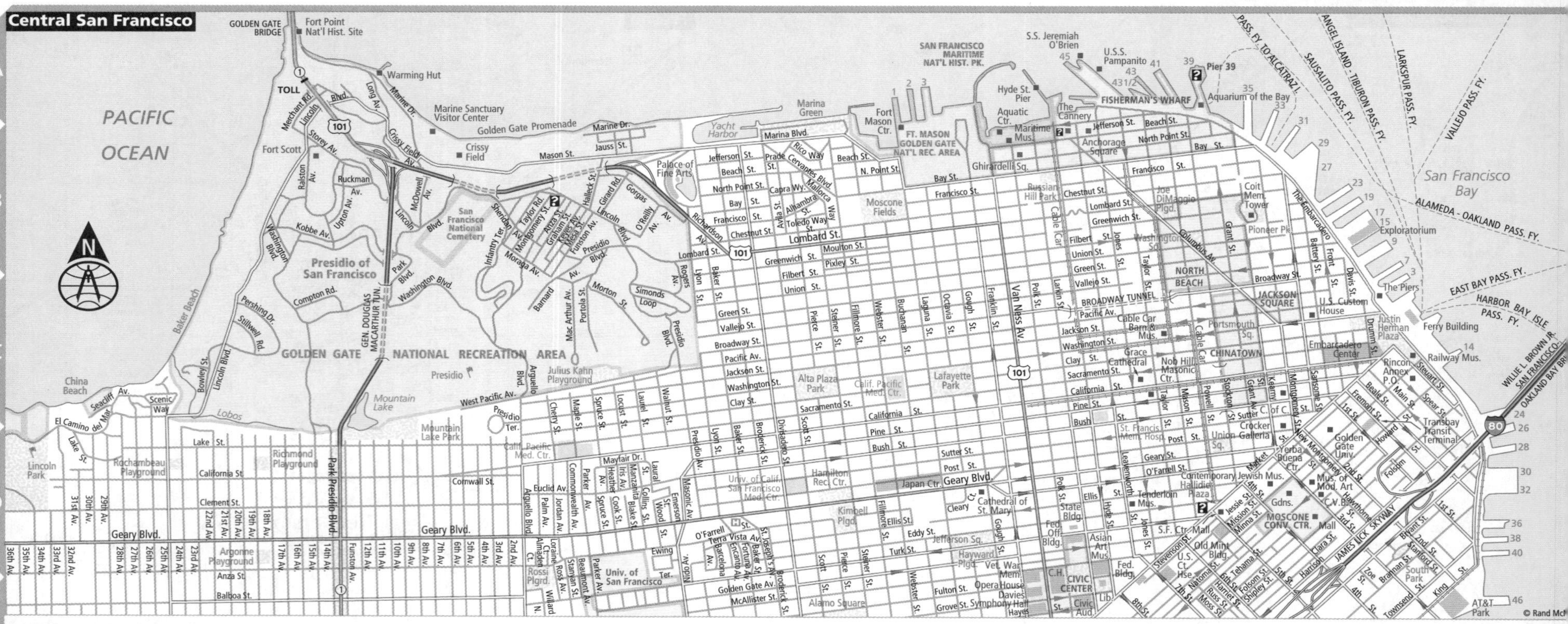

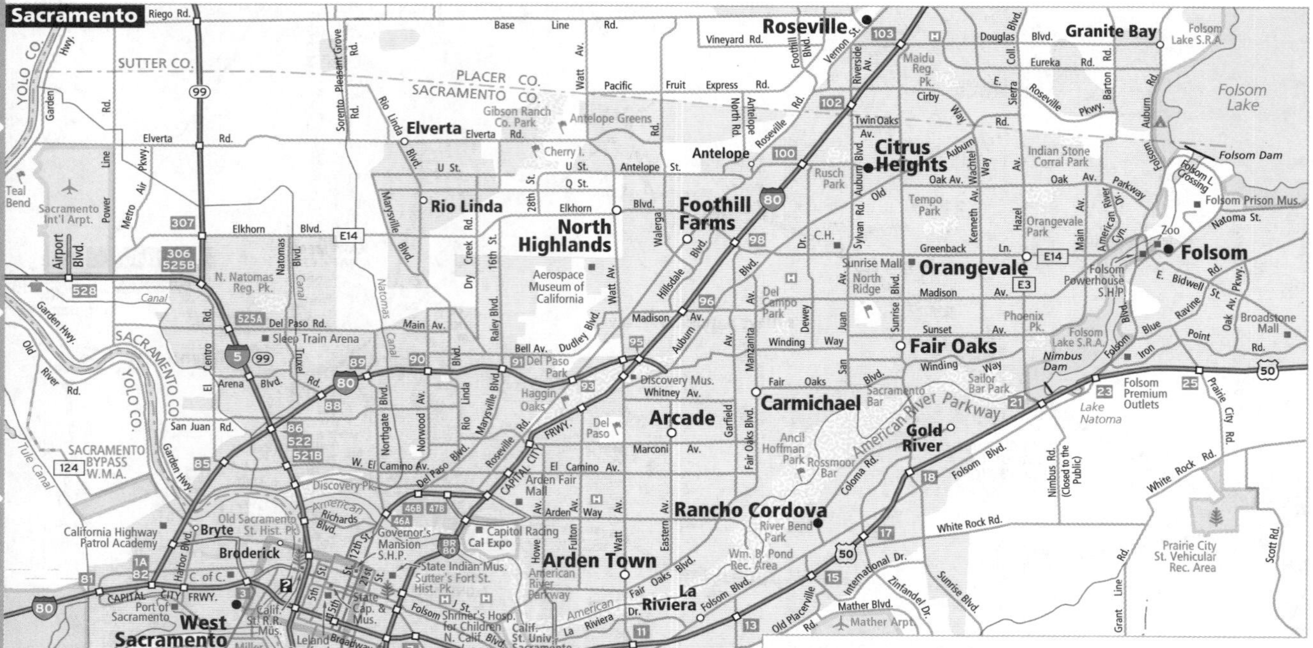

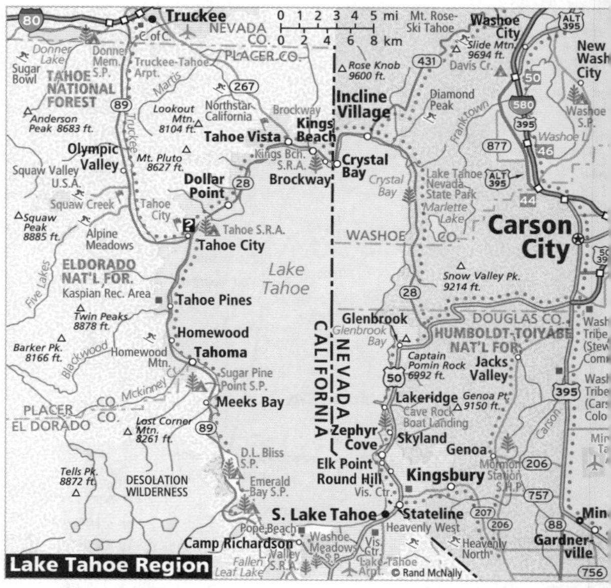

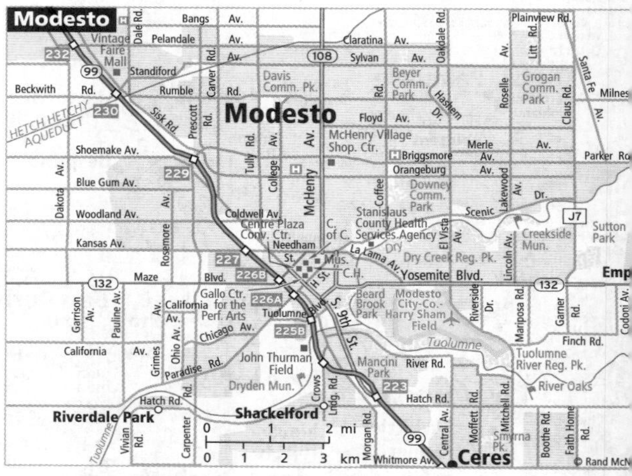

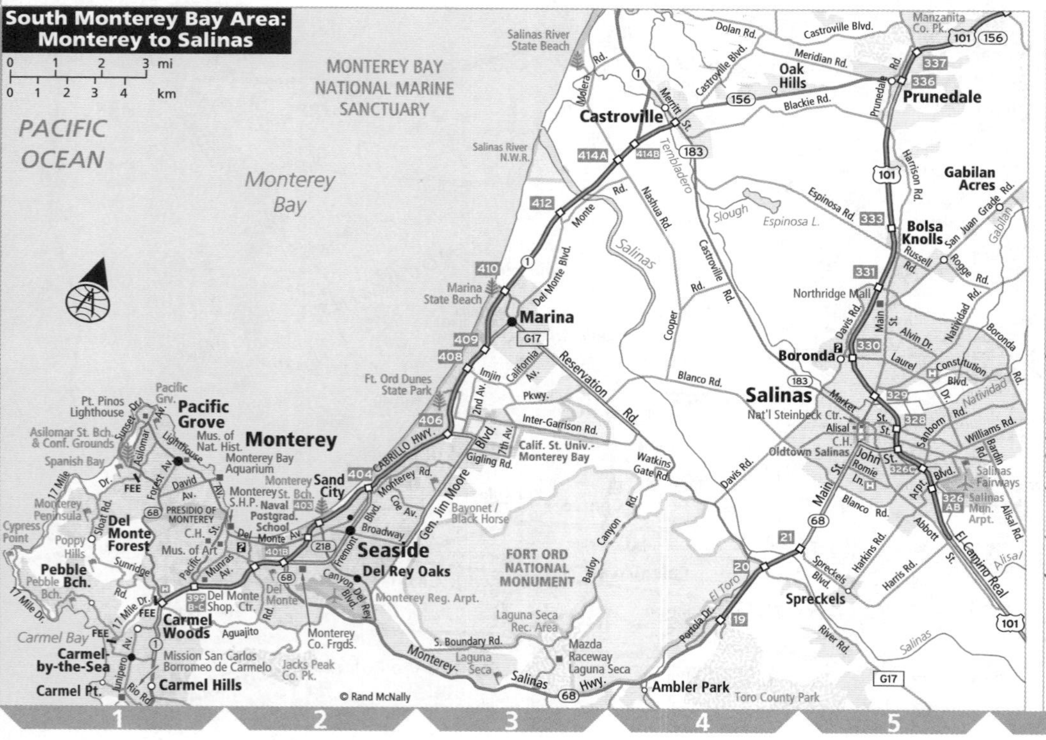

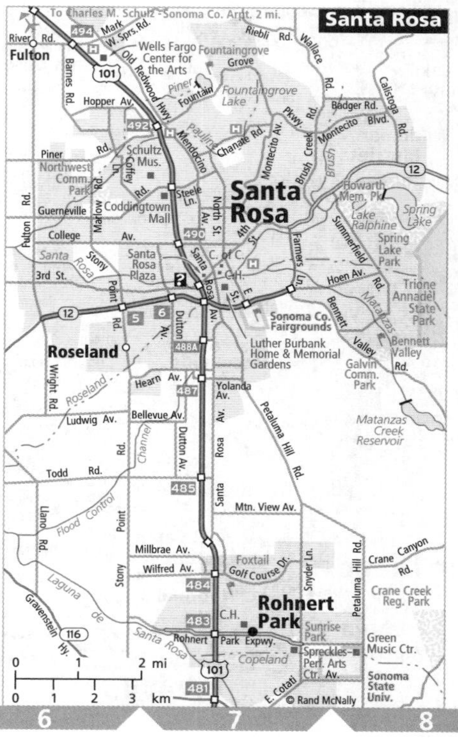

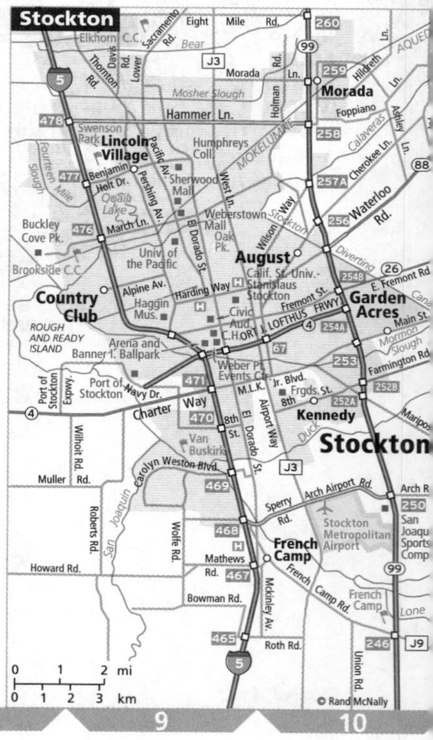

Central San Francisco

PACIFIC OCEAN

Sacramento

Central Sacramento

Lake Tahoe Region

Modesto

South Monterey Bay Area: Monterey to Salinas

PACIFIC OCEAN

MONTEREY BAY NATIONAL MARINE SANCTUARY

Santa Rosa

Stockton

© Rand McNally

Santa Barbara harbor and coastline

Sights to see

- Balboa Park, San Diego.........................K-10
- Birch Aquarium at Scripps Institute, San Diego G-1
- Cabrillo National Monument, San Diego K-1
- Gaslamp Quarter Historic District, San Diego M-9

- Legoland California, Carlsbad J-8
- The Living Desert Nature Preserve, Palm Desert G-10
- Museum of Contemporary Art, San Diego L-8
- Palm Springs Art Museum, Palm Springs..........E-7

- San Diego Air & Space Museum, San Diego K-9
- San Diego Zoo, San Diego J-3
- SeaWorld, San Diego............................I-1
- Stearns Wharf, Santa Barbara B-5

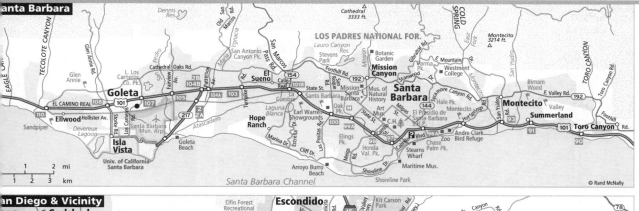

Santa Barbara

Oxnard / Ventura

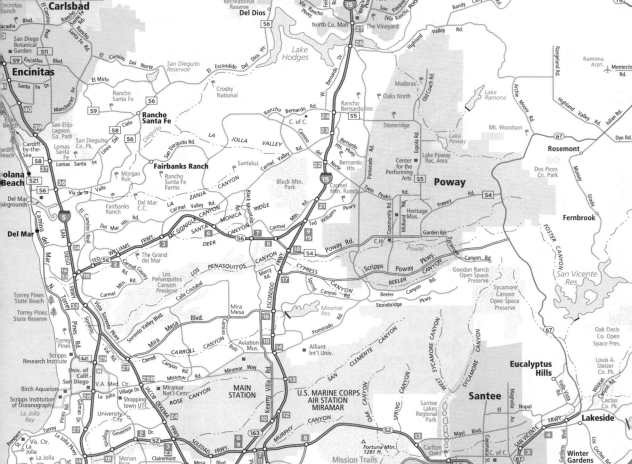

San Diego & Vicinity

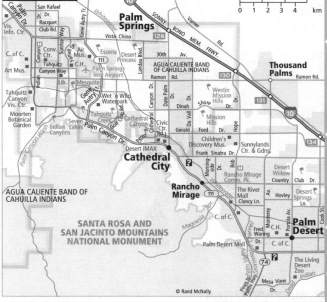

Palm Springs

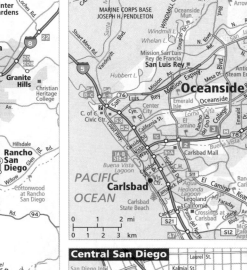

Oceanside

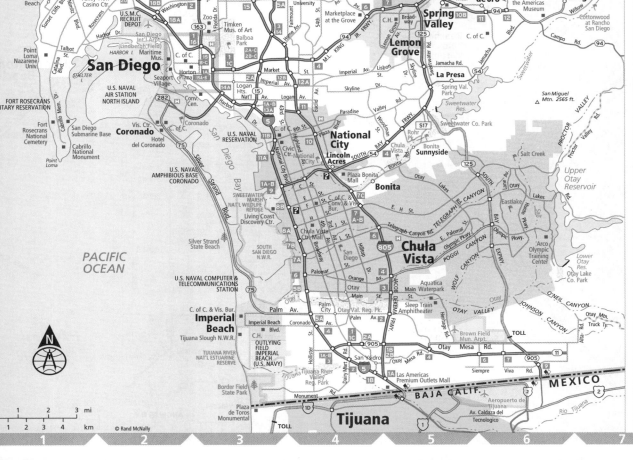

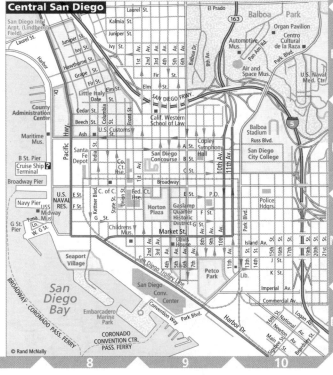

Central San Diego

Sights to see

Walt Disney Concert Hall

Huntington Beach Pier, Huntington Beach

Sights to see

- Mission San Juan Capistrano, San Juan Capistrano . . M-14
- Old Pasadena, Pasadena D-8
- Oldest Winery in California, Rancho Cucamonga . . . D-14
- The Queen Mary, Long Beach J-8
- Richard M. Nixon Library & Birthplace, Yorba Linda H-12
- Santa Monica Pier, Santa Monica F-4
- Universal City D-5
- Venice Boardwalk F-4
- Walt Disney Concert Hall K-1
- Warner Bros. Studio, Burbank D-6
- Will Rogers State Historic Park, Pacific Palisades E-4

© Rand McNally

Nickname: The Centennial State
Capital: Denver, E-13
Land area: 103,642 sq. mi. (rank: 8th)
Population: 5,029,196 (rank: 22nd)
Largest city: Denver, 600,158, E-13

Index of places Pg. 129

Travel planning & on-the-road resources

Tourism Information
Colorado Tourism Office:
(800) 265-6723; www.colorado.com

Toll Road Information
E-470 (Denver metro) (*ExpressToll*): (888) 946-3470, (303) 537-3470; www.expresstoll.com
Northwest Parkway (Denver metro) (*GoPass*): (303) 533-1200; www.northwestparkway.org

Road Conditions & Construction
511, (303) 573-7623, (303) 639-1111
www.cotrip.org

Determining distances along roads

Highway distances (segments of one mile or less not shown):
Cumulative miles (red): the distance between red arrows
Intermediate miles (black): the distance between intersections & places

Interchanges and exit numbers
For most states, the mileage between interchanges may be determined by subtracting one number from the other.

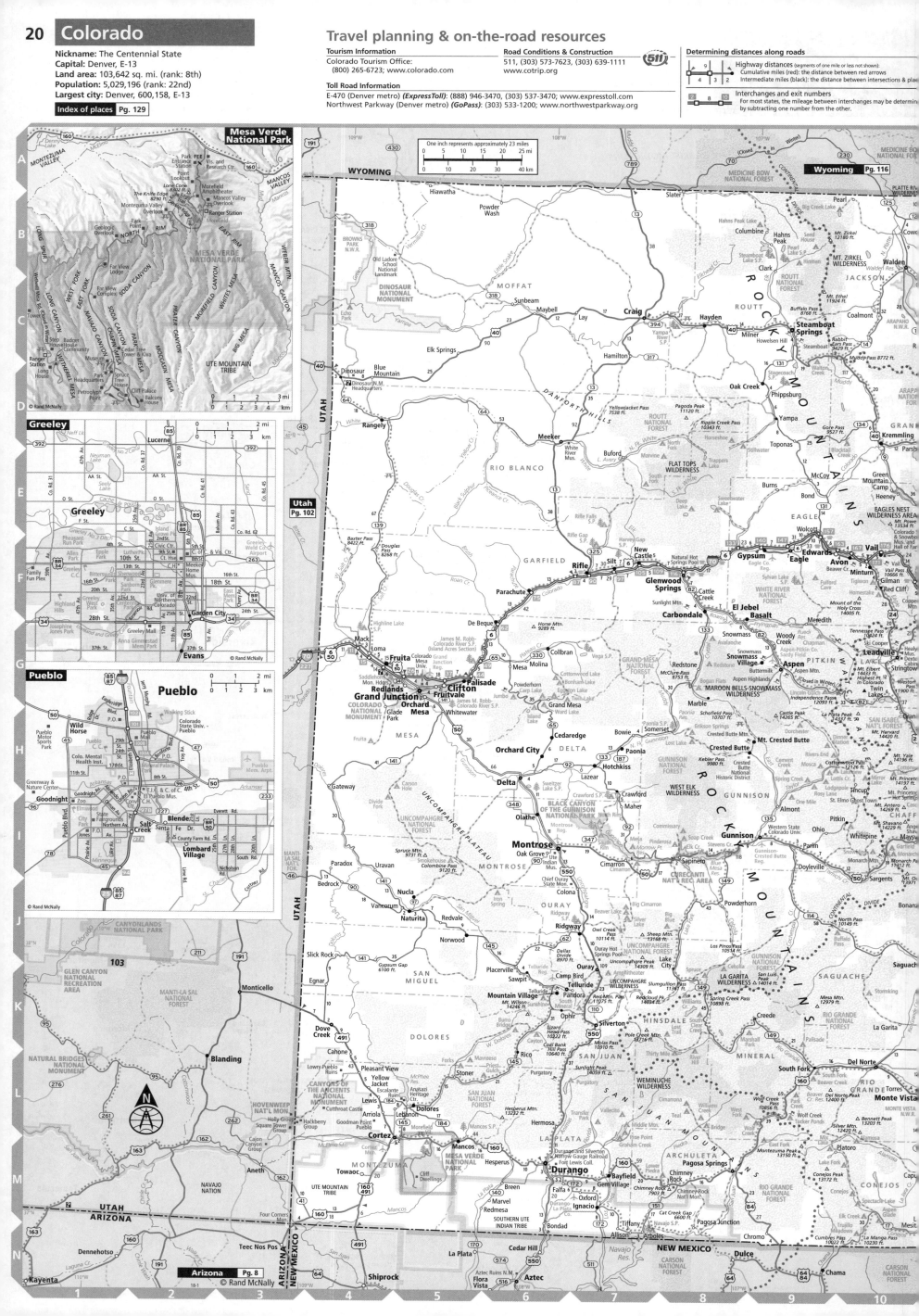

One inch represents approximately 23 miles

© Rand McNally

Mileages between cities

	Alamosa	Aspen	Burlington	Colorado Springs	Craig	Denver	Durango	Estes Park	Fort Collins	Grand Junction	Gunnison	Lamar	Leadville	Pueblo	Sterling	Trinidad
Burlington	311	363		151	363	166	460	222	220	408	324	108	265	189	142	230
Colorado Springs	163	155	151		264	69	313	133	133	309	166	158	121	42	194	128
Denver	234	197	166	69			336	64	63	243	200	208	99	112	125	198
Durango	149	246	460	313	312	336		402	396	168	142	351	253	269	458	258
Fort Collins	296	258	220	133	201	63	396	42		303	261		160	175	102	261
Grand Junction	247	128	408	309	151	243	168	258	303		126	448	174	222	364	370
Leadville	135	58	265	121	145	99	253	143	160	174	102	276		154	222	204
Trinidad	109	232	230	128	392	198	258	262	261		209	136	204	85	322	

Total mileages through Colorado

- 25   300 miles
- 70   451 miles
- 75   185 miles
- 50   467 miles

More mileages at www.randmcnally.com/MC

Garden of the Gods

Sights to see

- Black American West Mus. & Heritage Ctr., Denver....L-3
- Cave of the Winds, Colorado Springs G-1
- Colorado History Museum, Denver M-2
- Colorado State Capitol, Denver M-2
- Denver Art Museum, Denver M-2
- Denver Museum of Nature & Science, Denver I-7
- Garden of the Gods, Colorado Springs G-1
- National Center for Atmospheric Research, Boulder...D-4
- Old Town National Historic District, Fort Collins B-9
- ProRodeo Hall of Fame, Colorado Springs F-2
- United States Mint, Denver M-2
- World Figure Skating Hall of Fame, Colorado Springs..I-2

The Pepsi Center, Denver

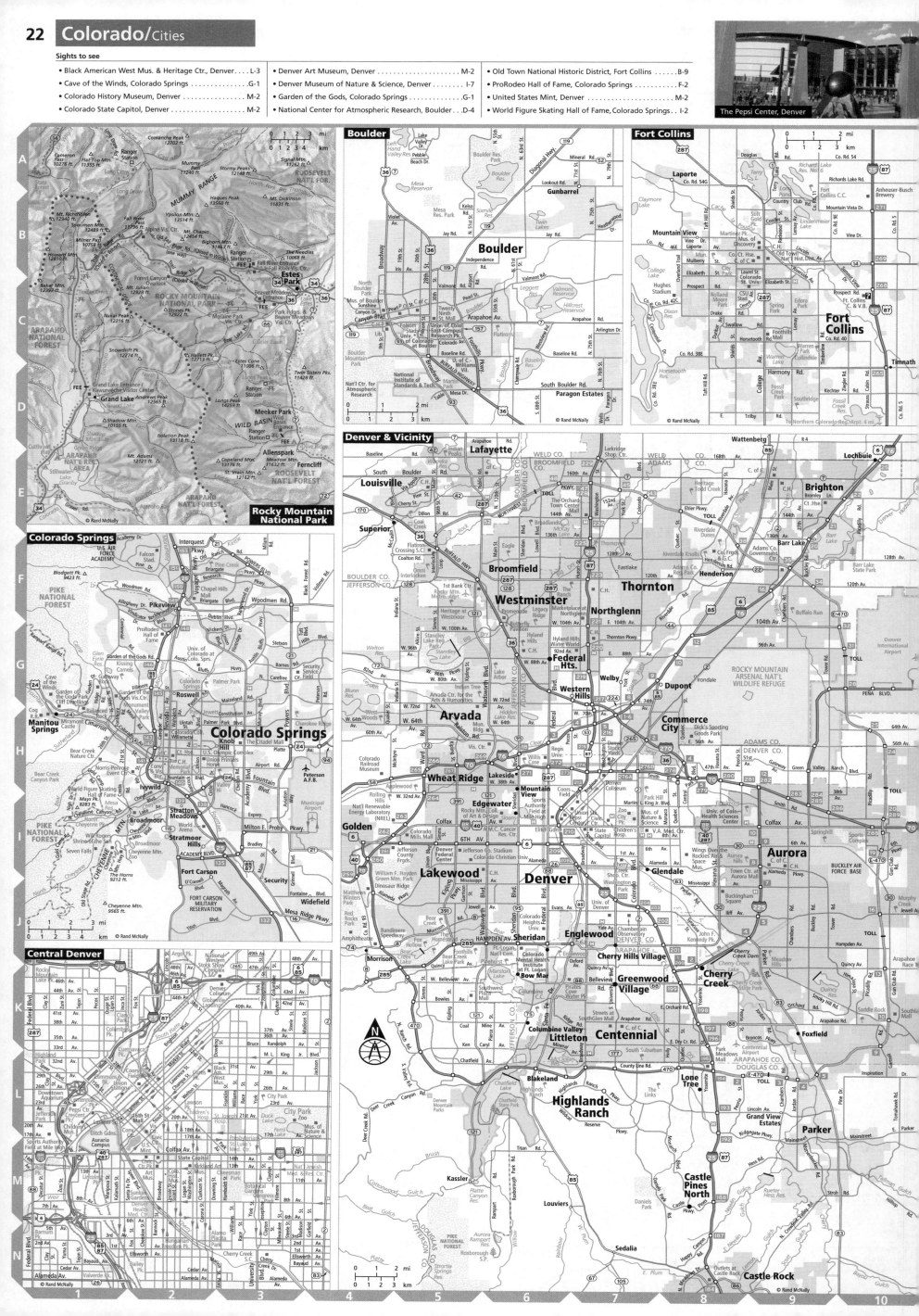

ravel planning & on-the-road resources

urism Information
nn. Office of Tourism:
(88) 288-4748,
(60) 256-2800
www.ctvisit.com

Road Conditions & Construction
(860) 594-2000, (860) 594-2650
www.ct.gov/dot
www.i-84waterbury.com

Determining Distances

Road Information
toll roads

Total mileages through Connecticut
84 — 98 miles   95 — 112 miles
91 — 58 miles   395 — 55 miles
More mileages at randmcnally.com/MC

Mileages between cities	Bridgeport	Hartford	New Haven	New London, NY	New York,	Putnam	Torrington	Waterbury
Bridgeport		55	18	64	54	107	50	30
Danbury	29	57	35	81	62	104	47	27
Hartford	55		38	45	108	47	26	30
New Haven	18	38		46	72	89	43	22
New London	64	45	46		118	47	79	63
Putnam	107	47	89	47	162		73	78
Torrington	50	26	43	79	109	73		20
Waterbury	30	30	22	63	89	78	20	

Nickname: The Constitution State
Capital: Hartford, C-9
Land area: 4,842 sq. mi. (rank: 48th)
Population: 3,574,097 (rank: 29th)
Largest city: Bridgeport, 144,229, H-5

Index of places Pg. 129

© Rand McNally

the beach at St. Petersburg/Clearwater

Sights to see

- Art Deco National Historic District, Miami Beach......L-9
- Busch Gardens, Tampa.............................B-4
- Hugh Taylor Birch State Park, Fort Lauderdale.......H-9
- Marie Selby Botanical Gardens, Sarasota...........H-3
- Miami Seaquarium, Miami.........................M-9
- Norton Museum of Art, Palm Beach...............B-10
- Ringling Center for the Cultural Arts, Sarasota......G-3
- Salvador Dali Museum, St. Petersburg.............D-2
- St. Petersburg Museum of History, St. Petersburg.....D-2
- Thomas A. Edison & Henry Ford Winter Estates, Fort Myers...................................M-2
- Vizcaya Museum and Gardens, Miami.............M-8

Nickname: The Sunshine State
Capital: Tallahassee, B-2
Land area: 53,625 sq. mi. (rank: 26th)
Population: 18,801,310 (rank: 4th)
Largest city: Jacksonville, 821,784, C-9

Index of places Pg. 129

Travel planning & on-the-road resources

Tourism Information
Visit Florida: (888) 735-2872,
 (850) 488-5607; www.visitflorida.com

Road Conditions & Construction
511
www.fl511.com, www.dot.state.fl.us

Toll Road Information
Central Florida Expressway Authority (Greater Orlando) *(E-Pass or SunPass)*: (407) 823-7277; www.cfxway.com
Florida's Turnpike Enterprise (all other state toll routes/bridges) *(SunPass)*: (800) 749-7453; floridasturnpike.com
Miami-Dade Expressway Authority *(SunPass)*: (855) 277-0848; www.mdxway.com
Osceola Co. Expressway Authority *(E-Pass)*: (407) 742-0200; www.osceolaxway.com
Tampa-Hillsborough Co. Expressway Authority *(SunPass)*: (813) 272-6740; www.tampa-xway.com

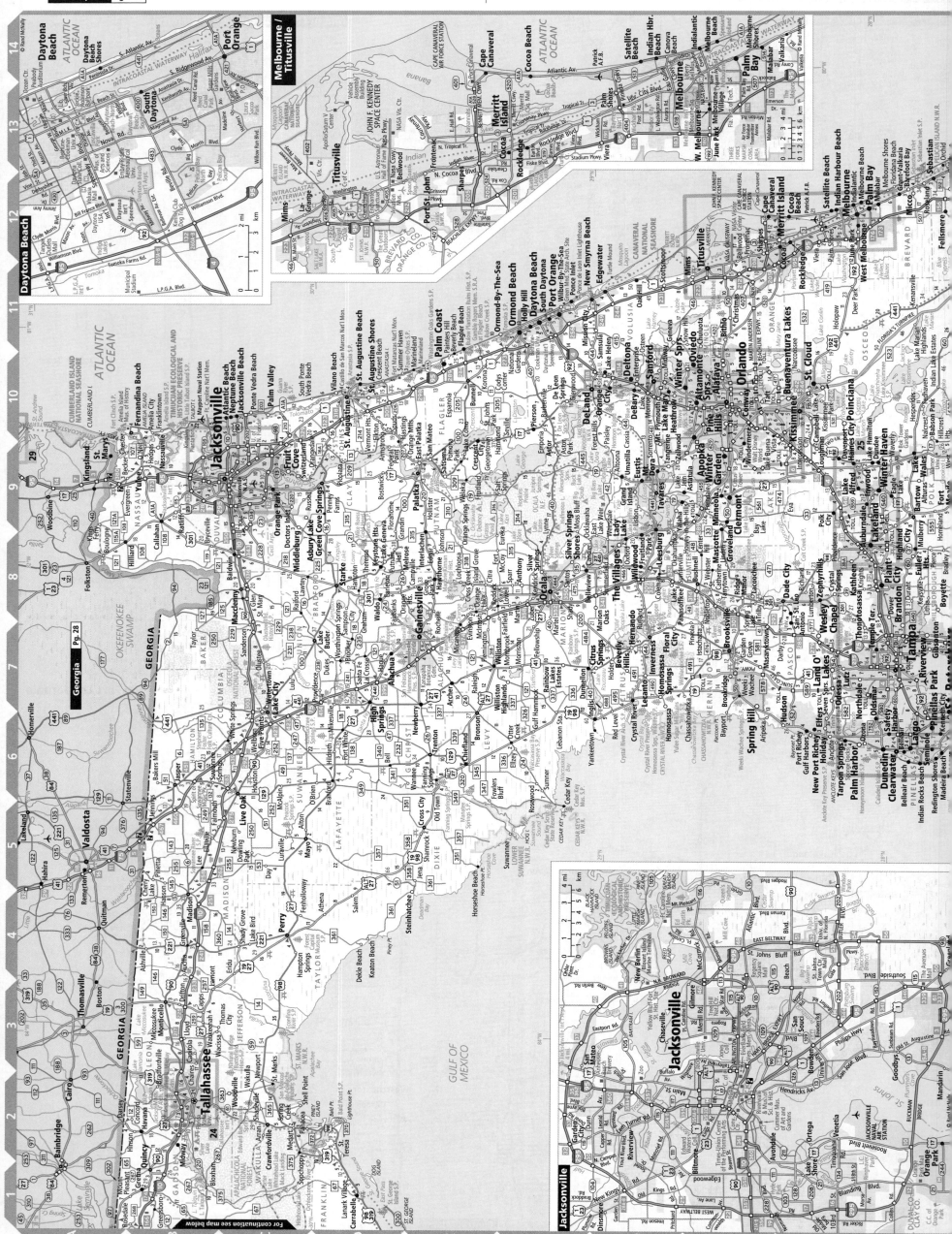

Jacksonville

Mileages between cities	Daytona Beach	Fort Myers	Fort Pierce	Gainesville	Jacksonville	Key West	Miami	Orlando	Panama City	Pensacola	St. Petersburg	Sarasota	Tallahassee	Tampa	Titusville	West Palm Beach
Fort Myers	225		128	254	312	279	152	171	497	589	117	80	397	130	209	124
Jacksonville	92	312	227	72		507	349	141	264	355	222	253	164	198	136	284
Key West	414	279	284	483	507		162	387	727	821	390	352	402	371		231
Miami	256	152	123	336	349	162		229	579	663	262	225	479	255	213	68
Orlando	54	171	110	144	141	387	229		357	451	106	132	257	84	39	159
Pensacola	442	589	549	338	355	821	663	451	102		458	511	193	459	487	594
Tallahassee	253	397	364	148	164	627	479	257	96	193	257	328		273	295	413
Tampa	137	130	151	127	198	402	255	84	373	628	23	60	273		124	202

Total mileages through Florida

- ④ 132 miles
- ⑩ 362 miles
- ㊀75 471 miles
- 382 miles

More mileages at randmcnally.com/MC

Nickname: The Peach State
Capital: Atlanta, E-4
Land area: 57,513 sq. mi. (rank: 21st)
Population: 9,687,653 (rank: 9th)
Largest city: Atlanta, 420,003, E-4

Index of places Pg. 130

Travel planning & on-the-road resources

Tourism Information
Visit Georgia: (800) 847-4842; www.exploregeorgia.org

Road Conditions & Construction
511, (888) 635-8287, (877) 694-2511, (404) 635-8000; www.511ga.org

Toll Road Information
No toll roads

Determining distances along roads

Highway distances (segments of one mile or less not shown)
Cumulative miles (red): the distance between red arrows
Intermediate miles (black): the distance between intersections & p

Interchanges and exit numbers
For most states, the mileage between interchanges may be determ
by subtracting one number from the other.

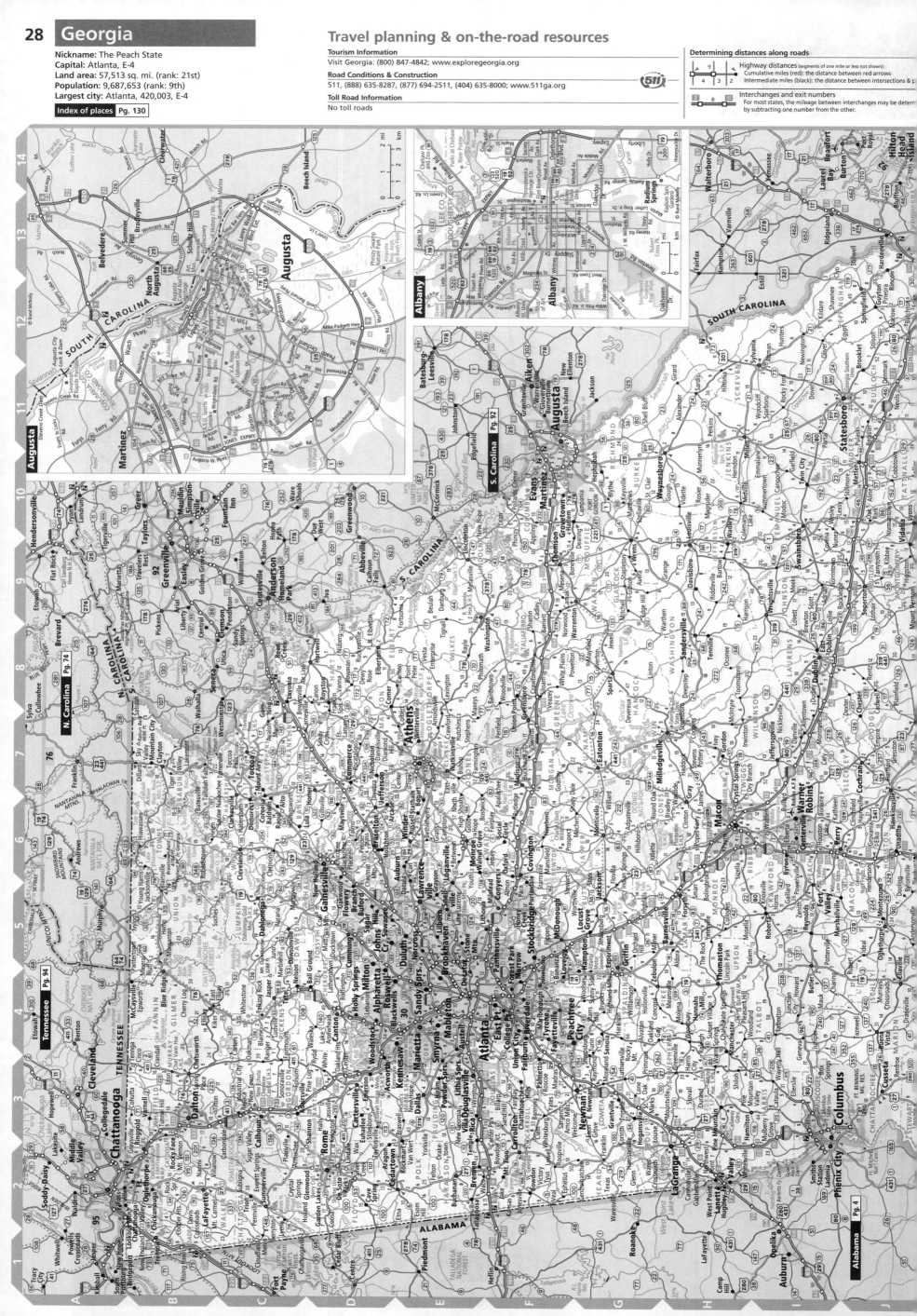

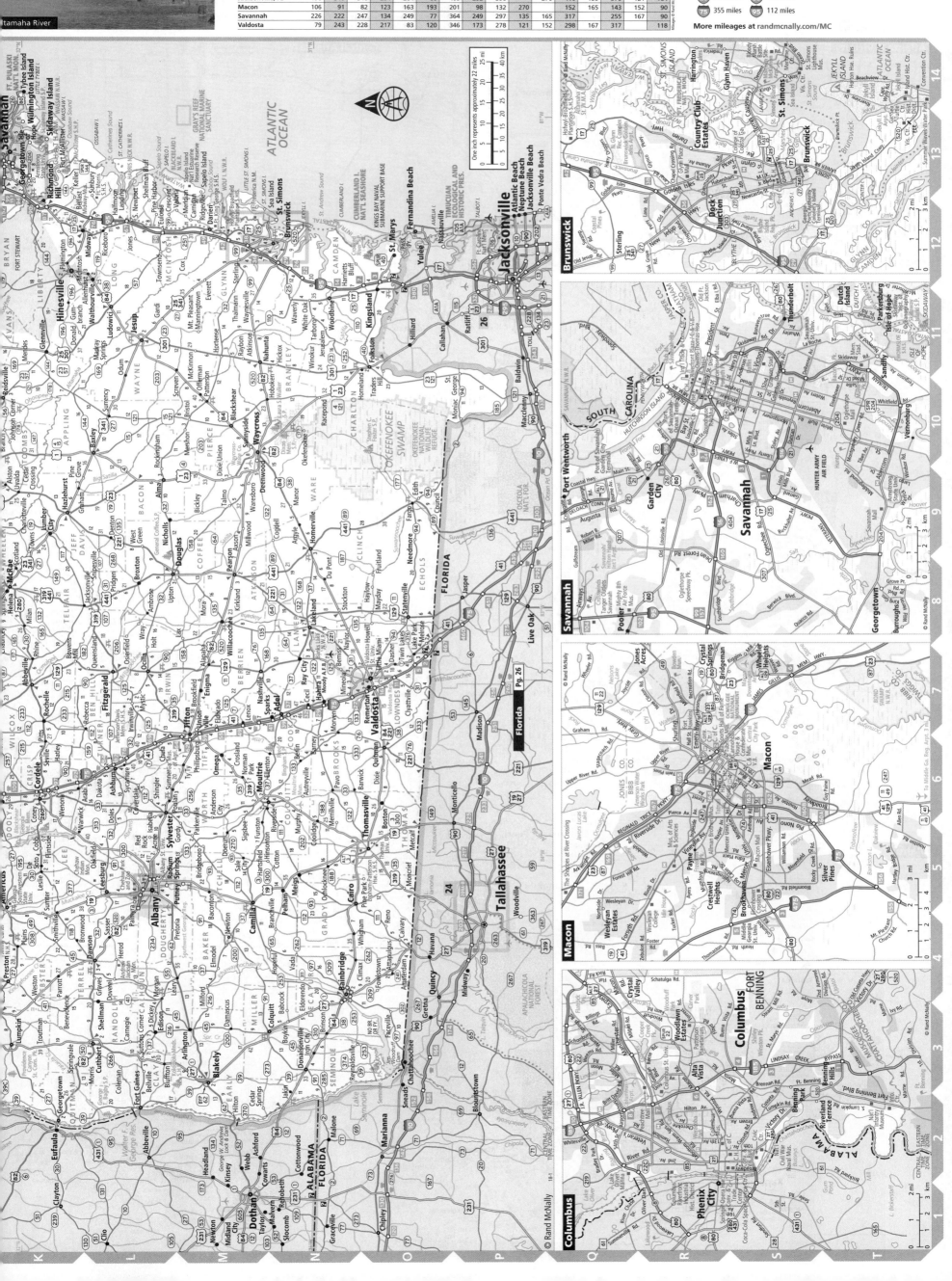

Mileages between cities	Albany	Athens	Atlanta	Augusta	Bainbridge	Brunswick	Chattanooga, TN	Columbus	Gainesville	Jacksonville, FL	Macon	Rome	Savannah	Toccoa	Valdosta	Vidalia
Atlanta	182	69		148	240	275	117	106	54	346	82	70	247	94	228	172
Augusta	211	98	148		268	193	265	249	140	254	123	217	134	132	217	99
Chattanooga, TN	300	172	117	265	348	397		219	121	465	201	71	364	155	346	289
Columbus	85	171	106	249	128	258	219		161	292	98	144	264	201	173	175
Jacksonville, FL	198	310	346	254	204	66	465	292	396		270	416	135	375	121	164
Macon	106	91	82	123	163	193	201	98	132	270		152	165	143	152	90
Savannah	226	222	247	134	249	77	364	249	297	135	165	317		255	167	90
Valdosta	79	243	228	217	83	120	346	173	278	121	152	298	167	317		118

Total mileages through Georgia

20 203 miles   85 180 miles
75 355 miles   95 112 miles

More mileages at randmcnally.com/MC

Nickname: The Aloha State
Capital: Honolulu, N-4
Land area: 6,423 sq. mi. (rank: 47th)
Population: 1,360,301 (rank: 40th)
Largest city: Honolulu, 337,256, N-4

Index of places Pg. 130

Mileages between cities

	Hilo	Honolulu	Kahului	Kailua Kona	Kapa'a	Lahaina	Wahiawā
Hilo		225'	127'	237'	74	337'	149'	236'
Honolulu	225'		108'	11	177'	116'	130'	20
Kahului	127'	108'		22	93'	214'	22	119'
Kailua Kona	74	177'	93'		188'	283'	116'	188'
Kapa'a	337'	116'	214'	128'		283'	236'	128'
Kaunakakai	177'	68'	55'	79'	144'	174'	77'	79'
Lahaina	149'	130'	22	43'	116'	236'		141'
Wahiawā	236'	20	119'	26	188'	128'	141'	

'Via plane

Total mileages through Hawaii

H1 27 miles   H3 15 miles
H2 8 miles

More mileages at randmcnally.com/MC

Travel planning & on-the-road resources

Tourism Information
Hawaii Visitors & Convention Bureau:
(800) 464-2924, (808) 923-1811; www.gohawaii.com

Road Conditions & Construction
(808) 587-2220; hidot.hawaii.gov

Toll Road Information
No toll roads

Determining Distances

Cumulative miles (red): the distance between red marks
Intermediate miles (black): the distance between intersections & places

Atlanta & Vicinity

Central Atlanta

Honolulu

KAUA'I

Maui

O'ahu

MAUI

MOLOKA'I

LĀNA'I

KAHO'OLAWE

HAWAI'I

PACIFIC OCEAN

© Rand McNally

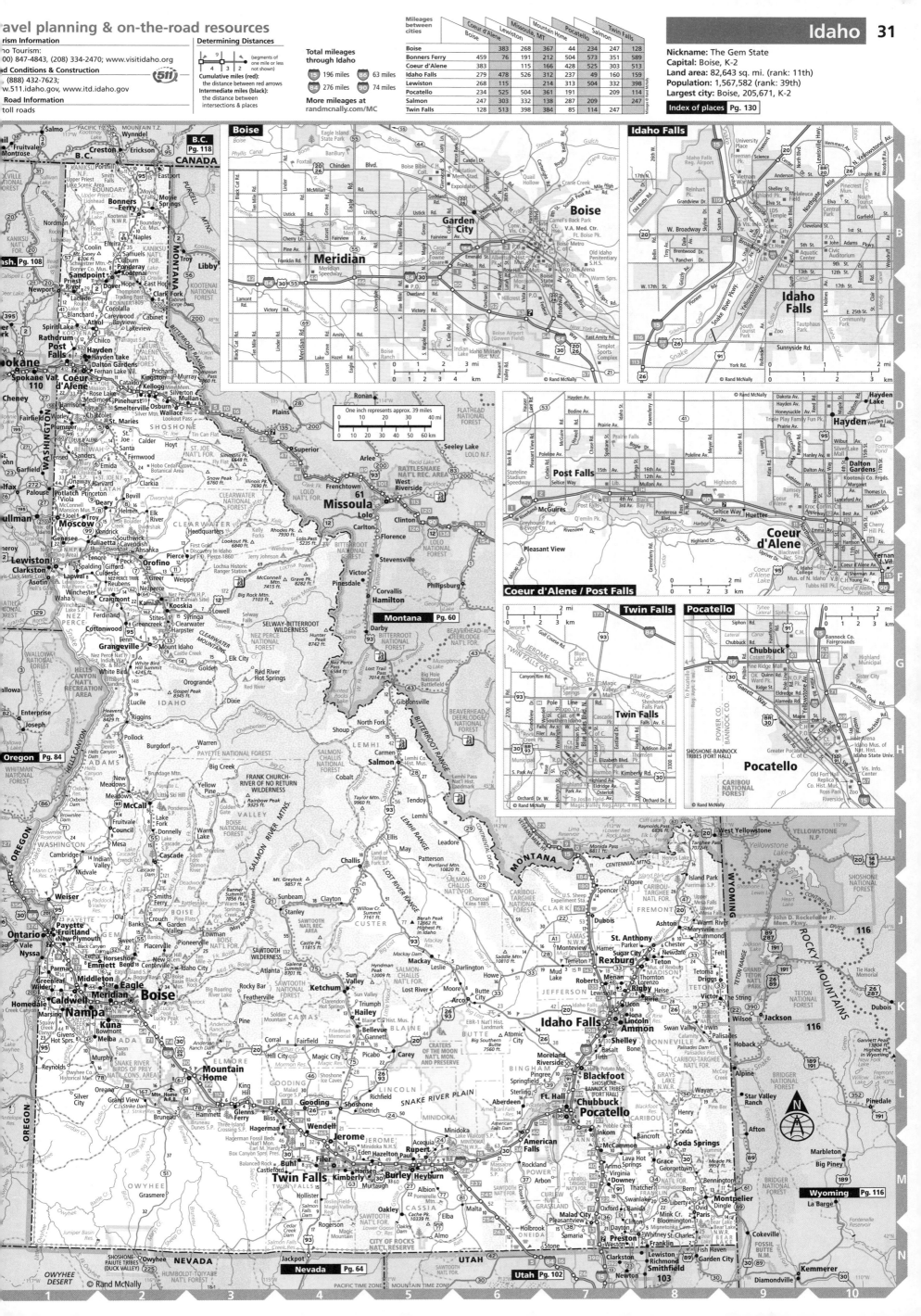

Nickname: Land of Lincoln
Capital: Springfield, J-8
Land area: 55,519 sq. mi. (rank: 24th)
Population: 12,830,632 (rank: 5th)
Largest city: Chicago, 2,695,598, C-13

Index of places Pg. 130

Travel planning & on-the-road resources

Tourism Information
Illinois Office of Tourism:
(800) 226-6632; www.enjoyillinois.com

Toll Road/Bridge Information
Illinois Tollway (all other toll roads): (800) 824-7277; www.illinoistollway.com
Skyway Concession Co. (Chicago Skyway): (312) 552-7100; www.chicagoskyway.org

Road Conditions & Construction
(800) 452-4368
www.gettingaroundillinois.com, www.dot.il.gov

(all use I-Pass)

Determining distances along roads

Highway distances (segments of one mile or less shown):
Cumulative miles (red): the distance between red arrows
Intermediate miles (black): the distance between intersections & places

Interchanges and exit numbers
For most states, the mileage between interchanges may be determined by subtracting one number from the other.

Wisconsin Pg. 114
Iowa Pg. 38
Ind. Pg. 36

One inch represents approximately 19 miles

Mileages between cities	Bloomington	Carbondale	Champaign	Chicago	Decatur	Dubuque, IA	Kankakee	Lawrenceville	Moline	Mt. Vernon	Peoria	Quincy	Rockford	St. Louis, MO	Springfield	Waukegan
Carbondale	245		200	330	176	406	272	146	332	57	240	240	379	104	170	374
Champaign	51	200		135	48	256	78	130	182	147	89	194	185	180	85	180
Chicago	132	330	135		179	177	58	247	166	277	154	309	84	296	198	38
Moline	131	332	182	166	171	75	158	307		308	93	148	120	261	164	190
Peoria	38	240	89	154	78	167	168	214	93	215		130	138	168	71	184
Rockford	132	379	185	84	180	93	139	309	120	268	138		268	294	197	73
St. Louis, MO	162	104	180	296	135	335	252	144	261	79	168	139	294		98	326
Springfield	66	170	85	198	38	238	157	153	164	138	71	112	197	98		229

Total mileages through Illinois

- 55 313 miles
- 70 156 miles
- 80 164 miles
- 90 124 miles

More mileages at randmcnally.com/MC

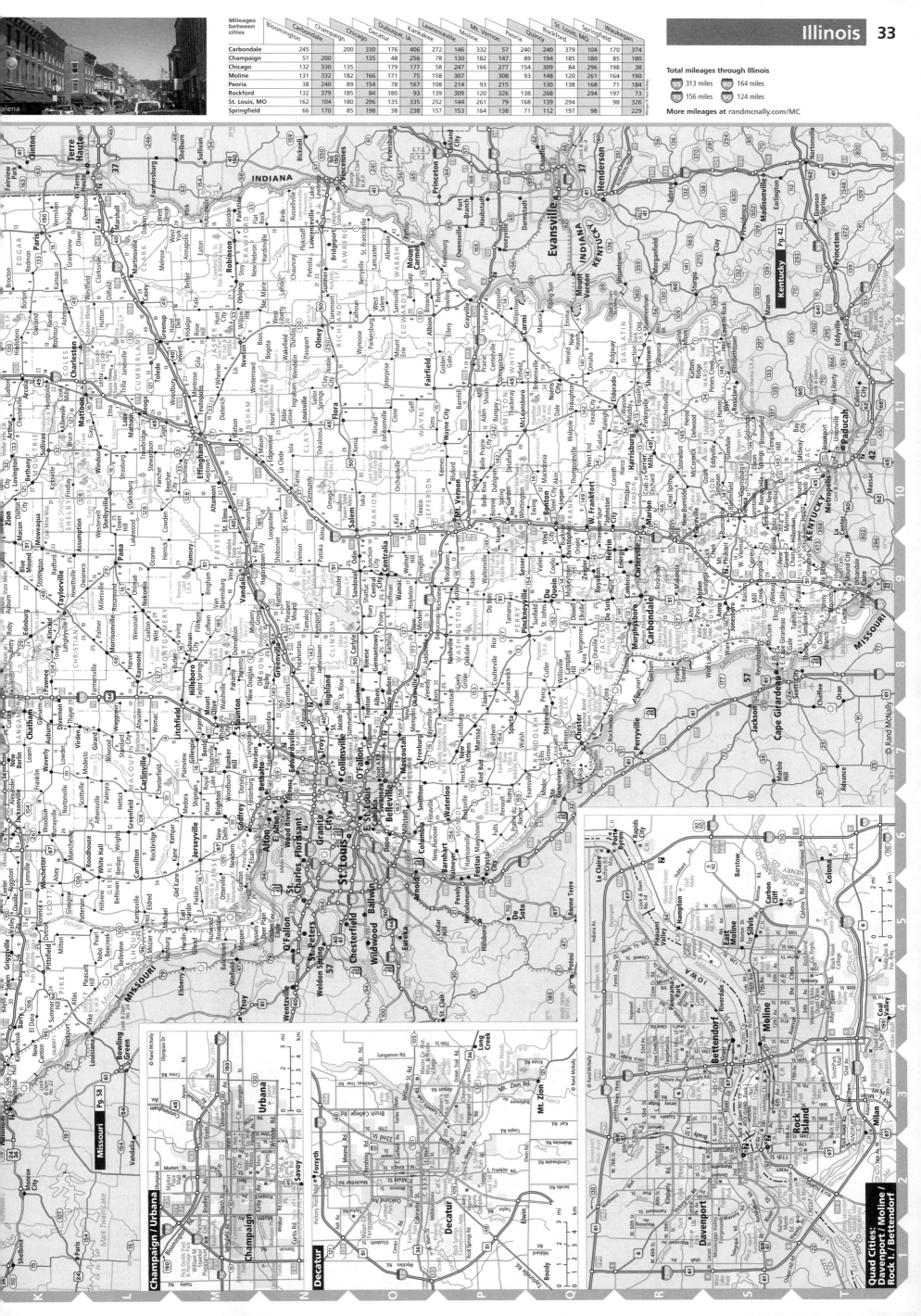

Sights to see

Chicago Cultural Center

Chicago & Vicinity

LAKE MICHIGAN
El. 579 ft. above sea level

Children's Museum of Indianapolis

Sights to see

- Abraham Lincoln Presidential Library & Museum, Springfield M-16
- Buckingham Fountain, Chicago F-13
- Children's Museum of Indianapolis, Indianapolis D-18
- Fort Wayne Children's Zoo, Fort Wayne L-19
- Illinois State Capitol Complex, Springfield M-16
- Indiana State Capitol, Indianapolis H-19
- Indiana State Museum, Indianapolis H-19
- Indianapolis Motor Speedway and Hall of Fame Museum, Indianapolis D-16
- NCAA Hall of Champions, Indianapolis H-18
- President Benjamin Harrison Home, Indianapolis F-20

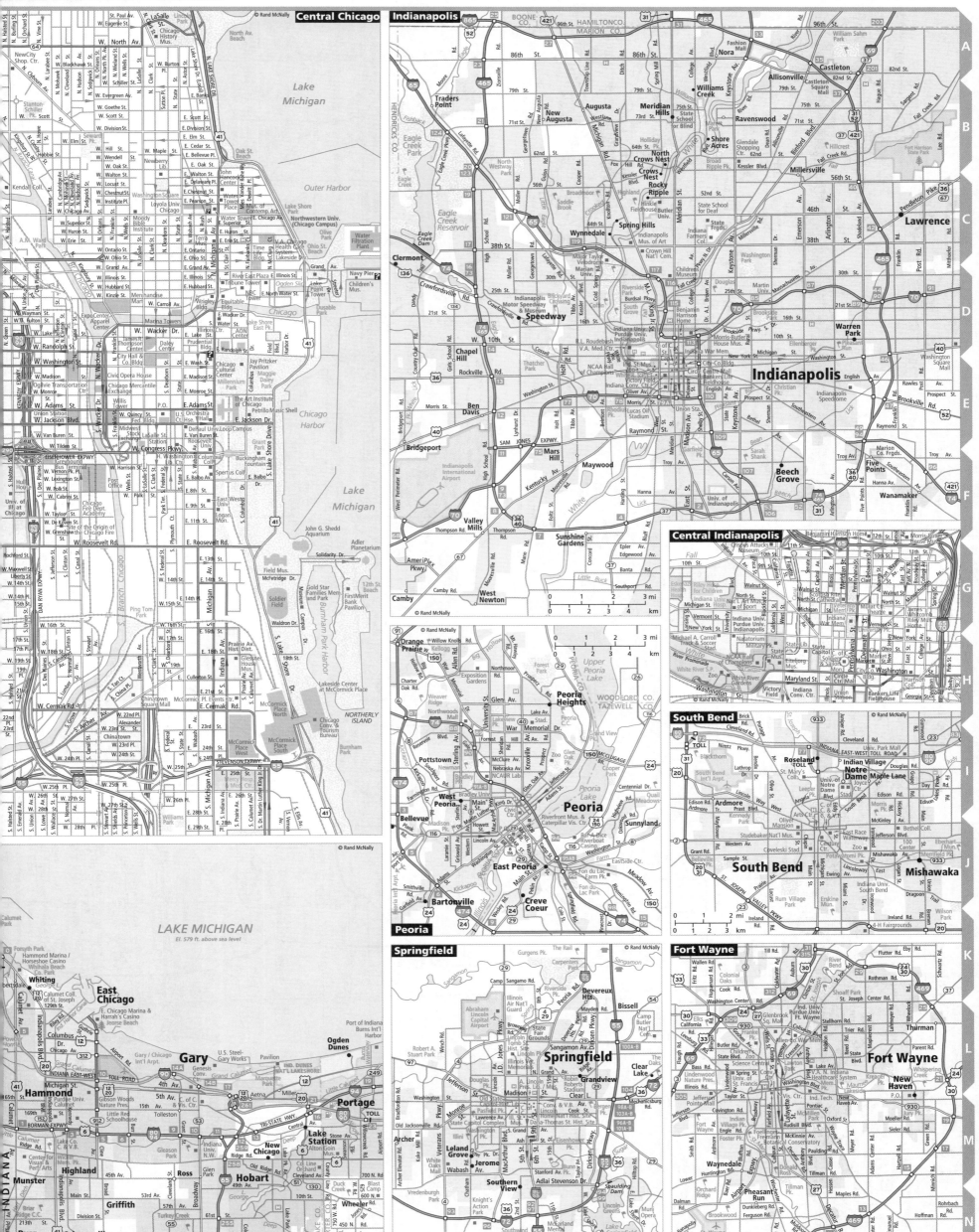

Nickname: The Hoosier State
Capital: Indianapolis, J-9
Land area: 35,826 sq. mi. (rank: 38th)
Population: 6,483,802 (rank: 15th)
Largest city: Indianapolis, 820,445, J-9

Index of places Pg. 130

Travel planning & on-the-road resources

Tourism Information
Indiana Office of Tourism Development: (800) 677-9800; www.visitindiana.com

Road Conditions & Construction
(800) 261-7623, (866) 849-1368; www.in.gov/dot, www.in.gov/indot/2420.htm

Toll Road Information
Indiana Toll Road Concession Co. (E-ZPass): (574) 675-4010; www.ezpassin.com
RiverLink (Louisville area toll bridges) (RiverLink or E-ZPass): (855) 748-5465; www.riverlink.com

Determining distances along roads
Highway distances (segments of one mile or less not shown):
Cumulative miles (red): the distance between red arrows
Intermediate miles (black): the distance between intersections & places

Interchanges and exit numbers
For most states, the mileage between interchanges may be determined by subtracting one number from the other.

Michigan Pg. 50

Ohio Pg. 78

Chicago

Elkhart

Lafayette

West Lafayette

Anderson

Muncie

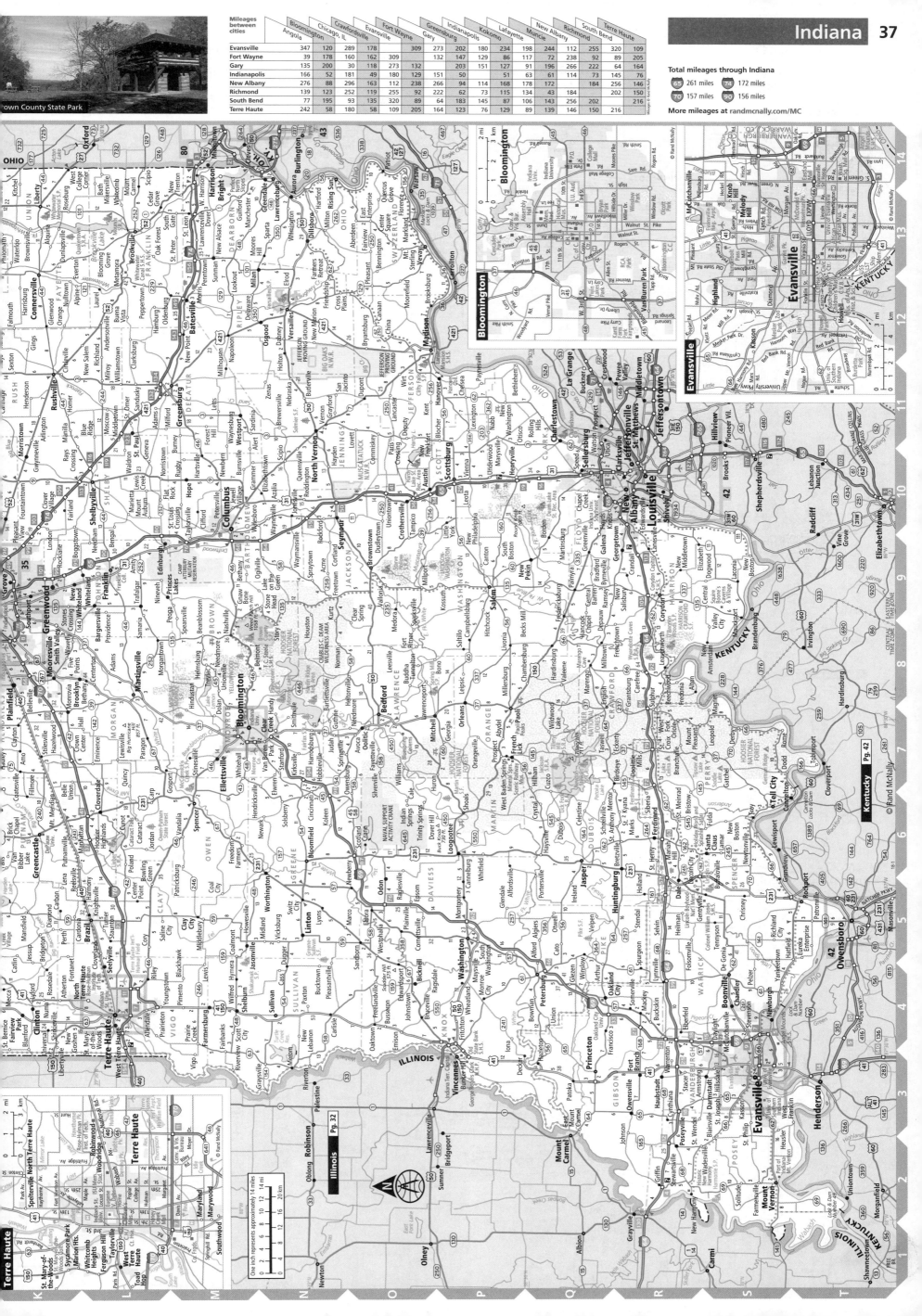

Mileages between cities

	Angola	Bloomington	Chicago, IL	Crawfordsville	Evansville	Fort Wayne	Greensburg	Gary	Indianapolis	Kokomo	Lafayette	Muncie	New Albany	Richmond	South Bend	Terre Haute
Evansville	347	120	289	178	—	309	273	202	180	234	198	244	112	255	320	109
Fort Wayne	39	178	160	162	309	—	132	147	129	86	117	72	238	92	89	205
Gary	135	200	30	118	273	132	203	—	151	127	91	196	222		64	164
Indianapolis	166	52	181	49	180	129	50	151	—	51	63	61	114	73	145	76
New Albany	276	88	296	163	112	238	266		114	168	178	172	—	184	256	146
Richmond	139	123	252	119	255	92	62	222	73	115	134	43	184	—	202	150
South Bend	77	195	93	135	320	89	64	183	145	87	106	143	256	202	—	216
Terre Haute	242	58	180	58	109	205	164	123	76	129	89	139	146	150	216	—

Total mileages through Indiana

- 65 261 miles
- 74 172 miles
- 70 157 miles
- 90 156 miles

More mileages at randmcnally.com/MC

Brown County State Park

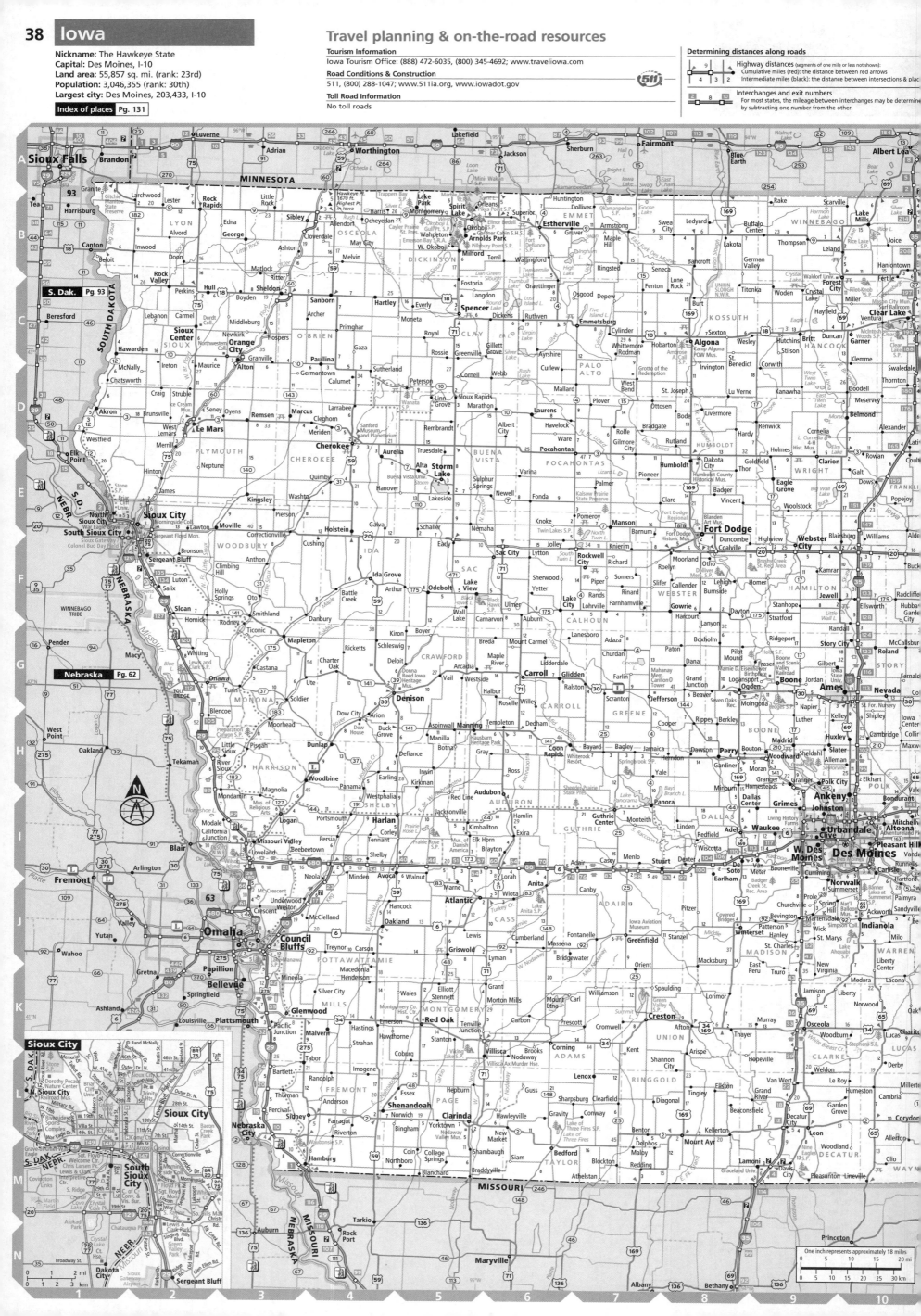

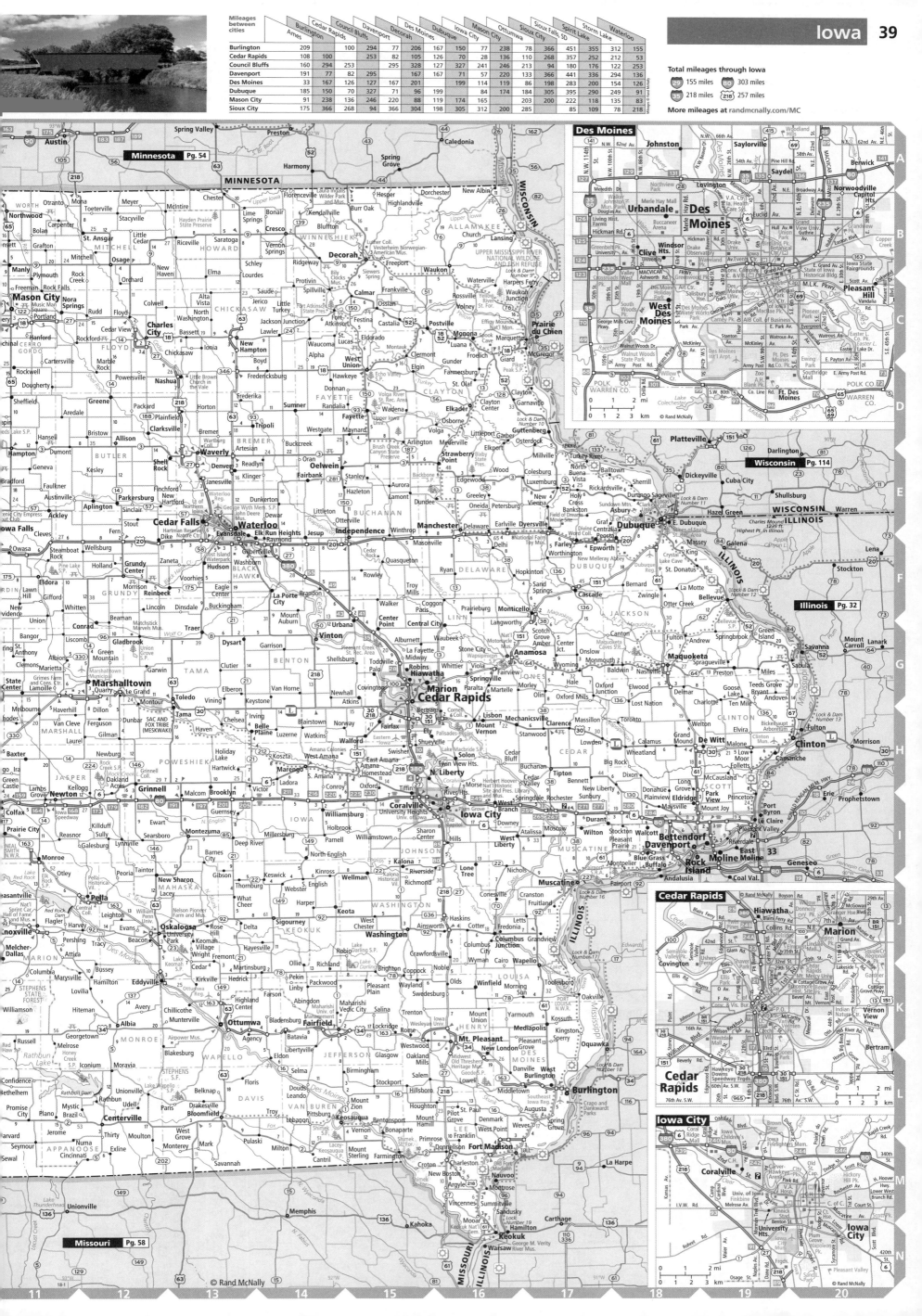

Mileages between cities

	Ames	Burlington	Cedar Rapids	Council Bluffs	Davenport	Decorah	Des Moines	Dubuque	Iowa City	Mason City	Ottumwa	Sioux City	Sioux Falls, SD	Spirit Lake	Storm Lake	Waterloo
Burlington	209		100	294	77	206	167	150	77	238	78	366	451	355	312	155
Cedar Rapids	108	100		253	82	105	126	70	28	136	110	268	357	252	212	53
Council Bluffs	160	294	253		295	328	127	327	241	246	213	94	180	176	122	253
Davenport	191	77	82	295		167	167	71	57	220	133	366	441	336	294	136
Des Moines	33	167	126	127	167	201		199	114	119	86	198	283	200	154	126
Dubuque	185	150	70	327	71	96	199		84	174	184	305	395	290	249	91
Mason City	91	238	136	246	220	88	119	174	165		203	220	118	135	83	
Sioux City	175	366	268	94	366	304	198	305	312	200	285		85	109	78	218

Total mileages through Iowa

- 29 — 155 miles
- 80 — 303 miles
- 35 — 218 miles
- 218 — 257 miles

More mileages at randmcnally.com/MC

Nickname: The Sunflower State
Capital: Topeka, D-16
Land area: 81,759 sq. mi. (rank: 13th)
Population: 2,853,118 (rank: 33rd)
Largest city: Wichita, 382,368, H-13

Index of places Pg. 131

Travel planning & on-the-road resources

Tourism Information
Kansas Dept. of Wildlife, Parks & Tourism: (800) 252-6727, (785) 296-2009; www.travelks.com

Road Conditions & Construction
511, (800) 585-7623, (785) 296-3585; 511.ksdot.org, www.ksdot.org

Toll Road Information
Kansas Turnpike Authority (K-TAG): (800) 873-5824, (316) 682-4537; www.ksturnpike.com

Determining distances along roads

Highway distances (segments of one mile or less not shown):
Cumulative miles (red): the distance between red arrows
Intermediate miles (black): the distance between intersections & places

Interchanges and exit numbers
For most states, the mileage between interchanges may be determined by subtracting one number from the other.

Nebraska Pg. 62

Colorado Pg. 20

Oklahoma Pg. 82

Salina

Hutchinson

Wichita

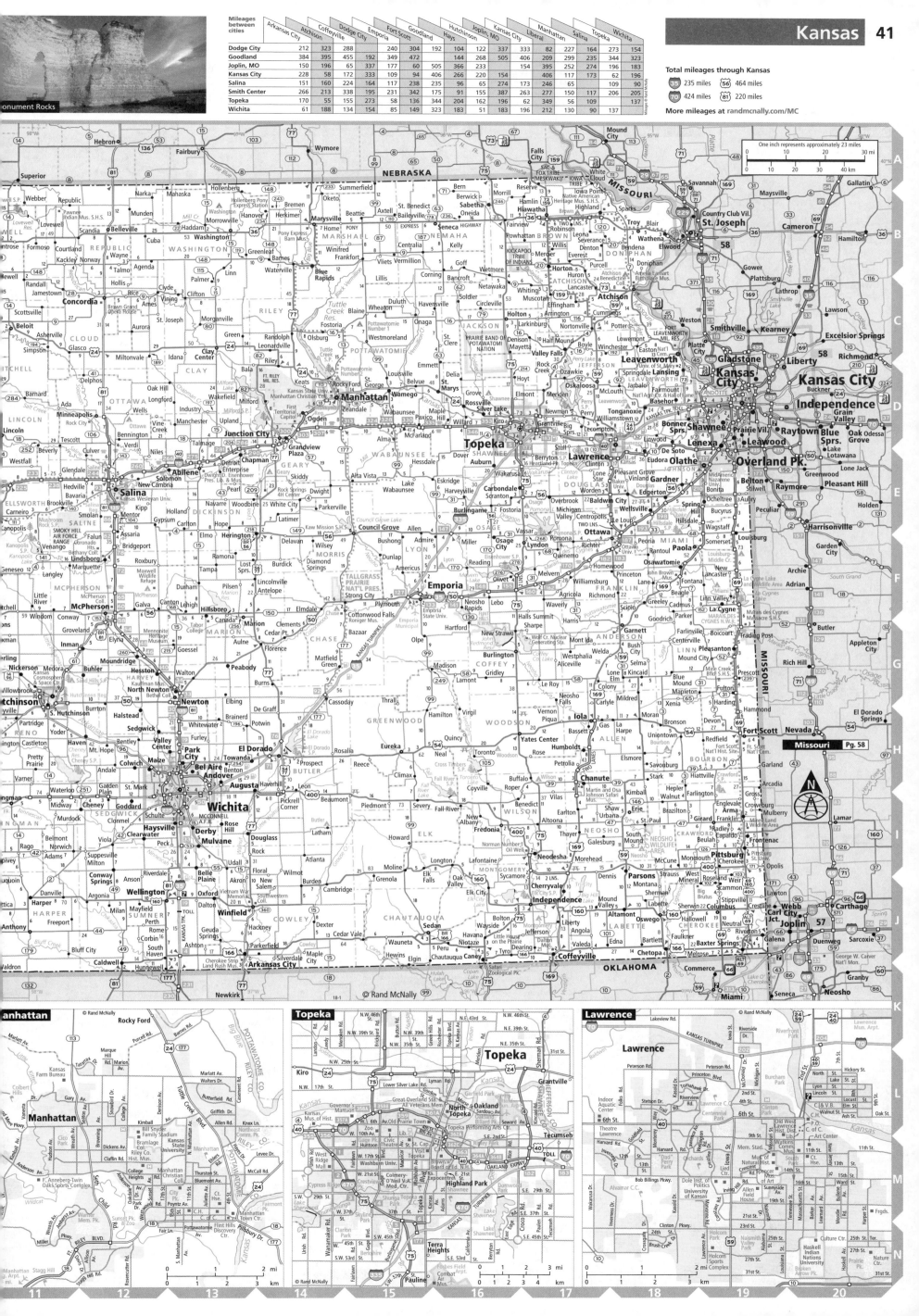

Monument Rocks

Mileages between cities	Arkansas City	Atchison	Coffeyville	Dodge City	Emporia	Fort Scott	Goodland	Hays	Hutchinson	Joplin, MO	Kansas City	Liberal	Manhattan	Salina	Topeka	Wichita
Dodge City	212	323	288		240	304	192	104	122	337	333	82	227	164	273	154
Goodland	384	395	455	192	349	472		144	268	505	406	209	299	235	344	323
Joplin, MO	150	196	56	337	177	60	505	366	233		154	395	252	274	196	183
Kansas City	228	58	172	333	109	94	406	266	220	154		406	117	173	62	196
Salina	151	160	224	164	112	238	235	96	65	274	173	246	65		109	90
Smith Center	266	213	338	195	231	342	175	91	155	387	263	277	150	117	206	205
Topeka	170	55	155	273	58	136	344	204	162	196	62	349	56	109		137
Wichita	61	188	134	154	85	149	323	183	51	183	196	212	130	90	137	

Total mileages through Kansas

35 235 miles 56 464 miles
70 424 miles 81 220 miles

More mileages at randmcnally.com/MC

One inch represents approximately 23 miles

42 Kentucky

Nickname: The Bluegrass State
Capital: Frankfort, G-11
Land area: 39,486 sq. mi. (rank: 37th)
Population: 4,339,367 (rank: 26th)
Largest city: Louisville, 597,337, G-8

Index of places Pg. 131

Travel planning & on-the-road resources

Tourism Information
Kentucky Department of Travel & Tourism: (800) 225-8747; www.kentuckytourism.com

Road Conditions & Construction
511, (866) 737-3767; www.511.ky.gov, transportation.ky.gov

Toll Road Information
RiverLink (Louisville area toll bridges) *(RiverLink or E-ZPass)*: (855) 748-5465; www.riverlink.com

Determining distances along roads

Highway distances (segments of one mile or less not shown):
Cumulative miles (red): the distance between arrows
Intermediate miles (black): the distance between intersections and places

Interchanges and exit numbers
For most states, the mileage between interchanges may be determined by subtracting one number from the other.

Inset maps: Owensboro, Bowling Green, Louisville, Paducah

© Rand McNally

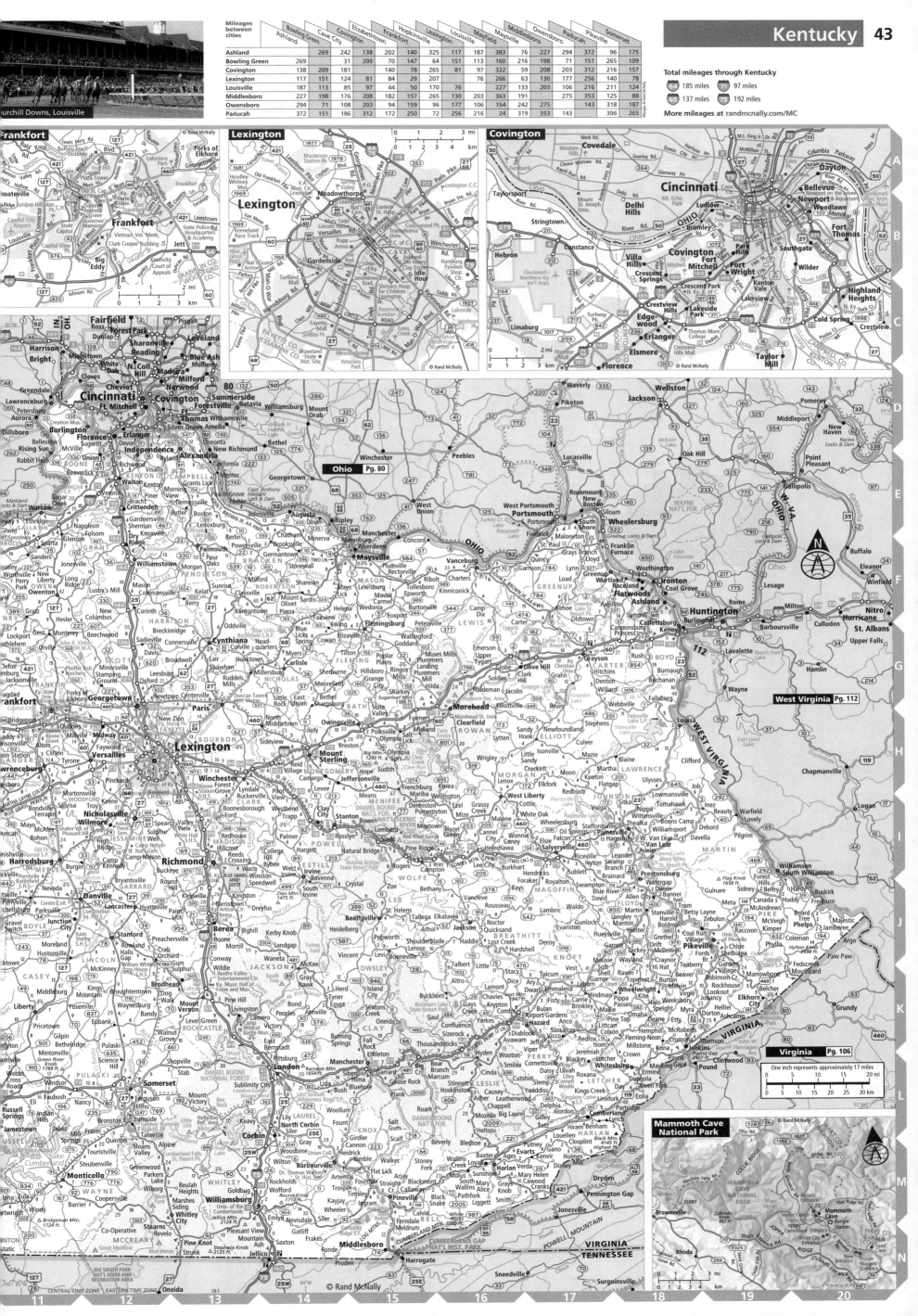

Churchill Downs, Louisville

Mileages between cities

	Ashland	Bowling Green	Cave City	Covington	Elizabethtown	Frankfort	Hopkinsville	Lexington	Louisville	Mayfield	Maysville	Middlesboro	Owensboro	Paducah	Pikeville	Somerset
Ashland		269	242	138	202	140	325	117	187	383	76	227	294	372	96	175
Bowling Green	269		31	209	70	147	64	151	113	160	216	198	71	151	265	109
Covington	138	209	181		140	78	265	81	97	322	58	208	203	312	216	157
Lexington	117	151	124	81	84	29	207		76	266	63	130	177	256	140	78
Louisville	187	113	85	97	44	50	170	76		227	133	203	106	216	211	124
Middlesboro	227	198	176	208	182	157	265	130	203	363	191		275	353	125	88
Owensboro	294	71	108	203	94	159	96	177	106	154	242	275		143	318	187
Paducah	372	151	186	312	172	250	72	256	216	24	319	353	143		396	265

Total mileages through Kentucky

64 = 185 miles   71 = 97 miles
65 = 137 miles   75 = 192 miles

More mileages at randmcnally.com/MC

Frankfort

Lexington

Covington

Mammoth Cave National Park

One inch represents approximately 17 miles

© Rand McNally

West Virginia Pg. 112

Virginia Pg. 106

Ohio Pg. 80

Nickname: The Pelican State
Capital: Baton Rouge, G-7
Land area: 43,204 sq. mi. (rank: 33rd)
Population: 4,533,372 (rank: 25th)
Largest city: New Orleans, 343,829, H-9

Index of places Pg. 131

Mileages between cities	Baton Rouge	Beaumont, TX	Houma	Lake Charles	Monroe	New Orleans	Shreveport	Vicksburg, MS
Alexandria	125	155	190	95	97	218	123	147
Baton Rouge		183	85	124	186	79	250	157
Gulfport, MS	134	318	131	258	276	78	375	201
Lafayette	55	133	102	73	182	134	211	212
Lake Charles	124	60	177		190	203	184	243
New Orleans	79	262	56	203	281		340	207
Shreveport	250	206	314	184	98	340		171
Vicksburg, MS	157	301	234	243	74	207	171	

Total mileages through Louisiana
10 274 miles   208 miles
20 190 miles   66 miles

More mileages at
randmcnally.com/MC

Travel planning & on-the-road resources

Tourism Information
Louisiana Office of Tourism: (800) 994-8626, (800) 677-4082; www.louisianatravel.com

Road Conditions & Construction
511, (877) 452-3683; www.511la.org, www.dotd.la.gov

Toll Bridges
Lake Ponchartrain Causeway *(TollTag)*: (504) 835-3118; www.thecauseway.us
Louisiana Dept. of Trans. & Development (La. Hwy. 1 Bridge) *(GeauxPass)*:
(866) 662-8987; www.geauxpass.com

ravel planning & on-the-road resources

urism Information
aine Office of Tourism: (888) 624-6345; www.visitmaine.com

ad Conditions & Construction
1, (207) 624-3000, (800) 675-7453;
w.511maine.gov, www.maine.gov/mdot

ll Road Information
aine Turnpike Authority (*E-ZPass*):
877) 682-9433, (207) 871-7771; www.maineturnpike.com

Determining Distances

(segments of one mile or less not shown)

Cumulative miles (red): the distance between red arrows
Intermediate miles (black): the distance between intersections & places

Total mileages through Maine
95 299 miles 2 273 miles
1 527 miles 201 164 miles
More mileages at randmcnally.com/MC

Mileages between cities	Auburn	Bangor	Bar Harbor	Eastport	Houlton	Millinocket	Portland	Rangeley
Bangor	107		47	120	118	72	128	120
Eastport	226	120	118		115	125	247	242
Houlton	225	118	167	115		69	246	238
Madawaska	326	219	267	218	102	170	347	339
Portland	35	128	174	247	246	181		118
Portsmouth, NH	81	180	225	301	298	231	51	165
Rangeley	84	120	165	242	238	153	118	
Waterville	53	55	101	174	173	107	75	77

Nickname: The Pine Tree State
Capital: Augusta, F-4
Land area: 30,843 sq. mi. (rank: 39th)
Population: 1,328,361 (rank: 41st)
Largest city: Portland, 66,194, H-3

Index of places Pg. 131

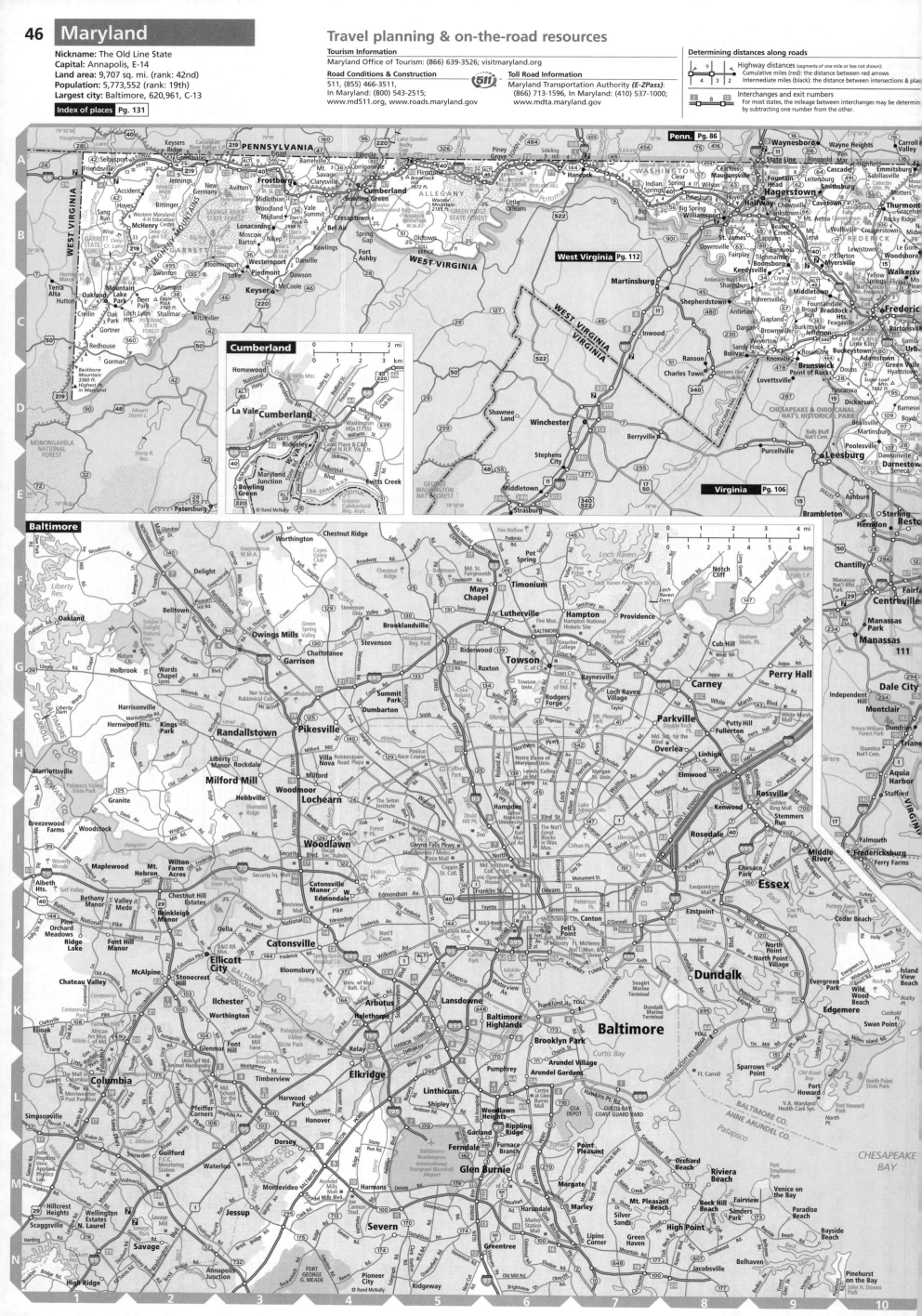

Nickname: The Old Line State
Capital: Annapolis, E-14
Land area: 9,707 sq. mi. (rank: 42nd)
Population: 5,773,552 (rank: 19th)
Largest city: Baltimore, 620,961, C-13

Index of places Pg. 131

Travel planning & on-the-road resources

Tourism Information
Maryland Office of Tourism: (866) 639-3526; visitmaryland.org

Road Conditions & Construction
511, (855) 466-3511,
In Maryland: (800) 543-2515;
www.md511.org, www.roads.maryland.gov

Toll Road Information
Maryland Transportation Authority (*E-ZPass*):
(866) 713-1596, In Maryland: (410) 537-1000;
www.mdta.maryland.gov

Determining distances along roads
Highway distances (segments of one mile or less not shown):
Cumulative miles (red): the distance between red arrows
Intermediate miles (black): the distance between intersections & places
Interchanges and exit numbers
For most states, the mileage between interchanges may be determined by subtracting one number from the other.

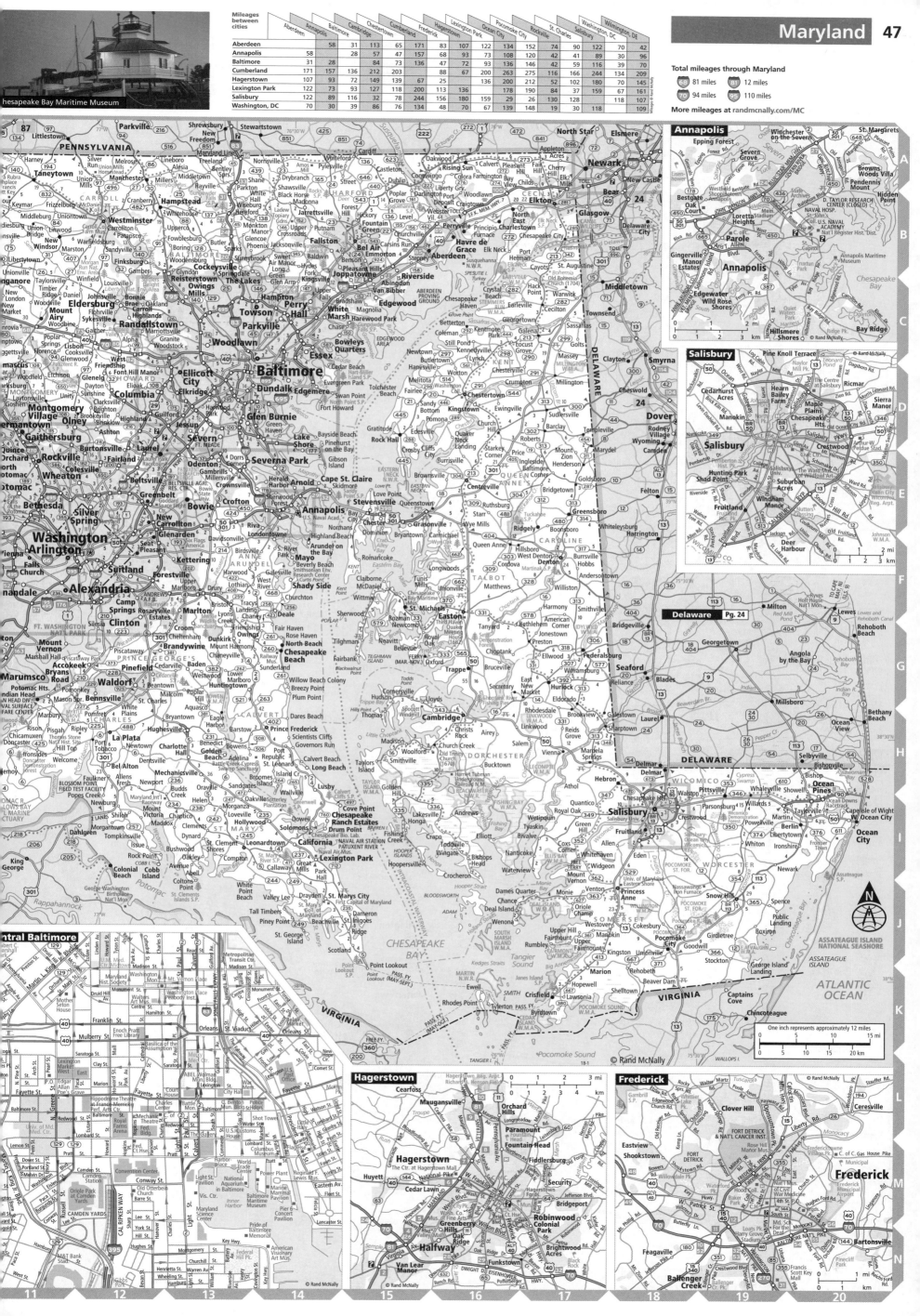

Chesapeake Bay Maritime Museum

Mileages between cities

	Aberdeen	Annapolis	Baltimore	Cambridge	Chestertown	Cumberland	Frederick	Hagerstown	Lexington Park	Ocean City	Pocomoke City	Rockville	St. Charles	Washington, DC	Wilmington, DE
Aberdeen		58	31	113	65	171	83	107	122	134	152	74	90	122	70	42
Annapolis	58		28	57	47	157	68	93	73	108	120	42	41	89	30	96
Baltimore	31	28		84	39	136	47	72	93	136	146	42	59	116	39	70
Cumberland	171	157	136	212	203		88	67	200	263	275	116	166	244	134	209
Hagerstown	107	93	72	149	139	67	26		136	200	212	52	102	180	70	145
Lexington Park	122	73	93	127	118	200	113	136		178	190	84	37	159	67	161
Salisbury	122	89	116	32	78	244	156	180	159	29	26	130	128	118	107
Washington, DC	70	30	39	86	76	134	48	70	67	139	148	19	30		118	109

Total mileages through Maryland

- 68 — 81 miles
- 81 — 12 miles
- 70 — 94 miles
- 95 — 110 miles

More mileages at randmcnally.com/MC

Nickname: The Bay State
Capital: Boston, E-14
Land area: 7,800 sq. mi. (rank: 45th)
Population: 6,547,629 (rank: 14th)
Largest city: Boston, 617,594, E-14

Index of places Pg. 131

Travel planning & on-the-road resources

Tourism Information
Massachusetts Office of Travel & Tourism:
(800) 227-6277, (617) 973-8500;
www.massvacation.com

Toll Road Information
Massachusetts Department of Transportation (E-ZPass):
(877) 623-6846, (857) 368-4636; www.massdot.state.ma.us/highway

Road Conditions & Construction
511, Metro Boston: (617) 986-5511;
Central: (508) 499-5511;
Western: (413) 754-5511;
www.mass511.com, www.mhd.state.ma.us

Determining distances along roads
Highway distances (segments of one mile or less not shown):
Cumulative miles (red): the distance between red arrows
Intermediate miles (black): the distance between intersections & places

Interchanges and exit numbers
For most states, the mileage between interchanges may be determined by subtracting one number from the other.

Cape Cod

Mileages between cities	Boston	Brockton	Falmouth	Fitchburg	Gloucester	Greenfield	Lowell	Nantucket	New Bedford	North Adams	Pittsfield	Plymouth	Providence, RI	Provincetown	Springfield	Worcester
Boston		24	76	47	39	94	29	101*	58	157	136	40	50	116	90	43
Gloucester	39	63	114	74		120	47	140*	97	157	169	78	90	154	122	75
Lowell	29	50	102	32	47	78		130*	84	115	139	69	69	145	92	41
New Bedford	58	37	40	94	97	148	84	77*		182	161	37	31	91	114	71
Pittsfield	136	150	189	124	169	79	139	226*	161	22		167	130	240	51	98
Provincetown	116	106	69	162	154	208	145	87*	91	262	240	77	119		194	146
Springfield	90	103	143	77	122	38	92	180*	114	73	51	121	83	194		51
Worcester	43	56	96	26		72	41	133*	71	120	98	74	40	146	51	

*Via ferry

Total mileages through Massachusetts

90 — 136 miles 93 — 47 miles
55 — 55 miles 95 — 92 miles

More mileages at randmcnally.com/MC

One inch represents approximately 9 miles

© Rand McNally

Nickname: The Great Lake State
Capital: Lansing, Q-9
Land area: 56,539 sq. mi. (rank: 22nd)
Population: 9,883,640 (rank: 8th)
Largest city: Detroit, 713,777, R-12

Index of places Pg. 131

Travel planning & on-the-road resources

Tourism Information
Travel Michigan:
(888) 784-7328; www.michigan.org

Road Conditions & Construction
(800) 381-8477, (517) 373-2090;
www.michigan.gov/drive

International Toll Bridge/Tunnel Information
Ambassador Bridge (Detroit): (800) 462-7434; www.ambassadorbridge.com
Detroit-Windsor Tunnel (NEXPRESS): (313) 567-4422 ext. 200, (519) 258-7424 ext. 200; www.dwtunnel.com
International Bridge Administration (Sault Ste. Marie): (906) 635-5255, (705) 942-4345; www.saultbridge.com
Michigan Department of Transportation: Blue Water Bridge (Port Huron): (810) 984-3131; www.michigan.gov/mdot

Michigan Toll Bridge/Tunnel Information
Mackinac Bridge Authority (Mac Pass): (906) 643-7600; www.mackinacbridge.org

© Rand McNally

Isle Royale National Park

Lansing

Saginaw

Wisconsin

Ontario Pg. 122

Wisconsin Pg. 114

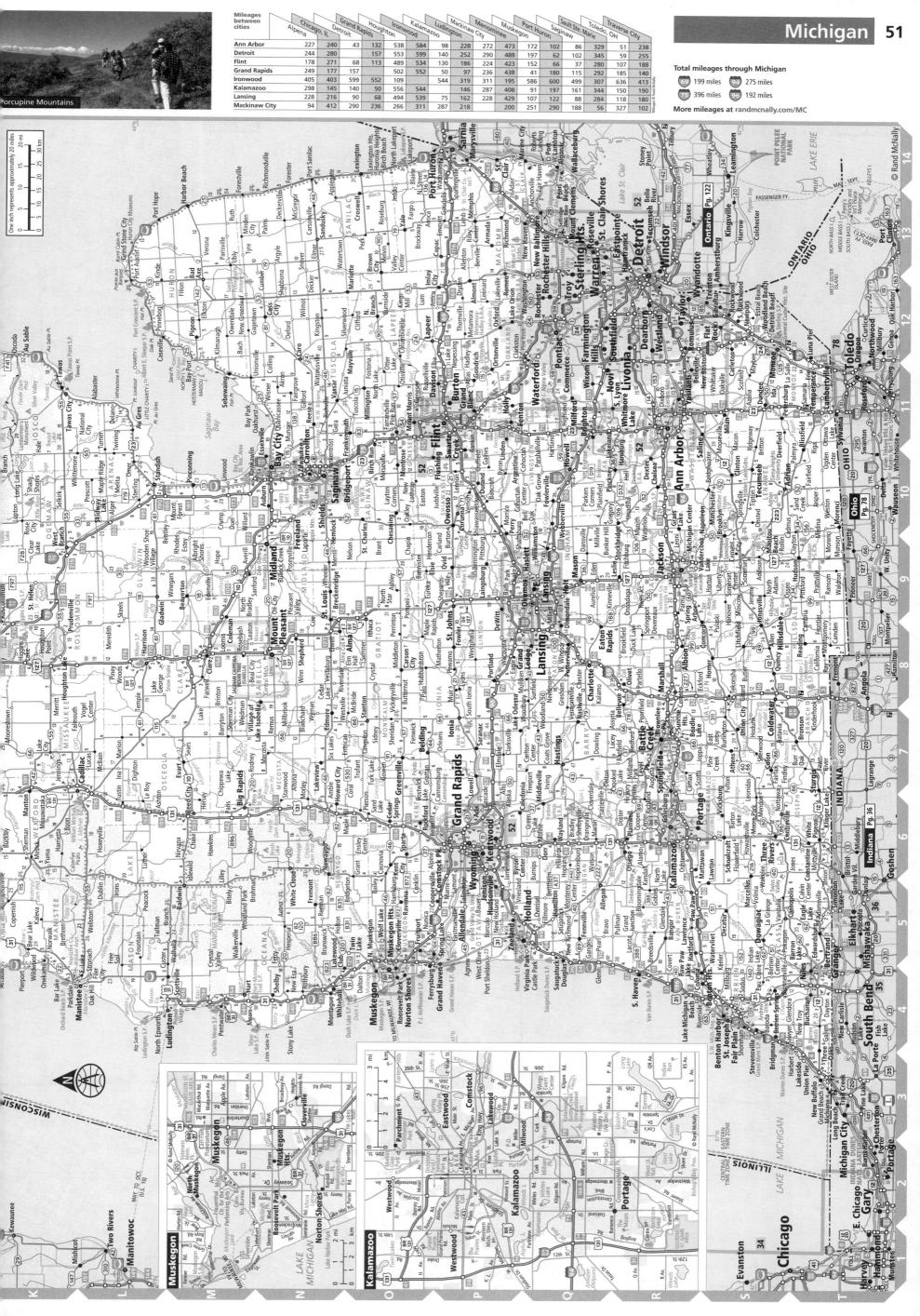

Porcupine Mountains

Mileages between cities	Alpena	Chicago, IL	Detroit	Grand Rapids	Houghton	Ironwood	Kalamazoo	Ludington	Mackinaw City	Menominee	Muskegon	Port Huron	Saginaw	Sault Ste. Marie	Toledo, OH	Traverse City
Ann Arbor	227	240	43	132	538	584	98	228	272	473	172	102	86	329	51	238
Detroit	244	280		157	553	599	140	252	290	488	197	62	102	345	59	255
Flint	178	271	68	113	489	534	130	186	224	438	152	66	37	280	107	188
Grand Rapids	249	157	157		502	552	50	97	236	438	41	180	115	292	185	140
Ironwood	405	403	599	552	109		544	319	311	195	586	600	499	307	636	413
Kalamazoo	298	145	140	50	556	544		146	287	408	91	197	161	344	150	190
Lansing	228	216	90	68	494	539	75	162	228	429	107	122	88	284	118	180
Mackinaw City	94	412	290	236	266	311	287	218		200	251	290	188	56	327	102

Total mileages through Michigan

69	199 miles	94	275 miles
75	396 miles	96	192 miles

More mileages at randmcnally.com/MC

Sights to see

- Cranbrook Art Museum, Bloomfield Hills G-5
- Detroit Zoo, Royal Oak H-6
- Edsel & Eleanor Ford House, Grosse Pointe Shores I-9
- Frederik Meijer Gardens, Grand Rapids A-3
- Gerald R. Ford Museum, Grand Rapids B-2
- Gerald R. Ford Presidential Library, Ann Arbor B-10
- Henry Ford Museum, Dearborn K-5
- Motown Historical Museum, Detroit J-7
- New Detroit Science Center, Detroit J-7
- Renaissance Center, Detroit N-10
- Sloan Museum, Flint B-6
- University of Michigan, Ann Arbor B-9

Detroit Institute of Art

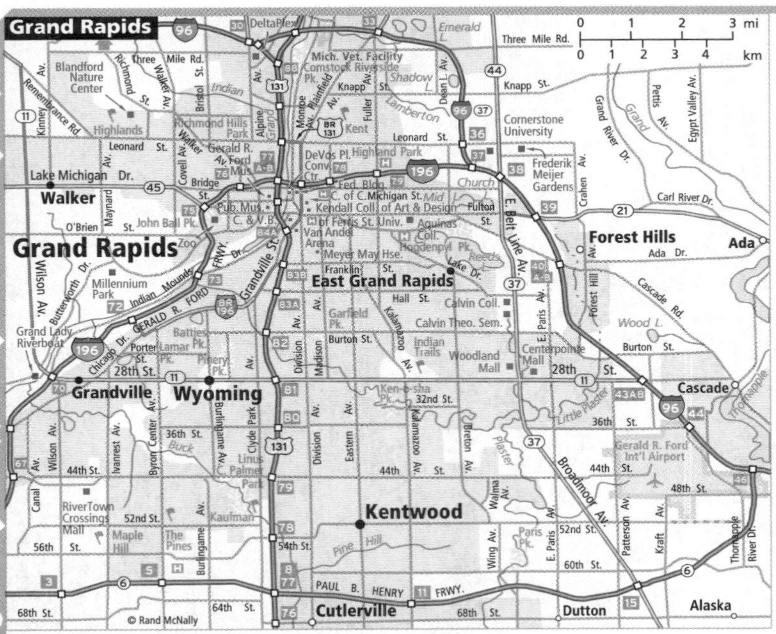

Grand Rapids

Flint

Ann Arbor

Detroit & Vicinity

Central Detroit

© Rand McNally

Walker Art Center, Minneapolis

Sights to see

- Bell Museum of Natural History, Minneapolis L-4
- Cathedral of St. Paul, St. Paul M-7
- Frederick R. Weisman Art Museum, Minneapolis M-4
- Mall of America, Bloomington I-5
- Mill City Museum, Minneapolis L-3
- Minneapolis Institute of the Arts, Minneapolis N-2
- Minneapolis Sculpture Garden, Minneapolis M-1
- Minnesota History Center, Minneapolis M-7
- Minnesota State Capitol, St. Paul L-7
- Ordway Center for the Performing Arts, St. Paul M-7
- Science Museum of Minnesota, St. Paul M-7
- Walker Art Center, Minneapolis M-1

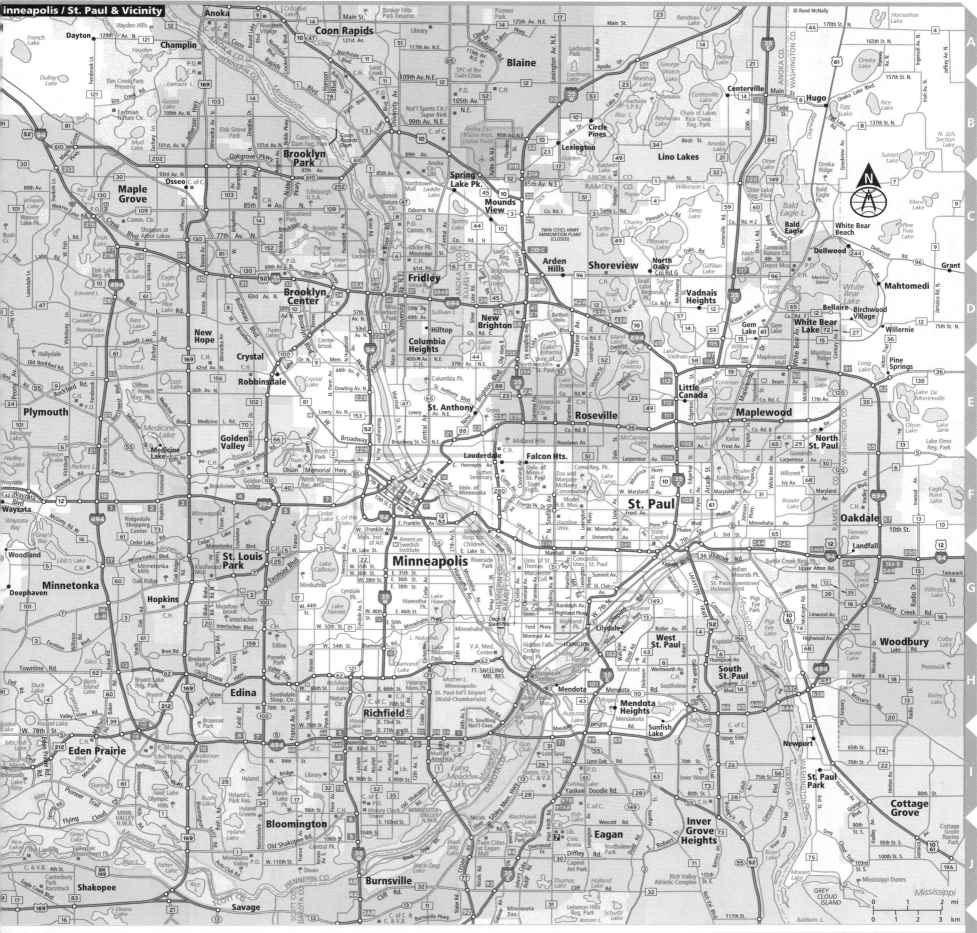

Minneapolis / St. Paul & Vicinity

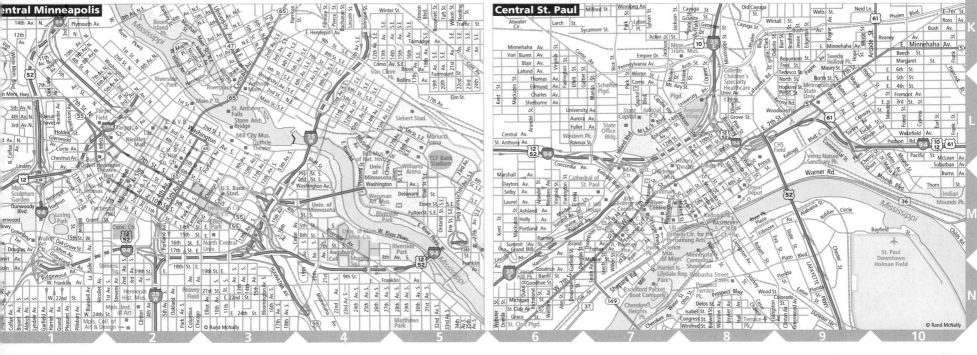

Central Minneapolis

Central St. Paul

© Rand McNally

Nickname: The North Star State
Capital: St. Paul, O-10
Land area: 79,627 sq. mi. (rank: 14th)
Population: 5,303,925 (rank: 21st)
Largest city: Minneapolis, 382,578, O-9

Index of places Pg. 132

Travel planning & on-the-road resources

Tourism Information
Explore Minnesota Tourism: (888) 847-4866, (651) 296-5029, (651) 757-1845; www.exploreminnesota.com

Road Conditions & Construction
511, (651) 296-3000, In MN: (800) 657-3774; www.511mn.org, www.dot.state.mn.us

Toll Road Information
No toll roads

Determining distances along roads

Highway distances (segments of one mile or less not shown):
Cumulative miles (red): the distance between red arrows
Intermediate miles (black): the distance between intersections & places

Interchanges and exit numbers
For most states, the mileage between interchanges may be determined by subtracting one number from the other.

© Rand McNally

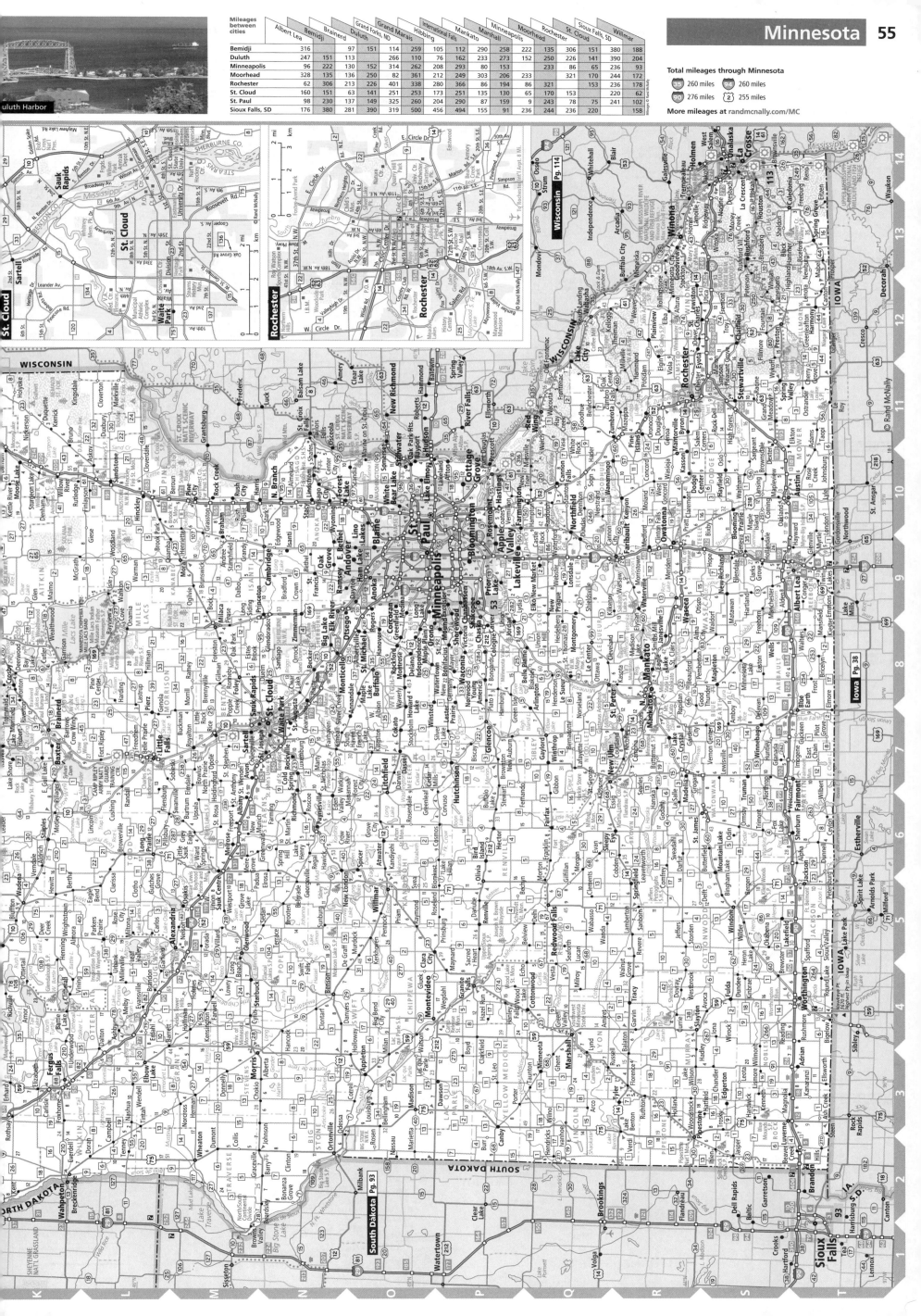

Duluth Harbor

Mileages between cities

	Albert Lea	Bemidji	Brainerd	Duluth	Grand Forks, ND	Grand Marais	Hibbing	International Falls	Mankato	Marshall	Minneapolis	Moorhead	Rochester	St. Cloud	Sioux Falls, SD	Willmar
Bemidji	316		97	151	114	259	105	112	290	258	222	135	306	151	380	188
Duluth	247	151	113		266	110	76	162	233	273	152	250	226	141	390	204
Minneapolis	96	222	130	152	314	262	208	293	80	153		233	86	65	236	93
Moorhead	328	135	136	250	82	361	212	249	303	206	233		321	170	244	172
Rochester	62	306	213	226	401	338	280	366	86	194	86	321		153	236	158
St. Cloud	160	151	63	141	251	253	173	261	135	130	70	170	153		220	62
St. Paul	98	230	137	149	325	260	204	290	87	159	9	243	78	75	241	102
Sioux Falls, SD	176	380	281	390	319	500	456	494	155	91	236	244	236	220		158

Total mileages through Minnesota

- 35 — 260 miles
- 90 — 276 miles
- 2 — 255 miles

More mileages at randmcnally.com/MC

Nickname: The Magnolia State
Capital: Jackson, H-6
Land area: 46,923 sq. mi. (rank: 31st)
Population: 2,967,297 (rank: 31st)
Largest city: Jackson, 173,514, H-6

Index of places Pg. 132

Mileages between cities	Batesville	Biloxi	Hattiesburg	Jackson	Memphis, TN	Natchez	Tupelo	Vicksburg
Biloxi	320		80	172	379	228	315	214
Greenville	112	293	210	121	152	152	177	91
Jackson	149	172	89		209	103	190	44
Memphis, TN	61	379	297	209		304	105	245
Meridian	176	172	89	91	234	194	142	134
New Orleans, LA	335	90	109	183	394	171	340	207
Tupelo	74	315	232	190	105	283		225
Vicksburg	188	214	131	44	245	70	225	

Total mileages through Mississippi
(10) 77 miles   (55) 290 miles
(20) 169 miles   (59) 172 miles
More mileages at randmcnally.com/MC

Travel planning & on-the-road resources

Tourism Information
Visit Mississippi:
(866) 733-6477, (601) 359-3297; www.visitmississippi.org

Road Conditions & Construction
511, (601) 359-7001;
www.mdot.ms.gov, www.mdottraffic.com

Toll Road Information
No toll roads

Determining Distances
Cumulative miles (red):
the distance between red arrows
Intermediate miles (black):
the distance between intersections & places

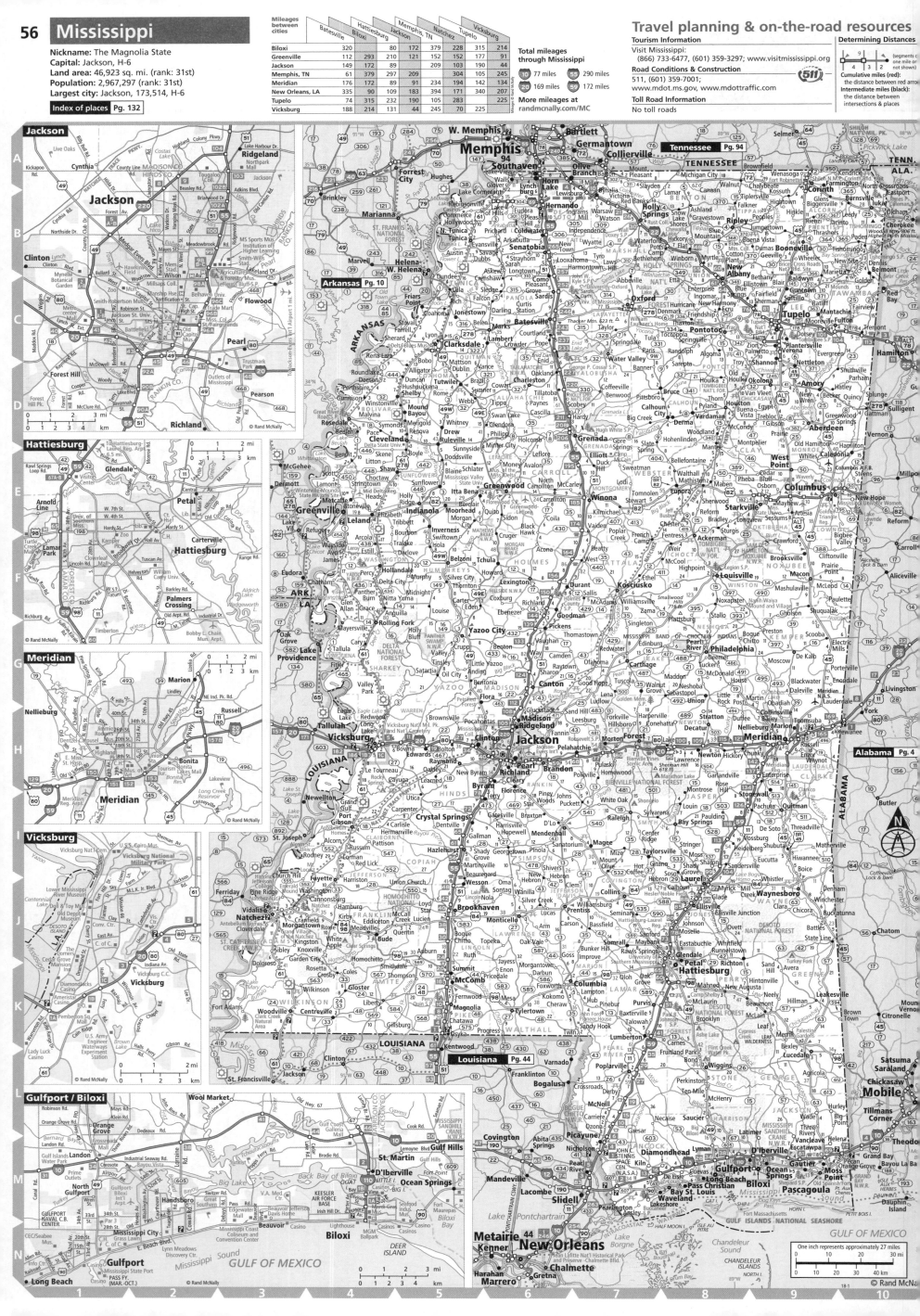

Gateway Arch, St. Louis

Sights to see

- Andy Williams Moon River Theatre, Branson M-8
- Anheuser-Busch Brewery, St. Louis ...I-7
- Bass Pro Shops® Outdoor World®, Springfield C-3
- Dolly Parton's Dixie Stampede, Branson M-9
- Gateway Arch, St. Louis L-4
- Laumeier Sculpture Park, St. Louis ...J-4
- Magic House, Kirkwood I-4
- Missouri Botanical Garden, St. Louis ...I-6
- Shoji Tabuchi Theatre, Branson L-7
- St. Louis Art Museum, St. Louis H-6
- St. Louis Science Center, St. Louis ...H-6
- St. Louis Zoo, St. Louis H-6
- Shepherd of the Hills, Branson K-6
- White Water, Branson M-7

Springfield

Joplin

Cape Girardeau

St. Louis & Vicinity

Central St. Louis

Branson

Nickname: The Show Me State
Capital: Jefferson City, G-14
Land area: 68,741 sq. mi. (rank: 18th)
Population: 5,988,927 (rank: 18th)
Largest city: Kansas City, 459,787, F-9

Index of places Pg. 132

Travel planning & on-the-road resources

Tourism Information
Missouri Division of Tourism: (573) 751-4133; www.visitmo.com

Road Conditions & Construction
(888) 275-6636, (573) 751-2551; www.modot.org

Toll Road Information
No toll roads

Determining distances along roads
Highway distances (segments of one mile or less not shown):
Cumulative miles (red): the distance between red arrows
Intermediate miles (black): the distance between intersections & places

Interchanges and exit numbers
For most states, the mileage between interchanges may be determined by subtracting one number from the other.

Central Kansas City

St. Joseph

Kansas City & Vicinity

Detailed road map of the Kansas City metropolitan area, St. Joseph, Central Kansas City insets, and surrounding counties in Missouri, Kansas, Iowa, Nebraska, and Oklahoma.

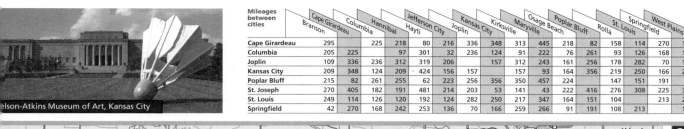

Nelson-Atkins Museum of Art, Kansas City

Mileages between cities	Branson	Cape Girardeau	Columbia	Hannibal	Jefferson City	Joplin	Kansas City	Kirksville	Maryville	Osage Beach	Poplar Bluff	Rolla	St. Louis	Springfield	West Plains
Cape Girardeau	295		225	218	80	216	336	348	313	445	218	82	158	114	270	182
Columbia	205	225		97	301	32	236	124	91	222	76	261	93	126	168	191
Joplin	109	336	236		312	319	206		157	312	243	161	256	178	282	70	175
Kansas City	209	348	124	209	424	156	157		157	93	264	356	219	250	166	275
Poplar Bluff	215	82	261	255	62	223	256	350	457	224		147	151	191	98
St. Joseph	270	405	182	191	481	214	203	53	141	422	222	416	276	308	225	336
St. Louis	249	114	126	120	192	124	282	250	217	347	164	151	104	213	202
Springfield	42	270	168	242	253	136	70	166	259	266	91	191	108	108	213	108

Total mileages through Missouri

- 35 = 115 miles
- 44 = 290 miles
- 55 = 210 miles
- 70 = 252 miles

More mileages at randmcnally.com/MC

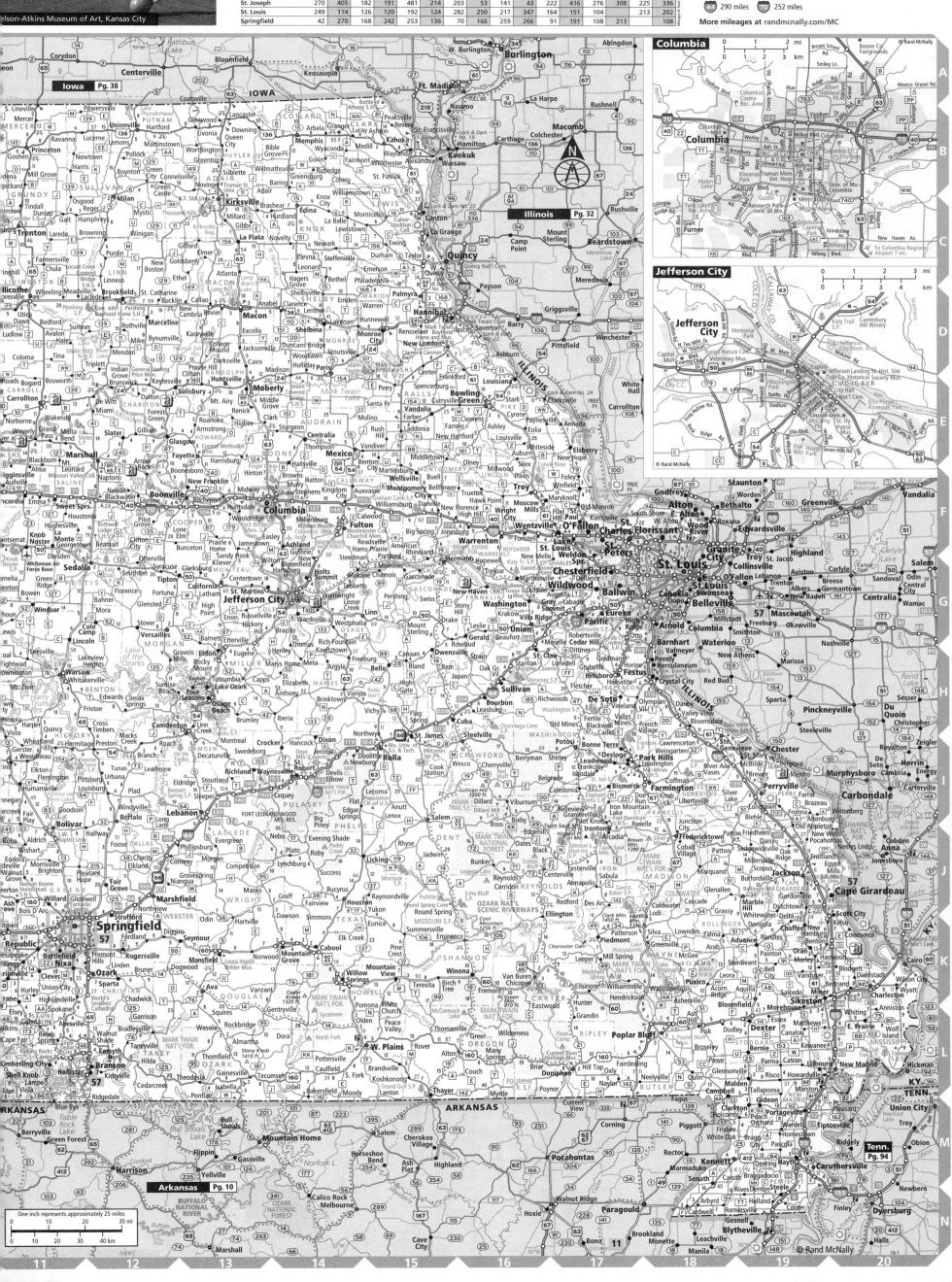

Nickname: The Treasure State
Capital: Helena, G-7
Land area: 145,546 sq. mi. (rank: 4th)
Population: 989,415 (rank: 44th)
Largest city: Billings, 104,170, I-13

Index of places Pg. 132

Travel planning & on-the-road resources

Tourism Information
Montana Office of Tourism: (800) 847-4868; www.visitmt.com

Road Conditions & Construction
511, (800) 226-7623, (406) 444-6200; www.mdt511.com, www.mdt.mt.gov

Toll Road Information
No toll roads

Determining distances along roads
Highway distances (segments of one mile or less not shown):
Cumulative miles (red): the distance between red arrows
Intermediate miles (black): the distance between intersections & place

Interchanges and exit numbers
For most states, the mileage between interchanges may be determined
by subtracting one number from the other.

Waterton-Glacier
Int'l Peace Park

Helena

One inch represents approximately 30 miles

St. Mary Lake in Glacier N.P.

Mileages between cities

	Belle Fourche, SD	Billings	Bozeman	Butte	Dillon	Glasgow	Great Falls	Havre	Kalispell	Lewistown	Libby	Miles City	Missoula	St. Mary	West Yellowstone	Sidney
Billings	261		143	223	256	276	218	247	451	125	536	144	343	375	269	232
Butte	486	223	82		54	425	154	267	224	244	309	367	120	269	494	149
Great Falls	481	218	186	154	219	271		113	224	106	312	317	166	158	375	264
Helena	500	238	98	66	132	360	90	202	193	193	281	383	113	205	463	177
Kalispell	711	451	308	224	278	419	224	261		330	88	593	121	82	558	371
Miles City	174	144	285	367	399	195	317	333	593	211	678		487	473	126	375
Missoula	606	343	202	120	172	437	166	280	121	272	191	487		203	614	267
Sidney	298	269	411	494	524	140	375	298	558	270	646	126	614	490	501	

Total mileages through Montana
- 15   396 miles
- 94   249 miles
- 90   552 miles

More mileages at randmcnally.com/MC

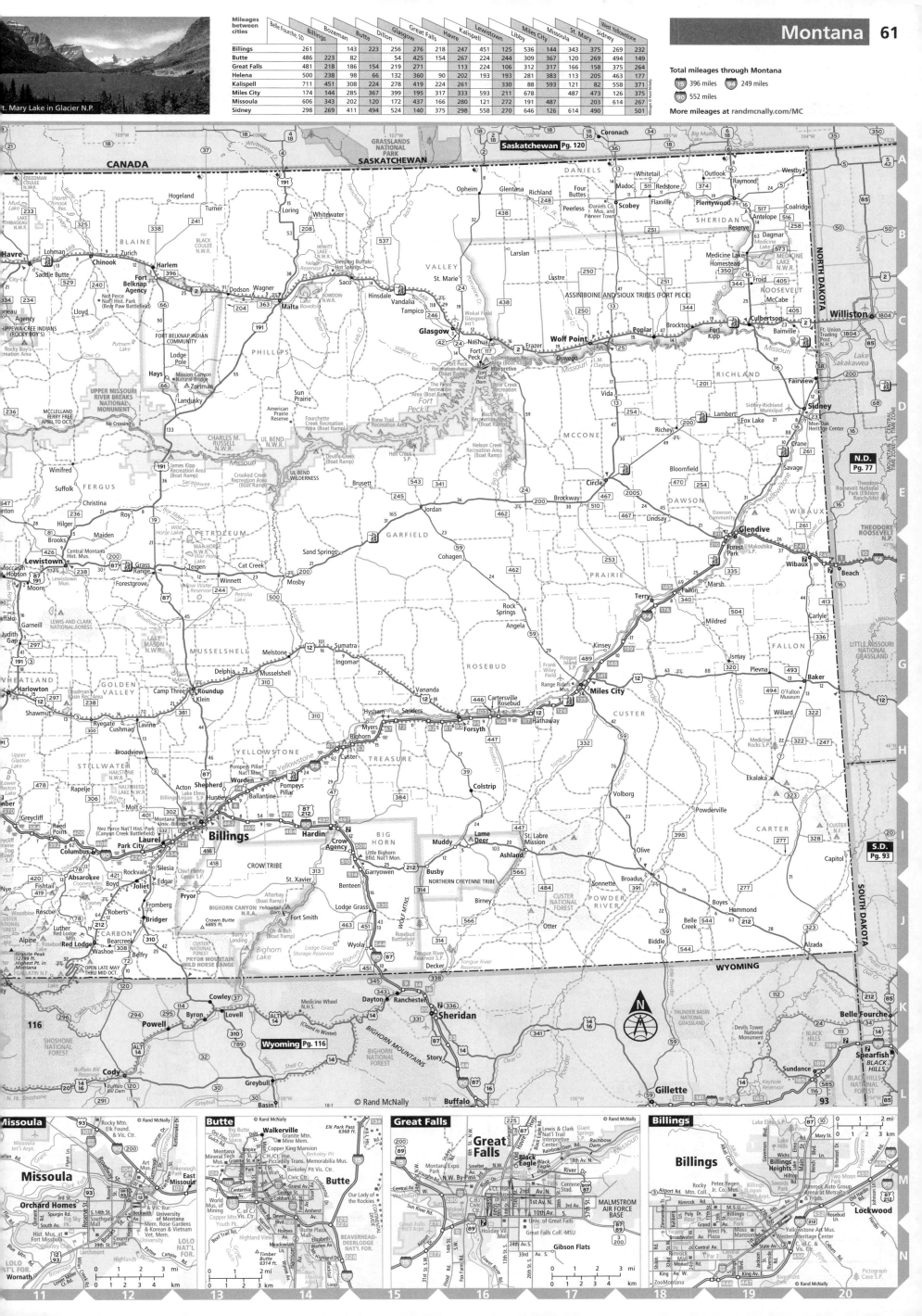

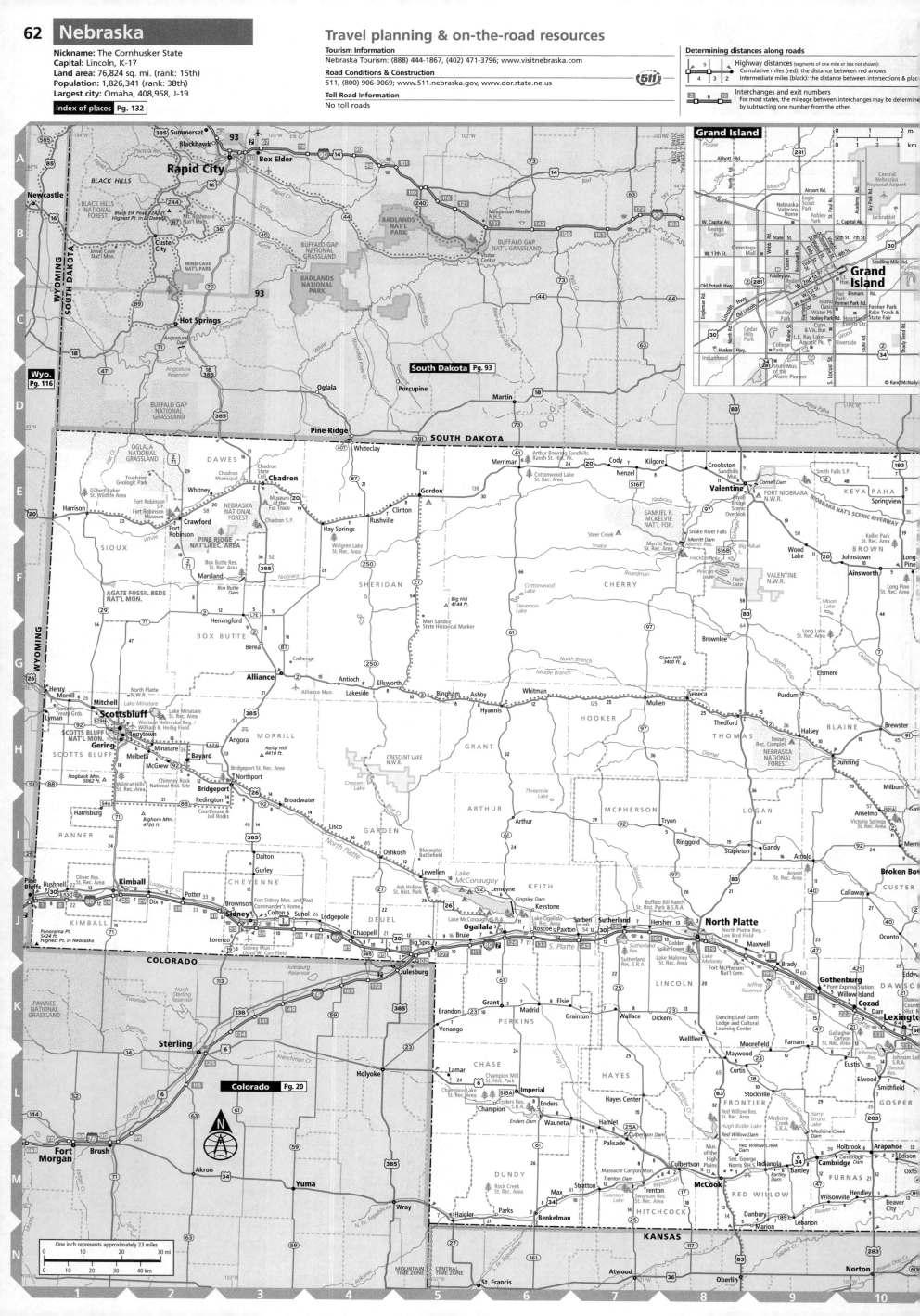

62 Nebraska

Nickname: The Cornhusker State
Capital: Lincoln, K-17
Land area: 76,824 sq. mi. (rank: 15th)
Population: 1,826,341 (rank: 38th)
Largest city: Omaha, 408,958, J-19

Index of places Pg. 132

Travel planning & on-the-road resources

Tourism Information
Nebraska Tourism: (888) 444-1867, (402) 471-3796; www.visitnebraska.com

Road Conditions & Construction
511, (800) 906-9069; www.511.nebraska.gov, www.dor.state.ne.us

Toll Road Information
No toll roads

Determining distances along roads
Highway distances (segments of one mile or less not shown):
Cumulative miles (red): the distance between arrows
Intermediate miles (black): the distance between intersections & places

Interchanges and exit numbers
For most states, the mileage between interchanges may be determined by subtracting one number from the other.

© Rand McNally

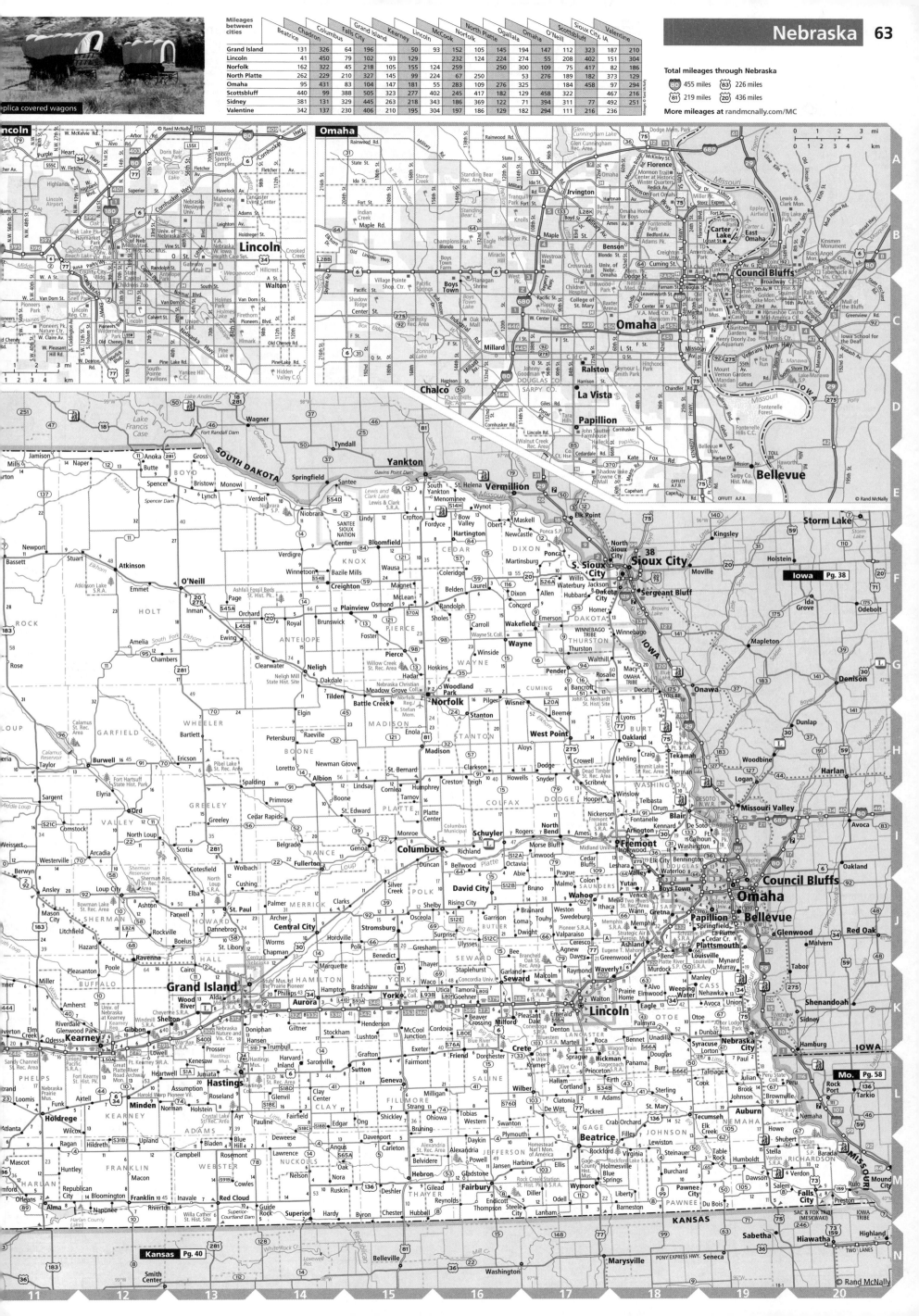

Replica covered wagons

Mileages between cities	Beatrice	Chadron	Columbus	Falls City	Grand Island	Kearney	Lincoln	McCook	Norfolk	North Platte	Ogallala	Omaha	O'Neill	Scottsbluff	Sioux City, IA	Valentine
Grand Island	131	326	64	196		50	93	152	105	145	194	147	112	323	187	210
Lincoln	41	450	79	102	93	129		232	124	224	274	55	208	402	151	304
Norfolk	162	322	45	218	105	155	124	259		250	300	109	75	417	82	186
North Platte	262	229	210	327	145	99	224	67	250		53	276	189	182	373	129
Omaha	95	431	83	104	141	181	55	283	109	276	325		184	458	97	294
Scottsbluff	440	99	388	505	323	277	402	245	417	182	129	458	322		467	216
Sidney	381	131	329	445	263	218	343	186	369	122	77	394	311	77	492	251
Valentine	342	137	230	406	210	195	304	197	186	129	182	294	111	216	236	

Total mileages through Nebraska

80 455 miles 83 226 miles
81 219 miles 436 miles

More mileages at randmcnally.com/MC

© Rand McNally

Nickname: The Silver State
Capital: Carson City, F-2
Land area: 109,781 sq. mi. (rank: 7th)
Population: 2,700,551 (rank: 35th)
Largest city: Las Vegas, 583,756, L-8

Index of places Pg. 132

Travel planning & on-the-road resources

Tourism Information
Nevada Commission on Tourism:
(800) 638-2328, (775) 687-4322; www.travelnevada.com
Road Conditions & Construction
511, (877) 687-6237, (775) 888-7000;
www.nevadadot.com, www.nvroads.com
Toll Road Information
No toll roads

Determining Distance
Cumulative miles (red): the distance between red and
Intermediate miles (black): the distance between intersections & places

Mileages between cities	Carson City	Elko	Ely	Jackpot	Las Vegas	Reno	Tonopah	Winnemucca
Elko	304		188	117	429	288	252	125
Ely	319	188		205	241	319	167	271
Las Vegas	435	429	241	446		447	210	472
Reno	32	288	319	405	447		237	163
S. Lake Tahoe, CA	27	332	347	450	451	60	237	163
Tonopah	225	252	167	373	210	237		261
West Wendover	414	120	120	125	361	397	288	232
Winnemucca	179	125	271	240	472	163	261	

Total mileages through Nevada
15: 124 miles 6: 307 miles
80: 411 miles 95: 652 miles

More mileages at randmcnally.com/MC

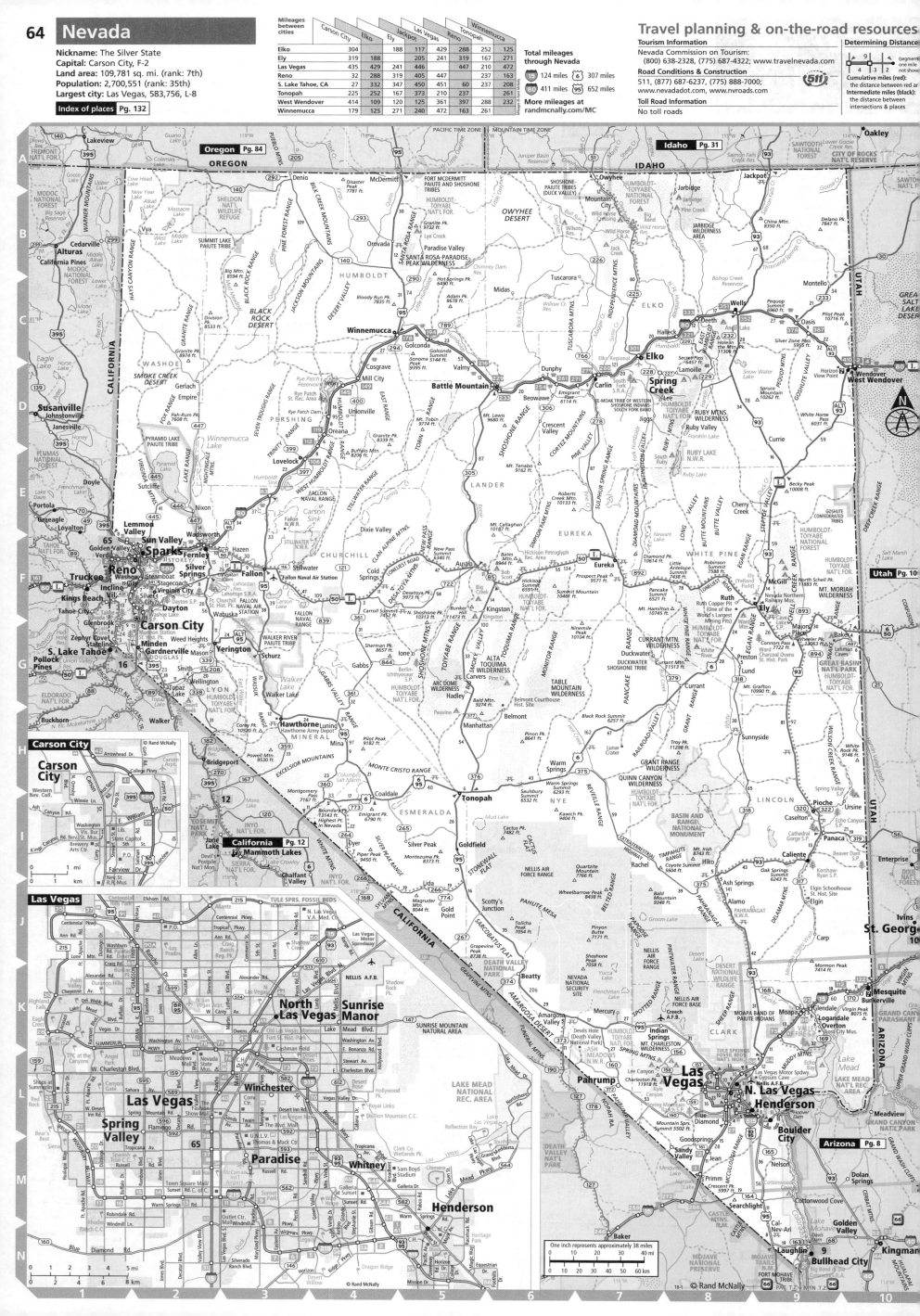

Travel planning & on-the-road resources

Tourism Information
New Hampshire Division of Travel & Tourism:
(603) 271-2665; www.visitnh.com

Road Conditions & Construction
(603) 485-3806; www.nhtmc.com, www.nh.gov/dot

Road Information
Bureau of Turnpikes: (603) 485-3806;
www.nh.gov/dot/org/operations/turnpikes

511
(E-ZPass)

Total mileages through New Hampshire

| 89 | 61 miles | 95 | 16 miles |
| 93 | 132 miles | 2 | 36 miles |

More mileages at randmcnally.com/MC

Mileages between cities

	Colebrook	Concord	Conway	Keene	Laconia	Littleton	Nashua	Portsmouth
Berlin	49	115	40	168	97	42	151	117
Concord	137		77	51	27	87	36	44
Conway	181	51		130	80	136	50	99
Lebanon	128	57	88	64	58	82	89	111
Littleton	56	87	54	136	66		121	129
Manchester	155	18	95	55	45	105	18	43
Nashua	172	36	113	50	63	121		54
Portsmouth	180	44	77	99	57	129	54	

New Hampshire 65

Nickname: The Granite State
Capital: Concord, K-7
Land area: 8,953 sq. mi. (rank: 44th)
Population: 1,316,470 (rank: 42nd)
Largest city: Manchester, 109,565, L-7

Index of places Pg. 132

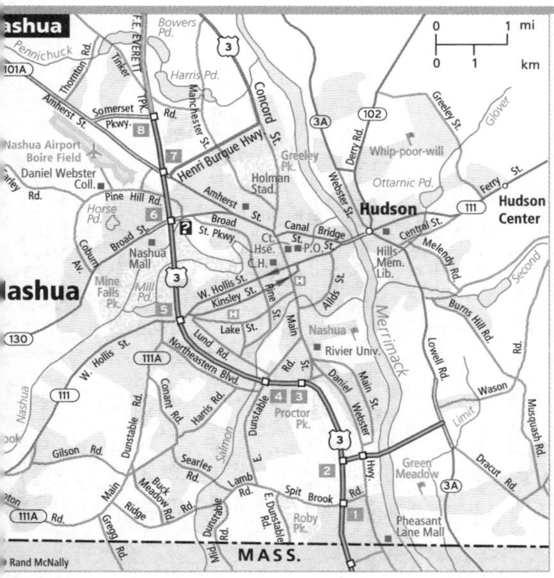

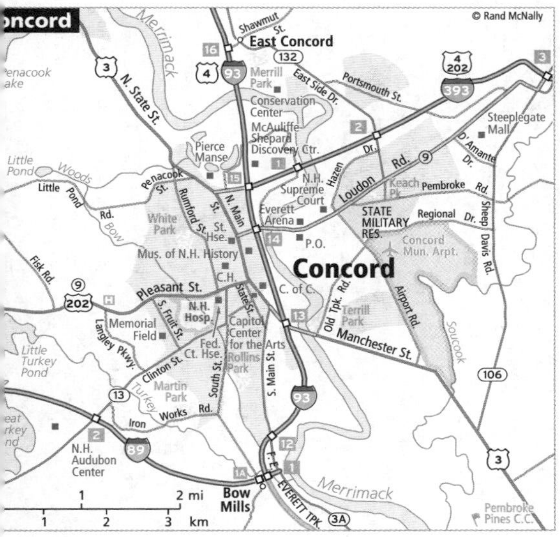

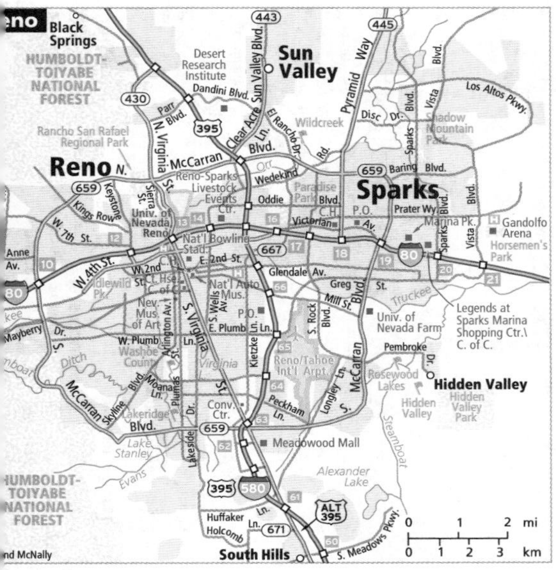

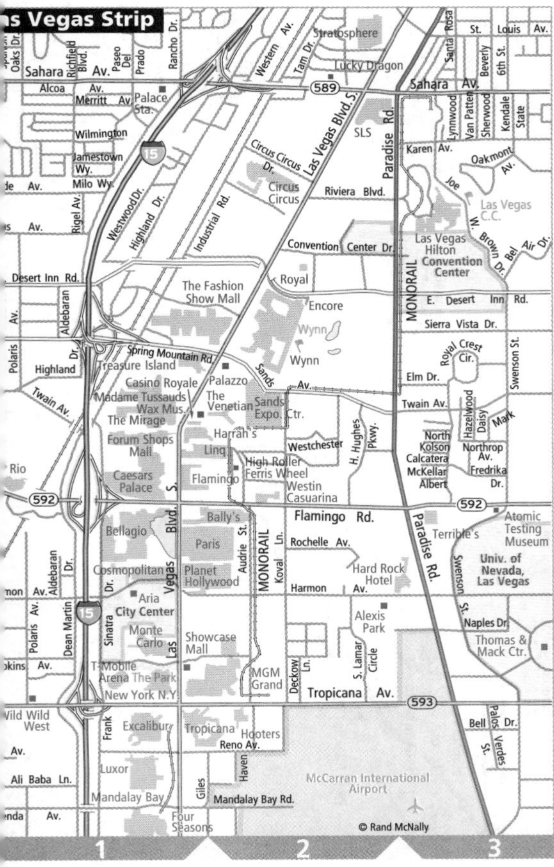

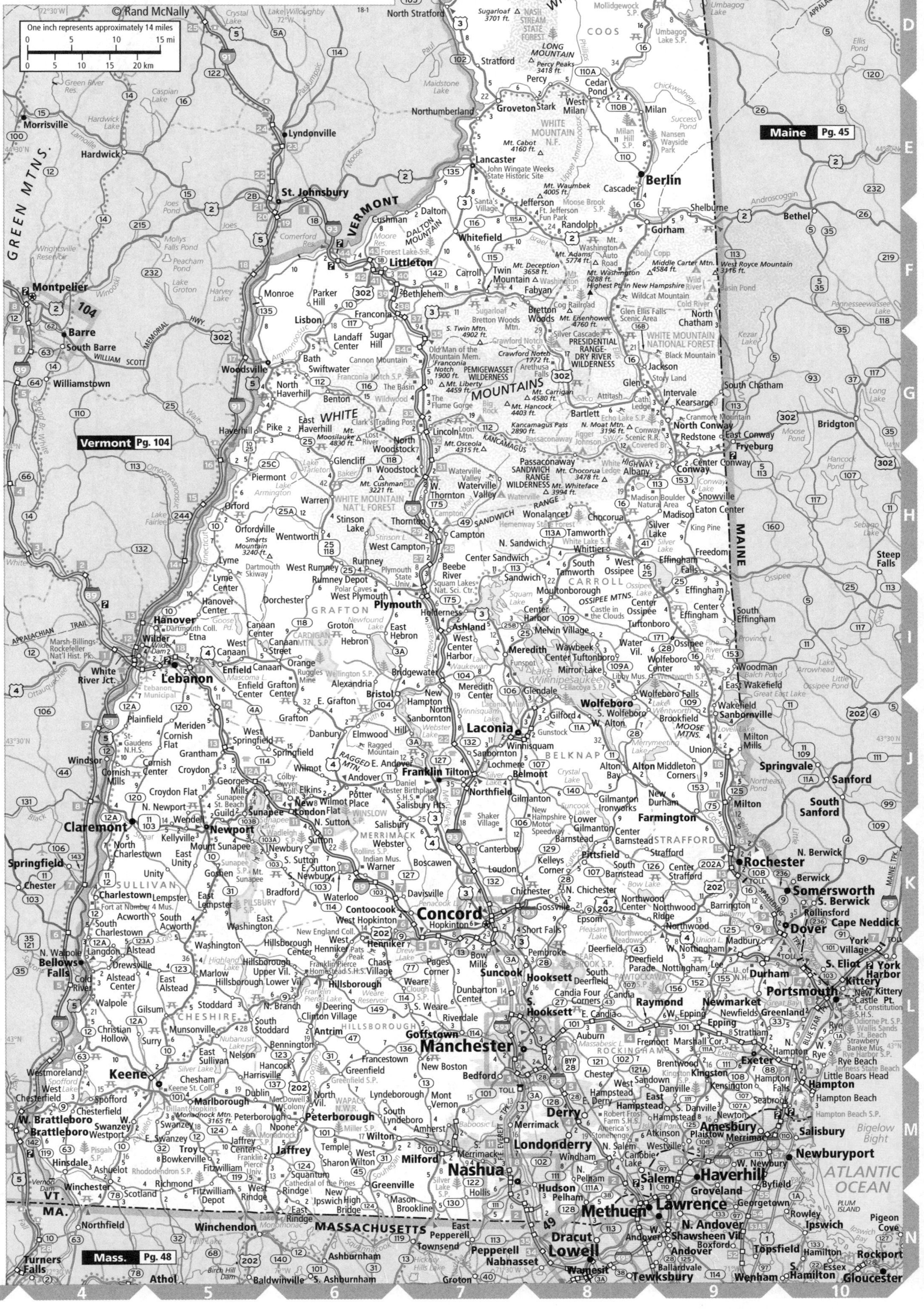

© Rand McNally

One inch represents approximately 14 miles

Québec Pg. 124

Maine Pg. 45

Vermont Pg. 104

Mass. Pg. 48

Nickname: The Garden State
Capital: Trenton, J-8
Land area: 7,354 sq. mi. (rank: 46th)
Population: 8,791,894 (rank: 11th)
Largest city: Newark, 277,140, F-12

Index of places Pg. 132

Travel planning & on-the-road resources

Tourism Information
New Jersey Travel & Tourism: (609) 599-6540; www.visitnj.org

Toll Road Information: *(all use E-ZPass)*
New Jersey Turnpike Authority (N.J. Turnpike, Garden St. Pkwy.):
(732) 750-5300; www.state.nj.us/turnpike
South Jersey Transportation Authority (Atlantic City Expressway):
(609) 965-6060; www.sjta.com

Road Conditions & Construction
511, (866) 511-6538; www.511nj.org, www.state.nj.us/transportation

Toll Bridge/Tunnel Information: *(all use E-ZPass)*
Burlington County Bridge Commission: (856) 829-1900, (609) 387-1480; www.bcbridges.org
Del. River & Bay Auth. (Del. Mem. Br., Cape May/Lewes Fy.): (302) 571-6300; www.drba.net
Del. River Port Auth. (Philadelphia area bridges): (877) 567-3772, (856) 968-2000; www.drpa.org
Del. River Joint Toll Br. Commission (other Del. River bridges): (800) 363-0049; www.drjtbc.org
Port Auth. of N.Y. & N.J. (NYC area inter-state bridges & tunnels): (800) 221-9903; www.panynj.gov

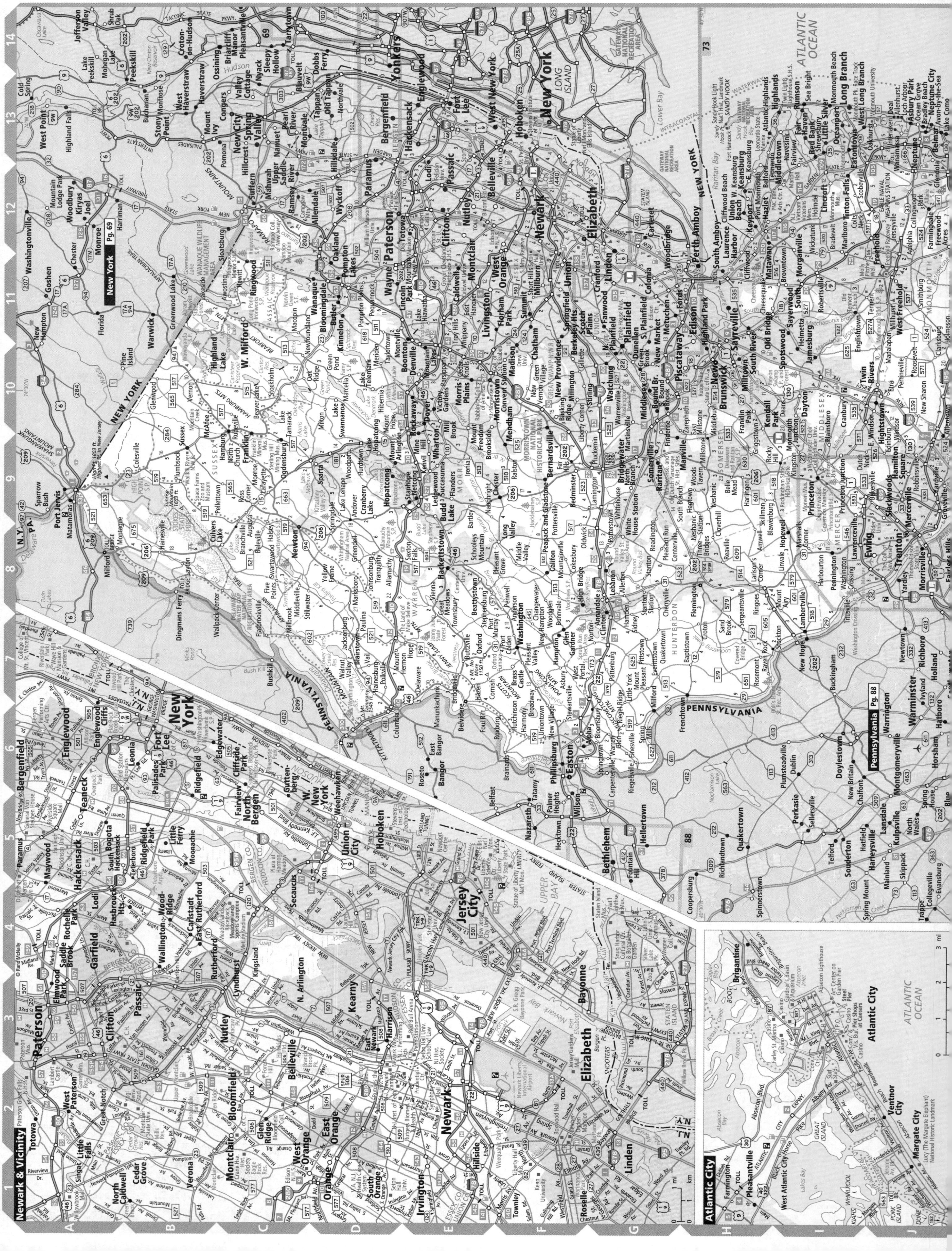

511

Pennsylvania Pg. 88
New York Pg. 69

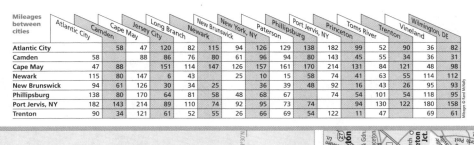

...ardwalk at Atlantic City

Mileages between cities	Atlantic City	Camden	Cape May	Jersey City	Long Branch	Newark	New Brunswick	New York, NY	Paterson	Phillipsburg	Port Jervis, NY	Princeton	Toms River	Trenton	Vineland	Wilmington, DE
Atlantic City		58	47	120	82	115	94	126	129	138	182	99	52	90	36	82
Camden	58		88	86	76	80	61	96	94	80	143	45	55	34	36	31
Cape May	47	88		151	114	147	126	157	161	170	214	131	84	121	48	98
Newark	115	80	147		6	43	25	10	15	58	74	41	63	55	114	112
New Brunswick	94	61	126	30	34	25		36	39	48	92	16	43	26	95	93
Phillipsburg	138	80	170	64	81	58	48	68	67		74	74	101	54	118	95
Port Jervis, NY	182	143	214	89	110	74	92	95	73	74		94	130	122	180	158
Trenton	90	34	121	61	52	55	26	66	69	54	122		11	47	69	61

Total mileages through New Jersey

78 68 miles   95 98 miles

80 68 miles

More mileages at randmcnally.com/MC

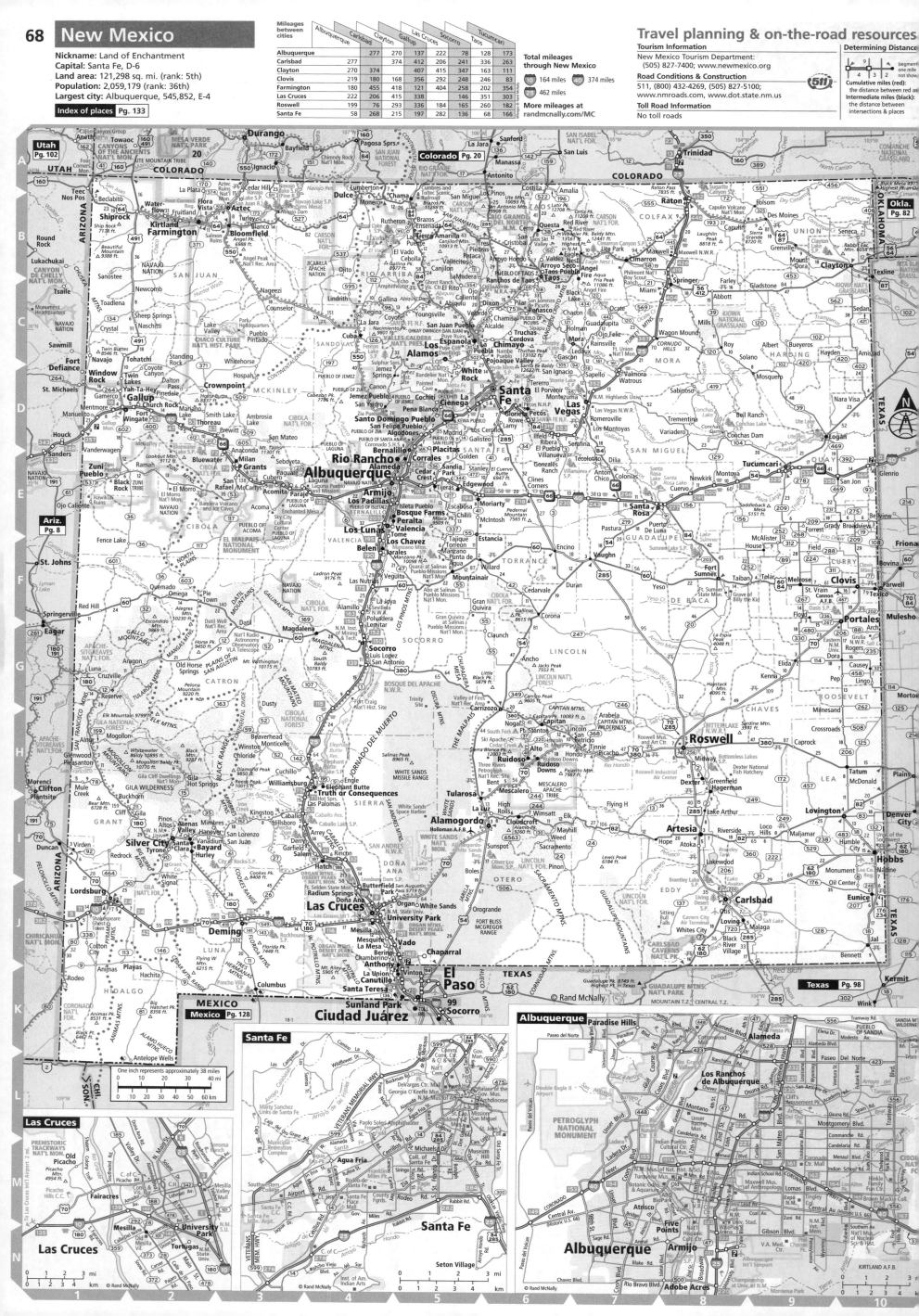

Nickname: Land of Enchantment
Capital: Santa Fe, D-6
Land area: 121,298 sq. mi. (rank: 5th)
Population: 2,059,179 (rank: 36th)
Largest city: Albuquerque, 545,852, E-4

Index of places Pg. 133

Mileages between cities	Albuquerque	Carlsbad	Clayton	Gallup	Las Cruces	Socorro	Taos	Tucumcari
Albuquerque		277	270	137	222	78	128	173
Carlsbad	277		374	412	206	241	336	263
Clayton	270	374		407	415	347	163	111
Clovis	219	180	168	356	292	246	246	83
Farmington	180	455	418	121	404	258	202	354
Las Cruces	222	206	415	338		146	351	303
Roswell	199	76	293	336	184	165	260	182
Santa Fe	58	268	215	197	282	136	68	166

Total mileages through New Mexico
10 164 miles   40 374 miles
25 462 miles
More mileages at randmcnally.com/MC

Travel planning & on-the-road resources

Tourism Information
New Mexico Tourism Department:
(505) 827-7400; www.newmexico.org

Road Conditions & Construction
511, (800) 432-4269, (505) 827-5100;
www.nmroads.com, www.dot.state.nm.us

Toll Road Information
No toll roads

Determining Distance
Cumulative miles (red): the distance between red and intermediate miles (black): the distance between intersections & places

ravel planning & on-the-road resources

rism Information
. State Division of Tourism:
00) 225-5697; www.iloveny.com

ad Conditions & Construction
(888) 465-1169;
www.511ny.org, www.dot.ny.gov
uway: (800) 847-8929; www.thruway.ny.gov

511

Toll Road Info
see next page for listings

Determining Distances

Cumulative miles (red):
the distance between red arrows
Intermediate miles (black):
the distance between intersections & places

Total mileages through New York

| 84 72 miles | 95 24 miles |
| 87 334 miles | 495 66 miles |

More mileages at randmcnally.com/MC

Mileages between cities	Albany	Buffalo	Hempstead	Newburgh	New York	Poughkeepsie	Riverhead	White Plains
Albany		289	167	87	156	75	219	138
Buffalo	289		423	361	395	362	471	394
Hempstead	167	423		78	12	92	59	34
Kingston	55	339	116	37	106	19	168	87
Montauk	260	513	97	172	107	184	42	126
Newburgh	87	361	78		72	19	130	49
New York	156	395	12	72		84	66	26
Poughkeepsie	75	362	92	19	84		143	60

Nickname: The Empire State
Capital: Albany, NK-19
Land area: 47,126 sq. mi. (rank: 30th)
Population: 19,378,102 (rank: 3rd)
Largest city: New York, 8,175,133, SF-6

Index of places Pg. 133

Nickname: The Empire State
Capital: Albany, NK-19
Land area: 47,126 sq. mi. (rank: 30th)
Population: 19,378,102 (rank: 3rd)
Largest city: New York, 8,175,133, SF-6

Index of places Pg. 133

Travel planning & on-the-road resources

Tourism Information
New York State Division of Tourism:
(800) 225-5697; www.iloveny.com

Road Conditions & Construction
511, (888) 465-1169;
www.511ny.org, www.dot.ny.gov
Thruway: (800) 847-8929; www.thruway.ny.gov

Toll Road Information: (all use E-ZPass)
MTA (N.Y. City in-state bridges & tunnels):
(877) 690-5116, N.Y. only: 511 and say "Bridges & tunnels";
www.mta.info/bandt
New York State Bridge Authority (Hudson River bridges):
(845) 691-7245; www.nysba.state.ny.us
New York State Thruway Authority:
(518) 436-2805; www.thruway.ny.gov

International Toll Bridge Information:
Buffalo & Ft. Erie Public Br. Auth. (Peace Br.) (E-ZPass):
(716) 884-6744; www.peacebridge.com
Niagara Falls Bridge Comm. (E-ZPass or ExpressPass):
(716) 285-6322; www.niagarafallsbridges.com
Ogdensburg Br. & Port Auth.: (315) 393-4080; www.ogdensport.com
Seaway Int'l Bridge Corp. (Seaway Transit Card): (613) 932-6601; www.sib
Thousand Islands Br. Auth. (Alexandria Bay): (315) 482-2501; www.tibridge

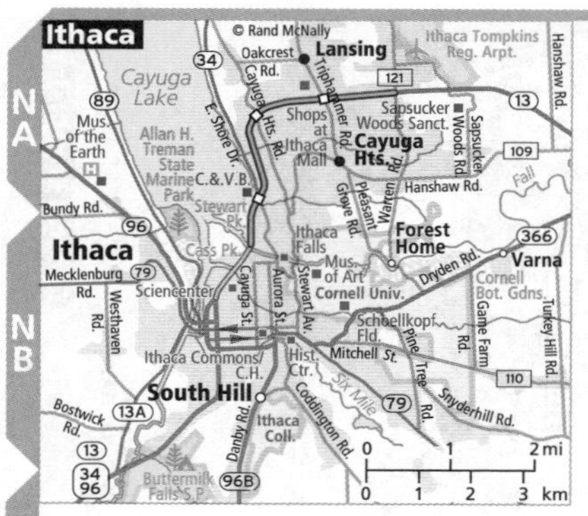

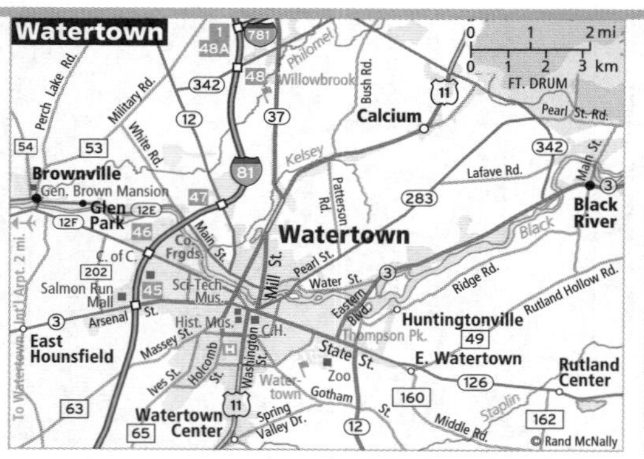

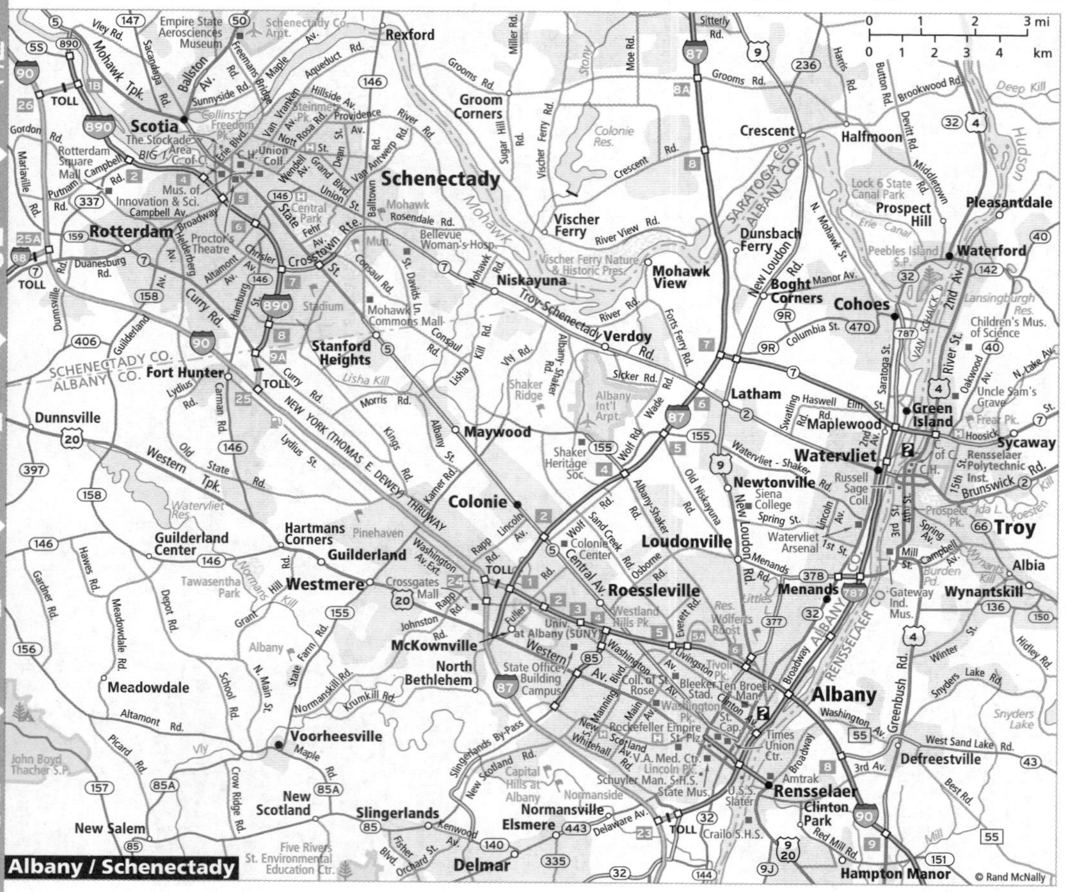

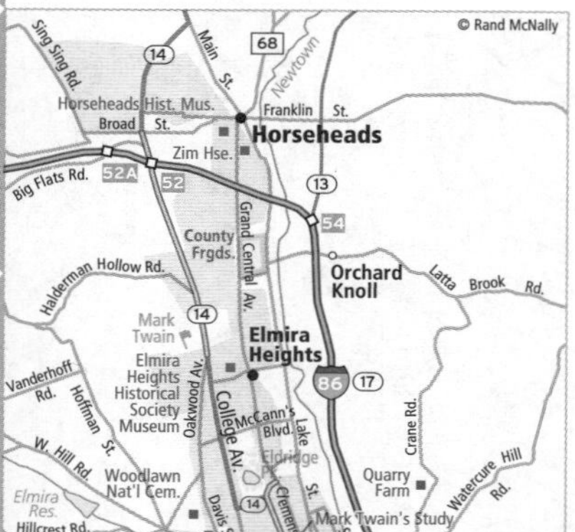

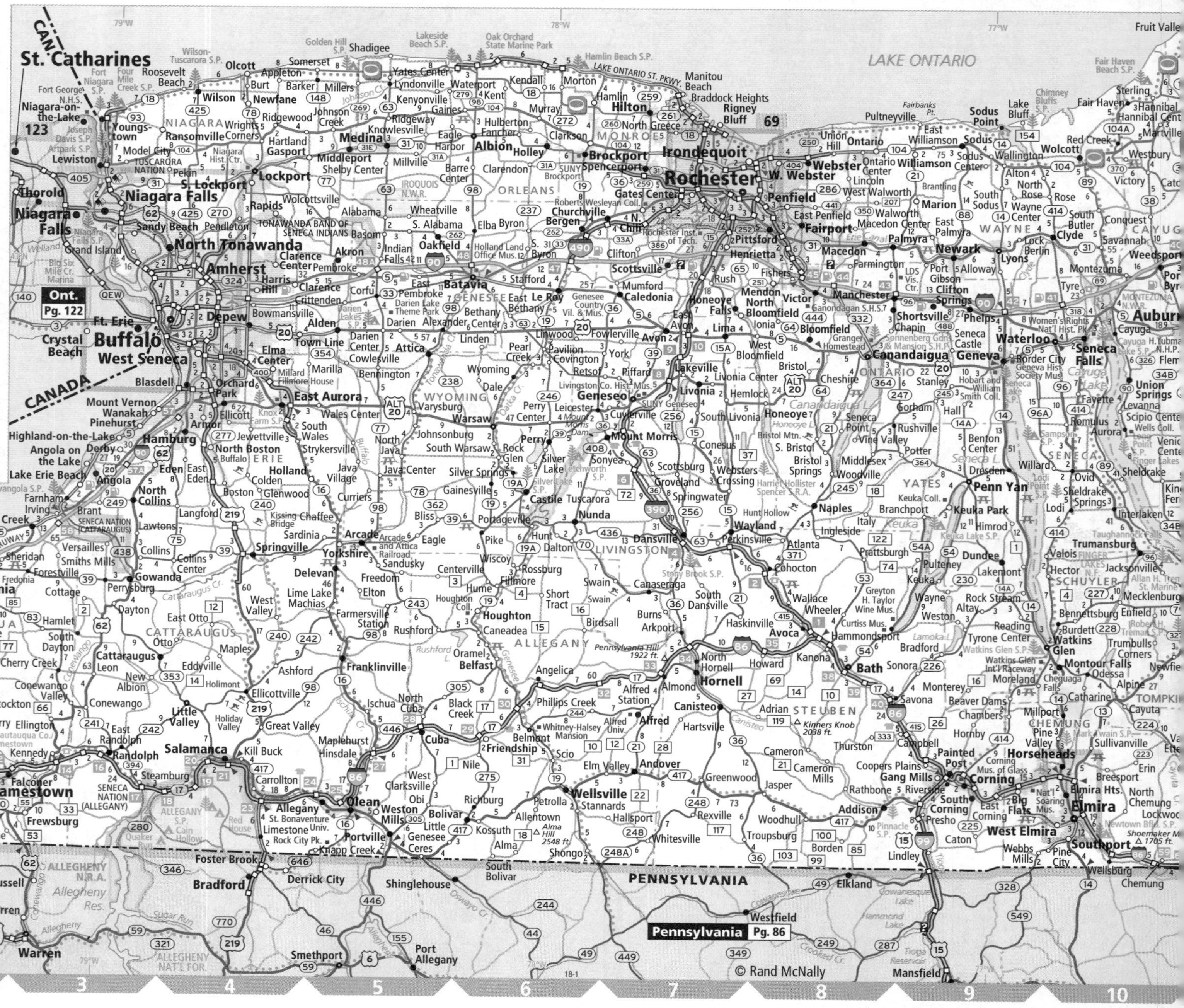

Ithaca

Watertown

Buffalo / Niagara Falls

Albany / Schenectady

Elmira

© Rand McNally

Niagara Falls

Mileages between cities

	Albany	Binghamton	Buffalo	Elmira	Glens Falls	Jamestown	Kingston	Lake Placid	Massena	New York	Niagara Falls	Plattsburgh	Rochester	Syracuse	Utica	Watertown
Albany		140	289	195	53	356	55	140	217	156	302	160	226	145	94	175
Binghamton	140		222	56	179	218	130	266	231	176	235	287	159	73	89	143
Buffalo	289	222		148	313	71	339	337	305	395	21	373	73	150	198	212
Jamestown	356	218	71	163	395		349	404	370	392	92	436	139	214	263	278
Plattsburgh	160	287	373	342	436	214		50	82	317	384		308	227	183	165
Rochester	226	159	73	120	248	139	277	275	242	332	87	308		86	135	149
Syracuse	145	73	150	90	160	214	195	159	246	162	227	86		53	70
Watertown	175	143	212	160	278	226	125	89	316	225	165	149	70	80	

© Rand McNally

Total mileages through New York

- 81 — 184 miles
- 86 — 176 miles
- 87 — 334 miles
- 90 — 385 miles

More mileages at randmcnally.com/MC

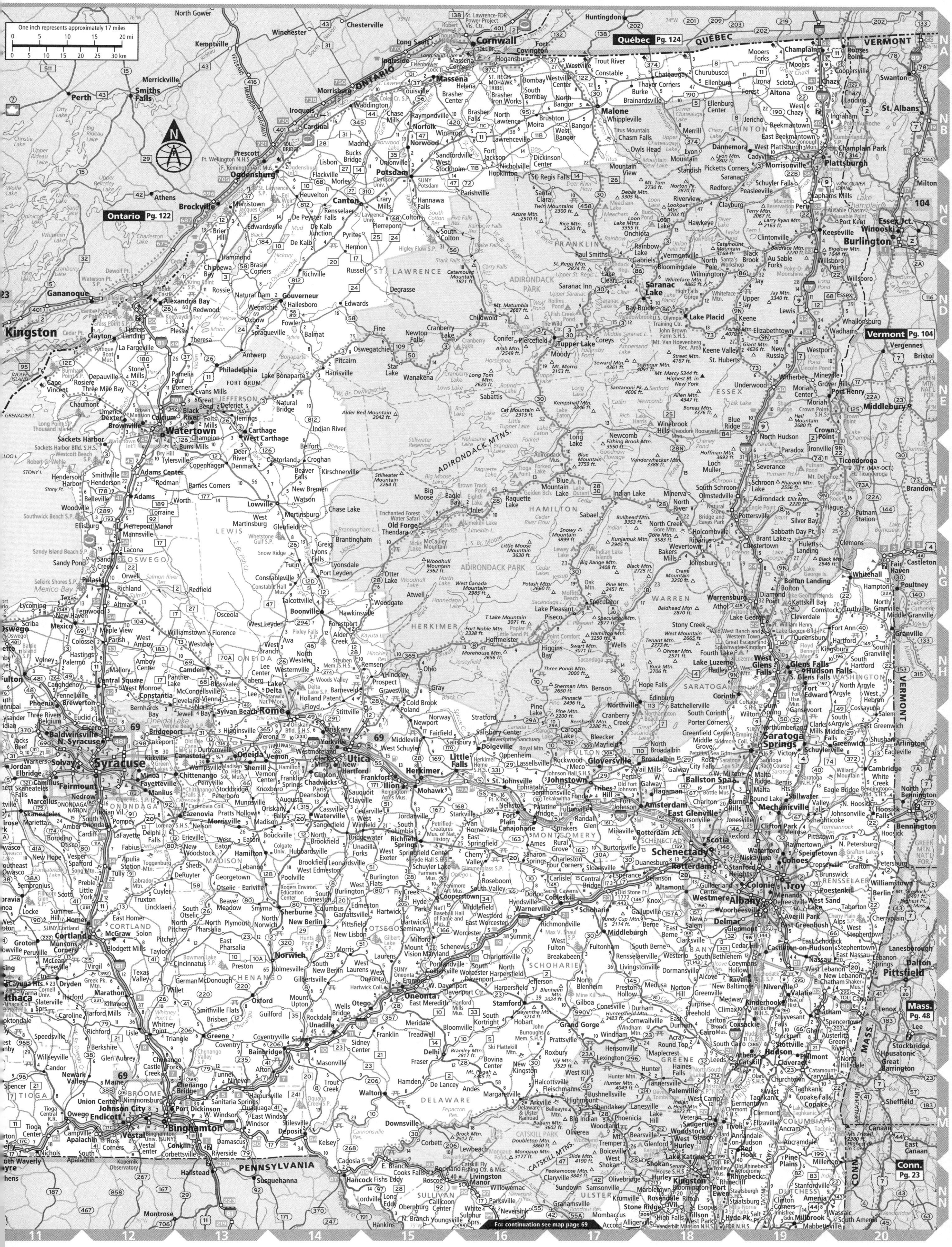

One inch represents approximately 17 miles

0 5 10 15 20 mi
0 5 10 15 20 25 30 km

Ontario Pg. 122

Québec Pg. 124

Vermont Pg. 104

Mass. Pg. 48

Conn. Pg. 23

For continuation see map page 69

Sights to see

• American Museum of Natural History A-4	• Carnegie Hall C-4	• Ellis Island I-9
• Battery Park I-1	• Central Park B-4	• Empire State Building D-3
• Bronx Zoo E-12	• Chrysler Building D-4	• Greenwich Village H-10
• Brooklyn Bridge H-2	• Coney Island L-10	• Grand Central Terminal D-4

Ellis Island Museum

Brooklyn Bridge, New York City

Sights to see

- Guggenheim Museum..........................A-5
- Intrepid Sea-Air Space Museum...............C-2
- Lincoln Center.............................B-3
- Madison Square Garden......................D-2
- Metropolitan Museum of Art.................B-5
- National September 11 Memorial.............H-1
- New York Stock Exchange and Wall Street.....H-1
- Rockefeller Center.........................C-4
- Staten Island Ferry..................I-2 and J-8
- Statue of Liberty..........................I-9
- Times Square..............................D-3
- Yankee Stadium............................E-11

ATLANTIC OCEAN

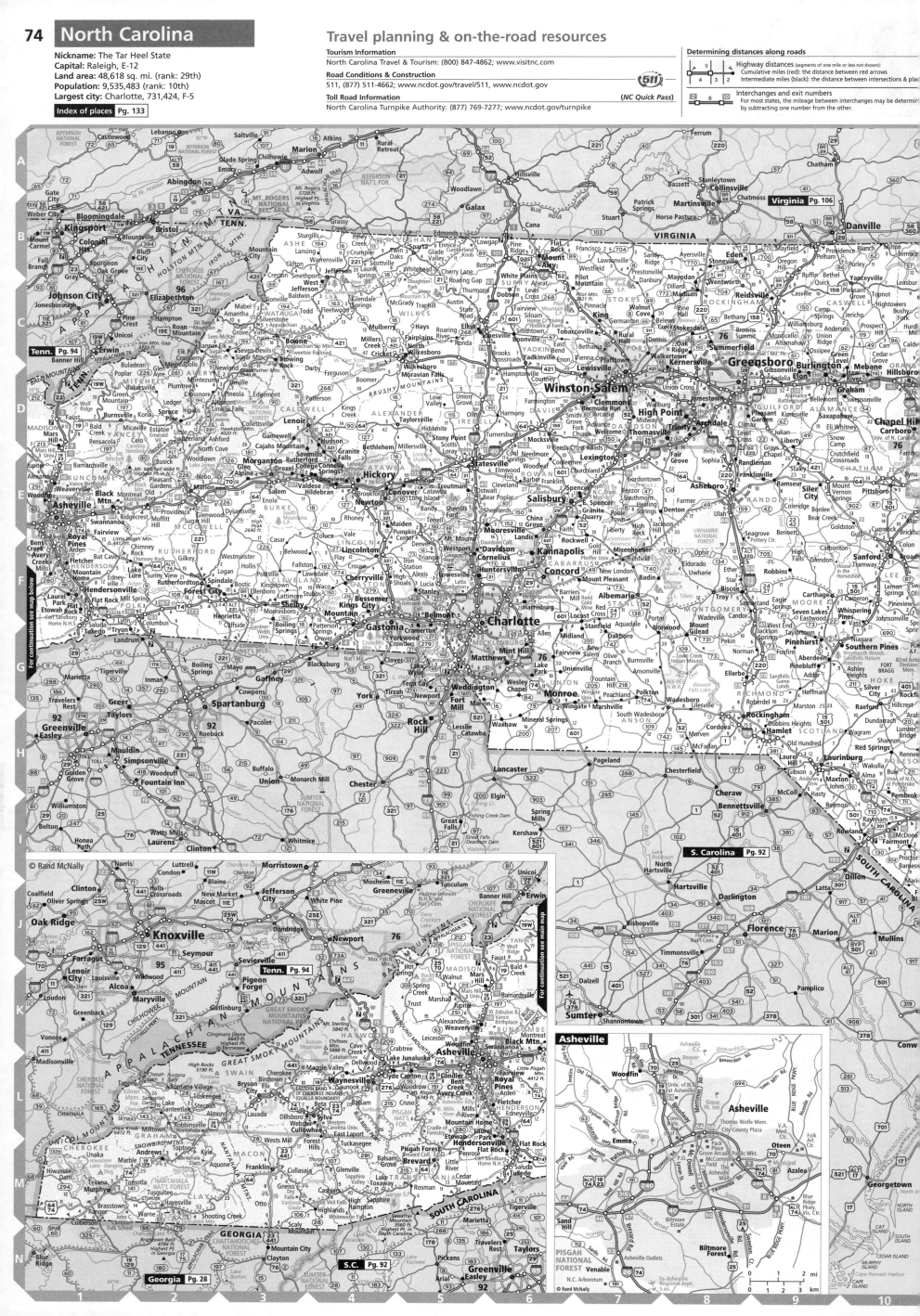

Nickname: The Tar Heel State
Capital: Raleigh, E-12
Land area: 48,618 sq. mi. (rank: 29th)
Population: 9,535,483 (rank: 10th)
Largest city: Charlotte, 731,424, F-5

Index of places Pg. 133

Travel planning & on-the-road resources

Tourism Information
North Carolina Travel & Tourism: (800) 847-4862; www.visitnc.com

Road Conditions & Construction
511, (877) 511-4662; www.ncdot.gov/travel/511, www.ncdot.gov

Toll Road Information
North Carolina Turnpike Authority: (877) 769-7277; www.ncdot.gov/turnpike

(NC Quick Pass)

Determining distances along roads
Highway distances (segments of one mile or less shown):
Cumulative miles (red): the distance between red arrows
Intermediate miles (black): the distance between intersections & pla

Interchanges and exit numbers
For most states, the mileage between interchanges may be determin
by subtracting one number from the other.

Virginia Pg. 106
Tenn. Pg. 94
S. Carolina Pg. 92
Georgia Pg. 28
S.C. Pg. 92
Tenn. Pg. 94

© Rand McNally

Asheville

Mileages between cities	Asheville	Boone	Charlotte	Durham	Elizabeth City	Greensboro	Hickory	Morehead City	Murphy	Nags Head	New Bern	Raleigh	Rockingham	Wilmington	Winston-Salem
Asheville		94	128	224	412	172	77	393	110	444	358	251	308	200	327	145
Charlotte	128	100		144	332	93	57	313	223	364	278	168	231	71	197	77
Elizabeth City	412	354	332	185		241	338	152	520	56	174	164	97	259	208	269
Fayetteville	261	202	137	89	203	94	189	138	520	369	234	130	63	127	64	89	119
Greensboro	172	113	93	53	241		97	98	223	279	271	188	80	138	93	207	29
Greenville	332	273	250	241	97	156		258	79	440	129	44	82	86	176	116	188
Raleigh	251	192	168	22	164	80	177	146	358	195	111		89	98	130	107
Wilmington	327	319	197	156	208	207	259	91	428	230	90	130	178	127		236

Total mileages through North Carolina
- (40) 419 miles
- (85) 233 miles
- (77) 102 miles
- (95) 182 miles

More mileages at randmcnally.com/MC

Linn Cove Viaduct

© Rand McNally

Sights to see

- Discovery Place, Charlotte........................H-4
- Duke Homestead State Historic Site & Tobacco Museum, Durham......................F-9
- Historic Bethabara Park, Winston-Salem...........A-1
- Mint Museum of Art, Charlotte...................H-5
- Morehead Planetarium & Science Center, Chapel Hill..H-8
- North Carolina Museum of History, Raleigh.........I-12
- North Carolina Museum of Life & Science, Durham..F-10
- North Carolina State Capitol, Raleigh.............I-13
- North Carolina State University, Raleigh...........I-13
- Old Salem, Winston-Salem......................B-2
- Reynolda House, Winston-Salem.................B-1

Old Salem, Winston-Salem

Greensboro / Winston-Salem / High Point

Raleigh / Durham / Chapel Hill

Great Smoky Mountains National Park

Charlotte & Vicinity

Travel planning & on-the-road resources

Tourism Information
North Dakota Tourism:
(800) 435-5663, (701) 328-2525; www.ndtourism.com

Road Conditions & Construction
511, (855) 637-6237;
www.dot.nd.gov, www.dot.nd.gov/travel-info-v2

Road Information
No toll roads

Determining Distances

Cumulative miles (red):
the distance between red arrows

Intermediate miles (black):
the distance between intersections & places

(segments of one mile or less not shown)

Total mileages through North Dakota

29: 218 miles	2: 359 miles
94: 352 miles	83: 265 miles

More mileages at
randmcnally.com/MC

Mileages between cities

	Bismarck	Bowman	Fargo	Garrison	Grand Forks	Jamestown	Williston	Winnipeg, MB
Bismarck		174	195	75	272	102	228	413
Devils Lake	180	354	167	89	99	245	230	
Dickinson	97	78	292	149	368	198	132	509
Fargo	195	368		266	80	94	422	222
Grand Forks	272	444	80	256		171	334	146
Minot	110	260	268	47	210	170	124	299
Wahpeton	243	416	54	315	131	142	470	273
Williston	228	170	422	144	334	293		424

Nickname: The Peace Garden State
Capital: Bismarck, H-7
Land area: 69,000 sq. mi. (rank: 17th)
Population: 672,591 (rank: 48th)
Largest city: Fargo, 105,549, H-13

Index of places Pg. 133

© Rand McNally

One inch represents approximately 30 miles

Nickname: The Buckeye State
Capital: Columbus, SB-9
Land area: 40,861 sq. mi. (rank: 35th)
Population: 11,536,504 (rank: 7th)
Largest city: Columbus, 787,033, SB-9

Index of places Pg. 133

Travel planning & on-the-road resources

Tourism Information
Tourism Ohio:
(800) 282-5393; www.discoverohio.com

Toll Road Information
Ohio Turnpike and Infrastructure Commission
(E-ZPass): (888) 876-7453, (440) 234-2081;
www.ohioturnpike.org

Road Conditions & Construction
(614) 466-7170;
www.dot.state.oh.us, www.buckeyetraffic.org;
Cincinnati metro area: 511;
www.ohgo.com/dashboard/cincinnati
Ohio Turnpike: (440) 234-2030, (440) 234-2081;
www.ohioturnpike.org

Determining distances along roads

Highway distances (segments of one mile or less not shown):
Cumulative miles (red): the distance between red arrows
Intermediate miles (black): the distance between intersections & pla

Interchanges and exit numbers
For most states, the mileage between interchanges may be determi by subtracting one number from the other.

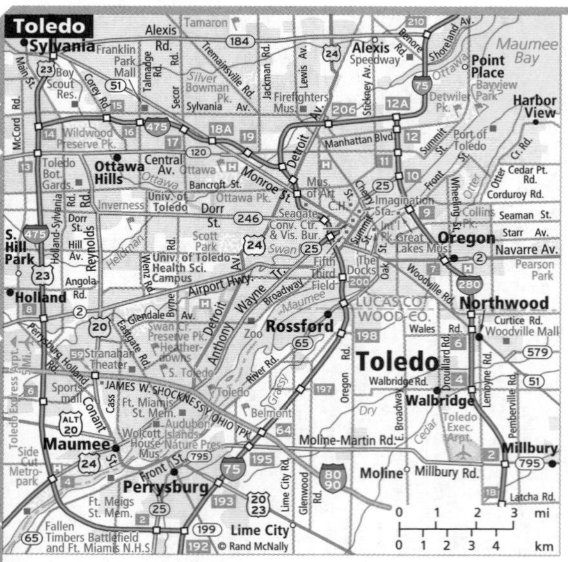

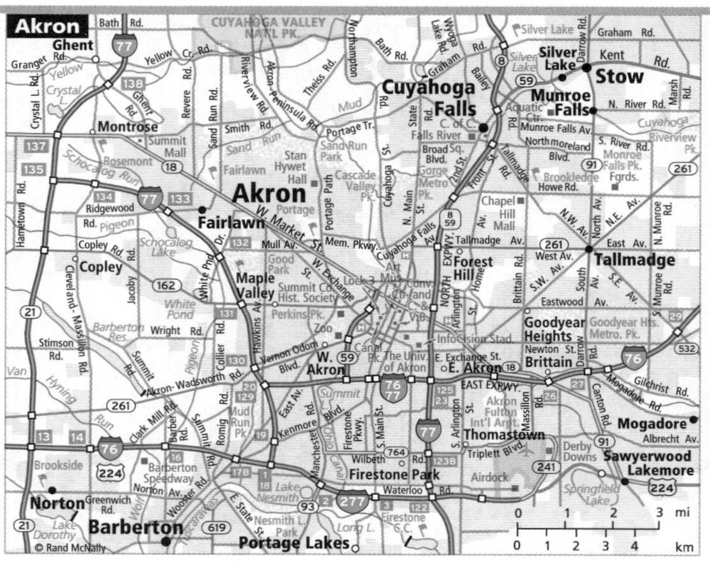

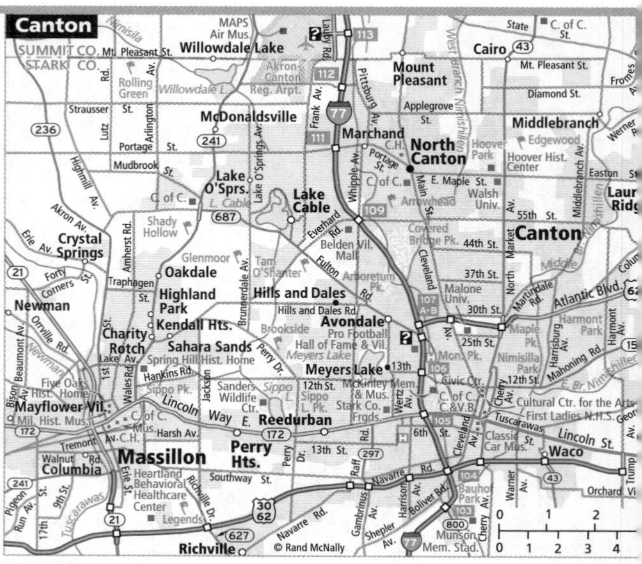

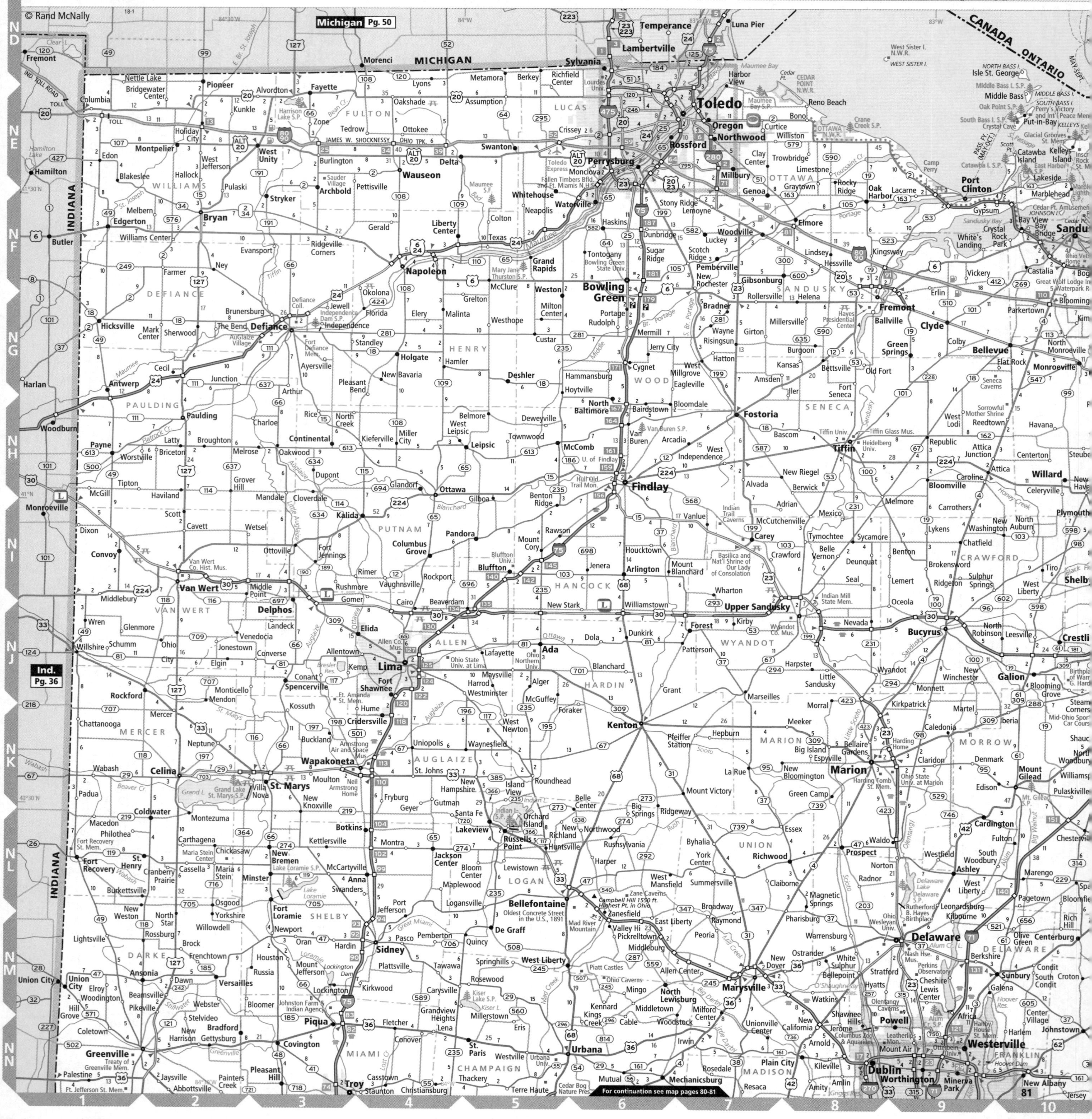

Toledo
© Rand McNally

Akron
© Rand McNally

Canton
© Rand McNally

© Rand McNally
Michigan Pg. 50
Ind. Pg. 36
For continuation see map pages 80-81
MICHIGAN
INDIANA
CANADA
ONTARIO
Toledo
Findlay
Lima
Marion
Delaware
Bowling Green
Defiance
Kenton
Sidney
Piqua
Marysville
Bellefontaine
Bucyrus
Tiffin
Fremont
Sandusky
Westerville
Dublin
Worthington

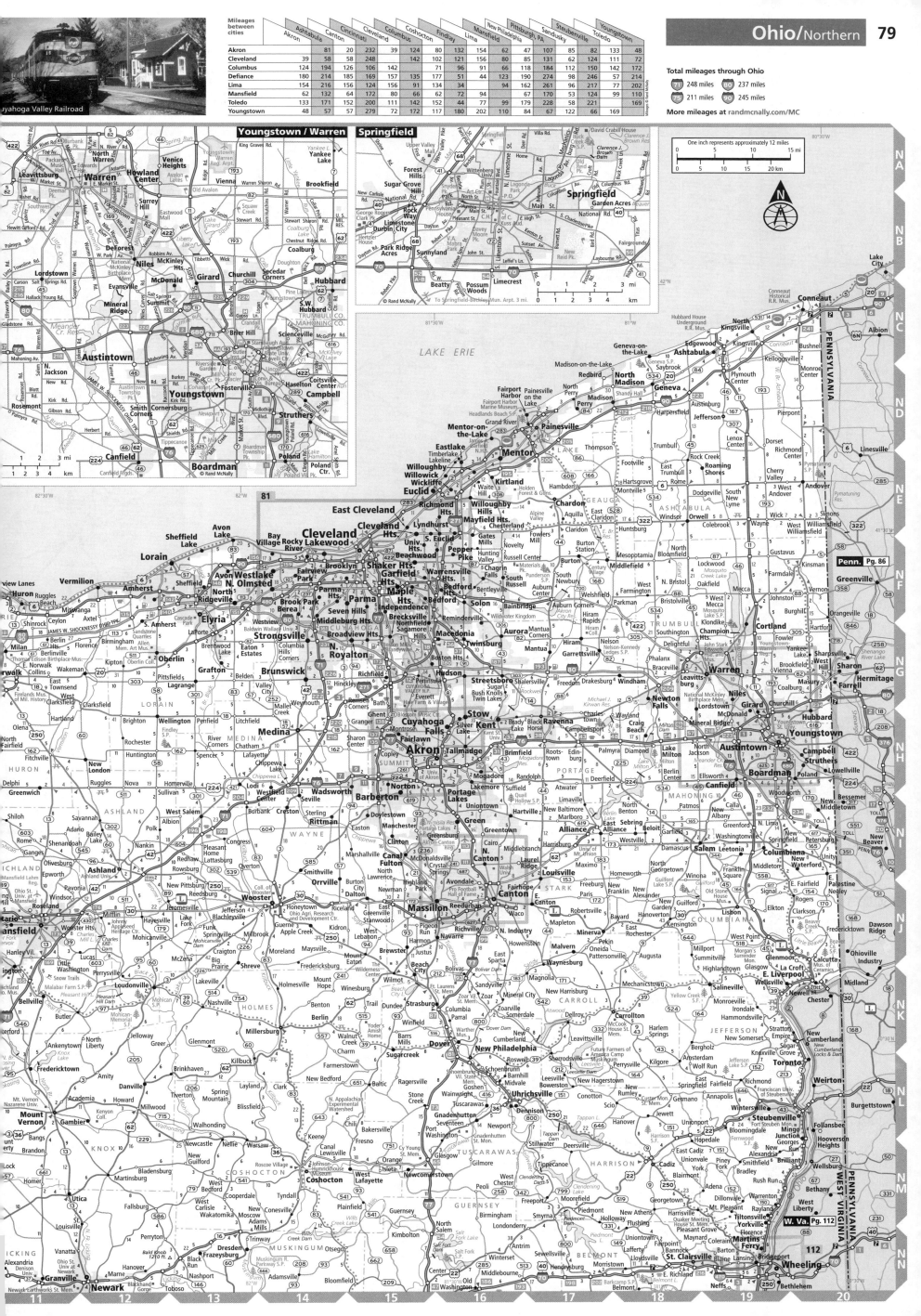

Nickname: The Buckeye State
Capital: Columbus, SB-9
Land area: 40,861 sq. mi. (rank: 35th)
Population: 11,536,504 (rank: 7th)
Largest city: Columbus, 787,033, SB-9

Index of places Pg. 133

Travel planning & on-the-road resources

Tourism Information
Tourism Ohio:
(800) 282-5393; www.discoverohio.com

Toll Road Information
Ohio Turnpike and Infrastructure Commission
(E-ZPass): (888) 876-7453, (440) 234-2081;
www.ohioturnpike.org

Road Conditions & Construction
(614) 466-7170;
www.dot.state.oh.us, www.buckeyetraffic.org;
Cincinnati metro area: 511;
www.ohgo.com/dashboard/cincinnati
Ohio Turnpike: (440) 234-2030, (440) 234-2081;
www.ohioturnpike.org

Determining distances along roads

Highway distances (segments of one mile or less not shown):
Cumulative miles (red): the distance between red arrows
Intermediate miles (black): the distance between intersections & places

Interchanges and exit numbers
For most states, the mileage between interchanges may be determined
by subtracting one number from the other.

Ind. Pg. 36

Kentucky Pg. 42

Central Cincinnati

Cincinnati

Dayton

© Rand McNally

Lebanon City Park

Mileages between cities

	Athens	Cambridge	Chillicothe	Cincinnati	Cleveland	Columbus	Dayton	Gallipolis	Huntington, WV	Lancaster	Marietta	Maysville, KY	Portsmouth	Wheeling, WV	Wilmington	Zanesville
Cincinnati	160	183	106		248	106	50	153	148	133	210	61	110	230	51	158
Columbus	74	79	47	106	142		71	106	137	30	124	112	91	126	62	55
Dayton	134	149	77	50	212	71		137	168	101	195	108	122	197	34	126
Gallipolis	42	114	60	153	235	106	137		39	86	66	111	55	162	112	94
Marietta	44	48	104	210	164	124	195	66	106	82		165	128	90	156	69
Portsmouth	81	162	44	110	233	91	122	55	46	80	128	52		201	79	138
Springfield	118	123	69	77	185	45		129	160	74	168	102	114	171	38	99
Zanesville	52	24	94	158	145	55	126	94	134	45		164	138	72	114	

Total mileages through Ohio
- 70 — 226 miles
- 75 — 211 miles
- 71 — 248 miles
- 77 — 160 miles

More mileages at randmcnally.com/MC

One inch represents approximately 12 miles

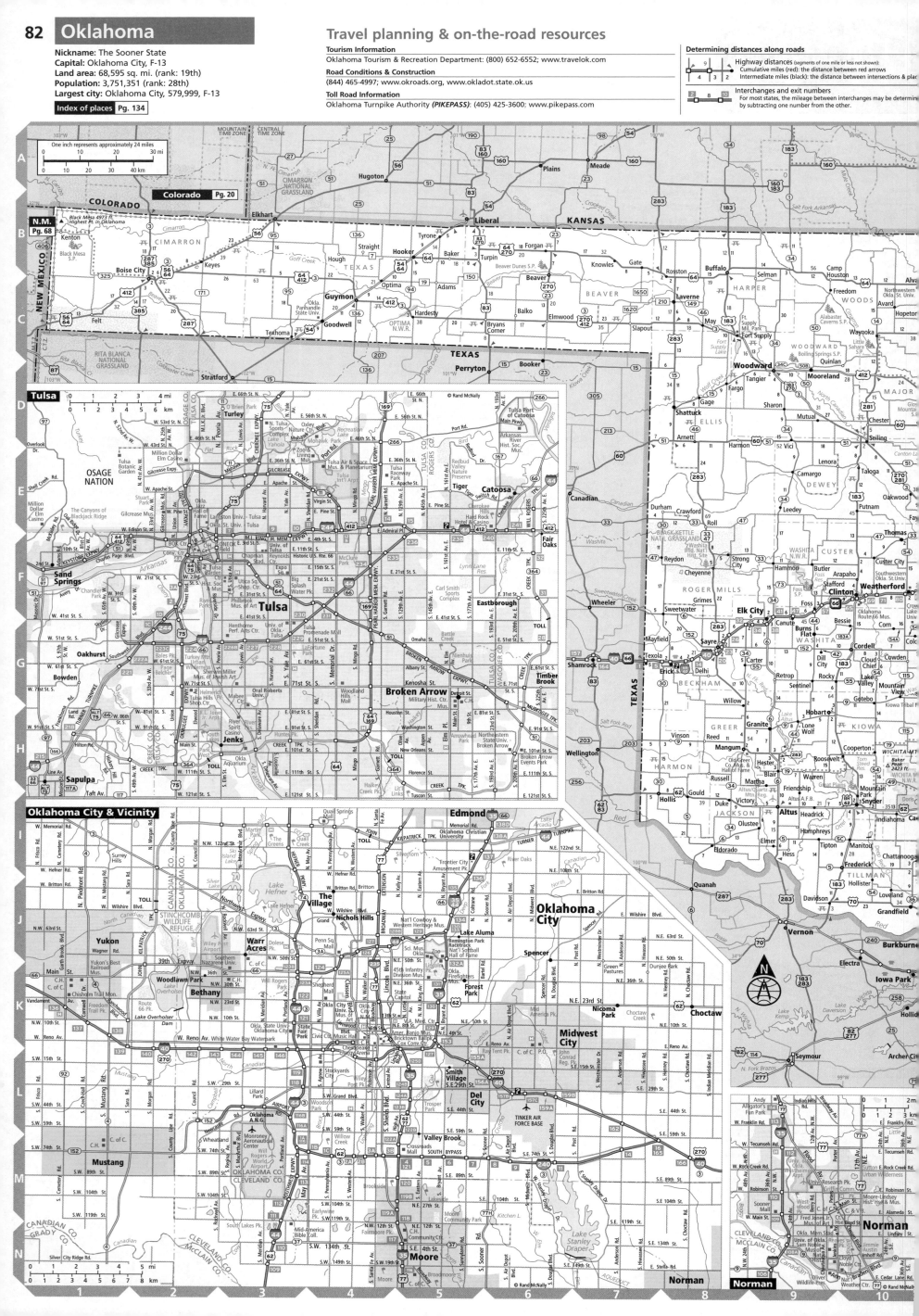

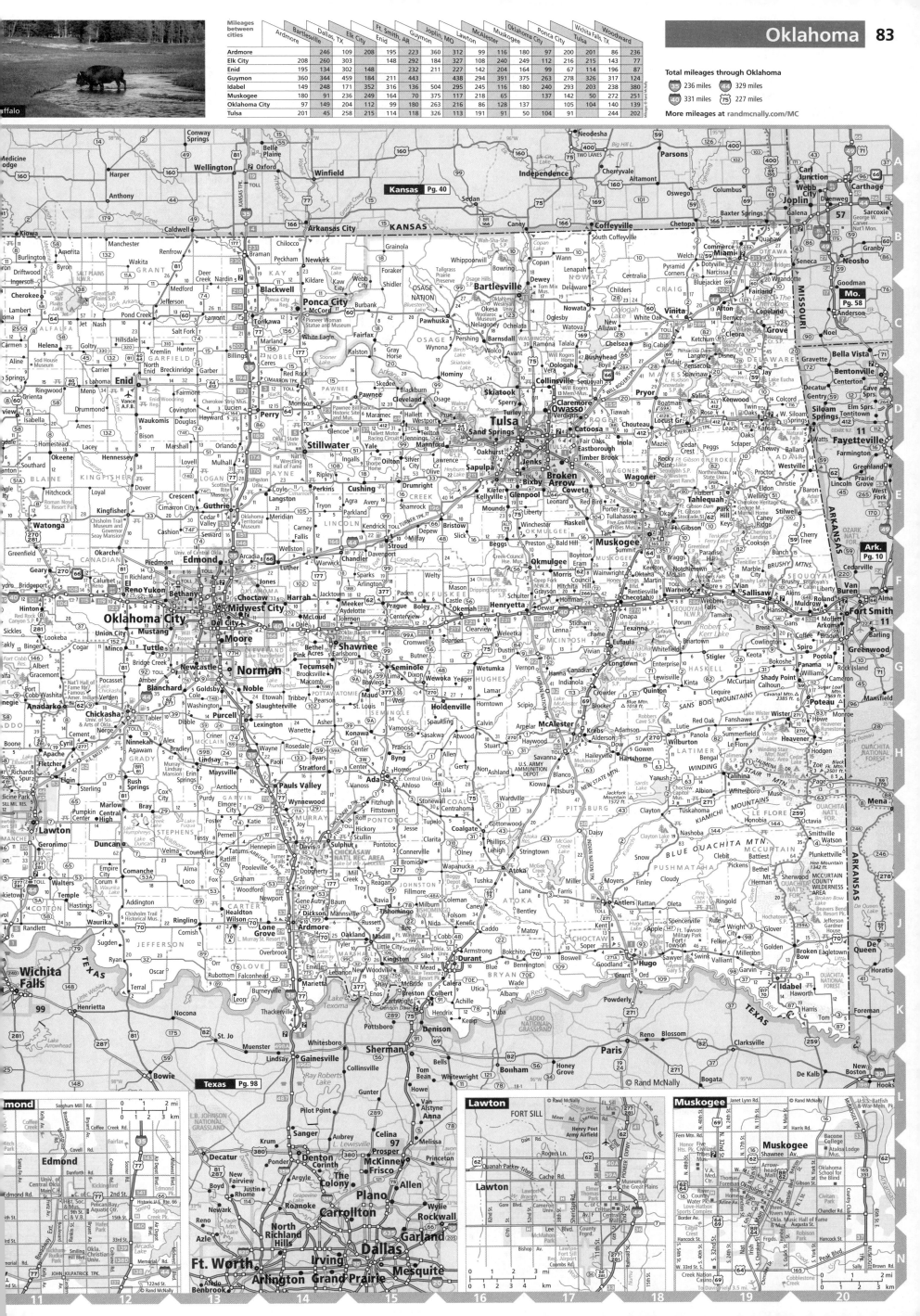

Mileages between cities

	Ardmore	Bartlesville	Dallas, TX	Elk City	Enid	Ft. Smith, AR	Guymon	Joplin, MO	Lawton	McAlester	Muskogee	Oklahoma City	Ponca City	Tulsa	Wichita Falls, TX	Woodward
Ardmore		246	109	208	195	223	360	312	99	180	97	200	201	86	236	
Elk City	208	260	303		148	292	184	327	108	240	249	112	216	215	143	77
Enid	195	134	302	148		232	211	222	142	204	164	99	67	114	196	87
Guymon	360	344	459	184	211	443		438	294	391	375	263	278	326	317	124
Idabel	149	248	171	352	316	136	504	245	116	180	240	293	203	238	380	
Muskogee	180	91	286	249	164	70	375	117	218	65		137	142	50	272	251
Oklahoma City	97	149	204	112	99	180	263	216	86	128	137		105	104	140	139
Tulsa	201	45	258	215	114	118	326	113	191	50	104	91		244	202	

Total mileages through Oklahoma

35	236 miles	44	329 miles
40	331 miles	75	227 miles

More mileages at randmcnally.com/MC

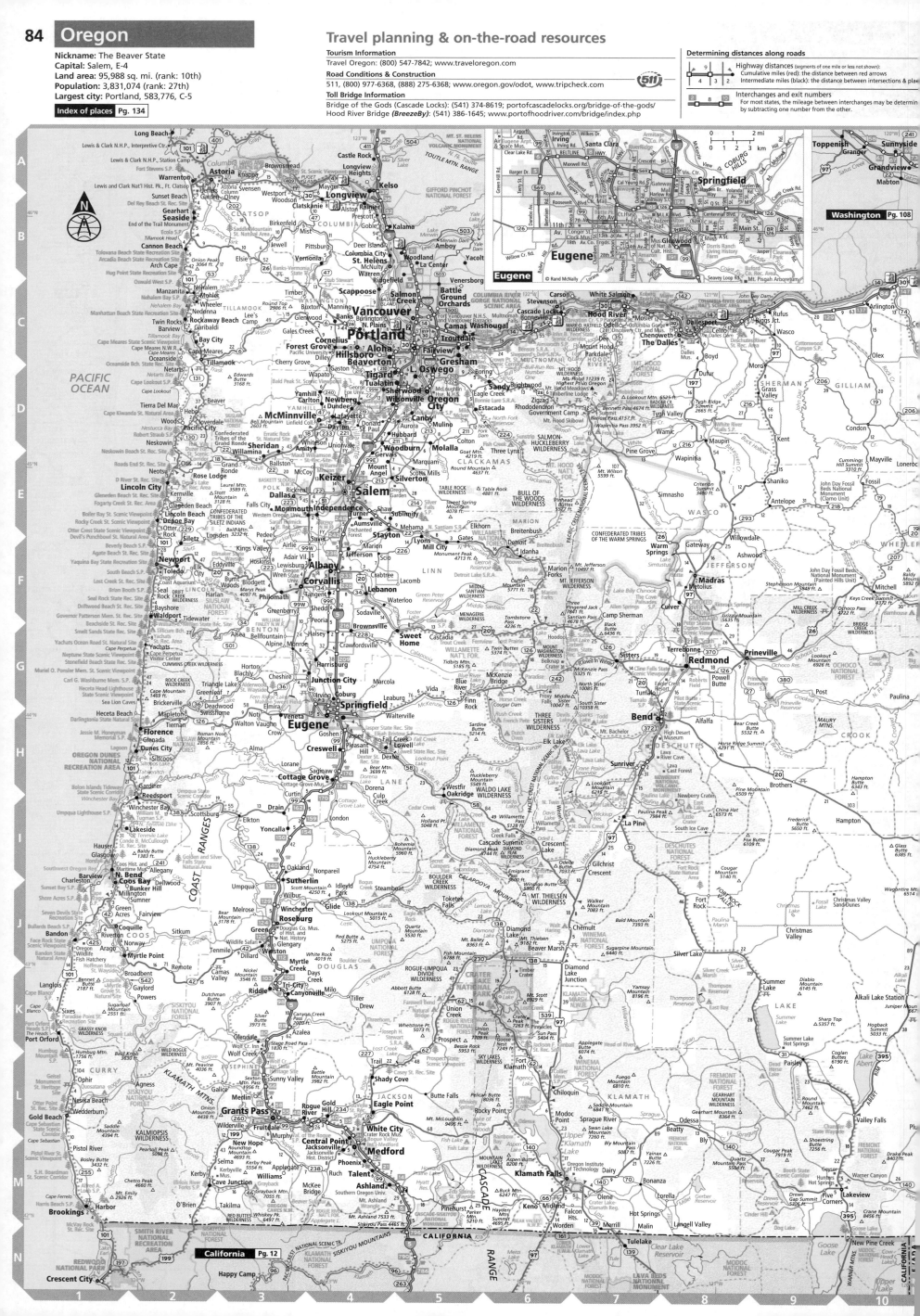

Oregon coast

Total mileages through Oregon
5 308 miles   84 375 miles
11 11 miles   348 miles
More mileages at randmcnally.com/MC

One inch represents approximately 24 miles

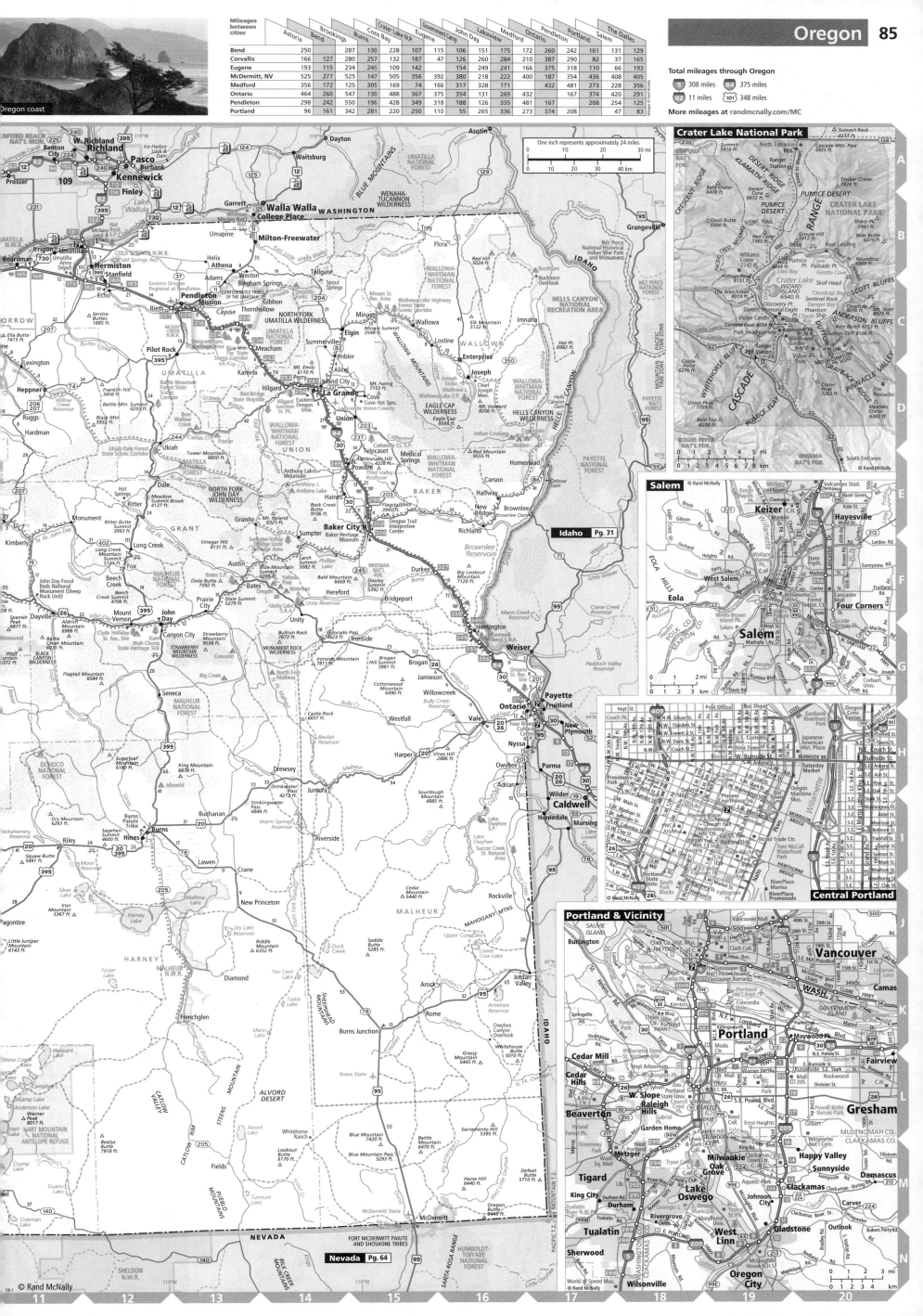

Crater Lake National Park

Salem

Central Portland

Portland & Vicinity

Idaho Pg. 31

Nevada Pg. 64

© Rand McNally

Nickname: The Keystone State
Capital: Harrisburg, EN-4
Land area: 44,743 sq. mi. (rank: 32nd)
Population: 12,702,379 (rank: 6th)
Largest city: Philadelphia, 1,526,006, EP-12

Index of places Pg. 134

Travel planning & on-the-road resources

Tourism Information
Tourism Office: (800) 847-4872; ww.visitpa.com
Road Conditions & Construction
511, (888) 783-6783; www.511pa.com; www.dot.state.pa.us
Toll Road Information
Pennsylvania Turnpike Commission (E-ZPass): (800) 331-3414; www.paturnpike.com

Determining distances along roads
Highway distances (segments of one mile or less not shown):
Cumulative miles (red): the distance between red arrows
Intermediate miles (black): the distance between intersections & place
Interchanges and exit numbers
For most states, the mileage between interchanges may be determined by subtracting one number from the other.

For continuation see map pages 88-89

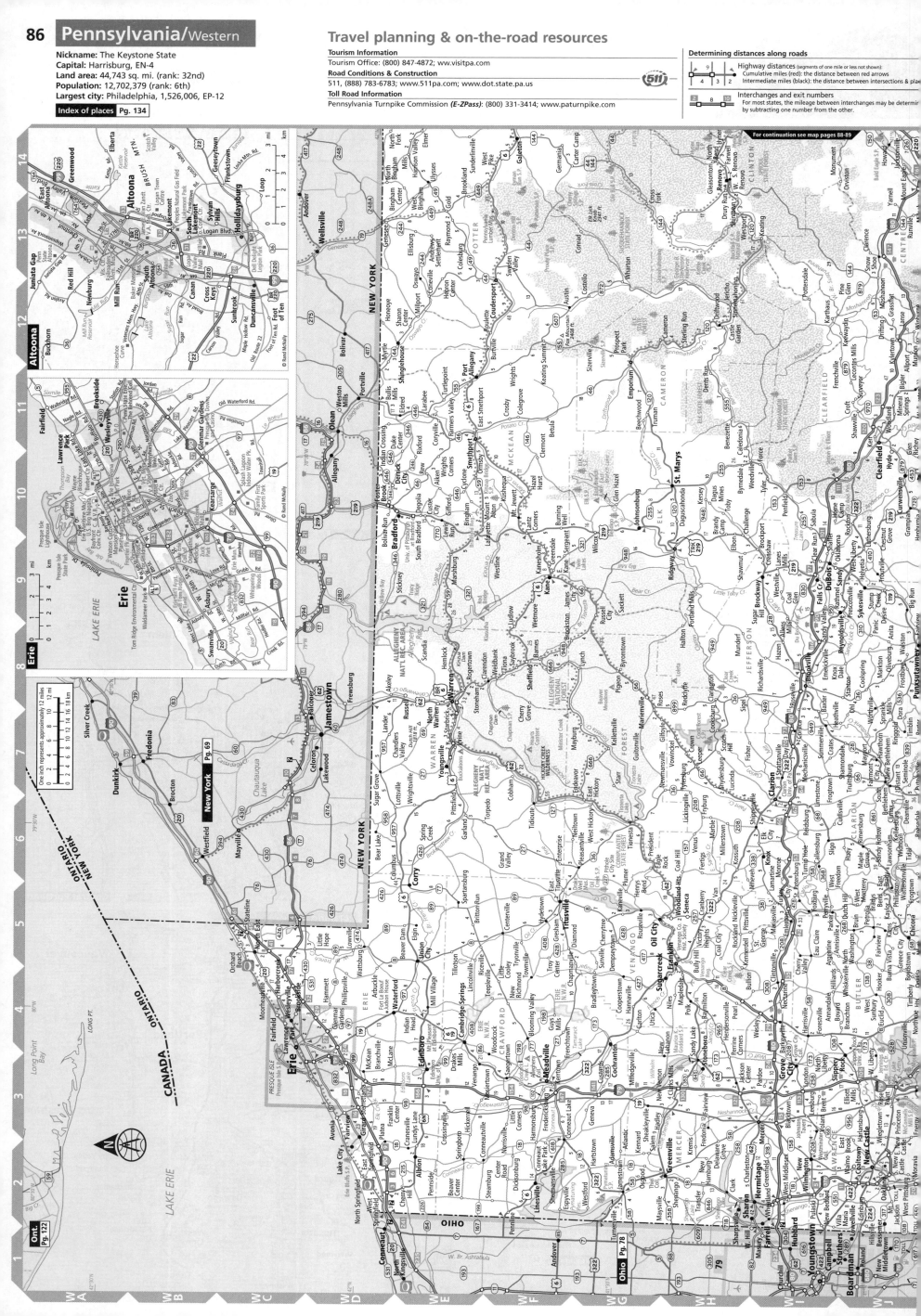

Mileages between cities

	Altoona	Chambersburg	Cumberland, MD	Du Bois	Erie	Galeton	Harrisburg	Johnstown	Kittanning	Meadville	New Castle	Philadelphia	Pittsburgh	State College	Uniontown	Warren
Altoona		90	66	71	202	135	134	46	79	165	127	234	96	41	112	130
Chambersburg	90		87	153	282	215	54	94	160	246	206	157	160	101	149	218
Erie	202	282	232	148		159	297	177	123	41	88	419	127	208	184	66
Johnstown	46	94	70	77	177	79	137		53	141	102	238	67	85	80	135
New Castle	127	206	156	110	88	197	250	102	48	52		350	52	171	108	120
Pittsburgh	96	160	111	101	127	200	203	67	42	91	52	304		55	51	148
State College	41	101	106	61	208	100	87	85	120	173	171	193	135		152	119
Williamsport	100	132	166	110	257	72	83	146	168	220	219	176	196	63	212	171

Total mileages through Pennsylvania

- 70 168 miles
- 79 183 miles
- 80 311 miles
- 90 46 miles

More mileages at randmcnally.com/MC

Brady's Bend, East Brady

York

Gettysburg / Gettysburg National Military Park

State College

Johnstown

© Rand McNally

Pennsylvania/Eastern

Nickname: The Keystone State
Capital: Harrisburg, EN-4
Land area: 44,743 sq. mi. (rank: 32nd)
Population: 12,702,379 (rank: 6th)
Largest city: Philadelphia, 1,526,006, EP-12

Index of places Pg. 134

Travel planning & on-the-road resources

Tourism Information
Tourism Office: (800) 847-4872; www.visitpa.com

Road Conditions & Construction
511, (888) 783-6783; www.511pa.com; www.dot.state.pa.us

Toll Road Information
Pennsylvania Turnpike Commission (E-ZPass): (800) 331-3414; www.paturnpike.com

Determining distances along roads

Highway distances (segments of one mile or less not shown):
Cumulative miles (red): the distance between red arrows
Intermediate miles (black): the distance between intersections & pl

Interchanges and exit numbers
For most states, the mileage between interchanges may be determ
by subtracting one number from the other.

Scranton / Wilkes-Barre

Allentown / Bethlehem

One inch represents approximately 12 miles

NEW YORK Pg. 69

© Rand McNally

For continuation see map pages 86-87

ferry rides on the Delaware River

Mileages between cities	Allentown	Gettysburg	Harrisburg	Lancaster	Mansfield	Philadelphia	Pittsburgh	Port Jervis, NY	Scranton	State College	Stroudsburg	Towanda	Trenton, NJ	Wilkes Barre	Williamsport	York
Allentown		121	81	67		62	282	81	74	175	40	126	75	60	127	92
Chambersburg	132	25	54	91	182	157	160	227	171	101	170	188	157	154	132	74
Harrisburg	81	38		36	39	133	107	203	176	120	87	119	139	127	104	83	26
Philadelphia	62	138	107	78		226	304	140	124	193	100	175	32	109	176	101
Reading	37	96	64	34	175	62	261	118	100	150	76	152	82	86	126	56
Scranton	74	160	120	132	102	124	279	59		150	46	64	137	16	101	146
State College	175	129	87	126	107	193	135	205	150		162	134	213	132	63	118
Williamsport	127	126	83	123	50	176	196	157	101	63	113	67	189	84		115

Total mileages through Pennsylvania

76 350 miles   81 232 miles
80 311 miles   95 51 miles

More mileages at randmcnally.com/MC

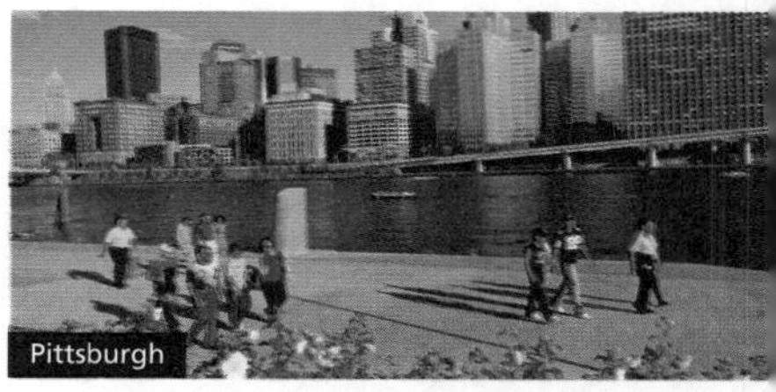

Sights to see

Pittsburgh

Philadelphia & Vicinity

Central Philadelphia

Pittsburgh & Vicinity

Central Pittsburgh

© Rand McNally

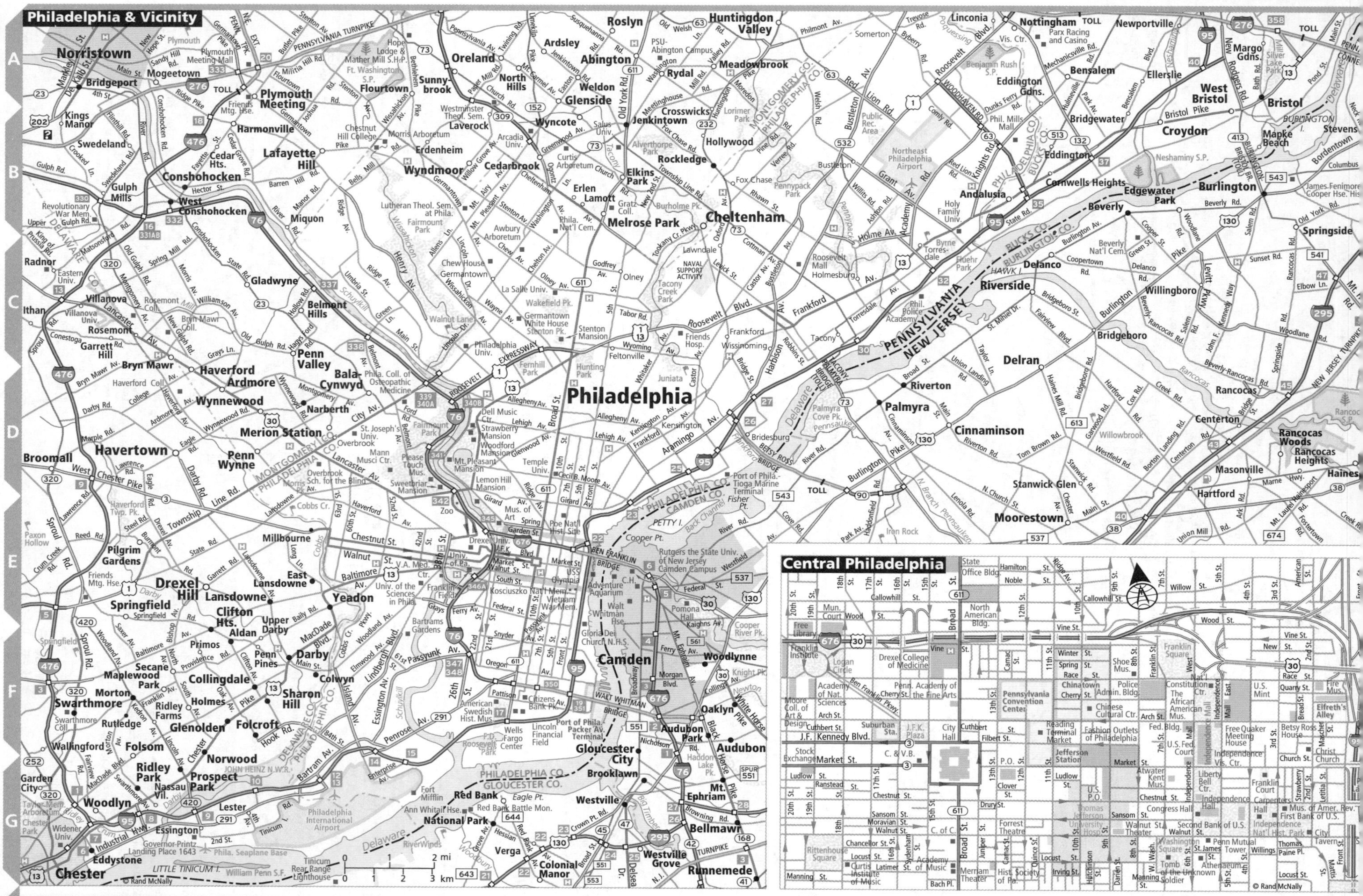

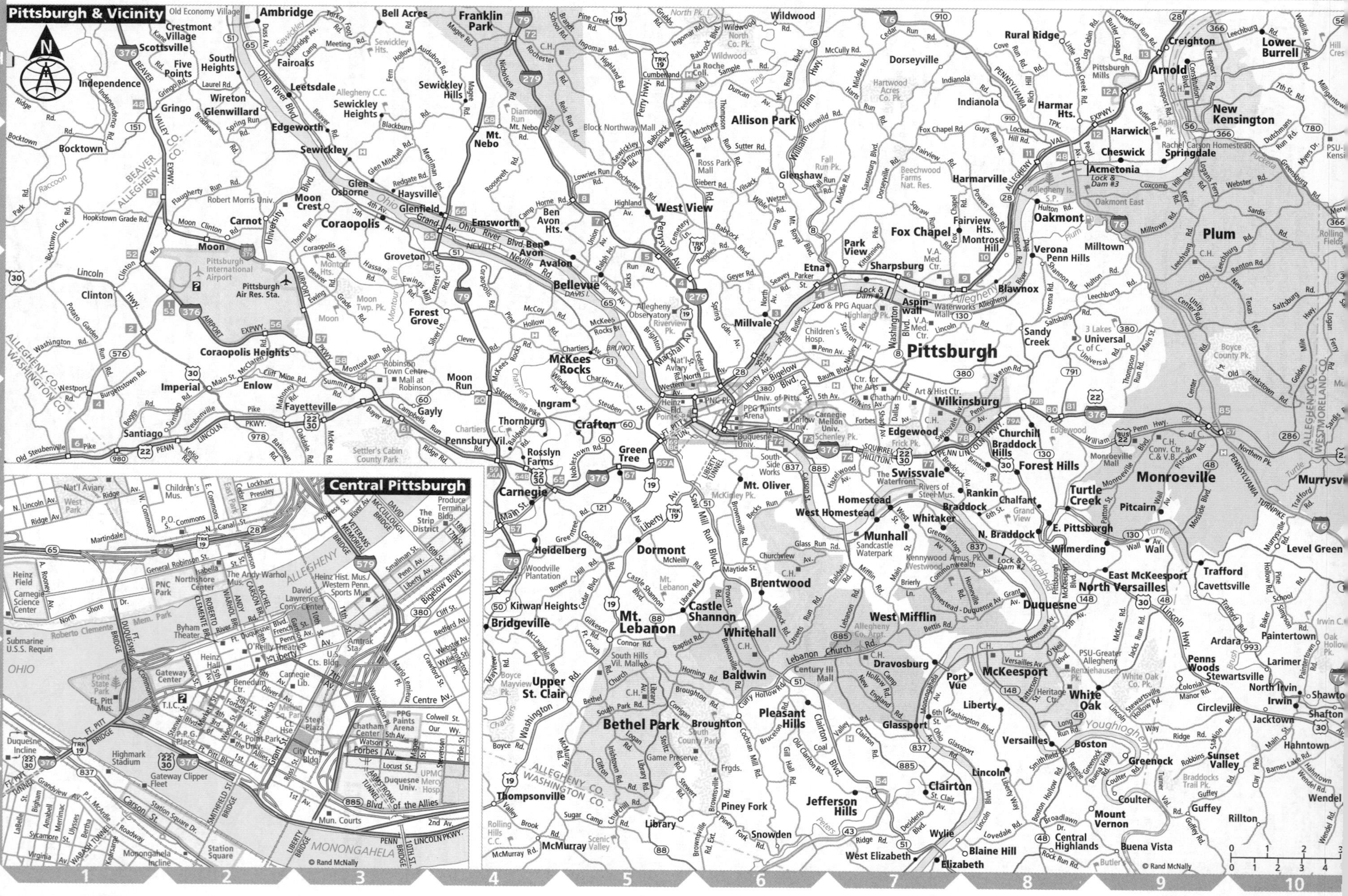

travel planning & on-the-road resources

rism Information
de Island Tourism Division:
1) 278-9100;
ww.visitrhodeisland.com

d Conditions & Construction
(888) 401-4511, (401) 222-2450;
w.dot.ri.gov/travel

Toll Bridge Info (EZ-Pass)
Rhode Island Turnpike
& Bridge Authority:
(401) 423-0800;
www.ritba.org

Determining Distances

(segments of one mile or less are not shown)

Cumulative miles (red):
the distance between red arrows

Intermediate miles (black):
the distance between intersections and places

Total mileages through Rhode Island
95 — 42 miles   6 — 31 miles
1 — 60 miles

More mileages at
randmcnally.com/MC

Mileages between cities	Fall River, MA	Kingston	Newport	Providence	Warwick	Westerly	Woonsocket	Worcester, MA
Chepachet	35	41	45	19	23	54	13	37
Fall River, MA		35	20	16	25	58	31	56
Newport	20	16		33	26	39	47	72
Providence	16	29	33		10	42	14	40
Warwick	25	23	26	10		37	24	50
Westerly	58	23	39	42	37		56	82
Woonsocket	31	43	47	14	24	56		27
Worcester, MA	56	68	72	40	50	82	27	

Nickname: The Ocean State
Capital: Providence, D-6
Land area: 1,034 sq. mi. (rank: 50th)
Population: 1,052,567 (rank: 43rd)
Largest city: Providence, 178,042, D-6

Index of places Pg. 134

One inch represents approximately 5.5 miles

© Rand McNally

Nickname: The Palmetto State
Capital: Columbia, D-7
Land area: 30,061 sq. mi. (rank: 40th)
Population: 4,625,364 (rank: 24th)
Largest city: Columbia, 129,272, D-7

Index of places — Pg. 134

Mileages between cities

	Anderson	Augusta, GA	Charleston	Charlotte, NC	Columbia	Hilton Head I.	Myrtle Beach	Spartanburg
Augusta, GA	92		175	160	72	151	216	120
Charleston	238	175		207	112	104	95	201
Charlotte, NC	128	160	207		93	253	176	72
Columbia	117	72	112	93		158	148	93
Florence	206	148	130	104	81	177	67	169
Myrtle Beach	273	216	95	176	148	200		237
Savannah, GA	282	134	106	251	156	34	202	246
Spartanburg	60	120	201	72	93	247	237	

Total mileages through South Carolina

- ▬ 142 miles
- ▬ 106 miles
- ▬ 221 miles
- ▬ 199 miles

More mileages at randmcnally.com/MC

Travel planning & on-the-road resources

Tourism Information
South Carolina Department of Parks, Recreation & Tourism:
(803) 734-1700; www.discoversouthcarolina.com

Road Conditions & Construction
511,
(877) 511-4672,
(855) 467-2368;
www.511sc.org, www.dot.state.sc.us

Toll Road Information (all use Palmetto Pa...
Cross Island Pkwy. (Hilton Head I.):
(843) 342-6718; www.crossislandparkway...
Southern Connector (Greenville Co.):
(864) 527-2143; www.southernconnector.

Tourism Information
South Dakota Department of Tourism: (800) 732-5682;
www.travelsd.com, www.travelsouthdakota.com

Road Conditions & Construction
(866) 697-3511;
www.sddot.com, www.safetravelusa.com/sd

511

Road Information
toll roads

Determining Distances

Cumulative miles (red):
the distance between red arrows
Intermediate miles (black):
the distance between
intersections & places

(segments of
one mile or less
not shown)

**Total mileages
through South Dakota**

29 253 miles   12 317 miles
90 413 miles   83 242 miles

More mileages at
randmcnally.com/MC

Mileages between cities	Aberdeen	Mobridge	Pierre	Pine Ridge	Rapid City	Sioux Falls	Watertown	Yankton
Aberdeen		100	160	360	333	203	96	236
Belle Fourche	312	212	206	172	60	362	362	421
Mobridge	100		108	308	243	303	196	332
Pierre	160	108		200	173	224	188	242
Rapid City	333	243	173	111		347	403	365
Sioux City, IA	285	384	305	358	428	85	184	63
Sioux Falls	203	303	224	356	347		103	81
Watertown	96	196	188	415	403	103		155

South Dakota

Nickname: The Mount Rushmore State
Capital: Pierre, D-7
Land area: 75,811 sq. mi. (rank: 16th)
Population: 814,180 (rank: 46th)
Largest city: Sioux Falls, 153,888, F-13

Index of places Pg. 134

Sioux Falls

Pierre

Rapid City

Black Hills Region

Rapid City

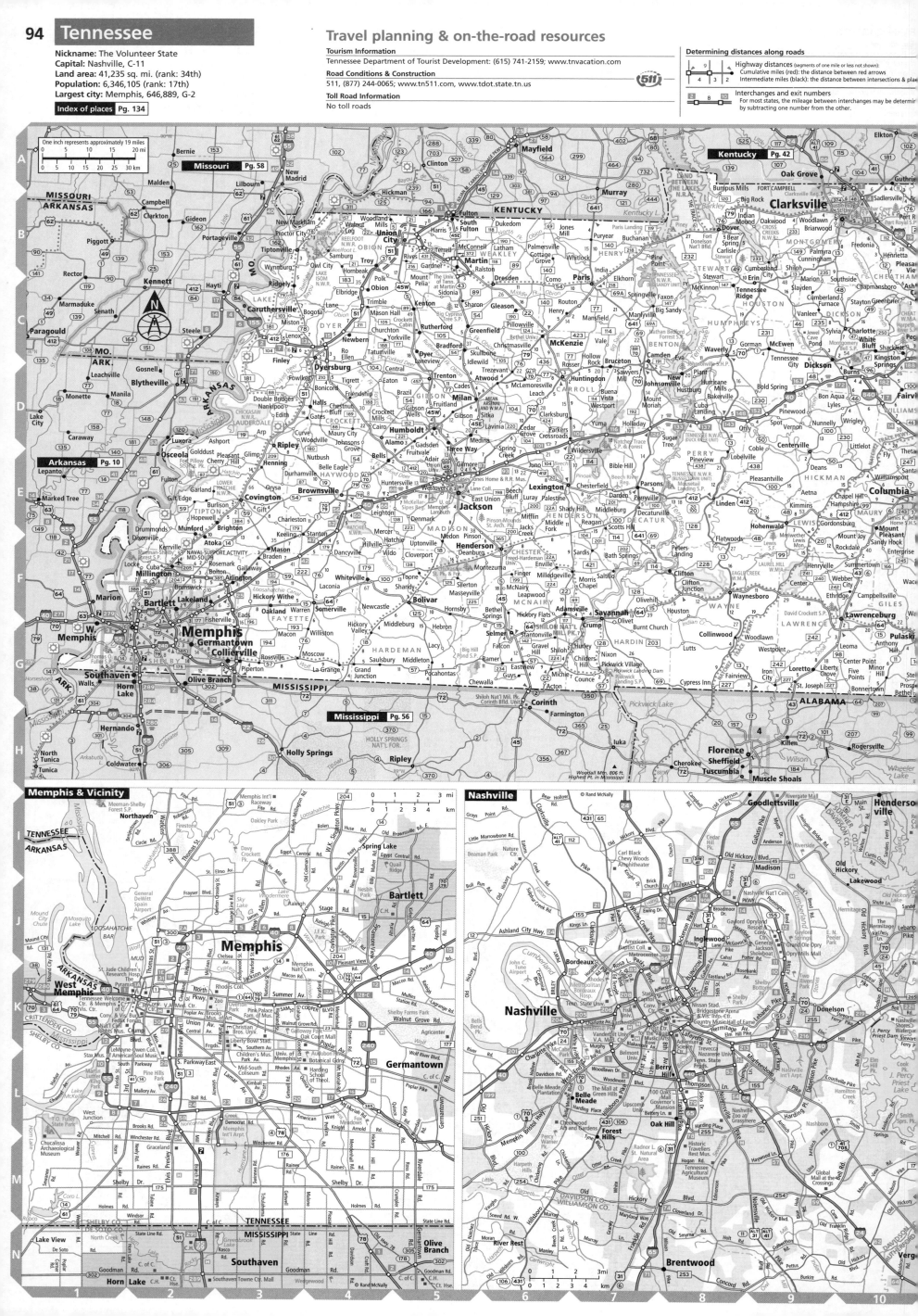

Mileages between cities	Atlanta, GA	Bristol	Chattanooga	Clarksville	Cookeville	Dyersburg	Fayetteville	Gatlinburg	Jackson	Johnson City	Knoxville	Memphis	Morristown	Nashville	Oak Ridge	Union City
Chattanooga	117	223		177	98	303	94	151	260	215	110	314	158	131	108	311
Clarksville	293	337	177		125	173	136	265	123	329	224	201	271	47	207	138
Dyersburg	418	463	303	173		252	229	392	47	455	351	76	398	172	334	34
Fayetteville	211	317	94	136	109	229		246	167	308	204	243	252	90	189	224
Johnson City	256	24	215	329	206	455	308	106	412		104	495	65	283	128	463
Knoxville	202	113	110	224	102	351	204	41	308	104		390	48	179	24	358
Memphis	380	502	314	201	291	76	243	431	87	495	390		437	212	373	113
Nashville	249	292	131	47	80	172	90	220	129	283	179	212	162			168

Total mileages through Tennessee
40 455 miles   75 161 miles
65 121 miles   81 76 miles
More mileages at randmcnally.com/MC

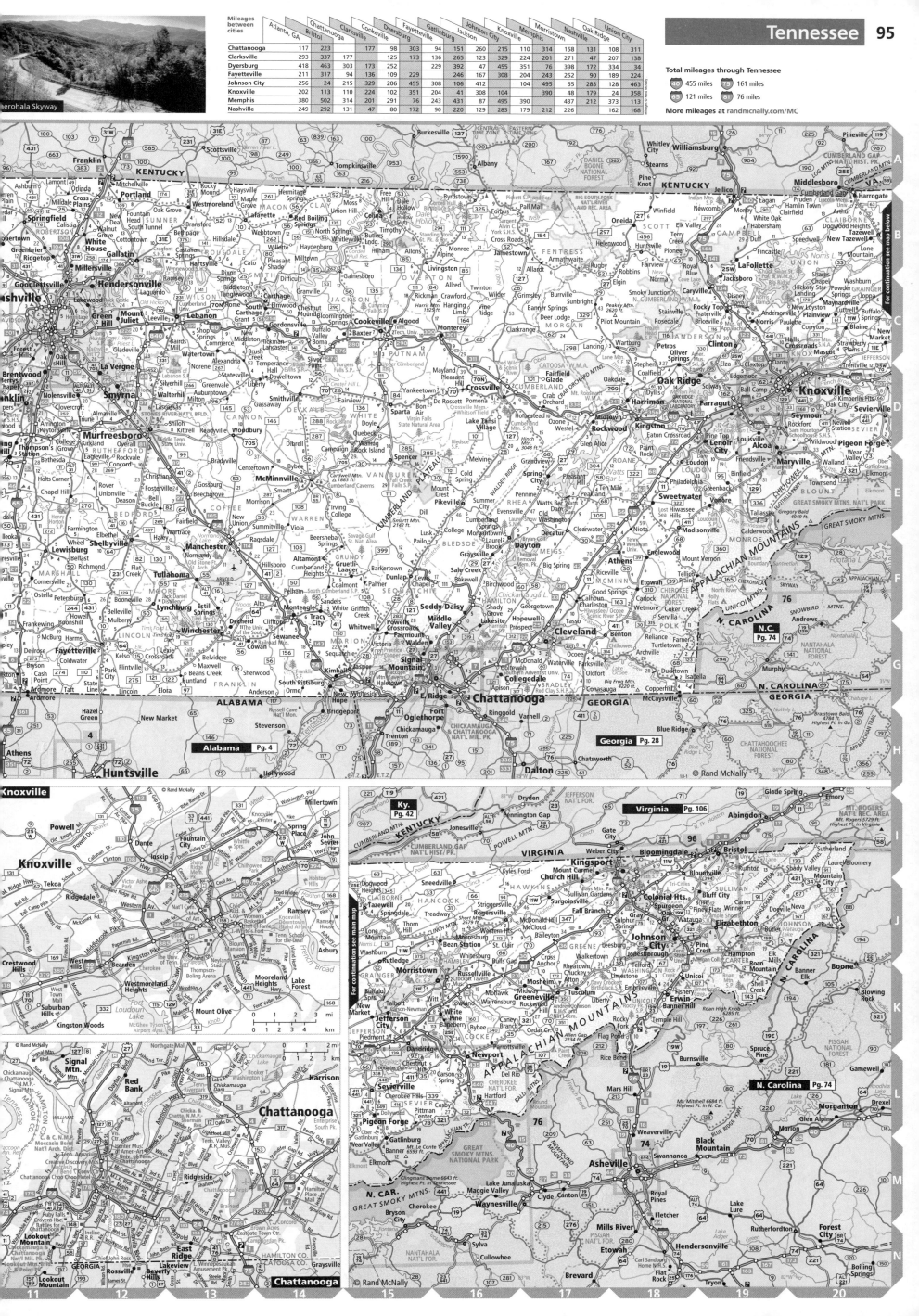

Cherohala Skyway

Sights to see

- Appalachian Caverns, Blountville...............K-3
- Battleship USS Texas, La Porte...............D-9
- Bayou Place, Houston...............K-8
- Bristol Caverns, Bristol...............J-6
- Bristol Motor Speedway, Bristol...............K-4
- Contemporary Arts Museum, Houston...............E-5
- Houston Fire Museum, Houston...............E-5
- Houston Zoo, Houston...............E-5
- Museum of Natural Science, Houston...............E-5
- Rocky Mount Museum, Piney Flats...............L-3
- Space Center Houston, Houston...............G-8
- Wortham Theatre Center, Houston...............K-8

Church Circle, Kingsport

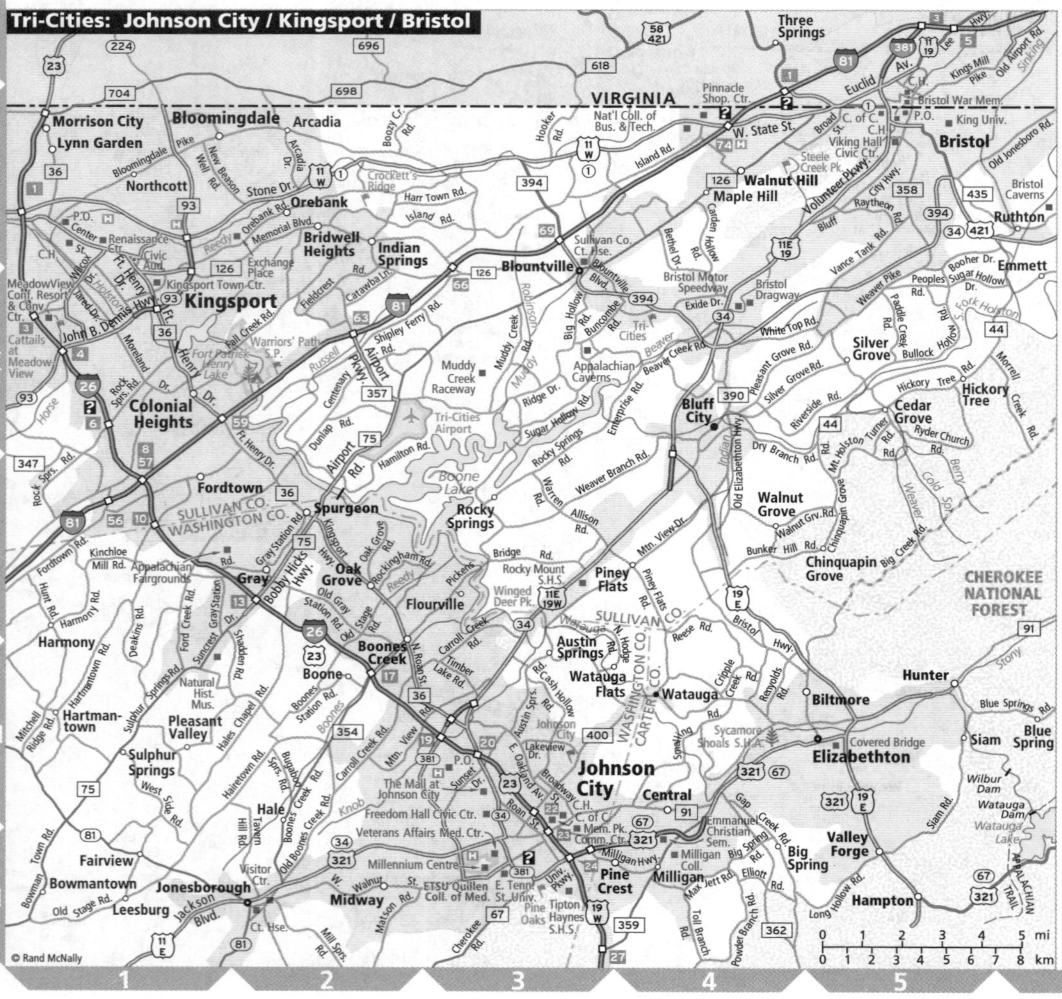

Houston & Vicinity

Texas City

Galvest[on]

Central Houston

Tri-Cities: Johnson City / Kingsport / Bristol

© Rand McNally

Space Center Houston

Sights to see

Nickname: The Lone Star State
Capital: Austin, EK-5
Land area: 261,231 sq. mi. (rank: 2nd)
Population: 25,145,561 (rank: 2nd)
Largest city: Houston, 2,099,451, EL-10

Index of places Pg. 135

Travel planning & on-the-road resources

Tourism Information

Texas Tourism:
(800) 452-9292; www.traveltex.com

Road Conditions & Construction

(800) 452-9292, (512) 463-8588;
www.txdot.gov, www.drivetexas.org

Toll Road Information

(continued on p. 100)

Cameron County Reg. Mobility Auth. (TX 550) (TxTag): (956) 621-5571; www.ccrma.org
Harris County Toll Road Authority (Houston area) (EZTAG or TxTag): (281) 875-3279; www.hctra.org
North Texas Tollway Authority (Dallas Metroplex) (TollTag or TxTag): (972) 818-6882; www.ntta.org
Texas Department of Transportation (all other toll roads in Texas) (TxTag): (888) 468-9824; www.txtag.org

Determining distances

Cumulative miles (red):
the distance between red arrows
Intermediate miles (black):
the distance between
intersections & places

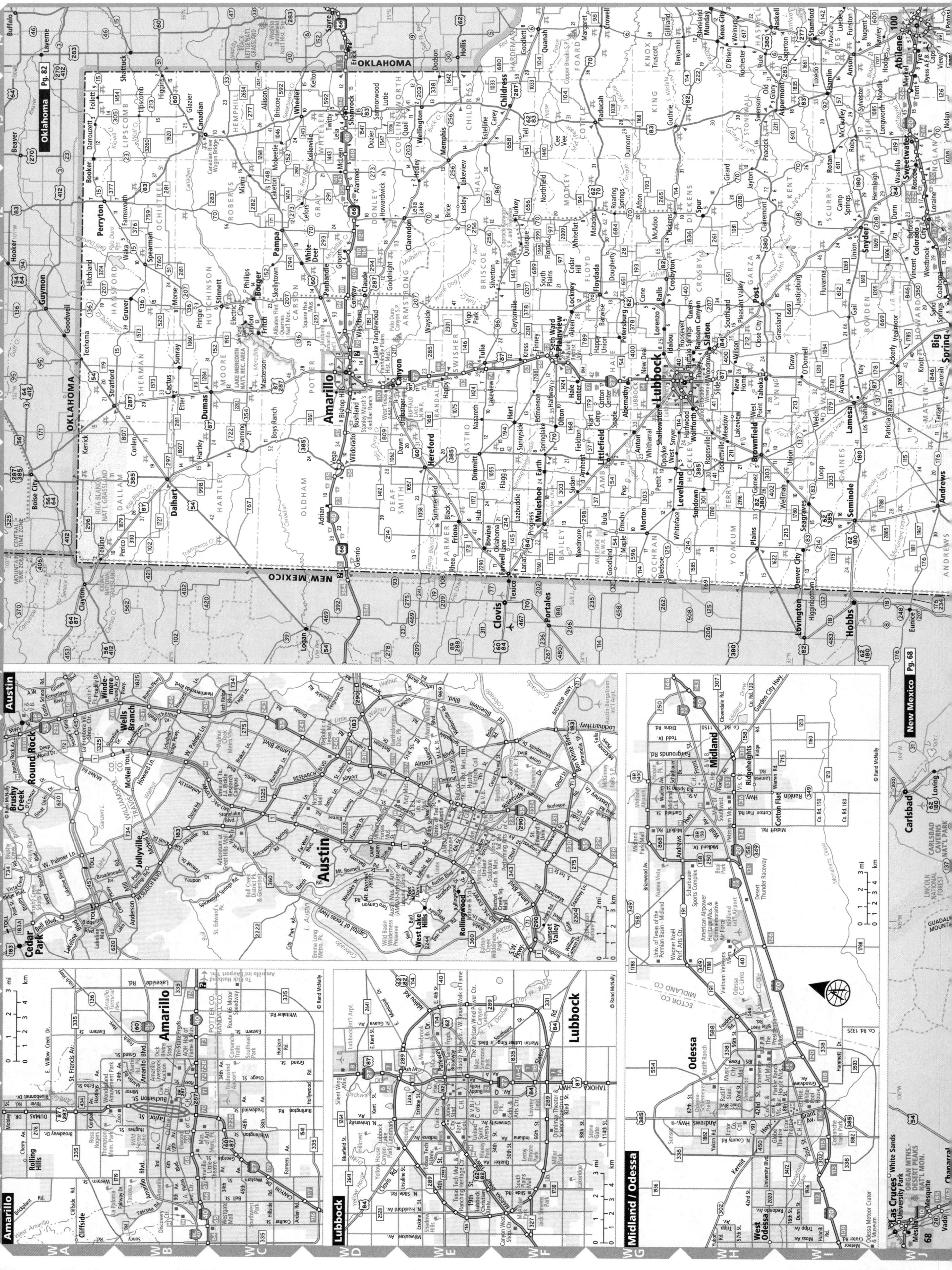

Big Bend National Park

Mileages between cities

	Abilene	Amarillo	Big Bend N.P.	Big Spring	Childress	Clovis, NM	Dallas	Eagle Pass	El Paso	Fort Stockton	Lubbock	Odessa	Perryton	San Angelo	San Antonio	Van Horn
Abilene		268	380	108	155	267	179	304	454	255	163	168	306	88	250	332
Amarillo	268		470	226	112	104	363	510	407	344	120	258	115	318	510	423
Del Rio	241	454	242	240	383	425	426	56	428		338	258	534	154	151	303
El Paso	454	407	325	346	482	301	635	484		240	343	258	516	440	554	121
Lubbock	163	120	454	106	141	103	343	390	343	240		138	194		390	302
Odessa	168	258	210	61	279	204	352	314	284	85	138		377	132	352	164
San Angelo	88	318							440		194	132			213	
San Antonio	250	510	404	299	408	493	276	143	554	315	390	352	556	213		434

Total mileages through Texas

- 10 — 881 miles
- 40 — 177 miles
- 20 — 636 miles

More mileages at randmcnally.com/MC

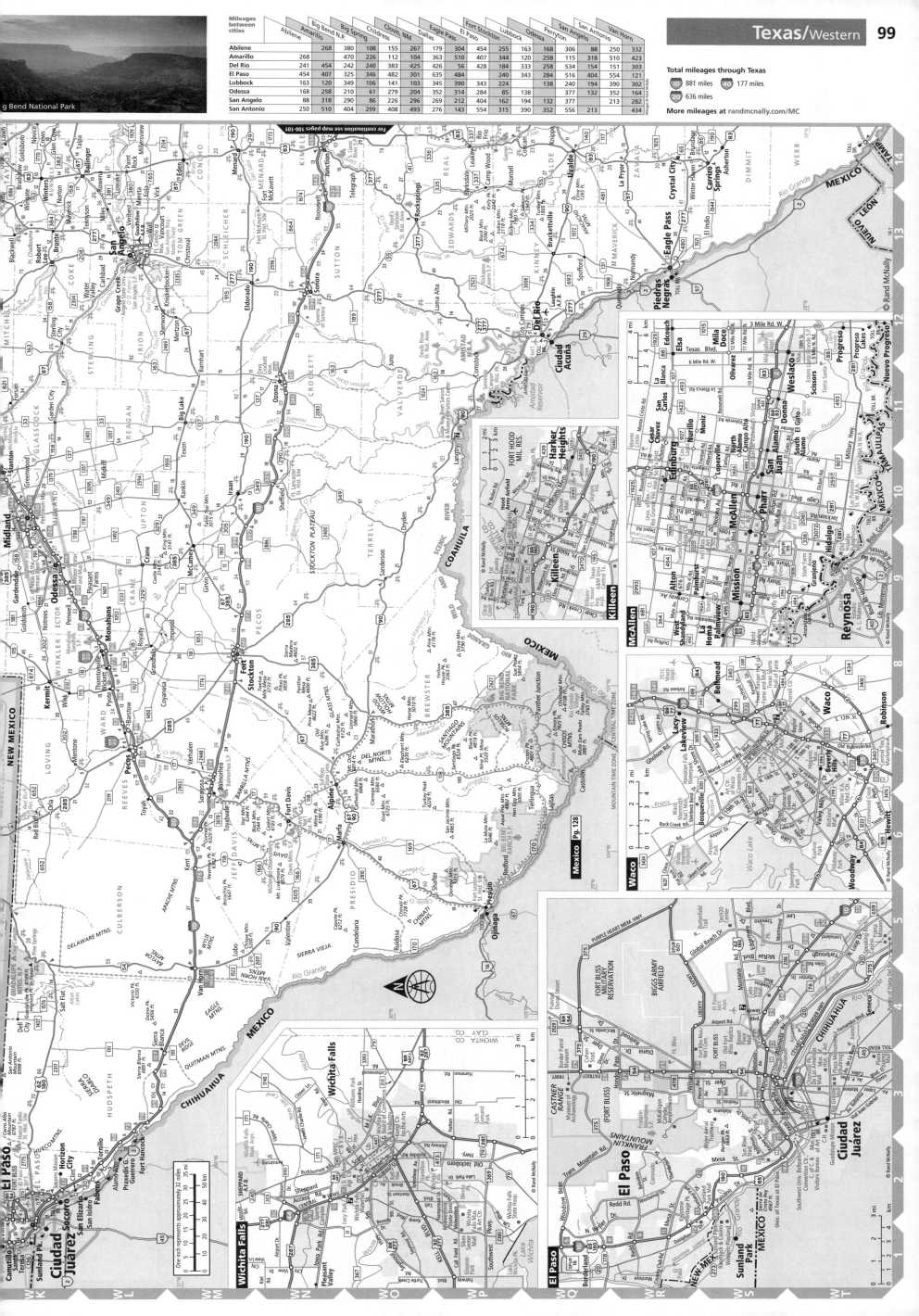

Nickname: The Lone Star State
Capital: Austin, EK-5
Land area: 261,231 sq. mi. (rank: 2nd)
Population: 25,145,561 (rank: 2nd)
Largest city: Houston, 2,099,451, EL-10

Index of places Pg. 135

Travel planning & on-the-road resources

Tourism Information
Texas Tourism:
(800) 452-9292; www.traveltex.com

Road Conditions & Construction
(800) 452-9292, (512) 463-8588;
www.txdot.gov, www.drivetexas.org

Toll Road Information
(list continued from p. 98)

Central Texas Regional Mobility Authority (Austin area) (*TxTag*):
(512) 996-9778; www.mobilityauthority.com
Fort Bend County Toll Road Authority (Houston area) (*EZTAG or TxTag*): (855) 999-2024; www.fbctra.com
North East Regional Mobility Authority (TX 49) (*TxTag*): (903) 630-7447; www.netrma.org
SH 130 Concession Co. (TX 130) (*TxTag*): (512) 371-4800; mysh130.com
Texas Department of Transportation (all other toll roads in Texas) (*TxTag*): (888) 468-9824; www.txtag.org

Determining distances
Cumulative miles (red):
the distance between red arrows
Intermediate miles (black):
the distance between intersections & places

For continuation see map pages 98-99

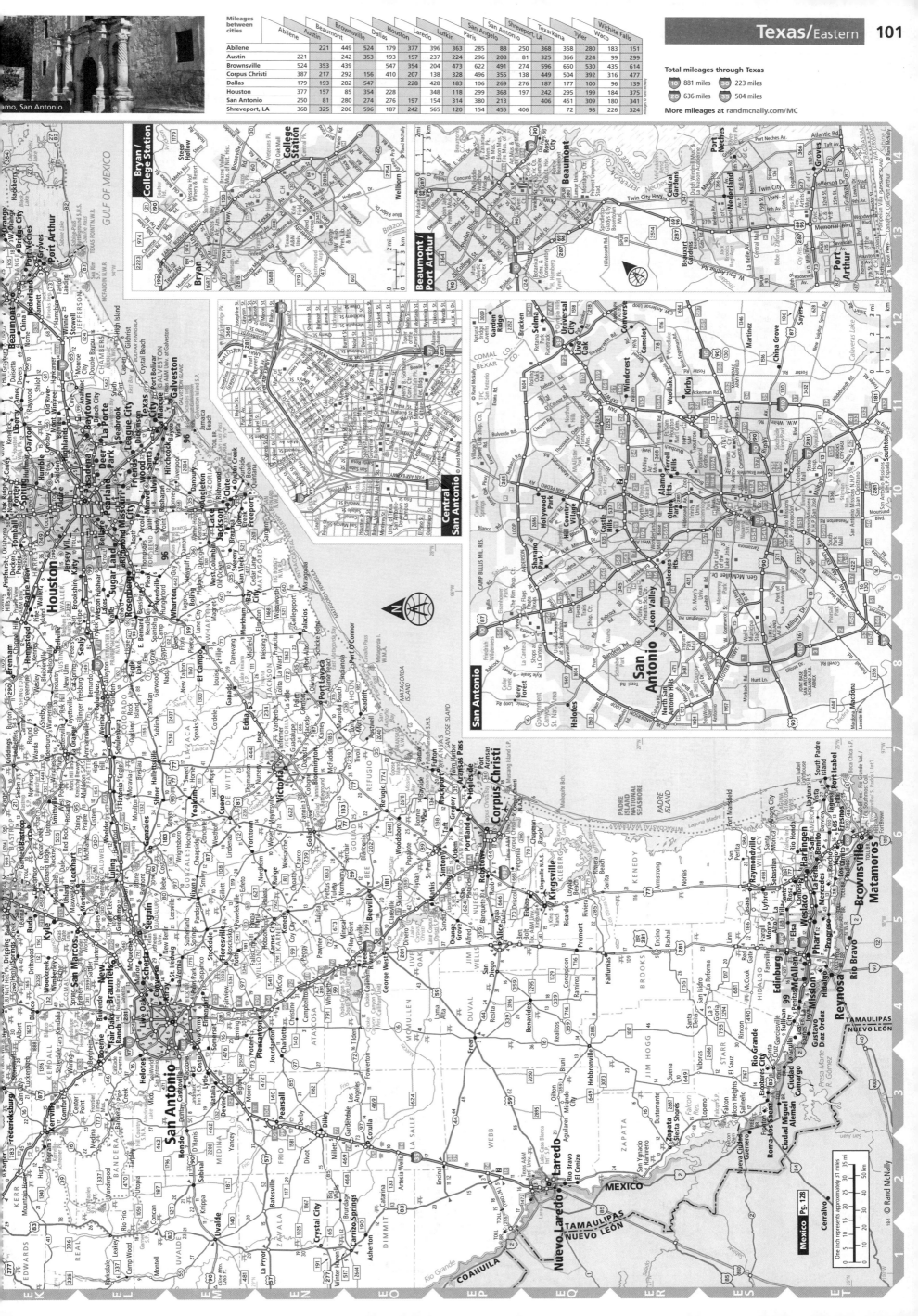

Mileages between cities	Abilene	Austin	Beaumont	Brownsville	Dallas	Houston	Laredo	Lufkin	San Angelo	Paris	San Antonio	Shreveport, LA	Texarkana	Tyler	Wichita Falls	Waco
Abilene		221	449	524	179	377	396	363	285	88	250	368	358	280	183	151
Austin	221		242	353	193	157	237	224	296	208	81	325	366	224	99	299
Brownsville	524	353	439		547	354	204	473	622	491	274	596	650	435	614	
Corpus Christi	387	217	292	156	410	207	138	328	496	138	449	504	392	316	477	
Dallas	179	193	282	547		228	428	183	106	269	276	187	177	100	96	139
Houston	377	157	85	354	228		348	118	296	368	197	242	295	199	184	375
San Antonio	250	81	280	274	276	197	154	314	380	211		406	451	309	180	341
Shreveport, LA	368	325	206	596	187	242	565	120	154	455	406		72	98	226	324

Total mileages through Texas
- 10 881 miles
- 20 636 miles
- 30 223 miles
- 35 504 miles

More mileages at randmcnally.com/MC

Utah

Nickname: The Beehive State
Capital: Salt Lake City, D-8
Land area: 82,169 sq. mi. (rank: 12th)
Population: 2,763,885 (rank: 34th)
Largest city: Salt Lake City, 186,440, D-8

Index of places Pg. 135

Travel planning & on-the-road resources

Tourism Information
Utah Office of Tourism: (800) 200-1160, (800) 882-4386, (801) 538-1900; www.visitutah.com

Road Conditions & Construction
511, (866) 511-8824, (801) 887-3700; www.udot.utah.gov, www.utahcommuterlink.com

Toll Road Information
Adams Av. Pkwy., Inc. (Washington Terrace): (801) 475-1909; www.adamsavenueparkway.com

(ExpressCard)

Determining distances along roads

Highway distances (segments of one mile or less not shown):
Cumulative miles (red): the distance between arrows
Intermediate miles (black): the distance between intersections & places

Interchanges and exit numbers
For most states, the mileage between interchanges may be determined by subtracting one number from the other.

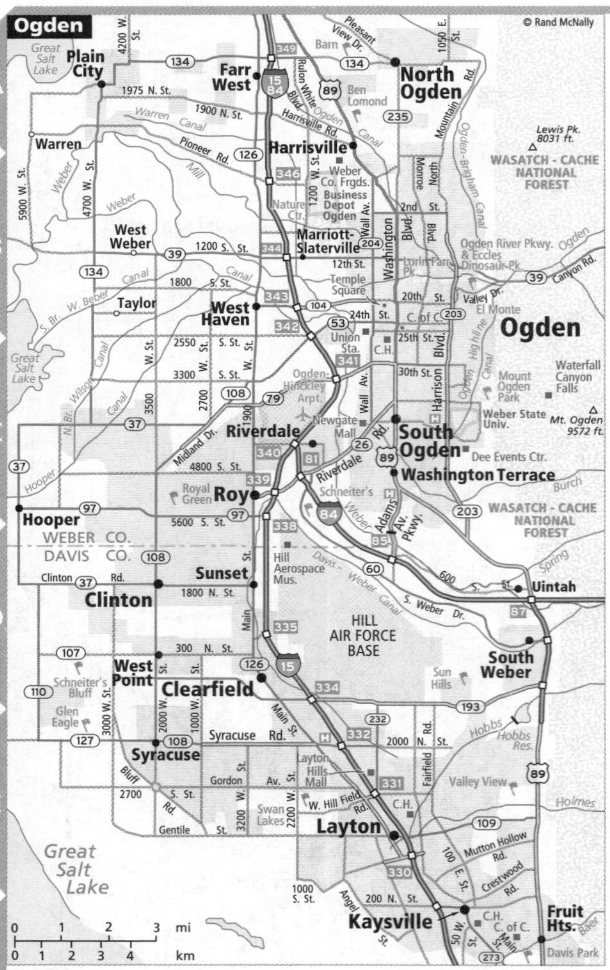

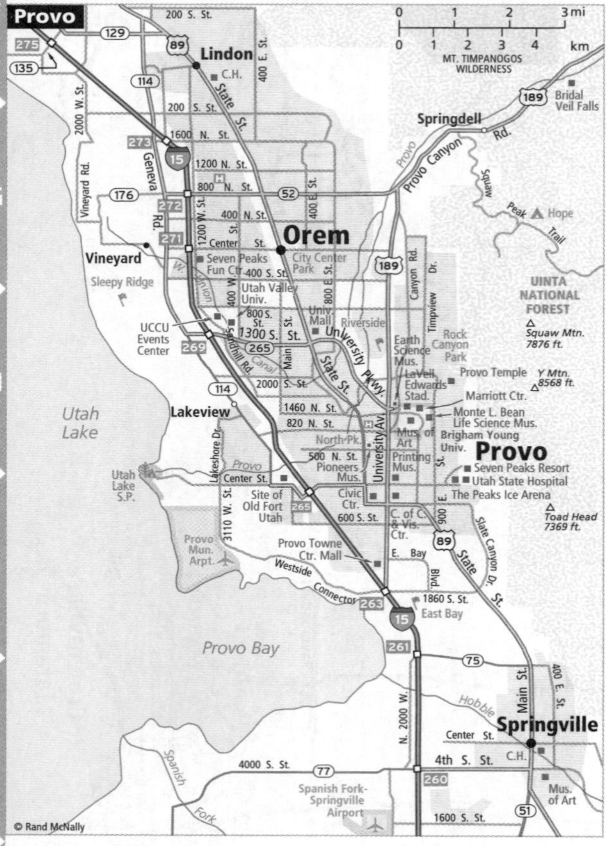

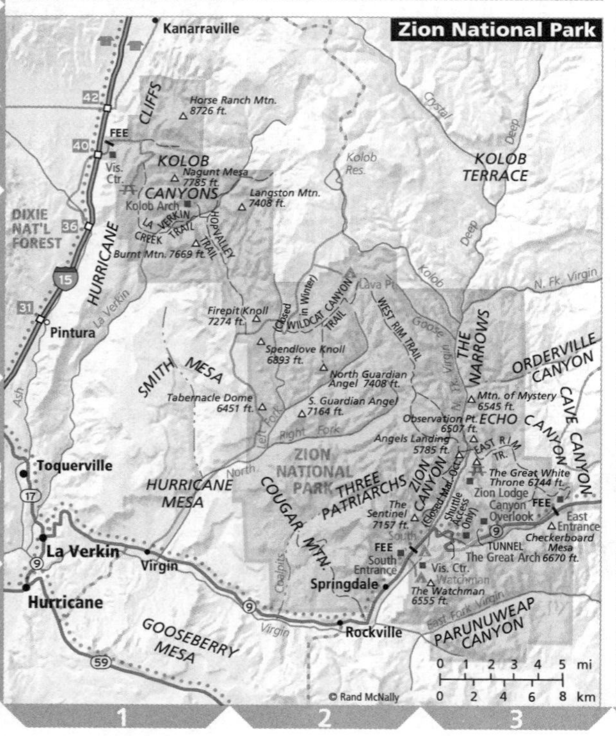

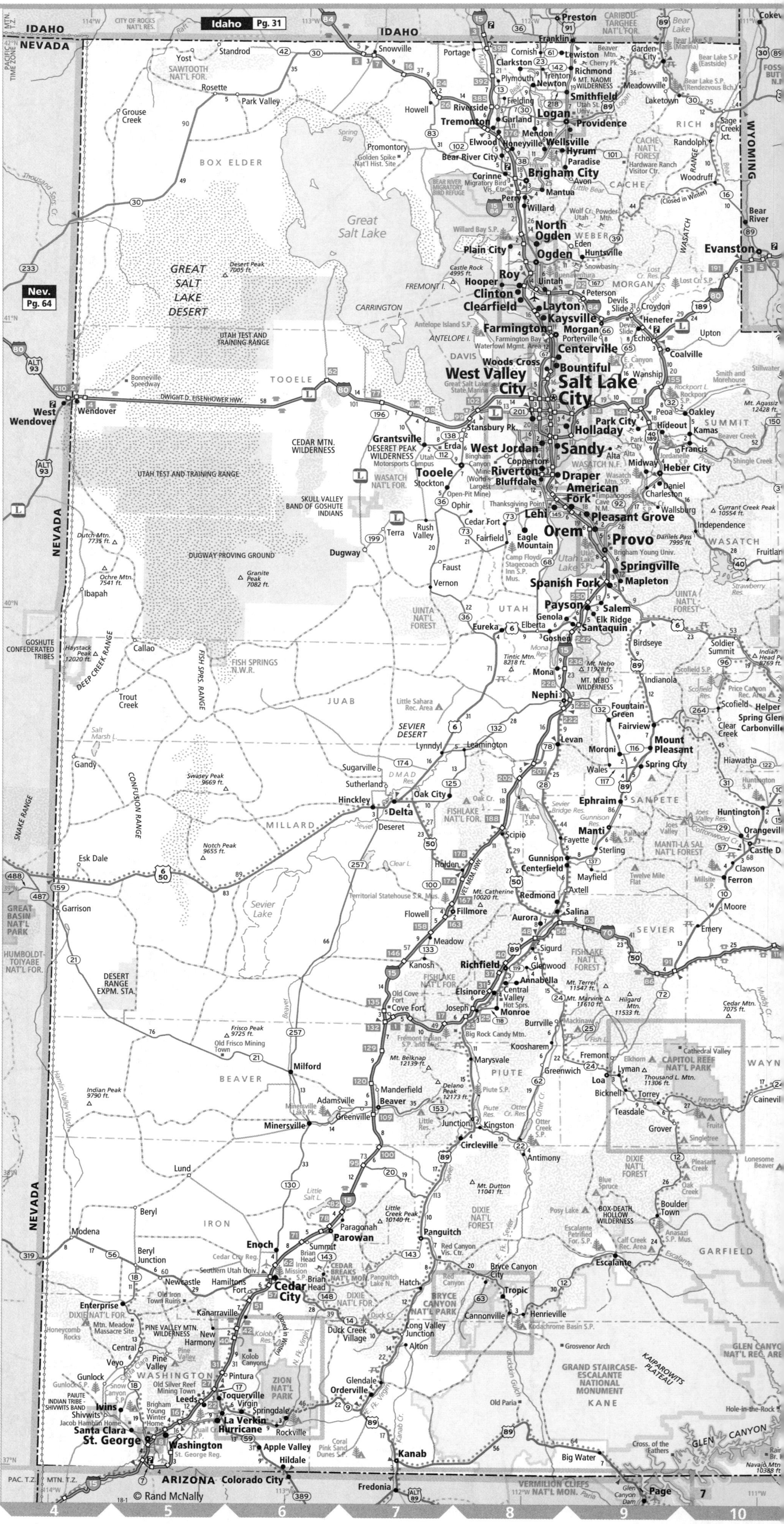

Ogden

Provo

Zion National Park

© Rand McNally

Delicate Arch

Mileages between cities

	Blanding	Cedar City	Grand Jct. CO	Las Vegas NV	Logan	Moab	Ogden	Page AZ	Park City	Price	Provo	Richfield	Salt Lake City	Vernal	Wendover
Grand Junction, CO	186	335	—	506	363	112	380	286	164	240	224	389	283	140	401
Logan	388	330	363	499	—	313	46	457	113	199	124	239	82	252	199
Moab	74	287	112	456	313	—	269	268	238	115	190	174	234	207	352
Richfield	249	114	224	282	239	174	194	219	166	121	121	—	159	232	270
St. George	415	55	389	117	385	341	341	154	308	286	261	169	304	401	401
Salt Lake City	308	250	283	419	82	234	37	377	30	119	43	159	—	172	121
Vernal	281	345	140	514	252	207	207	420	145	112	154	232	172	—	291
Wendover	426	317	401	361	199	352	154	503	150	237	161	270	121	291	—

Total mileages through Utah
- 15 — 401 miles
- 80 — 196 miles
- 70 — 232 miles
- 84 — 119 miles

More mileages at randmcnally.com/MC

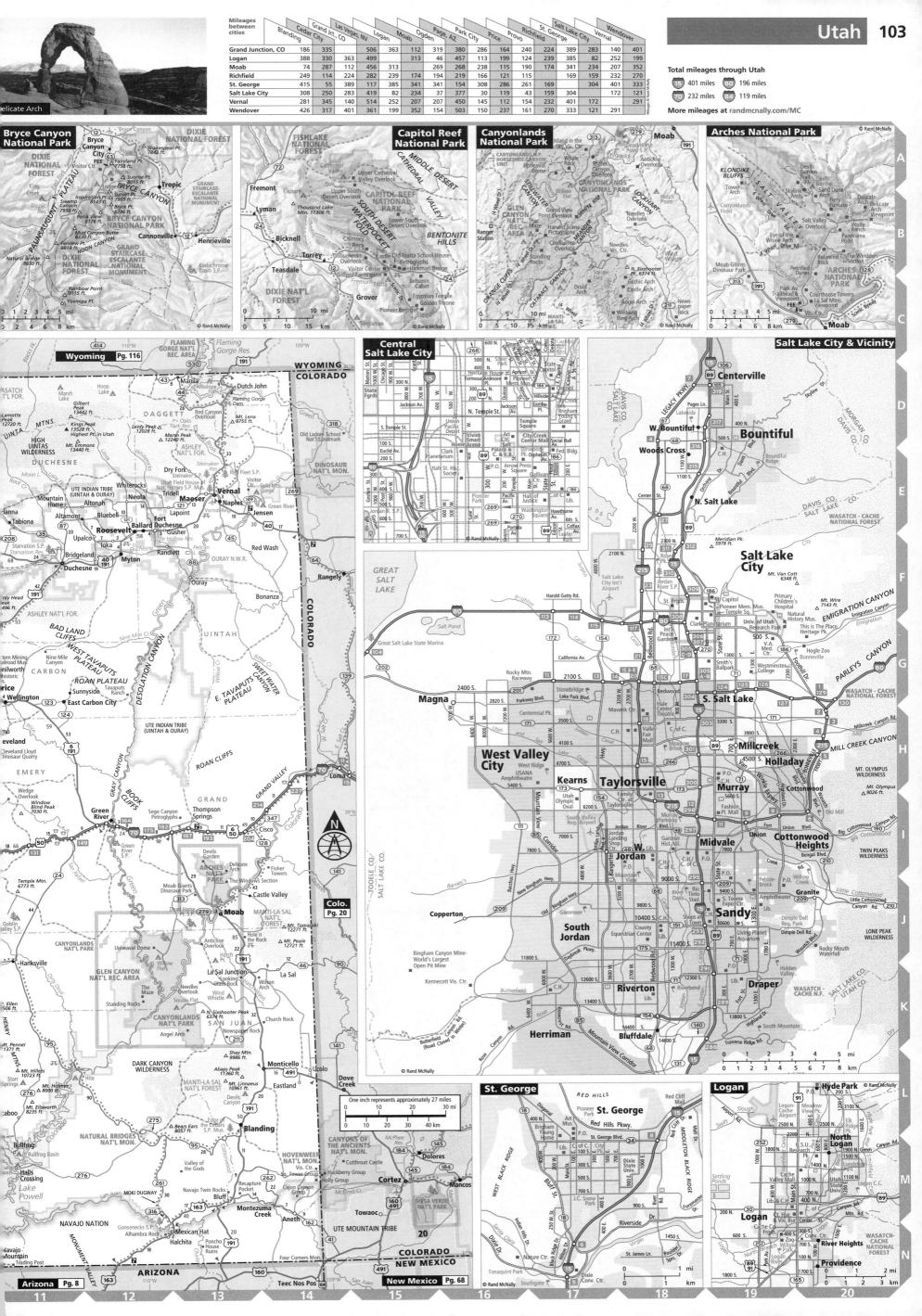

Bryce Canyon National Park — Capitol Reef National Park — Canyonlands National Park — Arches National Park

Salt Lake City & Vicinity — Central Salt Lake City — St. George — Logan

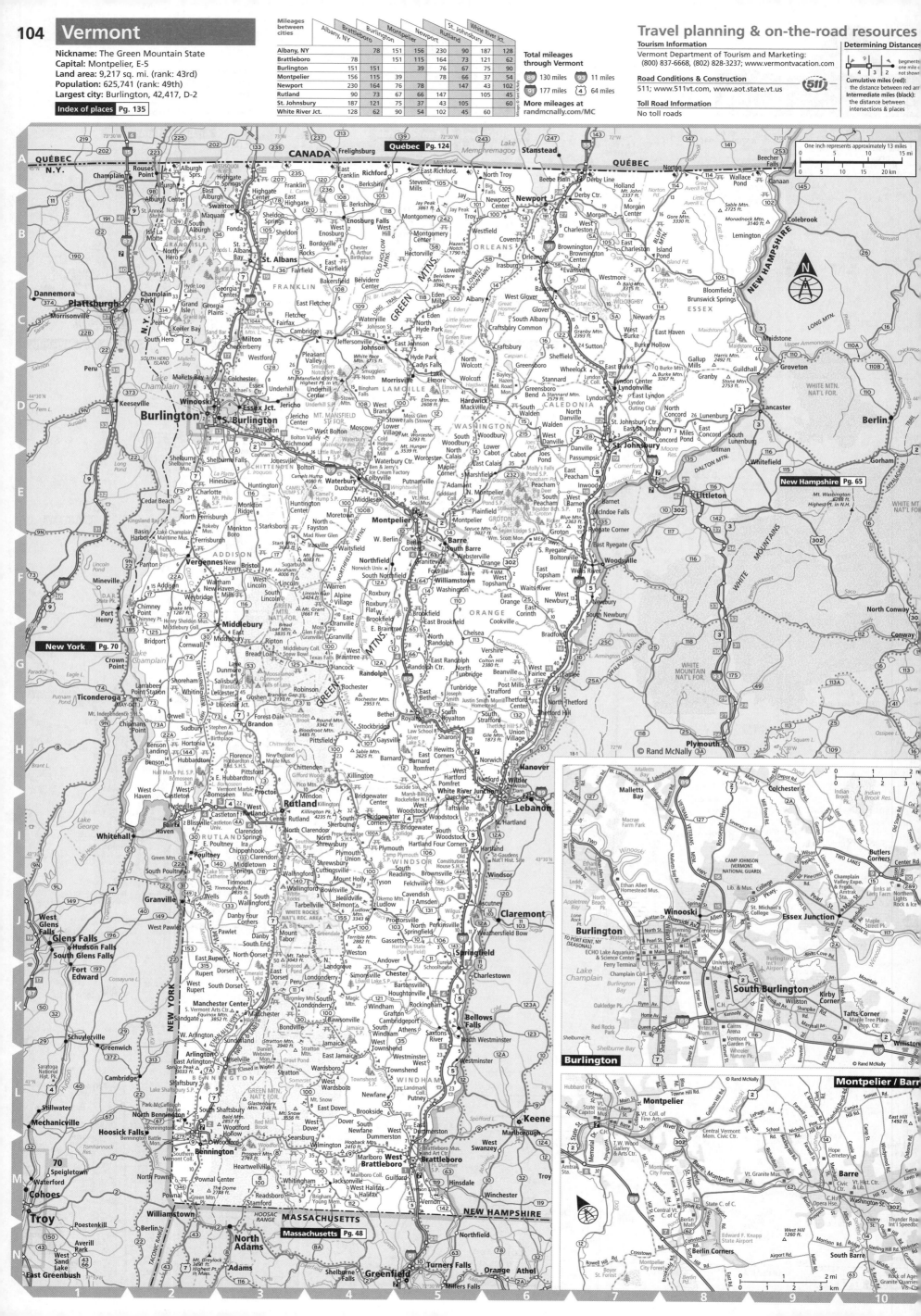

Historic Downtown Mall, Charlottesville

Sights to see

Nickname: Old Dominion
Capital: Richmond, J-14
Land area: 39,490 sq. mi. (rank: 36th)
Population: 8,001,024 (rank: 12th)
Largest city: Virginia Beach, 437,994, L-18

Index of places Pg. 135

Travel planning & on-the-road resources

Tourism Information
Virginia Tourism:
(800) 847-4882; www.virginia.org

Road Conditions & Construction
511, (866) 695-1182, (800) 367-7623;
www.511virginia.org,
www.virginiadot.org/travel

Toll Road Information *(all use E-ZPass)*
Chesapeake Expwy. (VA 168, in Chesapeake): (757) 204-0010; www.chesapeakeexpressway.com
Dulles Greenway: (703) 707-8870; www.dullesgreenway.com
Metro. Wash. Airports Authority (Dulles Toll Rd.): (877) 762-7824; www.dullestollroad.com
Pocahontas Pkwy. (Richmond): (866) 428-6339; www.pocahontas895.com
Richmond Metro. Trans. Auth. (toll rds. within Richmond): (804) 523-3300; www.rmaonline.org
Virginia Dept. of Transportation (all others): www.virginiadot.org/travel/faq-toll.asp

Toll Bridge/Tunnel Info. *(all use E-ZPass)*
Chesapeake Bay Bridge-Tunnel:
(757) 331-2960; www.cbbt.com
Elizabeth River Tunnels (Hampton Rds.):
(855) 378-7623; www.driveert.com
S. Norfolk Jordan Bridge:
(855) 690-7652; www.snjb.net

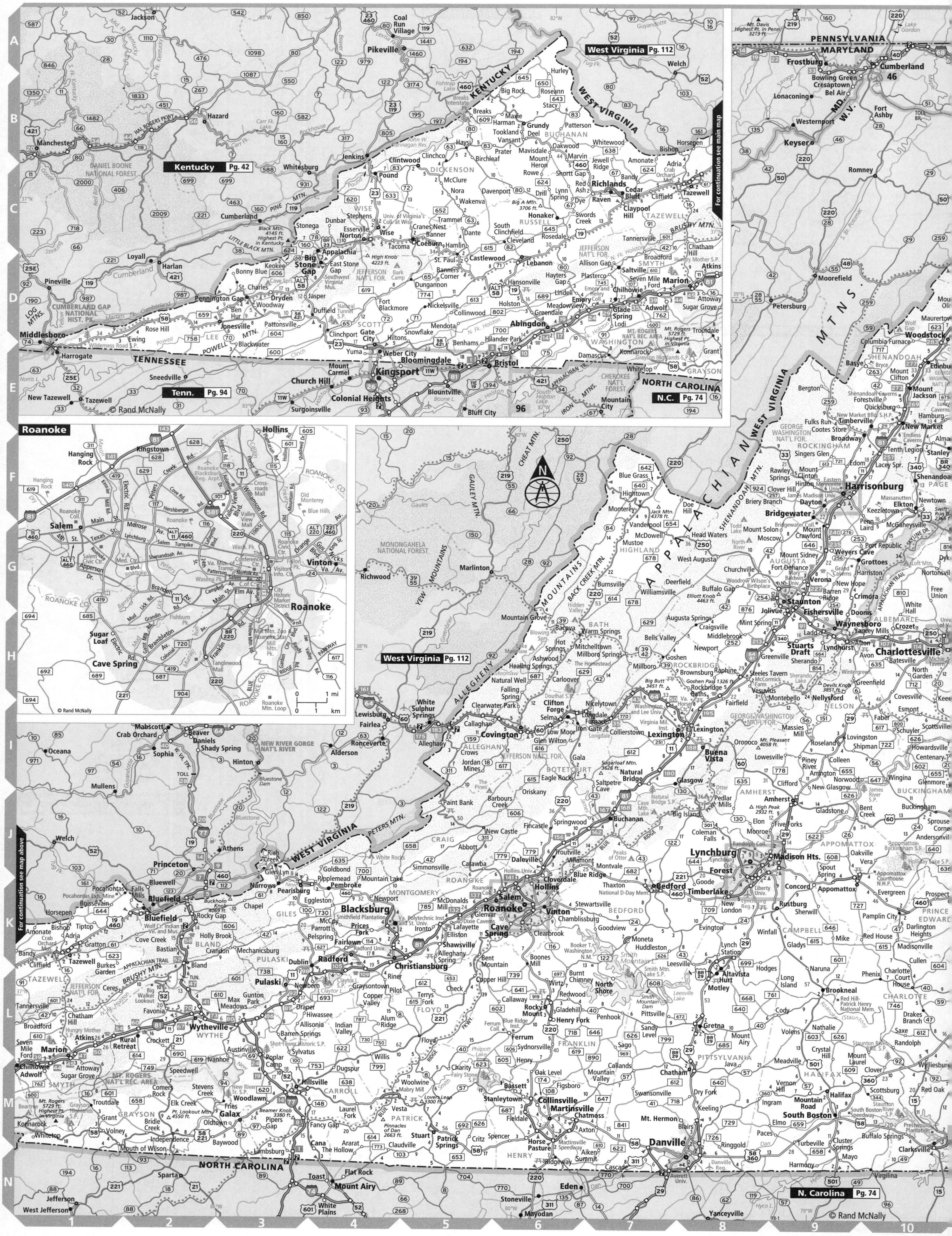

© Rand McNally

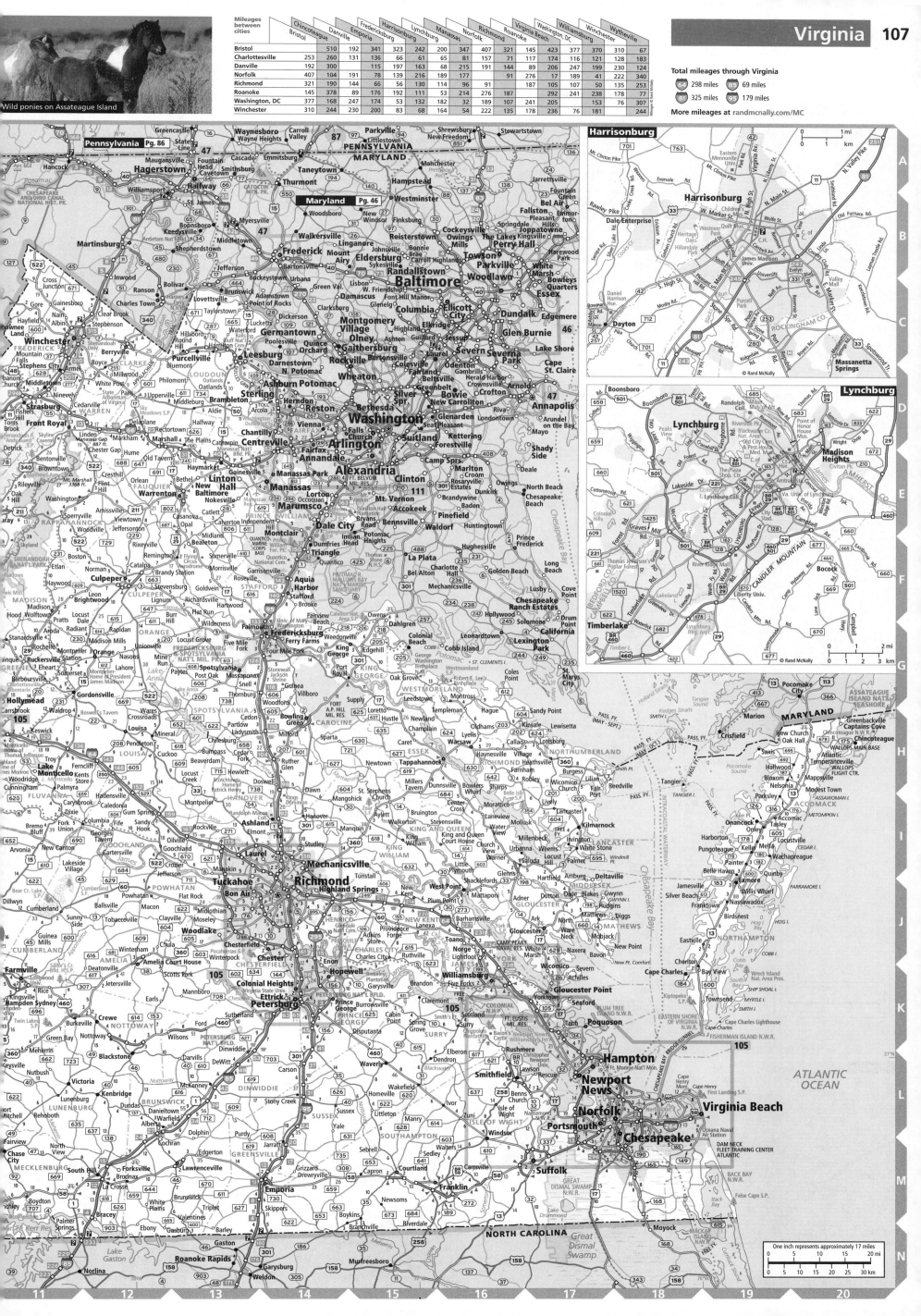

Wild ponies on Assateague Island

Mileages between cities	Bristol	Chincoteague	Danville	Emporia	Fredericksburg	Harrisonburg	Lynchburg	Manassas	Norfolk	Richmond	Roanoke	Virginia Beach	Washington, DC	Williamsburg	Winchester	Wytheville
Bristol		510	192	341	323	242	200	347	407	321	145	423	377	370	310	67
Charlottesville	253	260	131	136	66	61	65	81	157	71	117	174	116	121	128	183
Danville	192	300		115	197	163	68	215	191	144	89	206	247	199	230	124
Norfolk	407	104	301		78	139	216	189	177	91	276	17	189	41	222	340
Richmond	321	190	144	66		92	130	114	96	91	187	105	107	50	135	253
Roanoke	145	378	89	176	292	111	53	214	276	187		292	241	238	178	79
Washington, DC	377	168	247	174	53	132	182	32	189	107	241	205		153	76	307
Winchester	310	244	230	200	83	68	164	54	222	135	178	236	76	181		244

Total mileages through Virginia
64 298 miles   85 69 miles
81 325 miles   95 179 miles

More mileages at randmcnally.com/MC

Nickname: The Evergreen State
Capital: Olympia, H-6
Land area: 66,455 sq. mi. (rank: 20th)
Population: 6,724,540 (rank: 13th)
Largest city: Seattle, 608,660, F-7

Index of places Pg. 135

Travel planning & on-the-road resources

Tourism Information
Washington Tourism: (800) 544-1800; www.experiencewa.com

Road Conditions & Construction
511, (800) 695-7623; www.wsdot.wa.gov/traffic

Toll Bridge Information
Wash. St. Dept. of Trans. (Tacoma Narrows Br., SR 520 Br.): (866) 936-8246; www.wsdot.wa.gov/tolling

511 (Good to Go!)

Determining distances along roads

Highway distances (segments of one mile or less not shown):
Cumulative miles (red): the distance between red arrows
Intermediate miles (black): the distance between intersections & places

Interchanges and exit numbers
For most states, the mileage between interchanges may be determined by subtracting one number from the other.

One inch represents approximately 20 miles
0 5 10 15 20 mi
0 10 20 30 km

18-1 © Rand McNally

Olympia (inset map)

Oregon Pg. 84

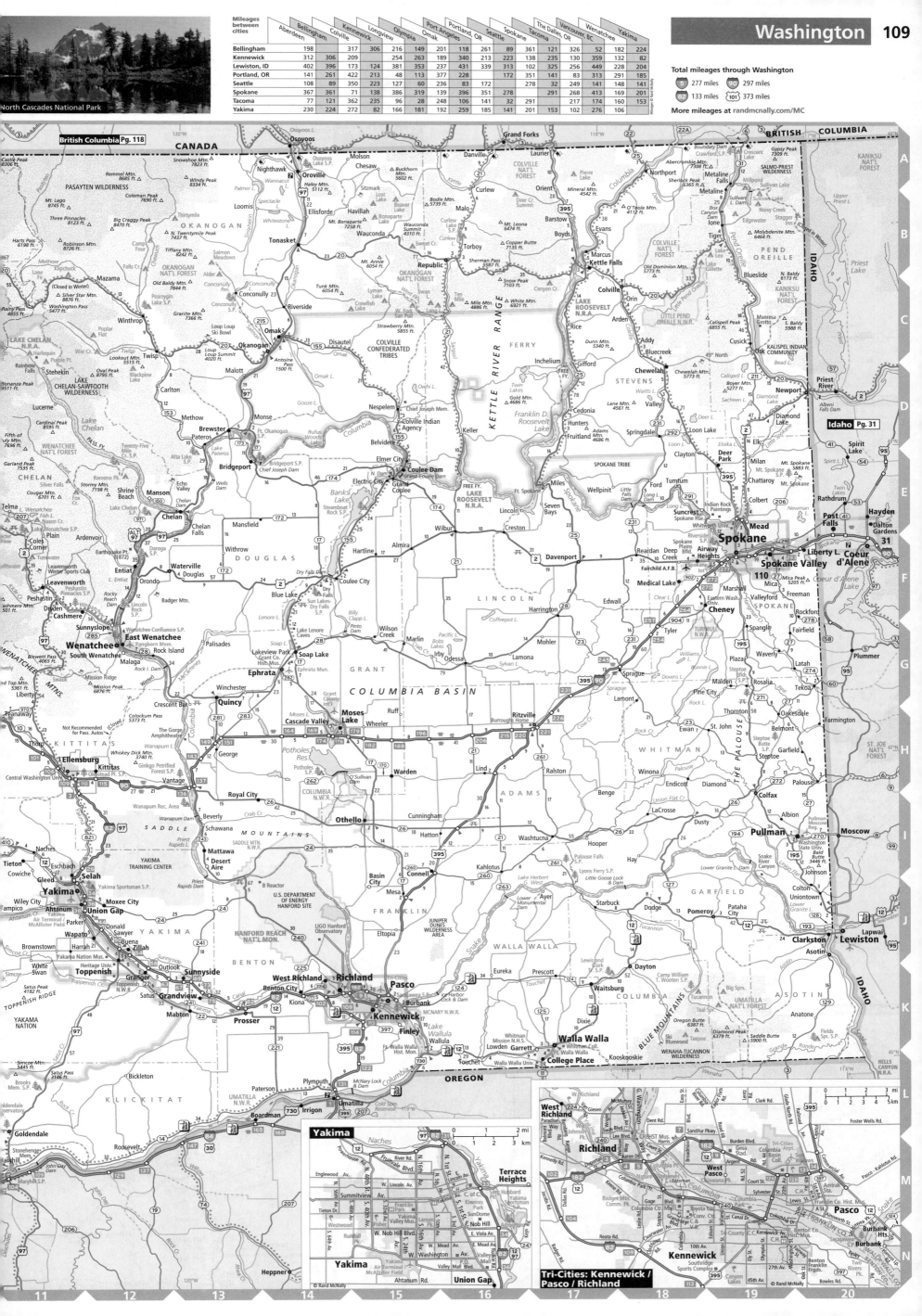

North Cascades National Park

Mileages between cities

	Aberdeen	Bellingham	Colville	Kennewick	Longview	Olympia	Port Angeles	Portland, OR	Seattle	Spokane	Tacoma	The Dalles, OR	Vancouver, BC	Wenatchee	Yakima
Bellingham	198		317	306	216	149	201	261	89	361	121	326	52	182	224
Kennewick	312	306	209		254	263	340	213	223	138	235	130	359	132	82
Lewiston, ID	402	396	173	124	381	353	431	237	339	102	325	256	449	228	204
Portland, OR	141	261	422	213	48	113	377		172	351	141	83	313	291	185
Seattle	108	89	350	223	127	60	236	172		278	32	249	141	148	141
Spokane	367	361	71	138	386	319	396	351	278		291	268	413	169	201
Tacoma	77	121	362	235	96	28	106	141	32	291		217	174	160	153
Yakima	230	224	272	82	166	181	259	185	141	201	153	102	276	106	

Total mileages through Washington

- 5 — 277 miles
- 90 — 297 miles
- 82 — 133 miles
- 2 — 373 miles

More mileages at randmcnally.com/MC

British Columbia Pg. 118

Idaho Pg. 31

Spokane 110

Yakima

Tri-Cities: Kennewick / Pasco / Richland

Sights to see

- Experience Music Project, Seattle................H-1
- Frye Art Museum, Seattle......................J-3
- Klondike Gold Rush National Historical Park, Seattle ..K-2
- Museum of Glass, Tacoma......................L-6
- Nordic Heritage Museum, Seattle C-7
- Pacific Science Center, Seattle..................H-1
- Pike Place Market, Seattle J-2
- Point Defiance Zoo & Aquarium, Tacoma............K-5
- Seattle Aquarium, Seattle.........................J-1
- Space Needle, Seattle.............................H-1
- Washington State History Museum, Tacoma L-6
- Woodland Park Zoo, Seattle.......................C-7

Elliott Bay, Seattle

Spokane

Bellingham

Central Seattle

Mount Rainier National Park

Seattle / Tacoma & Vicinity

On-the-road resources

Tourism Information

Destination DC:
(800) 422-8644, (202) 789-7000; www.washington.org

Road Conditions & Construction
(202) 737-4404, (202) 673-6813; ddot.dc.gov

Road Information
For toll roads in District of Columbia see Maryland or Virginia pages for toll road information

Sights to see

- Arlington National Cemetery, Arlington, VA N-1
- Frederick Douglass National Historic Site.. . G-7
- John F. Kennedy Center for the Performing Arts. L-3
- Martin Luther King Jr. Memorial.... M-4
- National African American Museum.. L-6
- National Arboretum F-7
- National Mall. M-7
- National Zoological Park F-6
- The Pentagon, Arlington, VA G-6
- The Supreme Court of the United States M-9
- United States Botanic Garden M-8
- The White House K-5
- Wolf Trap National Park for the Performing Arts, Vienna, VA E-2

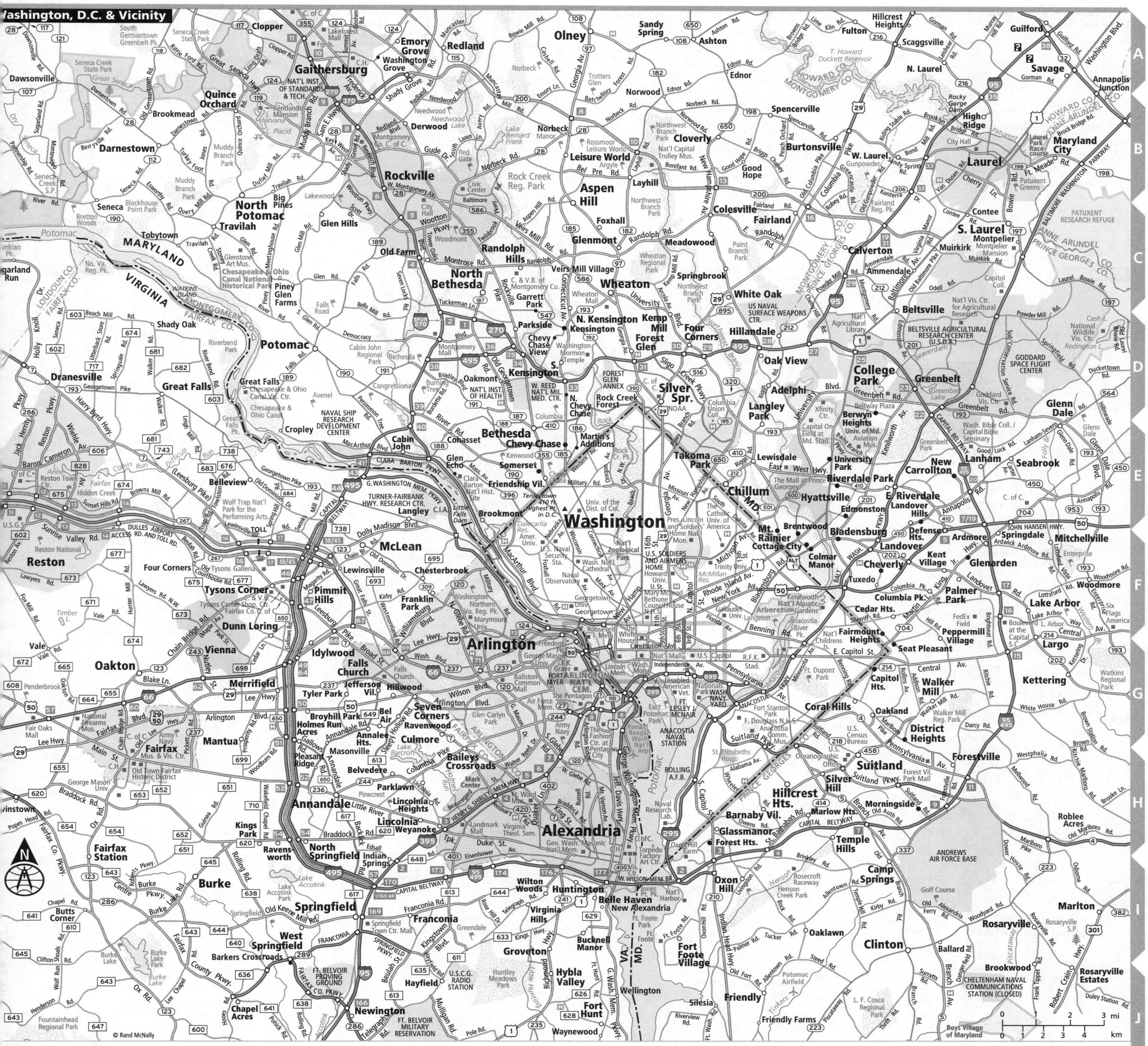

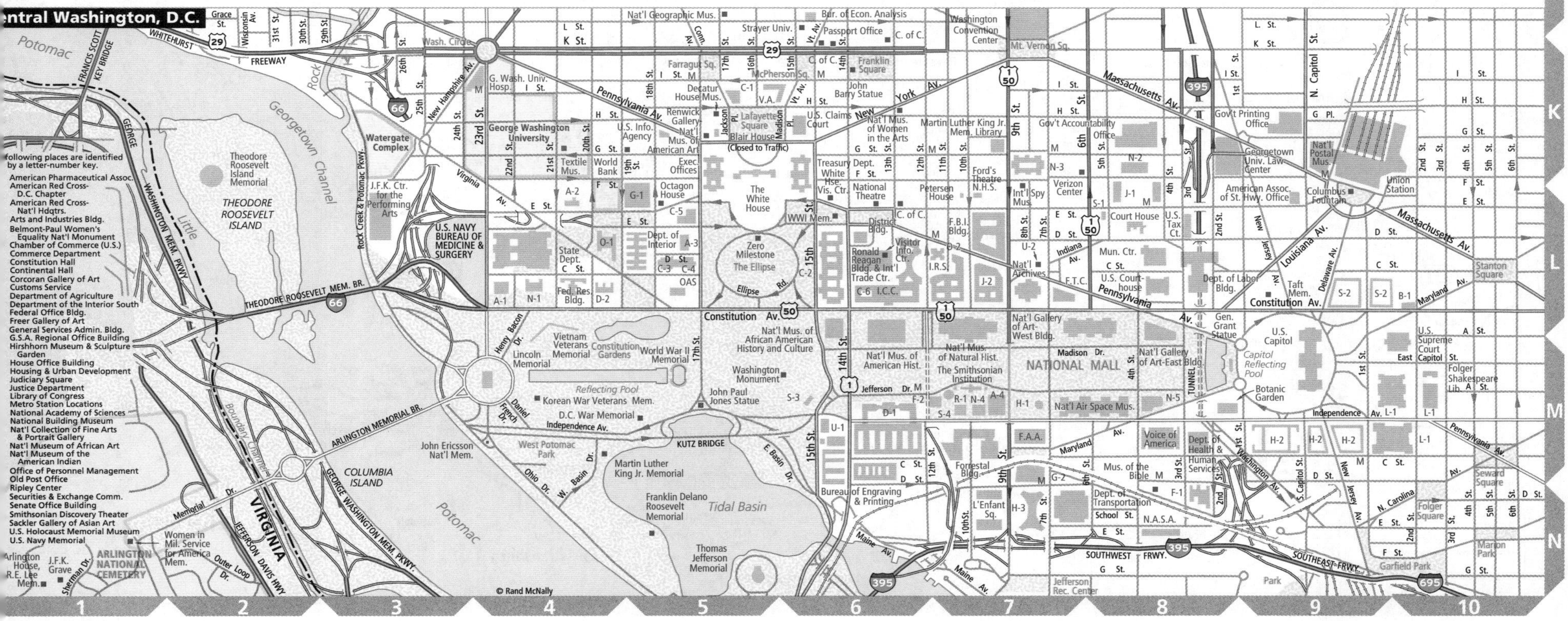

Washington, D.C.

Land area: 61 sq. mi. | Population: 601,723

Washington, D.C. & Vicinity

Central Washington, D.C.

© Rand McNally

Nickname: The Mountain State
Capital: Charleston, J-3
Land area: 24,038 sq. mi. (rank: 41st)
Population: 1,852,994 (rank: 37th)
Largest city: Charleston, 51,400, J-3

Index of places Pg. 135

Mileages between cities

	Bluefield	Charleston	Clarksburg	Cumberland, MD	Martinsburg	Petersburg	Wheeling	White Sulphur Sprs.
Beckley	50	59	136	239	267	184	236	59
Charleston	106		123	225	304	193	177	120
Cumberland, MD	288	225	109		79	66	155	194
Huntington	158	51	174	276	355	244	228	172
Morgantown	218	164	38	73	151	103	78	187
Parkersburg	183	76	72	181	259	172	104	198
Wheeling	283	177	114	155	225	179		262
White Sulphur Sprs.	79	120	155	194	208	125	262	

Total mileages through West Virginia

54 — 189 miles   77 — 187 miles
64 — 14 miles   79 — 161 miles

More mileages at randmcnally.com/MC

Tourism Information
West Virginia Division of Tourism:
(800) 225-5982, (304) 558-2200; www.wvtourism.com, gotowv.com

Road Conditions & Construction
511, (877) 982-7623; www.wv511.org, www.transportation.wv.gov

Toll Road Information (E-ZPass)
W.V. Parkways Authority: (304) 926-1900; www.transportation.wv.gov/turnpike

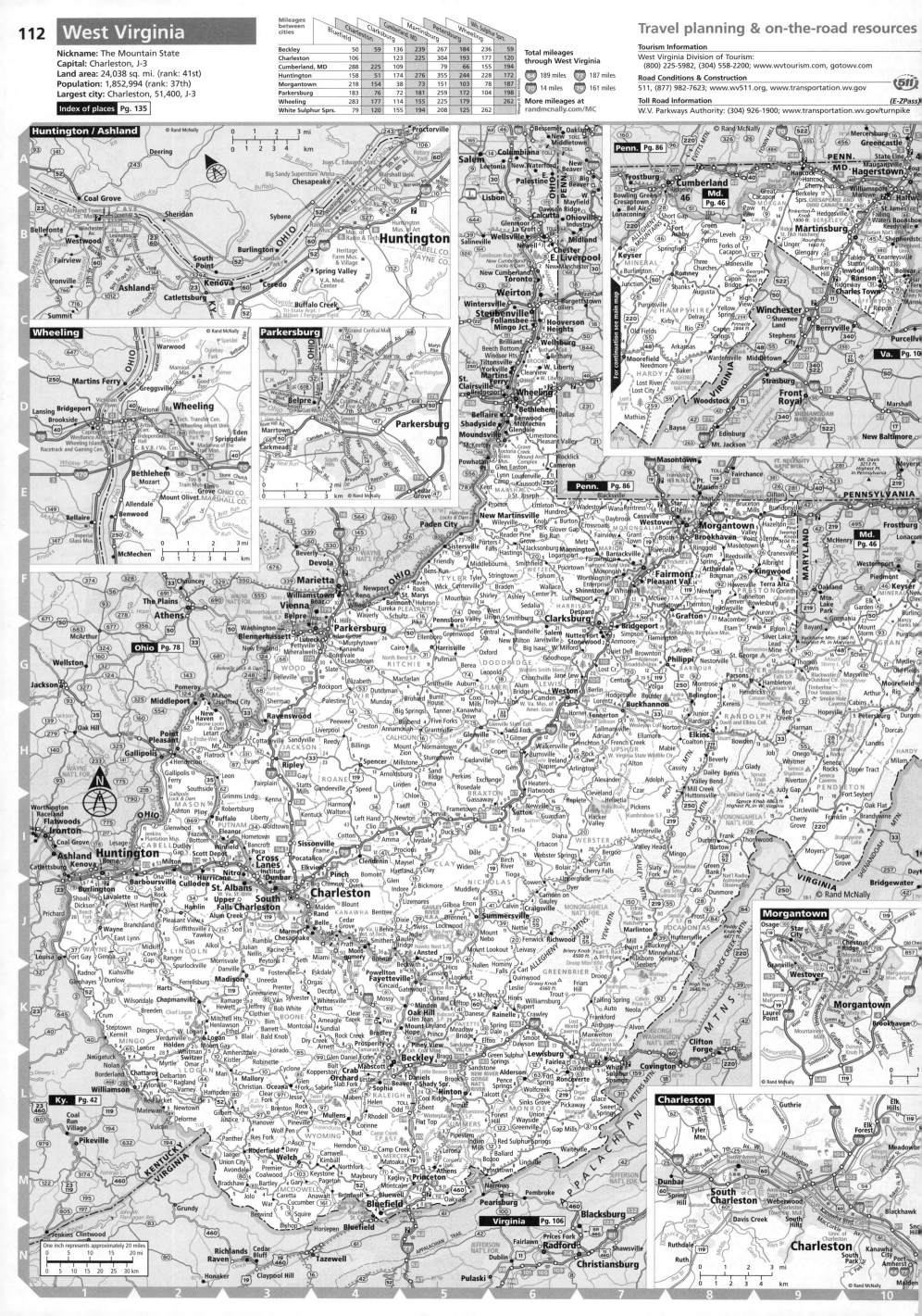

One inch represents approximately 20 miles
© Rand McNally

arborPark promenade, Kenosha

Sights to see

Milwaukee & Vicinity

La Crosse

Sheboygan

Kenosha / Racine

Janesville / Beloit

Central Milwaukee

Nickname: The Badger State
Capital: Madison, N-9
Land area: 54,158 sq. mi. (rank: 25th)
Population: 5,686,986 (rank: 20th)
Largest city: Milwaukee, 594,833, N-13

Index of places **Pg. 136**

Travel planning & on-the-road resources

Tourism Information
Wisconsin Department of Tourism: (800) 432-8747, (608) 266-2161; www.travelwisconsin.com

Road Conditions & Construction
511, (866) 511-9472; www.511wi.gov

Toll Road Information
No toll roads

Determining distances along roads

Highway distances (segments of one mile or less not shown):
Cumulative miles (red): the distance between red arrows
Intermediate miles (black): the distance between intersections & places

Interchanges and exit numbers
For most states, the mileage between interchanges may be determined by subtracting one number from the other.

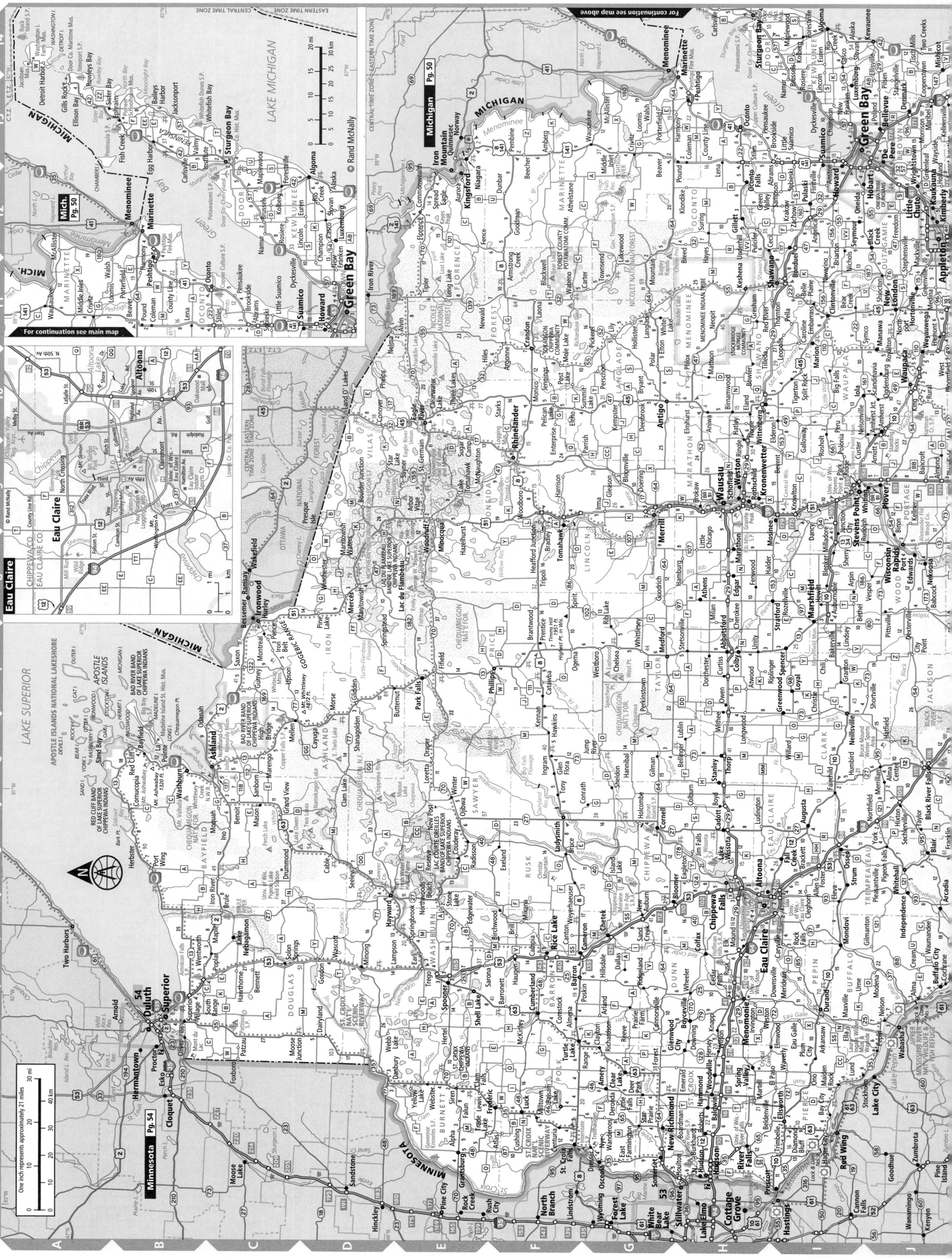

© Rand McNally

(Map of Wisconsin showing cities, highways, lakes, and geographic features including Lake Superior, Lake Michigan, Green Bay, Door County, Eau Claire, Madison, Milwaukee area, and surrounding regions of Michigan and Minnesota.)

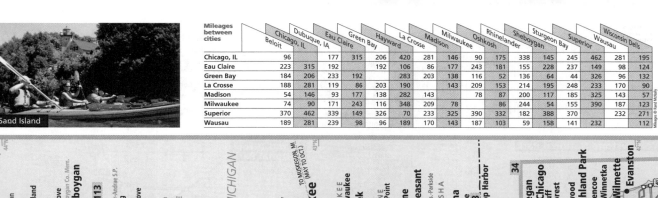

...ghthouse, Sand Island

Mileages between cities

	Chicago, IL / Beloit	Dubuque, IA	Eau Claire	Green Bay	Hayward	La Crosse	Madison	Milwaukee	Oshkosh	Rhinelander	Sheboygan	Sturgeon Bay	Superior	Wausau	Wisconsin Dells
Chicago, IL	96	177	315	206	420	281	146	90	175	338	145	245	462	281	195
Eau Claire	223	315		192		192	420	86	177	243	181	228	237	149	98	124
Green Bay	184	206	233	192		283	203	138	116	52	64	44	326	96	132
La Crosse	188	281	119	86	203		190	143	209	153	214	195	248	233	170	90
Madison	54	146	93	177	138	282	143		78	200	117	185	325	143	57
Milwaukee	74	90	171	243	116	209	78		86	224	54	155	390	187	123
Superior	370	462	339	149	326	70	233	325	390	332	182	388	370	232	271
Wausau	189	281	239	98	96	189	170	143	187	103	59	158	141	232	112

Total mileages through Wisconsin

- (39) 182 miles
- (90) 189 miles
- (94) 192 miles
- (43) 341 miles

More mileages at randmcnally.com/MC

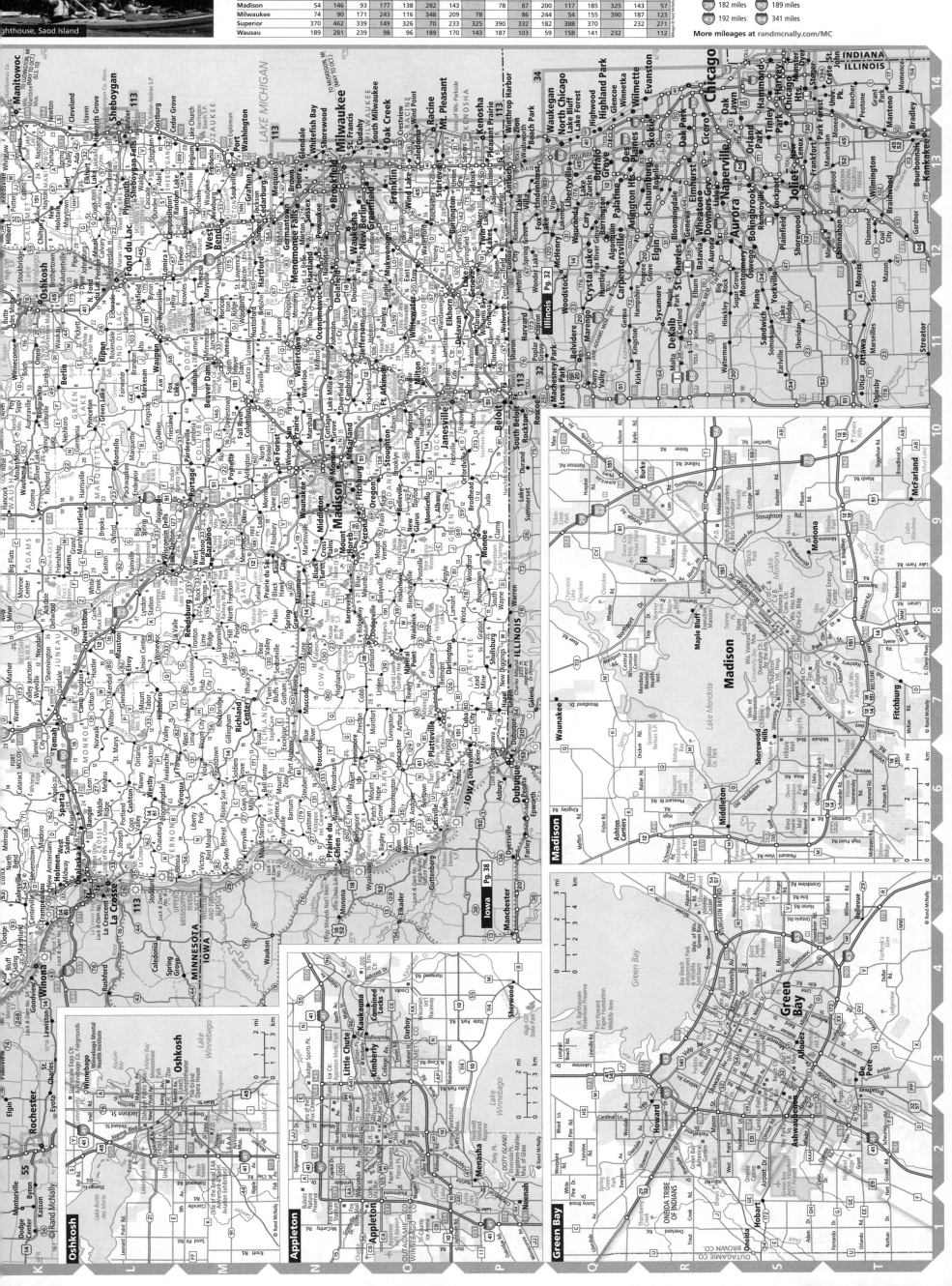

Nicknames: The Equality State
Capital: Cheyenne, M-9
Land area: 97,093 sq. mi. (rank: 9th)
Population: 563,626 (rank: 50th)
Largest city: Cheyenne, 59,466, M-9

Index of places Pg. 136

Mileages between cities	Casper	Cheyenne	Cody	Evanston	Gillette	Laramie	Sheridan	Spearfish, SD
Casper		178	213	325	126	147	148	219
Cheyenne	178		392	357	244	49	324	290
Cody	213	392		376	250	363	148	344
Jackson	283	432	177	190	411	383	325	504
Riverton	119	272	138	238	248	213	213	341
Rock Springs	225	257	278	100	351	207	373	444
Sheridan	148	324	148	473	103	294		196
Spearfish, SD	219	290	344	544	93	296	196	

Total mileages through Wyoming

- 301 miles
- 209 miles
- 403 miles
- 505 miles

More mileages at randmcnally.com/MC

Travel planning & on-the-road resources

Tourism Information
Wyoming Office of Tourism: (800) 225-5996,
(307) 777-7777; www.wyomingtourism.org

Road Conditions & Construction
511, (888) 996-7623; www.wyoroad.info

Toll Road Information
No toll roads

Determining Distance
Cumulative miles (red): the distance between red intersections
Intermediate miles (black): the distance between intersections & places

Selected National Park locations

Banff National Park G-3	Gros Morne National Park F-13	Kootenay National Park G-3	Prince Edward Island Nat'l Park H-12
Cape Breton Highlands Nat'l Park . .G-13	Jasper National Park F-3	Mount Revelstoke National Park G-3	Pukaskwa National Park H-8
Fundy National Park H-12	Kejimkujik National Park H-12	Parc National de la Maurice H-11	Riding Mountain National Park H-6
Glacier National Park H-3	Kluane National Park & Reserve C-2	Prince Albert National Park F-5	St. Lawrence Islands National Park . . I-10

Capital: Ottawa, I-10
Land area: 3,511,023 sq. mi.
Population: 33,476,688
Largest city: Toronto, 2,615,060, I-10

Index of places Pg. 136

Mileage between principal cities
Miles in red; kilometers in blue

Cities listed: CALGARY, AB · DAWSON CREEK, BC · EDMONTON, AB · HALIFAX, NS · HAVRE-ST-PIERRE, QC · MONTRÉAL, QC · PRINCE RUPERT, BC · QUÉBEC, QC · REGINA, SK · SAINT JOHN, NB · SAULT STE. MARIE, ON · THUNDER BAY, ON · TORONTO, ON · VANCOUVER, BC · WHITEHORSE, YK · WINDSOR, ON · WINNIPEG, MB

Glossary of French terms

Aéroport	Airport
Arrondissement	District
Baie	Bay
Barrage	Dam
Basilique	Basilica
Bibliothèque	Library
Bois	Woods
Cap	Cape
Centre de recherches	Research centre (or center)
Centre des congrès	Convention centre (or center)
Chemin	Road
Chenal	Channel
Chutes	Falls
Débarquement	Landing
Détroit	Strait
Fleuve	Major river (that flows to the sea)
Hippodrome	Race track
Hôtel de Ville	City or town hall
Île	Island
Jardin	Garden
Jardin botanique	Botanical garden
Jardin zoologique	Zoological garden (or Zoo)
Lac	Lake
Lieu historique	Historic site
Hôtel du Parlement	Parliament building
Lieu historique national	National historic site
Lieu natal	Birthplace
Mont	Mountain
Musée	Museum
Oratoire	Oratory
Parc	Park
Parc marin	Marine park
Parc national	National park (or provincial park in Québec)
Pont	Bridge
Promenade	Boulevard
Réserve faunique	Wildlife reserve
Réserve indienne	Indian reserve (or Reservation)
Rivière	River
Rue	Street
Stade	Stadium
Tribunal	Court house
Université	University

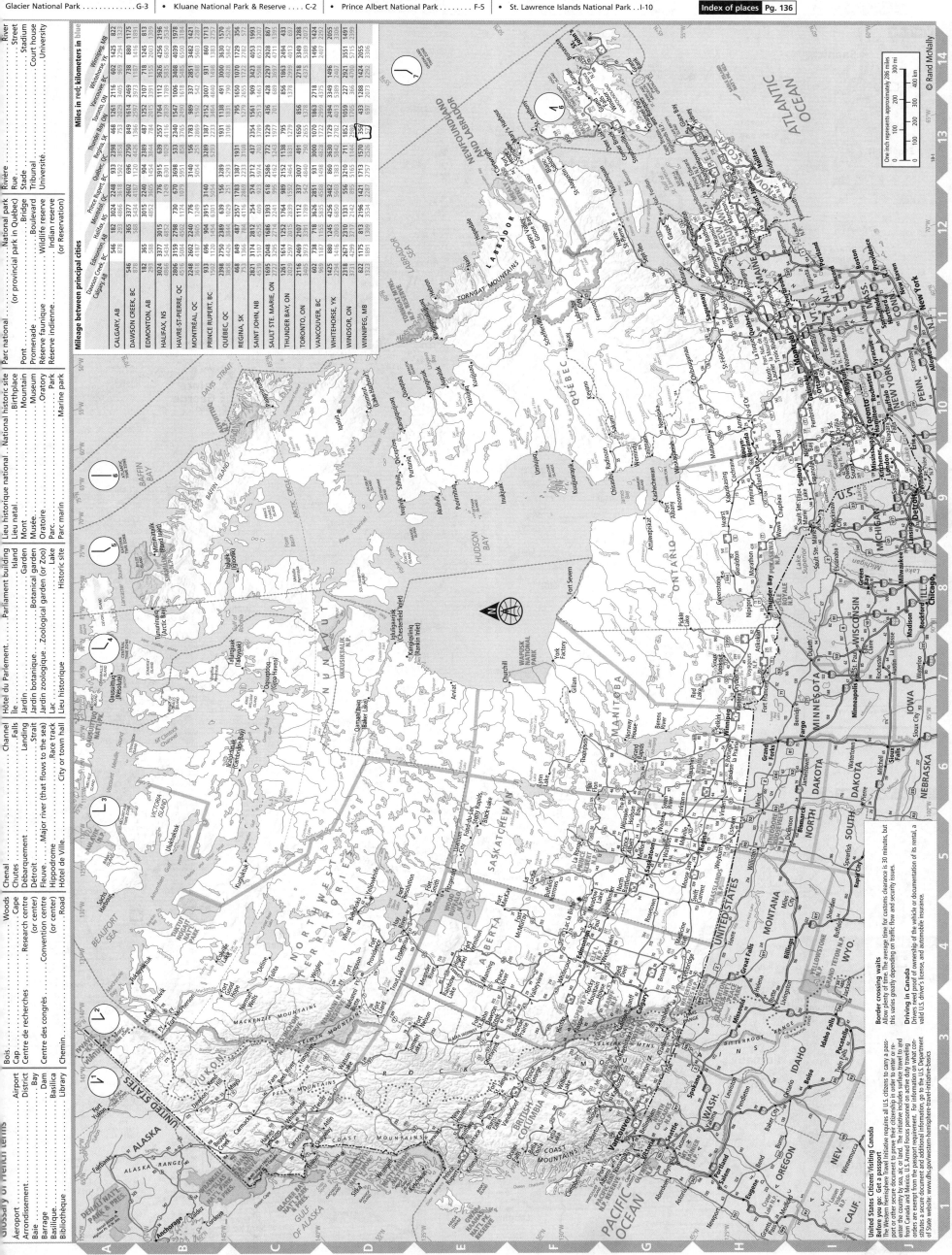

© Rand McNally

British Columbia
Capital: Victoria, M-7
Land area: 357,216 sq. mi. (rank: 4th)
Population: 4,400,057 (rank: 3rd)
Largest city: Vancouver, 603,502, L-7

Index of places Pg. 136

Mileages between cities

	Banff, AB	Dawson Creek, AB	Jasper, AB	Port Hardy	Prince Rupert	Vancouver	Victoria	Williams Lake	*Via ferry
Banff, AB		503	178	808*	855	524	578*	483	
Cranbrook	173	638	312	806*	989	521	575*	553	
Dawson Creek	503		326	1022*	696	738	791*	399	
Kamloops	307	576	275	502*	769	217	271*	177	
Kelowna	299	671	376	526*	865	242	295*	272	
Prince George	408	250	231	772*	447	488	542*	149	
Prince Rupert	855	696	677	307*		931	985*	592	
Vancouver	524	738	492	285*	931		72*	339	

Total mileages through British Columbia
[1] 538 miles
[16] 658 miles
More mileages at randmcnally.com/MC

Travel planning & on-the-road resources

Tourism Information
Destination British Columbia:
(604) 660-2861; www.hellobc.com

Road Conditions & Construction
(800) 550-4997; www.drivebc.ca

Toll Bridges
TransLink (Golden Ears Bridge, Vancouver) (QuickPass, TreO):
(877) 299-0599; www.translink.ca
Transportation Investment Corp.: (Port Mann Bridge, Vancouver) (TreO):
(604) 516-8736; www.treo.ca

One inch represents approximately 46 miles
0 10 20 30 40 50 mi
0 10 20 30 40 50 60 70 80 km

© Rand McNally

Saskatchewan
Capital: Regina, K-8
Land area: 228,445 sq. mi. (rank: 7th)
Population: 1,033,381 (rank: 6th)
Largest city: Saskatoon, 222,189, G-6

Index of places Pg. 136

Mileages between cities	La Loche	La Ronge	Medicine Hat, AB	N. Battleford	Prince Albert	Regina	Saskatoon	Yorkton
Estevan	668	498	391	371	350	125	285	159
Lloydminster	331	347	289	85	214	331	171	375
Meadow Lake	217	232	370	98	162	343	183	388
Prince Albert	318	148	365	129		225	88	233
Regina	543	373	289	246	225		160	116
Saskatoon	379	236	277	86	88	160		205
Swift Current	505	403	139	190	255	151	167	266
Yorkton	551	382	405	290	233	116	205	

Total mileages through Saskatchewan
1 413 miles
16 437 miles
More mileages at randmcnally.com/MC

Travel planning & on-the-road resources

Tourism Information
Tourism Saskatchewan: (877) 237-2273, (306) 787-2300;
www.sasktourism.com, www.tourismsaskatchewan.com

Toll Road Info
No toll roads

Road Conditions & Construction
In Saskatchewan only: (888) 335-7623,
Saskatoon area: (306) 933-8333, Regina area: (306) 787-7623;
www.saskatchewan.ca/residents/transportation/highways/highway-hotline

© Rand McNally

travel planning & on-the-road resources

Tourism Information
Travel Manitoba: (800) 665-0040, (204) 927-7800;
www.travelmanitoba.com

Road Conditions & Construction
511
MB, (877) 627-6237, (204) 945-3704;
www.manitoba.ca/roadinfo

Road Information
toll roads

Determining Distances
(segments of one mile or less not shown)
Cumulative miles (red), km (blue):
the distance between red arrows
Intermediate miles (black):
the distance between intersections & places

Total mileages through Manitoba
1 306 miles
16 166 miles

More mileages at
randmcnally.com/MC

Mileages between cities

	Ashern	Brandon	Dauphin	Flin Flon	Grand Rapids	Pine Falls	Thompson	Winnipeg
Brandon	200		104	444	355	217	558	134
Dauphin	127	104		342	282	267	485	198
Flin Flon	368	444	342		255	546	244	483
Morden	184	129	216	552	338	167	542	87
Portage la Prairie	119	80	144	485	274	136	477	53
Swan River	233	208	106	236	211	372	385	303
Virden	245	47	148	419	399	262	568	178
Winnipeg	114	134	198	483	269	81	472	

Manitoba
Capital: Winnipeg, L-17
Land area: 213,729 sq. mi. (rank: 8th)
Population: 1,208,268 (rank: 5th)
Largest city: Winnipeg, 663,617, L-17
Index of places Pg. 136

One inch represents approximately 38 miles

Ontario Pg. 122
N. Dakota Pg. 77
Minnesota Pg. 54

Capital: Toronto, I-10
Land area: 354,342 sq. mi. (rank: 5th)
Population: 12,851,821 (rank: 1st)
Largest city: Toronto, 2,615,060, I-10

Glossary of common French terms found on these maps: pg. 117

Travel planning & on-the-road resources

Tourism Information
Ontario Travel: (800) 668-2746; www.ontariotravel.net

Road Conditions & Construction
511, (800) 268-4686, Toronto area: (416) 235-4686; www.mto.gov.on.ca/english/traveller

Toll Road Information:
407 ETR (Toronto): (888) 407-0407; www.407etr.com

Ontario–Michigan Toll Bridge Information:
Ambassador Bridge (Detroit): (800) 462-7434; www.ambassadorbridge.com
Federal Bridge Corp. (Blue Water Bridge, Sarnia):
  (866) 422-6346; www.bluewaterbridge.ca
Detroit-Windsor Tunnel (NEXPRESS):
  (313) 567-4422 ext. 200, (519) 258-7424 ext. 200; www.dwtunnel.com
International Bridge Administration (Sault Ste. Marie):
  (705) 942-4345, (906) 635-5255; www.saultbridge.com

Ontario–New York Toll Bridge Info
Buffalo & Ft. Erie Public Br. Authority
  (Peace Bridge) (E-ZPass):
  (716) 884-6744; www.peacebridge.com
Niagara Falls Bridge Commission:
  (E-ZPass or ExpressPass) (716) 285-6322;
  www.niagarafallsbridges.com
For St. Lawrence River crossings, see New York, p. 70

Niagara-on-the-Lake

Mileages between cities	Bracebridge	Hamilton	Kenora	Kingston	Montréal, QC	Niagara Falls	Ottawa	Owen Sound	Pembroke	Sarnia	Sault Ste. Marie	Sudbury	Thunder Bay	Timmins	Toronto	Windsor
Kingston	223	204	1285		180	243	120	269	154	335	555	369	983	509	161	381
London	213	47	1255	274	450	127	360	143	360	68	525	339	953	535	121	116
Niagara Falls	185	44	1227	243	419		329	163	328	168	497	311	925	507	83	233
Ottawa	237	290	1207	120	124	329		338	91	421	494	301	905	445	247	467
Sudbury	153	272	925	369	424	311	300	238	209	401	195		623	182	242	446
Thunder Bay	767	886	303	983	989	925	905	852	814	1015	436	623		517	856	1060
Toronto	116	44	1158	161	337	83	247	118	246	182	428	242	856	438		227
Windsor	319	187	1361	381	556	233	467	259	466	96	631	445	1059	641	227	

Total mileages through Ontario

69 & 400 & QEW 323 miles   401 513 miles

17 & 417 1358 miles

More mileages at randmcnally.com/MC

Capital: Québec, J-11
Land area: 527,079 sq. mi. (rank: 2nd)
Population: 7,903,001 (rank: 2nd)
Largest city: Montréal, 1,649,519, M-8

Glossary of common French terms found on these maps: pg. 117

Index of places Pg. 136

Travel planning & on-the-road resources

Tourism Information
Tourisme Québec: (877) 266-5687, (514) 873-2015;
www.bonjourquebec.com

Road Conditions & Construction
511, (888) 355-0511;
www.quebec511.gouv.qc.ca/en

Toll Road Information
Concession A25 (Pont Olivier-Charbonneau, Montréal) (*A25 Smart Link*):
(855) 766-8225, (514) 766-8225; www.a25.com
A30Express (near Montréal) (*A30 Express*):
(855) 783-3030, (514) 782-0800;
www.a30express.com

Determining distances along roads

Highway distances (segments of one mile or less not shown):
Cumulative miles (red): the distance between red arrows
Cumulative kilometers (blue): the distance between red arrows
Intermediate miles (black): the distance between intersections & places

Comparative distance: 1 mile = 1.609 kilometers   1 kilometer = 0.621 mile

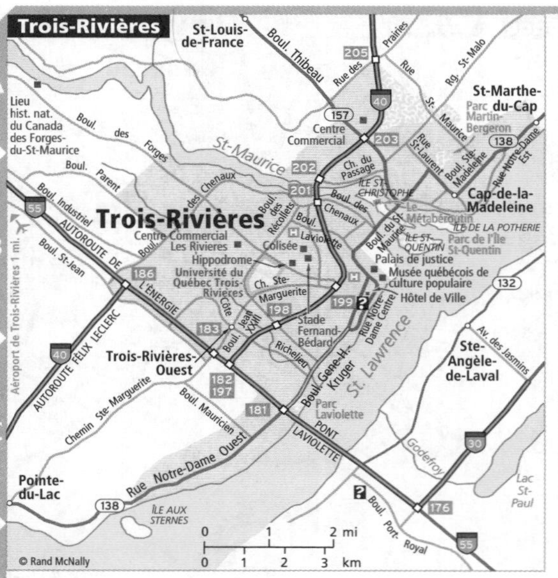

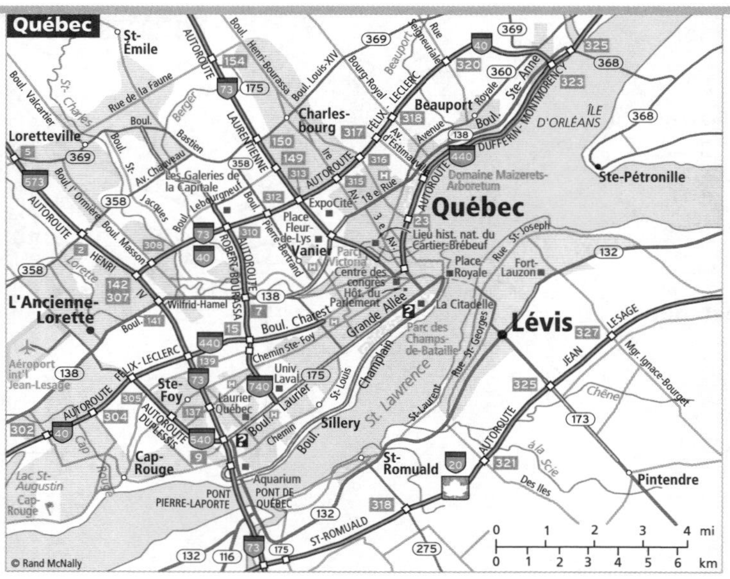

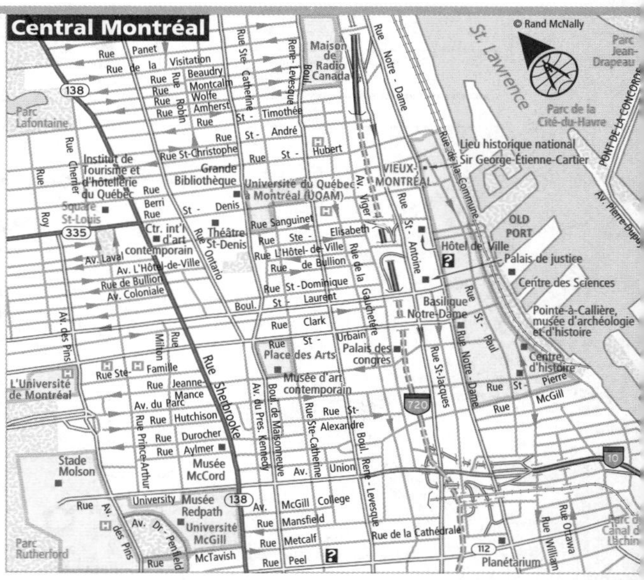

Trois-Rivières

Québec

Central Montréal

Sherbrooke

Ontario Pg. 122

New York Pg. 70

Vermont Pg. 104

© Rand McNally

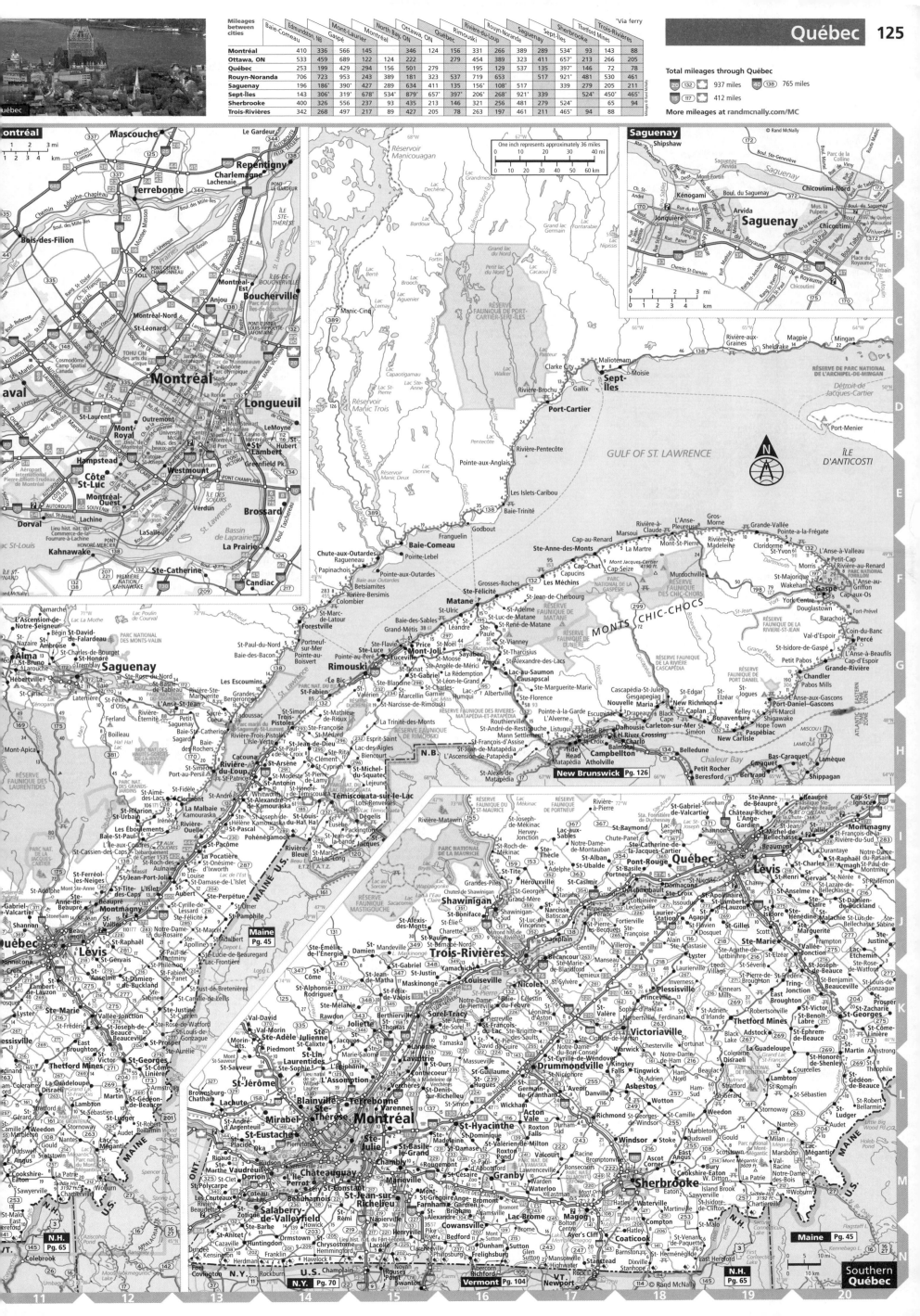

New Brunswick
Capital: Fredericton, H-4
Land area: 27,587 sq. mi. (rank: 11th)
Population: 751,171 (rank: 8th)
Largest city: Saint John, 70,063, J-5

Index of places **Pg. 136**

Travel planning & on-the-road resources

Tourism Information
Tourism New Brunswick:
(800) 561-0123;
www.tourismnewbrunswick.ca
Nova Scotia Tourism Agency:
(800) 565-0000, (902) 425-5781;
www.novascotia.com

Prince Edward Island Tourism:
(800) 463-4734;
www.tourismpei.com
Newfoundland &
Labrador Tourism:
(800) 563-6353, (709) 729-2830;
www.newfoundlandlabrador.com

Road Conditions & Construction
New Brunswick:
511, (888) 747-7006,
(506) 453-3939;
www.gnb.ca/roads
Nova Scotia:
511, (902) 424-3933
In Canada: (888) 780-4440;
511.gov.ns.ca/map

Prince Edward Island:
511, (902) 368-4770,
In Canada: (855) 241-2680;
www.gov.pe.ca/roadconditions
Newfoundland & Labrador:
Avalon: (709) 729-2382, Eastern: (709) 466-4120,
Central: (709) 292-4300, Western: (709) 635-4217,
Labrador: (709) 896-7840; www.roads.gov.nl.ca

Toll Road Information
Strait Crossing Bridge Ltd:
(Confederation Bridge) *(StraitPass)*:
(888) 437-6565; www.confederationbridge.com
Atlantic Hwy. Management Corp. Ltd.
(Cobequid Pass, N.B. (Hwy 104)) *(E-Pass)*:
(902) 668-2211; www.cobequidpass.com
Halifax Harbor Bridges (Halifax): *(MACPASS)*:
(902) 463-2800; www.hdbc.ca

(Map of the Atlantic Provinces — New Brunswick, Nova Scotia, Prince Edward Island, and parts of Québec and Maine)

© Rand McNally

18-1

*Via ferry

	Amherst, NS	Bathurst, NB	Campbellton, NB	Charlottetown, PE	Corner Brook, NB	Edmundston, NB	Fredericton, NB	Grand Falls, NB	Halifax, NS	Moncton, NB	New Glasgow, NS	Saint John, NB	St. John's, NL	St. Stephen, NB	Sydney, NS	Yarmouth, NS
...lottetown, PE	82	214	280		461*	392	222	354	205	112	63	204	888*	274	215	389
...unundston, NB	319	160	125	392	817*		176	39	442	283	419	239	1244*	215	571	353
...dericton, NB	149	160	248	222	647*	176		138	272	113	249	65	1074*	80	401	183
...ifax, NS	122	286	353	205	496*	442	272	403		162	98	254	923*	323	250	188
...nt John, NB	39	137	203	112	537*	283	113	244	162	139	95		964*	164	291	346
...ohn's, NL	925*	1088*	1155*	888*	433	1244*	1074*	1205*	923*	825*	1056*	964*		1125*	688*	1107*
...ney, NS	252	415	482	215	261*	571	401	532	250	291	152	383	688*	452		434

Nova Scotia
Capital: Halifax, K-9
Land area: 20,594 sq. mi. (rank: 12th)
Population: 921,727 (rank: 7th)
Largest city: Halifax, 390,096, K-9

Prince Edward Island
Capital: Charlottetown, G-10
Land area: 2,185 sq. mi. (rank: 13th)
Population: 140,204 (rank: 10th)
Largest city: Charlottetown, 34,562, G-10

Newfoundland & Labrador
Capital: St. John's, F-20
Land area: 144,353 sq. mi. (rank: 10th)
Population: 514,536 (rank: 9th)
Largest city: St. John's, 106,172, F-20

More mileages at randmcnally.com/MC

Glossary of common French terms found on these maps: pg. 117

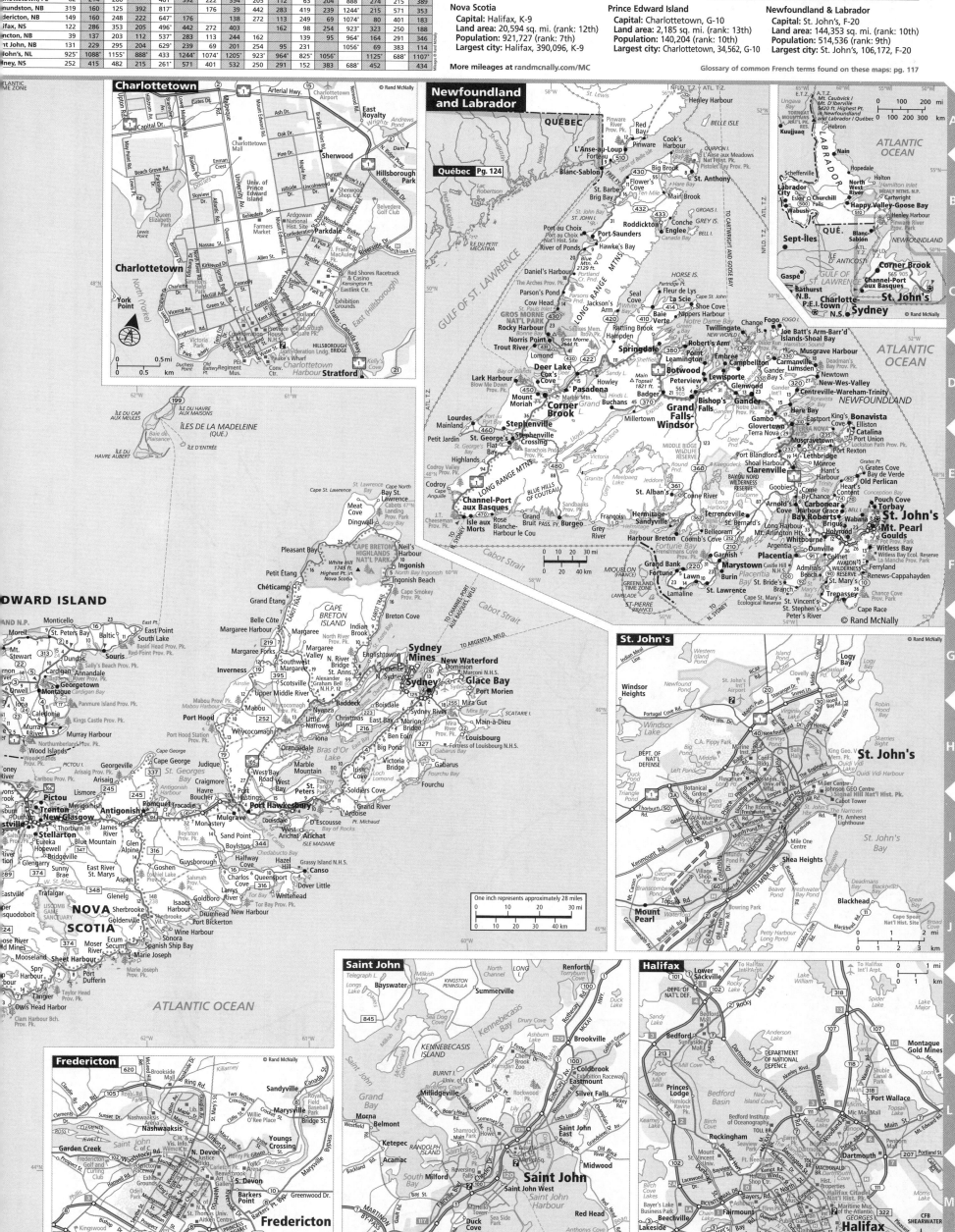

On-the-road resources

Mexico
Capital: Mexico City, G-8
Land area: 758,450 sq. mi.
Population: 112,336,538
Largest city: Mexico City, 8,851,080, G-8

Puerto Rico (U.S.)
Capital: San Juan, A-13
Land area: 3,425 sq. mi.
Population: 3,725,789
Largest city: San Juan, 381,931, A-13

Index of places Mexico: Pg. 136; Puerto Rico: Pg. 134

Sights to see

Mexico
- Chichen Itza Ruinas G-13
- Barranca del Cobre C-4
- Grutas de Cacahuamilpa H-8
- Parque Ecológico de Xochimilco I-3

Puerto Rico
- Bahía Fosforescente B-10
- Castillo del Morró A-13

- Parque Internacional del Río Bravo C-7
- Plaza de la Constitucion G-2
- Teotihuacán Ruinas G-8
- Tulum Ruinas G-14
- Museo de Arte de Ponce B-11
- Submarine Gardens A-13

Mexico Tourism Information
Mexico Tourism Board:
(800) 446-3942;
www.visitmexico.com/en

**Mexico Toll Information,
Road Conditions, & Construction**
www.gob.mx/carreteras (in Spanish)

Puerto Rico Tourism Information
Tourism Company of Puerto Rico:
(800) 866-7827; www.puertorico.co

**Puerto Rico Toll Information,
Road Conditions, & Construction**
(800) 981-3021, (787) 977-2200
www.dtop.gov.pr

United States Citizens Visiting Mexico

Before you go: Get a passport
The Western Hemisphere Travel Initiative requires all U.S. citizens to carry a passport or other secure document to prove their citizenship in order to enter or re-enter the country by sea, air, or land. The initiative includes surface travel to and from Canada and Mexico. U.S. Armed Forces personnel on active duty traveling orders are exempt from the passport requirement. For information on the U.S. Department of State website: www.dhs.gov/western-hemisphere-travel-initiative-basics

Border crossing waits
Allow plenty of time. The average time for customs clearance is 30 minutes, but this varies greatly depending on traffic flow and security issues.

Driving in Mexico
According to the U.S. Department of State, tourists traveling beyond the border zone must obtain a temporary import permit or risk having their car confiscated by Mexican customs officials. To acquire a permit, submit evidence of citizenship, title

for the car, car registration certificate, driver's license, and a processing fee to either a Banjercito (Mexican Army Bank) branch located at a Mexican Customs office at the port of entry, or at one of the Mexican consulates in the U.S. Mexican law also requires posting a bond at a Banjercito branch to guarantee departure of the car from Mexico within a period determined at the time of application. Carry proof of car ownership (the current registration card or a letter of authorization from the finance or leasing company). Auto insurance policies, other than Mexican, are not valid in Mexico. A short-term liability policy is obtainable at the border.

Tourist cards
Tourist cards are valid up to six months, require a fee, and are required for all persons, regardless of age, to visit the interior of Mexico. Cards may be obtained from Mexican border authorities, Consuls of Mexico, or Federal Delegates in major cities. Cards are also distributed to passengers en route to Mexico by air.

Mileage between principal cities

Distances in miles (red: kilometers in blue)

Glossary of Spanish terms

Avenida (Av.)	Avenue
Bahía (B.)	Bay
Barranca	Canyon
Cabo (C.)	Cape
Calzada (Calz.)	Highway
Canal	Canal, strait
Carretera	Highway
Castillo	Fort
Centro Comercial	Shopping center
Cerro	Mountain
Ciudad	City
Deportes	Sports
Estadio	Stadium
Golfo	Gulf
Grutas	Caves
Hipódromo	Race track
Isla (I.)	Island
Lago (L.)	Lake
Parque Nacional (Nac.)	National park
Parque Natural	Wildlife park
Paseo	Drive
Playa	Beach
Presa	Reservoir
Punta (Pta.)	Point, headland
Sierra	Mountain
Via	Road

© Rand McNally

ndex

nited States Counties, cities, towns & places

populations are from the 2010 U.S. Census or Rand McNally estimates

dex to Canada and Mexico cities and towns, page 136

Alabama

Map pp. 4 – 5

Alaska

Map p. 6

Arizona

Map pp. 8 – 9

* City keyed to p. 7

Arkansas

Map pp. 10 – 11

California

Map pp. 12 – 15

Map keys	Atlas pages
NA – NN	12 – 13
SA – SN	14 – 15

* City keyed to p. 16
† City keyed to p. 17
‡ City keyed to pp. 18 – 19

Colorado

Map pp. 20 – 21

* City keyed to p. 22

Connecticut

Map p. 23

Delaware

Map p. 24

District of Columbia

Map p. 111

Washington, 601723........A-5

Florida

Map pp. 26 – 27

* City keyed to p. 24
† City keyed to p. 25

*, †, ‡, § See explanation under state title in this index. County and parish names are listed in CAPITAL LETTERS and in boldface type. Independent cities (not in any county) are shown in italics.

Idaho
Map p. 31

Georgia
Map pp. 28 – 29
*City keyed to p. 30
†City keyed to p. 95

Hawaii
Map p. 30

Illinois
Map pp. 32 – 33
*City keyed to pp. 34 – 35
†City keyed to p. 57

Indiana
Map pp. 36 – 37
*City keyed to p. 35

Iowa
Map pp. 38 – 39
§ City keyed to p. 63

Kentucky
Map pp. 42 – 43
† City keyed to p. 112

Kansas
Map pp. 40 – 41
* City keyed to p. 58

Louisiana
Map p. 44

Maine
Map p. 45

Maryland
Map pp. 46 – 47
* City keyed to p. 111

Massachusetts
Map pp. 48 – 49

Michigan
Map pp. 50 – 51
* City keyed to p. 52

*, †, ‡, § See explanation under state title in this index. County and parish names are listed in CAPITAL LETTERS and in boldface type. Independent cities (not in any county) are shown in italics.

Minnesota
Map pp. 54 – 55
* City keyed to p. 53

Mississippi
Map p. 56

Missouri
Map pp. 58 – 59
* City keyed to p. 57

Montana
Map pp. 60 – 61

Nebraska
Map pp. 62 – 63

Nevada
Map p. 64
* City keyed to p. 16
† City keyed to p. 65

New Hampshire
Map p. 65

New Jersey
Map pp. 66 – 67
† City keyed to pp. 72 – 73
‡ City keyed to p. 90

New York
Map pp. 69 – 71

Map keys   Atlas pages
NA – NN   70 – 71
SA – SJ   69

* City keyed to pp. 72 – 73

Ohio
Map pp. 78 – 81

Map keys   Atlas pages
NA – NN   78 – 79
SA – SN   80 – 81

* City keyed to p. 112

Oklahoma
Map pp. 82 – 83

Oregon
Map pp. 84 – 85

Pennsylvania
Map pp. 86 – 89

Map keys Atlas pages
EA – ET 88 – 89
WA – WT 86 – 87

* City keyed to p. 24
† City keyed to p. 67
‡ City keyed to p. 90

Puerto Rico
Map p. 128

Rhode Island
Map p. 91

South Dakota
Map p. 93

South Carolina
Map p. 92

* City keyed to p. 28

Tennessee
Map pp. 94 – 95
* City keyed to p. 96

Texas

Map pp. 98 – 101
Map keys   Atlas pages
EA – ET   100 – 101
WA – WT   98 – 99

* City keyed to p. 96
† City keyed to p. 57

Virginia

Map pp. 106 – 107
* City keyed to p. 105
† City keyed to p. 111

Utah

Map pp. 102 – 103

Vermont

Map p. 104

Washington

Map pp. 108 – 109

West Virginia

Map p. 112
* City keyed to p. 46

*, †, ‡, §   See explanation under state title in this index.   County and parish names are listed in CAPITAL LETTERS and in boldface type.   Independent cities (not in any county) are shown in italics.

Canada Cities and Towns
Populations are from latest available census or are Rand McNally estimates

Alberta
Map pp. 118 – 119
* City keyed to p. 117

Manitoba
Map p. 121
* City keyed to p. 117

British Columbia
Map pp. 118 – 119
* City keyed to p. 117

New Brunswick
Map p. 126 – 127

Newfoundland & Labrador
Map p. 127

Nova Scotia
Map pp. 126 – 127

Northwest Territories
Map p. 117

Nunavut
Map p. 117

Ontario
Map pp. 122 – 123

Québec
Map pp. 124 – 125
* City keyed to p. 117

Prince Edward Island
Map pp. 126 – 127

Saskatchewan
Map pp. 120 – 121
* City keyed to p. 117

Yukon
Map p. 117

Mexico Cities and Towns (map p. 128)
Populations are from 2010 Mexican Census or are Rand McNally estimates

Aguascalientes
Baja California
Baja California Sur
Campeche
Chiapas
Chihuahua
Coahuila
Colima
Distrito Federal
Durango
Guanajuato
Guerrero
Hidalgo
Jalisco
México
Michoacán
Morelos
Nayarit
Nuevo León
Oaxaca
Puebla
Querétaro
Quintana Roo
San Luis Potosí
Sinaloa
Sonora
Tabasco
Tamaulipas
Tlaxcala
Veracruz
Yucatán

Wisconsin
Map pp. 114 – 115
* City keyed to p. 113

Wyoming
Map p. 116

CONTRIBUTORS AND CREDITS

EDITORS: Laura M. Kidder (Editorial Director), Linda Pappalardo (Managing Editor)

CONTRIBUTORS: Michele Bigley, Bob Blake, Linda Cabasin, Kelsy Chauvin, Lori Erickson, April Maher, Gary McKechnie, Kimberly Thompson, Jane Zarem, Rebecca Zito

DESIGNERS: Jodie Knight (Art Director), Joerg Metzner (Design Director), Joe Rockey, Jenii Stewart

CARTOGRAPHERS: Greg Babiak, Robert Ferry (Project Manager), Justin Griffin, Marc Kugel, Steve Wiertz, Tom Vitacco (Director)

PRODUCTION: Carey Seren

California coastline near Big Sur

Mileage Chart

This handy chart offers more than 2,400 mileages covering 90 North American cities and U.S. national parks. Want more mileages? Visit **randmcnally.com/MC** and type in any two cities or addresses.

	Albuquerque, NM	Amarillo, TX	Atlanta, GA	Baltimore, MD	Billings, MT	Birmingham, AL	Boise, ID	Boston, MA	Branson, MO	Brownsville, TX	Buffalo, NY	Charleston, SC	Charleston, WV	Charlotte, NC	Cheyenne, WY	Chicago, IL	Cincinnati, OH	Cleveland, OH	Columbus, OH	Dallas, TX	Denver, CO	Des Moines, IA	Detroit, MI	El Paso, TX	Fargo, ND	Grand Junction, CO	Hartford, CT	Houston, TX	Indianapolis, IN	Jackson, MS	Jacksonville, FL	Kansas City, MO	Las Vegas, NV
Acadia N.P., ME	2490	2206	1366	671	2507	1448	2935	283	1704	2469	728	1241	1014	1112	2198	1254	1142	911	1034	2035	2242	1570	997	2626	1900	2484	372	2115	1208	1683	1417	1692	2988
Albuquerque, NM		284	1386	1887	998	1241	938	2219	864	990	1782	1703	1543	1626	546	1333	1387	1598	1457	647	446	983	1570	260	1318	380	2118	884	1279	1047	1636	784	572
Amarillo, TX	284		1102	1602	965	957	1243	1935	580	788	1498	1419	1259	1342	515	1049	1103	1314	1173	363	424	765	1286	407	1002	607	1834	589	995	762	1352	570	857
Anchorage, AK	3672	3641	4338	4321	2660	4284	2707	4495	3788	4430	4155	4532	4111	4389	3128	3617	3914	3965	3975	4097	3227	3450	3905	3940	2935	3288	4513	4339	3804	4302	4689	3572	3424
Atlanta, GA	1386	1102		682	1831	146	2177	1095	652	1145	894	317	502	244	1439	715	461	714	567	780	1404	902	722	1418	1361	1643	996	794	533	380	346	800	1959
Baltimore, MD	1887	1602	682		1952	780	2378	400	1079	1801	372	571	361	442	1644	699	513	369	409	1368	1673	1015	524	2003	1346	1916	300	1448	584	1017	744	1068	2420
Big Bend N.P., TX	592	470	1344	1929	1393	1201	1530	2325	973	625	1939	1661	1610	1588	938	1442	1495	1755	1614	561	838	1182	1678	325	1525	949	2226	637	1388	964	1505	988	1043
Billings, MT	998	965	1831	1952		1780	620	2236	1241	1758	1786	2132	1742	1990	453	1246	1546	1596	1606	1425	551	946	1535	1257	607	662	2143	1652	1435	1688	2182	1026	971
Birmingham, AL	1241	957	146	780	1780		2126	1177	507	1020	908	463	564	390	1386	660	464	716	569	636	1329	848	724	1274	1307	1573	1078	668	478	237	434	749	1814
Boise, ID	938	1243	2177	2378	620	2126		2660	1588	1928	2214	2473	2123	2336	736	1693	1943	2020	2013	1702	830	1360	1960	1205	1227	620	2566	1930	1835	2048	2528	1372	624
Boston, MA	2219	1935	1095	400	2236	1177	2660		1433	2198	453	970	744	841	1927	983	870	638	763	1764	1970	1299	724	2373	1629	2210	101	1844	937	1412	1146	1421	2714
Branson, MO	864	580	652	1079	1241	507	1588	1433		1005	995	968	755	868	851	545	601	808	668	435	806	400	784	985	816	1049	1327	602	493	432	968	209	1437
Brownsville, TX	990	788	1145	1801	1758	1020	1928	2198	1005		1853	1459	1525	1388	1303	1474	1409	1669	1528	547	1213	1230	1673	814	1614	1370	2099	354	1379	793	1225	1036	1550
Buffalo, NY	1782	1498	894	372	1786	908	2214	453	995	1853		866	435	656	1478	533	434	190	326	1378	1521	849	273	1908	1180	1762	397	1499	500	1125	1037	984	2266
Calgary, AB	1542	1511	2357	2332	541	2305	747	2615	1783	2299	2165	2542	2122	2400	998	1627	1925	1976	1985	1967	1096	1461	1915	1809	956	1154	2524	2209	1814	2239	2703	1567	1284
Charleston, SC	1703	1419	317	571	2132	463	2473	970	968	1459	866		471	207	1740	908	620	721	636	1099	1706	1199	826	1734	1557	1946	871	1105	726	697	235	1103	2276
Charleston, WV	1543	1259	502	361	1742	564	2123	744	755	1525	435	471		264	1389	491	196	250	162	1049	1355	788	352	1684	1136	1595	644	1171	312	801	642	752	2099
Charlotte, NC	1626	1342	244	442	1990	390	2336	841	868	1388	656	207	264		1600	769	477	514	426	1023	1566	1057	616	1662	1414	1810	742	1038	583	624	379	961	2199
Cheyenne, WY	546	515	1439	1644	453	1386	736	1927	851	1303	1478	1740	1389	1600		960	1210	1288	1281	971	100	628	1227	807	787	340	1834	1202	1104	1316	1792	634	829
Chicago, IL	1333	1049	715	699	1246	660	1693	983	545	1474	533	908	491	769	960		289	342	354	926	1002	332	280	1455	641	1242	888	1085	181	738	1068	526	1746
Cincinnati, OH	1387	1103	461	513	1546	464	1943	870	601	1409	434	620	196	477	1210	289		248	106	934	1187	580	259	1569	937	1427	767	1055	108	686	796	584	1932
Cleveland, OH	1598	1314	714	369	1596	716	2020	638	808	1669	190	721	250	514	1288	342	248		142	1194	1330	659	168	1721	990	1570	562	1315	315	937	892	799	2073
Columbus, OH	1457	1173	567	409	1606	569	2013	763	668	1528	326	636	162	426	1281	354	106	142		1039	1261	653	191	1578	1000	1501	661	1174	176	790	812	657	2004
Crater Lake N.P., OR	1307	1595	2580	2772	1033	2528	422	3054	1990	2305	2609	2866	2515	2736	1129	2086	2336	2413	2406	1976	1223	1753	2353	1473	1640	972	2959	2212	2227	2375	2931	1775	754
Dallas, TX	647	363	780	1368	1425	636	1702	1764	435	547	1378	1099	1049	1023	971	926	934	1194	1039		880	683	1163	635	1079	1124	1665	228	873	402	992	489	1220
Denver, CO	446	424	1404	1673	551	1329	830	1970	806	1213	1521	1706	1355	1566	100	1002	1187	1330	1261	880		670	1270	707	873	243	1876	1035	1083	1226	1756	603	747
Des Moines, IA	983	765	902	1015	946	848	1360	1299	400	1230	849	1199	788	1057	628	332	580	659	653	683	670		599	1124	475	909	1206	938	474	828	1253	193	1413
Detroit, MI	1570	1286	722	524	1535	724	1960	724	784	1673	273	826	352	616	1227	280	259	168	191	1163	1270	599		1702	930	1508	668	1319	288	945	1002	764	2013
El Paso, TX	260	407	1418	2003	1257	1274	1205	2373	985	814	1908	1734	1684	1662	807	1455	1569	1721	1578	635	707	1124	1702		1370	642	2300	744	1398	1038	1619	929	718
Fargo, ND	1318	1002	1361	1346	607	1307	1227	1629	816	1614	1180	1557	1136	1414	787	641	937	990	1000	1079	873	475	930	1370		1115	1538	1321	825	1265	1708	600	1579
Grand Canyon N.P., AZ	400	684	1786	2294	1072	1641	861	2618	1264	1390	2182	2102	1943	2025	774	1729	1786	1997	1857	1047	676	1344	1969	600	1546	433	2518	1284	1679	1446	2036	1184	275
Grand Junction, CO	380	607	1643	1916	662	1573	620	2210	1049	1370	1762	1946	1595	1810	340	1242	1427	1570	1501	1124	243	909	1508	642	1115		2115	1279	1324	1470	1994	844	506
Grt. Smoky Mts. N.P., TN	1440	1151	189	536	1806	289	2142	940	684	1310	705	333	313	190	1408	585	293	548	406	882	1375	873	561	1522	1230	1614	843	962	399	528	510	771	2010
Halifax, NS	2865	2581	1742	1046	2878	1823	3306	660	2079	2844	1103	1616	1390	1488	2569	1624	1517	1286	1409	2410	2612	1940	1335	3042	2271	2854	747	2490	1583	2059	1792	2067	3358
Hartford, CT	2118	1834	996	300	2143	1078	2566	101	1327	2099	397	871	644	742	1834	888	767	562	661	1665	1876	1206	668	2300	1538	2115		1745	834	1313	1047	1318	2619
Houston, TX	884	589	794	1448	1652	668	1930	1844	602	354	1499	1105	1171	1038	1202	1085	1055	1315	1174	228	1035	938	1319	744	1321	1279	1745		1021	439	871	732	1457
Indianapolis, IN	1279	995	533	584	1435	478	1835	937	493	1379	500	726	312	583	1104	181	108	315	176	873	1083	474	288	1398	825	1324	834	1021		671	874	482	1828
Jackson, MS	1047	762	380	1017	1688	237	2048	1412	432	793	1125	697	801	624	1316	738	686	937	790	402	1226	828	945	1038	1265	1470	1313	439	671		590	664	1620
Jacksonville, FL	1636	1352	346	744	2182	434	2528	1146	968	1225	1037	235	642	379	1792	1068	796	892	812	992	1756	1253	1002	1619	1708	1994	1047	871	874	590		1152	2210
Kansas City, MO	784	570	800	1068	1026	749	1372	1421	209	1036	984	1103	752	961	634	526	584	799	657	489	603	193	764	929	600	844	1318	732	482	664	1152		1349
Key West, FL	2099	1815	809	1251	2646	905	2992	1659	1431	1688	1544	742	1149	886	2256	1534	1275	1399	1325	1455	2222	1726	1515	2082	2178	2466	1560	1334	1348	1053	507	1617	2673
Las Vegas, NV	572	857	1959	2420	971	1814	624	2714	1437	1550	2266	2276	2099	2199	829	1746	1932	2073	2004	1220	747	1413	2013	718	1579	506	2619	1457	1828	1620	2210	1349	
Little Rock, AR	877	593	515	1050	1407	370	1786	1447	172	794	1061	831	732	754	1055	650	617	868	724	319	965	573	885	954	988	1207	1348	439	583	261	832	381	1450
Los Angeles, CA	786	1072	2174	2670	1240	2029	842	2983	1651	1630	2535	2491	2330	2414	1102	2015	2172	2342	2244	1437	1015	1682	2281	796	1848	774	2888	1550	2068	1838	2421	1616	270
Louisville, KY	1300	1016	420	604	1539	366	1877	978	510	1314	540	613	244	470	1144	296	97	347	206	836	1109	586	361	1474	944	1349	877	960	113	586	772	507	1854
Memphis, TN	1008	720	379	914	1477	234	1825	1312	274	929	922	696	597	619	1091	531	482	729	587	453	1097	617	742	1089	1054	1340	1213	575	464	209	677	451	1581
Mexico City, DF	1392	1332	1718	2372	2301	1592	2330	2768	1548	570	2424	2029	2095	1962	1846	2017	1979	2239	2098	1090	1756	1790	2254	1124	2158	1772	2669	924	1963	1364	1796	1598	1755
Miami, FL	1952	1668	661	1082	2497	746	2844	1482	1284	1538	1385	583	990	728	2107	1381	1127	1240	1164	1307	2069	1567	1354	1934	2025	2308	1385	1186	1198	905	349	1466	2525
Milwaukee, WI	1354	1132	809	792	1173	754	1732	1074	630	1557	630	1002	589	867	1000	90	381	434	445	1010	1042	371	374	1497	569	1282	980	1163	272	830	1163	565	1786
Minneapolis, MN	1225	1009	1127	1112	838	1072	1461	1396	643	1475	946	1323	902	1180	865	408	703	756	766	928	913	242	696	1377	235	1152	1304	1171	591	1040	1474	436	1656
Mobile, AL	1234	949	328	1003	1874	258	2236	1427	620	821	1166	602	816	571	1504	917	721	973	826	589	1414	998	978	1215	1451	1657	1328	468	733	188	403	850	1808
Montpelier, VT	2203	1919	1165	498	2207	1247	2636	179	1417	2268	428	1068	813	928	1899	954	855	611	747	1824	1942	1270	718	2347	1601	2184	198	1914	921	1482	1245	1405	2688
Montréal, QC	2129	1845	1218	548	2099	1299	2523	310	1342	2311	393	1118	822	980	1790	847	824	578	714	1722	1832	1163	560	2261	1496	2072	328	1884	847	1517	1294	1330	2576
Nashville, TN	1219	932	248	703	1586	192	1925	1099	464	1140	712	549	388	407	1192	469	273	525	378	664	1158	656	534	1300	1116	1397	1000	786	287	414	596	555	1792
New Orleans, LA	1165	881	468	1124	1868	343	2216	1520	597	700	1248	742	908	712	1488	923	804	1057	910	519	1398	1008	1066	1095	1445	1638	1421	347	818	183	547	844	1739
New York, NY	2001	1716	882	192	2041	960	2465	207	1201	1981	395	768	530	641	1733	787	637	460	533	1548	1775	1105	613	2201	1438	2014	108	1632	707	1198	939	1196	2518
Norfolk, VA	1910	1632	558	228	2132	715	2525	569	1158	1716	569	437	403	328	1792	878	605	551	570	1350	1758	1196	704	1986	1529	1997	470	1362	720	948	613	1155	2486
Oklahoma City, OK	542	256	844	1346	1203	699	1497	1678	323	738	1242	1160	1002	1084	720	792	846	1057	917	204	631	545	1029	660	875	870	1577	437	739	603	1160	348	1112
Omaha, NE	863	647	992	1153	845	939	1225	1436	402	1192	987	1293	943	1151	492	470	722	797	792	656	534	137	736	1004	420	774	1345	898	613	852	1343	187	1278
Orlando, FL	1730	1446	440	889	2275	534	2622	1288	1062	1319	1184	380	792	526	1885	1153	905	1043	954	1086	1851	1339	1144	1712	1807	2095	1189	965	968	683	141	1246	2303
Philadelphia, PA	1924	1640	780	98	2011	880	2435	306	1138	1900	388	668	466	539	1703	757	571	428	468	1467	1732	1074	583	2102	1405	1975	207	1547	643	1115	844	1127	2480
Phoenix, AZ	462	746	1844	2349	1210	1700	914	2681	1326	1259	2245	2165	2005	2088	1008	1795	1849	2060	1920	1066	908	1445	2032	424	1780	571	2580	1178	1742	1466	2050	1246	285
Pittsburgh, PA	1641	1357	684	246	1713	748	2137	570	851	1708	216	654	225	446	1405	459	288	131	184	1221	1447	777	285	1774	1107	1686	469	1354	359	971	825	840	2190
Portland, ME	2315	2031	1192	496	2333	1274	2761	110	1529	2294	553	1066	840	938	2024	1079	967	736	859	1861	2067	1395	825	2455	1726	2309	197	1940	1034	1509	1243	1518	2813
Portland, OR	1363	1669	2603	2804	891	2551	428	3086	2013	2354	2639	2904	2554	2761	1161	2118	2369	2446	2439	2128	1256	1786	2385	1630	1497	1046	2992	2356	2260	2473	2954	1797	1022
Québec, QC	2283	1999	1372	694	2257	1455	2681	396	1497	2472	552	1264	979	1134	1948	1004	979	735	870	1876	1991	1320	715	2416	1650	2230	427	2123	1001	1676	1440	1484	2734
Raleigh, NC	1761	1474	408	302	2067	555	2444	702	1003	1556	637	278	322	168	1712	816	521	572	486	1191	1678	1107	677	1826	1460	1917	602	1202	628	789	449	1074	2334
Rapid City, SD	843	714	1508	1616	323	1456	942	1900	920	1515	1450	1811	1410	1670	298	912	1208	1260	1270	1061	397	626	1200	1110	550	639	1808	1291	1100	1371	1860	704	1039
Regina, SK	1284	1253	1904	1882	472	1850	1092	2090	1321	2046	1721	2066	1674	1937	740	1151	1445	1503	1510	1510	838	1016	1441	1551	513	1080	2080	1753	1337	1805	2220	1104	1443
Reno, NV	1019	1304	2396	2599	956	2262	422	2881	1806	1998	2433	2698	2342	2555	956	1913	2163	2240	2234	1668	1051	1581	2180	1166	1564	799	2786	1904	2056	2067	2748	1591	447
Saint Louis, MO	1037	752	555	829	1278	501	1622	1182	249	1177	746	856	506	714	888	296	348	560	421	630	854	354	533	1157	841	1095	1080	784	243	491	906	250	1600
Salt Lake City, UT	599	883	1878	2081	552	1826	339	2365	1288	1589	1915	2180	1829	2037	437	1398	1647	1725	1718	1403	533	1065	1664	866	1160	283	2271	1634	1541	1749	2229	1073	419
San Antonio, TX	712	510	986	1642	1480	861	1651	2039	708	274	1654	1300	1324	1230	1025	1202	1210	1457	1314	276	935	960	1439	554	1343	1092	1940	197	1149	635	1066	766	1272
San Diego, CA	810	1097	2138	2695	1301	1994	958	3046	1675	1552	2596	2459	2354	2381	1162	2080	2196	2407	2269	1359	1077	1747	2346	718	1908	835	2930	1472	2089	1759	2343	1597	331
San Francisco, CA	1086	1370	2472	2816	1173	2327	639	3098	1950	2010	2650	2789	2564	2712	1172	2130	2380	2458	2451	1734	1268	1798	2397	1175	1781	968	3004	1929	2273	2133	2723	1808	569
Sault Ste. Marie, ON	1777	1493	1040	852	1273	1014	1893	923	991	1918	514	1156	683	947	1411	471	577	496	521	1370	1428	710	347	1910	665	1692	904	1527	540	1180	1333	951	2196
Savannah, GA	1634	1350	247	605	2078	393	2418	1014	900	1320	909	106	514	251	1687	951	664	764	680	996	1651	1150	870	1632	1609	1890	915	971	770	580	135	1048	2206
Seattle, WA	1438	1743	2649	2770	818	2597	503	3054	2059	2428	2604	2950	2560	2808	1225	2063	2363	2414	2424	2193	1320	1764	2353	1705	1424	1121	2960	2431	2253	2537	3000	1844	1128
Shenandoah N.P., VA	1794	1488	556	119	1951	634	2399	519	1016	1655	382	516	260	317	1650	698	474	368	389	1223	1614	1014	523	1863	1345	1855	420	1306	563	872	687	1012	2359
Spokane, WA	1320	1505	2369	2491	540	2318	425	2774	1780	2296	2325	2671	2281	2528	993	1785	2084	2135	2144	1964	1091	1484	2075	1587	1147	1002	2682	2192	1973	2229	2720	1564	1138
Tampa, FL	1746	1462	451	942	2291	537	2638	1342	1078	1329	1235	433	840	578	1901	1166	916	1091	1007	1102	1860	1354	1178	1728	1813	2099	1242	980	984	699	198	1252	2319
Thunder Bay, ON	1566	1348	1376	1288	1049	1322	1670	1298	983	1830	942	1570	1118	1382	1210	656	949	932	957	1270	1253	583	784	1718	441	1492	1305	1522	840	1361	1728	776	1996
Toronto, ON	1800	1516	963	472	1771	968	2194	548	1014	1919	98	964	535	756	1462	519	493	290	426	1393	1504	834	232	1932	1167	1744	490	1551	518	1186	1135	1001	2247
Tucson, AZ	449	735	1732	2320	1326	1588	1030	2669	1314	1145	2233	2052	1994	1975	995	1784	1836	2048	1908	952	895	1433	2020	312	1769	687	2569	1066	1728	1353	1936	1234	401
Vancouver, BC	1574	1878	2785	2906	953	2733	638	3188	2195	2564	2740	3086	2696	2944	1372	2198	2499	2548	2560	2338	1465	1900	2487	1841	1559	1256	3094	2565	2389	2675	3136	1980	1264
Washington, DC	1885	1600	637	39	1951	744	2375	439	1078	1765	382	530	362	398	1642	697	512	367	407	1332	1671	1014	522	1966	1344	1914	340	1411	582	980	706	1066	2428
Wichita, KS	591	382	955	1260	1064	810	1338	1613	292	896	1176	1272	945	1092	608	724	779	992	851	361	519	391	964	730	685	759	1512	595	674	707	1272	193	1164
Winnipeg, MB	1538	1222	1582	1570	723	1532	1345	1729	1033	1834	1403	1779	1360	1638	1006	864	1158	1214	1222	1298	1092	699	1153	1590	222	1334	1760	1541	1049	1484	1932	817	1692
Yellowstone N.P., WY	963	977	1904	2145	175	1852	418	2410	1316	1813	1960	2207	1906	2076	469	1418	1710	1772	1787	1436	563	1094	1710	1229	782	632	2315	1664	1602	1826	2256	1100	769
Yosemite N.P., CA	989	1289	2391	2695	1129	2246	594	2979	1868	1939	2529	2708	2403	2619	1051	2012	2264	2339	2335	1636	1045	1680	2279	1104	1735	802	2888	1858	2155	2052	2642	1649	415

	Little Rock, AR	Los Angeles, CA	Louisville, KY	Memphis, TN	Miami, FL	Milwaukee, WI	Minneapolis, MN	Mobile, AL	Montpelier, VT	Nashville, TN	New Orleans, LA	New York, NY	Norfolk, VA	Oklahoma City, OK	Omaha, NE	Orlando, FL	Philadelphia, PA	Phoenix, AZ	Pittsburgh, PA	Portland, ME	Portland, OR	Raleigh, NC	Rapid City, SD	Reno, NV	Saint Louis, MO	Salt Lake City, UT	San Antonio, TX	San Diego, CA	San Francisco, CA	Savannah, GA	Seattle, WA	Spokane, WA	Tampa, FL	Washington, DC	Wichita, KS
Acadia N.P., ME	1718	3256	1249	1583	1760	1348	1667	1698	293	1370	1791	478	840	1949	1707	1559	577	2952	841	172	3360	972	2171	3154	1453	2636	2310	3317	3371	1285	3325	3045	1613	710	1884
Albuquerque, NM	877	786	1300	1008	1952	1354	1225	1234	2203	1219	1165	2001	1910	542	863	1730	1924	462	1641	2315	1363	1761	843	1019	1037	599	712	810	1086	1634	1438	1320	1746	1885	591
Amarillo, TX	593	1072	1016	720	1668	1132	1009	949	1919	932	881	1716	1632	256	647	1446	1640	746	1357	2031	1669	1474	714	1304	752	883	510	1097	1370	1350	1743	1505	1462	1600	382
Anchorage, AK	3959	3412	3919	4093	5004	3545	3165	4486	4318	4093	4485	4428	4506	3894	3391	4782	4380	3681	4082	4443	2448	4436	2995	3026	3825	3006	4152	3532	3084	4585	2276	2387	4798	4319	3736
Atlanta, GA	515	2174	420	379	661	809	1127	328	1165	248	468	882	558	844	992	440	780	1844	684	1192	2603	408	1508	2396	555	1878	986	2138	2472	247	2649	2369	451	637	955
Baltimore, MD	1050	2670	604	914	1082	792	1112	1003	498	703	1124	192	228	1346	1153	889	98	2349	246	496	2804	302	1616	2599	829	2081	1642	2695	2816	605	2770	2491	942	39	1260
Big Bend N.P., TX	880	1128	1400	1015	1820	1525	1427	1102	2395	1226	981	2128	1912	650	1102	1598	2028	757	1794	2422	1956	1753	1190	1491	1145	1191	404	1050	1507	1558	2021	1912	1614	1892	807
Billings, MT	1407	1240	1539	1477	2497	1173	838	1874	2207	1586	1868	2041	2132	1203	845	2275	2011	1210	1713	2333	891	2067	323	956	1278	552	1480	1301	1173	2078	818	540	2291	1951	1064
Birmingham, AL	370	2029	366	234	746	754	1072	258	1247	192	343	960	715	699	939	534	880	1700	748	1274	2551	555	1456	2262	501	1826	861	1994	2327	393	2597	2318	537	744	810
Boise, ID	1786	842	1877	1825	2844	1732	1461	2236	2636	1925	2216	2465	2525	1497	1225	2622	2435	914	2137	2761	428	2444	942	422	1622	339	1651	958	639	2418	503	425	2638	2375	1338
Boston, MA	1447	2983	978	1312	1482	1074	1396	1427	179	1099	1520	207	569	1678	1436	1288	306	2681	570	110	3086	702	1900	2881	1182	2365	2039	3046	3098	1014	3054	2774	1342	439	1613
Branson, MO	172	1651	510	274	1284	630	643	620	1417	464	597	1201	1158	323	402	1062	1138	1326	851	1529	2013	1003	920	1806	249	1288	708	1675	1950	900	2059	1780	1078	1078	292
Brownsville, TX	794	1630	1314	929	1538	1557	1475	821	2268	1140	700	1981	1716	738	1192	1319	1900	1259	1708	2294	2354	1556	1515	1998	1177	1589	274	1552	2010	1320	2428	2296	1329	1765	896
Buffalo, NY	1061	2535	540	922	1385	630	946	1166	428	712	1248	395	569	1242	987	1184	388	2245	216	553	2639	637	1450	2433	746	1915	1654	2596	2650	909	2604	2325	1235	382	1176
Calgary, AB	1958	1557	1930	2028	3018	1555	1221	2481	2380	2116	2419	2438	2516	1763	1386	2797	2390	1524	2093	2505	787	2446	865	1276	1820	869	2021	1617	1500	2620	678	424	2833	2330	1606
Charleston, SC	831	2491	613	696	583	1002	1323	602	1068	549	742	768	437	1160	1293	380	668	2165	654	1066	2904	278	1811	2698	856	2180	1300	2459	2789	106	2950	2671	433	530	1272
Charleston, WV	732	2330	244	597	990	589	902	816	813	388	908	530	403	1002	943	792	466	2005	225	840	2554	322	1410	2342	506	1829	1324	2354	2564	514	2560	2281	840	362	945
Charlotte, NC	754	2414	470	619	728	867	1180	571	928	407	712	641	328	1084	1151	526	539	2088	446	938	2761	168	1670	2555	714	2037	1230	2381	2712	251	2808	2528	578	398	1092
Cheyenne, WY	1055	1102	1144	1091	2107	1000	865	1504	1899	1192	1488	1733	1792	720	492	1885	1703	1008	1405	2024	1161	1712	298	956	888	437	1025	1162	1172	1687	1225	993	1901	1642	608
Chicago, IL	650	2015	296	531	1381	90	408	917	954	469	923	787	878	792	470	1153	757	1795	459	1079	2118	816	912	1913	296	1398	1202	2080	2130	951	2063	1785	1166	697	724
Cincinnati, OH	617	2172	97	482	1127	381	703	721	855	273	804	637	605	846	722	905	571	1849	288	967	2369	521	1208	2163	348	1647	1210	2196	2380	664	2363	2084	916	512	779
Cleveland, OH	868	2342	347	729	1240	434	756	973	611	525	1057	460	551	1057	797	1043	428	2060	131	736	2446	572	1260	2240	560	1725	1457	2407	2458	764	2414	2135	1091	367	992
Columbus, OH	724	2244	206	587	1164	445	766	826	747	378	910	533	570	917	792	954	468	1920	184	859	2439	486	1270	2234	421	1718	1314	2269	2451	680	2424	2144	1007	407	851
Crater Lake N.P., OR	2178	738	2270	2235	3246	2126	1874	2562	3038	2318	2494	2858	2917	1889	1618	3025	2828	1039	2530	3156	250	2837	1351	310	2015	691	2028	858	410	2810	422	493	3041	2768	1731
Dallas, TX	319	1437	836	453	1307	1010	928	589	1824	664	519	1548	1350	204	656	1086	1467	1066	1221	1861	2128	1191	1061	1668	630	1403	276	1359	1734	996	2193	1964	1102	1332	361
Denver, CO	965	1015	1109	1097	2069	1042	913	1414	1942	1158	1398	1775	1758	631	534	1851	1732	908	1447	2067	1256	1678	397	1051	854	533	935	1077	1268	1651	1320	1091	1860	1671	519
Des Moines, IA	573	1682	586	617	1567	371	242	998	1270	656	1008	1105	1196	545	137	1339	1074	1445	777	1395	1786	1107	626	1581	354	1065	960	1747	1798	1150	1764	1484	1354	1014	391
Detroit, MI	885	2281	361	742	1354	374	696	978	718	534	1066	613	704	1029	736	1144	583	2032	285	825	2385	677	1200	2180	533	1664	1439	2346	2397	870	2353	2075	1178	522	964
El Paso, TX	954	796	1474	1089	1934	1497	1377	1215	2347	1300	1095	2201	1986	660	1004	1712	2102	424	1774	2455	1630	1826	1110	1166	1157	866	554	718	1175	1632	1705	1587	1728	1966	730
Fargo, ND	988	1848	944	1054	2025	569	235	1451	1601	1116	1445	1438	1529	875	420	1807	1405	1780	1107	1726	1497	1460	550	1564	841	1160	1343	1908	1781	1609	1424	1147	1813	1344	685
Grand Canyon N.P., AZ	1277	490	1699	1408	2351	1716	1586	1634	2603	1619	1565	2406	2314	942	1208	2130	2324	218	2041	2715	1286	2160	1070	722	1436	522	1112	551	788	2033	1351	1243	2146	2285	990
Grand Junction, CO	1207	774	1349	1340	2308	1282	1152	1657	2184	1397	1638	2014	1997	870	774	2095	1975	571	1686	2309	1046	1917	639	799	1095	283	1092	835	968	1890	1121	1002	2099	1914	759
Grt. Smoky Mts. N.P., TN	567	2224	286	430	862	682	996	520	1015	220	633	716	485	896	964	624	637	1903	496	1042	2577	326	1479	2371	527	1852	1151	2249	2528	378	2624	2344	640	502	908
Halifax, NS	2093	3627	1624	1958	2145	1724	2037	2073	668	1745	2166	853	1216	2324	2078	1935	952	3328	1216	550	3731	1348	2541	3524	1828	3006	2685	3688	3741	1661	3695	3416	1988	1085	2259
Hartford, CT	1348	2888	877	1213	1385	980	1304	1328	198	1000	1421	108	470	1577	1345	1189	207	2580	469	197	2992	602	1808	2786	1080	2271	1940	2930	3004	915	2960	2682	1242	340	1512
Houston, TX	439	1550	960	575	1186	1163	1171	468	1914	786	347	1632	1362	437	898	965	1547	1178	1354	1940	2356	1202	1291	1904	784	1634	197	1472	1929	971	2431	2192	980	1411	595
Indianapolis, IN	583	2068	113	464	1198	272	591	733	921	287	818	707	720	739	613	968	643	1742	359	1034	2260	628	1100	2056	243	1541	1149	2089	2273	770	2253	1973	984	582	674
Jackson, MS	261	1838	586	209	905	830	1040	188	1482	414	183	1198	948	603	852	683	1115	1466	971	1509	2473	789	1371	2067	491	1749	635	1759	2133	580	2537	2229	699	980	707
Jacksonville, FL	832	2421	772	677	349	1163	1474	403	1245	596	547	939	613	1160	1343	141	844	2050	825	1243	2954	449	1860	2748	906	2229	1066	2343	2723	135	3000	2720	198	706	1272
Kansas City, MO	381	1616	507	451	1466	565	436	850	1405	555	844	1196	1155	348	187	1246	1127	1246	840	1518	1797	1074	704	1591	250	1073	766	1597	1808	1048	1844	1564	1252	1066	193
Key West, FL	1294	2884	1238	1159	162	1632	1944	866	1758	1063	1010	1446	1120	1623	1807	387	1357	2514	1332	1756	3417	956	2326	3211	1370	2693	1529	2806	3186	642	3464	3185	402	1213	1735
Las Vegas, NV	1450	270	1854	1581	2525	1786	1656	1808	2688	1792	1739	2518	2486	1112	1278	2303	2480	285	2190	2813	1022	2334	1039	447	1600	419	1272	331	569	2206	1128	1138	2319	2428	1164
Little Rock, AR		1665	520	137	1147	724	815	449	1506	348	425	1230	1035	335	574	925	1150	1340	905	1543	2211	889	1093	1898	345	1488	594	1676	1963	763	2275	1948	941	1014	446
Los Angeles, CA	1665		2085	1794	2735	2055	1925	2014	2957	2006	1894	2787	2707	1326	1546	2515	2713	370	2428	3082	963	2548	1312	470	1821	688	1357	120	380	2422	1134	1215	2525	2670	1377
Louisville, KY	520	2085		384	1085	390	710	620	962	174	705	740	649	759	699	858	676	1762	388	1074	2310	568	1214	2104	263	1586	1111	2109	2321	658	2357	2077	872	606	701
Memphis, TN	137	1794	384		1012	622	831	382	1369	212	394	1094	898	466	641	778	1014	1471	768	1408	2245	753	1160	2029	283	1524	727	1819	2095	626	2299	2018	779	879	577
Mexico City, DF	1364	1839	1884	1500	2111	2100	2032	1392	2838	1710	1272	2571	2286	1282	1735	1889	2471	1469	2279	2865	2756	2126	2139	2202	1721	1991	821	1700	2218	1906	2830	2711	1905	2335	1440
Miami, FL	1147	2735	1085	1012		1475	1791	719	1587	913	861	1288	950	1476	1658	229	1180	2362	1173	1585	3260	797	2173	3063	1221	2544	1379	2656	3038	483	3315	3035	255	1044	1587
Milwaukee, WI	724	2055	390	622	1475		336	1011	1054	564	1015	879	969	875	509	1258	849	1817	551	1176	2062	914	840	1953	379	1437	1285	2118	2170	1045	1990	1712	1260	788	763
Minneapolis, MN	815	1925	710	831	1791	336		1224	1367	881	1223	1204	1295	788	372	1573	1171	1687	874	1492	1727	1227	575	1818	563	1308	1205	1986	2040	1374	1655	1377	1578	1110	634
Mobile, AL	449	2014	620	382	719	1011	1224		1497	447	144	1202	887	791	1038	497	1101	1643	1000	1523	2661	737	1557	2255	645	1936	662	1936	2320	502	2727	2478	509	965	894
Montpelier, VT	1506	2957	962	1369	1587	1054	1367	1497		1160	1589	306	668	1662	1408	1387	405	2666	612	220	3061	800	1871	2854	1166	2336	2096	3018	3071	1113	3025	2746	1440	538	1597
Montréal, QC	1451	2845	931	1314	1646	938	1262	1549	133	1105	1640	381	717	1588	1302	1436	454	2591	603	258	2948	850	1766	2743	1092	2228	1998	2912	2960	1162	2916	2638	1490	587	1529
Nashville, TN	348	2006	174	212	913	564	881	447	1160		532	884	688	677	747	683	802	1682	560	1196	2357	542	1262	2151	310	1633	939	2030	2306	495	2404	2124	700	666	688
New Orleans, LA	425	1894	705	394	861	1015	1223	144	1589	532		1304	1026	722	1032	641	1222	1523	1090	1616	2642	878	1551	2186	675	1920	541	1816	2252	642	2716	2409	651	1087	880
New York, NY	1230	2787	740	1094	1288	879	1204	1202	306	884	1304		370	1460	1245	1089	97	2463	369	304	2891	502	1708	2685	954	2170	1822	2809	2902	811	2858	2580	1138	228	1391
Norfolk, VA	1035	2707	649	898	950	969	1295	887	668	688	1026	370		1366	1335	755	270	2373	425	666	2962	183	1799	2744	911	2238	1557	2730	2973	481	2949	2671	808	189	1349
Oklahoma City, OK	335	1326	759	466	1476	875	788	791	1662	677	722	1460	1366		452	1254	1384	1005	1100	1775	1922	1218	857	1563	496	1200	468	1351	1627	1092	1948	1710	1270	1343	158
Omaha, NE	574	1546	699	641	1658	509	372	1038	1408	747	1032	1245	1335	452		1436	1212	1325	914	1533	1650	1266	525	1445	439	930	920	1613	1662	1239	1663	1383	1445	1151	298
Orlando, FL	925	2515	858	778	229	1258	1573	497	1387	683	641	1089	755	1254	1436		986	2145	975	1385	3048	597	1956	2841	999	2323	1160	2436	2816	280	3093	2814	84	849	1365
Philadelphia, PA	1150	2713	676	1014	1180	849	1171	1101	405	802	1222	97	270	1384	1212	986		2387	304	402	2861	399	1675	2656	888	2140	1742	2738	2873	703	2828	2550	1040	137	1319
Phoenix, AZ	1340	370	1762	1471	2362	1817	1687	1643	2666	1682	1523	2463	2373	1005	1325	2145	2387		2104	2778	1332	2224	1305	733	1499	653	985	352	749	2091	1414	1381	2153	2348	1053
Pittsburgh, PA	905	2428	388	768	1173	551	874	1000	612	560	1090	369	425	1100	914	975	304	2104		666	2563	499	1378	2357	604	1842	1495	2452	2574	697	2530	2252	1023	244	1035
Portland, ME	1543	3082	1074	1408	1585	1176	1492	1523	220	1196	1616	304	666	1775	1533	1385	402	2778	666		3186	798	1996	2979	1279	2461	2136	3143	3196	1111	3150	2871	1438	535	1710
Portland, OR	2211	963	2310	2245	3260	2062	1727	2661	3061	2357	2642	2891	2962	1922	1650	3048	2861	1332	2563	3186		2897	1214	578	2050	765	2076	1083	635	2844	172	351	3064	2800	1764
Québec, QC	1606	3003	1086	1470	1792	1096	1417	1703	259	1262	1795	524	863	1742	1457	1582	600	2745	760	275	3107	996	1921	2901	1246	2386	2152	3067	3119	1308	3074	2795	1636	733	1683
Raleigh, NC	889	2548	568	753	797	914	1227	737	800	542	878	502	183	1218	1266	597	399	2224	499	798	2897		1735	2690	830	2172	1397	2551	2847	322	2885	2605	648	262	1227
Rapid City, SD	1093	1312	1214	1160	2173	840	575	1557	1871	1262	1551	1708	1799	857	525	1956	1675	1305	1378	1996	1214	1735		1167	959	649	1242	1372	1384	1756	1141	862	1960	1615	699
Regina, SK	1525	1712	1454	1594	2570	1078	743	2009	1914	1659	1985	1994	2037	1307	927	2348	1946	1682	1619	2039	1120	2002	532	1428	1360	1024	1774	1773	1645	2117	1046	767	2360	1878	1149
Reno, NV	1898	470	2104	2029	3063	1953	1818	2255	2854	2151	2186	2685	2744	1563	1445	2841	2656	733	2357	2979	578	2690	1167		1844	518	1720	558	217	2644	720	793	2857	2595	1558
Saint Louis, MO	345	1821	263	283	1221	379	563	645	1166	310	675	954	911	496	439	999	888	1499	604	1279	2050	830	959	1844		1326	906	1845	2061	802	2096	1817	1008	827	442
Salt Lake City, UT	1488	688	1586	1524	2544	1437	1308	1936	2336	1633	1920	2170	2238	1200	930	2323	2140	653	1842	2461	765	2172	649	518	1326		1311	750	735	2125	839	720	2339	2079	1042
San Antonio, TX	594	1357	1111	727	1379	1285	1205	662	2096	939	541	1822	1557	468	920	1160	1742	985	1495	2136	2076	1397	1242	1720	906	1311		1278	1736	1161	2150	2018	1170	1606	625
San Diego, CA	1676	120	2109	1819	2656	2118	1986	1936	3018	2030	1816	2809	2730	1351	1613	2436	2738	352	2452	3143	1083	2551	1372	558	1845	750	1278		501	2356	1256	1468	2447	2693	1401
San Francisco, CA	1963	380	2321	2095	3038	2170	2040	2320	3071	2306	2252	2902	2973	1627	1662	2816	2873	749	2574	3196	635	2847	1384	217	2061	735	1736	501		2720	807	874	2832	2812	1775
Sault Ste. Marie, ON	1089	2465	649	972	1685	398	538	1268	740	823	1355	921	1037	1236	850	1475	911	2240	614	871	2165	1007	1118	2364	740	1848	1646	2502	2581	1201	2090	1812	1492	851	1150
Savannah, GA	763	2422	658	626	483	1045	1374	502	1113	495	642	811	481	1092	1239	280	703	2091	697	1111	2844	322	1756	2644	802	2125	1161	2356	2720		2896	2616	333	575	1202
Seattle, WA	2275	1134	2357	2299	3315	1990	1655	2727	3025	2404	2716	2858	2949	1948	1663	3093	2828	1414	2530	3150	172	2885	1141	720	2096	839	2150	1256	807	2896		278	3109	2768	1828
Shenandoah N.P., VA	904	2582	506	768	1035	798	1111	886	618	558	978	320	181	1233	1155	847	217	2238	245	616	2824	263	1615	2604	768	2107	1496	2586	2842	567	2769	2490	885	82	1207
Spokane, WA	1948	1215	2077	2018	3035	1712	1377	2478	2746	2124	2409	2580	2671	1710	1383	2814	2550	1381	2252	2871	351	2605	862	793	1817	720	2018	1468	874	2616	278		2830	2490	1600
Tampa, FL	941	2525	872	779	255	1260	1578	509	1440	700	651	1138	808	1270	1445	84	1040	2153	1023	1438	3064	648	1960	2857	1008	2339	1170	2447	2832	333	3109	2830		902	1381
Thunder Bay, ON	1156	2265	957	1153	2041	585	341	1547	1121	1130	1545	1349	1473	1127	720	1822	1339	2028	1049	1246	1938	1443	913	2006	870	1648	1547	2326	2224	1613	1866	1588	1828	1286	974
Toronto, ON	1120	2517	601	983	1483	609	933	1222	465	774	1306	489	669	1259	974	1284	497	2262	316	592	2620	737	1438	2414	763	1899	1669	2583	2632	1007	2588	2310	1333	482	1188
Tucson, AZ	1271	485	1749	1406	2250	1805	1675	1530	2654	1617	1410	2448	2303	990	1313	2029	2383	116	2092	2766	1447	2142	1293	848	1485	776	871	407	864	1949	1529	1496	2040	2283	1040
Vancouver, BC	2421	1275	2493	2437	3451	2125	1790	2894	2982	2540	2851	2993	3084	2083	1799	3229	2963	1550	2665	3286	313	3021	1277	890	2232	973	2286	1398	947	3032	141	413	3245	2903	1973
Washington, DC	1014	2670	606	879	1044	788	1110	965	538	666	1087	228	189	1343	1151	849	137	2348	244	535	2800	262	1615	2595	827	2079	1606	2693	2812	575	2768	2490	902		1258
Wichita, KS	446	1377	701	577	1587	763	634	894	1597	688	880	1391	1349	158	298	1365	1319	1053	1035	1710	1764	1227	699	1558	442	1042	625	1401	1775	1202	1828	1600	1381	1258	
Winnipeg, MB	1208	1965	1164	1273	2252	791	456	1721	1552	1336	1664	1659	1749	1095	640	2029	1629	2000	1331	1677	1474	1684	745	1684	1062	1277	1562	2025	1912	1829	1401	1121	2047	1568	905
Yellowstone N.P., WY	1519	1037	1611	1624	2569	1345	1016	2014	2381	1658	1950	2213	2314	1182	958	2356	2182	1002	1892	2506	833	2178	497	755	1356	351	1535	1098	972	2151	760	481	2356	2142	1072
Yosemite N.P., CA	1870	308	2159	2009	2957	2051	1922	2239	2950	2212	2162	2802	2811	1533	1547	2735	2754	678	2457	3075	751	2762	1263	214	1899	615	1665	429	189	2639	923	967	2751	2695	1564